THE POLITICS OF MEDICAID

COLUMBIA

UNIVERSITY

PRESS

New York

THE
POLITICS
OF
MEDICAID

Laura Katz Olson

Columbia University Press
Publishers Since 1893
New York   Chichester, West Sussex
Copyright © 2010 Columbia University Press
All rights reserved

Library of Congress Cataloging-in-Publication Data

Olson, Laura Katz, 1945–
The Politics of Medicaid / Laura Katz Olson.
p. cm.
Includes bibliographical references and index.
ISBN 978-0-231-15060-6 (cloth : alk. paper) — ISBN 978-0-231-52159-8 (ebook)
1. Medicaid—Political aspects.   I. Title.

RA412.4.O47 2010
368.4'200973—dc22
2009050497

Columbia University Press books are printed on permanent and durable acid-free paper.
This book is printed on paper with recycled content.
Printed in the United States of America

c 10 9 8 7 6 5 4 3 2

References to Internet Web sites (URLs) were accurate at the time of writing. Neither
the author nor Columbia University Press is responsible for URLs that may have expired or
changed since the manuscript was prepared.

FOR MY SISTER ANNIE

CONTENTS

ABBREVIATIONS

ADA	American Dental Association
AFDC	Aid to Families with Dependent Children
AHA	American Hospital Association
AHCA	American Health Care Association
AHIP	America's Health Insurance Plans
AMA	American Medical Association
BBA	Balanced Budget Act
CMS	Centers for Medicare and Medicaid Services
CNA	certified nurse's aide
DRA	Deficit Reduction Act of 2005
DSH	Disproportionate Share Hospital
EPSDT	early and periodic screening, diagnosis, and treatment
FCA	False Claims Act
FDA	U.S. Federal Drug Administration
FPL	federal poverty level
GAO	U.S. Government Accountability Office (previously Government Accounting Office)
HCBS	home and community-based services
HEW	U.S. Department of Health, Education, and Welfare
HHS	U.S. Department of Health and Human Services

HIFA	Health Insurance Flexibility and Accountability Initiative
HIPP	Health Insurance Premium Payment Program
HOA	Health Opportunity Account
HSA	Health Savings Account
ICF	Intermediate Care Facility
ICF-MR	Intermediate Care Facility for the Mentally Retarded
LTC	long-term care
MCO	managed-care organization
MFCU	Medicaid Fraud Control Unit
NACDS	National Association of Chain Drug Stores
NCPA	National Community Pharmacists Association
OBRA	Omnibus Budget Reconciliation Act
OECD	Organization of Economic Cooperation and Development
OHP	Oregon Health Plan
OIG	Office of Inspector General
PACE	Program of All-Inclusive Care for the Elderly
PCN	Primary Care Network
PhRMA	Pharmaceutical Research and Manufacturers of America
PRWOR	Personal Responsibility and Work Opportunity Reconciliation
REIT	Real Estate Investment Trust
SCHIP	State Children's Health Insurance Program
SSI	Supplemental Security Income
TANF	Temporary Assistance for Needy Families
UPL	upper payment limit

ACKNOWLEDGMENTS

I owe a great professional and intellectual debt to Joe Hendricks, whose generosity of spirit, inspiration, and insights have been an important influence in my career and thinking. I also thank William O. Winter, my Ph.D. dissertation adviser at the University of Colorado, Boulder, for his caring, kindness, and assistance over the past thirty-nine years.

Many people have shared their ideas, thoughts, and knowledge with me as I wrote this book and have helped make it a reality. I am particularly indebted to Mark E. Rushefsky, an expert on health policy, who read the manuscript in its entirety and provided me with critical suggestions for revisions. Colleen Grogan graciously looked at the chapter on the early history of Medicaid and gave me sound advice about clarifying my arguments. Her large body of scholarship on welfare medicine has enormously influenced my thoughts about the subject. Miriam Laugesen, with an eye for clarity, offered me critical feedback on organizing chapter 5 more effectively. I greatly benefited from the suggestions given to me by Daniel Gitterman, whose own work on Medicaid lobby groups is an important contribution to the field. Because of Michael Gussman's perceptive comments, I was forced to rethink and revise certain parts of chapter 9. I owe a debt to Cynthia Massie Mara, who, with her usual sharpness, pointed out ways to improve the chapter on long-term care. She has been a good friend and collaborator on aging issues over the years. Two anonymous reviewers' close readings greatly influenced the final version of the book. One reviewer in particular recommended detailed restructuring of the entire work, which I resisted at first but soon accepted, realizing the enormous importance of the suggestions.

I also am blessed with a remarkable community of scholars in the Lehigh Valley Feminist Research Group. I am particularly appreciative of the useful observations and advice from Judy Lasker, Myra Rosenhaus, Annette Benert, Elizabeth Bodien, and Cheryl Dugan. I also acknowledge the students in Judy Lasker's health care seminar, who read portions of the book and provided me with their opinions. I especially thank Lehigh University's hard-working and considerate librarian, Pat Ward, for her efforts in making sure that I had the books I needed as quickly as possible. I do not know how I would have managed without her.

I appreciate the efforts of Columbia University editor Anne Routon, who shepherded the manuscript along so effectively and supportively. I am grateful to Annie Barva for her careful and expeditious copyediting of the manuscript.

My daughter, Alix, a performance poet and graduate student in political science, has always played an important role in my life, as well as engaging me in thoughtful conversation and pushing me to think in new ways. My husband, George, gave me his ongoing encouragement and patience as I laboriously wrote and revised the manuscript. He discussed many of the ideas with me from beginning to end and at the same time managed a great number of the household obligations, which allowed me to pursue the project with single-mindedness. I dedicate this book to the memory of Annie, my loving sister, a talented artist and passionate political activist.

THE POLITICS OF MEDICAID

1

INTRODUCTION:
THE MEDICAID STORY

This book is an attempt to make sense of Medicaid, a program that encompasses a labyrinth of fifty separate state government plans that are regularly in flux (as some students of the subject famously observe, "If you've seen one Medicaid program, you've seen one Medicaid program"); countless national rules and regulations, many of which are repeatedly waived; myriad, volatile funding sources; a large range of health industries, professionals, and their trade associations, representing hundreds of thousands of private contractors with diverse agendas, stakes in the program, and levels of integrity; and a patchwork of categorical and financial participation standards that differentiate within and among the millions of low-income families, regardless of their medical needs. Add to the mix the numerous other entities that to varying extents affect and are affected by welfare medicine[1] (including employers, workers, and their communities) and the ever-changing political winds steering its policies. No one designed the existing program; rather, it is a perplexing Rube Goldberg of incremental adjustments and periodic enhancements or cutbacks, at both the national level and the state level, which rarely work in concert.

Perhaps it is for these reasons that so few comprehensive books have been written about Medicaid, especially relative to Medicare, a national plan with hardly any state variations and less-complicated qualification requirements, funding mechanisms, and administration. The small number of books on welfare medicine tends to focus on specific, separate pieces of the puzzle, as do the more voluminous research efforts by scholars, foundations, agencies, and others.[2] Despite this piecemeal approach, these investigations have not only rendered the study of Medicaid more manageable, but provided me with a rich source of data and information. As I quickly discovered, however, assembling the tangled parts into a coherent whole is a daunting task. Regardless, I pushed forward in an attempt to confront the Medicaid story in its entirety.

Medicaid was initially considered Medicare's friendless stepchild, created in its shadow and catering to a politically powerless clientele. It soon became evident, however, that the sleeper program would awaken with a start, and over the years it has become a formidable force of its own. From a cost of $1.2 billion in its first year, the annual price tag of Medicaid had jumped to $333 billion by 2007, accounting for 15 percent of the nation's total spending on health services, nearly reaching Medicare's $375 billion, or 16 percent. In fact, welfare medicine rose faster than any other federal

+ +

program, 10 percent on average since its inception. In 2001, its enrollment surpassed that of Medicare, and in the past five years the caseload swelled by another 40 percent, providing medical and long-term care (LTC) services to roughly 15 percent of the U.S. population. The program, which tends to grow faster than the overall economy, is now 2.3 percent of the gross domestic product.[3]

The Political Economy of Welfare Medicine

Public policy and its consequences highly depend on how a problem is defined. Almost from the start, Medicaid has been characterized as a budget buster, and, as such, fiscal issues have dominated its strategies, courses of action, and outcomes. Even as the program expanded—whether because of medical inflation, greater coverage, or broader services—officials sought to rein in funding, most often to the detriment of participants. They have squeezed physician fees, thus contributing to less access to medical services; mandated managed care, seriously undermining consumer choice and quality of care; added premiums and higher copayments, forcing some families to forgo treatments or even withdraw from the program entirely; and established drug formularies and restrictions on the number of monthly prescriptions, endangering patients' health and well-being.

Dogged economizing has been accompanied by an admixture of rhetoric, obfuscation, facades, and marketplace illusions. As with other social ills, Medicaid policies are steeped in the American marketing craze, wherein elected leaders advocate ever more private solutions to public problems. In the name of privatization, they are audaciously unleashing commercial forces on a program that is already heavily reliant on—and in certain cases controlled by—entrenched economic interests. As part of the incarnation of antistatist values, officials have also pushed for greater individualism, personal responsibility, consumer empowerment and choice, and familism. With the imprimatur of the George W. Bush administration and his congressional supporters, such precepts progressively set the terms of the debate over welfare medicine during the early twenty-first century, nationally and locally.

The glorification of the marketplace, client autonomy, and self-reliance were translated into the blaming of people for their own illnesses, a rationing of services, divergent benefit packages that discriminate against certain categories of beneficiaries, enrollment caps, ceilings on individual funding amounts, heavy burdens for family caregivers, and other consequences that undermined the low-income health program and its entitlement status. Policy deliberations, couched in business terms to an unprecedented extent, bent beneficiary needs to commercial ends. To be sure, a few states—such as Florida—began endeavoring to privatize the entire Medicaid program, but with disastrous results for the poor.

Enrollees predictably did not respond as policymakers anticipated to the assortment of "choices" and "empowering" inducements that, despite being cloaked in marketplace assurances, fell far short in their realities. Hard-to-sell incentives were accordingly tied to controls, and options were transformed into mandates. Grounded in personal responsibility jargon, many of the new proposals confounded logic and decency. As the drone of the privatization rhetoric intensified, beneficiaries lost ground. Even the modest consumer-directed assistance programs, now offering the disabled greater independence, have not been backed by sufficient resources to meet clients' actual needs.

As privatization deepens, costs are boosted, thereby taking Medicaid full circle. The ascendancy of commercial establishments ensures that Medicaid is not only paying for medical services per se, but also for high, sometimes exorbitant profits and stockholder gains, lavish executive salaries, mergers and acquisitions, administration, marketing, as well as, at times, lobbying, campaign contributions, and lawsuits. Quite a few nonprofit players display profit-maximizing behavior as well. Although painted as paragons of innovation, flexibility, and efficiency, the health industries—insurance companies, pharmaceutical manufacturing firms, hospitals, nursing homes, home health agencies, and the like—have in fact contributed measurably to escalating welfare medicine outlays.

Even when policymakers seek to combat fraud and abuse, they concentrate on the financial aspects of the problems. As Victoria Wachino astutely points out, the definition of Medicaid program integrity is quite narrow, fixed mostly on recovering improper payments to providers and uncovering their deceptive billing practices; it does not embrace human concerns such as consumer rights or the impact of illicit activities on clients' health and well-being.[4] The grim irony is that because of the way Medicaid is currently structured, greater attention to the quality of care—and to the more stringent rules and regulations that it would require—may undermine other aspects of the program crucial to participants, especially access to services.

Devolution of Power

Unlike the other entitlements (Social Security and Medicare), Medicaid is entangled in a complex and at times contentious web of relationships between the federal government and the states. Because spending has overshadowed other issues, including access to and quality of care, the funding of welfare medicine has been a political football: the central government has sought to lower its share, but the states have endeavored to maximize national allocations or pass portions to their local entities or do both. The states have been particularly adept at designing schemes to draw in extra federal dollars by taking advantage of regulatory loopholes and oversights. Some of them also have cashed in on the unrestricted nature of Medicaid's cost-sharing provision: there is no set limit to total federal payments to a state, thus encouraging certain places (such as New York) to offer a large number of nonmandated services; they can choose from among thirty-four alternatives. This provision not only allows states to expand benefits to their residents at federal expense, but provides them greater outside dollars to spur their local economies. Although the states may complain about the financial burdens of welfare medicine imposed on them by national mandates, nearly two-thirds of all Medicaid spending is at their option.[5]

In response, regulations and directives from Washington have mounted over the decades. In their turn, governors have sought—and achieved—more control over their low-income health plans. However, the ongoing devolution of decision-making power to the states through the waiver process, later augmented by the Deficit Reduction Act (DRA) of 2005, was not linked to enhanced federal dollars. Thus, the states were granted "new flexibilities," but without the resources to improve or even sustain their plans effectively. In many jurisdictions, they utilized their greater latitude to quash national guarantees for current enrollees and to limit benefit packages, although the retrenchments were more measured and nuanced at first. The extension of welfare medicine to more families has also suffered measurably from a dearth of local money, notwithstanding a prevailing (and in this case misguided) notion in some circles that you cannot throw (government) money at problems.

The (Many) Hands in the Till

Medicaid is the quintessential program detested today by radical conservative forces: its entitlement status signifies an open-ended right to benefits, in this case by America's impoverished households. It is the fourth-largest program in the federal budget (following Social Security, national defense, and Medicare)[6] and among the top two in the vast majority of states.[7] In contrast, relatively few resources have been devoted to cash-assistance payments for young families, nationally or locally. Yet Aid to Families with Dependent Children (AFDC), despite its limited funding, elicited outrage and antagonism among a significant number of policymakers who viewed it as violating American values of self-sufficiency and the work ethic, furthering "Big Government," and rewarding the "undeserving" poor, in particular unmarried mothers. Financial support for "welfare" has always been grudging, culminating in its elimination as a national entitlement in 1996.[8] Although the financially more burdensome low-income health program enrolls many of the same recipients, especially children, it has not generated similar opposition. Indeed, like the Energizer Bunny, it just keeps going; despite periodic political obstacles, budgetary constraints, and other setbacks, its enrollment and funding have continued to escalate over the decades.

The stark contrast between support for Medicaid and resistance to other programs for low-income families—including food stamps, public housing, legal aid, and supportive services—was a curiosity that sparked my journey into the politics and policies of welfare medicine. What I found, as this book explores, is a sweeping program that helps sustain many of the main commercial interests in the United States. To varying extents, health providers and other types of contractors not only feed off the program, but press for its expansion. Together, they form a powerful Medicaid medical industrial complex.[9] For some entities, especially the states, Medicaid is an ongoing source of budgetary strain; for the health industries, it is a cash cow.

Eligibility thresholds, the scope and intensity of services, and, most important, reimbursement rates are decided at the state level, where special interests tend to have a decided advantage in lobbying, financing electoral campaigns, and making personal political contacts. These interests can also hold legislators hostage if they are among the several vendors vital to the continuation of specific services or even the program itself. Since the 1980s, not only have the number and assortment of groups that lobby local legislators expanded, but certain commercial enterprises have strengthened their clout, most notably those profiting from welfare medicine—especially hospitals, nursing homes, and medical insurance companies.[10] Researchers found, for example, that in 2002 state officials viewed nursing homes and hospitals as the most influential forces in twenty-one states and as the second most effective in eighteen states.[11]

Health-related businesses and professionals not only have stepped up their spending on traditional means of influencing state officials, but also commonly organize ad hoc coalitions, grassroots movements, and public-relations drives to preserve and further their separate financial interests in the program. Collectively and independently, they regularly issue jeremiads about inadequate fees, in general conflating their own needs with those of Medicaid recipients and their communities, although such arguments tend to be more illusory than real. Their main goal is to claim more public-sector dollars to feed their bottom line; the poor may gain only marginally.

Medicaid stakeholders also include large numbers of newly impoverished white middle-class elders relying on the program for LTC, especially nursing home services. Along with younger (mainly white) low-income disabled adults,[12] these "protected" sectors of the welfare medicine population have contributed measurably to Medicaid's escalating outlays over the decades; in fact, LTC comprises roughly one-third of program costs. As several knowledgeable observers suggest, the coalition of interest between the nursing home industry and the families of frail elders who need care is a strikingly powerful force at the state level.[13] It also helps explain Medicaid's preferred status as compared to that of income-support programs for young, poor families—AFDC and, later, Temporary Assistance for Needy Families (TANF).

The Disregarded Stakeholders: Low-Income Households

Another major goal of the book is to explore whether and to what extent Medicaid meets the needs of the low-income people it was intended to serve. After all, the program ostensibly is about making health services available to families who cannot afford private insurance. It is the basic safety-net health plan in the United States; without it, we would have even more than the 47 million medically uninsured individuals that we have today. Despite its many shortcomings, is welfare medicine better than nothing, both for economically disadvantaged households and for the nation at large? In other words, how well does it serve its clients, and which segments of the population are left out? Given all of the high-powered fingers in the Medicaid pie, is the program sufficiently advancing health in the country, and are we on the whole receiving our money's worth?

In order to qualify for welfare medicine, individuals must be more than indigent; they must meet stringent income thresholds that vary by state and are generally far below the official federal poverty level (FPL): in 2005, only two-fifths of the nonelderly poverty population participated in Medicaid.[14] It does not, then, serve as a safety net for everybody who is poor and is of less benefit to workers who have low earnings. Recipients must also fit specific categorical criteria wherein the program privileges the aged (mostly for LTC) and children. Policymakers are curiously tone-deaf when it comes to the medical requirements of nondisabled, low-income adults younger than age sixty-five, despite their low coverage rates: in 2005, fully 20 percent of them lacked health insurance, but only 8 percent were enrolled in welfare medicine. In contrast, one-fourth of all children received benefits through the low-income health plan or the State Children's Health Insurance Program (SCHIP).[15]

Access to care and the quality of services are also at issue. Initially guaranteeing mainstream medical care, Medicaid rapidly developed into a second-class health system. Program money goes directly into the hands of contractors, with enrollees having little or no control over the value of the assistance they receive. Managed-care organizations (MCOs)[16] steadily captured the Medicaid market and, with the advent of mandatory enrollment in the 1990s, participants have had even less ability to negotiate where and when they can obtain services or the type, amount, and quality of care provided to them.

The vast majority of chronically ill elders covered under the program, notwithstanding the expansion of home- and community-based services (HCBS), is still shunted into institutions. Nursing homes, at least as they are constituted at present, are sadly incapable of delivering the kind of care our frail older people deserve. These facilities are "big business": their main incentive is and has always been to reap high monetary returns, whether through real estate schemes, mergers and acquisitions, stock-market manipulations, financial fraud, skimping on essential patient and staff needs, or all of the above. They embody the worst aspects of the privatization that so many of our elected officials have championed. Over the decades, the nursing home industry's transgressions have been and will continue to be papered over with ineffective hearings, regulations, and enforcement procedures.[17]

Social Location: Gender and Race

Any analysis of Medicaid should be first and foremost about class—the have-nots in American society who compose the program's clientele. Because welfare medicine concerns poverty, it also is inextricably linked to issues of gender, race, ethnicity, and age. Women not only are more likely than men to endure financial hardship, experience low-wage jobs lacking pensions and health benefits, and reside alone or in single-parent households, but are apt to outlast them in old age.[18] Marital status is a significant predictor of economic well-being, and women are far less likely to be married than men. In 2006, only 5 percent of married couples had incomes at or below the FPL as compared to 28 percent of female-headed families with no husband present and 13 percent of male-headed families without a wife.[19] Women's health status also tends to be worse than men's, in part an effect of their increased risk of indigence. What is more, women comprise nearly two-thirds of older people with severe disabilities.

Roughly 70 percent of adult Medicaid participants are women, whether qualifying as mothers or as frail elders in need of LTC. They make up three-fourths of nursing home residents, mostly subsidized by welfare medicine, and 65 percent of the program's HCBS clients.[20] Nevertheless, Medicaid does not protect females during their entire life cycle: it clearly favors those who are in their reproductive years and at the tail end of their life, while falling short for the middle-aged poor. Divorced and widowed women whose children are grown, for example, are generally not among the categorically eligible, regardless of their generally low-income status. Only 16 percent of women participating in Medicaid are between the ages of forty-five and sixty-four; they clearly are not viewed as among America's "worthy" poor. Nor does the low-income health care program safeguard the vast majority of women in need; only 21 percent of females with incomes at or below 200 percent of the FPL are enrolled.[21]

Because various interlocking locations of social oppression cut across gender lines, minority women experience their socioeconomic disadvantages in different ways. Most important, poverty among black and Latina women is significantly more prevalent than among white women. And although the former groups disproportionately rely on welfare medicine for their health care needs, they are less likely to have access to quality health professionals, hospitals, nursing homes, and other services, while simultaneously suffering from more infirmities and chronic disabilities.[22]

Indeed, minorities of both sexes tend to depend on Medicaid to a greater extent than whites do, primarily because they typically earn far lower wages, are poorer, and have less access to employer-sponsored insurance for themselves and their children.[23] Blacks compose 12.8 percent of the U.S. population but make up roughly one-fourth of welfare medicine participants. Nearly 15 percent of Americans are Latino, but they represent more than one-fifth of the Medicaid population.[24] More people of color than whites do not have any health insurance at all, public or private. In 2006, one-fifth of all blacks and Asians/South Pacific Islanders and one-third of Latinos and American Indians/Alaskan Natives lacked coverage, as compared to 13 percent of non-Latino whites.[25]

According to an Institute of Medicine report, which assessed more than 100 studies pertaining to minorities and medical care, insurance status is strongly associated with the quality of their services; the privately insured tend to receive better care than those individuals who are insured through Medicaid. Even when certain ethnic and racial minorities have access to the low-income health program, they tellingly experience fewer diagnostic and other routine services than do other sectors of society. Not only are blacks, Latinos, and other minorities more likely than other population groups to be funded through welfare medicine, but they also are more apt to be served in public hospitals and clinics or community health centers, where quality of care is lower than other places; about two-thirds of health center patients are nonwhite.[26]

It is well documented that on average black Americans tend to receive less adequate care than white Americans, resulting in poorer clinical outcomes.

Insufficiently managed chronic conditions and neglected diagnostic screenings frequently lead to needless complications, morbidity, disability, lost productivity, and even death.[27] The Institute of Medicine inquiry discovered that in such areas as cardiovascular disease, cerebrovascular disease, cancer, end-stage renal disease, diabetes, some surgical procedures, pediatric care, rehabilitation, and mental illness, there are clear disparities between the two racial groups in diagnosis and treatment.[28] The annual *National Health Disparities Report*, which also compares medical services among racial, ethnic, and socioeconomic groups, consistently finds that inequality of care is pervasive throughout the health care system.[29] In the main, because of a disproportionate access to quality services—along with socioeconomic inequities, discriminatory practices, cultural and language barriers, and a host of other risk factors—large disparities in health status exist between white Americans and racial/ethnic minorities.[30]

Public Opinion and Partisan Politics

Medicaid tends to be a low-profile issue, with only limited coverage by the mass media.[31] Except during periods of severe budgetary stress or intense partisan conflict, the topic is conspicuously absent in local and national newspapers, magazines, and television or radio newscasts. At times, it is tucked away in the back pages of newspapers, accompanied by sensationalist or alarmist headlines emphasizing financial fraud, fiscal crises, escalating costs, or catastrophic events. Typical of such captions in 2008 are "Hynes: Illinois' Medicaid System Is Broke," "Pharmacist Indicted for Alleged Medicaid Fraud," "Hospital Would Lose $6.5 Million in Medicaid Cuts," "Medicaid Close to Running out of Money," "Scam Alert: Medicaid RX Fleecing Bank Accounts," "Medicaid Agrees to Pay for Life-Saving Surgery After Channel 9 Report," "Georgia Medicaid Program Challenged in Court," "Arizona a Prime Example of Financial Ruin by Medicaid," "Medicaid Cuts Hurting Disabled," "Medicaid Program Losing Providers," and "Nursing Home's Threats Violate Many Regulations." Media exposés periodically make it to the front pages. Such investigations, which tend to center on financial abuses and patient exploitation in nursing homes, momentarily capture the public's attention.

The generally negative tone of the reportage, fostering images of a program run amuck, is stoked by certain elected officials and various other policy elites who are intent on undermining Medicaid. Welfare medicine is regularly embroiled in partisan politics: from its start, there has been a political tug of war between Democrat and Republican leaders over its policies, procedures, and especially its funding and benefit levels. At various times, the acrimonious debates have pitted Congress against the president, the House of Representatives against the Senate, governor against state assembly, or the two local chambers against each other. The wrangling has heated up over time and is now grounded in fundamental divisions regarding what values and principles should guide, shape, and restrict the Medicaid conversation, along with the parameters of discussion over national health care more broadly. This politics of dissensus, as Fay Lomax Cook and Meredith B. Czaplewski label it,[32] has stirred up fears of fiscal disaster and images of unworthy clients taking advantage of taxpayer dollars.

The mass media, policymakers, and political analysts generally convey few particulars about Medicaid policies, the benefits or drawbacks for its recipients, or the quality of care. It is no wonder, then, that a significant number of people confuse the Medicaid and Medicare programs as to which age groups are covered, the qualification requirements in general, the services they offer (especially LTC), and funding sources.[33] Nevertheless, despite both the misunderstandings and the crossfire, Medicaid is surprisingly a popular program among the general public.[34] As indicated by public-opinion polls and focus groups, the degree of approval is almost—though not quite—as high as the widely supported Social Security and Medicare social insurance programs, both of which, unlike Medicaid, are viewed as "rights" that have been "earned" by deserving individuals through work and individual contributions over the years.

Studies in the early 1990s, such as those by Fay Cook and Edith Barrett, found that although the public may not approve of welfare per se, they do have a positive opinion of the low-income health plan: overall, respondents were relatively pleased with Medicaid's effectiveness. The researchers found that 47 percent of the adults polled would increase its funding levels, and another 46 percent would maintain them, thus indicating a large commitment to the program.[35] Their survey data suggest that the most appreciated programs, in order of support, were Social Security, Medicare, Supplemental

Security Income (SSI), and Medicaid; AFDC had the least backing.[36] Other surveys confirm these results, even during the fierce battles over Medicaid between President Bill Clinton and the Newt Gingrich Republican Congress during the mid-1990s.[37]

Since entering the twenty-first century, the public has been steadfast in their overall endorsement of welfare medicine's objectives. A 2005 Henry J. Kaiser Family Foundation national survey on "the public's views about Medicaid," for example, found that 74 percent of the respondents regarded Medicaid as a "very important" program, just below the 88 percent for Social Security and 83 percent for Medicare. Even when the public perceived that their state was experiencing budgetary shortfalls, relatively few adults were inclined to lower Medicaid funding or reduce its coverage.[38] In New York, although the vast majority of residents in a 2008 poll viewed the state's fiscal condition as the worst it has been since the economic crisis in the 1970s, most of them were not in favor of cutting their welfare medicine plan.[39]

In another nationwide poll, commissioned by AARP in 2006, 85 percent of the respondents indicated that they would either increase federal Medicaid funding in the next budget cycle (51 percent) or keep the expenditures the same (34 percent); only a small minority would decrease the amount of money allocated to the program. Notably, agreement with boosting welfare medicine outlays compared positively with that of choosing higher outlays for education (74 percent), Medicare (61 percent), and Social Security (60 percent), and in contrast to defense (35 percent), transportation (33 percent), and agriculture (42 percent).[40]

The fact that an overwhelming majority of Americans apparently backs welfare medicine should not obscure partisan disparities, however. As with other issues in American society, since the beginning of the twenty-first century the public has become more polarized in their preferences, a trend that is tied to a greater identification with political parties and their policy positions, particularly in the realm of social concerns.[41] In the 2005 Kaiser survey, for instance, although people of various political persuasions regarded Medicaid as a very important program, Democrats (81 percent) and Independents (79 percent) approved of it far more than Republicans (61 percent).[42] In a poll assessing the public's views on the 2007 reauthorization controversy over SCHIP, Democrats again were more likely to uphold an expansion of the program (82 percent) than were either Independents (69 percent) or Republicans (54 percent).[43] Indeed, similar partisan differences exist on a range of health care issues, including the role that the government should play in ensuring that everyone has adequate access to services.[44]

Nevertheless, support remains strong for welfare medicine across the political spectrum. A major reason may be that most Americans know individuals—whether themselves or others—who have depended on the program for their medical needs. In addition, they accurately and approvingly view it as more than just a health care program: sixty-eight percent of the respondents in the 2005 Kaiser poll indicated that the need for LTC was a main reason why people have health insurance through Medicaid. An overwhelming percentage considers the program essential for meeting the LTC needs of chronically ill older people.[45] To be sure, the public may assume that even more frail elderly avail themselves of LTC benefits than is actually the case.

Race, of course, plays a significant role as well, as it does in social welfare policy in the United States generally. Certain policymakers see income supports for young, poor families as programs that serve indolent, dependent minority households, even though the majority of recipients has been Caucasian.[46] As discussed earlier, such government assistance has been more open to political attack and retrenchment than Medicaid, in part because welfare medicine also serves a frail older white population.

Overview and Organization of the Book

Chapter 2 briefly describes the trajectory of Medicare and Medicaid's enactment, including the role of powerful industry groups and conservative Republicans and southern Democrats in preventing more comprehensive national health care. I argue that Medicare was carefully crafted, but that Medicaid was a hastily conceived afterthought, leaving it susceptible to the many contradictions, conflicts, inadequacies, and inconsistencies the program has displayed over the years. Indeed, Medicaid's myriad vulnerabilities materialized immediately, setting the stage in the 1960s and 1970s for what was in store for everyone concerned in the years ahead.

The chapter details the early political troubles of welfare medicine, including inequities among the states, inadequate coverage of needy families, perpetuation of the two-tier medical system, insufficient access to health professionals, the fiscal tug-of-war between the national and state governments, ongoing budgetary shortfalls, cost-cutting approaches, the catch-22 of reimbursement policies, pervasive financial fraud, and poor quality of care. I show how powerful sectors of the medical industrial complex, despite their initial opposition to Medicaid, not only became entrenched stakeholders in it, but through a variety of strategies were also able to hold political leaders hostage to their demands.

Chapter 3 first examines President Ronald Reagan's struggle not only to curtail the federal share of Medicaid funding, but also to end the program as an entitlement. His administration ushered in an era of fiscal austerity and retrenchment in social programs in general, especially those serving the poor, but it ultimately failed to keep welfare medicine in check. Although abandoning the idea of abolishing Medicaid as a basic social right, George H. W. Bush also persisted in pursuing measures to rein in overall program expenditures. The chapter shows how—regardless of these attempts by the administration—congressional mandates, rising unemployment, greater poverty, and judicial decisions led to a steady expansion in coverage and improved benefits, especially for pregnant women, children, older people, and the disabled.

The chapter next addresses the range of tactics state policymakers have utilized to cope with their growing Medicaid case loads, the escalation in the program's price tag, and mounting fiscal pressures on local budgets. It concentrates on their early use of waiver authority—urged by the Reagan White House under the pretext of greater state autonomy and flexibility—to sidestep national regulations and consumer protections.

The chapter then turns to an exploration of the Bill Clinton years, beginning with the emergence of the "New Right" Republicans as a powerful force in both chambers of Congress and their ideological, decidedly partisan fervor to crush social welfare programs, including Medicaid. Again, welfare medicine ultimately proved highly resistant to assaults on its national budget but became subject to ever greater control by the states. This section of the chapter also describes the contrasting status of AFDC and the severing of its linkage to the low-income health program. I also discuss additional expansions to Medicaid, especially under the newly enacted SCHIP program and, to a lesser extent, initiatives to assist low-income working adults. At the same time, armed with waivers, the states increasingly approved economizing measures, especially managed care, which in due course would undermine the program's efficacy.

Chapter 4 evaluates the policies of the George W. Bush administration in the first eight years of the new millennium, which sought to dismantle welfare medicine, shrink funding levels, and scale back federal standards by devolving ever-increasing program authority to the states. After exploring the early Bush years, this section considers the implications of the 2005 DRA as well as the president's endeavors to make an end-run around Congress and others opposed to his Medicaid strategies.

The chapter analyzes the states' fiscal condition and their varying responses to the "new flexibilities," including greater cost sharing for Medicaid participants and the vital role of mandated managed care in their restructurings of the program. It first explores local attempts to broaden welfare medicine but without commitments of sufficient resources to maintain earlier offerings for the extended populations or, at times, for existing clientele. This section then turns to state officials who are intent on undermining Medicaid, exploring such tactics as Health Opportunity Accounts, behavioral controls, greater marketization, and targeted, sharp reductions in benefits. It concludes with a look at the situation of children and their future prospects for attaining the health insurance that they require to meet their medical needs.

Chapter 5 critically evaluates how well the low-income health program serves the poor. It begins with an exploration of who is eligible and then analyzes barriers to participation among covered households, including procedural constraints, cost-sharing requirements, and citizenship status. The chapter next addresses fundamental issues related to program adequacy, access to health practitioners, and the scope of benefit packages. The narrative concludes with a discussion of welfare medicine's dubious role in responding to a wide range of societal ills and political controversies, ranging from drug abuse and AIDS to abortion and natural disasters.

Chapter 6 takes up the politically thorny questions concerning LTC for the frail elderly and disabled younger adults, the single most expensive item in state Medicaid budgets. It starts with an outline of LTC users, who pays the bill, and the preponderant role of nursing homes in the narrow arsenal of welfare medicine service choices. The next section considers the several measures aimed at curbing program outlays, first tackling the politically charged issue of asset transfers by middle-class elders seeking to qualify for Medicaid. Focusing next on HCBS, now the darling of politicians determined to slash costs, the chapter attempts to explain how the rash of state waivers and the even greater "flexibilities" established under the 2005 DRA have chipped away at the LTC entitlement, imposing immense burdens on unpaid caregivers, mostly wives and daughters.

The final section of chapter 6 assesses the latest market-based solutions for elder care—MCO pilot projects, LTC insurance, the Partnership for Long-Term Care Program, tax incentives—and it attempts to demonstrate that they bolster mostly the insurance industry and well-off families but fail to serve the vast majority of older and disabled people or even to lower Medicaid expenditures.

Chapter 7 scrutinizes quality of care, starting with a discussion of the medical treatment and health outcome disparities among individuals who are privately insured, uninsured, and covered under Medicaid. It moves on to explore the role of MCOs, arguing that they short-change patients by rationing services and offering limited access to specialists; operate with few meaningful government standards; impose inappropriate restrictions on health professionals; and engage in a host of other medical misdeeds in order to enhance their "bottom line." The chapter next tackles the seamy sides of LTC, concentrating on the prevalence of patient neglect and abuse in nursing homes, the poor quality of waiver HCBS, and emergent concerns about assisted-living facilities.

The last part of the chapter focuses on two interrelated issues. First, it describes the financial exploitation of Medicaid by an assortment of providers and the sorely deficient mechanisms for preventing, detecting, and punishing fraud at the state and national levels of government. Second, it takes up the question of whether policymakers take consumers into account in their oversight activities, arguing that financial con games and other illicit activities adversely affect Medicaid enrollees' safety, health, and well-being. It argues that policymakers tend to be more focused on the program's fiscal integrity, thus at times leaving vulnerable welfare medicine clients at risk.

Chapter 8 highlights the primary stakeholders in the program, the corporate and professional groups that compose the Medicaid medical industrial complex: nursing homes, hospitals, drug manufacturers, pharmacies, MCOs, doctors, dentists, as well as other companies and professionals. It shows the extent to which each of these powerful health industries both depend on Medicaid dollars and influence its policies. The chapter also seeks to disentangle the financial realities (Medicaid as economically advantageous for them) from the general gloom-and-doom rhetoric (i.e., the program as economically detrimental to their bottom line) as they all demand ever greater fees for their services. This section of the chapter moves on to discuss how these groups frequently work together—along with business, labor, and advocacy groups on behalf of the aged, children, and disabled—to defend and expand their assorted vested interests in welfare medicine.

The chapter ends by illustrating how the states have become reliant on the program and on the outside federal dollars it draws in for their economic growth, employment, and tax income. Financed heavily by Medicaid, health care providers are among the leading employers and purchasers of goods and services across the United States and in certain areas are the most essential ones.

Chapter 9 delineates the ways in which health care costs are shifted between and among various players and the ripple effects of these maneuvers throughout the economy. It first sketches out state strategies for maximizing federal Medicaid dollars and then turns to national measures for minimizing its share of the costs. The chapter also summarizes the impact of Medicare policies on welfare medicine obligations; funding controversies between the states and their localities; the transfer of financial responsibilities among providers, employers, and the low-income health program; and cost-sharing requirements that pass on expenses from state treasuries to low-income beneficiaries and their families. The main argument is that although Medicaid is supported by large sectors of American society, nobody wants to pick up the tab.

Concluding the book, chapter 10 summarizes the main themes developed in the book. It then takes up the question of whether the low-income health program is a suitable vehicle for extending coverage to the medically uninsured. It outlines the arguments for such a decentralized approach but contends that, for a variety of reasons, states do not have the fiscal or political capacity to sustain universal coverage. The next section in the chapter looks at the overall American health care system in which Medicaid is embedded, pointing out its dysfunctional, inequitable characteristics, fragmented bases of funding, and spiraling costs. It also shows that the United States already has sizable taxpayer-supported health insurance expenditures despite the antigovernment rhetoric. The section then compares both our health outlays and our health outcomes with those of other industrialized nations, revealing that we spend far more than most of them but have a poorer record on a wide range of health indicators.

The final section of this chapter compares the market-based solutions of contemporary conservative Republicans with the public/private models advanced by President Barack Obama and other Democrats, all building on Medicaid to varying degrees. The chapter ends by arguing that national and local policymakers should recognize quality health care as a basic human right, collective responsibility, and social good rather than as a commercial product. They must muster the political will to enact fundamental reform that ensures affordable, comprehensive coverage to everyone.

2

THE LAUNCHING
OF MEDICAID:
1965 TO 1980

National Health Care: Early Failures

Medicaid emerged in 1965 after a turbulent journey over several decades, first as a stingy alternative to national health care in the form of the Kerr-Mills legislation and later as a postscript to Medicare. Comprehensive medical insurance, which has long been a goal of a significant number of progressive leaders, faced formidable obstacles from the start. Beginning in 1916, social reformers, including the American Association for Labor Legislation, began promoting the idea of compulsory health insurance. Focusing at the local level, they introduced a model bill into a number of state legislatures, including New York and California, but opposition was strong and their proposals fizzled.[1] The issue was revived in the 1930s through various congressional measures, along with President Franklin D. Roosevelt's short-lived vision that national health care would be included in his Social Security legislation. Intense pressure by the American Medical Association (AMA), the most powerful lobby in the United States at the time, along with opposition by southern Democrats and most Republicans, convinced Roosevelt that he had to leave medical care out of his pet program if it were to be enacted.[2]

National health insurance continued to be debated throughout the 1940s, but again was forcefully crushed by self-serving stakeholders. With a well-funded media campaign, the AMA (along with insurance companies and other allies) succeeded in defeating the various Wagner-Murray-Dingell bills and President Harry S. Truman's proposal for national health insurance by equating government-funded medical services with "socialism." As a result, the subject became embroiled in McCarthyism.[3] Public support for Truman's legislation rapidly deteriorated, from 75 percent of the population in 1945 to a meager 21 percent by 1949.[4] Indeed, Truman viewed health care as one of his most important domestic initiatives and its decisive defeat as one of the greatest failures of his administration.[5]

National health insurance floundered, but as the need for affordable medical services grew, it became evident that Congress—however grudgingly—had to do something, at least for the neediest groups. In order to sidestep direct federal intervention, it offered states, under the Social Security Amendments of 1950, some limited cost sharing for hospitals, nursing homes, and certain health professionals serving individuals and families on public assistance. In keeping with the primacy of the private sector, the legislation stipulated that payments would be made directly to providers.

Not surprisingly, the gains for recipients were relatively meager. Medical vendor payments for the welfare population expanded in a few states but remained sparse in others or were not offered at all. Fees under the public program were considerably lower than those paid privately, further restricting the availability of services; quality of care suffered as well. For the most part, the indigent population was dependent on underfunded, often substandard state, city, or county hospitals and clinics, where available: such facilities were scarce in rural areas and the poorer states. Moreover, in most places, doctors, hospitals, nursing homes, and other professionals were expected to deliver at least some charity care.

Reformers in the 1950s, lacking the power to achieve their larger goal of universal health care, advocated special assistance for elders, a group they viewed as having the greatest political appeal. Through no fault of their own, a significant majority of them experienced inadequate private coverage, low incomes, and heavy medical needs.[6] Nevertheless, endeavors on their behalf were tempered by the ongoing opposition of powerful groups—in particular the AMA, its business associates, conservative Republicans, and southern Democrats—to any national approach, comprehensive benefits, or entitlements. These groups stood firm against even modest congressional measures that offered only hospital services for older people, financed under the contributory Social Security program. One prominent act, proposed by Representative Aime Forand (D–R.I.), was soundly defeated in the House Ways and Means Committee in 1957 and 1959; the AMA spent a quarter of a million dollars fighting it.[7] This organization, along with its allies in the insurance industry, continued to use fear of "socialism" as its major weapon against these bills. Such legislation was ironically denounced as akin to socialism even though in some countries, such as Germany and Japan, national health care was launched as a means of impeding the spread of socialism.[8]

Eventually placated, the adversaries acquiesced to the Kerr-Mills Act, put forth in 1960 by Wilbur Mills (D–Ark.), chair of the House Ways and Means Committee, as a conservative alternative to the Forand bill.[9] Its state-centered features and circumscribed eligibility pool—the aged poor—satisfied southern Democrats. Because payments would be made through state health agencies, controlled largely by doctors, the AMA was mollified as well.[10] Perceiving Kerr-Mills as taking over some of its burdensome, uncompensated services, the American Hospital Association (AHA), especially its nonprofit affiliates, also supported the measure.

Kerr-Mills was not a milestone even for the aged, nor was it far-reaching. For the most part, it broadened the existing system of vendor payments by offering states more liberal federal matching funds for older welfare recipients. It also added a new eligibility criterion, "medical indigence," for the elderly poor with income too high to qualify for Old Age Assistance but in need of support for their medical expenses.[11] Significantly, Kerr-Mills retained stringent eligibility tests in every participating state and forced participants to spend down their assets in order to participate in the new Medical Assistance to the Aged plans. By 1965, forty states had set up programs, although they varied considerably. Only a few offered the full range of benefits, and five of them (California, New York, Massachusetts, Minnesota, and Pennsylvania) received nearly 62 percent of the federal funding. In fact, New York's Medical Assistance to the Aged program, the largest in the nation, served roughly one-third of all national Kerr-Mills recipients. Moreover, many of the states with already established medical services for the poor used Kerr-Mills to shift part of their state funding burdens to the federal government, foreshadowing their ability to capitalize on Medicaid.[12]

The Social Security Amendments of 1965: Medicare and Medicaid

Unlike Medicare, Medicaid was enacted not with a bang, but a whimper. It emerged in the shadow of Medicare, after only limited debate and discussion. The real center of controversy was the elderly, not indigent younger families. Despite the passage of the Kerr-Mills Act, the question as to whether access to medical services should be extended to the entire sixty-five and older population persisted; Medicaid was merely an afterthought.

In an ongoing effort to impede passage of a more comprehensive plan, leading health care groups, such as the AMA, the National Association of Blue Shield Plans, the Health Insurance Institute, and the American Dental Association, as well as many important Republican officials, vigorously defended the program. In some places, Kerr-Mills elicited additional support because it boosted the income of providers who had previously offered free care or services at reduced fees. In Pennsylvania, for instance, hospitals had received state subsidies of only $10 per day for indigent patients; eligible elders now brought in a daily rate of $25.[13]

For many other people, however, the program clearly did not meet the needs of the aged, a group that they increasingly touted as special, needy, and worthy. The National Council of Senior Citizens—created by the American Federation of Labor and Congress of Industrial Organizations—and other newly established senior and social welfare organizations particularly objected to the means-testing aspect of the act. At the same time, hospital costs were steadily growing, rendering it increasingly difficult for older people to pay their medical bills. Two years after the passage of Kerr-Mills, public support for a more comprehensive "Medicare" bill reached 69 percent.[14]

Congress resisted any expansions, despite initiatives by President John Kennedy, who, as part of his New Frontier domestic agenda, strongly endorsed some form of universal health insurance for the aged. Introduced as the King-Anderson bill in 1962 and again in 1964, the chief executive's Social Security–based legislation narrowly focused on certain hospital expenses and nursing home benefits, conspicuously excluding physician and other outpatient services.[15] Even so, Wilbur Mills and his powerful House Ways and Means Committee repeatedly defeated the president's proposals.

Political conditions altered, however, with the overwhelming electoral triumph in 1964 of President Lyndon Johnson, who embraced health care for the aged as part of his Great Society agenda. Wilbur Mills relented in his opposition and instead used his savvy political skills, along with Johnson's high-pressured leadership tactics, to enact a two-part Medicare program under Title XX of the 1965 amendments to the Social Security Act. Medicare Part A (a version of the King-Anderson bill), which would be supported by employer and employee payroll taxes, provides hospital and some limited nursing home care for older people covered under Social Security. Originally put forward as a Republican alternative to King-Anderson, Medicare Part B, a premium-based benefit that is partly funded by general revenues and beneficiary copayments, pays for physician and other services.[16]

Mills sculpted the legislation carefully, meeting the needs of the various provider opposition groups. The plan left many service holes that insurance companies could fill. Blue Cross and Blue Shield would have an administrative role as fiscal intermediaries. Not only would doctors be paid their "usual and customary" fees for much of what they had previously performed as charity work, but their participation in the program would be voluntary. Hospitals, too, were accommodated: they received payments for

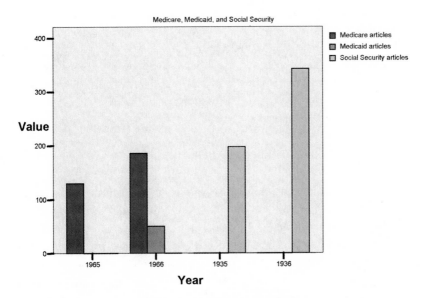

Figure 2.1. Number of *New York Times* Articles, Selected Years.

the full costs of care.[17] The legislation, based on an insurance concept, notably avoided any semblance of a "socialist" solution to health care.[18]

The third piece of what Mills labeled a "three-layer cake," Medicaid (Title X1X of the 1965 Social Security Act) was more hastily devised, emerging after only minimal debate. He developed it from an earlier scheme, Eldercare, proposed by the AMA in 1964 as part of yet another of its concerted efforts to defeat the King-Anderson bill. Mills reworked the association's original plan, an expanded Kerr-Mills program for the elderly poor, into health services for impoverished Americans in general.

Contrary to the observation that "Title X1X was signed into law on July 30, 1965, with a blaze of publicity,"[19] the evidence suggests that there was little, if any, fanfare about the Medicaid legislation. Figure 2.1 shows that Medicaid was not even mentioned in the *New York Times* throughout 1965, as compared to 130 articles on Medicare; the latter was featured in 24 front page stories and 19 editorials that year. In 1966, when Medicaid was first implemented, there were 50 articles regarding the program, as compared to 186 for Medicare. Figure 2.1 also presents comparable information for the 1935 Social Security Act. During the year of its passage, 198 articles were written about that program, with 35 on the front page and 33 presented as editorials; in the following year, the *New York Times* published 343 articles on Social Security. Consequently, few people in 1965 were fully aware of the complex nature of Medicaid, its inherent contradictions and looming controversies, or anticipated its imminent financial debacle.

Medicaid: More Than a Welfare Program?

As constructed, Medicaid was a conservative, sparse, uneven, and stigmatized program, but, as will be shown, it was potentially sweeping at the same time. It connoted dependence, relied on a demeaning and stringent means test, and, aside from the mandated groups and services, was funded only by dint of national and state officials' annual good will. Over the years, their "benevolence" was sorely challenged. In contrast, Medicare, based on the concept of social insurance, was contributory and therefore deemed a national entitlement or "right" for the working classes and eligible elderly. Its benefits were uniform and guaranteed.

Welfare medicine also preserved the status quo in that it was institutionally fragmented, continuing the well-established state-focused approach to health care that was integral to earlier programs. The federal government required five basic benefits: inpatient hospital care, excluding psychiatric assistance; outpatient hospital treatments; laboratory and X-ray work; skilled nursing home care for individuals age twenty-one and older; and physician services. States retained the power to choose the scope of services and additional ones—if any—they would provide.[20] Thus, beneficiaries could obtain only those services that were offered in their area, regardless of their actual needs.

Eligibility for the mandated categorically eligible population (families participating in Aid to Families with Dependent Children [AFDC], the aged, blind, and permanently and totally disabled) would be based on each state's welfare levels, thereby perpetuating the lopsided access to benefits across the nation.[21] States with the most impoverished populations often had the least ability or inclination to pay for such assistance. The availability and extent of services for the medically needy—defined as people who are able to pay everyday living expenses but cannot afford their health care bills—also depended on state largesse. Unless states included the medically needy option in their plan, they would receive federal reimbursement for only those individuals covered under existing public-assistance cash programs. Congress reinforced Medicaid's restricted scope by stipulating that "medically needy" households would first have to impoverish themselves by spending down their own assets and income on medical costs until they reached the state-established qualification level.

In most places, Medicaid did not include a significant percentage of the poor and near-poor populations. The program was certainly never intended to function as a catch-all system for all economically deprived people in need of health insurance.[22] By the mid-1970s, it served only about 60 percent of America's poor,[23] although some states were considerably more parsimonious than others. Eligible households often found it both difficult and humiliating to sign up for the program, further reducing the number of covered individuals.

As would be expected, there were wide variations among the states in terms of protected populations, financial eligibility levels, and access to services. To be sure, Medicaid itself fostered some of the stark disparities in the availability of services, with certain areas of the nation encountering acute shortages. According to Jonathan Engel, by relying primarily on the private sector, the program actually reduced access in certain instances: not only did patients lose much of the free care that certain physicians had offered previously, but public hospitals suffered from declining government subsidies. Because of the overall scarcity of general practitioners, mainly a by-product of AMA decisions, pressures, and interventions, foreign-educated doctors provided much of the care to welfare medicine recipients in many areas.[24] In addition, when Medicaid participants did locate a doctor, dentist, or other health professional, they often experienced poor-quality care, including assembly-line medicine.

Racism, too, played its role. Minorities experienced a shortage of black medical practitioners: such physicians and dentists represented less than 3 percent and 2 percent, respectively, of their professions. Moreover, a significant number of them earned their livelihood in middle-class and high-income suburbs. Decent hospitals and nursing homes catering to racial and ethnic minorities also were conspicuously lacking.[25]

Robert Stevens and Rosemary Stevens contend, however, that the program's most basic weakness at this time was its lack of specific goals.[26] Indeed, some conservatives saw Medicaid, together with Medicare, as a means of curtailing more comprehensive national health care. For them, welfare medicine did not represent a commitment to medical care as a basic right. To the contrary, they anticipated that because Medicare removed the "deserving" elderly population from public debate,[27] the Medicaid welfare population, along with uninsured working-class families, would be isolated and politically vulnerable. In other words, conservatives were assuming that the program's scope would be kept in check by its clients' lowly status. They failed to appreciate that other, more powerful stakeholders, such as nursing homes, hospitals, and physicians, would soon embrace the program as their own. It was inevitable that the pursuit of profits would take precedence over better ways of meeting the medical needs of the poor because Medicaid and Medicare were superimposed on the existing, sorely inadequate U.S. health care system. By keeping medical services in private hands and as free as possible from government supervision and public accountability, health care providers were given free rein.

However, the program had some far-reaching implications. Medicaid could arguably be considered an entitlement, at least to a certain degree: if the states chose to establish a program, they had to include everyone who was both income and categorically eligible (and to serve all recipients equally within each category). Without a section 1115 waiver,[28] states could not impose waiting lists or enrollment caps. They also had to treat all of their localities uniformly. Furthermore, the legislation stipulated that they had to provide sufficient services—in "amount, duration, and scope"—to accomplish a recipient's medical goals, an objective that proved unattainable.

Just as significant, the federal government offered cost-sharing dollars for a comprehensive array of services to those states that could—or chose to—avail themselves of the opportunity.[29] Congress had set rock-bottom levels for Medicaid funding, but not an upper limit; there were no federal caps on expenditures. Thus, in some states, the poor, especially children and pregnant women, had much greater access not only to the health care system than ever before, but also to a broader range of medical benefits.

Medicaid early on assumed a major role in long-term custodial services for the elderly and disabled, the politically favored groups, one of the ways it was distinguished from other welfare programs. By the end of the 1960s, a significant and growing percentage of welfare medicine outlays were spent on newly impoverished frail older people for their nursing home care. There is some debate as to whether the framers of the program intended this development. Nevertheless, over the decades, previously middle-class elders consumed a disproportionate and mounting share of program costs.

What is more, the initial legislation did attempt, albeit not entirely with success, to allow recipients opportunities to benefit from mainstream health services rather than be forced into clinics or county institutions.[30] In establishing the freedom-of-choice requirement, the 1967 amendments ostensibly gave welfare medicine participants the opportunity to select from a wide variety of providers. At least one observer argues that a major difficulty in achieving this goal can be attributed to the American public's ambivalence on the issue.[31] Other students of the subject point to the growing disparity in provider fees between the low-income health program and commercial plans. Regardless, as shown in later chapters, the barriers were—and are—systemic, inevitably generating a two-tiered system of medical care that provided separate services for poor families and better-off families. As managed-care organizations (MCOs) steadily took over state Medicaid programs during the ensuing decades, even the pretense of "choice" faded away.[32]

Finally, progressive reformers viewed Medicaid as the "camel's nose in the tent"; they would achieve piece by piece the all-inclusive coverage that they were not able to achieve in one fell swoop. The enactment of the Early and Periodic Screening, Diagnosis, and Treatment (EPSDT) Program in 1967 was encouraging in this regard: welfare medicine was extended to include preventive care for poor children, even if their parents did not qualify. However, by 1978 less than one-third of eligible youngsters were participating.[33] Liberals also took some comfort in a federal mandate requiring states to broaden their programs progressively by 1975 in order to maintain federal funding. They anticipated that all medically needy households, including the working class, would eventually be protected by a comprehensive array of health services.[34] Such optimism faded as the deadline was extended to 1977 and then eventually dropped. At any rate, by the early 1970s the future of Medicaid appeared linked to larger, federal approaches to health care. Public officials of both parties, from President Richard Nixon and New York governor Nelson Rockefeller to Senator Edward Kennedy (D–Mass.) and Representative Wilbur Mills, all agreed that Medicaid had to be replaced—with something more far-reaching it was hoped. That expectation, too, fizzled out.

Cost Shifting: Paying Welfare Medicine's Bill

From day one, there was an ongoing tug-of-war, still prevalent today, between the federal and state governments over which one would get stuck with the Medicaid bill. On the one hand, the states viewed the low-income health program as a way of garnering federal dollars; the national budget was open-ended, providing matching funds ranging from 50 to 83 percent, depending on a state's per capita income.[35] The federal government, on the other hand, continuously struggled not only to prevent the leakage, but to reverse the course. As Robert and Rosemary Stevens dryly note, some states were "smelling easy federal money under the new Title X1X . . . [and] . . . rudely jostled their way towards the Title XIX trough, to the increasing consternation of legislators and administrators in Washington."[36]

Although many state officials understood Medicaid's inherent shortcomings, they did not want to risk obstructing the influx of outside income.[37] A few states immediately set up programs, often with little or no debate, in order to be eligible for national funds as soon as possible. The deadline had been set for January 1, 1970; after that time, states without a program for their categorically eligible population would lose all prior federal grants for their indigent health services. For a number of states, the rush was on: at the end of 1966, twenty-five of them had approved programs; by October 1967, another ten had joined up.

The struggle between the national and state governments emerged immediately over such issues as substituting federal for state dollars, high income-eligibility levels, and expansive plans generally. Localities with well-entrenched, relatively generous Kerr-Mills programs plunged readily and lustily into the Medicaid largesse so as to subsidize health care for the poor with federal dollars instead of with their own money.[38] Although regulations were in place to prevent states from using national funding for any of their previously supported health services, a number of localities ignored them.[39] Certain states, such as New York and California, further capitalized on the program by adding new eligibility groups and broadening medical services measurably, thus creating sizeable welfare medicine plans that were well beyond what the framers of Title XIX had intended.[40] By the end of 1967, twenty-two states had enlarged their programs to include the medically needy, and several of them set their qualification levels sufficiently high so as to maximize the amount of federal money transferred into their treasuries.[41] Other states that had been parsimonious in their own earlier support of health care for the poor were now forced to offer a Medicaid program in order to tap the national coffers. A number of them offered services either at minimum levels or with modest expansions.[42] Sixteen states limited their programs to the welfare population but were still eager to take advantage of the federal cash.[43]

The mood soon turned more sanguine among the states that had not yet signed on as they witnessed the problematic financial experiences of the earlier programs. The temporary shut down of Medicaid in New Mexico in 1968 was particularly worrisome. Despite the hesitation, the potential monetary bonanza, along with the fear of losing federal subsidies for the health services the states already provided, eventually drew nearly all of them in. These states hopped on board more slowly and cautiously, and the poorest among them, mostly in the South, established particularly sparse programs.[44] By the end of 1969, all of the states, except Arizona and Alaska, had committed themselves to some sort of Medicaid program.[45]

Stemming the Cash Flow

As national officials watched both the states and health care providers pick the federal treasury's pocket, they became wary and almost immediately initiated measures to control spending. Cost overruns were rampant everywhere, with total Medicaid expenditures reaching more than $1.2 billion the first year, well over the estimated amount.[46] In response, Congress enacted the Social Security Amendments of 1967, which, among other goals, attempted to curb the flood of money to the states by placing a ceiling on their eligibility levels for the medically needy.[47] Several lawmakers wryly pointed out that any state could continue with the higher qualification standards by paying for the extra benefits on its own: every affected state shifted to the new, lower amounts. As a result, the number of Medicaid recipients nationwide dropped significantly, by 750,000 in 1968 and by 900,000 in 1969.[48]

The legislators sought to "encourage" cutbacks in other ways. The 1967 amendments granted states greater "flexibility" in their choice of services: instead of requiring the basic five, they could now offer any seven of the fourteen allowable ones. The legislation also introduced a new category of nursing homes, Intermediate Care Facilities (ICFs), in order to lower long-term care (LTC) payments. Several states exploited this provision by reclassifying patients who required skilled services, situating them in lower-cost intermediary institutions instead. In some cases, places that could not meet the regulatory standards, however meager, of the skilled nursing homes started calling themselves ICFs.[49]

Despite the latest amendments and other endeavors to save money, the federal share of Medicaid outlays continued to escalate, reaching $2.7 billion by 1970. Particularly uneasy about the financial implications of its mandated expansion of state programs, Congress moved the deadline for states to achieve the modifications up to 1977 and later abandoned it altogether. The incoming Richard M. Nixon administration was also concerned about the growing federal share. Viewing Medicaid as a "bottomless pit," the president recommended program cuts in his first budget proposal. The U.S. Department of Health, Education, and Welfare (HEW) also imposed a freeze and a few months later a national ceiling on fees paid to physicians and dentists.[50] Among Washington's most pressing concerns were the soaring inflation of medical services, program mismanagement among the states, client overutilization of services, fraudulent vendor payments, and a paucity of federal controls in general. Over the next several years, national officials engaged in a continuing round of task forces, special study groups, congressional hearings, reports and legislative proposals, culminating in the Social Security Amendments of 1972.

The focus was again on reducing the rush of money to the states. Among the more important changes, the legislation repealed many of the congressional mandates that had fostered, in some places, high eligibility levels and expansive programs.[51] For the first time, it also allowed "nominal" cost sharing and deductibles to be placed on the medically needy population (for all services) and the categorically eligible groups (for nonmandatory services), provided that the charges were reasonably related to the recipient's financial circumstances.[52] In implementing the amendment the following year, HEW unsuccessfully endeavored to require the states to impose a monthly income–based premium on all nonwelfare Medicaid recipients.[53]

Nevertheless, welfare medicine costs continued to spiral throughout the country. Although the United States experienced high inflation overall, health expenses—especially for hospital services—escalated even more dramatically.[54] Because of declining economic conditions, Medicaid enrollments also grew considerably.[55] The federal share of program outlays rose commensurately, reaching $16 billion at the end of the decade. Throughout the 1970s, Washington continued to grapple with ways to shut off the spigot. The Gerald R. Ford administration even attempted to cut the federal match for the most affluent states. President Jimmy Carter, focusing on limiting hospital expenses, vainly proposed the Hospital Cost Containment Act of 1977, which included a 9 percent cap on hospital outlays as well as greater use of MCOs.

By the end of the 1970s, more than 200 proposals for changes in Medicaid had been made at the national level alone, including those that would abolish the program entirely. The states, in contrast, continued to seek ways to reap a greater share of federal dollars for themselves. In some instances, they were challenged in court; at other times, they led a charge against the onslaught of new federal rules designed to slow down the flow of resources to them.

National Health Care Strikes Again

Medicaid inevitably became enmeshed in the debate over national health care, which emerged once more at the forefront of political concerns in the early 1970s. As early as 1969, New York governor Nelson Rockefeller had called for a national contributory health insurance plan as the best way out of his state's Medicaid financial mess. Numerous congressional and industry proposals emerged, ranging from the conservative AMA voluntary plan employing tax incentives to the more liberal schemes offered by Martha Griffiths (D–Mich.) and Edward Kennedy. At least twenty-two bills were on the table by 1974, all with different roles for welfare medicine.

Griffiths, for example, would substitute universal coverage for all health insurance arrangements to date. Kennedy's Health Security Act would fall back on Medicaid only as a backup for any noncovered services. Wilbur Mills proposed replacing Medicaid with uniform national coverage for low-income households, along with help for the middle-class through standardized employer plans and for the self-insured through risk pools. Nixon's Family Health Insurance Plan, designed primarily to nationalize Medicaid, included utilization controls and fewer benefits. Even President Carter had an ill-fated plan of his own, which, among other features, would federalize Medicaid and join it—at least administratively—with Medicare.

Both political parties supported national health insurance, albeit in vastly different forms, and although its implementation appeared inevitable, the schemes once again met fierce resistance from influential stakeholders.[56] Health professionals and provider groups, other business organizations, and even unions attacked one or the other offered plans. They would allow only the type of reform that would serve their own self-interests. By the 1970s, Medicaid, along with Medicare, was doing just that: as shown later, nearly every conceivable category of health care supplier already had its hands in the piggy jar. With the election of Ronald Reagan in 1980, interest in universal health insurance fizzled out.

Disillusionment

Despite the potential windfall of federal dollars, the states themselves were on guard. Even in its first year of operation, the "sleeper" program was waking up local politicians with a jolt, generating howls of protest from all quarters. Medicaid became increasingly unpopular as elected officials had to face fiscal realities, especially the need for additional state or county taxes, or both, to fund the program. They also were forced to consider the potential backlash of the working poor, many of whom had no health insurance themselves or were forced to contribute to or fully pay for their premiums.

As the number of Medicaid recipients steadily grew, demand for services rose and medical inflation soared, welfare medicine outlays exploded, siphoning off an ever-growing share of state resources. Nearly everywhere, to a greater or lesser extent, expenditures began to exceed budget estimates, with some places especially hard hit. By 1969, most of the thirty-five states that had implemented a plan either curtailed it or were considering doing so. The National Governors Association and National Conference of State Legislative Leaders were even urging the federal government to take over the full cost of the program.

In the earliest years, the states endeavored to control their Medicaid budgets without inordinately offending providers. State legislatures and governors across the nation engaged in a variety of budget-cutting strategies aimed primarily at the poor, such as lowering eligibility levels, reducing services, eliminating drug coverage, lowering permissible in-patient hospital stays, and dropping the medically needy option from their plan altogether. They eventually launched attacks on the medical establishment as well.

New York had the most expensive program in the country, dwarfing the others; it accounted for almost 37 percent of total costs nationally, followed by California (14 percent).[57] Offering all of the options allowed under Medicaid law and with no limits on the number of services, New York's plan also had one of the highest eligibility levels in the nation. Early estimates, never entirely realized, indicated that fully one-third of the population, half of them children, potentially could meet program criteria.[58] Costs grew commensurately, vastly exceeding budget estimates. From the outset, the New York State legislature attacked the program from all sides.[59] In particular, the Republican-controlled Senate, along with upstate Democratic supporters, immediately chipped away at benefits and qualifying guidelines, especially for the medically needy. Further, what was originally envisioned as a program that would cover both the welfare population and the working poor was increasingly restricted.[60] The lawmakers soon took aim at providers, although not without adversely affected groups' ongoing protests and resort to the courts to delay or block many of the initiatives.

Beginning in 1967, California, under its new governor, Ronald Reagan, attempted sharp reductions in its plan, including restrictions on the number of allowable hospital days per year. Without delay, the state was brought to court, and the cutbacks were temporarily halted. Officials watched in dismay as Medi-Cal's budget continued to soar.[61] In Michigan, too, Medicaid rapidly exceeded anticipated costs during its first year, and Governor George Romney (R) delayed full implementation of the program.[62] Even so, outlays continued to rise at alarming rates. Similarly, with expenses doubling in just two years, Massachusetts postponed a planned expansion of its program.[63] Other states followed suit during the late 1960s.[64]

Throughout the following decade, nearly all of the states—to varying degrees—experienced an ongoing fiscal crisis in their plans. In fact, Medicaid was the most rapidly escalating item in state general budgets and had become one of the largest expenditures for many of them.[65] At one time or another in the 1970s, several localities were forced to come up with supplementary annual appropriations. The states accordingly stepped up their efforts to roll back their programs. More of them restricted coverage exclusively to the welfare population and reduced discretionary services. In 1975 alone, twenty states lowered benefits or decreased the number of recipients.[66] By the mid-1970s, only twenty-seven jurisdictions included the medically needy, and only New York and Minnesota offered all of the options allowed under federal Medicaid law.[67] The financial situation in the states had become so desperate that in 1976 the National Governors Conference set up the Medicaid Task Force, describing welfare medicine as one of the states' highest priorities. Among other proposals, they sought to limit recipients' choice of providers and to add copayments, without the need for federal waivers.[68]

State policymakers continued to target beneficiaries but now appreciably enlarged their assault on providers as well. They imposed new reimbursement mechanisms or cut fees outright and, as shown later, began challenging financially fraudulent activities more forcefully. Nearly all of these actions were counterattacked—usually successfully—by various provider groups, workers, and even welfare organizations.[69] A few states resorted to experimenting with managed-care models by applying for section 1915(b) waivers; it allowed them to put aside Medicaid's freedom-of-choice requirement, thereby limiting an individual's right to select his or her provider.[70]

Regardless of their approach for controlling program costs, the states continued to face an ever-growing pool of eligible people, mostly due to high unemployment, expanding welfare rolls, and other adverse conditions in the larger economic realm. Indeed, the number of people on AFDC nationally increased by nearly 9 percent annually throughout the 1970s.[71] Medicaid grew commensurately, from 4 million people in 1966 to more than 22 million by 1980. Costs rose even more dramatically than enrollment, mostly because of soaring medical inflation. Greater use of the low-income health program to pay for LTC and ever-expanding provider profiteering, as discussed later, also contributed to the states' financial woes.

Reimbursement and Provider Participation

The Status of Hospitals

Reimbursement policies have raised some of the main dilemmas and challenges of Medicaid. Public officials had to figure out how to set rational and reasonable rates without discouraging provider participation. For hospitals,[72] the original legislation mandated a cost-based formula, with the rates set to those of Medicare: they would be reimbursed for all of their expenses, including capital costs, lobbying, and professional association dues. The upshot was that Medicaid was forced to pay for just about anything the hospitals insisted on.[73] As a result, not only was hospital participation assured, but the institutions benefited by a guaranteed, steady flow of cash and a substantial lowering of their charity-care expenditures.

Private hospitals profited handsomely in the wake of Medicare and Medicaid, generating an accelerating expansion of for-profit institutions—especially chains—along with a twenty-year building and spending spree, inflated costs, and a glut in beds.[74] Outlays for hospitalization became the fastest-growing item in the low-income health program; between 1970 and 1980, spending on hospital services increased nearly 14 percent annually.[75] Alarmed, the 1976 governors' Medicaid Task Force proposed a fee schedule, set by the federal government. Congress eventually settled on a "reasonable cost" standard that would be determined by the states. During the 1980s, states implemented a variety of methods for achieving this criterion, including negotiated rates, capped budgets, and average patient formulas.

Government health care establishments, in contrast, consisted of a limited number of poorly subsidized community hospitals, clinics, and rehabilitation centers as well as certain national institutions for war veterans. Many cities—including New York, Baltimore, Washington, D.C., and Chicago—had large, entrenched municipal hospitals, most of which included outpatient health centers. Such places were funded primarily by local and county governments as well as by various philanthropic organizations. After the enactment of Medicaid, these facilities, which were already second rate, had to compete with proprietary institutions for public-sector dollars. As a result, they became increasingly overcrowded and understaffed, drawing from the least-trained and experienced doctors and nurses. Medicaid also substantially curbed the free care previously provided by a number of private hospitals; program recipients, viewed initially as paying customers, now added to the "bottom line."[76]

Nonetheless, as hospital expenditures continued to escalate, and states reacted by reducing their Medicaid reimbursement rates, the situation began to alter. In New York City, as hospital fees were lowered, many private institutions began turning Medicaid patients away. Not only did municipal facilities have to pick up the slack, but many of the private places actually began referring the poor to them.[77] In California, which had turned its extensive county hospitals into a state-run system, Medicaid recipients were given access to hospitals of their choice, both private and public. As a result, they increasingly avoided county institutions, leaving them underutilized; however, welfare medicine patients were now encountering overcrowded conditions in privately run institutions.[78] In contrast, rural states faced a paucity of both private and public hospitals.[79] Capitalizing on Medicaid money, some of these jurisdictions began establishing county hospitals and community clinics. By the end of the 1970s, public hospitals and health centers were providing 20 percent of all Medicaid services nationwide and more than 40 percent of charity treatments.[80]

Physicians, Dentists, and Other Professional Providers

The problem of participation by other types of providers, sufficient to ensure adequate access to health services, loomed large, both then and today. Questions about optimum reimbursement levels raised additional questions: Do the poor "deserve" mainstream health services, and if so, how can such standards be achieved without costs running out of control? Because states were given the power to set their own reimbursement formulas for physicians,[81] dentists, and other professionals, they had to deal with these quandaries on their own. The approaches varied widely: in California, for instance, doctors received their "usual and customary" fees, whereas New York paid them and dentists based on a fee schedule. By the mid-1970s, more and more states imposed fee schedules and at increasingly lower amounts relative to the private sector.

Jurisdictions with the highest payments to medical professionals predictably had fewer participation problems but faced the heaviest outlays. In places with more austere compensation and thus limited physician (or dentist) involvement, recipients were often forced into high-priced hospital emergency rooms, poorly funded government health centers, or substandard private medical practices. Many families simply went without medical services entirely. Moreover, because physicians everywhere received their "usual and customary" fees under Medicare, they were especially reluctant to serve welfare medicine clients in places where reimbursement rates were substantially lower.

New York is a case in point. Lawmakers were particularly challenged in their approach to physician fees because they had to balance recipients' health care needs, physicians' demands, and public costs. Significantly, the state faced a serious shortage of Medicaid-participating doctors. Diminishing numbers of physicians and dentists—about 8 percent and 5 percent, respectively—were now serving the bulk of welfare medicine patients, especially in the poorest neighborhoods. Some of these providers, lured by the easy money, offered perfunctory care through unlicensed and unregulated clinics, known as "Medicaid mills," which proliferated during the 1970s.[82] Composed of three or more types of medical practitioners, who shared equipment and buildings, these medical practices tended to be unsavory places.[83] Because of low physician participation in welfare medicine, patients often had no place else to go for care, though. More conventional physicians not only contested what they viewed as inadequate compensation for their services, but also were opposed to the audits, the paperwork, slow reimbursements, controls over utilization, and the program as a whole, which they viewed as "socialized medicine." Over the years, New York officials, who continued to encounter fierce opposition from physicians and dentists over Medicaid reimbursement rates, had to cope with an ongoing shortage of health professionals who would participate in the program.

The Burgeoning Nursing Home Industry

Medicaid was instrumental in the explosive growth of nursing homes throughout the nation, and the industry soon became dependent on the program for the bulk of its income. Initially subsidized by the Medical Assistance Program under Kerr-Mills, which had no maximum federal assistance to the states for institutional care, commercial LTC interests received an even greater financial boost through the new welfare medicine plan; it even financed the construction of new facilities. The number of institutions grew rapidly, in particular those established by for-profit companies.[84] Such places served nearly all of the LTC needs of chronically ill older Medicaid participants, especially the medically needy. Throughout the first two decades of Medicaid, nursing home care remained the primary alternative for them. For the most part, both the frail elderly and disabled younger people depended on relatives or had to pay privately for any home care services they required.[85] In addition, residents of state mental hospitals, whose care was financed through state and local budgets, were released en masse during the 1970s so as to take advantage of federal welfare medicine dollars. Many of them were shunted into Medicaid-subsidized nursing homes.[86]

When Medicaid was first launched, most states paid a flat per diem rate. But because this payment scheme apparently was fostering scandalous cutbacks in patient services, in 1972 Congress required states to adopt a "cost plus" method of reimbursement within four years.[87] Nursing home owners consequently changed tactics: to keep the money flowing their way, they generated ever-increasing expenses.[88] LTC Medicaid outlays spiraled. By 1970, nursing homes represented fully 30 percent of total program spending nationally. Concerned about the rising welfare medicine budget, President Nixon attempted but failed to decrease the federal share of these costly facilities. Outlays continued to climb steadily, reaching slightly more than 40 percent of the Medicaid budget by the end of the 1970s.

The Powerful Stakeholders

Researchers early on underestimated the structure of support for welfare medicine because its recipients were the defenseless poor; such observers tended to view Medicare, which serves the elderly, as the more politically powerful of the two programs. Nonetheless, both government plans have always relied on the private sector to supply services and administer payments, mostly paid for by the public treasury, and are subject to similar pressures by their commercial stakeholders. These various interests were either already highly organized prior to 1965 or quickly formed new associations.

Many of these groups have been formidable forces, especially at the state and local levels. From the start, they developed cozy relationships with public officials and regulatory bodies[89] and vigorously lobbied legislators with their vast resources and clout. These prominent and politically connected groups donated generously to candidates at all levels of government.[90] Providers sometimes wielded enormous political power not only as part of their professional associations, but also as individuals. In a few instances, leading public officials themselves owned nursing homes in their states.[91]

When stakeholders' will was thwarted, they frequently resorted to the judicial system, which by the early 1970s was playing a vital role in preventing states' initiatives to control costs. With their considerable resources, these stakeholders could tie up legislative action in court for long periods; administrative hearings and appeals sometimes took years.[92] When all else failed, organized interests effectively utilized boycotts, often justifying their self-seeking actions by invoking the needs of the poor. At times, certain groups threatened to leave the program altogether, stranding vulnerable recipients who desperately required services.[93] Their power was bolstered in some areas by a dearth of providers, such as physicians and especially specialists.[94] In most places, nursing home beds, too, were in short supply. Because state policymakers viewed themselves and their Medicaid programs as dependent on providers' good will, they were anxious not to antagonize health professionals and industry groups, whenever feasible. The national and state governments treaded lightly when faced with industry ultimatums.

Established health care interests have thus clearly wielded considerable power over welfare medicine policies from the start, thwarting most efforts made to control them. In addition, Medicaid generated new power relationships within the states, unlikely alliances that bolstered support for a wide range of often mutually self-serving enterprises. These partnerships often included organizations representing the poor.[95] They were sometimes joined by unionized workers, especially those employed in hospitals and nursing homes, as well as by associations for the elderly. These ad hoc coalitions, which emerged in the earliest years, have surfaced regularly in the twenty-first century.[96]

Combating Fraud

Emerging National Concerns

Financial fraud across the nation plagued Medicaid from the start. Reaching back to 1967, newspapers were regularly reporting overcharging and other malfeasance by providers, including physicians, nursing homes, dentists, clinical labs, hospitals, and factoring companies. Congress, too, especially the House Ways and Means Committee, confronted ongoing complaints about profiteering. However, HEW proved to be both weak and ineffectual in dealing with it. Unlike the agency's Medicare division, which at least had a limited auditing staff, its Medicaid section had no investigative unit until 1976 and only one part-time inspector. Understaffed in both its national and its regional offices and with few federal regulations, it could not provide sufficient program oversight. As a result, the agency left such control over Medicaid primarily to the states.

After the enactment of the 1967 amendments, and as costs continued to escalate beyond expectations, more attention was paid to regulating the program. HEW, Congress, and the Nixon administration began addressing fraudulent practices more seriously, focusing on both providers and recipients. Overutilization of services developed into a national rallying cry, allowing political leaders to place at least part of the blame for cost overruns on the beneficiaries themselves.[97] As a result, prior authorization for procedures and other types of control over service consumption became central to national fraud-control endeavors.[98]

Physicians, who were targeted by the national government as one of the primary scoundrels, also became a center of attention.[99] Beginning in the late 1960s, the Senate Finance Committee and the U.S. Government Accounting Office (now the Government Accountability Office) began taking serious stock of physicians' behavior. They documented the prevalence of a wide range of illicit activities, including extraordinary earnings among some practitioners;[100] kickback arrangements involving nursing homes, doctors, and drug suppliers; duplicate payments; excessive rates and fees; unwarranted prescriptions; other erroneous charges; and overutilization of services. It became clear that Medicaid fraud had become deeply embedded in a number of physician practices.[101]

By the mid-1970s, the scandals had become even more commonplace: newspapers everywhere were reporting more or less weekly accounts of financial exploitation among all types of providers, from clinical labs to neighborhood pharmacies. A series of hearings ensued in both chambers of Congress, which exposed further abuses.[102] The Senate took an especially aggressive role in pursuing Medicaid fraud. One of the more influential investigations was undertaken by Senator Frank Moss (D–Utah), chair of a subcommittee of the Senate Special Committee on Aging. Posing as

Medicaid patients in eight major cities, the senator and his six aides found profiteering Medicaid mills, involving doctors, dentists, optometrists, and chiropractors, to be commonplace in the low-income areas visited. They uncovered rampant fraud among Medicaid staff and health officials as well.[103] MCOs were not exempt from deceitful activities : headed by Senator Henry Jackson (D–Wash.), the Senate's Permanent Subcommittee on Investigations began examining California's prepaid plans, finding that less than one-half of its welfare medicine allocations actually aided patients; the rest of the money funded a variety of nonmedical items benefiting the insurance companies. It also determined that the companies' net profits reached as high as 33 percent.[104]

Vastly underestimating the profiteering, HEW had initially approximated fraud and "errors" at about 1 percent of total Medicaid costs. As the deceptions became more exposed, the agency was forced to raise its calculation steadily. Acknowledging in 1976 that criminal misconduct might be responsible for about 5 percent of total outlays, the agency had to revise the figure upward to 9 percent the following year.[105] Others speculated that as much as 25 percent of total welfare medicine outlays were lost on financial fraud, "mistakes," and poor-quality care.[106] Public officials clearly still were not sure of the full magnitude of the problem.

Few prosecutions or convictions were carried out prior to the mid-1970s. Under federal law, Medicaid (and Medicare) fraud constituted a misdemeanor rather than a felony. At best, when providers were found guilty of cheating the system, they had to return the ill-gotten gains.[107] In 1977, however, Congress enacted the Medicare-Medicaid Anti-fraud and Abuse Amendments, after several earlier attempts had failed. The legislation made fraud in the government health care programs a felony, established both a special national office of investigations and the Office of Inspector General (OIG), and mandated Medicaid antifraud control units in each of the states to investigate and prosecute Medicaid offenses.[108]

Designating Medicaid fraud as a top priority, HEW secretary Joseph Califano—under President Carter—assembled his new office of investigations, adding additional staff.[109] For the remainder of the decade, scandals and probes were ubiquitous. The most prominent investigation by the newly created OIG, Project Integrity, began phase one by concentrating on dishonest doctors and pharmacists. Winding up these activities in 1978, the OIG next targeted (phase two) dentists and laboratories, the latter notorious for the clinical lab scandals of 1976.[110] However, the mission resulted in relatively few convictions, sanctions, or even substantial restitutions.[111] Phase three did not become fully operational until 1980, at which time the agency's investigative staff honed in on nursing homes, home health agencies, and especially hospitals.[112] Overall, Project Integrity revealed that the large industrial states did not have a monopoly on financial fraud, but that it was pervasive throughout the United States. As costs continued to soar and federal officials increasingly viewed crackdowns on Medicaid fraud as a vital means of controlling outlays, they began pressing the states to take a tougher stand against program theft.[113]

The States Weigh In

California was home to some of the earliest reports of widespread illegal activities, and almost all providers were assailed. In 1968, the state had announced a massive investigation of doctors, pharmacists, and nursing homes.[114] Investigations by other states soon followed, each one unearthing massive egregious practices.[115] Nevertheless, although acknowledging that Medicaid was financially exploited by nearly everyone involved with the program, most states did not provide the resources (money, equipment, or personnel) to monitor the program effectively.

As federal investigative activities picked up nationwide, some of the states began beefing up their own staff and conducting more audits. In 1975 and 1976 alone, ongoing inquiries took place in New York, California, Minnesota, Florida, Illinois, Georgia, New Jersey, Michigan, and Massachusetts, all focusing on ways in which both providers and clients were bilking Medicaid. More providers were accordingly taken to court, although the total remained relatively small.[116]

As in other places, Medicaid fraud had become a central concern to New York politicians, who approximated program losses at between 10 and 20 percent of expenditures.[117] The legislature, which in 1971 had created the Inspector General Office to root out AFDC cheaters, soon turned its attention to Medicaid. As at the national level and in several other states, New York officials persisted in inveighing against dishonest welfare medicine recipients, but they also began pursuing contractors, especially hospitals: by the mid-1970s, there were five separate investigations.[118] New York City, which embarked on its own inquiries, found widespread improprieties by nearly all Medicaid providers. Particular attention was paid to the rapidly spreading Medicaid mills that not only engaged in deplorable and shoddy treatment of patients, but also kept poor—or no—records of services rendered; many of them were sham organizations.

National, state, and local officials, to greater or lesser extents, went on the offensive with increasing vigor against both recipients and providers whom they viewed as preying on the welfare medicine program. The panoply of congressional and state hearings and investigations, legislative mandates, new and revised regulations, improved and expanded agencies, and staff and newspaper disclosures was ultimately dwarfed by the enormity of the problem. And in some places, the antifraud activities amounted to little more than blustering by elected officials. By the end of the 1970s, the pilfering of Medicaid funds continued unabated and had possibly even worsened.

The Nursing Home Profiteers

Nursing homes arguably manipulated the system the most but received the least oversight. Indeed, the free flow of public money had encouraged investment in extended care facilities by real estate firms, insurance companies, and others outside the health field. A Medicaid-inspired building and stock-market boom led to ever-increasing financial returns, sometimes reaching 40 percent or higher.[119] Regional and national chains emerged and prospered by the late 1960s, although a number of them overextended themselves.[120] By 1979, from 25 to 30 percent of all beds were owned by chains.

These Medicaid-subsidized nursing homes were mired in a morass of tangled real estate transactions: proprietors would sell their properties to a corporation, often owned by themselves or a relative, and then lease them back or purchase services from the new company at higher prices. Many operators became wealthy simply by selling nursing homes back and forth among themselves to inflate their value or, in some cases, to reduce certain taxes.[121] Sophisticated real estate machinations and subcontracting deals allowed the owners to conceal profits and avoid taxes.[122] Conglomerates also set up wholly owned subsidiaries to provide services to the homes: they constructed buildings, sold pharmaceutical supplies, and furnished food and the like on a noncompetitive basis at elevated prices—the profit then became a cost to the home and was thus reimbursed by the government.

Nursing home proprietors also enriched themselves through payoffs and kickbacks from their contractors.[123] Over the next several decades, such unethical manipulation of the program not only became more complex, but intensified.

For the most part, understaffed and poorly funded agencies did not have the resources—or in many cases the political will—to pursue illegal nursing home activities aggressively.[124] Contending that they could not meet the high cost of hiring enough auditors to survey each and every home meticulously, the states continued to provide only slipshod inspections at best.[125] For example, New York, which began to inspect its facilities in 1971, did not seriously scrutinize industry crimes until a few years later.[126] The *New York Times* initiated its own two-month probe in 1974, uncovering extensive profiteering, kickbacks, nepotism, phony bills, staff shortages, patient abuse, and neglect.[127] To be sure, a significant number of facility owners in New York and the surrounding region was associated with criminals and thugs, some of whom were protected through their political connections.[128] Nonetheless, as late as 1975 no nursing home operator in the state had been taken to court for Medicaid fraud. That year, a special state prosecutor began tracking the industry's criminal practices, including secret syndicates of nursing home ownership.[129] He audited nearly all of the facilities, but despite discovering unlawful behavior in each and every one of them, as in other states, he indicted or convicted relatively few perpetrators.[130] On the whole, policymakers' antifraud activities nationwide were not sufficiently far-reaching to put even a dent into the nursing home industry's illegal behavior. As chapter 9 shows, they would prove equally deficient in the decades ahead.

Quality of Care

As unease over exploding Medicaid costs grew, increasingly attributed to wrongdoings among providers and recipients alike, any concern regarding quality of care was relegated to a secondary status. At the same time, because of the severe shortage of available health professionals, nursing homes, and hospitals, Medicaid participants could not take full advantage of the "free-choice" federal principle that allowed them to select their own provider. In some rural and urban areas, certain services were not available at all. In effect, the dual system of care for the indigent and better-off families, prevalent prior to Medicaid, not only continued but was reinforced under the program.

Just as important, the vital linkages between financial and patient abuse were for the most part ignored from the start. A substantial number of health providers not only raided Medicaid, but also mistreated and neglected their clients. Among other injurious practices, they subjected recipients to improper testing, medical services performed by unlicensed and untrained personnel, dangerous overuse of certain procedures and tests, and shortfalls in pill counts, sometimes at great risk to patients' lives. In some jurisdictions, physicians, dentists, and other professionals were seeing as many as 100 patients daily and not providing even minimal care. The inextricable connection between financial misdeeds and substandard services was clearly evident in the situation of nursing home residents. Unlike for Medicare, requirements for Medicaid-funded facilities were left largely to the states, which tended to be more concerned with financial fraud than with patient needs. There were not even basic national standards against which to measure the homes.

Congress was eventually jolted into action in 1970, following a series of fires and salmonella poisoning that took the lives of a number of residents across the nation. Senate hearings held that year indicated just how lax federal and state regulations and inspections were. They also revealed the extreme shortages of nurses and aides everywhere.[131] Similarly, Representative David Pryor (D–Ark.) investigated several facilities with his staff, disguising themselves as volunteers.[132] Despite findings of sorely inadequate conditions, including hunger and squalor, inhumane care, and an appalling lack of services, national legislators chose to limit their attention mostly to bricks and mortar. They set criteria for fire resistance and corridor widths (to allow greater removal of people in wheelchairs during an emergency), along with a few other health and safety features, as part of the federal life-safety code. Furthermore, skilled nursing homes now had to have at least one registered nurse on duty. In reality, few facilities could fulfill even these minimum requirements. Any attempt by HEW to force them to do so set off a wave of successful litigation by the nursing home industry. State officials' implementation of the rules was perfunctory, anyway.[133] As a result, most Medicaid-certified homes persisted in their failure to comply with basic federal safety regulations.[134]

Local policymakers also proved reluctant to enact regulations or impose sanctions that would improve patient care. In places where there were acute bed shortages, officials were particularly unwilling to take on the industry.[135] Even where there were egregious conditions, they would not shut down a facility because its inhabitants had no other place to live.[136] Thus, the owners could hold elected leaders hostage because "throwing old people out of nursing homes was scarcely politically acceptable, unless organized alternatives were available—and they were not."[137] Burdensome court procedures proved an ongoing obstacle as well: inspectors and prosecutors recognized that it could take three to five years of litigation to close down a facility—and even that seldom happened. Across the nation, as with other provider organizations, nursing homes used the courts effectively against any attempt to improve the dire situation of their welfare medicine clients.[138] Medicaid-subsidized nursing home residents, who generally lived in the worst facilities, thus continued to experience substantial and extensive care problems.

Conclusion: Emerging Questions

Medicaid was enacted not with a bang, but a whimper: emerging in Medicare's shadow, it soon loomed large as a political issue. From the start, escalating costs became the primary focus of public debate, dwarfing concerns over beneficiaries' needs and rights. Cost shifting became a central pursuit as governments at all levels endeavored to provide welfare medicine to their constituents at someone else's expense. States chased ever greater shares of federal dollars, while the central government in turn grappled with ways to hand more of the Medicaid bill over to them. Private institutions vied with public facilities, and states contended with each other, all struggling over who ultimately would have to pick up the check.

Although opposed to the program at the outset, providers nevertheless immediately helped themselves to the Medicaid largesse. They developed into powerful stakeholders as many of them increasingly became dependent on welfare medicine for financial gains. The program also facilitated the steady growth of profit-making facilities and chains, especially in the nursing home and hospital industries. Fraud was prevalent everywhere, from physicians, dentists, and pharmacists to transportation companies and institutional facilities—all contributing to the swelling Medicaid budget.

In desperate efforts to control expenditures, the states first targeted beneficiaries, seeking to limit eligibility and reduce the array of benefits. They soon expanded their attacks to include providers, limiting their reimbursement levels and eventually investigating illicit activities, albeit without much force. Hospitals, physicians, dentists, pharmacists, nursing home proprietors, and other suppliers vigorously and effectively fought back through the courts, boycotts, alliances, lobbying, campaign contributions, and the like, often holding Medicaid hostage to their ultimatums. These powerful groups held their ground, unfailingly insisting on more money while decrying the program's failure to meet their persistent demands.

Quality of care was questionable from the start. Medicaid mills proliferated in urban areas around the nation, providing perfunctory and sometimes unnecessary physician and dental services that jeopardized client health and well-being. A substantial number of nursing homes, although collecting nearly half of their income from the public treasury, neglected and mistreated their frail residents. Among all types of vendors, Medicaid financial abuse was associated with substandard services. At the same time, in many areas of the country beneficiaries were facing an inadequate supply of medical professionals and LTC beds. Despite the initial goal to provide mainstream medicine to America's poor, Medicaid in reality perpetuated our two-tiered medical system.

Throughout these early years, the program was attacked from all sides. Liberal reformers were disappointed in its low coverage, but especially in the failure to spark universal health care. Conservatives lambasted the mounting dollars devoted to welfare medicine. Providers railed at what they viewed as sorely inadequate fees, and unions joined industry groups in demanding greater compensation. Recipient groups decried inadequate access to providers and low-quality care. The working class, resenting tax obligations for benefits that they themselves often lacked, also disapproved of the program.

The 1960s and 1970s set the stage for nearly every thorny question that reared its head during the following decades. To a large extent, the problems stemmed from the underlying structure of the program itself, which, among other factors, sustained and in some cases worsened inequalities among the states; relied on a demeaning means test; induced impoverishment as a basis of eligibility, especially for the medically needy; lacked national goals, financing, coherence, and accountability; depended on the private for-profit sector for services; and avoided a social insurance financing scheme. Superimposed on an already inequitable health care system that placed profits over patient care, Medicaid sustained and at times exacerbated many of the system's inherent flaws. Regardless, it offered vital and sometimes life-saving medical services to many indigent families and elders that they would not have obtained otherwise.

3

FROM REAGAN TO CLINTON:
THE LOW-INCOME HEALTH
PROGRAM ON TRIAL

Over the next two decades, Medicaid cycled between campaigns to restrict the program and struggles to enhance it. Presidential hostility in the 1980s was met with congressional support. During the 1990s, the situation was reversed: the chief executive fought to strengthen welfare medicine, whereas majority-party legislative leaders aimed to dismantle it. In these twenty years, the program experienced a succession of cuts for some groups and expansions for others. To varying extents, however, all national officials sought to lower total program expenditures both by reigning in federal grants to the states and by giving them greater control over their plans. As I argue in this chapter, the localities characteristically responded with schemes to maximize their federal dollars. Given the multiple financial constraints at the local level, which are exacerbated during hard economic times, greater policy devolution concomitantly fostered cost-saving measures that have weakened client rights and access to services, but, as in prior times, ultimately failed to control escalating program outlays.

Welfare Medicine on the Defensive

Ronald Reagan, intent on curbing social programs in the United States, immediately set his sights on Medicaid, especially the national government's share of the outlays.[1] However, although the president was generally successful in his efforts aimed at the poor, he failed to cut back welfare medicine materially. As with programs designed primarily for the white middle class, such as Social Security and Medicare,[2] the low-income health program proved politically resilient. The White House particularly could not achieve one of the primary goals under its "new federalism" approach to social welfare, the conversion of Medicaid into block grants to the states, which would have terminated the program as an entitlement and imposed federal spending caps.[3] The objectives were to shift a larger portion of Medicaid expenditures to the states, forcing them to scale down their plans; keep eligibility and benefits contained through predetermined program costs; lessen national regulations; and ultimately abolish welfare medicine as a basic "right."

Reagan had persuaded Congress, under the Omnibus Budget Reconciliation Act (OBRA) of 1981, to combine seventy-six different categorical programs into nine block grants, accompanied by a more than 15 percent reduction in their combined funding levels. By substantially downsizing a variety of social services, this act was the most far-reaching assault on low-income people in decades.[4] Since that time, these public benefits have experienced considerable legitimacy issues. The president could not, however, broaden the scope of these consolidations—and severe cuts—to include welfare medicine because of forceful bipartisan congressional and gubernatorial resistance.[5] Instead, the legislators agreed to a temporary, lesser decrease in the federal match in exchange for greater state autonomy and flexibility over their programs.[6]

Throughout his presidency, Reagan continued to press for greater limits on federal obligations for the low-income health care program, along with a variety of "swap" schemes involving other welfare benefits, but did not succeed.[7] Faced with intense opposition, especially from state policymakers, none of his exchange plans was ever seriously considered by Congress. The governors, demanding that the national government pay a larger share of their Medicaid costs, were particularly unwilling to shoulder any greater burdens for other social welfare programs.

The George H. W. Bush administration did not fare any better at paring down welfare medicine outlays. Bush unsuccessfully urged Congress to impose caps on the growth of entitlements, including Medicaid, and considered the idea of Medicaid block grants, but quickly abandoned that suggestion as politically unrealistic. The new president particularly encouraged privatization measures, including an abortive proposal that would have permitted recipients to buy coverage in the private market at public expense if it proved less costly than Medicaid.[8] However, his main thrust was to crack down on the states' increasing maneuvers to maximize their national share of program funding. All told, despite the ongoing presidential attacks on welfare medicine in the 1980s, the program not only remained intact, but continued to grow.

Congress, Mandates, and Expansionary Politics

Although Congress, too, was concerned about what it viewed as unconstrained Medicaid outlays, it did not place any limits on the program's overall growth. To the contrary, beginning in the mid-1980s national policymakers approved a series of gradual, targeted expansions aimed primarily at older people, pregnant women, and young children.[9] Despite opposition from the Reagan and Bush administrations as well as a large number of congressional Republicans, Democratic leaders were quietly able to permit and later often require the states to expand Medicaid to these groups by using an array of hidden legislative maneuvers and deals, including slipping in certain provisions through the congressional budget reconciliation process; the mandated coverage of all pregnant women receiving welfare merely squeaked by in conference committee.[10] Many of the changes, however, also had the effect of gradually severing Medicaid eligibility from Aid to Families with Dependent Children (AFDC) qualifications, chipping away at welfare medicine's entitlement status.[11] What is more, the incremental expansion of Medicaid occurred during a period of fiscal austerity and declining resources for social programs overall, forcing affected groups to fight over a shrinking pie.[12]

The legislature also enlarged the Early and Periodic Screening, Diagnosis, and Treatment (EPSDT) Program, despite a concerted attempt by the Reagan administration to jettison it.[13] Dating back to the late 1960s, the EPSDT Program had mandated preventive medical services for children, including a complete physical examination. Now, under OBRA 1989, federal policymakers directed the states to boost their EPSDT enrollments[14] and pay for any necessary follow-up treatments, even if such care was not covered under their Medicaid plan.[15] The states also had to set reimbursement rates for health professionals high enough so that children participating in the low-income health program would have access to medical services similar to those of youngsters whose family could afford to pay privately. Indeed, a few states were taken to court for not meeting one or more of these provisions.[16]

Health services for low-income pregnant women, infants, and children were supported by a large number of policymakers who viewed such an inexpensive broadening of coverage as cost effective: it would prevent larger medical expenditures in the coming decades as well as foster a healthier population and more vigorous future workforce.[17] Youngsters and expectant mothers' greater participation in welfare medicine also was endorsed by a broad coalition of groups, each with its own, often self-interested financial motives. The powerful Children's Medicaid Coalition, for example, consisted of advocates for children, labor unions, business organizations, health insurance associations, and a variety of professional health groups, and it lobbied dynamically and effectively for OBRA 1990, which ordered the states to expand Medicaid to all indigent children up to age eighteen by 2002.[18] In addition, supporters of older people were instrumental in fostering a succession of buy-in legislation, beginning in 1986, aimed at protecting low-income elders (dual eligibles) from some of the burdens of Medicare's premiums, copayments, and deductibles.[19]

Partly as a result of these expansionary measures, welfare medicine enrollments climbed perceptibly, alarming governors and state legislators of both parties.[20] However, other factors were at work in fostering the rising numbers of participants, including high unemployment generated by the recession, growing poverty, the mounting AIDS epidemic, the 1990 Supreme Court decision in *Sullivan v. Zebley*, requiring retroactive determination of Medicaid eligibility to 1980 for disabled children, and especially an enlargement in the number of blind and disabled participants covered under Supplemental Security Income (SSI), encouraged by advocacy groups.[21] Medicaid coverage of the adult welfare population did not expand, though, and the percentage of these beneficiaries actually dropped relative to the number of people living in poverty.[22]

Medicaid outlays were increasing not only because of swelling case loads. The nation also was experiencing an aging of the population and a subsequent demand for high-priced nursing home care. Double-digit medical inflation, set in motion during the 1970s, was a factor as well.[23] Welfare medicine costs—which had grown about 10 percent annually during the first half of the decade, more slowly than Medicare and private insurance—escalated in the late 1980s, averaging about 21 percent per annum between 1988 and 1995.[24] The low-income health program was consequently absorbing a growing share of the federal budget, reaching 5.9 percent of the total that year.[25]

Devolution: Fiscal Crisis in the States

As part of its "new federalism," the Reagan administration sought to cut Medicaid costs through a determined advocacy of "states rights." Since the early years of the American Republic, such a stance has generally been used to obscure other, more problematic objectives. In this instance, under the guise of greater "autonomy" and "flexibility," the states not only lost some federal money, but also received permission to disregard a number of national policies, regulations, and safeguards currently in place. Local officials simultaneously had to contend with the new expansionist congressional mandates—and administrative rules—that threatened to increase their Medicaid costs even further.

Most important, by 1988 the national economic situation had seriously deteriorated—similar to the recession a decade earlier—again demonstrating one of the greatest weaknesses of the Medicaid program. In times of financial stress, particularly when unemployment is high, enrollments inevitably expand, but at the same time state tax revenues plunge. Thus, local policymakers have the least money to pay for welfare medicine plans when their residents need benefits the most. Along with these events, a growing antipathy toward new taxes, perpetuated in part by the Reagan administration itself, compounded the budgetary problems. Indeed, voter initiatives, such as those in California, Massachusetts, and Oregon, either had cut taxes or restricted expenditures. Furthermore, in many places court judgments had forced legislators to increase their funding for mental health programs, prisons, and education for disadvantaged populations.[26]

The growth in the states' own-source dollars predictably declined relative to their obligations, and in a growing number of jurisdictions the shortages were significant, especially in 1991 and 1992.[27] In the latter year, the level of "overspending" in seventeen states, largely blamed on welfare medicine, was nearly 10 percent of their budgets.[28] As early as 1981, Medicaid had emerged as the fastest-growing program in many states. Over the course of the decade, it consumed a steadily increasing share of funding from their own revenue sources, reaching an average of 12 percent by 1993.[29] Including federal and other funding, the low-income health plan represented about 17 percent of their aggregate annual outlays.[30] In many places, welfare medicine had become the second-costliest program.

The states' greater "independence," along with their enhanced welfare medicine enrollments, recent national directives, federal cuts, and especially the economic downturn, would translate into efforts to devise alternative, less-expensive ways of serving clients, to control both provider and consumer utilization rates, to restrain reimbursements, and to trim down or eliminate optional services. With unique Medicaid plans, histories, tax bases, cultural and ideological attitudes, resources, political composition, and the like, each of the states struggled independently—and distinctively—in dealing with climbing welfare medicine outlays.

Similar to the 1970s but now with even greater license—and with increasing urgency by the early 1990s—nearly every state revamped its Medicaid plan to a certain extent. Many took advantage of the section 1115 waiver that allowed them to offer benefits to specific geographic areas or to target selected Medicaid-eligible groups. At Reagan's urging, states were encouraged to devise alternative ways of paying for and delivering services by applying for freedom-of-choice (section 1915[b]) waivers as well, thereby ushering in more experiments with or expansions of prepaid, market-based plans. Although several states had sponsored managed-care organizations (MCOs) during the 1970s, reaching 6 percent of the Medicaid population nationwide by 1976, total enrollments actually declined to less than 2 percent by the time of Reagan's election; only five states—California, Maryland, Michigan, Utah, and Oregon—had signed up more than 5 percent of their caseloads, and even in these places such coverage was minimal.[31]

In 1982, under the authority of a section 1115 waiver, Arizona launched the first and only Medicaid program that mandated managed care statewide.[32] To a lesser extent, other states began testing greater use of voluntary enrollment in various types of capitated plans during the ensuing years; by the early 1990s, at least some of the Medicaid beneficiaries in each state, except Alaska, was served through these plans. Moreover, with section 1915(b) waivers in hand, about 20 percent of the states tentatively moved toward forcing a small portion of their beneficiaries to rely on such arrangements for their health services.[33]

Also with the goal of saving money, under OBRA 1981 states could request other exemptions from national Medicaid rules, including a section 1915(c) home- and community-based services (HCBS) waiver that allowed them to substitute limited amounts of at-home and other assistance in lieu of institutional care. For the first time, they could provide targeted populations with such supports as homemakers, home health aides, personal care attendants, adult day care, respite care, and case management. These programs were carefully shaped so as to be cost effective; the states had to ensure that they would assist only eligible recipients who would otherwise be placed in a nursing home or an Intermediate Care Facility for the Mentally Retarded (ICF-MR) and that their home-based services would be budget neutral. Local officials, uncertain of the actual financial implications, approached this option gingerly.[34]

As in earlier years, the vast majority of states attempted to economize through a mix of provider and beneficiary curtailments, depending on the power of their local stakeholders. As certain populations gained access to Medicaid for the first time through federal mandates, other populations were paradoxically either cut from the rolls or received fewer benefits.[35] Likewise, state policymakers began to ration the use of services. By 1991, twenty-two states had decreased the number of allowable hospitalization days.[36] Several jurisdictions also curbed the number of physician visits; capped the number of prescriptions allowed per year; restricted the types of medicines to prescribed formularies; or took all of these steps. These measures, however, were successfully resisted at times.[37]

Seeking to restrain what they viewed as clients' misuse of health services, officials in certain places began charging them at least a small share of their medical and dental bills. In a few areas, they raised eligibility levels. In response to the new federal mandates and reductions in their Medicaid grants, many states eliminated some of their optional services, in particular those with high Medicaid coverage.[38] By the mid-1990s, only New York, California, Massachusetts, Washington, and Wisconsin offered twenty-six or more of the thirty-one discretionary benefits.[39]

When politically feasible, a number of states took aim at providers. The most common strategy for reining in Medicaid outlays—especially when facing an imminent budget shortfall—was to reduce or freeze reimbursements.[40] States were now more empowered to do so, having been provided, through the 1980 Boren amendment, greater discretion in setting fees for institutional care.[41] Hospitals were a prime target, particularly because they generated one of the highest charges under Medicaid, slightly more than one-fourth of total outlays. Determined to lower payments, most of the states revised their compensation formulas during the 1980s, typically eliminating cost-based approaches.[42]

Nursing homes posed more of a dilemma, primarily because of the seemingly incompatible problems associated with a shortage of beds and poor-quality care. Nevertheless, policymakers were set on lowering costs because long-term care facilities, at an average of nearly 40 percent of expenditures, had become the most expensive item in most state welfare medicine plans.[43] Each jurisdiction developed a different payment method, ranging from flat rates and case mixes to retrospective and prospective procedures. The variation in fees was considerable, but nearly all of the states were committed to paying enough money to attract sufficient nursing home participation in their program.[44] In 1987, Congress simultaneously enacted comprehensive nursing home reforms that included a requirement that the states must compensate facilities for any additional costs they incurred in meeting the new standards.[45] Despite these changes, the vast majority of nursing homes across the nation continued to provide substandard care even though they were paid to improve their services.

In dealing with physician fees, legislators had to consider the impact on participation rates, which were already relatively low. States always had the authority to establish these payments, but since 1979 they were supposed to be sufficient to ensure the availability of services. Disregarding such concerns, more than a few places steadily reduced fees throughout the decade; for their 1985 budgets, fully seventeen states froze their rates.[46] Sorely inadequate previously, reimbursements in most states deteriorated even further.[47] As states lowered or froze their compensation, doctors withdrew from the program in greater numbers.[48]

In contrast, hospitals and nursing homes—more dependent on government health program clients for their financial well-being—appealed to the judiciary, contending that the states were not meeting the terms of the Boren amendment, which stipulated that fees had to be sufficient to cover their costs. Although the courts had upheld the various local rates for institutional services in the early 1980s, by the end of the decade they were repeatedly ruling that the states were not reimbursing hospitals and nursing homes adequately and ordering the local legislators to raise compensation levels.[49] In June 1990, the U.S. Supreme Court upheld the federal jurisdiction of "Boren lawsuits," declaring that hospitals and nursing homes have a judicially enforceable right to sue for "reasonable and adequate" payments under Medicaid. According to a *New York Times* report, this decision gave "the nursing homes a potent tool to squeeze more money out of the Medicaid program."[50]

Accordingly, states temporarily gave up in their aggressive endeavors to contain hospital and nursing home costs through rate-setting strategies. In 1990 alone, at least thirteen states were in court over their reimbursement rates; in the following year, that number increased to twenty-four. In some places, policymakers simply augmented the amounts in order to settle cases.[51] Even the mere threat of a Boren amendment lawsuit intimidated elected officials, fostering increased compensation in a number of cases.[52] Institutional expenditures consequently accelerated in the 1990s. At the same time, governors—who were united in their opposition to the Boren amendment—continued to lobby Congress for its repeal, which they eventually achieved in 1997.[53] Henceforth, although certainly not ending the battle with providers over funding, the states would be allowed to initiate new, lower-cost reimbursement methods.

Despite their retrenchment policies, few states cut their welfare medicine plans sharply, and costs continued to expand everywhere. Across the nation, Medicaid spending from state-generated funds escalated an average of 16.7 percent in 1991 and 19.6 percent the following year.[54] The mounting expenditures began to put pressure on their other obligations, including public schools, income supports, law enforcement, prisons, transportation, roads, water supply, and sewage treatment. Because nearly all of the states require a balanced budget,[55] a number of them were forced to reduce government jobs and slash other items in their budgets, especially higher education, AFDC, and other income-assistance programs.[56] Officials were particularly alarmed that the low-income health program was squeezing out support for elementary and secondary education, their largest financial commitment.[57] Indeed, public schools lost ground in a few places, including Connecticut, Florida, and Massachusetts.[58] A few states even had to increase general taxes in the early 1990s, such as those on sales, personal income, and corporations,[59] and to earmark or increase special taxes for Medicaid, such as in California and Florida, where they were levied on cigarettes.

Despite the financial turmoil, many governors and legislators were clearly unwilling to impose draconian reductions in their Medicaid programs, in part because of resistance from stakeholders, who were more than willing to use every means at their disposal to prevent such cuts, including the courts.[60] Elected officials also were highly reluctant to lose the federal grants that Medicaid generated: they could provide health services to their low-income residents partly—or in some states mostly—at the expense of the national government. To be sure, as discussed in the next section, a number of states sought to resolve their economic woes by drawing on even more federal dollars through creative financing methods.

The States Strike Back

As the federal government shifted costs to the states, the latter began devising innovative methods to reverse the flow, endeavors that intensified during the recession years. The more inventive the state, the more resources it was able to attain from the national treasury. An unquestionable boon for the localities and hospitals alike, the new contrivances generated yet another round in the state–federal struggle over who would pay the escalating welfare medicine bill.

When Congress applied the Boren amendment to hospitals in 1981, it allowed states to pay additional compensation to hospitals serving a disproportionate number of Medicaid or uninsured patients. Under the Disproportionate Share Hospital (DSH) arrangement, because a state was not subject to any federal limits, it could boost DSH provider payments, at its own discretion, to whatever level the local policymakers chose.[61] During most of the early 1980s, only a few states were taking advantage of the program; under OBRA 1987, they were required to do so but maintained their authority to designate DSH hospitals, establish reimbursement levels, and determine the magnitude of funding.

In a related development, in 1985 the U.S. Health Care Financing Administration permitted a state to receive donations from private health providers to fund, in part, its share of DSH payments, a practice that was first utilized by West Virginia to leverage federal Medicaid money. It soon spread rapidly to other places across the nation, particularly in the Southeast.[62] In addition, some states began to tax certain contractors, similarly using the money to draw in extra federal matching funds.[63] The original donations or taxes—and sometimes a little more—would then be returned to the institutions in the form of enhanced reimbursement rates (or DSH payments), and the state would retain the remainder of the federal contribution for its general fund.

Beginning in the late 1980s, as the states were stymied in their bids to restrain hospital reimbursement rates because of the Boren amendment, and they experienced the full effects of the Medicaid mandates and the economic downturn, their expenses continued to exceed revenues. As a consequence, many of them turned to provider taxes, donations, and the DSH program as a means of transferring a larger portion of their Medicaid expenditures to the federal government. By the early 1990s, thirty-eight states were engaging in these strategies. In fact, such policies possibly contributed to the rising Medicaid price tag itself.[64] During a relatively short period, DSH payments increased to a whopping $17 billion in 1992, adding to the rapid growth in hospital costs.[65] The DSH program now accounted for fully 15 percent of all Medicaid spending, up from 2 percent just two years earlier.[66] New York, as usual, received the most from the schemes, followed by California.

DSH payments developed into more than just a way to fund safety-net providers and welfare medicine; in one survey, it was found that, on average, states were retaining fully one-third of the money for their own coffers.[67] Although the program to some extent assisted medically uninsured populations and hospitals providing indigent care, much of the money was used to offset state budgetary shortfalls and, significantly, to forestall the need to raise taxes. It also kept many states from drastically downsizing their Medicaid programs, and some legislatures depended on the additional dollars for other vital financial obligations.[68]

What is more, DSH funds were windfalls for many private-sector hospitals. A number of states were giving the enhancements even to facilities that provided extremely limited care to welfare medicine or uninsured indigent patients or were bestowing amounts that surpassed the facilities' actual costs in caring for such patients. In some places, the extra money that providers collected was even greater than their entire annual Medicaid compensation.[69] New Hampshire, which was particularly aggressive in exploiting DSH funds, used the flood of federal dollars not only to balance its budget, but also to assist certain hospitals with their finances; the facilities did not even have to account for how the money was spent.[70] Then again, states such as Alabama gave the entire federal match back to the hospitals, favoring those that offered services to a disproportionate number of the poor.[71]

Labeling these creative-financing arrangements as "scams," the George H. W. Bush administration attempted in 1991 to cap DSH payments as well as to limit the number of eligible hospitals under the program. Governors and a bipartisan coalition of congressmen, however, recognized that many of the states had become financially dependent on the extra DSH money, for both Medicaid and other fundamental services. A compromise was struck: Congress sanctioned the use of voluntary donations for another year, allowed the states to continue taxing hospitals and nursing homes, up to 25 percent of its share of Medicaid costs, and capped DSH payments at 12 percent of national Medicaid spending after October 1992.[72] States also could apply for a waiver, especially if they needed the additional money to expand health services for the poor, and many states did so. In addition, blocked in their ability to use provider donations and taxes to the fullest extent, the localities increasingly turned to innovative approaches for raising their share of federal money. In response, as discussed in chapter 9, the national government has continued to wage periodic battles against these schemes.

Confrontation: Emergence of the "New Right"

Welfare medicine found itself at the center of national debate in 1995, at which time the newly elected Republican Congress set out to confront both the low-income health program and the Clinton administration head on. By then, the debate over national health insurance, a central issue during the 1992 presidential campaign, had abated. The new president's 1993 Health Security Act—indeed, any national health care measure—was clearly politically unattainable. At the same time, in part because of the proposal's debacle, the Republicans had achieved a majority in both the U.S. House of Representatives (for the first time in nearly forty years) and the Senate (which they had achieved only twice in sixty years). Composed of a significant number of "new right" conservatives, they intensified the ever-increasing hostility to social benefits and spearheaded an ideological crusade to privatize public services systematically, including the low-income and old-age entitlement programs.

Ostensibly committed to lowering taxes while also balancing the budget— somewhat diametrically opposed objectives—the new Republican majority immediately enacted spending-reduction targets. High among their major goals were a decrease in the growth of Medicare and especially Medicaid, mainly through caps on federal outlays, and a further devolution of policy-making to the states. Through the budget reconciliation process, they accordingly pushed through a somewhat revised version of Reagan's block grants that would have repealed Medicaid as an entitlement, replaced it with "Medi-grants," and provided for significantly greater local control over the program.[73] Endeavoring to cut the growth rate of welfare medicine expenditures in half,[74] the Republicans expected to generate billions in savings and lower payments to the states by 30 percent.

Unlike the earlier Reagan measures, which the states had unanimously opposed, the latest block-grant proposal developed into a highly partisan and ideologically divisive issue, supported by congressional Republicans[75] and nearly all of the Republican governors.[76] Although local Democratic leaders backed fewer federal mandates and more authority to design and run their own Medicaid plans, positions clearly articulated at the 1995 Annual Governors Conference, they favored maintaining the low-income health program's entitlement status, as did congressional Democrats. The block-grant proposal, because of its stark reduction in federal funds, also encountered resistance from many of the major health care lobby groups, whose members would be negatively affected.

Clinton famously vetoed the 1995 budget act, which included the Republican's Medicaid provisions, thereby temporarily and partially shutting down the federal government twice. The president stood firm in his defense of welfare medicine, which, as one source sardonically put it, "had evidently ascended to the status of most beloved federal programs."[77] He was supported by the Democrats in Congress, who by November not only were a cohesive force, but also were persevering in their protection of Medicaid's entitlement status.[78] Because of the resultant financial and political chaos, the Republicans were forced to capitulate, leaving Medicaid virtually intact, at least for the moment. All the same, contentious disagreements over the low-income health care programs resumed almost at once.

The president, although supportive of Medicaid as an entitlement, was not equally committed to maintaining its level of funding. In fact, because he had pledged to balance the national budget, in conjunction with tax cuts, he envisioned control over federal outlays for the low-income health program as a major key to his success. With the resumption of budget negotiations, Clinton quickly responded with Medicaid reductions of his own, albeit at lower amounts than the Republicans. His proposal, which set annual limits on federal Medicaid spending per beneficiary but did not restrict overall program growth, would have opened the way for greater enrollments over the years.[79] Opposed by governors across party lines, who rejected any loss of federal Medicaid money, Clinton's initiative would have placed considerable financial burdens on the states.

Budget talks between the president and Congress continued, notwithstanding several breakdowns in their discussions. Clinton remained resolute in his determination to prevent any basic restructuring of Medicaid (and Medicare); the idea of fundamentally reforming welfare medicine or converting it into block grants eventually petered out. Regardless, throughout the rest of the decade congressional Republicans strove to slash the program sharply and end its entitlement status, although with less resolve and lowered anticipation of success. Enthusiasm among Republican governors for block grants was also abating as the financial realities of what such a change would entail for their states set in.[80] Besides, by 1997 the economy was flourishing, medical inflation had slowed down, and Medicaid costs were rising at more moderate levels.

In their struggle to balance the budget, the president and Congress ultimately settled on substantial cuts to Medicare,[81] which, under the Balanced Budget Act (BBA) of 1997,[82] relied mostly on greater privatization and lower compensation to providers as the means of decreasing federal outlays.[83] The legislation notably did not call for sizeable reductions in Medicaid, which remained relatively unscathed.[84] Indeed, national officials expected the moderate decline in federal contributions to come from keeping state DSH funding maneuvers in check.[85]

BBA 1997 also further loosened up federal regulations, expanding the states' discretion over their Medicaid plans and removing some basic protections for their low-income participants. The provisions regarding commercial insurance companies would prove to one of the more precarious revisions: the act allowed local jurisdictions to mandate managed care, without waiver authority, and permitted payment to MCOs that served Medicaid clients exclusively.[86] The BBA also repealed the Boren amendment, thereby eliminating minimum-compensation standards for hospitals, nursing homes, and community health centers and allowing the states to structure their own reimbursement formulas.

The End of Welfare as We Know It

The national debate over welfare both paralleled and intersected with conversations about Medicaid.[87] Despite President Clinton's support for the low-income health program as an entitlement, his lack of enthusiasm for income assistance, mainly AFDC, ultimately undermined them both. To be sure, the eventual dismantling of welfare by Congress removed the relationship between the two programs and, with it, guaranteed access to medical services.

The United States has always been stingy with its use of tax dollars on collective needs, especially assistance for the poor. Among other factors, our meager provision or expansion of such benefits, compared to that of western Europe and other industrialized nations, is often attributed to the nation's antistatist political culture.[88] Furthermore, America's generally individualist national character and its long-held assumption that welfare is not a social right reinforce long-held notions that blame certain disadvantaged people for their own plight. Over the decades, political leaders—to a lesser or greater extent—have added force to these views through both rhetoric and law.

The way we define a particular problem limits how it is perceived, the parameters of public debate, and any potential outcomes or solutions. Poverty in the United States is characterized as stemming from personal inadequacies, with welfare recipients viewed as "lazy and shiftless," "welfare queens," "deceitful," "immoral," and "conniving." For the most part, it is assumed that young adults receiving income assistance are gaming, cheating, and abusing the system. Government's main role has thus been to "motivate," "educate," "control," and even "punish" individuals and their families who have not attained sufficient funds to meet their basic needs. Blaming victims, especially black and Hispanic low-income, single mothers, has become the national norm among Democrats and Republicans alike.

Rhetoric isn't necessarily grounded in reality; although particularly troublesome under the George W. Bush administration, the manipulation of popular beliefs about poverty and its causes has been endemic in American political life. Public officials also have employed politically useful distortions when communicating welfare costs, mainly those related to AFDC. In exaggerating the scope of these outlays, they have held the poor at least partly responsible for economic woes ranging from growing national deficits and state budgetary crises to greater taxation on the middle and working classes.[89] By depicting actual program costs, however, we can expose the obvious and purposeful misperceptions that are perpetuated by our social, economic, and political elites.

Until its termination in 1996, AFDC was the primary cash-assistance program in the United States for young, impoverished mothers. As for Medicaid, each state set its own qualification and benefit standards, sharing costs with the federal government. A powerful backlash against welfare mothers and the welfare program that served them emerged, intensifying in the 1980s and 1990s. A succession of presidents, governors, and legislatures—across party lines—slashed benefits, introduced various workfare inducements, penalties, and mandates, and generally made it more difficult to qualify for the program and receive checks. In some places, a recipient's payment was reduced—or eliminated—if she failed to apply for a set number of jobs per week or if a partner moved in with her. The nation was on a rampage against "freeloaders" living off of the taxes of "hard-working Americans."

Despite cyclical shifts in employment opportunities, economic downturns, an increase in single motherhood and poverty, and the ongoing loss of decent-paying jobs, AFDC funding levels were relatively fixed over the years. Benefits remained stagnant, and in some cases declined; only a few states attempted to keep up even marginally with inflation. From 1970 to 1990, the purchasing power of welfare allowances dropped by fully 39 percent.[90] During the following two years, even with increasing caseloads, forty-four states froze or cut their levels of support.[91] In most places and in sharp contrast to Medicaid, AFDC steadily shrank as a share of their overall budgets, consuming only about 3 percent of state spending, on average, at the time of its demise.[92]

Notwithstanding the ubiquitous diatribes against budget-busting single moms on the dole, welfare outlays at the national level have not been particularly burdensome. Representing 1.7 percent ($2.7 billion) of the federal budget in 1967, AFDC payments fell to 1.0 percent of total expenditures ($9.2 billion) in 1985 and to 1.1 percent ($17.1 billion) by 1995. In the latter year, the cash-assistance program for impoverished young families, mainly single women and their children, amounted to only 0.28 percent of the gross domestic product.[93]

Regardless of these facts, President Clinton kept up an onslaught on the program, vowing in his presidential campaign to "end welfare as we know it." Despite his vetoes and firm resolve to maintain Medicaid as a basic social right, he did not display such steadfastness with AFDC. He eventually acquiesced to Republican demands and reluctantly signed the stringent Personal Responsibility and Work Opportunity Reconciliation (PRWOR) Act of 1996: the legislation simultaneously converted income assistance into block grants and terminated welfare as an individual entitlement. Under the new law, which set up Temporary Assistance for Needy Families (TANF), states were directed to reduce their welfare rolls substantially, mostly by shifting people into jobs. Among other federal restrictions, family benefits were limited to two consecutive years, with an overall maximum of five years (states could impose stricter limits if they chose to do so). Legal immigrants lost their eligibility (although it was restored in 1997 for those who had entered the country in 1996 or earlier), and newly arrived immigrants would be disqualified for five years. Because the states were given a set level of appropriations under the PRWOR Act and permission to reduce their coverage and spending levels, many of them raised their income-qualification standards or slashed benefits measurably or both.[94]

Welfare caseloads dropped precipitously, by 27 percent nationally between 1996 and 1999.[95] In some states, the drop was even greater: Georgia, for example, experienced a 50 percent decline in enrollment.[96] Many people were removed from the rolls either for failing to comply with the PRWOR Act's burdensome requirements or because of more stringent qualification criteria—including the new restrictions regarding immigrants—and others found intermittent employment, mostly in low-wage sectors of the economy.[97]

Because TANF recipients would no longer be automatically entitled to health care benefits under the legislation, the linkage between income supports for young households and their entitlement to health services was completely severed.[98] As a result, after the enactment of the PRWOR Act, fewer low-income families were eligible for welfare medicine.[99] Medicaid caseloads were also affected by complicated new administrative procedures, strict workfare requirements, documentation constraints, questions over unpaid medical bills, language barriers, and other bureaucratic deterrents— all of which discouraged a high number of qualified families from seeking Medicaid assistance after it was split off from cash assistance. Moreover, many people who lost their eligibility for income support did not realize that their children still had access to welfare medicine.[100]

Resumption of Expansionary Medicaid Politics

Children First

Determined to downsize social supports, conservatives had made major inroads by eliminating cash assistance as an entitlement. However, by 1997 the national economic situation had improved, paving the way for liberal reformers to press for expansion of medical insurance coverage. Now that the prospect for universal health insurance was politically unattainable, they aspired to transform welfare medicine incrementally into a more comprehensive program.[101] With a booming economy, low unemployment, and a declining annual federal budget deficit, it seemed a propitious time to do so. Once more, even as the federal government was reducing TANF recipients' Medicaid coverage, it was simultaneously increasing the availability of welfare medicine for certain other groups.

As in earlier years, children were regarded as the most appealing target and the one most likely to achieve legislative success. They also had lost ground due to the recent welfare reform, particularly among the poorest families.[102] What is more, there were at least 10 million uninsured children nationally, the vast majority of them living in low-income households with working parents. Health care advocates pressed Congress to address these young people's medical needs. In a critical move, President Clinton used his annual State of the Union message in 1997 to request increased coverage of the medically uninsured, underlining his concern for kids. As part of BBA 1997, Congress accordingly established the State Children's Health Insurance Program (SCHIP), aimed at children living in households with incomes up to 200 percent of the federal poverty level (FPL) who do not qualify for Medicaid.

The new program, however, was both financially restricted and time limited: established as a block grant, with a cap of $40 billion over ten years, it clearly was not intended as an entitlement,[103] nor did it have many of the protections that Congress had mandated under Medicaid. The states had a large amount of latitude in their use of SCHIP money: they could establish a separate program, with fewer benefits and services, or affix SCHIP to their ongoing welfare medicine plan;[104] they also were allowed to impose premiums, deductibles, and copays (limited to 5 percent of total household income).[105]

After 1997, very few states were facing immediate budgetary problems. Along with their enhanced financial circumstances, inflation in health care had slowed down, and the growth in Medicaid enrollments—and costs— had declined markedly.[106] As a result, many states engaged in an unprecedented effort to expand coverage to new populations. They were particularly interested in taking advantage of SCHIP, which had somewhat higher federal matching rates than those for Medicaid.

The launching of SCHIP was slow, but most places had implemented their programs by mid-1998: sixteen states included the full SCHIP package in their ongoing Medicaid program (sometimes adding services); another sixteen enacted new, reduced schemes; and nineteen embarked on a combination of the two approaches. Regardless of party control or type of plan, the majority of states set their SCHIP eligibility levels relatively high, at or above 200 percent of the FPL. New Jersey established its qualification at 350 percent of the FPL and did so even under a Republican governor and Republican-controlled legislature.[107]

Medicaid/SCHIP enrollments, consisting mostly of children, began to climb, further boosted by the phasing in of the earlier federal mandates, which had directed the states to cover more youngsters in their regular plans. Between 1998 and 2001, coverage under the two health plans grew by roughly 30 percent across the states;[108] two-thirds of the new participants lived in households with at least one working parent. Despite these developments, however, only 2 million additional low-come children were served, considerably short of the anticipated 5 million.[109] In these early years, nearly one-fourth of the states exceeded their annual allotments before the year was out; later on, even more of them would regularly run out of federal money. In some places, state legislators would simply freeze enrollments, as they did repeatedly in Utah, or threaten to do so (e.g., in Georgia).[110]

Nevertheless, impoverished kids (about 40 percent of the total), if not their parents, now had greater access to basic medical care. As chapter 4 argues, because the national grants were circumscribed and there were relatively few federal regulations, SCHIP played out differently in each state, depending on local elected officials' good will. It also confronted ongoing fiscal constraints everywhere and ultimately became a political football between President George W. Bush and his Democratic Congress. Although eventually rescued by the Barack Obama administration, the program remains subject to the political vagaries of the times.

The Growth of Managed Care

Other groups besides children clearly fared less well, especially low-income adults. Even though more children were now eligible for publicly funded health insurance, nearly half of their parents lacked any protection at all. The number of uninsured adults had been climbing throughout the 1980s, reaching alarming rates by the 1990s. Comprising 35 million people by 1991, or 14 percent of the population, this group remained an enduring and critical problem. President Clinton proposed but failed to achieve his FamilyCare program, which would have extended Medicaid to a greater number of employed, low-income households.[111] Republican legislators (and many Democrats) were more interested in privatization measures than in direct government assistance to such families. They concentrated on tax credits and deductions, in conjunction with market-driven policies, to foster greater private-sector coverage. During the rest of the decade, there was a surge of tax-related health care proposals of various types.[112] In addition, Congress enacted legislation to induce disabled adults to leave the Medicaid rolls.[113]

Nevertheless, the medically uninsured population continued to expand, placing the burden squarely on the states. Seeking greater flexibility in their Medicaid programs, governors complained fervently about "cumbersome" federal regulations. President Clinton, who met with them almost immediately after taking office, was highly sympathetic and directed the U.S. Department of Health and Human Services (HHS) to expedite the approval process for relaxing the rules. Through section 1115 waivers, the previously small-scale Medicaid research and demonstration projects of the previous decade were expanded to allow states more control over their magnitude, structure, and funding sources.[114] Local policymakers began experimenting, albeit cautiously, with alternative ways to cover more of their employed low-income residents, either through welfare medicine, the private sector, or both, while simultaneously continuing to contain costs, improve "efficiency," lower provider fees, and—as always—shift the price tag to the federal government.

A few states utilized waivers to test whether subsidies to small firms would encourage them to offer insurance to their low-wage workers. Places such as New York provided financial assistance to a limited number of needy families who had lost their health coverage because of unemployment or had their benefits terminated by employers. In 1994, Minnesota broadened eligibility to all residents who had been uninsured for four months and had no access to a company-based plan.[115] California partly financed commercial policies for some people with high-cost illnesses, such as AIDS, cardiovascular diseases, and chronic diabetes, who could no longer work or whose employers had dropped their insurance.[116] Nonetheless, states that experimented with broader coverage for the most part had to scale back their programs or do away with them before long.[117] To be sure, endeavors to extend publicly supported health care services to previously ineligible populations were seriously restricted from the start and became increasingly more so as states confronted yet another economic downturn in the early twenty-first century.

A number of states turned to managed care as the primary means of serving additional low-income adults, and the Clinton administration gave them greater license to do so.[118] Advocates of this approach argued that it would generate enough cost savings to finance the section 1115 demonstration projects and other programs extending welfare medicine coverage to new populations. Indeed, nearly all of the expanded state Medicaid programs in the 1990s included provisions for broadening managed care.[119] Although states had been somewhat cautious about enrolling low-income health recipients in commercial prepaid plans in Medicaid's early years, they now began using waivers to move their Medicaid population (mostly welfare participants at first) steadily into them.

Participation became increasingly mandatory as states sought "freedom-of-choice" waivers from the Health Care Financing Administration. A few states sought to compel participation statewide, an arrangement used only by Arizona up to that time. Under the Clinton administration, Tennessee's new Medicaid plan (TennCare), approved by HHS in 1993, proposed to steer into MCOs all of the state's low-income health plan recipients, along with a large number of uninsured individuals with incomes up to 400 percent of the FPL.[120] Oregon's statewide waiver, which President George H. W. Bush had rejected in 1992, was now authorized.[121] Hawaii, one of the more successful states in achieving near-universal coverage since 1994, initially relied on managed care for children and nonelderly adults but later turned its noninstitutionalized elderly, disabled, and blind beneficiaries over to commercial companies as well.[122]

However, most state policymakers progressively pursued mandatory enrollments in MCOs as an economizing measure, but without enlarging welfare medicine coverage,[123] which served to lower overall payments to providers and to limit client access to services, in particular the more expensive ones.[124] Such efforts were facilitated by BBA 1997 because, as noted earlier, states could now force certain Medicaid enrollees into capitated plans without permission from the federal government. In some areas, policymakers utilized waivers to launch schemes that moved at least some of their higher-cost populations, such as nonelderly disabled recipients, into MCOs.[125] At the end of the 1990s, there were considerably greater caseloads of already participating clients relying on managed care, but not a considerable expansion of welfare medicine to additional households.[126]

In 1997, roughly 48 percent of all Medicaid clients were in some type of managed-care plan, and as mandatory enrollments accelerated, that proportion reached 56 percent by 2000. That year it spread to more than 80 percent of welfare medicine participants in twelve states.[127] The floodgates, now ajar, would spring wide open in the early twenty-first century. At the same time, the number of for-profit MCOs swelled, rising from less than 20 percent of all plans in 1981 to 75 percent by the end of the 1990s; nearly 23 percent of them were Medicaid-only organizations.[128] Of striking importance, however, is the fact that the escalating Medicaid enrollment in MCOs moved forward without serious political debate about the repercussions for the people served by them.[129]

Conclusion: The Ebb and Flow of Welfare Medicine

The occupants of the White House during the 1980s and early 1990s were determined to roll back the social welfare programs of earlier decades, especially those serving the poor. Although largely successful in achieving their overall goal, neither Ronald Reagan nor George H. W. Bush could abolish welfare medicine as an entitlement or reign in its costs. Not only did Medicaid prove highly resistant to presidential retrenchment measures, but Congress began an incremental extension of the program that—together with rising unemployment, mounting poverty, judicial rulings, an aging population, high medical inflation, and other factors—engendered expanded caseloads and escalating expenditures. The vast majority of the states, to varying extents, accordingly confronted severe budget pressures, especially beginning in the late 1980s.

As the chapter demonstrates, state policymakers—armed with states' rights rhetoric, waiver authority, and other new measures—proceeded to revamp their Medicaid plans by introducing market-based service and delivery systems; weakening federal rules, regulations, and safeguards; chipping away at recipient benefit packages; raising program eligibility levels;

and curtailing provider reimbursements—most of which the courts disallowed. Overall, however, elected state officials were unwilling to impose deep reductions in their welfare medicine plans. Indeed, they were increasingly more inclined to coax additional dollars from the federal treasury through creative use of provider taxes, donations, and the DSH program.

The emergence of the "new Right" and its grip on Congress in 1994 again threatened public benefits, including Medicaid. Nevertheless, as in the 1980s, welfare medicine emerged relatively unscathed financially, although, as the chapter emphasizes, the erosion of AFDC undercut low-income mothers and children's access to the program. In tandem with these developments, national policymakers transferred even greater power to the states over their Medicaid plans.

As economic stagnation turned into a boom during the late 1990s, the national legislature once more expanded coverage to low-income children. A number of local jurisdictions took advantage of the situation by providing more health insurance to needy youngsters and, to a lesser degree, to working adults, while simultaneously endeavoring to rein in their overall budgetary outlays. At first, they launched voluntary managed-care options but eventually turned to mandatory coverage as a means to drive down their expenditures. As we will see in the next chapter, the ever-rising managed-care caseloads and greater policy devolution in the Medicaid program in general were on shaky ground.

In transferring ever-increasing decision-making power to the states, the Clinton administration counted on more than just cost controls; it viewed waivers as yet another vehicle for expanding health coverage to the uninsured. Overall, however, the growing need for medical protection among low-income families proved far greater than any endeavors to assist them.

4

WELFARE MEDICINE IN THE
TWENTY-FIRST CENTURY

As the United States entered the twenty-first century, the nation experienced a severe economic crisis, culminating in the recession of 2001. The consequent loss of jobs translated into decreased tax revenues and stricter eligibility requirements for social programs. The George W. Bush administration's trillion-dollar tax cut enacted that year, followed by another one in 2003, along with increased military spending (especially for the wars in Afghanistan and Iraq) compounded the fiscal problems, generating huge annual national budget deficits.[1]

The dire economic situation presented the president with a propitious climate in which to undermine national welfare medicine guarantees and advance the deep cuts he was aiming for. Utilizing whatever tools he had at his disposal to meet his Medicaid goals—legislation, waivers, regulations, and other administrative means—Bush pressed for greater market-based initiatives, leaner Medicaid benefit packages, more self-sufficiency among recipients, further state control over their plans, and, most important, lower federal outlays.

Although state officials often had a similar mindset, they also sought to leverage *additional* national dollars. Faced with an admixture of budgetary shortages, growing numbers of medically uninsured residents, rising Medicaid costs, and pressures against raising taxes or imposing new ones, they responded with a variety of strategies, utilizing both expansive and restrictive policies. They regardless nearly always strove to curb their own spending and resorted to cost-containment measures that chipped away at the program's entitlement status. After a brief economic reprieve, beginning in 2008 they confronted yet another recession, this time steeper and more severe.

Destabilizing Medicaid

The Early Bush Years

During the George W. Bush administration, Medicaid policy was subsumed under the largest retrenchment of the welfare state since the 1930s. The president, along with House and Senate Republicans, engaged in a long-term strategy of transforming Medicare and Medicaid to meet their overall goals of lower taxes for upper-income families; greater decentralization and devolution; privatization of social programs; and the dismantling of entitlements. In an approach to the political economy similar to Reagan's in the 1980s and renewed by the New Republican Congress in 1995, they were determined to reshape social policies to their own ends. Their general outlook about Medicaid was supported, at least initially, by Republican governors, who clamored for greater flexibility to alter their welfare medicine plans and reduce national requirements, along with additional money. Democratic governors similarly demanded autonomy and funds, but they were also interested in expanding coverage to the medically uninsured.[2] In contrast, the president viewed "more freedom for the states" as a catch-phrase for reduced national funding.

Bush, like Reagan, was not successful in his block-grant approach to welfare medicine. Labeling it a "Medicaid modernization plan," he had proposed offering the states more power to design their benefit packages in exchange for federally capped allotments and loans.[3] Because of ongoing resistance by national Democratic leaders (who were concerned about Medicaid's loss of entitlement status) and by most governors and state officials (who were concerned about ceilings on the federal money), the administration's block-grant initiatives never moved forward.

Unsuccessful in his attempts to undermine Medicaid legislatively, Bush turned to alternative administrative means to achieve his ends, a modus operandi he increasingly relied on throughout his eight years. In order to achieve devolution, privatization, cost reductions, and even possibly mini block grants, he forcefully promoted section 1115 and 1915(b) waivers by accelerating the approval process and significantly raising the number of demonstration projects granted. The president also pushed his agenda through his 2001 Health Insurance Flexibility and Accountability Initiative (HIFA), which further eased and expedited the Medicaid and State Children's Health Insurance Program (SCHIP) waiver application process and was even more open-ended. It not only permitted state policymakers to expand Medicaid to more of their low-income uninsured residents by providing only basic primary-care services and imposing higher out-of-pocket costs on certain beneficiaries, but also allowed them to streamline Medicaid for many current participants.[4] The demonstrations were first encouraged and eventually mandated to include projects that integrated Medicaid and SCHIP with private health insurance plans (such as premium assistance programs).

Regulatory Politics: Circumventing Congress

In addition to pushing waivers, the Bush administration relied increasingly on rule-making activities to impose its will. In his 2005 budget proposal, the president had supported a steep retrenchment in the growth of entitlement spending, including large decreases in Medicaid, but he received a lesser amount than what he had put forward. The following year, pressured by the governors,[5] pharmacy trade organizations, and other affected groups, Congress rejected additional cuts sought by the White House.[6] In response, Bush opted to evade Congress by instructing the Centers for Medicare and Medicaid Services (CMS) to issue regulations that would meet his cost-saving goals. Pressing even further, he planned to achieve roughly half of his proposed budget cuts to Medicaid in 2007—which were higher than ever—through additional directives.[7] Again, the administration intended to promulgate these cuts on its own, including a few of the previous year's targets that had not yet been implemented. As usual, most of the savings would shift costs to the states.[8]

Protests emerged from all sides almost immediately. The pharmaceutical trade associations reacted forcefully to CMS's proposed rule that would lower their members' compensation for generic drugs. A coalition of hospitals and governors, supported by 64 U.S. senators and 263 representatives, similarly contested the reductions to government-run nursing homes and hospitals. The National Governors Association wrote to congressional leaders, requesting them to prepare legislation to block the rule, and they did so: it was put on a one-year hold in a supplementary appropriations bill later that year.[9] The medical school cuts, along with restrictions affecting public schools and rehabilitation services, were also temporarily suspended because of energetic lobbying by the Association of American Medical Colleges, education lobbies, officials of school districts, disability groups, and other interested parties. In several short months, nearly all of the regulations had been incorporated into a congressional measure delaying their implementation for a year.

Undeterred, the Bush administration not only reinstated the previous rules, but issued some new ones the following year.[10] Again, a mix of special-interest groups, governors of both parties, and the National Conference of State Legislators fervently opposed them. Congress voted to postpone six of the seven regulations for another year; although the president had vowed to veto the provisions, the legislature slipped the moratorium into its 2009 supplementary appropriations bill, forcing him to sign it. Shortly after Barack Obama's election in 2008, Congress continued the moratorium as part of the American Recovery and Reinvestment Act, and, several months later, the U.S. Department of Health and Human Services (HHS) issued rules permanently rescinding implementation of four of them.[11]

The Deficit Reduction Act of 2005

With larger Republican majorities in 2005, Congress enacted the Deficit Reduction Act (DRA), legislation that promoted the most far-reaching and profound changes to Medicaid since its passage.[12] Authorizing the states to transform their plans with far less interference by the national government, it engendered a fundamental restructuring of welfare medicine across the nation. The DRA notably passed without a single Democratic vote, receiving a slim majority in the House and requiring Vice President Dick Cheney to break a tie in the Senate.[13]

The driving force underlying the act was cost reduction, to be achieved by restricting and controlling Medicaid participants and their services. It thus sharply abridged prior guarantees: legislators now could redesign and downsize their benefit packages to "benchmark" basic services as well as tailor them to different subsets of enrollees. The DRA also allowed the states to force certain beneficiaries to pay premiums for their plans and substantially higher copayments for their medical services.[14] Critically, for the first time in the program's history, not only could states end Medicaid coverage for families who did not pay their premium, but the legislation empowered providers to deny services to anyone who failed to fund their share of the costs. Immigrants, too, bore the brunt of the DRA cost-saving measures: in order to participate in welfare medicine, they had to prove their citizenship with a passport or birth certificate.

The aged and younger disabled populations lost some ground as well. In an attempt to restrict eligibility for nursing home care, the DRA tightened rules on asset transfers. In addition, states were given greater leeway to shape their provisions regarding long-term care (LTC) provisions, including the ability to offer home- and community-based services (HCBS) without a waiver and, most important, to cap the number of older and disabled people served. They also could maintain waiting lists and limit services to specific geographic areas. In order to promote greater privatization, the DRA opened up more avenues for attaining commercial LTC insurance.[15]

Welfare Medicine in the States

Fiscal Crisis: 2001 to 2004

Few states, of course, were prepared for the turn-of-the-century financial upheavals. Beginning in 2001, they now confronted annual budgetary crises that simultaneously affected and were affected by Medicaid. As usual, due to the program's countercyclical nature, its eligible population expanded measurably as more people lost their jobs and with those jobs their employer-based health coverage, at a time when the states could least afford to cover them through Medicaid.[16] The ongoing shift from industrial to marginal service jobs, an aging population, increasing numbers of people with disabilities, and prior state Medicaid expansions that became fully effective in the early years of the twenty-first century also contributed to higher welfare medicine caseloads.[17] At the same time, medical inflation, which had slowed down in the late 1990s, began to escalate again, especially for prescription drugs, hospital services, and nursing home care. Medicaid costs consequently grew considerably;[18] already a significant percentage of the states' own outlays, welfare medicine increased to nearly one-fifth of their overall budgets by 2004.[19]

Nevertheless, the main cause of state budgetary problems was deteriorating revenues, in some cases because they had enacted tax cuts during earlier, more prosperous times.[20] The proceeds from income and sales taxes declined precipitously because of the rise in unemployment and especially a decline in the stock market,[21] thus fostering large and continuing budget deficits in nearly every state. Constrained by constitutional requirements for a balanced budget and constituent resistance to higher taxes, local officials relied on a patchwork of stopgap financial gimmickry to meet their expenses: they issued new bonds, drew on tobacco settlement money, enacted or increased "sin" taxes on cigarettes and alcohol, and spent down any available "rainy-day" reserves.[22] The federal government also was forced to provide temporary financial relief, although at a sum far lower than it would make available during the next economic downturn in 2008.[23] In most places, these makeshift budget-balancing efforts simply pushed the fiscal problems into the future.

Despite the fiscal distress, during the early years of the crisis lawmakers were more likely to single out budget items other than Medicaid. A number of states decreased spending on public safety, environmental protection, transportation, economic development, and especially aid to public education. Attempts to rein in the low-income health program, however, were comparatively restrained in most places. In a few states, it was a larger target, often depending more on the elected officials' political views than on the severity of the state's economic woes.[24]

During these early years of the twenty-first century, the majority of legislatures enacted only modest benefit reductions (focusing on prescription drugs, but also for such services as vision and dental care) and restricted income eligibility to some extent, engendering substantial declines in enrollment in a few places. At least one-third of the states instituted new or slightly higher copayments, but federal regulations hampered more sizeable cost sharing.[25] Nearly all states reduced the growth of provider fees, at least temporarily.[26] In a number of places, policymakers initiated certain structural changes, especially with regard to managed care.

The Rising Medically Uninsured Population

Although the Balanced Budget Act (BBA) of 1997 had led to increased welfare medicine coverage for low-income children and some of their parents, along with pregnant women, it had not dealt with the nation's large and escalating pool of medically uninsured people, amounting to 47 million by the end of 2006, a 22 percent increase since 2000.[27] That year, nearly 16 percent of the population had no health insurance,[28] and many more were underinsured. State officials were particularly concerned about their low-income residents, who, despite having jobs, did not have access to an employer plan or could not afford to participate in one because of high and rapidly rising premium costs.[29] Nongroup commercial insurance, with its even more exorbitant price tag, was certainly not an option for them.[30] To be sure, the vast majority of uninsured adults could not pay for insurance on their own, were denied protection, or had a proviso excluding their particular medical condition(s) from coverage. Thus, although the states were under pressure to reign in Medicaid costs, they felt compelled to provide at least some assistance to their growing number of medically uninsured residents, especially workers and their families.

Responses to the "New Flexibilities"

After 2004, state policymakers increasingly sought permission to take advantage of the new national "flexibilities," some to rein in spending, others to tackle the thorny issue of medical coverage for the uninsured or to reinstate earlier reductions or to do both. The majority of states endeavored to achieve both improvements and savings simultaneously. Privatization, along with various cost-cutting strategies, promoted through the Bush administration's Medicaid waiver policies, was central to these local pursuits. Although the rebound in the national economy had improved the states' budgetary condition, and the growth in their Medicaid caseloads and overall program outlays had temporarily stabilized, local officials still faced fiscal constraints, which worsened a few years later.[31]

The variations across the states were marked: according to one study, in 2005 alone nineteen states expanded eligibility through section 1115 Medicaid waivers, but six of them restricted access; twenty-nine states broadened optional benefits, five decreased them, and three implemented some expansions while also restricting others.[32] The following year, one-third of the states attempted to cover more of their uninsured residents through SCHIP or Medicaid, mostly taking advantage of the recently enacted DRA provisions; others were working on such proposals.[33] For the most part, however, elected officials seeking to extend coverage to new populations took only incremental steps, usually centered on children's needs, and offered only modest improvements in eligibility or benefits for their parents and other adults.

The spread of health insurance to previously uninsured populations was also inextricably linked to an undermining of national guarantees. Because states had to demonstrate that their enlarged Medicaid programs would be budget neutral (i.e., not increase federal spending), a restriction tied to both section 1115 and HIFA waivers, any expansions necessarily entailed a restructuring of their current plans, reductions for current participants, lean benefit packages for new beneficiaries, greater cost sharing for everyone, and frequently a combination of all of these approaches.

Furthermore, although some governors and legislators eagerly sought waivers to expand coverage to their residents, they intended to do so by leveraging more federal dollars. None of them was willing to raise state income or sales taxes. Indeed, in addition to attaining more national money, they again tapped new revenue sources, especially the "sin" taxes, notorious for falling most heavily on the poor, and their tobacco settlement money.[34]

Local officials also continued to target health care providers: some states raised reimbursements, anticipating greater access for clients, whereas others froze or even reduced rates, rendering the adjustments either across the board or by selection.[35] As usual, when the affected industries were dissatisfied with their fees, they generally fought back with organized protests, lobbying, and court action.

Greater Privatization: Managed Care

As in the 1990s, but now with greater intensity, state and federal officials alike viewed managed care as the "magic bullet" for controlling Medicaid outlays or expanding coverage to the medically uninsured or both. As advocates touted "efficiency," "flexibility," "modernization," and "reform," more states initiated or enlarged mandatory managed care, sometimes dramatically, in an ongoing abandonment of welfare medicine's "freedom-of-choice" provision.[36] Several of them—Ohio, Kentucky, Indiana, Louisiana, Missouri, Florida, South Carolina, and Texas—aimed to turn their entire Medicaid programs over to insurance companies through waivers. Some states with bare-bones programs, such as Georgia and Nevada, pushed nearly everyone into privately run plans without improving their benefit packages.[37]

Many places were now compelling some of their frail elders and disabled young adults to join managed-care organizations (MCOs) as well. By mid-2006, about 65 percent of all recipients nationwide were enrolled in some form of managed care and the numbers are still growing.[38] As discussed later in this chapter, states such as Florida even began empowering the commercial companies to determine the benefit packages. If Louisiana governor Bobby Jindal (R) receives his waiver, he currently (2009) intends to do the same in his state.[39]

Expanding Coverage

Chipping Away at Welfare Medicine: Utah and Oregon

As suggested earlier, expansion of Medicaid to new populations was generally accompanied by a substantial undermining of national guarantees, as
was most evident in states such as Utah and Oregon.[40] In 2002, Utah became the first place to use a waiver to provide basic benefits for previously
ineligible, low-income adults.[41] Through its newly established Primary
Care Network (PCN), clients would be entitled mainly to primary and preventive physician services and emergency-room care: the program did not
include hospitalization or specialists (e.g., cardiologists). It also limited
drugs to only four prescriptions per month and excluded follow-up services. Recipients would have to pay a $50 enrollment fee, along with from
$5 to $30 in copayments. It was assumed that hospitals and other doctors
would provide charity care to PCN participants as needed.[42] At the same
time, the state reduced benefits (i.e., eliminated dental and vision services)
and increased cost sharing for some current Medicaid clients, mostly mothers
on welfare.

The program also was capped, thereby serving only a fraction of eligible
families in need of services.[43] In a survey of beneficiaries in both the traditional program and the PCN, researchers tellingly found that, among other
problems, the majority of participants, especially households enrolled in
the PCN plan, used or required services beyond the scope of their coverage;
nearly one-third of them had been contacted by a collection agency in the
past year for unpaid medical bills. In addition, compared to equivalent
families relying on Medicaid across the United States, more PCN respondents were foregoing or delaying medical treatments—36 percent versus 12
percent of those on Medicaid.[44]

Oregon, too, expanded Medicaid eligibility even as it reneged on federal
guarantees. Indeed, the state had a long history of broadening coverage for
its residents through an admixture of rationing services and market-based
approaches, beginning with its first such venture in 1994. Early in the
twenty-first century, taking advantage of the eased waiver process, its
greater openness to privatization, and the ability to provide different benefits to diverse Medicaid populations, Oregon raised the eligibility level

from 100 percent of the federal poverty level (FPL) to 185 percent, but now with leaner benefit packages for everyone.[45]

The state established two plans. Oregon Health Plan (OHP) Plus covered people who qualified for welfare medicine under federal law, about 75 percent of whom were in managed care; their available services were sparser than what had been provided previously. OHP Standard, designed for "optional" families, offered even more meager benefits; moreover, recipients would be charged sizeable copayments and premiums, and providers could refuse services to people who did not pay up. Only six months after the implementation of the cost-sharing provisions, about 44 percent of OHP Standard clients lost coverage, and the numbers in this plan steadily decreased thereafter. At the same time, lawmakers reduced benefits, including dental care, outpatient mental health services, and chemical dependency services. As Jonathan Oberlander aptly puts it, "It is no longer a tradeoff of covering fewer services in order to cover more people; the OHP is now covering fewer services *and* fewer people."[46]

Maximizing the Commercial Market: Premium Subsidies

Both HIFA and the DRA, especially in HHS implementation guidelines, have furthered privatization by encouraging the states to maximize the use of premium assistance programs, if cost effective, for Medicaid-eligible recipients in the labor force. Under such schemes, public money pays a share of medical insurance costs, enabling workers to purchase employer-sponsored plans or, in some places, other types of policies in the private market. In a quest to cut outlays from their state-generated resources or to meet the needs of their medically uninsured workers, officials have viewed this subsidized approach not only as another opportunity to secure more federal dollars, but also as a means of inducing employers to contribute to their workers' health care expenses. Like George W. Bush, many local policymakers are intent on reinforcing the employer-based system of medical insurance and encouraging a progressive shift from welfare medicine to commercial coverage. Since 2001, nearly half of the states have established some form of premium assistance program, and a few of them have used it as a major tool for extending coverage to uninsured low-income people.[47]

Significant numbers of employers, too, have welcomed the initiatives, especially small firms, because financial support to workers—and to themselves, if self-employed—might reduce their own obligations. Other businesses would benefit as well, including certain large companies, such as Wal-Mart, that have encountered growing criticism about the fact that a high percentage of their workforce participates in welfare medicine. Hospitals, too, regard subsidized premiums as a boon because they relieved them of a portion of their uncompensated care costs.

States are permitted to establish premium subsidies through one of three means: the earlier 1990 Health Insurance Premium Payment (HIPP) Program (a component of the regular Medicaid plan), their SCHIP plan, or the newer HIFA waiver.[48] If executed under the HIPP Program or SCHIP, which comprise mandatory welfare medicine populations, the initiatives must save the federal government money while also offering packages comparable to traditional Medicaid, a seemingly tricky task. Needless to say, these efforts have not been far reaching. Under HIFA, however, which applies to clients in optional or expansion eligibility groups, there are no service guarantees or cost-sharing limitations. As a consequence, these schemes, functioning under the new, less-demanding national requirements, tend to offer meager benefits and require that enrollees shoulder significant out-of-pocket costs.[49] They also rely heavily on commercially provided managed care.

Officials also are struggling to implement the programs without adding to their state's financial obligations. An increasing number of jurisdictions are substituting new revenue sources, such as increased "sin" taxes, for the state share.[50] Others are relying primarily on tobacco settlement money or enhanced federal dollars, to support their initiatives.[51] Overall, local lawmakers have been financially cautious; a few of them have placed caps either on enrollments or on the level of subsidies.[52] Some places, such as Maine, New Jersey, and Michigan, have been reluctant even to promote their programs.[53]

Some states have also endeavored to prevent employers from using such schemes as vehicles for dumping their own health insurance commitments. To this end, legislators have incorporated exclusions into their programs, prohibiting companies that already offer insurance or who have dropped their coverage within a certain time period (in general twelve months) from joining in.[54] They also have been reluctant to set the income-eligibility thresholds high enough to enroll a significant number of workers, in part because of costs, but also to discourage companies that already offer plans from taking advantage of government supports. A few states, such as Montana and Massachusetts, offer tax credits to small businesses as an inducement for them to maintain their existing plans.[55]

For the most part, premium-subsidized programs are small, most of them assisting few participants relative to the employed uninsured population.[56] It also is unlikely that these efforts will work or effectively meet family needs. In the main, the states are only willing to subsidize bare-bones plans. At the same time, premium costs for small firms tend to be higher than those for larger companies, all of which are experiencing a steep inflation in annual charges. To be sure, the escalating price tag is threatening the programs themselves. Most important, a reliance on employer-based insurance for medically uninsured low-income workers is particularly problematic because of the rapid turnover in their jobs. Subsidized insurance tends to be largely unaffordable for them as well—with premiums, copayments, and deductibles representing a significant percentage of their salary.[57]

Universal Coverage with Limited Resources:
Massachusetts, Maine, and Vermont

In the past several years, Massachusetts, Maine, and Vermont have enacted legislation to implement medical coverage for everyone in their states, but their elected officials are assuming that it can be accomplished without garnering more state-generated dollars. Indeed, these policymakers depend on being able to squeeze costs from their existing programs—for instance, through managed care—as well as to use "sin" taxes and provider taxes, to leverage federal dollars, or to raid funds that previously had been committed elsewhere; none of them is entertaining an increase in state income or corporate taxes. Further, although each of the programs relies on welfare medicine to some extent, the legislators are depending, to varying degrees, on subsidized premiums for employer-sponsored plans as the centerpiece of their efforts. However, they are not demanding sizeable contributions from employers. All three New England states have had a long history of interest, if not achievement, in bringing universal coverage to fruition, relatively low levels of uninsured residents, and grassroots demands for improving the situation.

Although several states in the past had tested various types of far-reaching health care reforms to draw in more of their low-income uninsured population—statewide global budgets, employer mandates, uncompensated care pools, a gross revenue tax on providers —most of these endeavors had to be downsized or discarded shortly after their ratification owing to a mix of economic and political factors. These cases demonstrate the precariousness of such initiatives at the state level.[58] Only Hawaii had been successful in achieving near universal coverage, and even that state, faced with budgetary shortfalls in the 2008 recession, has been forced to downgrade some of its goals.

More recently, despite Governor Mitt Romney's (R) determined opposition, Massachusetts launched its new, comprehensive program in 2006. Relying on both an enlargement of Medicaid and premium assistance to low-income workers, the Massachusetts Health Care Reform waiver includes individual and employer mandates: all residents must obtain medical insurance (the first state in the nation ever to require such coverage),[59] and every company will have to offer some type of plan. With private indemnity firms as its cornerstone, the newly established Commonwealth Health Insurance Connector Authority (Connector) will facilitate insurance pooling and the purchase of "affordable" policies for individuals outside of the workplace through schemes designed by four MCOs.[60]

Employers can, if interested, use the Connector as the source of their insurance. Companies are not forced to pay any premiums; instead, businesses with more than eleven employees must contribute $295 per worker annually into the government pool, certainly a paltry amount. Workers with incomes up to 300 percent of the FPL are eligible for subsidies, based on a sliding scale; they also receive tax benefits on any premiums they pay.[61] In order to limit payments from the state's general budget, lawmakers have used resources from its free-care pool to finance a portion of the assistance; such money had previously been paid to medical facilities for their care of uninsured patients. In an attempt to placate the hospitals, officials had expected to raise their Medicaid fees but were stopped short, at least temporarily, by poor economic conditions.

According to the latest Public Citizen Health Research Group survey, Massachusetts already had the preeminent Medicaid program in the nation prior to the 2006 health care reform.[62] And the Bay State now appears close to achieving universal medical insurance, a laudable accomplishment. By 2009, slightly less than 3 percent of the state's population did not have any insurance, down from roughly 11 percent before the new plan commenced.[63] Nonetheless, the situation is precarious as medical costs escalate, residents experience high and growing out-of-pocket health expenses, Medicaid participants and other low-income patients have greater difficulty in obtaining services,[64] and lawmakers contend with acute and growing budget problems during the latest national economic crisis. All told, it is unlikely that a state on its own can sustain universal coverage over time.

Vermont, too, intends to render health insurance available to all of its residents through a blend of private and public resources, but its waiver program—Global Commitment to Health—entails a block grant, an idea long sought by Republican presidents, including George W. Bush, and their congressional counterparts. Governor James Douglas (R), in effect, received free rein from the federal government to redesign his state's Medicaid program in exchange for accepting an overall $4.7 billion, five-year federal funding cap. As in a number of other places, Vermont intends to enhance welfare medicine by controlling costs, especially through managed care.

Already rated as having the third-best Medicaid program overall,[65] and with nearly one-third of its population enrolled in some type of public program, Vermont officials are seeking to lower the uninsured population to 3 percent, down from 11 percent in 2007.[66] Vermont accordingly established the Catamount Health Plan to serve residents who did not have health insurance. The state provides varying levels of premium assistance to low-income workers whose income is less than 300 percent of the FPL, allowing them to buy a state-sanctioned private benefit package. Any company that does not already contribute to its employees' health care costs (or if a worker chooses not to purchase a policy) is required to pay minimal amounts (about $365 per employee annually) into the program.[67]

Like Massachusetts, the Green Mountain State is confronting challenging economic conditions but also is working within the confines of ceilings on its federal grants. Elderly and disabled Medicaid clients are already on waiting lists for LTC. In 2009, the governor proposed a series of reductions that will adversely affect the state's welfare medicine participants, and a planned expansion to the Catamount Health Plan is in jeopardy.[68] Thus far, despite its well-intentioned goals, Vermont has not reduced its uninsurance rate materially, millions of citizens remain underinsured, and progress toward universal health care is at risk.[69]

Maine's endeavors toward universal coverage have been even more problematic. Relying on premium assistance and greater Medicaid coverage, Governor John Baldacci (D) strove to achieve comprehensive insurance for everyone in the state by 2009. Policymakers initially expanded eligibility for adults through MaineCare, the state's traditional welfare medicine program.[70] In 2005, they established the Dirigo Choice Health Plan to assist low-income uninsured workers and the self-employed.[71] Subsidies are based on household income; employers are required to pay 60 percent of premium costs, both for their covered staff and those eligible for Medicaid.

Again, seeking to limit the state's own outlays, the legislature began replacing its contributions to Dirigo Choice with an assessment fee on the gross revenues of medical insurance firms. These charges immediately prompted a series of lawsuits by the industry. Indeed, funding mechanisms for the program have always been unstable and insufficient to meet the intended goals, especially as medical costs soared. In 2007, policymakers were forced to cap enrollments, engendering a growing waiting list among families most in need of assistance. The following year, the program had to borrow money from the state's general fund, which it must pay back with interest. By 2009, only a fraction of the projected number of enrollees had signed up, some because of the high cost of purchasing a policy. The fiscal setback since then, especially the large loss of jobs, undoubtedly does not bode well for more widespread health insurance in Maine.

Lawmakers elsewhere—including in Connecticut, Illinois, Indiana, California, New Mexico, New York, Pennsylvania, Maryland, and Wisconsin— also have been interested, to varying extents, in providing health care coverage to everyone in their state. New Mexico's governor Bill Richardson (D), for example, put forward "Insure New Mexico!" Indiana, which has an especially large number of uninsured residents because of the steady loss of its manufacturing jobs, is scrambling for ways to insure its population through such means as provider taxes, greater cigarette taxes, and special levies on employers. Wisconsin, which has a relatively low medically uninsured population in general (less than 10 percent), is seeking to expand Medicaid to every household in need by offering separate benefit packages.[72] California has toyed with a number of schemes for achieving universal health care, but it has been caught among a legislature that prefers a state-run, single-payer health insurance system, a governor, Arnold Schwarzenegger (R), who is insisting on a private-based approach, and a small majority of the electorate that has refused to impose an employer mandate. Nearly all of these initiatives, however, have been thwarted by the 2008 recession as states simultaneously struggle to maintain current welfare medicine obligations and to balance their budgets.

Dismantling the Program

Slashing Coverage and Benefits:
Tennessee, Missouri, Mississippi, and Rhode Island

Even as a number of states were making efforts to enhance benefits or improve coverage, a few of them wasted little time in using their augmented waiver authority to enact deep reductions in welfare medicine. Tennessee and Missouri led the pack, cutting people and services outright, and Mississippi and a few other states followed suit, although with less-drastic measures. Rhode Island is chipping away at guarantees through a recent wholesale revamping of its plan.

Armed with permission from the Bush administration, Tennessee governor Philip Bredesen (D) attempted massive disenrollment from its Medicaid program (TennCare) in 2005 by restricting the eligibility of nearly half of the program's adults and by reducing optional benefits for the remaining participants, including children; prescription drugs were also limited to five prescriptions per month.[73] The governor succeeded in removing about 120,000 people—mainly the working poor and medically needy— from the rolls, although this number was far short of his original objective.[74] According to a Families USA report, the cuts had devastating effects on and in some cases were life threatening for many of those who lost coverage or services.[75]

In that same year, Missouri's new governor, Matt Blunt (R), and his solidly Republican legislature sought to slash welfare medicine benefits and coverage drastically.[76] They lowered the eligibility ceiling for working parents from 82 percent to 42 percent of the FPL: about 90,600 people were immediately dropped from the rolls, and more were disqualified shortly thereafter. Missouri officials also eliminated its Medical Assistance for Workers with Disabilities Program (based on the federal Ticket to Work Act).[77] In addition, older and disabled recipients lost funding for certain durable medical equipment (including wheelchair batteries, bed rails, communication devices, walkers, crutches, eyeglasses, hearing aids, and bath benches),[78] dental care, optical services, and physical therapy. Medicaid premiums were raised as well; although modest, the increase fostered a 30 percent decline in the enrollment of children participating in the state's Managed Care Plus for kids plan.

Most important, the Missouri legislature authorized the closure of its entire Medicaid plan, establishing instead a restructured, considerably leaner one in 2007.[79] Grounded in a market-based approach, MO Health-Net mandated managed care for all participants by 2013, established a pilot program for subsidized employer-based insurance, and authorized state tax credits for families who purchase medical insurance on their own. It also permitted physicians to collect copayments from beneficiaries. Not surprisingly, the new plan did not restore coverage for most of the low-income people who had been cut from Medicaid in prior years, although it did reinstate eye care and dental services.

Mississippi, too, endeavored to lower welfare medicine outlays at the expense of its low-income residents. Despite the state's dubious distinction of already having the most deficient Medicaid program in the nation,[80] in 2004 Governor Haley Barbour (R) eliminated benefits for a significant number of elderly and disabled recipients. He also decreased the number of allowable prescription drugs from seven to five[81] and shortly thereafter required annual enrollment and recertification through face-to-face interviews, thus fostering a large drop in caseloads.[82] Since then, Mississippi has experienced considerable budgetary shortfalls, and there has been a standoff between the governor and the legislature over how to fill the revenue gaps.[83]

Rhode Island is undermining its low-income health program's entitlement status by capping federal and state expenditures through its Consumer Choice Global Compact plan. Unlike Vermont, which sought a lump sum from Congress to extend health insurance to more residents, Rhode Island is interested primarily in using its block grant to control welfare medicine spending. Pushed forward by Governor Donald Carcieri (R) and approved in the waning days of the George W. Bush administration, the agreement provides a fixed $12 billion in federal money over five years in exchange for full state authority over eligibility, scope of services, and the degree of cost sharing.[84] One of the main goals is to lower expensive LTC services: the state will guarantee institutional care only to those frail elders at the highest risk; others will receive HCBS that are contingent on the availability of funds. Lawmakers also intend to move all beneficiaries into managed care, reduce prescription drug coverage, institute higher copayments, ration certain treatments, and possibly eliminate some services, such as dental and mental health care as well as medical-related transportation. Given the current economic climate, the prospects appear dim for the Ocean State's low-income Medicaid clients: sharp reductions in benefits, along with waiting lists, are inevitable.

Subverting the Entitlement: Health Opportunity Accounts and Behavioral Controls

Using such catchwords as *greater choices, personal responsibility, patient empowerment,* and *competition* in their restructuring of welfare medicine, many states are using waivers to dismantle traditional Medicaid guarantees through the use of flexible benefit accounts. Modeled after the commercial, tax-deferred Health Savings Accounts (HSAs) promoted by the Bush administration for the middle class,[85] the Medicaid versions are yet another attempt both to control Medicaid costs and to undermine welfare medicine. Until the passage of the DRA and its general license to undercut national standards and consumer protections, several states were already using section 1115 waivers to promote such schemes. Beginning in 2006, availing themselves of the "new flexibilities," more and more states have enacted policies to make clients more responsible for their health services through either pilot HSAs or Health Opportunity Accounts (HOAs).[86] Under these "consumer-directed" approaches, Medicaid recipients receive money at capped amounts to purchase their own medical care in the private market.[87]

In promoting these types of programs, elected officials allege that welfare medicine participants, with little incentive to make cost-effective medical decisions, have been carelessly "overusing" services and making poor medical budgetary choices. The dubious if not simplistic assumption underlying the sponsorship of these accounts is that low-income people will be "empowered" with more "choices." In reality, many Medicaid recipients will be forced to forgo essential health services for themselves and their children or to decide between medical care and other basic needs, such as

food and heating. HSAs and HOAs are certainly among the more questionable market-based approaches gaining support among political leaders intent on sabotaging the right of the poor to health care. For the most part,
they turn welfare medicine from a defined benefit program, with open-
ended services, into a defined contribution plan that will inevitably and
severely restrict the types and amount of services people receive, regardless
of their medical needs.

Several states are also establishing other types of programs aimed at
controlling what their lawmakers deem "irresponsible" behavior, but, again,
without considering the consequences for their welfare medicine clients.
Montana has imposed one of the most disciplinary measures: launched in
2005 as a pilot program and expanded the following year, Team Care was
established for people who are designated as "overusing" Medicaid; such
individuals have to choose a primary-care provider and pharmacy, and
call Nurse First before they can receive any medical assistance or medications. Nurse First decides when, how, and where services can be provided.[88]
Although lawmakers have applauded the significant decline in visits to
doctors and emergency rooms, they have shown less interest in whether
recipients' health care needs have been compromised.

Some places are blaming clients for their own poor health and incorpo-
rating various types of "healthy behavior" initiatives into their HSAs or
HOAs; others are establishing such schemes separately. Using "carrots" and
"sticks," more and more states are seeking to control Medicaid recipients'
behavior and lifestyle.[89] West Virginia, in one of the boldest—and more
punitive—examples of such "healthy behavior" initiatives, restructured
nearly its entire Medicaid program around incentives. Promoted by Governor Joe Manchin (D) and targeted to families receiving cash-assistance
welfare, the revised plan (Medicaid Design) offers a special benefits package, Mountain Health Choices, to clients who sign an enforceable agreement to lead a healthy lifestyle, seek routine medical checkups and screenings, attend all doctor appointments, take their medications as directed,
and visit the emergency room only for urgent situations.[90] Forced into an
MCO, which must ensure compliance with the pact, enrollees receive a few
new services, such as weight-management and nutritional education, in addition to those covered under the previous program. Families who do not
sign or abide by the terms of the covenant are penalized, however: they are
placed in a basic plan and thus receive just the minimum benefits required

by federal law and only up to four prescriptions per month. Not surprisingly, given the complicated arrangements, a mere 15 percent of eligible adults had signed up their families as of 2009. As a result, most enrollees, including children, had their benefits restricted.[91]

A few places have combined HOAs and healthy behavior initiatives. Seeking deep savings in Medicaid and basing the sweeping revision of its plan on individual responsibility and incentives, Oklahoma centered its pilot program on encouraging patients to use medical resources more prudently. It offers recipients vouchers, based on their age and health status, to purchase insurance privately or to take part in an employer-sponsored plan. The initiative is coupled with a Personal Health Account; participants who engage in a variety of "healthy behaviors" can use it to pay for noncovered services, cost sharing, and wellness activities.[92] With similar guiding principles based on consumer empowerment and choice, New Hampshire set out to "modernize" its Medicaid program.[93] The resultant GraniteCare Enhanced Care Coordination Program, launched as a demonstration in 2007, comprises HSAs as well as inducements and bonuses for recipients who achieve particular health-related goals and spend less than their allotted amount of money.

Michigan, too, has applied a personal responsibility approach for its optional Medicaid population. In return for quitting smoking, losing weight, seeking routine checkups, and keeping their doctor appointments, clients pay lower copays and receive expanded benefits (e.g., dental services and more prescription drugs). Iowa engages in a similar strategy for its discretionary welfare medicine participants but has drastically reduced their benefits package. Offering only basic hospital and physician services provided by a restricted network of health professionals, most of whom practice in just a few clinics, the new program also imposes premiums and copays on enrollees. Overweight participants who diet successfully are exempt from the cost-sharing provisions.[94]

Rewards for "healthy behavior" or, even worse, penalties for not achieving weight-loss or smoking-cessation goals, treat low-income people like children and make them accountable for conduct not demanded of individuals who can pay for their own insurance. It also renders the poor "responsible" for their own and their children's illnesses and forces them to pay a price for factors that may be beyond their control. Typical of such absurdity is a warning from Angus King, former governor of Maine and cochair of the Federal Medicaid Advisory Commission: "We're so afraid of violating the social insurance principle, there's no advantage to people being healthy. . . . We've taken the personal responsibility piece from all this."[95] What is more, in blaming low-income Medicaid participants for medical neglect, we are failing to remedy situations that might ultimately improve low-income families' health and well-being.

Privatizing Medicaid: Florida

With the intentions of forcing nearly all Medicaid clients into market-based health insurance and empowering the companies covering them, Florida governor Jeb Bush (R) pushed through one of the more aggressive efforts to end Medicaid as an entitlement; in 2005, HHS endorsed his section 1115 waiver with little fanfare in a mere sixteen days.[96] Up to that time, the state had a relatively small Medicaid managed-care population, but, even so, its experience with the commercial insurance industry had been plagued by widespread abuses, including fraudulent marketing practices, falsification of applications, and poor-quality care.[97]

Nevertheless, by the end of 2006, not only had Governor Bush mandated managed care for nearly everyone,[98] but this time participating firms would have an unprecedented authority to determine which services—and how many—would be covered, along with the ability to exclude "optional" services that were once offered in the state. Labeled "empowered care," the plan provided recipients a subsidy—based on their health status and prior use of medical services—with which to purchase their own insurance or, for low-income workers, to opt out of Medicaid and buy into an employer-sponsored policy if one was available to them. Participants also received rewards for "healthy behavior" to use for the purchase of additional health-related benefits, such as nonprescription medications.[99]

From the start, the state's pilot programs were beset with problems, including inordinately low physician-participation rates, restrictions on medically necessary services,[100] instability of coverage,[101] fraudulent practices, and violations of federal regulations.[102] Deep concerns about the managed-care experiment were reinforced by research findings that a significant percentage of doctors had either withdrawn from Medicaid entirely or considerably lowered the number of welfare medicine patients in their practice.[103]

A report by Florida's inspector general confirmed that the waiver demonstrations were severely flawed. It cautioned that the MCOs have "too few specialists, untimely access to care, inaccurate information about resources and patient needs, and inaccessible drug coverage information and consumer service phone numbers." The evidence also suggested that enrollees, especially individuals with mental illness or complex medical conditions, encountered difficulty in obtaining all of the prescription drugs and medical services that they required. Just as troubling, the state had not instituted a consumer complaint procedure. In fact, there was only limited government oversight of the program generally. Even though the inspector general urged political officials to refrain from expanding such a defective program to the rest of Florida's counties,[104] and despite the morass of horror stories and considerable protest, lawmakers added three more counties in 2007 and expect the plan to take effect statewide as scheduled.[105]

Targeting Populations: Kentucky

States are increasingly taking advantage of the DRA's permission to undermine national standards and ration services by targeting benefits to particular low-income populations. Although a few states had already established small pilot programs in that vein under HIFA and section 1115 waivers, Kentucky was one of the first to respond to the DRA's more broadly based authorization—and encouragement—to do so by overhauling its entire Medicaid plan.[106] Its new, leaner low-income health program, KyHealth Choices, includes four separate benefit packages, each tailored to different categories of people, including parents, pregnant women, frail children, and Supplemental Security Income recipients (Global Choices); most children (Family Choices); the elderly and disabled in need of LTC (Comprehensive Choices); and the mentally disabled (Optimal Choices).[107] It also provides premium assistance for employer-sponsored coverage, allowing low-income workers to opt out of Medicaid entirely.

To varying extents, all of Kentucky's Medicaid participants are subject to higher out-of-pocket expenses and trimmed benefits. Global Choices, for example, imposes premiums and higher copayments on certain items, including in-patient hospital care and nonpreferred prescription drugs.[108] It also rations services: clients are limited to four medications per month and a maximum of fifteen visits per year for physical, speech, and occupational therapy. Restrictions have been placed on some procedures as well, such as radiology. Beneficiaries can secure "rewards" through the Get Healthy Benefits program by participating in and complying with a disease-management regimen (diabetes, asthma, heart disease) for a year; the "rewards" include limited dental and vision services or access to selected "wellness" programs.[109] Governor Ernie Fletcher (R), who launched the state's revamped plan in anticipation of massive savings, was instead confronted with higher Medicaid outlays in the project's first year.[110] Kentucky is apparently yet another state that is seeking to save money by restricting its low-income residents' access to medical care and is winding up instead with a downsized but costlier plan.

Children First

Toward Universal Coverage

Most states have already increased—or intend to expand—the number of medically insured children, and some are seeking to cover all their youngsters. By 2006, forty states had enrolled children in families with incomes up to 200 percent of the FPL, and many of them have drawn the line even higher.[111] Most notably, by mid-2007, seven states had enacted measures to extend health insurance to every child, and six more were proposing to do so.[112] To be sure, several of them are initiating such expansions as a first step toward universal health care. Few places, however, propose to fund their enlarged programs through their own resources.

In Illinois, All Kids—launched by Governor Rod Blagojevich (D) while he was still in office and building on an already strong base of coverage—offers subsidized insurance to uninsured children who are not eligible for Medicaid or SCHIP. As usual, policymakers expect to move forward with their plans through cost savings as a result of a newly enacted managed-care mandate and disease-management projects, along with funds derived from the program's substantial cost-sharing provisions.[113] The state is also steadily expanding insurance to adults through its FamilyCare program.[114]

Before his political demise, Governor Eliot Spitzer (D) of New York had endorsed universal coverage for children, also with the ultimate goal of providing access to insurance more broadly. The state's SCHIP program

(Child Health Plus), already the largest in the nation, was expanded even further; in 2007, New York policymakers raised the income-eligibility level to 400 percent of the FPL, thereby qualifying nearly every uninsured child. As discussed in the next section, the Bush administration rejected New York's waiver.

Not all states are improving their young residents' situation, and many of them are struggling just to maintain their existing coverage under SCHIP. What is more, because of declining numbers of families enrolled in employer-based plans, children lost ground for the first time in 2005. Until then, the steady growth of Medicaid caseloads had compensated both for the deterioration of private insurance and the leveling of SCHIP enrollments. More children were now medically uninsured, slightly more than 11 percent of the total nationwide, and a much higher proportion receives only sporadic coverage.[115]

The State Children's Health Insurance Program: Caught in the Crossfire

The Bush administration's lukewarm support of SCHIP and its initiatives to starve the program not only limited any expansion in the number of children served, but kept the program from protecting everyone who was eligible.[116] A number of states continued to encounter shortfalls in their plans, which forced them to freeze enrollments; Congress provided them with only limited, supplementary funds to meet their existing obligations.[117] When it was time to reauthorize the program itself, lawmakers who were intent on expanding it—Democrats, some Republicans, and the majority of governors—met considerable resistance, especially from the White House. HHS secretary Michael Leavitt demeaned it as a "big-government approach that would pave the way for socialized medicine," despite the large number of participants covered through commercial insurance companies.[118] To him, the president, and other Republicans, it was just another middle-class government entitlement that they needed to ward off. After a long, heated battle, Congress eventually agreed to reauthorization legislation; Bush promptly vetoed it, along with a second measure. At the end of 2007, he ultimately signed a bill that barely maintained the program at its current level for another eighteen months.

Meanwhile, in order to circumvent the legislature, preempt expansive SCHIP policies in the states,[119] and ensure that the government health program would not substitute for (or "crowd-out") commercial insurance, the administration issued new directives in an August 17, 2007, letter to the states.[120] These rules limited participation of children living in households with incomes higher than 250 percent of the FPL and penalized states with more liberal income thresholds. They also raised cost-sharing requirements and prevented families from replacing any private coverage with welfare medicine.[121]

In keeping with the August 17 regulations, the White House held state attempts to boost coverage of youngsters at bay. New York's request to increase its SCHIP eligibility ceiling to 400 percent of the FPL was turned down; its elected officials went forward anyway, paying out of the state's own resources. Other states, such as Ohio, Louisiana, Montana, and Oklahoma, were also denied permission to raise their income thresholds above the 250 percent level. As a result, at least seven states were forced to downsize or even abandon, at least temporarily, their goal of enlarging the number of children participating in welfare medicine. The administration expected to block additional jurisdictions as well: states that already covered children in families that earned higher than 250 percent of the FPL would have to conform to the new rules by August 2008 or pay for the extended coverage out of their own budgets.[122] In his ongoing efforts to privatize as many public benefits as possible, Bush advocated tax credits or tax deductions in lieu of any growth in SCHIP. Along with other conservative policymakers, he also sought to eject the relatively few adults covered under the program.

Barack Obama will now leave his mark on the health care debate, including what role the low-income health plans should play in insuring children and adults alike. Along with his stronger Democratic majorities in both Houses of Congress, the president may even progress toward more comprehensive health insurance generally. During his first month in office, he had already signed SCHIP extension legislation (the Children's Health Insurance Program Reauthorization Act) that added nearly 4 million more children to the program, including legal immigrants; at a cost of $33 billion over five years, the broadened program is funded almost entirely by an increase in the federal tobacco tax. The bill also permits states to raise their eligibility levels up to 300 percent of the FPL. The economic stimulus package contributes a whopping $87 billion for Medicaid, and even more money is being set aside for a larger health initiative.

+ +

Conclusion: Smokescreens and Mirrors

In the first decade of the twenty-first century, in order to "sell" their assault on Medicaid and the poor to the public, the George W. Bush administration, New Republican conservatives, and certain Democrats framed the issues in terminology that defied reality. Doggedly promoting "new flexibilities" for the states, more "choices" and "individual responsibility" for beneficiaries, and increased commercialization of health care services, they pressed the states to follow suit. Although enthusiastic about abolishing the "one-size-fits-all" philosophy, most governors and state legislators were wary of the financial consequences: greater local policy authority most often translated into fewer federal dollars.

For Medicaid beneficiaries, *empowerment* and *greater choices* have been insidious code words for leaner benefit packages, lower services, reduced access to health professionals, and fewer consumer protections. Because one of the most prominent goals for elected officials in the George W. Bush years was less government and more market-based services, Medicaid *reform, enhanced efficiency,* and *improved competition,* the popular phrases of the day, were all catchwords for shrinking welfare medicine while subordinating the program to insurance companies' interests. In earlier years, Medicaid participants were coaxed into managed care; under the new Medicaid rules, more people were mandated to join.

Demands that welfare medicine clients take charge of their own health and health care, dubbed "personal responsibility," are based on the core American values of work and self-reliance. In the case of Medicaid, policymakers were implying that recipients and their uninsured neighbors act irresponsibly and irrationally in their medical decisions. Such language is reminiscent of general attitudes toward welfare recipients, who have been demonized as "lazy and shiftless": in the mid-1990s, they lost their entitlement to cash assistance. Scapegoating the poor, an enduring American pastime, was increasingly tied to Medicaid policymaking. New "consumer-directed" initiatives, such as HOAs, became an essential part of the "empowerment" rhetoric but, in reality, were instituted to slash Medicaid. Higher cost sharing was alleged to "encourage" recipients into making "better medical budgetary choices," but it, too, was intended primarily to shift more program costs to low-income families who cannot afford them.

The Bush administration's general approach to health care and its "solutions" to the growing number of medically uninsured families were firmly anchored in the private sector. Whenever the president could, he undercut local efforts to extend Medicaid to the uninsured, promoting the subsidization of commercial insurance—primarily managed care—instead.[123] Market-based remedies, which rely primarily on fuzzy math, were just another pretext for turning over even more social responsibilities to the business community and low-income workers themselves.

Later chapters discuss how it is not enough to increase Medicaid caseloads; policymakers must pay attention to the scope and quality of services as well. In addition, as national and state officials strive to lower public outlays, they have been targeting additional welfare medicine populations and overhauling more pieces of the low-income health care program, especially LTC. People in need, as usual, are paying the price.

5

BETTER THAN NOTHING?
WHO GETS WHAT, WHEN,
HOW, AND WHERE

In order to assess the adequacy of welfare medicine in meeting the health needs of the low-income nonelderly population, this chapter first examines *who* is actually covered under the program. It finds not only that a significant percentage of impoverished people is excluded, but that there are substantial barriers to participation, even among eligible families. Next, it addresses the question of *where* services are obtained, focusing in particular on Medicaid enrollees' inability to gain sufficient access to quality private medical practices and, at times, to any services at all. This section concentrates on the causes of the problem and how it has perpetuated a two-class medical system in the United States. It also takes up the issue of *how* and *when* participants get benefits, drawing attention to the circumstances that impede both the application and the recertification processes, leading to a discontinuous, uncertain environment of medical care.

The third part of the chapter highlights *what* recipients receive, underscoring that benefit packages often depend on factors peripheral to their health needs. Geographic location, political climate, and budgetary concerns are among the dynamics determining many of the nonmandated services available in a particular state. The final segment considers the larger role that welfare medicine plays in dealing with societal ills, arguing that policymakers try to resolve a number of these issues through Medicaid dollars because of the federal match, thereby providing only partial, generally superficial results.

Who Is Covered: Barriers to Participation

Restricted Income Eligibility

Medicaid does not make even a dent in covering the total number of low-income people who need health insurance. Eligibility is so stringent that the vast majority of states does not include everyone living in poverty. Apart from its long-term care (LTC) provisions, Medicaid is a program mainly for needy children, and yet that group, too, conspicuously lacks full protection: roughly one-fifth of youngsters living in official poverty are medically uninsured.[1] Nonelderly adults are particularly underserved: qualifying criteria in most states are inordinately low, averaging merely 65 percent of the federal poverty level (FPL), and in a number of places are stingier.[2]

Indeed, a parent in a family of three, working full-time at minimum wage, would not qualify for Medicaid in twenty-five states.[3]

Despite initiatives by a number of localities to extend welfare medicine to their uninsured residents, the low-income health program enrolls a little more than one-third of the nation's impoverished adults.[4] Nonetheless, even the officially defined indigent population can scarcely meet their family's basic needs. A disproportionate share of blacks, Latinos, and other groups on the margins of American society, along with female-headed households and the children in them, are particularly at risk.[5] In most states, certain groups of low-income people are excluded entirely, regardless of their income, including undocumented foreigners, some legal immigrants, and childless adults or those with grown children. The near elderly population (citizens between the ages of fifty-five and sixty-four) are particularly vulnerable because they are not yet old enough to qualify for Medicare, may be retired (and therefore without access to job-related insurance), and are more likely than younger adults to experience serious medical disorders.[6]

Medicaid has never safeguarded all poverty-stricken families but has done so even less comprehensively over the decades. Despite a rise in caseloads during the 1980s, only about half of the officially defined poor participated in the program, a decrease from 63 percent a decade earlier.[7] The "reform" of Aid to Families with Dependent Children in 1996 and the severing of its linkage to welfare medicine contributed to a steady erosion in the participation of female-headed households.[8] As more impoverished mothers continue to be forced into low-paying jobs that do not offer affordable health insurance, the vast majority of them lacks any medical coverage for themselves and often their children.[9]

Constraints on Participation

There is a marked difference between qualifying for Medicaid and actually gaining entry to it, primarily because several barriers block signing up for the program. As a consequence, a substantial percentage of eligible children, their parents, and dual-eligible elders who are entitled to welfare medicine are not receiving any assistance.[10] One major reason for nonparticipation is the system's often daunting complexities, which deter people from seeking coverage. Depending on the state, families confront confusing bureaucracies and demanding, complicated application processes that involve income verification and other documentation requirements; lack of or inadequate outreach; language barriers; transportation problems; misconceptions or lack of knowledge about the program; long waiting periods; high premiums and other cost-sharing provisions; and, since the 2005 Deficit Reduction Act (DRA), proof-of-citizenship requirements.

Recent investigations show that complicated and sometimes overwhelming procedures can serve as a substantial deterrent to remaining on welfare medicine as well. Bureaucratic hurdles can at times be more significant than eligibility rules in fostering disenrollment. Indeed, the percentage of people dropped from Medicaid because they no longer meet the income threshold in their state is actually quite small, especially among children.[11] One researcher discovered that in 2006 fully 40 percent of youngsters entitled to Medicaid or the State Children's Health Insurance Program (SCHIP) had been removed from the rolls during the previous year mainly because of obstacles in maintaining their qualification, and this number has increased since 2000.[12] What is more, coverage of children is often linked to their parents' participation: dropout rates for youngsters tend to be lower when their mothers, too, acquire benefits.[13] Nevertheless, only a few states include adults in their SCHIP programs, and, as noted in chapter 4, the George W. Bush administration energetically discouraged their participation.[14]

Frequency of the renewal process apparently has a large impact on the stability of coverage. Federal law requires reenrollment at least every twelve months, but in misguided attempts to purge allegedly ineligible households,[15] nearly 20 percent of the states have mandated reenrollment more often for children, and around 33 percent of them have required it for parents, generally twice a year. However, a few localities, such as New Mexico, had to revert to their earlier annual procedures after experiencing overly sharp drops in participation.[16] In contrast, when lawmakers in Florida lengthened the time period for SCHIP renewals, they fostered a more stable caseload. Louisiana, too, experienced substantially less loss of coverage when it adopted a similar policy change.[17]

Other administrative and bureaucratic impediments abound, including a patchwork of diverse rules for individuals within families. Parents sometimes have to apply for and recertify every member of their household separately. In doing so, not only must they navigate through different criteria for each person, but they may discover that although some members are eligible, others are not.[18] Furthermore, a few states require face-to-face interviews in order to renew children, and nearly one-third of the states demands them of adults, even though mail-in or phone procedures have proven much less problematic for clients.[19]

States often have stringent documentation requirements as well, including income, asset, and identity verifications. In one nationwide survey, investigators found that, in addition to the complications of the process, one of the major stumbling blocks was obtaining the required papers.[20] Even so, some states, such as Georgia, are imposing more stringent validation policies.[21] Furthermore, as I show later in this chapter, the DRA mandated a rigorous proof of citizenship and identity that has generated massive disenrollments everywhere.

The history of Washington State demonstrates the vital importance of the screening process in participation rates. After steadily easing regulations in the 1990s, lawmakers in the state reversed course in 2003; they issued stricter income-verification guidelines and abolished the continuous twelve-month eligibility for children. A study of the earlier and later rule modifications found that they had a measurable impact on coverage: according to the researchers, "As the state adopted a number of changes to streamline the re-enrollment process, there was a decline in the rates of individuals leaving Medicaid enrollment. As requirements were increased, retention rates declined."[22] In fact, the actual reduction in caseloads after 2003, primarily among children, was far higher than had been anticipated.

An inadequate understanding of Medicaid, SCHIP, and their requirements, compounded by limited state outreach efforts, also discourages families from joining the programs and continuing their coverage. In many cases, families do not realize that they have to renew their eligibility on a regular basis, or they have difficulty understanding the forms and filling them out.[23] One survey that compared eligible but uninsured children with those actually participating in Medicaid identified lack of knowledge about how welfare medicine functions as one of the more considerable barriers. More than 70 percent of the parents whose youngsters were not enrolled believed inaccurately that the program had time limits similar to cash-assistance welfare, and more than 50 percent did not know that their child qualified, were unsure of how to apply or where to go, or found the rules confusing and complicated. The investigation highlighted additional obstructions: a significant minority of families had difficulty finding transportation to the Medicaid agency, meeting its office hours, or waiting the long hours that the certification process entailed, mostly because of job constraints. Furthermore, about half of those who spoke Spanish experienced language difficulties.[24]

Because of these myriad impediments, families tend to cycle on and off the low-income health programs, rendering it difficult, if not impossible, for them to keep up their medical treatments. The problem of discontinuity is exacerbated by sometimes inconsistent household income, stemming from the instability of low-wage employment, which can affect eligibility. The convoluted rules, restrictions, and penalties associated with the Temporary Assistance for Needy Families program can have an impact as well, periodically triggering a temporary loss of coverage.[25] The situation is worsened in those states that impose waiting periods—specified amounts of time that people must be uninsured before they can be certified or reinstated in the plan.

Nearly half of all Medicaid or SCHIP beneficiaries have had interruptions in their benefits, forcing them to do without their prescription drugs, postpone preventive services, and forgo medical care for chronic conditions (i.e., diabetes, cancer, and heart disease), all of which can result in seriously deteriorating health or even death. Low-income families paying for medical services on their own during these interludes may be forced to sacrifice other basic needs or to accumulate huge debts from which they most likely will never recover. Although some eligible people who are dropped from welfare medicine on procedural grounds eventually regain coverage, sometimes within a few months, a significant percentage of them never enrolls again. Nor do they gain access to private insurance, thus swelling the ranks of the medically uninsured in the United States.

Client Cost Sharing

As lawmakers impose greater cost sharing on Medicaid recipients and justify the measures with convenient explanations, they have encumbered the poor with increasingly unaffordable fees that have had a harmful effect on their ability to seek medical treatment or even participate in welfare medicine itself. The imposition of more and higher patient out-of-pocket outlays is first and foremost a niggardly measure that aims to save the government money at the expense of low-income and indigent families. Nevertheless, state officials typically contend that premiums, copayments, and deductibles force participants to become more "engaged" in their health care and to render more cost-conscious medical decisions. Such assertions advance the ill-founded notion that the poor consume unnecessary and overly expensive services. As Families USA points out, however, there is no evidence at all that low-income families utilize health services needlessly.[26] Some proponents of greater cost sharing also insist that it serves to prevent workers from dropping their employer-sponsored coverage, when available, because virtually all private plans impose some financial responsibility on participants.

In actuality, greater economic burdens on Medicaid participants limit their ability to gain access to services, thus endangering their health and well-being. As several knowledgeable observers tell us, "A longstanding body of research demonstrates that when cost sharing is increased significantly for low-income people, their use of essential health care services declines and their health status worsens."[27] The vast majority of affected families cannot afford the cost-sharing fees. In an analysis of budgets for a family of four living at the FPL, researchers concluded that essentials— housing, utilities, transportation, food, and child care—absorb every available resource, not allowing for higher medical outlays.[28] For individuals already hedging about taking their medications, such as the mentally ill, an increase in out-of-pocket expenses may tip the balance against the drugs.

Such an increase in client payments also discourages some people from enrolling in Medicaid or forces them to drop their coverage, leading to a greater uninsured population. In a study of Washington, Hawaii, and Minnesota, investigators determined that only about 57 percent of people without insurance would enroll in a government health program if families were charged a premium equivalent to one percent of their income, and only 18 percent would join if the fee was equivalent to 5 percent.[29]

The actual experience in several states corroborates these findings. As part of its Medicaid waiver, Oregon increased out-of-pocket costs for adults in 2003 and instituted a six-month loss of coverage for people who did not pay their premiums.[30] As a result, nearly half of the individuals affected by the new requirements left the program. Researchers found that individuals who dropped out because they could not afford the charges ultimately experienced less access to health services and more financial difficulties than people who stayed on the program or withdrew for other reasons. The former participants also often reported a greater deterioration in their health.[31] New cost-sharing provisions have had similar effects elsewhere. Almost immediately after Rhode Island imposed a premium on certain families, about one-fifth of them lost coverage because they did not pay it; nearly half of them claimed that they could not come up with the money.[32] Similar enrollment losses stemming from increased premiums, especially among the lowest-income households, occurred in Vermont, Missouri, and several other jurisdictions.[33]

Immigrants

Over the decades, the national government has endeavored to conserve Medicaid dollars by steadily whittling away at medical benefits for low-income foreign-born families. With the exception of "emergency" services, undocumented immigrants have been barred from the program entirely, although what exactly characterizes an emergency varies from place to place. On the one hand, states may press for more expansive definitions in some cases so as to maximize federal Medicaid dollars, thus fostering yet another controversy between the two levels of government over financing issues.[34] On the other hand, local policymakers are also often reluctant to finance expensive medical treatments for undocumented households.[35]

Beginning in 1996 (under the Personal Responsibility and Work Opportunity Reconciliation Act), the states were precluded from receiving federal Medicaid matching funds for legal immigrants, including children, who had lived in the country for less than five years, although they could provide their own assistance to this group.[36] Ten years later, in order to prevent undocumented families from obtaining benefits illicitly, a problem that could not even be verified, Congress mandated (under a provision of the DRA) that all Medicaid recipients must submit proof of their citizenship and identity. Implemented in 2006, everyone subject to the new law has to produce a birth certificate, passport, certificate of naturalization, or other designated papers.[37]

By adding to the documentation requirements, Congress not only has undercut efforts by those states endeavoring to increase participation among their Medicaid-eligible residents, but has contributed to a decline in the number of caseloads overall. Shortly after the new DRA regulations took effect, welfare medicine caseloads dropped nationwide for the first time since the late 1990s. Thousands of Medicaid applications, including those of children, have been either delayed or denied, and many more people continue to be removed from the program during the renewal process.[38]

The truth, however, is that most individuals who lose access to the government health programs are American citizens, not illegal immigrants. Research data suggest that low-income families who are native born may have difficulty in obtaining the proper documents expeditiously, thus forcing them out of Medicaid and SCHIP for at least some period of time.[39] Administrators of state Medicaid programs, including officials in Iowa, Kansas, Louisiana, and Wisconsin, reached similar conclusions: Kevin Concannon, director of the Iowa Department of Human Services, warned: "The largest adverse effect of this policy has been on people who are American citizens. . . . [W]e have not turned up many undocumented immigrants receiving Medicaid in Waterloo, Dubuque or anywhere else in Iowa."[40] One study predicts that nearly 10 percent of U.S. nationals who are enrolled in Medicaid will eventually be forced from the program because of the DRA requirements.[41] Certain sectors of society will be affected disproportionately, including minorities; people who are mentally ill, homeless, or severely disabled; individuals who are not residing in their state of birth; and citizen children of illegal immigrants.

Significant numbers of income-eligible families who are not participating in the government health programs because of the DRA rules are waiting to enroll or receive recertification. Delays in coverage—sometimes for several months or more—are now widespread as families scramble to obtain (and pay for) the necessary documentation and as Medicaid agency workers struggle to cope with the overwhelming numbers of verifications, amounting to an estimated 10 million applicants and 38 million renewals nationally. In several states, considerable backlogs have developed.[42] Although many households will eventually be covered, they are being forced to endure long periods without health insurance, a particularly dire situation for individuals with chronic disorders. Children must do without preventive care, vital medical treatments, and medications that even for a short interval of time may have dangerously adverse effects on their health.[43]

More families are now relying on hospital emergency rooms and struggling public clinics, which are shouldering at least part of the financial burdens of caring for families who are waiting to enroll in Medicaid or

SCHIP. In an initial assessment of the new requirements' impact on community health centers, one study reported that 60 percent of them were providing services to individuals who had lost welfare medicine coverage; more than 20 percent had a simultaneous decrease in Medicaid-funded patients and a growth in the number who were uninsured.[44]

Impediments to Obtaining Services

Inadequate Access to Providers

Not surprisingly, qualifying for the low-income health program is not a guarantee of obtaining services: for many families, it is difficult to find a provider, at least one within a reasonable distance from their home, who will accept them as patients. Indeed, welfare medicine enrollees often discover that when they attempt to make an appointment for an office visit, and the receptionist asks what type of insurance they have, they are most likely to hear that they are not welcome based on their response. Professional health groups, such as the American Medical Association and the American Dental Association, have contended over the years that inadequate fees are the primary reason for the shortages of practitioners willing to treat Medicaid patients. Nonetheless, rather than a direct causal link between low reimbursement rates and access problems, as the professionals claim, most research on the subject suggests that other factors play a role as well. In one major study of the issue, researchers learned that although compensation levels are strongly associated with the probability that doctors will admit new welfare medicine patients, the effects of these fees are tempered by practice type and size, the extent of managed care in an area, physician characteristics, Medicaid policies, and community traits.[45]

Raising or lowering payments may not be the only factor affecting the supply of physicians available to participants in an area, but it is a vital one. Because physician and dental care in the United States—and the insurance companies that fund them—are mostly profit-making enterprises, and such providers do not have to participate in the government health insurance programs, low reimbursements substantially curtail the availability of services. In the main, whenever states have endeavored to control high and spiraling Medicaid costs, they have alternated between focusing on participants (by raising eligibility, trimming benefit packages, increasing copayments) and zeroing in on providers (by freezing or lowering fees, revising rate-setting methodologies, creating new payment and service structures), and they sometimes take aim at both simultaneously. Nonetheless, when officials freeze or lower practitioner fees, they adversely affect recipients as well: more private medical practices will opt out of the program or stop accepting new public-aid patients.

The scarcity of health professionals willing to serve families covered under welfare medicine is inconsistent with national Medicaid guarantees, including those related to the Early and Periodic Screening, Diagnosis, and Treatment (EPSDT) Program. Under federal law, all children enrolled in the low-income health care program are entitled to periodic EPSDT services, including appropriate immunizations. Likewise, Congress early on had appended to the Medicaid statute the "equal access provision" requiring high enough fees to ensure an adequate supply of quality providers. It held that state plans must "provide such methods and procedures relating to the utilization of, and the payment for, care and services . . . to assure that payments are consistent with efficiency, economy, and quality of care and are sufficient to enlist enough providers so that care and services are available under the plan at least to the extent that such care and services are available to the general population in the geographic area."[46] In other words, welfare medicine recipients are entitled to an amount—and quality—of services in their communities similar to those available to people enrolled in Medicare and private insurance.

Over the decades, state officials clearly have not been sufficiently attentive to either the EPSDT Program or "equal access" Medicaid provisions. Few welfare medicine participants, including children, have ever had unhampered entrée to mainstream medical care, and since the 1990s hardly any political leaders even bring up the subject.[47] Inadequate access to high-quality, private-sector medical practitioners reaches back to Medicaid's earliest years and is even worse today.

Provider Shortages: Physicians

Doctor shortages have been endemic to the Medicaid program: at the outset, state policymakers were not prepared to pay physicians a rate equivalent to that of Medicare and were even less inclined to meet commercial fees. During the 1980s, reimbursements generally decreased, along with a declining number of doctors ready to serve welfare medicine patients.[48] In many places, especially low-income urban areas, those practitioners who did take part in the program were organized into poor-quality "Medicaid mills." By the end of the decade, the gap between Medicaid and other payers (i.e., Medicare and private insurers) had widened, and there was a considerable dearth of doctors enlisted in the program. Specialists were in particularly short supply. For instance, the proportion of pediatricians nationwide that turned away low-income health plan clients jumped from 26 percent in 1979 to 39 percent in 1989.[49]

Since then, physician fees have ebbed and flowed, depending on state officeholders' political will and the annual status of their respective budgets. Regardless, they have never been good enough to satisfy the practitioners and rarely match fees paid for equivalent services to other customers. As a consequence, families participating in Medicaid still do not have sufficient access to private medical practices: by the early twenty-first century, almost one-third of primary-care physicians were not accepting any new Medicaid patients at all.[50] The results of a 2005 nationwide survey by Peter Cunningham and Jessica May indicated that roughly 35 percent of solo practice physicians and 24 percent of small group practices rejected welfare medicine enrollees, up from 29 percent and 16 percent, respectively, in 1997. Indeed, the investigators reported that physicians who work in large group practices, community health clinics, academic medical centers, or public hospitals are the most willing to treat such clients.[51]

Specialists are conspicuously absent in the program: across the United States, Medicaid recipients generally wait longer for appointments and must travel greater distances for their services than other insured consumers. Regulations in some states give health plans a wide berth in how far enrollees can travel for care. Incredibly, Florida requires only that its plans provide specialists within sixty miles or a sixty-minute drive of participants' homes. A 2006 *Palm Beach Post* investigation of two counties in the state uncovered yet another major problem, one that is prevalent everywhere: even if a physician is listed as a participating provider, it does not necessarily mean that he or she actually treats welfare medicine clients. In the study area, of the 750 doctors on Florida's official Medicaid registry, fully one-third of those contacted by newspaper staff, including 43 percent of the specialists, indicated that they in fact would not accept such patients.

The problem among certain specialists was even more acute: only two out of twenty-four orthopedic surgeons and eleven of the forty-six cardiology practices on the list were willing to serve low-income health program recipients.[52] In a similar study in Utah, only three of twenty-six urologists on the state's Medicaid provider rolls billed the program in 2006 and 2007. Other specialists—such as abdominal surgeons, cardiovascular surgeons, geriatricians, hand surgeons, head and neck surgeons, pediatric radiologists, and therapeutic radiologists—performed no Medicaid-funded services at all.[53]

Managed-care organizations (MCOs) only exacerbate the problem because they tend to be particularly stingy in their payments and exacting in their demands on practitioners. In Pennsylvania, for example, few specialists have been willing to join Medicaid MCOs. According to the state's Department of Public Welfare, nearly 33 percent of Medicaid enrollees surveyed in 2005 said they had a problem seeing a specialist, as compared to 21 percent only two years earlier.[54] Although MCOs often rely on public funding and are entirely dependent on it in the case of Medicaid-only plans, they incredibly do not always have to disclose key information about such issues as fee schedules and rejection rates for services and prescription drugs. In many places, the commercial insurers forbid their medical providers from discussing what they view as "contractual matters." In Connecticut, elected officials, legal aid groups, and others who were concerned that overly low physician payments were generating severe access-to-care problems sought information on how much doctors were being compensated by the four Medicaid-funded MCOs operating in the state. The companies resisted, asserting that the agreements were private and that the specific figures involved "trade secrets." An ongoing battle ensued among the governor, certain legislators, and insurance firms over state Freedom of Information Act stipulations.[55]

The evidence suggests that, for the most part, welfare medicine participants are increasingly forced to depend on community health centers, public hospitals, and other institutional-based outpatient facilities for their medical needs.[56] But government-supported clinics may not be available in certain communities or within easy reach of Medicaid clients. At times, there are waiting lists as well. In quite a few areas of the country, hospital emergency rooms, mostly those that are nonprofit facilities, consequently function as the family doctor or, in more cases, attend to conditions that have deteriorated due to lack of preventive or ongoing care. Recent data indicate that Medicaid and SCHIP enrollees have far higher emergency-room visitation rates than individuals with other types of insurance and even the uninsured.[57] Contrary to political officials' self-serving claims, most of these visits are prompted by a genuine need for medical assistance: of the total emergency-room visits by Medicaid participants in 2004, 10 percent were for an emergency and 61 percent for urgent or semiurgent health conditions; only 14 percent of them were not pressing.[58]

Provider Shortages: Dentists

Far fewer dentists participate in Medicaid than physicians, and it is more difficult for public-aid youngsters to gain access to oral health services.[59] A National Conference of State Legislatures survey documented that in most areas of the country only a small percentage of dentists signs up for Medicaid, an even smaller segment treats any recipients, and a still smaller fraction will serve a significant number of them.[60] Thus, few children receive the oral care for which they are entitled under the EPSDT Program.[61] The data tellingly indicate that only about 33 percent of Medicaid-enrolled children receive any dental services in a given year, and even fewer obtain actual treatments for their disorders; at least 13 percent of the young participants have never seen a dentist at all.[62] Moreover, state Medicaid managed-care contracts do not usually mandate specific interventions, such as fluoride or sealant treatments.[63] As Burton Edelstein, a professor of dentistry, so aptly puts it, "In the majority of states, Medicaid dental coverage is little more than an unfulfilled promise—adequate coverage but inadequate services."[64]

Children covered under SCHIP confront even greater hurdles, despite the fact that, as of 2006, every state offers them a dental option. However, officials tend to restrict the benefits substantially by imposing ceilings on the number of examinations and cleanings or maximum amounts for annual payments per child (e.g., $350 in Montana). Several states place restrictions on specific procedures, demand expensive cost sharing, stipulate waiting periods, or require other allowable SCHIP controls on spending.[65]

The situation is direr for adults, especially in their inability to obtain specialty care such as root canals. Because states are not required to provide a dental benefit to them, some jurisdictions have not included it in their plans. Even where it is offered, most places cap total outlays, and many legislators have reduced or eliminated such services whenever they experience budgetary shortfalls.[66] Forty-one states provide parents only emergency procedures such as tooth extractions.[67] In the more generous states, adults confront the formidable access problems that children do. To make matters worse, relatively fewer dentists than physicians provide services at community health clinics or other government-run facilities.[68] Several states have experimented with alternative solutions to the paucity of participating dentists, but none has been particularly successful in measurably boosting treatment rates.[69]

The limited availability of dental care has led to serious but preventable health problems, particularly among low-income children. In 2000, U.S. surgeon general David Satcher released the report *Oral Health in America*, which identifies tooth decay as the most common chronic disease among youngsters. In it, he notes that children living in households with incomes less than 200 percent of the FPL had three times the incidence of tooth decay than that of their higher income peers and that their cavities were much more likely to go untreated.[70] Roughly one-third of children covered under welfare medicine in 2005 had neglected tooth decay, and youngsters without any health insurance at all fared even worse.[71]

Among other complications, untreated oral disease can cause wrenching pain and infection; exacerbate disorders such as diabetes; impair people's speech, learning, and behavior; mar their appearance; restrict their productivity; obstruct their ability to eat properly; worsen their overall quality of life; and increase the risk of life-threatening illnesses, including cardiovascular disease and strokes. And even though cavities are avoidable through the use of fluoridated water and individualized applications of topical fluorides and dental sealants, and completely curable with restorative care, only a fraction of impoverished children receive such preventive measures compared to those children living in families with higher incomes.[72]

The urgency of the situation was highlighted in 2007 by the death of Deamonte Driver, a twelve-year-old Maryland boy, from a brain infection resulting from an untreated, decayed tooth. A subsequent investigation and hearings, launched by U.S. House Representative Dennis Kucinich (D–Ohio), scrutinized United Health Care,[73] one of Maryland's largest MCOs operating under the state's mandatory Medicaid managed-care program (HealthChoice). The congressman's staff discovered that of the twenty-four participating dentists listed as serving the boy's immediate geographic area, twenty-three of them were either impossible to contact or did not actually accept public-aid patients.

Not surprisingly, the subcommittee also uncovered chronic underutilization of dental services by the company's clients in general.[74] What is more, the hearings revealed that not only were there considerably fewer dentists treating Medicaid enrollees than had been assumed, but care was highly concentrated in only a few locations.[75] For example, in one county, three dentists at a single practice provided 35 percent of all Medicaid services. As one witness scathingly testified, these dentists would have had to treat sixty children per day to submit the number of annual claims that they did.[76]

The Courts

In many places, provider and consumer advocacy groups are challenging inadequate practitioner fees in court under the federal EPSDT Program and "equal access" provisions. The federal appellate courts, which have differed widely over the interpretation of these requirements, have occasionally ordered the states to increase their rates. In one instance, Medicaid recipients and their supporters filed suit against Texas, claiming that physician reimbursements were so low that the state was not meeting the federally mandated access obligations for EPSDT services. Children participating in welfare medicine experienced lengthy delays in obtaining appointments, endured extended periods of time in waiting rooms, and sometimes traveled unacceptably long distances for care. Although the 1993 case was first settled three years later, the state did not comply fully with the deal, leading to an even worse situation: the number of physicians accepting new public-aid patients, including children, actually declined.[77] After vast expenditures of time and money by all parties involved in the suit, a second pact was ultimately reached: in 2007, state officials reluctantly agreed to increase practitioner fees,[78] provide beneficiaries with transportation to their appointments, improve managed care, and expand outreach activities. Nonetheless, as of 2009, still too few dentists were treating welfare medicine participants, and officials had spent only a fraction of the money promised.

Several other recently settled lawsuits have challenged low compensation and its adverse effects on children. In Michigan, a deal was reached that will dramatically raise Medicaid payments to physicians and dentists serving youngsters and improve outreach to them.[79] After several years of litigation and negotiations over the paucity of basic oral care, New Hampshire was forced to ensure that every child covered under its low-income health plan would be able to attain dental services.[80] In Illinois, despite the state's new All Kids program, children had restricted access to physician services: in three counties, the Tri-County Health Community Center, operated by nurse practitioners, was one of the few places that would treat them.[81] The state—which had both low provider rates and traditionally long delays in payments—settled a lawsuit against it by agreeing to pay more money to doctors and dentists providing care to youngsters. During the past several years, federal judges have ordered authorities in Oklahoma and Pennsylvania, among other places, to boost compensation to medical practitioners. Similarly expensive and time-consuming class-action lawsuits are pending throughout the nation while large numbers of poor children and their parents do without the medical and dental services they are entitled to.[82]

Restricted Benefit Packages

In most states, Medicaid recipients are not offered a full range of services, regardless of their particular health status. Each locality decides which "optional" benefits to provide, depending on its financial circumstances, political makeup, ideology, generosity, and other factors unrelated to medical care. Benefit packages may or may not include more than thirty "elective" services, including speech and hearing therapies, psychiatric care, rehabilitation (occupational and physical therapy), dental services, dentures, optometric services, eyeglasses, hearing aids, medical equipment and supplies, and prosthetic devices. Thus, welfare medicine patients' ability to secure a treatment regimen tailored to their particular situation is not tied to their actual needs, but rather to geographic location: they can be denied crucial care simply because they reside in the wrong place.[83] Some states with particularly bare-bones programs, such as Colorado, Mississippi, South Carolina, and Alabama, offer scarcely more than the basic benefits required under federal law.

At the same time, the various Medicaid plans and their MCOs are now allowed to provide services selectively, thus denying certain types of treatment to particular sectors of the population or forcing them to pay greater costs for their care. They also can limit medical aid to particular conditions, restrict the types of procedures, and control the quantity, frequency, and duration of service provision. A person with a severe mental illness, for example, may be allowed only a few visits with a psychiatrist, which may imperil his or her well-being. In a similar scenario, the establishment of different prescription drug formularies, ever-changing lists of what is covered, and even varying constraints on the number of permitted medications can endanger the health and safety of vulnerable Medicaid participants, depending on which state they live in.

Not only are Medicaid clients denied many of the services they require, but the assistance they do receive is not always assured: over the decades, many states have tended to treat optional benefits cavalierly, adding new ones or cutting and restoring them in accordance with annual budget fluctuations. At times, these services are slashed or augmented because of swings in political party power configurations.[84] Thus, welfare medicine benefits can be a moving target, even when essential to participants' care. In addition, there are long waiting lists for services in capped waiver programs, despite the fact that disease does not wait for someone's number to come up.

Welfare Medicine: Universal Problem Solver

Tackling Societal Ills: Partial Solutions

Not only is Medicaid one of the few relatively popular welfare programs, but it also has a sizeable stream of federal dollars, thereby inducing state lawmakers to take advantage of it for a wide range of problems they cannot or will not pay for otherwise. Because our current employer-sponsored health insurance system, administered by commercial companies, neither provides for everyone in need nor covers many of the services required by their policyholders, substantial pressure has been placed on Medicaid to fill in the gaps. The program also has become a veritable "dumping ground" for a plethora of other community requirements. As such, officials have periodically enlarged its targeted population to meet new challenges, sustained certain types of providers or sectors of the population, and counterbalanced particular deficiencies in the private-sector marketplace.

However, rather than put together a coherent, carefully thought-out approach to social questions, officeholders have used welfare medicine to tackle them piecemeal. Drug abuse and its treatment present one such example. In lieu of confronting fundamental issues, policymakers have financed billions of dollars to hospitalize Medicaid-covered addicts. According to one report, in 2005 alone the program paid for more than 1.3 million hospital stays related to dependency on cocaine, heroin, opiate-based pain relief drugs, marijuana, and amphetamines, at a cost of more than $10 billion.[85] Unfortunately, these institutional services tend to be isolated from the larger, complex difficulties that impoverished people encounter. Despite the fact that New York spends more than $300 million a year on hospitalization to detoxify welfare medicine enrollees, officials have observed that such patients do not recover; instead, they return to the hospital again and again. A core problem appears to be a paucity of outpatient drug, alcohol, and mental health treatment programs, along with a shortage of housing for the low-income and homeless populations.[86]

In a similar vein, prisoners have access to an array of medical services that are paid for by local governments. However, regardless of their health status, they are on their own upon leaving jail. Even if they are eligible for Medicaid, it is difficult for them to obtain coverage expeditiously, a particularly thorny problem for released felons in immediate need of medications and psychiatric care. In the latter case, not only are they a danger to themselves and others, but the lack of such assistance may contribute significantly to their high recidivism rates.

Treatment for HIV and AIDS is yet another example of welfare medicine's partial approach to societal ills. As early as 1990, financial support for the treatment of this disorder had shifted rapidly from private insurance to welfare medicine. At that time, about 40 percent of the people diagnosed with AIDS had become dependent on Medicaid, many of them because they could no longer work.[87] By 2007, the low-income health program had become the primary payer, providing medical coverage to more than 230,000 poor or disabled people with the disease. Regardless, not all of the states offer the comprehensive services required: nearly half of them do not pay for one or more of the drugs commonly used to treat AIDS or AIDS-related infections, and many places provide medications to eligible individuals who test positive for the illness *only* if they have advanced symptoms (full-blown AIDS).

Welfare medicine policies are also enigmatic, patchy, imbalanced, or simply unfair in many cases, especially given that certain groups of people and types of benefits have been included over the years, but others of equal importance are not. For example, since 2000 the states have permission to cover medically uninsured women for the treatment of breast or cervical cancer, even if they are otherwise ineligible for Medicaid, but not for the care of other life-threatening cancers or conditions such as heart disease. Men who do not qualify for the low-income health program are not eligible for any medical services. Just as problematic, thirteen states fund tuberculosis services for the medically uninsured,[88] but they do not provide them with assistance for their other health care needs. Seniors are better protected than the middle-aged, parents more than childless adults, and mothers more than fathers, regardless of income. Qualifying elders are automatically entitled to institutional services, but not to home-based care. Thus, although the provided benefits may be vital to families obtaining them, their inequitable—and at times limited—distribution clearly disregards larger concerns affecting the health, safety, and well-being of Americans in general.

Medicaid Warfare

Over the years, low-income people with a wide variety of divergent needs have become embroiled in fierce political battles over certain benefits, also involving special-interest groups and the courts. In a number of cases, they have successfully added new types of services to state Medicaid benefit packages. These expansions range from sex-change operations, breast implants, the provision of medications for erectile dysfunction,[89] and circumcisions to bariatric surgery (gastric bypass surgery for people who are obese), liver transplants, and treatments administered by Christian Scientist practitioners. Even marriage of and civil unions between gay men or women, a particular bête noire of the Religious Right, have sparked struggles over whether same-sex partners are entitled to protections under welfare medicine, especially for institutional care.

Medicaid has in particular been at the epicenter of disputes over reproductive rights, resulting in a denial of specific services to low-income women. Family planning, a federally mandated service, has generated recurring flare-ups by the Religious Right and other conservative factions, many of whom consider certain types of birth control as tantamount to abortion. Among the methods they particularly object to is emergency contraceptive Plan B, approved by the U.S. Food and Drug Administration for nonprescription sales in 2006, and they have fought aggressively against covering it; as of January 2007, only New York, Washington, and Illinois fund the drug under the low-income health program.

Even more controversial from the start has been the political tug of war over abortion, which has dominated debates over welfare medicine since the 1970s. Although Medicaid itself slipped through Congress, antiabortion groups almost immediately raised its visibility in a storm of unremitting protests. After the U.S. Supreme Court decision *Roe v. Wade* in 1973, legalizing a woman's right to terminate her pregnancy within the first twelve weeks, "pro-life" organizations began pressing the states to prohibit abortion coverage under the low-income health program. Where they were successful in doing so, such as in Connecticut, New Jersey, and Pennsylvania, the courts consistently struck down the new, restrictive policies. In response, Congress enacted the Hyde amendment (effective 1977) to prohibit Medicaid-funded abortions, which was upheld by the Supreme Court in *Harris v. McRae* (1980). Since that time, the exceedingly divisive question regularly unleashes an explosion of controversy within Congress, generating an ongoing addition to or removal of exceptions to the ban. The national government currently will pay for its share of Medicaid abortion costs only if the mother's life is endangered or in cases of rape or incest.

Abortion issues have been bitterly played out in the states over the decades as well, fostering an adverse situation for low-income women. If local officeholders do not abide by the federal regulations, they risk losing their Medicaid matching funds, thereby influencing at least part of the overwhelming conformity to the national rules: roughly two-thirds of the states cover abortions only in the most extreme circumstances.[90] Another seventeen states pick up the tab for a wider variety of medical reasons, many of them as a result of court rulings. Medicaid-related abortion concerns resurface annually, along with the antagonism surrounding the issue.[91] Pro-choice groups, and their allies, continue in their efforts to rescind the Hyde amendment and to add an abortion option to state plans. The religious groups and their conservative supporters concurrently still seek to prevent the use of welfare medicine funds for the procedure at all.[92] The Radical

Right's war against Medicaid is of course only a piece, albeit a key one, of its general struggle to ban abortion for everyone.

In most places, then, poor women are effectively denied the right to terminate their pregnancy and accordingly have paid a substantial price: it has been estimated that from 18 to 35 percent of Medicaid participants who intended to have an abortion but could not afford it reluctantly became parents. Additional welfare medicine enrollees have had to go into debt or forgo basic necessities to finance their abortion. Still others may have experienced injury or even death from utilizing unsafe methods. And, as with so many other Medicaid-related questions, the program's payments to medical practitioners are so low that even in states that permit Medicaid funds for the procedure, eligible women may have difficulty finding a place willing to perform it. By not offering indigent women the same reproductive options as higher-income women, policymakers are violating their basic human rights.

Hurricane Katrina

Because welfare medicine is locally administered and financed, it is not equipped to cope with situations that cross state boundaries, as clearly revealed in the case of Hurricane Katrina. In September 2005, the Gulf of Mexico coast was devastated by the storm; nearly one million people living in Mississippi and Louisiana were forced to leave their homes, many relocating to another state. Facing additional Medicaid costs because of these migrations, places such as Texas, Florida, Arkansas, Alabama, and Mississippi demanded federal assistance. Instead of disbursing supplementary subsidies as needed, the Bush administration required state-by-state negotiations for emergency money through the waiver process. Seventeen localities ultimately reached deals that allowed them to pay evacuees who met Medicaid eligibility criteria, fully funded by the federal government, but only up to five months.

In addition to the inadequate response to displaced families, Louisiana policymakers were not even able to care for all of the distressed residents who stayed behind. Its waiver gave the state access to an uncompensated care pool to reimburse practitioners who furnished emergency treatments to families injured by Katrina, regardless of whether these households were enrolled in welfare medicine. It also extended coverage to certain low-income survivors who were not otherwise qualified, but again for only five months. Nevertheless, many people were denied health services because they did not meet the strict eligibility regulations in place: most of them had been forced out of work because their companies were shut down as a result of the storm. Concerned about a possible permanent enlargement of Medicaid, the president and his supporters in Congress generally resisted the inclusion of individuals who had lost their jobs and homes but were not income eligible for the program. Nor did they approve of providing benefits without sufficient documentation. As a result, many families, even those with prior medical insurance, were now financially on their own, regardless of their health status.

Conclusion: Good Enough?

This chapter has shown that welfare medicine has not met the goal of insuring the indigent population adequately and has shortchanged low-income adults who are under the age of sixty-five in particular. Poor children, pregnant women, and elders are the main beneficiaries, but even they must meet sometimes strict income-eligibility criteria, endure onerous and complex application and recertification procedures, and satisfy burdensome cost-sharing requirements—all of which raise substantial barriers to participation and can lead to discontinuous care. Once enrollees receive coverage and even if they can sustain it, they often encounter difficulty in locating decent practitioners who will treat them: Medicaid has maintained the two-class medical system in the United States, despite the program's "equal access" and EPSDT Program guarantees. At the same time, recipients frequently cannot obtain the types of services they require or use them for as long as needed. Their benefit packages depend on where they live and their state's political, ideological, and financial environment. Finally, the low-income health program finances certain services to the exclusion of others, some highly controversial, but many of them neglect to address basic issues, ignore low-income families' real needs, are short-sighted, and, in the case of reproductive rights, seriously harm low-income women.

A fundamental question, then, is whether Medicaid and SCHIP are better than nothing, even with all of their shortcomings and omissions. The available evidence seems to suggest that welfare medicine enrollees are to some extent more advantaged than people without any health insurance. In a survey of the program's effectiveness for women, for example, investigators found that only 10 percent of beneficiaries did not visit a doctor during the year, as compared to 33 percent of the uninsured. Welfare medicine participants were also less likely to forgo a breast examination (27 percent versus 48 percent) or Pap test (16 percent versus 40 percent). Although nearly one-third of the women on Medicaid delayed medical treatments that they viewed as essential or did not fill a prescription because of the expense, the situation was even worse for the uninsured: fully two-thirds of them postponed needed services, and 40 percent went without their medications.[93] Because individuals lacking medical coverage obtain preventive services at a much lower rate than those who are insured, they tend to be diagnosed at a later stage in their disease. When hospitalized, they often receive fewer medical services and are more likely to die.[94] Households without health insurance are also forced to pay fully or partially for their hospital services prior to receiving them. In fact, the costs for such families can be up to four times what private insurers and public programs normally pay and are a major cause of bankruptcy in the country.[95]

Not only do children participating in the low-income health programs tend to receive greater preventive and acute health services than uninsured children, but their parents also experience fewer financial burdens.[96] In addition, although Medicaid-enrolled children have limited access to dentists, nearly 33 percent of youngsters across the United States are not protected at all; without welfare medicine, therefore, the proportion would be even higher. Indeed, Medicaid and SCHIP pay for 25 percent of all dental expenses for children younger than the age of six.[97] Many private insurance policies conspicuously lack coverage for oral care, and their customers, in particular those with inadequate resources, are often forced to forego preventive treatments and neglect ongoing conditions.

Medicaid also funds medical services for nearly 10 percent of women of reproductive age, paying for more than one-third of U.S. births,[98] and is the largest financial sponsor of family-planning services and supplies.[99] Despite its insufficiencies, the program also plays a critical role in mental health services, representing nearly 20 percent of such costs.[100] Due to EPSDT Program requirements, it is particularly beneficial for children. To be sure, some youngsters covered under commercial plans encounter greater limits (i.e., caps on the number of visits), higher cost sharing, and more obstacles to attaining psychological services than those enrolled in welfare medicine; uninsured children are in an even more precarious situation. As the next chapter discusses, many older people benefit from Medicaid's coverage of LTC services and its subsidization of Medicare premiums, copayments, and deductibles.

From the perspective of low-income enrollees, especially pregnant women, infants, children, older people, and the disabled, the answer to whether welfare medicine is better than nothing is probably yes. We live in a nation that does not offer satisfactory alternatives for otherwise uninsured people, many of whom are forced to forgo medical services for themselves and their children, to accumulate ever-increasing debts, and to do without other essential needs, including proper nutrition. Given the failings of the costly, private insurance marketplace, welfare medicine is all there is for many families. The Medicaid and SCHIP glass is for them not half empty, but half full. Nevertheless, a larger question persists: given the limited reach and scope of welfare medicine's acute care services relative to public-sector costs, are we getting our money's worth, or can we do a great deal better?

6

LONG-TERM CARE:
MEDICAID'S
EIGHT-HUNDRED-POUND
GORILLA

Long-term care (LTC) costs, paid for mainly through Medicaid, are exploding primarily because of population aging and the high and growing expense of institutional care. Mandated under federal law, nursing home services have long been a key economic force driving the low-income health program's escalating expenditures and of paramount concern to office-holders seeking to control these costs. Yet it is not easy to streamline spending for older and disabled people, as has been accomplished for other groups: greater cost sharing, managed care, privatization, and Health Savings Accounts are all strategies that, to a large extent, are difficult to impose on vulnerable, destitute elders and physically or mentally impaired younger adults and children. Nor is it easy to muster the political will to reduce services that assist populations whom the American public traditionally has viewed as "deserving," even though the vast majority of spending for LTC is at state option.[1] It is rendered even more problematic because Medicaid's LTC "entitlement" also serves as a safety net for the middle-class aged and their family caregivers.

As seen in chapter 5, benefit reductions, privatization, and other program transformations aimed at reigning in expenditures have been concentrated mainly on younger, nondisabled populations, but they represent only one-third of total welfare medicine outlays. Care of the elderly and disabled poor is far more costly, representing the bulk of Medicaid spending: both per capita costs and total expenditures for all medical services—including physicians, hospitalization, and prescription drugs, but especially nursing homes—are higher for them than for any other group.[2] Because of their disproportionately large and rising share of welfare medicine dollars, these two sectors of society have proven a major stumbling block for policymakers, who must restructure LTC services with great caution.

This chapter begins with a look at who requires LTC, where it is provided, and how it is financed. The first section points out that most services are provided at home by family members, free of charge, but substantial numbers of frail elders ultimately end up institutionalized, supported by welfare medicine, despite the reluctance of everyone involved. The program has been biased toward high-priced nursing homes from the start, both propelling and sustaining the industry. The next section considers the ways in which Medicaid has increasingly served more moderate-income households, arguing that it now has the status of a middle-class entitlement for frail older and disabled people because of the relatively liberal standards for meeting state "medically needy" income levels or other criteria, at least for nursing home care. This aspect of welfare medicine has broadened support for the program considerably, despite the sharp attacks on nonpoor seniors who allegedly are taking advantage of the program.

As the final parts of the chapter show, national and state officials have tentatively explored various ways to lessen the growth of LTC expenditures, including greater home- and community-based services (HCBS) relative to nursing home care; tighter eligibility standards for institutionalization; preliminary attempts to force more frail and disabled recipients into managed care; the promotion of LTC insurance; additional tax benefits for employers and individuals purchasing LTC premiums; and the encouragement of reverse mortgages. Indeed, cost curtailment has been at the center of nearly all policy debates about LTC reform. Nevertheless, none of these initiatives to date has curbed escalating Medicaid costs, which has triggered more aggressive measures in recent years, in particular those aimed at middle-class elders. As I show, officials, in their zeal to rein in funding, have tended to skirt some central concerns, principally equity, effectiveness of services, responsiveness to family and recipient needs, the situation of direct-care workers, indirect and hidden burdens, and the quality of care.

Long-Term Care in the United States

Who Needs Assistance?

All people are at risk of requiring LTC or of having a family member who will depend on them for such services, although women tend to be in a more vulnerable position than men.[3] Millions of people, whether chronically ill or disabled, need help with the basic tasks of daily living or with other activities that allow them to maintain a certain level of autonomy,[4] require therapies that can enhance their functioning, or would benefit from certain devices and equipment that can further their independence. The actual number of people turning to paid or unpaid personal care continues to expand, primarily because of population growth and changing demographics, even though overall disability rates among the aged have been declining in recent years.

Since the enactment of Medicaid in 1965, the sheer number of elderly in the United States has risen from nearly 20 million people (10 percent of the population) to 37 million (12.6 percent of the population) in 2007.[5] The group most needing LTC—individuals age eighty-five or older—have been the fastest-growing segment, currently reaching more than 5 million seniors.[6] In the years following 2011, when the first of the 78 million U.S. Baby Boomers turn sixty-five, the demand for LTC will swell commensurately. Their oldest and frailest sector is expected to expand to 6.1 million in 2010 and to 7.3 million by 2020, a 44 percent increase from 2000.[7] Such changes portend not only a greater need for informal and formal caregivers, but also escalating pressures on Medicaid funding and policies.

The vast majority of older people with cognitive or physical disabilities resides at home, typically cared for by their spouses or adult children, mostly wives and daughters.[8] The aged and their families tend to dread the prospect of institutionalization and take that step only when there is no other viable choice: placement in a nursing home generally occurs when the primary caregiver is no longer available (he or she has died or is too sick and worn-out to continue) or the frail elder's needs have become too overwhelming, especially individuals suffering from dementia. In addition, since the introduction of stringent payment methods for hospitals (diagnosis-related groups, more commonly referred to as DRGs) under Medicare in the late 1980s, the aged have been forced out of hospitals "quicker and sicker," thus generating more intense and often crushing medical needs at home. Because of the high price of in-home services, most chronically ill older people cannot afford to pay for them on their own, and many who can manage it eventually impoverish themselves.

Despite population aging and the considerable societal impact of the nation's ongoing demographic transformation, policymakers have not developed a coherent approach to LTC, privileging nursing homes over other types of assistance. Although viewed only as a last resort, institutional facilities have become "home" to a substantial number of vulnerable seniors, mainly because Medicaid will fund their stays to a far greater extent than the services that would be required to keep them in the community. Today, about 14 percent of people age eighty-five or older, most of whom are female, live in a nursing home, for the most part either fully or partially subsidized through welfare medicine.[9] In contrast, disabled children and younger adults, whose enrollment in Medicaid more than tripled since the 1970s, are more likely to reside in noninstitutional settings. They currently represent about 45 percent of the program's total LTC users, mainly for HCBS and Intermediate Care Facilities for the Mentally Retarded (ICFs-MR).[10]

Medicaid and the Nursing Home Industry

As the U.S. population ages, and as the older and disabled sectors of society are living longer, paid LTC services have become a vital but often hidden piece of our health care system despite its astronomical price tag, totaling $206.6 billion in 2005. The bulk of the money is spent on nursing homes (63 percent), with the remainder on a variety of HCBS.[11] Institutional facilities are the most expensive form of care and have become increasingly more costly over time. In 2007, the average annual rate for a semiprivate room, the most common situation, was roughly $62,000. Single-occupancy rooms are much higher, averaging $75,000 and varying widely among the localities.[12] Home health services, too, are expensive: in 2007, the average hourly private pay rate for an aide from an agency was $25.47 (or $28,000 for one year of three hours of daily assistance).[13]

Medicaid is the foremost supporter of LTC, financing nearly half ($101.1 billion) of the nation's total costs.[14] Welfare medicine subsidizes 45 percent ($59 billion) of nursing home outlays and 55 percent ($42 billion) of home health spending.[15] In fact, it plays a significant role in filling the gaps left by private insurance and Medicare, both of which finance a relatively small share of the bill.[16] Indeed, because of the paucity in Medicare funding for LTC, dual eligibles—individuals entitled to both Medicaid and Medicare—represent one of the most expensive components of the low-income health insurance program: they make up less than 5 percent of beneficiaries, but 67 percent of LTC users and 42 percent of total costs.[17] To be sure, LTC has always been and continues to be the most expensive and fastest-growing segment of state Medicaid budgets, averaging 32 percent of the total.[18] There are wide variations among the states, however, in terms of the size of their older population and the extensiveness of their eligibility, coverage, and reimbursement policies.[19]

The public sector has long supported nursing homes, and the preponderance of Medicaid LTC spending has always been targeted to institutional care. Indeed, the earlier Kerr-Mills program and later Medicaid were instrumental in the growth of the industry itself, which expanded from a

$500 million operation in the mid-1960s to a $13 billion business in 1978.[20] By that time, welfare medicine was already funding more than half of all nursing home residents, with institutional costs representing one of the largest portions of total program outlays. Expenditures have continued to grow unabated, especially since the 1990s.[21] Today, welfare medicine devotes nearly one-third of its total dollars to skilled nursing homes and ICFs-MR and is the principal payer for 65 percent of their inhabitants.[22]

The Middle Class as Stakeholders

Filling the Institutional Care "Gap"

Medicaid has been a substantial payer of nursing home services from the start but increasingly became a major source of funding for the middle class. Grounded in the American approach to welfare generally, its original intent had been to provide services exclusively to the "needy," who had to satisfy stringent state income-eligibility standards. The program had mandated some skilled nursing home services and related supplies, but with restrictions similar to those of the earlier Kerr-Mills legislation.[23] The states eventually were allowed to expand LTC services to older and younger disabled individuals who met certain financial and functional eligibility criteria, depending on local guidelines. Under their various "medically needy" programs, states may cover a nursing home resident whose income exceeds their standard welfare medicine eligibility threshold—up to 133 percent of the state's maximum cash-assistance benefit—after deducting the recipient's out-of-pocket outlays toward her own care. Likewise, the special income rule has let policymakers include categorically eligible people whose earnings are up to 300 percent of Supplemental Security Income (SSI).[24] In order to receive LTC coverage, income-eligible individuals also must meet certain conditions related to their physical or cognitive functioning, or both, as well as strict asset requirements.

Most states have *not* shied away from broadening eligibility for older and younger disabled people, even though they are costly groups. Nearly every jurisdiction permits users of LTC, whether for institutional care or HCBS, to qualify for Medicaid under either the "300 percent rule" or the medically needy guidelines; sixteen states use both options for nursing homes, and eleven of them for home care.[25] The extension of welfare medicine to families with higher household income fostered a moderate but steady increase in the share of state Medicaid funding devoted to nursing home care; by the late 1980s, three-fourths of this money were spent on the nonwelfare population.[26] Both the medically needy and special income provisions currently account for nearly 90 percent of Medicaid's nursing home expenses and for 75 percent of the program's total spending on the elderly.[27] And local legislators have not been inclined to reduce their support for such a vulnerable sector of society.

As such funding grew in the 1990s, Medicaid LTC services for the first time became visibly identified with the white middle class. When Republicans began yet another round of attacks on welfare medicine in 1996, Democrats defended the program by presenting it as a mainstay of support for defenseless elders. As Colleen Grogan and Eric Patashnik point out, President Clinton "sought to cast Medicaid as a broad social entitlement" by emphasizing that it protected older people who had long histories of both employment and tax payments.[28] Democrats were joined by other policy elites and major news sources in the reframing of Medicaid from health care for the poor to "a core social entitlement for the mainstream aged."[29] To be sure, considerable and growing numbers of older people across the nation are potentially income eligible for Medicaid's nursing home services under the special rules.

Medicaid's high and escalating LTC outlays have turned into a broad social entitlement for America's frail middle-class elderly while paradoxically forcing them to impoverish themselves. Enrolled nursing home residents must apply their entire monthly income toward their care, except for a small personal allowance;[30] the program pays the remainder of the charges directly to the institution. Recipients also are forced to deplete nearly all of their assets to qualify as "medically needy," a situation that many moderate income seniors reach in short order. A relatively long stay in a nursing home can easily drain a lifetime of savings for nearly anyone.

Several studies show just how few assets older people actually hold. In one examination of frail elders living at home (2005), researchers found that 65 percent of them could not afford even a year of care and that 16 percent could pay for one to three years; only 19 percent had the funds for a longer duration.[31] Another survey, which measured the total resources of functionally or cognitively impaired single older people age eighty-five and older, discovered that 74 percent of them possessed less than $5,000. Just 9 percent of the respondents had sufficient money for one to three years of nursing home services, and only 7 percent could support themselves for a more prolonged period.[32] According to the U.S. Government Accountability Office (GAO), the median assets of the nation's 28 million aged households in 2002 were $51,500, and among the severely disabled they averaged a mere $3,200.

It obviously would not take long for residents who pay privately for an extended stay in an institution to deplete their assets.[33] About 60 percent of elders entering a nursing home initially pay entirely on their own, but between 25 and 50 percent of them soon deplete their resources and are forced to depend on Medicaid. About one-third is covered by the program at admission, although a significant number had already used up their available resources on privately paid home care services prior to entering the facility.[34] Individuals eventually requiring government-supported institutional care tend to be female, primarily because they are more likely than males to live to an advanced age, lack a partner to assist them, and have a lower income and net worth.

For many seniors, then, Medicaid is the de facto LTC insurance coverage that neither Medicare nor private indemnity plans cover. It has developed into a program for middle-class, mostly white frail female elders and, as such, elicits substantial political support. But the participants pay a steep price: they must bankrupt themselves by initially paying their own way in full. In addition, although receiving assistance from welfare medicine, the medically needy population continues to funnel all of their income—whether from Social Security or a private pension—directly into the coffers of the nursing home, with Medicaid picking up only the remainder of the tab.

Attacking the Middle Class

Not surprisingly, frail elderly and disabled Medicaid participants have not been entirely immune from attacks by elected officials who face steadily growing nursing home costs. Certain politicians, in an attempt to chip away at Medicaid's LTC benefit, assert that the middle class, assisted by estate planners, shelter their assets in order to qualify for institutional care. Limited challenges to welfare medicine for the middle class have occurred periodically, beginning with the Reagan administration's successful proposal to allow states to place liens against the homes of nursing home residents after the death of their surviving spouse.[35] However, the president intentionally did not confront the question of resource transfers. According to *New York Times* reporter Robert Pear, federal officials had "nothing to say" about such estate planning for Medicaid purposes. Although the general sense among them was that the program should be for the truly needy, "elderly people who used legal means to protect their assets were not regarded as cheats."[36]

By the early 1990s, the National Governors Association had become increasingly concerned that "estate planning" was a major force in the escalation of Medicaid LTC costs.[37] In response, Congress attempted to discourage the practice: in 1993, it stipulated that gifts of less than fair market value had to be signed over more than three years, up from thirty months, before a person could apply for Medicaid and tightened the rules for establishing certain types of trusts. Lawmakers also now mandated that the states recover LTC expenditures from the estates of deceased beneficiaries, a directive that few local officeholders pursued aggressively.[38]

Nevertheless, it was still relatively easy for elders to shift assets legally, galling the George W. Bush administration, Republicans in Congress, and most governors. Convinced that middle-class seniors and their families were "gaming" the system and using Medicaid as an "inheritance-protection plan," they lambasted the financial maneuvers with a vengeance, culminating in further restrictions under the Deficit Reduction Act (DRA) of 2005. Not only was the "look back" period for asset transfers increased to five years, but the penalty period would *now begin when elders applied for Medicaid* rather than when they transferred the money. Whereas previously the value of a primary residence had not been considered for eligibility purposes, the DRA now disallows home equity up to $750,000. In addition, recipients must name the state as the sole beneficiary, equal to the amount of Medicaid-funded assistance, for any annuities they hold; these annuities had previously been considered exempt assets.

The community spouse's situation also has been a long-standing issue: prior to the 1988 Medicare Catastrophic Coverage Act, the healthy partner frequently was forced into abject poverty. Since then, the well spouse has been guaranteed a higher minimum needs allowance; he or she is allowed to keep more of the couple's joint assets and income as well as all personal earnings.[39] Although an improvement over the hardship of earlier years, the healthy mate must still suffer monetarily as a condition of Medicaid nursing home assistance for his or her spouse. The DRA also mandates an "Income-First" Rule, which potentially can decrease the community spouse's allowable assets.[40]

The Bush administration and certain congressional and state policy-makers are disregarding the reality of the situation in their zeal to place greater financial burdens on chronically disabled elders and their families. Allegations about hordes of Medicaid estate-planning lawyers, huge cash gifts to children and grandchildren by middle-class and affluent seniors, and the extensive establishment of trusts to qualify for welfare medicine appear to be more anecdotal than based on actual facts. After reviewing the foremost research on the subject, Ellen O'Brien concluded that there is no support for "the claim that asset transfers are widespread or costly to Medicaid." Although some families may try to protect their modest resources for future needs or an inheritance, "most people who end up on Medicaid are already paying what they can. . . . The fact is that Medicaid is what it was intended to be, a safety net for those who cannot afford to pay for long-term care."[41]

Indeed, the evidence suggests that asset transfers by either current or potential nursing home users are not widespread. One national survey found that few residents enrolled in the low-income health program had given away substantial amounts of money. Among individuals who qualified for Medicaid prior to admission or within a year of placement, such shifts in funds were quite small, and only a fraction of individuals accounted for nearly all of the resources handed over. The researchers concluded that even those older people who made moderate transfers of money (generally $5,000 or less) were not particularly wealthy, most likely did not confer with a lawyer, and probably were not envisioning entry into an institution when they did so. To the contrary, nursing home residents who never enroll in Medicaid are the most likely to give away assets to their children, with roughly half of them distributing the money during the six years before they are admitted.[42] Another study similarly found that only from 9 to 15 percent of new Medicaid-eligible nursing home residents had shifted their resources to others, with the amount averaging only $4,000. In fact, the transfers were more common among the elderly who did not enter an institution.[43]

It would also appear that the formation of trusts by elders with modest resources for the purpose of avoiding nursing home costs is relatively rare and that the vast majority of people most likely to benefit from a trust in order to spend down to receive Medicaid did not even own a trust. Rather, trusts are most likely to be set up by wealthy families whose objective is to reduce taxes and evade probate.[44] What is more, instead of giving away funds in order to become eligible for welfare medicine, some older people are in actuality receiving money from their adult children. Many others are converting their house equity into cash so as to put off their enrollment in the program.[45] The data also show that a significant percentage of the sixty-five and older population with modest resources and declining health will hold on to their money, fearing future medical needs.[46] Furthermore, given that private-pay residents can choose from among the more desirable facilities, it would be counterproductive for individuals who eventually may become institutionalized to render themselves penniless. And since the late 1990s, under federal law these nursing homes must let them stay even after they are forced onto Medicaid because of a drop in their income or assets.

Age-Based Organizations

Age-based organizations, especially the AARP, have become a formidable force in American politics, lobbying vigorously and contributing liberally to political campaigns locally and nationally.[47] Although the AARP and other groups representing the elderly had only limited input into the initial construction of such programs as Social Security and Medicare or their early expansions, since the 1980s they have been able to exert considerable pressure on elected officials. By the 1990s, there were more than 1,000 senior groups at the local, state, and federal levels of government, and approximately 5,000 more if local chapters of national associations are included in the total. Several of them have a large membership base, sizeable resources, solid leadership, and strong political ties.[48] At the state level, the power of the elderly varies widely. According to Clive Thomas and Ronald Hrebenar, although businesses and the professions are the most commanding lobbying forces overall, and senior citizens rank well below them (thirty-seventh in 2002), in two states the latter are considered a leading power in politics, and in nine they demonstrate the second-most level of effectiveness.[49]

These senior organizations have undoubtedly had at least some influence in protecting government health insurance and retirement plans for the sixty-five and older population. Despite severe federal cutbacks in social welfare assistance during the 1980s, Medicare and Social Security emerged relatively unscathed. For the most part, the two programs have escaped similar challenges nationally during the 1990s and beyond. Because aging groups tend to have an overwhelmingly middle-class constituency, they have been less interested in programs serving the poor. However, they tend to regard LTC as a middle-class issue and are vitally interested in all aspects of it.[50] The evidence suggests that care of the frail elderly is one of the concerns that AARP, for one, is most united on. As such, it has devoted considerable energy into promoting Medicaid's LTC benefits, including the protections for healthy spouses of institutionalized people inserted in the 1988 Medicare Catastrophic Coverage Act. At times, groups for the elderly team up with the nursing home industry, which obviously also is interested in maintaining and expanding program eligibility for chronically ill, medically needy older people.[51]

Middle-age adults often support Medicaid as well. Unlike cash-assistance programs (such as Aid to Families with Dependent Children and Temporary Assistance for Needy Families), large segments of the white middle-class population view themselves, to varying degrees, as stakeholders in Medicaid LTC policies. They are at risk not only of having family members who may require assistance, but of being vulnerable themselves. Furthermore, welfare medicine protects them against filial responsibility for—and financial devastation from—the costs of institutionalization if it is required for their frail parents.[52]

The Growth of Home- and Community-Based Services

Long-Term Care Policymaking Through Waivers

The institutional bias in Medicaid policy and practice has precluded significant resources for in-home services. However, funding for HCBS has grown steadily since the 1980s, mainly because such services are viewed as a cost-saving measure if substituted for nursing home care. The argument is that in many cases they can delay or eliminate institutionalization. Even so, policymakers tend to fear the "woodwork effect," which assumes that a large number of families, many of whom are providing free care to their frail relatives, will take advantage of at-home services.

Although in the mid-1970s states were given the option to include a personal care or home attendant program as part of their standard Medicaid plan, the vast majority of outlays for HCBS, if not the number of people served, has been through 1915(c) waivers, established under the Omnibus Budget Reconciliation Act (OBRA) of 1981.[53] However, apprehensive that frail elders and disabled younger adults would flock to these programs, the federal government placed severe restrictions on their use. Eligibility is limited exclusively to people who are at risk of institutionalization. Local lawmakers also have to demonstrate that the overall costs of each of their waiver plans, which can include one or more of the allowed services, are budget neutral. As further protection against runaway federal payments, the localities must renew their program agreements periodically. As a result, HCBS waivers increased only slowly in the early years, serving less than 50,000 people nationwide throughout the 1980s.[54]

Relentless lobbying by groups representing the disabled played a large role in drawing attention to community-based care. In 1990, Congress enacted the Americans with Disabilities Act, which, among other objectives, instructed the states to take every reasonable step to avoid needless institutionalization of people with disabilities. For Medicaid, this directive implied that enrollees had to be provided with services in their own homes and communities to the maximum extent possible. Concerned over the legislation's financial ramifications, the states were still reluctant to push HCBS waivers forcefully. By the end of the 1990s, although there were 261 different 1915(c) waiver programs, they assisted a little more than a million participants, with most of the growth concentrated among younger, disabled people, especially the mentally and developmentally disabled population.[55] Even after the 1999 U.S. Supreme Court's *Olmstead v L.C.* (527 U.S. 581) ruling that the unnecessary institutionalization of persons with disabilities was unconstitutional under the Americans with Disabilities Act, local policymakers continued to implement waiver programs cautiously. The Court had added two caveats, thereby providing some cover for local officeholders: community placement is required only when it can be reasonably accommodated, and a state's economic ability to provide sufficient services can play a factor in the amount of assistance offered.

Undaunted, groups representing the disabled simultaneously instituted lawsuits based on the *Olmstead* decision and persisted in pressuring state officials. At the same time, home services became increasingly popular among policymakers themselves as a means of controlling escalating nursing home outlays. Under the 1915(c) waivers, local policymakers were allowed to tailor and restrict services delivered in community settings, which they could not do for institutional care. They could keep a tighter rein over LTC expenditures by imposing enrollment caps and limiting benefits to specific populations (the frail elderly, people with mental or developmental disabilities), certain geographic areas, or particular illnesses (i.e., AIDS, brain and spinal cord injuries). In short, the waivers were a license to undermine aspects of Medicaid's LTC entitlement. And because the primary goal in reducing institutionalization was to pare down expenses, several states carefully managed the growth of HCBS waivers by liberally utilizing the allowable cost-control measures, most commonly through enrollment limits and per capita spending caps.[56] Indeed, investigators report that ceilings on the number of enrollees have engendered substantial (and growing) waiting lists in many areas.[57] At the same time, when encountering fiscal pressures, states simply slash the number of openings, a course of action certain officials have not been hesitant to take.[58]

Since the mid-1990s, Medicaid plans have experienced a progressive shift in the percentage of LTC funding for HCBS relative to institutional care (both nursing homes and ICFs-MR). By 2005, assistance in community settings—including home health care, the personal assistance option, and 1915(c) waivers—represented 37 percent of the total Medicaid LTC bill, up from 14 percent in 1991.[59] All of the states (except Arizona) now participate in a variety of 1915(c) HCBS waiver programs, but, despite rising outlays, the number of people served continues to be quite small relative to the number of families that require help.[60] Moreover, because of the high cost of caring for individuals with mental impairments and developmental disabilities, roughly seven times the expense of seniors, they represent more than 70 percent of the total charges but are approximately only 40 percent of the waiver population. Although few people can afford to pay for HCBS on their own, and HCBS are the clear preference of individuals in need of aid, only about 14 percent of the elderly and 37 percent of younger people with severe disabilities receive Medicaid-funded assistance in community settings.[61]

In most places, despite efforts to rebalance institutional and community care, nursing homes remain the primary alternative for chronically ill elders who depend on welfare medicine for a number of reasons. Nearly one-quarter of the states has established more restrictive income standards for waivers than for institutional care. At the same time, because of spend-down provisions in jurisdictions offering medically needy programs, frail people with higher incomes can qualify for nursing home but not waiver services. Furthermore, the amount of resources that Medicaid enrollees dwelling in the community are permitted to keep is so low that it is very difficult to survive without considerable financial help from their families. One researcher argues that the insufficient maintenance allowance is likely one of the main reasons for Medicaid's institutional bias.[62] As chapter 8 shows, the power of the nursing home industry has played a considerable role in these outcomes as well.

As usual, there are large inequities among the states in the extent of HCBS relative to institutionalization, in the qualifying criteria for in-home assistance, and in the scope, type, and amount of services available.[63] New York, for example, has always offered both greater home-based support and more expensive nursing home care than any other state. As early as the 1970s, it devoted considerable resources to personal care programs such as Nursing Home Without Walls. In the 1990s, despite ongoing efforts by its governor George Pataki (R) to slash HCBS funding, legislators not only continued to provide a broad range of in-home aid to the frail elderly and disabled populations, but they also enacted relatively generous rules: it was the only state that had few limits on the number of weekly service hours per client.[64] New York's LTC costs continued to escalate, and in 2006 expenditures for institutional care ($7 billion) and HCBS ($9 billion) represented roughly 40 percent of the state's total Medicaid bill and 19 percent of all such program spending in the nation.[65]

The Deficit Reduction Act and Long-Term Care

As part of its overall objective to eliminate Medicaid's entitlement status and reduce the national share of welfare medicine funding at the same time, the George W. Bush administration had encouraged noninstitutional services and stark reductions in federal contributions to state plans. As such, it endorsed a DRA provision that offers localities the opportunity to deliver all in-home and community care without a waiver, allowing them even greater "flexibility" to restrict benefits. The legislation seriously undermines Medicaid LTC guarantees by allowing caps, waiting lists, and targeted populations to become standard provisions of state Medicaid plans. Even worse, localities have "adjustment authority" for the first time in Medicaid's history: they can change their qualifying criteria for home care if enrollments exceed their original projections.[66] The DRA has more restrictive eligibility thresholds for HCBS as well: only individuals who have household incomes of 150 percent of the federal poverty limit (FPL) or less are allowed to receive assistance, whereas most states had set their waiver ceilings somewhat higher.[67]

Although the new law eliminates the prior HCBS waiver requirement that beneficiaries must be at risk of institutionalization and that states adhere to strict budget neutrality, it also aims to cut LTC costs by restricting access to institutions. There are now more stringent functional (level-of-care) criteria for nursing home services.[68] Thus, the number of frail elders qualifying for institutional care is expected to decline in the coming years. For the most part, since 2006 the pressing and basic care needs of dependent seniors, the disabled, and their caregivers are clearly being disregarded even further.

Cost savings have been the driving force underlying many new home care options, with some states taking advantage of waivers for nursing home transition programs,[69] "choice" plans (enrollees can spend their LTC dollars by selecting among a variety of settings), self-directed care, and premium buy-in programs.[70] The Money Follows the Person Program, a leading Bush proposal under his 2001 New Freedom Initiative, was eventually established as part of the DRA. It allowed selected states to move certain enrollees from nursing homes to the community through small demonstration projects, beginning in 2007.[71] The federal government funds from 75 to 90 percent of the first-year costs for individuals who transfer, but the state must pick up its usual match in subsequent years and promise to continue supporting enrolled individuals for as long as they require home-based services.[72] As a consequence, local policymakers are pursuing the program warily. Concerned about steady increases in vacancy rates, the nursing home industry has also been less than enthusiastic about this program. Indeed, despite all of the fanfare, the Money Follows the Person Program represents less than one-half of one percent of LTC services.[73]

The drive for deinstitutionalization, without sufficient financial support for the individuals and families involved in the process, will face serious, often insurmountable barriers. In a study of nursing home transition programs in five states, for example, program administrators reported that unmarried individuals often do not have a place to live in the community because they are forced to sell their homes after a year of being institutionalized. There are few alternative housing options for low-income people, especially due to the generally long waiting lists for subsidized apartments. Moreover, a frail elder or disabled adult can be successfully deinstitutionalized only if there is an ample informal support system to supplement the limited Medicaid-funded in-home services offered. The officials also report that they encounter strong resistance to these types of programs from nursing home operators in their states, who are concerned about their bottom line.[74]

Another DRA initiative, the Cash and Counseling Option, allows self-directed care without the state's having to obtain a waiver. Initially established in the 1990s under section 1115 waiver authority and expanded under the Bush administration's Independence Plus Initiative in 2002, certain personal assistance services are "cashed out," allowing Medicaid recipients to hire their own aides, including relatives. The Cash and Counseling Option is limited to people who would otherwise qualify for personal care or HCBS waivers. As with other new allowable "flexibilities," the states can restrict services, cap funding or the number of recipients, and target selected populations or geographic regions at will. There also is serious concern as to whether a recipient's allowed Medicaid budget will be adequate to meet his or her real service needs.

The steady movement toward HCBS, the number one choice of the chronically ill aged and younger disabled populations, has had several ramifications. A lower percentage of dependent people, especially among young adults and children, is currently being institutionalized. Nevertheless, the cost savings from HCBS have for the most part not been realized. Not only is home care more expensive for individuals with extensive physical and emotional needs,[75] but the costs of nursing home services have spiraled in conjunction with rising vacancy rates. Policymakers have been whittling away at institutional care while LTC program costs continue to escalate overall. In many areas of the nation, instead of assisting more people at home with fewer dollars, the states are providing the same amount of services for more money. Facility owners are apparently now drawing in other vulnerable sectors of society, especially the mentally ill, which should boost expenditures even further. Quality of care also is at issue, for both nursing facilities and home health agencies. Finally, as the next section shows, insufficient HCBS funding places inordinate pressure on family and friends, who must fill the gaps.

Hidden Costs: Informal Caregivers

As suggested earlier, despite relatively large and increasing HCBS expenditures, Medicaid provides such assistance to relatively few older and disabled people requiring care, given the stringent qualification criteria, enrollment limits, and other barriers in nearly all of the states. Not only do large numbers of eligible people lack any services, but because of maximum payments per enrollee and/or meager funding generally, those participants actually receiving them tend to obtain far less aid than they need for their health and well-being. For the most part, government officials are promoting HCBS waivers while attempting to cut back on overall LTC outlays. The misguided assumption is that Medicaid-supported services in community settings are less expensive than those provided in institutional facilities. The evidence suggests, however, that at-home care is more cost effective for the government only if relatives and friends provide extensive, gap-filling, uncompensated assistance.[76]

Most seniors cannot afford to pay for supportive services on their own, and many who do purchase them experience a financial hardship that can lead to impoverishment. More than 80 percent of the frail elderly who live in the community thus rely either entirely or partially on family, friends, and volunteers for their mobility, functionality, and independence. The younger adult disabled population, whether born with a disorder or having experienced a devastating disease or injury later on, are generally in financial distress as well, mainly because of their inability to work full-time and the ongoing, expensive medical expenditures they must incur. More than 70 percent of them depend exclusively on informal care, and a smaller number (6 percent) receive a mix of unpaid and hired help.[77]

Recent strategies to save Medicaid money on LTC are clearly just shifting the costs elsewhere. More than 44 million people, about one-fifth of the adult population in the United States, already provide voluntary assistance to frail and disabled individuals, at times without any backing from others.[78] In an investigation of the subject, researchers found that nearly 33 percent of caregivers were aiding more than one person; they typically provided twenty-one hours of service per week for an average of 4.3 years, despite the fact that most of them were employed full-time. Tellingly, nearly 42 percent of the women and 34 percent of the men indicated that they did not have a choice as to whether they would provide the assistance or not.[79] The economic value of such aid has been estimated at roughly $350 billion annually.[80]

Policymakers tend either to ignore the immense and growing burdens placed on these caregivers (most of whom are adult daughters and wives) or to praise them by extolling the virtues of familism. Officials also are worried about what is labeled the "moral hazard" of Medicaid-funded HCBS, wherein individuals who provide uncompensated care to their relatives will demand Medicaid-supported services if the latter are more easily available. Thus, as suggested earlier, policymakers envision hordes of family and friends coming out of the "woodwork," resulting in vastly escalating HCBS outlays. I would argue, instead, that the paucity of paid HCBS for frail and disabled Medicaid-eligible individuals imposes a "moral infringement" on the rights and freedom of family caregivers. Studies show besides that hired services do not substitute for but rather only supplement informal care.[81]

Caregivers pay a price for assisting their frail family members or friends. Compared to other adults, they undergo more physical and mental stress, including symptoms of depression, chronic health conditions, medical debt, and other financial, psychological, and social difficulties. Those who are employed full-time face additional challenges. According to one study, a few must leave the labor force (9 percent), take early retirement (3 percent), or reduce their hours to part-time work (10 percent). Others take unpaid leave or experience workday interruptions, diminished wages, and reduced benefits (including health insurance, retirement savings, and Social Security). The toll on their employers can be significant as well: U.S. businesses suffer a productivity loss of roughly $34 billion annually because of employees' elder care obligations.[82] Rising numbers of chronically ill older people, a greater emphasis on HCBS, and policies that constrain Medicaid spending on LTC in general will only place even more—and increasingly untenable—demands on informal caregivers.

Déjà Vu: Counting on the Marketplace

Managed Care for the Frail and Disabled

The states have been aggressively turning their nonelderly welfare medicine beneficiaries over to commercial managed-care organizations (MCOs) but have been far more cautious with their chronically ill older and disabled populations, restricting such projects to relatively few participants. Implemented in the mid-1980s, the earliest managed LTC plans for the aged included the Frail Elder Option in Florida and the Program of All-Inclusive Care of the Elderly (PACE) initiatives, an outgrowth of San Francisco's On Lok Senior Health Services program.[83] Arizona established the only statewide mandated program, which pays contractors a fixed fee to provide a mix of LTC services to its low-income frail aged and disabled residents.[84] Other states instituted a few additional schemes in the early 1990s, but many of these attempts were unsuccessful and soon terminated. In these instances, both LTC providers, uneasy about the insurance companies setting low reimbursement rates, and age-based organizations, concerned over quality of care, successfully resisted such efforts.[85]

In recent years, policymakers' interest in capitated plans has been rekindled as yet another means of economizing on LTC. A few states are now viewing managed care as an alternative to the traditional fee-for-service programs for increasing numbers of their frail elderly and younger disabled Medicaid residents. Overall, however, qualification criteria are stringent, and there are still comparatively few enrollees nationwide. Although most of the ongoing waiver demonstration plans are voluntary, more states are requiring individuals to join.[86] To date, just 13 percent of such plans are run by commercial companies, mainly EverCare (an affiliate of United-Health Group) and Amerigroup,[87] but these companies and other proprietary firms are seeking to expand into what may prove to be a highly profitable market in the near future.

Long-Term Care Insurance

In accordance with the allure of market-based solutions to public problems prevalent under the Bush administration, elected officials, along with their allies in the insurance industry, began promoting private LTC insurance as the strategy of choice to reduce the burden on the Medicaid system. In the past, few companies offered such policies. Beginning in the mid-1980s, however, the industry began an aggressive search for new markets and, after studying the potential of LTC insurance, determined that it might develop into a lucrative enterprise.[88] Beginning in 2005, the federal government, in partnership with several states, initiated the Own Your Future consumer-awareness campaign illuminating Medicare's LTC restrictions while also advancing commercial coverage.

The DRA allowed another means for luring more people into the private sector, an expansion of the Partnership for Long-Term Care Program, which had been limited to four states since 1993.[89] Under the program provisions, policyholders can disregard an amount of their personal assets equal to the value of the insurance purchased when determining eligibility for Medicaid. Nursing home and HCBS users initially must rely on their private benefits, but when that funding has been exhausted, they can then turn to the low-income health program for assistance (if they meet the income and functional requirements).[90] The underlying premise is that Partnership for Long-Term Care Program arrangements will delay welfare medicine spending or avert it entirely for individuals who recover or die before depleting their commercial policies.

The evidence suggests, however, that these partnership schemes mainly boost the health insurance industry, subsidize high-income households, and may even increase Medicaid costs. In a survey of the initial four states offering the programs, the U.S. GAO found that 80 percent of policyholders said they would have bought LTC insurance anyway, and 20 percent would have otherwise paid for their own care.[91] According to policy expert Judith Feder, partnership LTC insurance purchasers might even be more likely *to use* LTC services, thereby adding to Medicaid expenditures.[92] Furthermore, at an annual cost of $2,300 or more, the plans are generally not affordable for low- and moderate-income households.[93] Despite the program's clear lack of success in attracting large numbers of buyers and the concerns about its efficacy, about half of the states have been developing such plans since 2006.

The national government also endeavored to stir up interest in LTC insurance through tax incentives. In particular, the Health Insurance Portability and Accountability Act of 1996 allowed LTC premiums and benefits to be treated like any other health insurance plan for income tax purposes.

According to most knowledgeable observers, similar to many of the other recent ventures, this feature of the act primarily helps high-income households, especially families who would have purchased insurance anyway.[94] The states also are considering or have launched a variety of similar enticements, including tax-exempt LTC Savings Accounts and tax credits for LTC insurance policyholders.

To be sure, private LTC insurance has not—and will never be—a way to drive down welfare medicine costs. Nor can it ever serve as the foremost solution to the care of our frail elderly. Several overwhelming obstacles, taken together, will make its extension to large sectors of the population unrealistic (and undesirable). For one thing, few employers offer such insurance, despite tax advantages provided to them, and where it is available only a few firms pay any part of the premium; just one-third of the total policies currently in force is employer sponsored.[95] Coverage is too expensive for most people, especially seniors, to pay on their own; only from 10 to 20 percent of the sixty-five and older population can afford high-quality plans.[96]

Most important, protection is often inadequate against future risks. Indeed, after assessing forty-seven policies offered by seven insurance companies, *Consumer Reports* found that only three of them were adequate. The contracts commonly have upper limits on daily payments, ceilings on the number of covered years, long waiting periods before the benefits take effect (in general ninety days), or all of these restrictions.[97] To date, few plans, if any, will pay the entire LTC bill for as long as services are required. Inflation can render the benefits even more insufficient, yet such protection, when provided, makes the agreements all the more unaffordable. Moreover, insurance companies, which peremptorily turn down people at risk of needing services, have rigorous underwriting screens; under the existing exclusions, fully one-fourth of all people age sixty-five would be deemed ineligible[98]

The insurance firms have come under attack for a number of other noxious practices. Some of them have hindered collection on their policies: strict disability criteria and fine-print details in the contracts can sometimes make it difficult to obtain benefits. Insurers also are allowed to hike premiums for an entire class of policyholders if their revised calculations indicate that the payments are inadequate for existing or future claims. In fact, beginning in 2003, many carriers raised their fees, some as much as by 30 percent.[99] The industry is moreover both volatile and uncertain as companies exit and enter the marketplace or merge with other firms. For some policyholders, the very solvency of their insurer may be in question. Needless to say, the private LTC insurance option has not been popular among Americans; few people have signed up, even among federal employees who have had access to such plans since 2002.[100] Private coverage accounts for only about 7 percent of LTC expenditures nationwide, a fraction of Medicaid outlays.[101]

Conclusion: Reckoning with Long-Term Care

LTC is obviously the 800-pound gorilla in Medicaid's policymaking arena: it is hugely expensive, and costs threaten to escalate even further. Most Americans arguably view the program's frail and disabled beneficiaries as the nation's most deserving poor, including many of its newly impoverished middle-class elders. The number of people who require LTC is swelling and will continue to do so in the upcoming years. Although high-priced nursing homes have dominated the LTC landscape over the decades, state policymakers—with a fixed gaze on their treasuries—are now increasingly (and virtuously) touting the value of in-home services, an alternative long preferred by caregivers and recipients alike. Nevertheless, the grim irony is that the slow but steady rebalancing of LTC options in favor of HCBS has come at a considerable price to Medicaid participants and their families: higher eligibility thresholds, enrollment ceilings, overall and per capita spending caps, waiting lists, a more limited mix of services, and a targeting of populations that favors certain low-income groups over others. The thinly transparent ideological fervor for "familism" and community-based care actually translates into greater, sometimes overwhelming burdens for unpaid caregivers, primarily wives and adult daughters.

Officials have also sought to economize by severely restricting the ability of middle- and upper-income older people to transfer assets to their children in order to qualify for welfare medicine, despite the lack of evidence that they do so to any great extent. The tightened rules have been yet another step in the ongoing erosion of Medicaid's LTC safety net and of its entitlement status more generally. Indeed, market-based solutions—both to lower Medicaid outlays and to substitute private benefits for government assistance—increasingly have become the foremost approaches on policymakers' radar screen, including managed-care demonstration projects, tax

++

incentives, and private LTC insurance. The data suggest, however, that such privatization measures in fact only buttress the insurance industry and advantage high-come households, but do not meet the needs of most older or disabled people and their families. Nor have they lessened LTC outlays. They certainly cannot serve as a substitute for universal LTC protection.

7

QUALITY OF CARE:
DOES WELFARE MEDICINE
MEASURE UP?

In this chapter, I concentrate on the quality of care received by eligible individuals who do manage to sign up for the program and obtain the services they require. I first address acute care, comparing a number of treatment and outcome results between welfare medicine and privately insured patients. I then turn to managed care, contending that in their relentless pursuit of cost efficiencies, states have been hastily forcing Medicaid participants into commercial plans without any concern for the compromised services they offer. In the third section of the chapter, I take a look at long-term care (LTC) alternatives to nursing homes and briefly assesses the nature of these services, finding that they, too, tend to be second rate, at least for low-income clientele. I also consider the inextricable linkage between staffing levels and quality of care.

Next, I deal with financial exploitation of Medicaid, along with the federal and state roles in combating the corruption. This fourth section explores the pervasiveness of the problem, explaining that the overseers of the program prefer to go after vendors that have "deep pockets" so as to maximize monetary recoveries, but in doing so they generally disregard the deleterious effects of financial fraud on program recipients. Throughout this section, I show how monetary returns trump the adverse impacts of inferior—or withheld—services, both in defining program integrity and as a priority for judicial action. In the last part, I discuss the potential of the federal False Claims Act (FCA) to bring to justice the owners of nursing homes with unsafe, deficient, and abusive conditions.

Second-Rate Care

A question often avoided by researchers and policymakers alike is whether Medicaid-funded services measure up to the standards of mainstream medicine. In other words, even if welfare medicine enrollees do not always receive medical and dental care conveniently or expeditiously, are they able to access services equivalent to those offered to people covered commercially or through Medicare? In actual fact, the data are surprisingly limited on whether the poor are being served well by the low-income health programs. Nevertheless, the available evidence paints a disconcerting picture of significant treatment and outcome disparities between Medicaid or State Children's Health Insurance Program (SCHIP) participants and patients insured elsewhere. As one investigator bluntly states, "Medicaid does not provide high-quality health care,"[1] a conclusion reached by most people who study the subject. Such inquiries are bolstered by innumerable nationwide newspaper accounts that are replete with "horror" stories about shoddy treatment and, at times, life-threatening medical neglect.

Since the inception of Medicaid, neither federal nor state policymakers have paid sufficient attention to quality concerns, centering their attention instead on ways to pare down expenses. At times, the U.S. Congress, the Centers for Medicare and Medicaid Services (CMS), and various localities have made half-hearted attempts to curb the more injurious practices, but the level of care has never been a prominent variable of the Medicaid/SCHIP equation. Political leaders have consequently permitted—and even sustained—highly concentrated group medical practices that engage in cursory, substandard patient care. In some places, then, welfare medicine participants may have sufficient access to physicians and dentists, but their choices are limited to practitioners who are second rate, at best; managed care has only exacerbated the situation. The quality of nursing homes, at-home services, and assisted-living facilities, too, falls far short of what program participants should expect and deserve.

Medicaid did not fare very well in two comprehensive appraisals of the program. In 1987 and again in 2007, Health Research Group, a unit of Ralph Nader's Public Citizen, Inc., assessed the fifty state programs according to four major criteria: eligibility, scope of services, provider reimbursement levels, and quality of care. Twenty years after the organization's initial evaluation, in which it determined that none of the states had a really outstanding Medicaid plan,[2] the group's researchers again came to the same conclusion. Their latest report tells us that state Medicaid programs are still severely deficient across the nation. The best plans scored only 646 out of 1,000 points; thirty-one states attained less than 500 points, and a few rated as low as 318, a grade of only 30 percent of the total.[3] Notably, even the top plans received their lowest ratings, by far, on quality of care; the mean score on this measure was only 28.2 points out of a maximum of 200.

Over the past several years, investigators who measured actual patient services and outcomes based on insurance type have found that services provided to welfare medicine recipients are not up to par. For example, in a comparison of pregnant women, evaluators at Alabama's Health Department discovered that individuals whose delivery was Medicaid-funded experienced a 40 percent higher probability of having a low-birth-weight baby and a 60 percent greater likelihood that their infant would die in the first year than mothers who were insured privately.[4]

Equally disturbing, although people with acute coronary syndromes can profit significantly from certain recommended interventions (medications, medical therapies, invasive cardiac procedures, and preventive measures), a recent study established that nonelderly welfare medicine participants were less likely to receive these treatments than privately insured patients. They also had poorer results, including greater mortality rates.[5] Similarly, in an exploration of the factors affecting the timing of treatment for laryngeal cancer, medical researchers ascertained that, at diagnosis, Medicaid patients had more than twice the risk of advanced-stage laryngeal cancer and were three or four times more likely to have large-volume tumors than people who were covered by commercial policies. After controlling for other variables, such as age, race, gender, and the like, they reported that the type of health insurance was "the strongest predictor of stage at diagnosis and tumor size."[6]

In some cases, Medicaid patients may be no better off than the uninsured. In one of the first nationwide studies of its kind, Michael Halpern and his colleagues at the American Cancer Center determined that both welfare medicine participants and people without any insurance were far more likely to be diagnosed with advanced-stage cancer of all types than people who were privately insured, mostly because of a paucity of screening, lack of timely diagnosis, and insufficient follow-up with doctors. As a consequence, they suffered from greater morbidity, an inferior quality of life, and lower survival rates.[7]

There even are differences among categories of Medicaid enrollees, with nursing home residents and dual eligibles apparently among the most disadvantaged. For example, researchers at Virginia Commonwealth University also addressed the issue of cancer care, in this case comparing Medicaid-insured institutionalized elders with those residing at home. They discovered that nursing home residents diagnosed with cancer experienced much greater late or undiagnosed stages of the disease, received appreciably fewer treatments (only 20 percent received surgery, and only 6 percent had chemotherapy and/or radiation treatments), had higher mortality rates, and were offered less hospice care than the community dwellers with cancer.[8] Another inquiry focused on the situation of dually eligible seniors living in their own homes or with family members. Using forty-four quality

indicators, the research group found that, despite eligibility for comprehensive services under both Medicare and Medicaid, they received only 65
percent of the recommended tests, medications, diagnostic evaluations,
and treatments for such illnesses as diabetes, heart disease, depression, and
osteoporosis.[9]

The overall evidence suggests that welfare medicine patients are frequently short-changed as to the nature of their care and, at times, lack early
diagnosis and treatment of diseases that potentially can be controlled or
cured. They are better off than the uninsured in many instances, but not
always, according to the data, especially specific sectors of the Medicaid
population. As the next section shows, the situation is often at its worst for
patients enrolled in managed care.

Skimping on Services: Managed Care

The dubious if not simplistic assumption among political leaders—or in
many cases simply the pretense— has been that managed-care organizations (MCOs) can deliver higher-quality services at a lower price than traditional Medicaid can. In actual fact, however, they achieve cost efficiencies
by rationing health care. Indeed, the payment mechanisms for capitated
plans create clear-cut inducements to skimp on patient services, in particular the more high-priced procedures. By restricting access to specialists,
expensive drugs, and costly treatments, MCOs profit at the expense of patients, sometimes barring them from essential services that can maintain
and possibly improve their health and well-being. The situation is even
more problematic for Medicaid managed-care participants because the insurers serving them are under intense economizing pressures by state policymakers who are seeking to rein in their own budgets.[10] What is more,
because welfare medicine patients frequently cycle in and out of coverage,
there is no incentive to invest in comprehensive preventive services, one of
the main justifications for managed care in the first place.

Although relatively few studies measure the quality of care provided
through Medicaid MCOs,[11] the available information indicates that these
organizations are not meeting high enough standards and in many cases
are delivering substandard medical services. In one of the first large com-
parisons between Medicaid and privately insured children, all participating

in prepaid plans, medical researchers documented that the welfare medicine enrollees frequently received a lower level of treatment on a number of performance indicators, even within the same insurance plan.[12]

Another group of researchers found similar problems. Using eleven measures of quality, they evaluated the services offered to private-sector participants versus Medicaid-covered households in three types of MCO plans: Medicaid only, commercial only, and mixed Medicaid/commercial arrangements. The Medicaid population experienced inferior care on ten of the indicators, regardless of plan type.[13] In another survey, this time of pregnant women and their infants who were forced to switch from Medicaid fee-for-service care to managed care, the data reveal a sharp decrease in services. Not only were the women less likely to start prenatal examinations early on, but their babies were more apt to suffer from low birth weight, premature delivery, and death.[14]

These capitated arrangements certainly did not have auspicious beginnings. One of the first large-scale Medicaid managed-care ventures was initiated in the late 1960s by California governor Ronald Reagan. Established commercial companies refused to enter the market at the time, viewing the undertaking as too risky. Instead, scores of new plans were rapidly constructed exclusively for welfare medicine clients. As one observer tells us, "By the early 1970s, many of these newly formed health plans were embroiled in scandals because of fraudulent marketing practices, inadequate capitalization, and substandard care."[15]

For-profit MCOs have since their expansion in the 1990s engaged in a wide range of objectionable activities, and their enrollees have lacked, for the most part, adequate access to decent, quality care. In 1996, an advisory "Quality Commission" established by the Clinton administration uncovered, among other unsavory practices, "gag rules" (controlling what physicians could disclose to their patients about treatment options, especially expensive ones); bonuses and other rewards to practitioners who limited services; a periodic denial of emergency care; and an unsatisfactory roster of doctors, in particular specialists. In response, the House and Senate offered a number of proposals for a patient bill of rights of varying strengths, but after two years of ideological and partisan strife they were unable to enact a single piece of legislation.[16] Moreover, despite the rampant and obvious problems, policymakers in 1997 allowed the states even greater flexibility to mandate managed care for Medicaid beneficiaries, generating a steady increase in such enrollments. Even worse, it rescinded the 75/25 rule requiring that at least 25 percent of managed-care patients in any plan had to be privately insured, an action that fostered the emergence of Medicaid-only arrangements and, with them, even greater care deficiencies.[17]

Pressed by other health-related issues, notably a large and increasing medically uninsured population in tandem with Medicaid budgetary concerns, most states have not placed high priority on setting their own consumer protections.[18] Instead, they have been charging forward with mandated managed care, regardless of the consequences. Georgia, for example, began experiencing serious problems with its MCOs (Centene, WellCare, and Amerigroup) shortly after its new program was launched in 2006 and was forced to fine at least one of them for negligence. At legislative hearings, medical practitioners, patients, and hospital administrators complained of delays in the delivery of care because of slow authorization procedures, denials of medically necessary treatments, impediments to preventive services, and sorely lacking provider networks.[19] Since implementing its new mandatory managed-care policy in 2006, Ohio began experiencing similar, serious problems as well, including lengthy waits for authorization of essential treatments. As discussed in chapter 4, Florida, too, has encountered extensive health-threatening practices among its MCOs, including a large withdrawal of physicians from the plans and patients' encountering difficulty in receiving timely medical services or medications.

MCOs increasingly are coming under greater scrutiny for their financial misdeeds, although the harmful consequences for welfare medicine participants continue to remain in the background. For example, in 2007, WellCare was under investigation, accused of not spending at least 80 percent of its Medicaid dollars on mental health services in Florida. The Connecticut Attorney General's Office concurrently accused the company of hiding the extent of its profits from the low-income health program. As a result, WellCare's CEO, finance chief, and general counsel resigned. The company also was under investigation in other states, including New York. Yet WellCare continues to prosper: despite the ongoing probes of illegal activities, in 2008 the insurance firm received contract renewals in Connecticut, Florida, Georgia, Illinois, and Louisiana, including an expansion of services in some of these places.[20]

Connecticut has experienced problems with another one of its four Medicaid MCOs, Health Net: in 2007, the company forwarded computer messages to pharmacies that fraudulently advised them to deny coverage of certain prescription drugs for children, and the MCO was subsequently sanctioned for its illegal activities.[21] In Illinois, Amerigroup was charged with shortchanging the state's Medicaid program. In 2002 and 2003, it paid out only 50 percent of its premium dollars on medical services, with obvious implications for the quality of care. In addition, as a result of a whistle-blower lawsuit, a jury found the MCO guilty of fraudulently discouraging unhealthy people and pregnant women from signing up and ordered it to pay $334 million in fines.[22] California's MCOs, too, are not measuring up to expectations. Economist Mark Duggan found that privatization of the state's Medicaid program raised costs substantially but without any improvement in health outcomes. He warned that the only way the commercial companies would save the government money would be to reduce the quality of care.[23] Other states are plagued with myriad managed-care problems as well. And many of them are spending more for services and receiving less in return.[24]

However, it is the poor who pay the ultimate price. MCOs serving Medicaid participants have grown dramatically, reaping stellar profits, but on the backs of low-income families. The firms are now paying out considerably fewer premium dollars on health care services. Since Medicaid is such a paltry payer to begin with, the obvious conclusion is that the health and well-being of welfare medicine enrollees are at risk. And where governments do save money, participants suffer even more from insufficient services and second-rate care. Their families also may experience greater burdens. Investigators recently found, for example, that MCOs could reduce state Medicaid outlays for the care of adults with severe mental illnesses, but these cost savings were at times offset by inferior health outcomes, along with additional financial and other hardships imposed on the patients and their caregivers.[25] MCOs have clearly not proved to be the "miracle elixir" for welfare medicine.

Serving Frail Elders and the Disabled

Home Care: Wavering on Quality

Even fewer federal requirements and sanctions are aimed at ensuring the quality of services for home- and community-based services (HCBS) waiver participants, and most states do not offer ample protections of their own. According to the U.S. Government Accountability Office (GAO), complaint systems, penalty mechanisms, and beneficiary satisfaction surveys are conspicuously lacking. The agency also discovered widespread quality problems, along with little interest in improving the situation. Among the more consequential findings was a failure to provide services already approved, most of which had been identified as essential to the enrollee's health and well-being. In addition, it uncovered insufficient monitoring of vulnerable elders by case workers, a paucity of aides relative to need, questionable worker credentials and training, and poor quality of care on the whole.[26]

Nor does CMS monitor the programs sufficiently, devoting few of its staff and only limited dollars to quality concerns. In both their waiver applications and annual reports, the states provide incomplete—and in many cases no information—on how they safeguard Medicaid recipients who receive assistance in their homes.[27] The HCBS waivers have evidently added "flexibility" for the localities to cut corners and without accountability for their actions. Thus, the full magnitude of the problems is not even known. By the same token, it is unclear to what extent home care agencies are answerable to policymakers for the quality of the services they provide, beyond meeting the bare minimum state certification requirements. As with our nation's nursing homes, nobody appears to be watching the store, and our frail elders and younger disabled people are paying the price.

Assisted Living: Out of the Frying Pan, into the Fire?

Emerging in the 1980s, the number of assisted-living facilities expanded rapidly in the following decade, leading to overbuilding, a rash of empty rooms, and bankruptcies. In recent years, however, the industry—which serves nearly a million people—has recovered: overall occupancy rates are now at 95 percent. Clients, however, are frailer and sicker than before; nearly half have cognitive impairments.[28] The vast majority of places caters almost exclusively to private-pay elders, most of whom view such housing as preferable to institutional care.

States, too, are turning to assistive living, albeit cautiously, as yet another cost-driven alternative to nursing homes because the average annual price per person is considerably less. To date, few assisted-living inhabitants (roughly 11 percent) are covered under welfare medicine, but forty states already have at least one Medicaid waiver program offering limited support for this option, and more states are joining in.[29] However, the expansion in the number of assisted-living beds and of initiatives to subsidize them through Medicaid has not been accompanied by policies to ensure the residents' safety and well-being. Thus far, no federal laws govern these facilities; each state establishes and enforces its own quality standards, most of which are sorely wanting. Conditions within many of them are no better—and in some cases worse—than in institutions. A *Consumer Reports* survey of assisted-living homes in 2005 found that poor care and neglect were rampant. The investigative staff reported that a preponderance of the residents were frail and sick, many suffering from dementia, but the facilities by and large were not equipped to take care of them. They noted that some states do not even require the provision of basic services or mandate minimum staffing or training levels.[30]

Other exposés also have provided searing descriptions of these board-and-care homes. A two-year investigation by *USA Today* divulged a pattern of unsafe conditions, neglect, and abuse, with only patchy local oversight of the facilities. In 2004, the newspaper's analysis showed a prevalence of staff-related problems, including serious shortages of direct-care aides, a lack of basic training, and inordinately low wages, leading to high turnover and vacancies. Reaching conclusions similar to those outlined in the *Consumer Reports* investigation, the researchers warned that in order to maintain high occupancy rates and profits, the facilities increasingly are marketing to and accepting elderly residents who require more care than the facilities are capable of providing.[31] An inquiry by the *Washington Post* found mistreatment, neglect, and exploitation of as well as violence against assisted-living residents in Virginia, along with serious injuries and life-threatening medication errors. In the paper's four-part series, the reporters describe exceedingly deficient staffing, overwhelmed inspectors, a pattern of intermittent compliance with regulations, and a lack of overall accountability for the perilous conditions.[32] The newspaper's editors scathingly observed: "It is called 'Assisted Living,' yet in an astonishing, depressing number of facilities across Virginia it is little more than neglected suffering and dying."[33]

Medicaid recipients, as usual, are at risk of placement in the worst places, especially because overall vacancy rates are now so low that the high-quality homes can target more affluent elders. At the same time, these financially better-off clients will be forced out if they exhaust their assets, which they generally do in about two and a half years. Therefore, frail elders who choose assisted living, even among the middle class, may find themselves in a catch-22 situation, ultimately ending up no better off than their low-income counterparts.[34]

Direct-Care Workers: A Vital Missing Link to Quality Care

According to most knowledgeable observers, the primary determinants of nursing home residents' quality of life are both the quantity of and their relationship with direct-care workers, but nearly all such institutions are critically understaffed.[35] A study commissioned by CMS found that more than half of the homes surveyed failed to meet all of the agency's minimum staffing-level recommendations, and fully 97 percent fell short of at least one of the recommendations, thus leading to a greater incidence of festering bedsores, urinary infections, malnutrition, weight loss, dehydration, pneumonia, and other critical conditions. Certified nurse's aides (CNAs), who provide nearly 90 percent of all hands-on assistance, are responsible for meeting just about all of the frail elder's physical, social, and emotional needs. Yet the researchers concluded that more than 40 percent of all facilities would need to increase their CNA staffing by 50 percent or more to conform to the government's lowest acceptable threshold.[36] Compounding the problem is inordinately high CNA turnover, a situation that also compromises continuity of patient care; in nineteen states, the annual turnover rate is greater than 80 percent, and in ten states it exceeds 100 percent.[37]

Although acknowledging the serious nature of the industry's staffing shortages, turnover, and vacancies, nursing home executives characteristically blame these problems, which have intensified in recent years, on low Medicaid reimbursement levels and the difficulty in recruiting direct-care workers. In actual fact, because LTC is labor intensive, and paid staff—especially CNAs—represent a nursing home's foremost expense, owners skimp on wages and benefits to enhance their profits. In 2008, the median hourly wage for CNAs was $10.61, compared to $12.59 for customer service representatives or $11.78 for receptionists in manufacturing and distribution. Roughly 20 percent of CNAs live in poverty, and slightly more than 50 percent of them earn incomes at near-poverty levels (less than 200 percent of the federal poverty level). Compared to other low-income workers, they are twice as likely to rely on Medicaid themselves, and 25 percent of CNAs have no health insurance at all. Hardly any of these frontline workers can afford the premiums and other cost-sharing expenses of employer-sponsored health coverage, even when it is offered to them.[38]

CNAs confront additional workplace struggles. For one, they experience an exceedingly high rate of on-the-job injuries, 18.2 per 100 workers, as compared to people engaged in coal mining (6.2), construction (10.6), and warehousing or trucking (13.8).[39] In fact, nurse's aides, attendants, and orderlies have the third-highest rate of nonfatal occupation-related mishaps in the nation.[40] Their concerns about safety are compounded by burdensome workloads, limited opportunities for advancement, inadequate training, lack of respect by supervisors, employers, and the public alike, and an exclusion from patient care planning. As a consequence, a significant number of these front-line employees abandon the industry entirely, most of them moving on to other low-wage jobs that offer comparatively better and healthier working environments.

As policymakers increasingly turn to community-based care in their chaotic search for money-saving alternatives to nursing homes, they face an even direr staffing situation in the home care industry. Nearly every state is struggling to find a sufficient number of workers for their HCBS waiver programs, although they are unwilling to assure that these workers are paid a living wage. Even where state legislators periodically increase reimbursement levels to home care agencies, these payments are not necessarily converted into higher earnings for their labor force. Indeed, home health aides and personal care assistants, in already the fourth fastest-growing occupations in the United States, receive even lower salaries, experience more challenging workplace conditions, have fewer opportunities, and therefore have greater annual turnover rates than CNAs. With a median hourly wage of $9.87 in 2008, nearly one-fourth of individuals employed in HCBS programs lives in poverty, and one-third has no health insurance.[41]

Under existing conditions, turnover, vacancies, and sorely inadequate direct-care staffing levels will clearly only worsen in the near future, generating an even more unfavorable situation for aides and residents alike. In 2006, 2.7 million people were employed in direct-care work;[42] from 2015 to 2050, as the overall labor force relative to the size of the eighty-five and older population markedly declines and the number of baby boomers requiring LTC grows, we will need to nearly double the number of such workers just to maintain the current ratio.[43] The gap undoubtedly will be even larger as women, who comprise nearly 90 percent of caregivers, continue to leave the occupation altogether. Among individuals working as CNAs, home health aides, or personal assistants in 2005, only 60 percent were still employed in such jobs a year later. Instead of improving wages and working conditions for these at-risk workers—consisting of a disproportionate number of blacks and Latinos—nursing homes, home health agencies, and assisted-living facilities, with policymakers' knowledge and apparent acquiescence, are limping along with a staff that is increasingly insufficient to meet the needs of frail elders and disabled younger clients. Already capitalizing on immigrant labor, industry lobbyists most likely will continue their pressure on elected officials to further expand the pool of foreign workers.[44]

Gaming the System

A program that has always been vulnerable to plunder by a vast array of providers, Medicaid has been a breeding ground for financial fraud since its inception. Medicare, too, was exploited early on by a wide range of providers, but welfare medicine experienced greater difficulties: it had much broader coverage, confusion over which level of government would or could control unscrupulous activities, and fifty different state programs to deal with. Yet even today policymakers have no precise knowledge of the extent of the problem, although they have sought an annual estimate for Medicare since 1996.[45] Even the Senate committee responsible for overseeing the low-income health program does not know exactly how much fraud, waste, and abuse occur.[46] There are varying conjectures among the states, but most of them acknowledge that at least 10 percent of total welfare medicine funding today are pilfered through criminal misconduct, and even more due to "errors" and "improper" payments. Some observers calculate the financial losses in a few localities, such as New York, as high as 25 to 40 percent.[47]

Medicaid not only continues to be "easy money" for legitimate vendors and con artists alike, but the scams have become more pervasive, complex, innovative, and audacious. Perpetrators include physicians, dentists, psychologists, psychiatrists, podiatrists, opticians, ophthalmologists, pharmacists, nurses, social workers, hospitals, nursing homes, assisted-living facilities, home health and personal care agencies, MCOs, pharmaceutical corporations, medical equipment and supply businesses, transportation firms, and ambulance companies. No health profession, agency, or institution has been entirely exempt from the temptation to exploit the Medicaid gold mine.

Most of the responsibility for preventing, detecting, and punishing fraud resides in the states. Their Medicaid agencies are supposed to ensure accurate spending, recover overpayments, identify potentially illegal activities, and perform preliminary investigations.[48] Substantiated cases are then forwarded to Medicaid Fraud Control Units (MFCUs), which further investigate and prosecute them as well as impose civil and criminal penalties when deemed appropriate. MFCUs, which tend to reside in state attorney general offices, also accept referrals from state and federal law enforcement agencies, insurance departments, consumers, legislators, whistle-blowers, and providers.[49]

At the national level, the Office of Inspector General (OIG) and the Department of Justice investigate and enforce federal fraud and abuse laws, including the FCA. The law's *qui tam* provision, strengthened in 1986, permits individuals (whistle-blowers) to bring suits on behalf of the federal government and awards them a share of any money recovered.[50] Individuals and companies convicted of cheating the system are subject to triple damages, along with fines for each false claim they submitted. In the past, the Department of Justice had used the FCA mostly against defense contractors, but since the late 1990s health care fraud has emerged as its primary target. On the whole, however, federal law enforcement agencies tend to favor perpetrators with "deep pockets," and Medicare over Medicaid-related cases.

States: The First Line of Defense

States have been less than vigilant in combating financial exploitation of their Medicaid programs. In the early years, few Medicaid cases were taken to court, and an even smaller number resulted in convictions. Despite intermittent spikes of activity in several places, many states have been cutting back on their antifraud pursuits, with lower budgetary outlays, hiring freezes, and staff reductions.[51] A recent OIG study found that, relative to the program's financial vulnerabilities, many state Medicaid agencies were not forwarding a large enough number of cases to their MFCUs for prosecution. More than half of the units received, on average, only one acceptable suit or less per month between 2002 and 2005, and in some places the number was actually declining. Rather than force individuals who engage in illicit activities to pay for their misdeeds, Medicaid agencies regularly attribute such fraud to "mistakes" and "instruct" the perpetrators on appropriate billing practices.[52] What is more, slightly more than 70 percent of MFCU referrals originated from other sources, commonly whistle-blowers.[53]

The MFCUs themselves are reluctant to pursue certain types of health providers vigorously. They generally take into account any potentially harmful effects of their actions on a range of interested parties, including contractors and their employees, shareholders, the community, and Medicaid clients—especially the latter's access to sufficient and appropriate services.[54] As a consequence, hospitals, nursing homes, pharmaceutical companies, and the like can hold law enforcement agencies hostage, despite looting Medicaid and preying on its recipients. In one such case, according to the New York Attorney General's Office, Staten Island University Hospital for the second time "knowingly embarked on a new plan to profit illegally from Medicaid." In an attempt to cover up the crime, hospital executives lied to both State Department of Health regulators and MFCU investigators. Nonetheless, the state attorney general asserted, "You do not and cannot destroy an entity as important to the delivery of health care as [Staten Island University Hospital]," and did not bring any charges against the executives or the hospital, deciding instead that the institution had to repay the illicit money and institute internal reforms.[55]

In the past several years, however, a few states have taken the lead in cracking down on waste and fraud. Texas has become the exemplar of the feisty guardian of taxpayer money, boasting that it saved 5 percent of its Medicaid budget in the first year of its war against illicit practices.[56] West Virginia, too, has been pursuing Medicaid thieves with a vengeance. In some places, newspaper disclosures have forced the issue, such as an inquiry by the Kansas City Star (Missouri) in 2005. The state legislature subsequently conducted hearings, established an inspector general, and enacted an FCA. A year later, its governor, Matt Blunt (R), identified antifraud activities among his key priorities.

That same year, a New York Times investigation disclosed that from 10 to 40 percent of state Medicaid money were either pilfered or paid erroneously. The staff researchers found that out of more than 400 million cases processed in 2004, inspectors had uncovered only 37 instances of suspected fraud. Moreover, the inspectors systematically ignored audits and other reports outlining the extent of the wrongdoings.[57] The newspaper's biting two-part series drew strong bipartisan responses from the New York State Assembly, including the purchase of a new IBM supercomputer to detect deception; establishment of an independent Medicaid inspector general office and millions more for additional staff; enactment of an FCA, along with tougher civil and criminal penalties; and initiation of the Medicaid Fraud Demonstration pilot authorizing twelve counties to pursue anti-fraud activities on their own.[58] In addition, in an unprecedented deal with CMS, the state agreed to engage in more aggressive recovery efforts, set at specific target amounts, in exchange for $1.5 billion from the federal government over five years.[59]

Scathing audit reports also have raised the visibility of Medicaid's vulnerability to financial exploitation in several states, including Massachusetts, Florida, and Ohio.[60] Additional jurisdictions are paying more attention to fiscal oversight by upgrading enforcement staff and performing on-site inspections (i.e., California and South Carolina), installing expensive, high-powered antifraud equipment (i.e., Ohio and South Carolina), and toughening penalties (i.e., New Jersey).[61] Furthermore, by 2008, about one-quarter of the states had enacted their own FCA, and more should gradually be doing so in coming years.[62] A few places are even hiring "bounty hunters," such as Des Varady's HWT, a Maine Company that retrieves money for eight Medicaid programs and retains from 5 to 15 percent of the salvaged funds. Whether because of their own urgent budgetary needs or because they are forced by outside investigators' disclosures, state policymakers are increasingly giving their attention to financial fraud.

Federal Oversight: Medicaid, Second-Class Citizen

The federal government's main role is to support state activities and provide oversight, but for most of Medicaid's history it has not taken an active role in tackling financial abuse of the program. In contrast, Congress established a federal inspector general in 1979 to combat exploitive practices associated with Medicare. The 1996 Health Care Fraud and Abuse Program, too, focused primarily on Medicare, as did its provision for a special

Medicare Integrity Program.[63] The GAO did not even officially list Medicaid as one of its high-risk programs until 2003, a designation that had been applied to Medicare in 1990. Under the George W. Bush administration, the limited amount of money allocated to welfare medicine through the Health Care Fraud and Abuse Program was used mostly against state attempts to maximize federal matching payments for their plans (see chapter 9).[64] Indeed, the GAO cast doubt as to whether the national government intended to crack down on Medicaid contractors at all, contending that CMS had shown relatively little interest in the matter.[65]

To engender a stronger federal presence at CMS and remedy some inequities between the two public-sector health programs, Congress launched the Medicaid Integrity Program, modeled on the Medicare approach, authorized under the 2005 Deficit Reduction Act (DRA). Among other provisions, the program provided for more staff to conduct federal reviews of state programs, boosted funding, established a new unit in CMS State Operations (the Medicaid Integrity Group), and, for the first time, mandated the development of a national Comprehensive Medicaid Integrity Plan every five years, beginning in 2006. In addition, CMS was required to enter into agreements with private entities—Medicaid integrity contractors—to conduct provider audits.[66] Even so, although the Medicaid Integrity Program indicated a stronger federal oversight of Medicaid fraud, the investment of resources was still comparatively moderate, especially given the enormity of the task, and represented only a fraction of the amount focused on Medicare.[67]

Fixing on the Mother Load

For the most part, state and federal Medicaid officials justify the costs of antifraud programs by calling attention to their "return on investment," which has become the primary gauge of accomplishment for welfare medicine law enforcement agencies.[68] Regulators consequently tend to take the greatest interest in cases that allow them to retrieve large amounts of money. The 2005 *New York Times* investigation, for instance, found that state watchdogs were much more interested in "recouping money through a few civil cases that have little deterrent value" than in preventing or fighting the problem itself.[69] Legal actions against providers, based on the FCA, plainly suggest that federal and state law enforcement authorities are targeting cases that maximize financial gains. In 2005, nearly 50 percent of all such settlements and judgments generated more than $2 million *each*, rising to 67 percent of the total the following year. In fact, six of the cases brought in $100 million or more apiece.[70] Drug companies, along with hospitals, have become the targets of choice not only because of their dogged ploys to game the system, but also on account of their comparatively "deep pockets." Indeed, about 80 percent of the Medicaid fraud settlements at the state and federal levels between 2000 and 2005 involved pharmaceutical firms.[71]

Recent activity, clearly with an eye on the money, has centered on inflated prescription drug pricing and the $10 billion rebate program. For a covered medication to be eligible for federal matching funds, the manufacturer must provide discounts to the state Medicaid programs, based on the firm's "best prices."[72] However, the refunds rely on manufacturer-reported data, with insufficient confirmation by government agencies, and scores of pharmaceutical companies have falsified their figures. Companies also participate in private labeling (marking down the cost of the drug to select purchasers and placing the latter's number on the package) so as to avoid the Medicaid rebate.

Firms have engaged in additional schemes to bilk Medicaid. For example, to facilitate greater sales, they discount medicine to pharmacists, doctors, and other providers, allowing them to sell the products at a higher profit. In addition, they have marketed prescription medicine for off-label usage (medical conditions not approved by the U.S. Federal Drug Administration [FDA]), with serious consequences for consumers. By the end of 2004, ten whistle-blower suits were settled against drug companies—mainly employing the joint resources of state MFCUs, the OIG, the Department of Justice, the FDA, and other local and national entities. Such illegal activities continue to be the foremost concern of Medicaid regulators, who are amassing huge amounts of money through financial settlements and judicial actions.[73]

Program Integrity

Taking Consumers into Account

Although state MFCUs and certain federal agencies clearly have investigative and enforcement authority over all aspects of Medicaid, they address fiscal oversight more willingly than consumer health and safety, which is far less likely to capture dollars for government treasuries. At the same time, economic deception is more easily documented and measured than poor-quality care, another deciding factor in whether to take legal action against a perpetrator. Furthermore, to prosecute a Medicaid case successfully, law enforcement agencies must amass vast resources, expend countless hours (that often run into years), draw on a significant percentage of their generally meager staff, and even coordinate with their counterparts elsewhere. Therefore, if they do take on a dishonest provider, they are more likely to negotiate a financial settlement, frequently disregarding the sometimes substantial emotional, physical, and social costs to vulnerable program recipients.

In Medicaid-related suits, the defendants commonly are charged with any number of crimes for exploiting the program monetarily, but the impact on clients tends to be overlooked. Yet nearly all of the ploys to steal welfare medicine money inevitably have severe adverse effects on consumers. Such offenses include billing for services not rendered or equipment not delivered; charging for more expensive services or equipment than the patient received (called "upcoding"); providing inappropriate, risky, or unnecessary treatments; requesting reimbursement for care provided by unlicensed or untrained workers; engaging in kickback arrangements, bribes, or other illegal marketing practices; forging prescriptions; promoting off-label drug use; offering flawed or nonexistent testing; and illegally adding tests or services that were not requested (bundling).

Although such Medicaid fraud and abuse cases abound daily across the nation, they generally go unnoticed; such accounts tend to be tucked away in local newspapers. The recent sampling of seriously injurious actions listed here can be multiplied many times over:

• Physicians bill for services not rendered, falsify medical records, and provide medically unnecessary services, risking the health, safety, and even lives of welfare medicine participants. In one case, an anesthesiologist's patients were either forced to do without their pain-management services because of illicit invoices or were subjected to unapproved procedures.[74] In another instance, a regional medical center (in Louisiana) performed unwarranted elective angioplasty and stenting, both extremely intrusive and risky surgical treatments.[75]

+ +

- Medical practices and hospitals allow unlicensed staff to practice medicine, again endangering Medicaid clients. The OIG and New York's MFCU found that physician fellows were performing endoscopic procedures unsupervised by a doctor and even at times when a patient's medical record indicated that the procedures were not medically necessary.[76] Just as damaging, a head injury firm billed for services it did not render to survivors of traumatic brain damage and for care performed by unqualified staff.

- Youngsters diagnosed with severe emotional disturbances were denied their much needed therapy because mental health providers billed Medicaid for sessions that never occurred. Adults, too, missed out on counseling for depression and other psychological disorders because psychotherapists, psychiatrists, and clinical social workers were financially abusing the program.

- Frail elders and disabled younger adults lingered unattended at home, forgoing their approved and paid-for assistance because home health companies and personal care attendants failed to make the scheduled visits. Others suffered from a lack of physical, occupational, and speech therapy essential to their well-being.

- Chronically ill children and adults were forced to utilize second-hand life-sustaining apparatuses such as feeding pumps and compressors because companies did not deliver new equipment, as required. Other places never even provided the already paid-for devices to their vulnerable customers.

- Dentists embezzled Medicaid dollars while denying recipients preventive and restorative treatments, leading to perilous but avoidable medical conditions.

- Pharmacists engaged in schemes that entailed the sale of expired or improperly stored medicine to unsuspecting customers, forcing them to take potentially impotent drugs.

- Because of false and illicit billings, recovering addicts lost out on their treatments for chemical dependency or, as in a recent case at a New York hospital, received substandard services from an unlicensed center.[77]

- Transportation companies left patients requiring urgent medical attention stranded, but they still submitted claims for the services.

- Clinical laboratories provided bogus, inaccurate, or incomplete tests, preventing clients from obtaining an early, potentially life-saving diagnosis of an illness or averting avoidable medical complications. Other Medicaid participants conversely experienced unnecessary screenings that engendered needless anxiety or false readings or both.[78]

+ +

- Pharmacies, including Rite Aid Corporation, Wal-Mart, and CVS, purposely short-filled prescriptions, causing some individuals to skip vital doses of their medication.[79]

What is more, in viewing Medicaid integrity mainly in financial terms, program overseers do not differentiate between offenses that jeopardize enrollees and those that result primarily in monetary losses. Wrongdoings that may be consequential but do not directly harm current recipients include double-billing (e.g., duplicate claims to Medicaid and Medicare); turning in claims for ineligible individuals or people who are deceased; the buying and selling of Medicaid cards or Social Security numbers; submitting false cost reports; billing for marketing or lobbying activities; and unbundling (an unwarranted separation of a service into smaller components to inflate fees). To be sure, because officials are concerned mostly with collecting money, they tend to treat the harmful impact of fraud on participants as of secondary importance and are less apt to punish either companies or their executives for the crimes they commit against clients.

Misconduct such as illegally marketing inappropriate or ineffective prescription medicine, which can injure consumers, is most likely to result simply in monetary penalties. As a case in point, in a ten-year marketing campaign dubbed "Viva Zyprexa," Eli Lilly promoted this highly profitable antipsychotic drug for the treatment of dementia, anxiety, sleep disruption, mood swings, and attention deficit disorder for all age groups, even though it was FDA approved only for bipolar disorder and schizophrenia in adults. Internal company documents showed that company officials also concealed Zyprexa's risks and known side effects, including diabetes, serious weight gain, and other metabolic problems as well as heart failure and pneumonia in older dementia patients. The company had previously marketed another one of its products, Evista, for the prevention of breast cancer and cardiovascular disease despite the fact that the drug was authorized only for treating osteoporosis; it also concealed Evista's risk of causing cancer.

For more than five years, the federal government, in coordination with several states, investigated the Zyprexa case, aiming to recover taxpayer money paid for the drug and secure additional funds to defray the costs of treating Medicaid and Medicare recipients injured by the medication. Despite the criminal activity that endangered thousands of people, company executives dodged personal responsibility and jail time. Lilly was forced only to pay monetary penalties and can continue to sell Zyprexa to welfare medicine enrollees, who represent a significant percentage of individuals purchasing it.[80] In the Evista case, the corporation was forced to pay a fine, but, once again, senior management was not held accountable for activities that harmed clients.[81]

There are numerous other instances in which pharmaceutical executives engaging in the most egregious practices have not been legally answerable for their crimes. Pfizer, for example, engaged in illegal marketing of Neurontin for the treatment of pain and psychiatric conditions, although the FDA had sanctioned the drug solely as an adjunct therapy for epilepsy. After several years of spectacular sales resulting from kickback schemes and false statements to physicians, with considerable repercussions for users of Neurontin, the company settled the case with monetary penalties. Characteristically, no company officers were charged,[82] as was the situation in two other recent off-label marketing cases: Merck Serono International illegally promoted its AIDS-wasting drug Serostim for unapproved applications; and Schering-Plough unlawfully pushed its hepatitis and cancer drugs Intron A and Temodar for superficial bladder cancer and certain brain conditions, respectively.[83] These cases and others like them show how Medicaid officials brush aside negative practices affecting clients living in the community. The next section addresses the inattention paid to our institutionalized elders.

Nursing Homes and the False Claims Act: A Potential Tool for Social Justice?

Unlike high-profile, revenue-yielding financial fraud cases, the federal Department of Justice, state attorney generals, and MFCUs generally do not view the situation of frail seniors languishing in nursing homes as warranting the high costs of legal proceedings. Federal OIG inspector general Daniel Levinson admitted in 2006: "MFCU cases involving abuse and neglect of beneficiaries in Medicaid-funded facilities, as well as board and care facilities, usually do not generate substantial monetary returns to a state's Medicaid program."[84] Yet, as suggested earlier, abuse and mistreatment of residents are ubiquitous. Incredibly, facility owners and administrators tend not to be held accountable for a resident's death, even if it is associated with their neglect. Nor are crimes within the institutions, including homicides, prosecuted.[85] In contrast, cases brought to court under the federal FCA, based on fraudulent *billings* to Medicaid, are more likely to produce heavier penalties to nursing homes than even the prevailing process of citations and sanctions and have forced some owners to be held responsible for their misdeeds.[86] Because proprietors can bilk Medicaid by submitting false claims for services never rendered, for equipment and supplies not provided, and for myriad other monetary improprieties, a few state prosecutors cautiously have begun to utilize this tack to prosecute them.[87]

In one of the first cases to convict a nursing home owner of Medicaid *financial fraud* because he failed to care for his residents adequately,[88] Melville Borne Jr. was charged with siphoning several million dollars for his own use from three facilities he owned in Louisiana, leaving them with hardly any basic supplies or even sufficient food. After six years and countless time, energy, and money, in 2004 Borne was sentenced to thirty-seven months in jail and fined $5 million in penalties for failing to meet the level of services actually funded by the government.[89] In a similar legal action that year, the Heritage nursing home and its owner, David Arnold, were found guilty of defrauding Medicaid as a result of having billed New York's welfare medicine program for services never provided, thus causing residents to experience a number of preventable medical disorders. In addition to restitution and fines, Arnold received a sentence of from four to twelve years in jail.[90] A few years later, American Healthcare Management, Inc., its CEO, and three nursing homes in Missouri also had to pay a heavy penalty for knowingly charging Medicare and Medicaid for improper care to its clients; the CEO was also sentenced to eighteen months in prison.[91]

But successful cases of this type are still relatively rare: although the FCA is one way to obtain large fines, it does not necessarily result in criminal prosecution of proprietors responsible for patient abuses. For example, Maxwell Manor nursing home in Chicago, along with ABS Long-Term Care Management Co. and MBA-LTC Inc., settled a suit that had accused them of withholding services that the government had paid for—what they did supply was deemed either inadequate or worthless. According to the two whistle-blowers, the facility was "a house of filth, terror and death." The mostly black residents "were routinely abused, neglected, mistreated, sexually assaulted, medicated as a form of punishment, unsupervised and otherwise untreated for their mental health, physical disability and substance abuse problems." They were subjected to detrimental environmental conditions that "included bulging ceilings, crumbling walls, rodent and insect infestations, pervasive mildew and hazardous fire alarm and electrical systems." In this case, the owners, a manager, and the companies paid a joint fine of $1.6 million, but no one was held personally accountable for the horrendous wrongdoings.[92]

The FCA has emerged as a back-door approach to penalizing nursing home owners for their misdeeds, over and above the use of the relatively ineffective citation-and-sanction process resulting from state surveys. It potentially can render the proprietors answerable for the abuse and neglect of their residents. However, it is still not the tactic of choice for MFCU officials and others who would rather tackle the types of cases that can capture massive amounts of money, especially because of the huge expenses and time required for prosecuting Medicaid offenses under the FCA. What is more, even when they do take such legal action, it is by necessity grounded in financial concerns—payment for services not rendered—rather than in the abuse and neglect of residents per se. The consumers of care, including the frailest among them, characteristically play second fiddle to monetary matters.

Conclusion: Disregarding the Poor

For the most part, welfare medicine participants do not have access to high-quality care and often suffer from more undiagnosed illnesses, fewer treatments, and poorer health outcomes than individuals insured privately—circumstances that are exacerbated by Medicaid MCOs. As states throw themselves headlong into managed care, more beneficiaries are confronting the adverse consequences of the industry's unsavory practices. Regardless, in their dogged but frequently fruitless attempts to economize, neither the states nor the federal government appears to be particularly concerned about the disturbingly compromised care these commercial plans offer.

Nor do policymakers seem ready to combat the egregious conditions prevalent in our nation's nursing homes, which include widespread mistreatment and neglect of residents. Subsidized predominantly by Medicaid, most of these facilities are simply not good enough for our frail seniors. As states cut corners by centering more on community-based assistance and to a lesser extent assisted living, they have ignored quality of care in these places, thereby putting vulnerable welfare medicine recipients at risk. Direct-care workers are the cornerstone of decent treatment wherever dependent elders or younger disabled people reside. Nevertheless, LTC providers have been unwilling to hire sufficient staff, pay them adequate wages and benefits, or improve their working environments, thus engendering high turnover and vacancy levels.

At the same time, unscrupulous providers have been able to coax millions out of the program through financial abuse of the system. Over the years, state Medicaid agencies and MFCUs, the first lines of defense against fraud, have not pursued the bad actors aggressively. Although many of them are becoming more forceful, "return on investment" is still a sacred cow, precluding greater emphasis on cases that yield lower revenue but which can have considerable deleterious effects on the very people the program is supposed to serve. At the national level, oversight by CMS has been relatively weak, and the U.S. Department of Justice has focused on company crimes with lucrative monetary recovery potential.

Despite its shortcomings, the FCA recently has emerged as a promising tool for rendering nursing homes and their proprietors more accountable for the often appalling conditions in their facilities. Although not ideal, it has allowed some law enforcement officials to move beyond the often weak fines and sanctions against patient mistreatment and neglect to the more potent penalties available to punish exploitive billing practices. Nevertheless, as chapter 8 shows, the industry has fought back by instituting even more complex ownership structures, rendering it especially difficult to establish accountability.

8

THE ENERGIZER BUNNY:
MEDICAID AND THE
HEALTH ECONOMY

In this chapter, I show the dominant forces in Medicaid policies and politics and how they not only protect the program, but shape it to their own advantages. Although ostensibly health coverage for the poor, welfare medicine has proven highly resilient, even when fiercely attacked by opponents of big government, because powerful corporate and professional stakeholders relentlessly defend it. I argue that the low-income health program has become an indispensable money machine, showering ever-increasing dollars at the Medicaid medical industrial complex and generating economic growth in many localities. Elected officials, although concerned about costs, have often found it politically advantageous to protect the program. As a result, unlike federally assisted income-maintenance payments and other support programs for the needy, which have experienced deep and far-reaching cuts since the 1960s, Medicaid outlays continue to escalate, at times dramatically.

I first look at the overall power of the health industries and their collective ability to influence policymakers. I then assess each of the vested interests in turn: nursing homes, hospitals, pharmaceutical companies, pharmacies, managed-care organizations (MCOs), health professionals (doctors and dentists), and other entities benefiting from welfare medicine. The subsections explore such factors as these interests' relationship to Medicaid, gains from the program, level of power, and tactics employed to achieve their ends. I close the chapter with a discussion of the linkages between the low-income program and state economic growth, particularly given the federal cost-sharing provisions.

The Medicaid Medical Industrial Complex

In his highly acclaimed book on Medicare, Jonathan Oberlander argues that "Medicare politics fundamentally differ from Medicaid politics. Medicaid has a political constituency comprised primarily of low-income women, children, and welfare recipients. There are few high-profile interest groups of Medicaid recipients organized around the program."[1] Welfare medicine clients clearly tend to be a powerless sector of society, with limited input into the policymaking process. Nevertheless, since its enactment, the program has proven to be a bottomless well for more than the needy. Providers—ranging from doctors, hospitals, nursing homes, and

MCOs to pharmacies, drug companies, durable medical equipment firms, and medical laboratories—have dipped into that deep well, often with an odd mix of enthusiasm and distaste.

Across the nation, sizeable and forceful groups—a Medicaid medical industrial complex—support welfare medicine, many of them becoming entirely or partially dependent on its funding for their financial viability. Their reliance on the low-income health program puts them at risk of adverse political decisions, but also drives them to exert disproportionate influence over policymakers. Medical providers and firms tend to be particularly well situated politically. Their high levels of financial resources and status allow them to sway elected officials, particularly by contributing substantially to campaigns. At the national level from 1990 to 2006, the health sector as a whole reported total contributions of $655 million. They generally donate to nearly all members of Congress, regardless of party, both through their business or professional associations and as individual firms.[2] They also pay sizeable dues to the trade groups, which hire legions of full-time staff, lobbyists, and attorneys.[3] Centering attention on the legislature, the White House, the U.S. Department of Health and Human Services (HHS), and the Centers for Medicare and Medicaid Services (CMS), a substantial percentage of the health industries is concerned exclusively with Medicare and Medicaid funding and policies, but the old-age program figures more prominently at the federal level.

Welfare medicine tends to be the target of choice locally, where the Medicaid medical industrial complex often finances even more substantial lobbying and political campaigns. In New York, for instance, a special commission found that roughly half of the largest spenders was made up of groups with a financial interest in Medicaid.[4] Vested interests—professionals, pharmaceutical firms, hospitals, MCOs, nursing homes, and the like—have wielded increasing clout over the years in tandem with the ongoing devolution of power over the program. In contrast, organizations advocating specifically for the medical needs of the poor have significantly less influence on state officials. Nor are many of the decisions affecting benefits and eligibility based on their wants, per se. Nevertheless, when provider and recipient concerns converge, as they often do with issues related to the low-income health plan, clients can secure some gains.

Medical providers are particularly adept at framing the public interest in ways that serve their own needs, especially with regard to government money, and have developed a panoply of stock phrases and clichés to that end. In an adaptation of former General Motors president Charles E. Wilson's infamous statement, "What's good for the country is good for General Motors, and vice versa,"[5] the health industries regularly equate their own financial protection with the well-being of Medicaid enrollees and the communities in which they live. In their perpetual appeal for ever-larger reimbursements, they contend that "inadequate" Medicaid fees negatively impact patient care and access to services. According to this rationale, often echoed by labor, aging, welfare, disability, and other organizations, greater fees would remedy the myriad problems experienced by recipients and providers alike. Regardless of whether the self-serving pronouncements reflect reality, they are often supported by the mainstream media.

Just as critical, providers are the mainstay of Medicaid plans, and, as a result, lawmakers tend to encounter difficulties in rendering policies that are objectionable to the health industries and medical professionals. Indeed, the various contractors can hold sway over both supply and demand. In many instances, if they perceive their fees as being too low, they can refuse to participate in the program. For those who opt to remain, their negative attitude or hurried, poor-quality care may deter patients from using their services, although clients have few choices in many areas. Most important, because of the vital nature of its "product"—medical services and supplies—the Medicaid medical industrial complex can hold elected officials hostage to its demands. Our most vulnerable populations—the low-income elderly, disabled younger adults, and children, many of them in poor health—depend on practitioners, health institutions, and specialized equipment for their well-being, safety, and sometimes even life itself.

At times, health care trade and professional associations mobilize "grassroots" support, eliciting hundreds of other powerful organizations to their cause. Although each member of the Medicaid medical industrial complex has its own concerns, level of vested interest in welfare medicine, and entry into the national and state political processes, which at times generates conflicts between and among them, on the larger matters they often rally together, especially to promote greater overall financing and coverage. They are often joined by other powerful groups, especially business organizations, unions, and advocates for the elderly, children, and the disabled. During the 1980s, for example, when the Reagan administration began its onslaught on Medicaid, including policies aimed at lowering provider compensation, the American Medical Association (AMA) organized the Health Policy Agenda for the American People, composed of 172 groups representing a wide variety of concerns.[6] In the 1990s, the Children's Medicaid Coalition, also consisting of broadly based enterprises, was instrumental in increasing the enrollment of low-income children, which was opposed by the George H. W. Bush administration.[7] Similarly, when the Republicans attempted deep cuts in Medicaid in 1995, an avalanche of lobbyists descended on Washington.[8] Two years later, when the health trade groups initially failed to defend their interests sufficiently, they engaged in comprehensive public-relations and lobbying campaigns, recovering their losses almost immediately; "givebacks" have become common practice in Medicaid (and Medicare) politics.[9]

Joint action has continued into the twenty-first century. George W. Bush's proposed Medicaid cuts in 2005 activated a number of opposition forces, including the American Nurses Association,[10] AARP,[11] national disability rights groups, the Coalition for Meaningful Medicaid Reform,[12] the Coalition on Human Needs, the American Friends Service Committee, labor groups, and the American Public Health Association. Likewise, composed of some of the most influential physician, hospital, business, insurance, pharmaceutical, and consumer groups, the Health Coverage Coalition for the Uninsured was formed in 2007 to expand Medicaid and the State Children's Health Insurance Program (SCHIP) eligibility to the nearly 47 million uninsured people in the United States.[13] Such coalitions are even more prevalent locally, where they have been formidable forces in maintaining their advantages and fostering ever-increasing Medicaid outlays.

Nursing Homes

For the nearly 16,000 nursing homes in the United States, the stakes in Medicaid policies are considerable, particularly because the program is their single-largest funding source and accounts for 45 percent of their revenues. Ostensibly a private-sector industry, composed mostly of for-profit businesses (about 67 percent), nursing homes appropriate billions from the public treasury annually.[14] The American Health Care Association (AHCA)—the primary trade organization for the proprietary facilities— has been a powerful presence nationally, although its main emphasis has been at the local level. In 2006, it reported spending $1.8 million on registered lobbyists, and another $1.3 million in contributions to federal candidates of both political parties.[15] The American Association of Homes and Services for the Aging—together with individual proprietary chains such as Kindred Healthcare, Manor Care Inc., Beverly Enterprises, Genesis HealthCare, Sun Healthcare, Vencor Inc., and the Alliance for Quality Nursing Home Care—also have spent millions on influencing officials.[16] For the most part, the companies have been able to prevent or recover from most congressional and presidential challenges to the bountiful, ongoing public-revenue stream they receive.

The industry—one of the most active and dominant at the local level—has relentlessly protected its advantages through fifty state AHCA affiliates. As suggested in chapter 6, institutional services represent a large and growing piece of state spending on Medicaid, roughly 16 percent of total costs. Providers vigorously defend their interests—mainly fees, medically needy provisions, and regulations—through lavish spending on local elections and lobbying. For example, two investigative journalists in Missouri revealed that nursing home owners invested thousands of dollars in 2002 to defeat a candidate who sponsored tough nursing home reforms.[17] In another inquiry, a *New Orleans Times-Picayune* reporter found, through an analysis of campaign finance reports in Louisiana, that nursing homes have been the most politically intrusive Medicaid contractors in the state at every stage of the policy process, focusing their attention primarily on long-term care (LTC) funding matters.[18]

The companies engage in highly organized, well-financed actions to prevent reductions or to promote increases. When actually threatened with revised reimbursement formulas that would lower their revenues, they have engaged in various counterattacks against the states. For instance, throughout the 1980s and 1990s nursing homes would take the states to court under the Boren amendment or merely threaten a lawsuit, thereby delaying any legislative enactments, burdening localities with high legal costs and, at times, forcing them to back down entirely.[19] After the amendment's repeal in 1997, and the states gained greater flexibility in setting rates, the industry endeavored to maintain—and improve—its advantages even more forcefully. The AHCA and its local affiliates, persistent in their claim that they are on the brink of economic ruin, have pointed primarily to sorely inadequate Medicaid reimbursements that they claim cover less than the actual costs of care.[20] They also blame the exploding price of malpractice insurance,[21] higher staffing mandates and other government regulations, and sicker, frailer patient populations as other sources of their financial predicament. At various times, nursing homes threaten that these growing burdens will force them to lower the quality of care, boycott new Medicaid patients, and, in the extreme, go bankrupt and thus foster a massive dislocation of their vulnerable residents.

Officials ironically also must meet industry demands because there tends to be a shortage of nursing home spaces, especially in certain urban and rural communities, a condition engendered by the states themselves.[22] Even facilities with inordinately poor quality of care have been able to maintain relatively high occupancy levels, averaging 85 percent nationwide, although this percentage has been declining in recent years. LTC companies do not have to participate in Medicaid and can withhold their services at will, forcing policymakers to induce their cooperation. Moreover, industry leaders recognize that a reduction in the number of Medicaid beds potentially may lead to more costly hospital stays, a situation that they take full political advantage of.[23]

As a consequence, despite the recent expansion of Medicaid's home- and community-based services (HCBS) waivers, state officials have continued to prop up the industry, funding nursing facilities at ever-increasing sums. They resisted the controls instituted by Congress in 1997 for Medicare nursing home outlays, and since then, although states have been allowed to establish their own formulas, many of them have continued to base their rates on actual facility costs, one of the most expensive approaches.[24] From 1998 to 2004, in more than three-fourths of the states the per diem rate grew, on average, by an amount greater than the skilled nursing facility market basket index.[25] In Michigan, for example, the state's budget advisory agency found that in the three years after 1997, reimbursements for LTC rose at not only almost twice the rate of the nursing home inflation indicator, but also more than for all other Medicaid providers.[26] Even during the recession of the first years of the twenty-first century, when nearly all of the states experienced severe fiscal pressures, nursing home compensation was largely unaffected, and where cuts were enacted, they tended to be small and short-lived. Local policymakers have reacted similarly during the more severe economic downturn since 2007.

Despite nursing homes' persistent complaints about paltry Medicaid payment levels, the evidence suggests that such enterprises can be hugely profitable. Concentrated in proprietary chains[27] and having a high level of acquisitions and mergers over the decades, these firms can earn millions for their stockholders and executives alike. For example, in a 2002 facility-by-facility survey of the finances of thousands of nursing homes across the nation, reporters for *U.S. News & World Report* found that many of the companies were obtaining substantial profits, frequently as high as 20 to 30 percent. Although the owners claimed substantial losses on their Medicaid patients, the study revealingly "found no relationship between a home's profits, or the size of its losses, and the portion of its patients covered by Medicaid." The journalists further noted that although the companies they examined reported serious, ongoing financial problems in their official reports to the government, 70 percent of them steered large amounts of their revenue elsewhere. Among other ploys, they paid high rental fees to other firms they own, offered consulting contracts to relatives and friends, bought services and supplies from related businesses, and compensated their chief executives generously.[28] According to Catherine Hawes, an expert in the field, "you never have anything show up as a profit. Instead . . . it's a 'management' expense, or it's buying food from yourself. They show these really skinny operating margins, so they can always plead poverty."[29] Such transactions not only mask actual earnings, but siphon dollars from patient care.

One-fifth of all the homes surveyed by the *U.S. News & World Report* notably spent 20 percent or more of patient revenues on administrative expenses.[30] The chains, in particular, pay enormous management fees and salaries to their company heads. An investigation in New York found that seventy executives of private nursing homes and clinics earned more than $500,000 in salary, and twenty-five received more than $1 million annually in 2002. In one case, the operator of Laconia Nursing Home, which was dependent on Medicaid for 90 percent of its revenues, obtained $3 million in salary and profit. At another place (the Grand Manor Nursing Home), also 90 percent financed through welfare medicine, the owner and three family members collected $2.4 million. Both facilities had staffing levels that were far lower than the mean across the states.[31] National *increases* alone for industry executives from 2002 to 2003 averaged 41 percent in total cash compensation (just less than $1 million) and even more in stocks.[32]

Nevertheless, substituting assertions for facts, the industry continues to insist on its financial vulnerability and to blame government policies for its economic woes. In particular, it points to Medicare's prospective payment system and other changes enacted under the Balanced Budget Act (BBA) of 1997, along with inadequate Medicaid reimbursements since then, as fostering the rash of bankruptcies beginning in the late 1990s, which included five large chains representing almost 11 percent of nursing homes in the nation.[33] To the contrary, government studies found that the Medicare prospective payment system fees not only were sufficient to meet patient costs, but were most likely far higher than the expenses actually incurred by many of the facilities; for-profit places, especially the largest chains, reaped the most excessive gains.[34]

Most significant, investigations of the bankrupt chains operating under Chapter 11 determined that the underlying financial problems did not stem from low Medicare or Medicaid rates; indeed, the chains' nursing operations were mostly profitable. Rather, the losses were caused by excessive capital-related expenditures and debts (buildings, equipment, depreciation, taxes, interest, rent), inflated purchasing prices for their recurrent acquisitions, overly leveraged ventures, the curbing under BBA 1997 of their use of unnecessary and costly ancillary services, losses in their other businesses, inefficient management practices, exorbitant administration costs, and lack of sufficient government oversight.[35]

Since emerging from bankruptcy, many of these chains, along with other LTC and medical facilities, have increasingly been taken over by Health Care Real Estate Investment Trusts (REITs), which are raising even greater nagging questions than ever about patient care. Specializing exclusively in nursing homes, assisted-living facilities, hospitals, and the like, REITs bought six of the largest nursing home chains in the United States between 2000 and 2007, along with a number of smaller ones, representing roughly 13 percent of all beds in the nation. They have been highly lucrative, benefiting at the expense of their residents; in 2005, large chains owned by investment companies were, on average, 41 percent more profitable than the typical facility across the nation.[36] According to *New York Times* investigators who compared nursing homes purchased by large investment groups with other facilities nationwide, the REITs immediately reduced costs, increased earnings, and then resold the properties at substantial monetary gains. The inquiry revealed that the companies cut expenses and staff, at times far below legal requirements. Compared to the other homes in the sample, residents were more likely to experience depression, lose their mobility and ability to dress themselves, encounter moldy food, be restrained for long periods of time, and receive incorrect medications. Moreover, the number of serious deficiencies for the REIT facilities, which earned worse than average national scores in twelve of fourteen quality indicators, was 10 percent higher than for the control institutions.[37]

Yet it is difficult to hold anyone accountable for the poor quality of care and the resultant illnesses and injuries, including deaths, because of the intricate corporate ownership webs that mask control of the homes. Focusing on a specific private equity firm, which bought forty-nine facilities in Florida, the New York Times attempted to disentangle the intricate network of nursing home ownership, leases, supplies, and services.[38] After plowing through the tangled maze, the researchers discovered that the interlocking companies engaged in a number of questionable financial practices, including inflating rents and prices.[39] Even worse, after the takeover of the properties by the private-equity firm, the nursing home managers had cut the number of registered nurses in half and severely reduced supplies and services. Overall, the investors and operators were earning millions from the facilities, but staff levels were well below mandatory minimum levels, the homes had unsanitary conditions, numerous patients suffered from bedsores infected by feces, and over a three-year period fifteen people had died from suspected negligence and unhealthy environments.

The industry obviously has progressively become a real estate business, seeking ever more properties for investor portfolios while draining nursing homes of their resources. The recent history of a number of large chains, including Vencor, Inc., Beverly Enterprises, and Genesis, exemplify some of the convoluted financial practices engaged in by these private equity firms.[40] Many of the deals are highly leveraged, as they had been prior to the earlier bankruptcies, which does not bode well for the years ahead. Most important, as shown earlier, quality of patient care suffers even more dramatically in these cases than under prior arrangements. Thus, the REITs protect their assets, earn sizeable profits, and pay high executive salaries and severance packages, a significant percentage accruing from welfare medicine funds, while siphoning money away from patient care and thereby putting residents seriously at risk.

One of the REITs' primary goals is to protect investors from both consumer lawsuits and government fines. The division of the cash-abundant real estate operations from the resource-deprived facility operations not only strips the nursing homes of their value and allows earnings to be hidden, but also limits malpractice liability. Lawyers who had previously sued nursing homes for patient abuse no longer do so because cases have become too complicated and expensive to pursue. It is also more difficult to collect any money if a suit is actually won because facility operators, separate from the real estate ventures, tend to have few assets. Powerful industry lobbyists have fiercely and successfully blocked any congressional attempts to render nursing home owners more accountable.[41]

Hospitals

Although hospitals rely on public money for a substantial share of their annual earnings, for most of them—in particular for-profit entities—Medicare is the more central source of their revenue stream. Medicaid accounts for 17 percent of the industry's overall income, up from 10 percent in the early 1990s, whereas Medicare represents fully one-third of the total.[42] As a result, the industry's political energy is focused less extensively than nursing homes on welfare medicine and more on the old-age program, particularly at the federal level. Nevertheless, hospitals are vitally concerned with Medicaid policies, regulations, coverage, and especially maximization of their fees.

Hospitals' trade organizations—most prominently the American Hospital Association (AHA) and its state affiliates, but also the Federation of American Hospitals, the National Association of Public Hospitals and Health Systems, the National Association of Children's Hospitals, and others—have enormous clout and pay out huge sums to influence elected officials nationally. In 2006, the AHA and allied individuals, subsidiaries, and affiliates reported spending $17.4 million to lobby Congress, CMS, HHS, the White House Budget Office, the Internal Revenue Service, and other agencies. The Federation of American Hospitals and the National Association of Public Hospitals paid an additional $0.7 million. AHA also contributed $1.9 million to federal candidates and parties; the other hospital trade associations and the large chains individually donated millions more.[43] At the state level, where Medicaid reimbursement policies are actually devised, AHA affiliates and other hospital organizations are also among the most powerful groups.

In addition to traditional tactics aimed at persuading political leaders, these alliances, like other Medicaid stakeholders, invoke the needs of vulnerable populations, workers, and local communities to protect their own special interests. Likewise, at times they use intimidation: when elected officials have targeted the industry in their efforts to control outlays, some hospitals threaten to stop serving Medicaid patients. Even worse, a number of them warn that they may be forced to shut down. According to the hospital trade associations, not only would the most disadvantaged people lose access to critical medical services, but health workers might experience loss of jobs.[44] These and similar coercive assertions arose in the earliest years of Medicaid policymaking, rendering it difficult to enact—or maintain—any significant cuts in their funding over time.

Hospitals regularly contend that their financial well-being is seriously jeopardized by unacceptably low Medicaid payments.[45] They have drawn on the fiscal crises they faced during the last two decades of the twentieth century to buttress their case for higher fees. For example, on the heels of a series of reduced rate increases and freezes in Illinois during the 1980s, twenty-two hospitals closed, affecting patients and workers alike. As a growing number of facilities nationwide verged on insolvency in the mid-1990s and onward, the industry blamed "insufficient" Medicaid (and Medicare) payments, claiming that unless the situation was rectified, an increasing number of hospitals would go out of business.[46]

Intimidating language has continued unabated. For example, in response to a Bush administration proposal in 2007 to slash Medicaid funding to hospitals drastically, the AHA, as usual, issued catastrophic warnings, reminding political leaders of "the serious challenges hospitals face." The trade group elicited opposition to the reductions by 223 representatives and 43 senators, culminating in the decisive rejection of the proposal by Congress.[47] In a typical local instance, when Ohio's governor suggested a second consecutive Medicaid rate freeze for hospitals in 2005, an official of the Ohio Hospital Association insisted, "'Disaster' is not too strong a word to describe what will happen to Ohio's fragile health care system if the Taft Administration fails to rethink a flawed plan to slash $168 million from the state's Medicaid program for hospitalized Ohioans."[48] He earlier had cautioned that the action "will jeopardize all Ohioans' access to quality health care."[49]

Nonetheless, the reality is that many private hospitals actually benefited from Medicaid patients in the 1990s and beyond.[50] In order to weigh the industry's denunciation of Medicaid payment levels against the veracity of their claims, Michigan's Senate Fiscal Agency decided to investigate the situation. As in many other places, the overall financial condition of hospitals was deteriorating during the mid- to late 1990s. In demanding a large increase in their Medicaid allocation for fiscal year 2000, the Michigan Health and Hospital Association claimed that the industry's main problem was Medicaid underfunding, which was engendering closures and employee layoffs as well as reducing access to care for everyone in the affected communities. The Senate Fiscal Agency research revealed, however, that although many of the state's facilities lost money on overall patient services, they actually showed a profit from Medicaid-supported care, which in effect lessened their shortfalls by nearly 20 percent. The agency concluded that the primary reason for the hospitals' financial distress was low occupancy rates.[51] In fact, Medicaid patients often filled up places that would otherwise have produced no income at all.[52]

The factors leading to a hospital's financial prosperity or, alternatively, the hardships that may foster layoffs and closures are multifaceted, defying any attempt to hold any single component responsible, including welfare medicine. Although I will not attempt to put forward all of the significant predictors of a hospital's financial condition, many of which are interrelated, the considerable research available on the subject suggests that they include ownership type; the number of medically uninsured people in the surrounding community; restrictiveness of a state's Medicaid eligibility criteria;[53] relative size of the institution; level of competition faced in the market;[54] teaching status; degree of indebtedness; urban or rural location; extent of managed-care penetration; method, scale, and pace of expansion, consolidation, acquisitions, and investments; administrative leadership and skill; the scale of health care–related planning in the community; and occupancy rates.

Medicaid emerges as a central actor mainly in the financial health of nonprofit and government facilities. Only particular types of hospitals are heavily financed through welfare medicine, including children's hospitals. Fully half of all these hospitals' patient care revenues currently accrue from the low-income health plan.[55] Other "safety-net" facilities also are sustained through welfare medicine: publicly run (state and local) hospitals, community health centers,[56] and certain private nonprofit facilities (generally through their outpatient departments) frequently receive nearly 40 percent of their income from the program, including Disproportionate Share Hospital (DSH) dollars.[57] Some institutions require Medicaid money for their very survival.[58] They serve not only a large percentage of Medicaid enrollees, but also other needy families who have no means of paying for their services. Less than 9 percent of hospitals nationwide provide more than 40 percent of all care to Medicaid participants and the medically uninsured; they also absorb more than 35 percent of the industry's bad debt.[59] Their burden for such patients has grown over the decades with the spread of proprietary facilities unwilling to serve them.[60] As a result, the "safety-net" providers are particularly affected by the vagaries of welfare medicine's reimbursement formulas and policies.

Proprietary establishments are the least in need of Medicaid funding for their financial viability, and as such can more easily refuse to participate in the program or threaten to pull out. Moreover, hospitals have experienced a vast shift in ownership to profit-making places since the late 1990s as well as a surge in merger activity, leading to large chains.[61] These corporate enterprises can drive local hospitals out of business, engendering even greater burdens for public-sector institutions. They also contribute less than other types of facilities to the community, especially in terms of services for low-income and uninsured households, even though they receive hefty welfare medicine subsidies. As a consequence, certain hospitals are increasingly dependent on welfare medicine funding. And when public officials lower or freeze rates *across the board*, our neediest communities and their citizens pay most of the price. They face closures of Medicaid-reliant institutions, especially state and local entities, and a lower level of services in those places that survive.[62] Such hospitals are most often located in rural areas and inner cities that already have a limited supply of beds.

Regardless, the hospital industry continues to insist that every hospital across the nation is in desperate need of higher Medicaid fees, a contention that its trade organizations have been able to "sell," for the most part, to elected officials. However, although welfare medicine reimbursement levels may play a significant part in the fiscal health of some places, they are only a piece of the economic puzzle for most, especially for the for-profit chains and a growing number of large-scale nonprofit systems.[63] The role that Medicaid plays in their earnings is often obscured by sensationalist rhetoric: the actual effects tend to be a mix of low fees and "smoke and mirrors," and it is often difficult to distinguish between the two.

Big Pharma

Pharmaceutical companies have developed into the most lucrative industry in the United States: their profit margins are about four times higher than the average of other Fortune 500 corporations. Shareholder returns, executive salaries, and bonuses have been spectacular as well.[64] Until 2006, Medicaid was the nation's single-largest drug purchaser, accounting for approximately 18 percent of industry sales, a figure that has dropped to 9 percent since then because of its lucrative stake in the new Medicare Part D legislation.[65] Nevertheless, the firms continue to take an acute and active interest in Medicaid policies and funding practices, especially at the federal level. Through its trade group, Pharmaceutical Research and Manufacturers of America (PhRMA), they fiercely defend their inflated charges for products, inordinately high profits, and exclusive rights over pricing mechanisms.[66] According to knowledgeable observers, pharmaceutical producers increasingly rely on price hikes to raise their profit levels. Their main goals are consequently to prevent cost controls and to limit the use of generic drugs. The industry, one of the most powerful in the nation, regularly uses "its wealth and power to co-opt every institution that might stand in its way."[67] In its concerted efforts to sway elected officials, particularly at the federal level, PhRMA has extremely huge resources at its disposal: in 2006, it reported $18.1 million in federal lobbying expenditures and another $10.6 million in funding to contenders for national office. Individual firms, including Pfizer, GlaxoSmithKline, and Eli Lilly, also press their cases independently.[68]

As with other major stakeholders in the Medicaid medical industrial complex, the pharmaceutical industry frames its self-interest in public-interest terminology. PhRMA contends that high drug prices are essential for the support of research and development activities that generate new and improved products that save lives, enhance people's well-being, combat diseases, reduce pain and suffering, and even lessen health spending on hospital and nursing home care.[69] The trade association subsidizes numerous organizations and think tanks as well as economists and other academics who write articles and opinion pieces that support drug company perspectives and even some that are against controlling drug prices. There also is a revolving door between government regulators and industry spokespersons.[70]

Drug coverage is an optional service that all of the states have chosen to extend to their Medicaid beneficiaries. As the rates increased dramatically over the decades, prescription medications became one of the more significant components driving spiraling welfare medicine outlays.[71] Demands by local policymakers for manufacturer discounts emerged early on, and in response Congress mandated rebates to state Medicaid programs, beginning in 1990.[72] The large pharmaceuticals, adamantly opposed to these payments, have limited their financial exposure by manipulating pricing data, much of which they claim is "protected" information. Because CMS relies entirely on information provided by the drug companies themselves, conducts few checks for errors, and has a lackluster system of control over the rebate program in general, the states have received back far less money than they are entitled to.[73]

Further efforts to reign in mounting drug costs have targeted welfare medicine clients as well. Under the original Medicaid regulations, beneficiaries had been guaranteed any prescription drug that their doctor prescribed. However, beginning in 1993, the states were allowed to establish formularies, and most of them now use such "preferred drug lists," which identify specific medications that can be prescribed.[74] Nearly all of the states have instituted additional economizing measures, including mandates for generic drugs, when available; greater control over utilization, including per capita limits on the number of allowable medications; higher copays; and the establishment of multistate purchasing pools to attain greater discounts. As the states became more aggressive in their attempts to control prescription drug costs, Big Pharma fought back. For example, it pursued legal action in federal court; although the industry did not always win, some states (i.e., Florida, Michigan, Vermont, and Maine) were forced to incur high legal fees.[75] Pharmaceutical companies also lobbied forcefully against the myriad restrictions, again with variable outcomes.

The companies' ultimate achievement, however, has been the enactment of the Medicare Prescription Drug Improvement and Modernization Act of 2003, which they, along with insurance firms, helped to design.[76] Implemented three years later, it shifted responsibility for a significant portion of prescription drug benefits from Medicaid to Medicare Part D. Among its provisions, dually eligible welfare medicine participants (along with other Medicare recipients) must now choose a Medicare-approved drug plan offered by private insurers. A windfall for Big Pharma, the legislation permits drug companies to hike their prices and boost their profits unabashedly. It fosters greater demand for prescription medications, avoids direct government administration of benefits, prevents legalization of drug reimportation, precludes CMS from exacting discounts, and, most important, prevents any price controls.[77] The act, then, shifts Medicaid spending for the dual eligibles to commercial providers, where costs are roughly 30 percent higher. The affected population has paid a considerable price as well: low-income elders now experience greater difficulty in accessing the particular drugs they require, pay higher out-of-pocket costs, and are subject to more plan volatility.[78]

Pharmacies

Retail pharmacies, also major stakeholders in the Medicaid medical industrial complex, have considerable interest in welfare medicine. States have sought to cut rising Medicaid prescription drug outlays over the years by reducing their payments, generally by lowering compensation and dispensing fees.[79] Reimbursement rates have been a particularly contentious issue because the localities have insufficient data on pharmacy drug-acquisition costs, which the industry tends to artificially inflate, thus boosting its profits considerably.[80] The firms have used a variety of techniques to stave off greater government controls over pricing and to maintain or even enhance their Medicaid earnings. Composed primarily of chain drug stores and mail order companies,[81] they have proven effective lobbyists through the National Association of Chain Drug Stores (NACDS) and state or regional councils, associations, and coalitions. In appealing for greater Medicaid payments, NACDS often joins with the National Community Pharmacists Association (NCPA), representing independent drug stores,[82] and the American Pharmacists Association.

As with other Medicaid providers, the trade associations effectively equate recipient and industry needs in presenting their case. Linking the size of Medicaid reimbursements with access to vital prescription drug services, they have insisted over the years that any economizing on payments to druggists will force more and more places to withdraw from the program, especially those located in low-income neighborhoods. As a typical example, the Coalition for Community Pharmacy Action—composed of both

NACDS and NCPA—commissioned a study that showed that their dispensing fees were inadequate, a conclusion also reached by the U.S. GAO. Deriding Medicaid payment levels, the group warned: "As a result of low reimbursement rates, many pharmacies will have trouble keeping their doors open or will be forced to reduce the number of pharmacists or pharmacy hours. . . . Inadequate dispensing fees, compounded by a cut to Medicaid prescription drug reimbursement, threaten patient access and the pharmacist's ability to continue to provide patients with quality health care."[83]

In another typical case, almost immediately after the George W. Bush administration proposed an administrative rule that would have substantially reduced pharmacies' payments for generic drugs, protests emerged from all sides. The national and state pharmaceutical trade associations energetically opposed the rule, claiming the revised formula would not even cover acquisition costs. NCPA argued that many of the establishments "will drop Medicaid or close their doors. . . . People on Medicaid—the poor, disabled and children—may have to find a different pharmacy to get their generic prescriptions filled, a daunting task in rural communities."[84] Industry groups enlisted forty-six senators and seventy-two House members to sign a letter in protest. When CMS did not back down, the trade associations filed a suit against the agency, winning a court order against implementation of the regulation. Congress eventually passed legislation postponing the action indefinitely. The several pharmacy associations have frequently resorted to lawsuits and boycotts of Medicaid prescriptions over the decades, generally forcing the national and local governments to capitulate.[85]

Managed-Care Organizations

MCOs have grown steadily over the decades, now cover the vast majority of Medicaid's nondisabled younger adults and children, and garner more than 16 percent of total Medicaid outlays.[86] Subsidiaries of multiline insurers are the biggest players in welfare medicine. These insurers include Well-Point Health Networks, one of the largest Medicaid MCO providers in the United States,[87] and AmeriChoice (a Medicaid-only subsidiary of United-Health Group, Inc.). The latter is the nation's leading health insurer, but much of its recent high growth and profit levels are due to its Medicaid business.[88] AmeriHealth Mercy affiliates also have experienced relatively large increases in Medicaid/SCHIP participants, mainly because of managed-care expansions in South Carolina and Indiana.[89] Another large-scale firm, Aetna, has boosted its Medicaid managed-care enrollments in recent years as well. Fostered by the federal government's abolishment of the 75/25 rule in 1997, four new firms have emerged (Amerigroup, Centene Corporation, Molina Healthcare, Inc., WellCare Health Plans, Inc.), which now serve 22 percent of the welfare medicine market, up from 14 percent in 1999. Focusing their businesses exclusively on public-sector health programs, their profits have surged over the past several years: despite volatility, their individual stocks have risen at a greater rate than the S&P 500 since their initial offerings.[90]

MCOs have considerable stakes in and are key players on policy issues concerning government health insurance programs (Medicare, Medicaid, and SCHIP) and private-sector plans. Their main trade organization, America's Health Insurance Plans (AHIP),[91] consists of some of the most powerful corporations in the nation, including the insurance, financial services, and health care industries. These corporations contribute generously to political campaigns at all levels of government. Together with its member organizations, AHIP spends millions to influence national officials, reporting $7.1 million in federal lobbying expenses in 2006.[92] It also retains local lobbyists across the nation, along with policy and state affairs teams. The trade group peppers elected leaders and consumers with news releases, special reports, booklets, a bimonthly periodical (*AHIP Coverage*), industry-subsidized research studies, and media advertising; provides spokespersons to testify at congressional, state, and local hearings; offers grants; and funds a foundation. An affiliated group composed of plans serving only Medicaid enrollees—Medicaid Health Plans of America—supplies additional research and other promotional materials for the industry. Individual companies also are bountiful donors in the states where they do the most business. WellCare has been particularly open-handed in its efforts to secure and safeguard its Medicaid enterprises, including large campaign donations to state leaders in Florida and elsewhere. The company also has countless political connections, at times based on a rotation of its personnel into influential government positions.[93]

MCOs and their trade organizations' main policy goals for Medicaid are higher reimbursement rates, fewer controls over service provision, more extensive coverage, and other measures to enhance enrollments and profits. Nevertheless, they, too, typically phrase such interests in terms of the needs of state governments and the vulnerable populations they serve. According to AHIP president Karen Ignagni, managed care not only allows beneficiaries greater access to providers and "more affordable, high-quality care than the Medicaid fee-for-service program," but is cost-effective, saving state Medicaid plans significant amounts of money. And, of course, AHIP argues that in order to ensure continued access to health care for low-income populations, the states must enhance reimbursement rates. Its adamant opposition to national regulations, requirements, and mandates— such as "patient rights" legislation—is translated into, as Ignagni puts it, the need to "preserve flexibility for states and health plans to meet the unique needs of the beneficiaries they serve." According to the industry, such "onerous" and "unnecessary" rules just add costs and administrative burdens to an already efficient and effective industry.[94]

The stark reality, however, is that the Medicaid MCOs are thriving, whereas their low-income clients are encountering restrictions on medical tests, prescription drugs, and other benefits; a limited number of participating providers at convenient locations; difficulty in obtaining timely treatments; and often perfunctory and substandard care. Such obstacles to quality medical services enhance the companies at the expense of beneficiary needs. They not only enrich shareholders, but also reward executives handsomely with exorbitant salaries, stock options, and perks.[95] In fact, direct health care costs as a percentage of premium revenues are identified as the medical *loss* ratio;[96] the industry views a for-profit MCO with a medical loss ratio of 85 percent "as adequately managing its patient base," although financially successful companies tend to have even lower percentages.[97] Thus, administrative costs (including executive compensation), entertainment, political contributions, lobbying, interest, profits, taxes, and other non-health-related expenses for commercial MCOs are much more than 15 percent of the premium dollar, as compared to 10 percent for non-profit entities. In the case of Medicaid-only plans, they tend to be even higher than the overall industry norm and significantly more than traditional Medicaid plans, which generally average from 4 to 6 percent.[98] In some states, the commercial plans pay even less of their publicly financed revenues on actual patient services.[99]

Many state policymakers, ignoring the actual situation, continue to have faith that MCOs can save them money without endangering the health of

Medicaid enrollees. When officials do freeze or lower the growth of their fees, the companies just ration services even more. What is more, because MCOs are highly concentrated among a few firms, they can threaten to pull out of the local programs when their demands are not met, and at times they do so, fostering instability and uncertainty for Medicaid patients.[100] Regardless, managed-care coverage steadily grows, the problems persist, and the companies enrich themselves.

Health Care Professionals

As a group, physicians tend to have only a limited stake in Medicaid because few of them take on its enrollees, and most who do treat them receive a relatively small percentage of their income from the program. The care of Medicaid patients also has become progressively more concentrated among fewer and fewer practitioners who generally work in large group practices, hospitals, academic medical centers, and community health clinics. All the same, a significant minority of doctors is highly dependent on welfare medicine dollars.[101]

Physicians' major trade group, the powerful AMA, spends lavishly on political campaigns and deploys an impressive number of lobbyists at all levels of government. It is one of the leading disperser of funds to influence political leaders: in 2006, it reported contributing $2.2 million to federal candidates and parties, and paid out an additional $19.7 million to sway national officials.[102] Because most physicians are more heavily reliant on Medicare (which represents 25 percent of their collective income) and private insurance (which accounts for fully 48 percent of the total),[103] the AMA devotes its greatest attention to these lucrative pieces of the health care pie. Nevertheless, along with such specialty groups as the American Academy of Family Physicians and the Federation of Pediatric Organizations,[104] it is an active presence on issues related to Medicaid and SCHIP.

Armed with data associating low access to care with insufficient Medicaid fees, averaging about 69 percent of Medicare payments and even less relative to private insurance, the physician organizations have predominantly pressed for higher rates to doctors as well as greater benefit coverage and less onerous paperwork. They also tend to link their efforts with other stakeholders in the Medicaid medical industrial complex. When their demands are fully or partially rejected, especially among states determined to curb welfare medicine budgets, doctors can—and do—pull out of the program, closing their practices to Medicaid patients. As suggested in chapter 5, lack of access to physicians, especially specialists, has consequently become a dire problem for low-income health program recipients, many of whom increasingly must rely on community clinics, emergency rooms, and practitioners who offer only perfunctory, substandard care.

Dentists, too, are highly active politically, although not on the same scale as physicians with regard to Medicaid.[105] Their major professional organization, the American Dental Association (ADA), tends to be more concerned over health policies affecting the private sector than with welfare medicine: only 3 percent of dentists' annual income accrue from the program.[106] Even so, the ADA has aggressively advocated for greater Medicaid compensation for practitioners, which currently tends to range from 40 to 60 percent of their standard fees, as a means of attracting more dentists into the program.[107] The association also lobbies for increased dental coverage among the states (an optional service under federal Medicaid policy). To this end, the ADA emphasizes the essential part that oral health plays in individuals' overall well-being—a fact that policymakers often do not recognize—and the high costs of hospital emergency-room care for people who cannot afford to pay for preventive dental services on their own. The group and its state affiliates appeal particularly to the unmet needs of children, who elicit the most support among voters.

More Hands in the Till

To a greater or lesser extent, additional vendors have benefited from the Medicaid medical industrial complex, also fueling the program's expansion. Home health agencies, for example, have become increasingly engaged in Medicaid politics, both pressing for and taking advantage of the developing interest in HCBS. Mostly for-profit firms, they now have access to ever-growing welfare medicine dollars, roughly 15 percent of the total Medicaid budget. These companies rely on Medicare and Medicaid, which, together, account for more than half of their revenues (38 percent and 18 percent, respectively).[108]

Providers ranging from nurses and home care aides to durable medical equipment suppliers and hospice organizations also have an intense interest in welfare medicine's HCBS money. These multifarious stakeholders tirelessly advocate on behalf of their particular Medicaid claims, employing both umbrella trade organizations and individual group resources; they all demand greater funding. The major groups, the National Association for Home Care and Hospice and the American Association for Homecare, have extensive lobbying networks and contribute generously to political campaigns everywhere.[109] Affiliates of the former represent the full array of home care industries and interests, and keep abreast of the varying federal regulatory and government policies affecting their specific concerns.[110] The latter, also composed of assorted health services industries, similarly attempts to influence federal, state, and local officials. Both organizations have active state associations that focus on local advocacy, networking, and grassroots political activities.

Greater outsourcing of Medicaid broker services—including consumer education on managed-care options, call centers, and customer support—has brought in more vested interests. Maximus, Inc., the leading firm in the field, furnishes 65 percent of such work in roughly eleven states, reaping more than half a billion dollars annually. Another firm, Accenture, provides similar assistance, including call centers for eligibility screening in Texas,[111] "choice counseling" in Florida, and care supervision, case-management, and prior-authorization functions in Pennsylvania. With contracts in twenty states since 1999, APS Healthcare offers case- and disease-management services for Medicaid beneficiaries with chronic conditions. Pfizer Health Solutions administers Florida's disease-management plan, Healthier Florida, and Zynex Medical Holdings, Inc., provides electrotherapy devices (pain-management systems) in sixteen jurisdictions.

Fiscal agents and information technology contractors have a substantial stake in welfare medicine as well, earning multimillions of dollars. Already the nation's largest provider of computer systems for the low-income health program, Ross Perot's Electronic Data Systems has lucrative contracts in about twenty states.[112] Affiliated Computer Services, Inc., supplies information technology and claims processing and management services for a number of other Medicaid plans, including Hawaii, Colorado, Montana, Massachusetts, and North Carolina.[113] Additional firms—including Unisys Corporation (in West Virginia),[114] CNSI (in Maine),[115] and Computer Sciences Corporation (in New York)—design, build, and implement locally procured computer systems. CMS also purchases data-management and other technological services for the federal government.[116] Still more companies cash in on welfare medicine, such as the highly profitable Logis-tiCare, which coordinates nonemergency medical transportation for Med-icaid patients in eighteen states.[117] Fraud detection also can be an especially lucrative endeavor. For example, HMS Holdings Corp. uncovers provider billing errors and false claims, receiving a contingency fee based on the actual amount of money recouped; from 2006 to 2007, the firm doubled the value of its stock.[118]

As discussed in the next chapter, Medicaid increasingly has become a major player in sustaining community mental health centers, substance abuse treatment services, maternal health, child welfare, foster care, job training, counseling, rehabilitation, and other social provisions, many of which had previously been paid for by state and local governments, federal grants, or charitable organizations. According to Steven Smith, social workers, nonprofit community agencies, certain proprietary firms, newly covered participants and their families, agency social workers, and case managers have become a significant political constituency, both resulting from and fueling the expansion of social services under the low-income health program. Smith argues that these interested parties tend to lobby state legislators as a group, within each service category, seeking higher Medicaid rates, greater eligibility, and ever-growing benefit packages.[119]

Economic Engine for the States

As the Medicaid medical industrial complex expanded over the years, it became a significant source of employment across the nation and, as such, was used as yet another justification to fend off welfare medicine cutbacks. Health services and supplies now represent the largest sector within the U.S. economy. Rising steadily from 5 percent of gross domestic product in 1960 to more than 16 percent by 2006, this sector is projected to reach 20 percent by 2015.[120] Medicare, Medicaid, and SCHIP currently account for nearly half of all such spending. Ambulatory health services (physician office visits, outpatient care centers, and home health) represent roughly 40 percent of health jobs nationally, closely followed by hospitals (36 per-cent).[121] Nursing homes (and other long-term residential services), compos-ing 24 percent of the total, are the fastest-growing source of occupational opportunities today.[122]

In some areas, health industries depend heavily on government health programs for their income, while, simultaneously, the localities rely on them for their own economic viability or even survival. Hospitals, for example, rank among the top ten businesses in several cities, including Boston, New York City, Detroit, and Cleveland. In certain rural areas, where jobs are scarce, nursing homes or hospitals serve as major employers. As a case in point, in Hazard, Kentucky, a poor Appalachian town of 4,800 people, Medicaid money has become its main source of support, mainly shoring up the Hazard A. R. H. Regional Medical Center. In fact, many of the communities in eastern Kentucky that survived the loss of coal mining have turned to health services, which in turn are dependent on welfare medicine funding.[123]

Medicaid dollars not only purchase actual health care goods and services, but also produce a multiplier effect, generating spending and jobs in other sectors of the economy. According to researchers at Families USA, for every million dollars a state invests in Medicaid, there is, on average, a $3.35 million return in new business activity. In some jurisdictions with particularly large welfare medicine budgets, the gains in jobs have been sizeable.[124] Significantly, much of the beneficial effects can be attributed to the matching federal dollars, which bring considerable outside capital into local economies.[125] Since the program's enactment, the states have used it as a means of attaining extra money from the central government to meet their everyday budgetary needs and foster economic growth. In fact, James Fossett and Courtney Burke argue that a key factor motivating local policymakers to expand Medicaid eligibility in the late 1990s was to increase their access to such resources.[126] Medicaid and SCHIP are now the leading source of national grants to the states, representing fully 45 percent of the total.[127]

Many investigations have demonstrated the stimulating effect of these external funds, findings that have been used to fight against state Medicaid reductions. One researcher, for example, argues that the main fiscal advantage of Medicaid for localities stems from the inflow of new cash.[128] In South Carolina, for example, analysts examined the federal portion of the state's plan and found that it generated at least $2.1 billion in additional economic activity per year. They not only noted that this amount was "a substantial sum for an economy the size of South Carolina," but warned that state officials should consider the "serious economic implications" of any curtailment in funding because of the lost federal match: a 4 percent cut in the state's Medicaid budget and its commensurate forfeiture of national contributions would lead to a decline of 2,472 jobs and more than $60 million in income. A 10 percent cut would be even more disastrous: 6,181 fewer jobs and more than $150 million in lost income. The investigators concluded, "The money the state would 'save' by reducing Medicaid allocations could have significant repercussions for the economy."[129]

Policymakers have often been forced to weigh their Medicaid cost-containment measures against the adverse effects of lost federal revenues. In Ohio, for example, the low-income health program, including its national match, brought in $13 billion to the health industries in 2005, and accounted for more than 3 percent of the state's gross domestic product. In turn, because of the multiplier effect, welfare medicine produced even greater value to Ohio's overall fiscal health. An evaluation of potentially large budgetary cuts in its welfare medicine plan for 2006 and 2007 indicated that the state would forgo $1.21 billion in federal money, resulting in a $2.4 billion loss to the economy, 24,000 fewer jobs, and a $33 million shortfall in taxes—with even more losses in city and county income—over the two years.[130]

Assessments in other places also have shown the considerable impact of welfare medicine spending on the local economy, underscoring the windfall generated by federal money.[131] Given the steady erosion of Michigan's automobile manufacturing sector, its legislators are particularly dependent on Medicaid money for the state's fiscal well-being. Researchers determined that a $100 million cut in the state's Medicaid spending, which would sacrifice $131 million in federal dollars, most likely would lead to $180.6 million in lost income and 6,300 fewer jobs. Like many other investigators, they caution against lowering Medicaid outlays as a way to balance the budget because of the large adverse effects on employment and tax earnings.[132]

Medical providers are clearly vital employers and purchasers of goods and services, financed to a large extent by government health programs. To be sure, Medicaid has been a foremost target for President Obama's $787 billion 2009 economic stimulus package, which devotes $87 billion (11 percent) of the total to the program.[133] The portion of money invested in welfare medicine is intended not only to maintain or enhance eligibility and benefit levels and assist states with their budgetary shortages during the recession, but also to spur hard-pressed local economies. Its specific role in the recovery process is underlined by the fact that the largest share of the Medicaid money accrues to states with the highest unemployment rates rather than to those having the most residents in poverty or the greatest percentage of welfare medicine enrollees. Supporters expect the Medicaid portion of the stimulus plan to help prop up jobs in both the health industries and derivative sectors of the economy. Despite escalating costs, then, welfare medicine is not just a source of strain for the states; a major reason policymakers have supported the program and have been so unwilling to decrease its funding substantially is its positive impact on economic growth, employment, and revenues.

Conclusion: Stakeholders and Welfare Medicine

Certain observers have described the low-income health program as Medicare's stepchild, but, to the contrary, it has had a leading role in fueling a medical industrial complex. Although generally suspicious of social welfare measures, suppliers of medical goods and services—ranging from doctors, hospitals, nursing homes, MCOs, and home health agencies to pharmaceuticals, drug companies, durable equipment companies, and medical laboratories—have capitalized on the program with a vengeance. They have adopted apocalyptic scenarios and other types of self-serving rhetoric and have spent plentiful campaign and lobbying cash to keep the dollars flowing. Members of the medical marketplace are frequently supported by organizations representing other businesses, labor, consumers, the disabled, older people, and a range of other constituencies. Stakeholders individually and collectively defend welfare medicine during budgetary crises and seek to broaden it when times improve.[134] Over the years, Medicaid's financial growth may have slowed down periodically, but it rarely was subject to draconian retrenchment measures.[135] Nevertheless, the needs of recipients—who have limited, if any, input into program policymaking—tend to be subject to the demands of the Medicaid medical industrial complex.

State governments are for the most part simultaneously overwhelmed by and reliant on Medicaid financially. Their ambivalence toward welfare medicine, especially when experiencing fiscal distress, can be overridden not only by the power of providers, but by the lure of federal money. The influx of massive national Medicaid dollars into their economies stimulates

+ +

economic growth, employment, and tax revenues. Some states and localities have become dependent for their financial prosperity on the government health insurance programs and the business establishments they subsidize. And stakeholders are not reluctant to remind legislators of this relationship whenever their special interests are at risk.

9

THE BUCK STOPS WHERE?

In this chapter, I seek to show the dynamics of Medicaid cost-shifting strategies and some of the ways in which the program is interlinked with other pieces of our health care system. As welfare medicine outlays have escalated, policymakers, agencies, and private concerns alike have endeavored to get someone else to pay at least a portion of the bill. I begin by examining the fiscal battle between the federal government and the states, a conflict that emerged at the program's inception but has intensified over the years. I then look at ways in which Medicare policies affect Medicaid obligations, especially for the dually eligible population. A number of states, too, wrangle with their localities over welfare medicine funding, the focus of the following section. Next, I turn to the rise in out-of-pocket client costs, one of the latest measures for transferring state Medicaid burdens elsewhere. I conclude the chapter with a discussion of the interrelationship between and among various private-sector stakeholders, including hospitals, nursing homes, employers, and managed-care organizations (MCOs), along with the ripple effects of their actions.

Tug-of-War: Paying the Bill

As welfare medicine outlays spiraled, state policymakers sought innovative approaches for financing their programs at the expense of the federal government. A key means of drawing in more of these outside dollars, beginning in the mid-1980s, has been the use of provider donations and taxes as part of the state match, generally returning the original payments to the vendors. The Disproportionate Hospital Share (DSH) program provided even greater opportunities to maximize national funds because these funds were not subject to upper payment limits (UPLs). Through creative accounting practices employing such devices as intergovernmental transfers and UPLs, states began to leverage increasing amounts of national money. As they gradually and fully appreciated their ability to lower their percentage of Medicaid outlays via these financing arrangements, they pursued them even more aggressively.[1]

Political pressure has made it difficult to curb the states' exploitation of these opportunities. Federal officials made a number of attempts to alter DSH arrangements during the 1990s, such as closing some loopholes, imposing hospital-specific caps, limiting the use of provider taxes and donations as financing mechanisms, and curtailing the overall growth of payments.[2] Nevertheless, the states effectively resisted, blunting the impact. To varying extents, they had become reliant on the extra money and, along with the powerful hospital and nursing home trade organizations, forced the national government to capitulate repeatedly.[3] Many members of the U.S. House and Senate themselves equivocated, torn between slowing down welfare medicine outlays and assisting the folks at home, for which they would get political credit.[4] This vacillation set in motion legislative ambiguity as Congress alternated between measures curbing loopholes and those enlarging DSH funding.[5] The various financing schemes continued to spread, with more and more states amassing billions in additional federal Medicaid revenues.[6] The George W. Bush White House, even more zealous than previous administrations in its opposition to state cost-shifting practices, issued regulations that curtailed some of them but could not eliminate them altogether. Costs continued to rise, albeit at a slower pace.[7]

Under the various federal-dollar maximization strategies, states have been able to help themselves to the national treasury, investing very little, if any, of their own money, but they do not always spend the surplus income on health services. To be sure, in a survey of thirty-four states, researchers found that states frequently contributed very little of their locally generated revenues into DSH programs.[8] In a few places, policymakers were engaging in more extreme "recycling" ploys, thereby drawing in even more federal cash.[9] Yet, instead of using the enhanced income to improve benefits for welfare medicine recipients, enlarge payments to safety-net providers, and extend Medicaid eligibility, many states deposit the money into their general budgets for non-Medicaid purposes or apply it to their mandated share of program costs.[10] Certain elected officials also have used the windfall dollars to avoid raising taxes or to cut them.[11] Indeed, the evidence suggests that the UPL shell games, to a greater or lesser extent, have been at the expense of public-sector institutions and their impoverished patients. Audits of several states revealed that much of the supplementary payments that under UPL rules should have gone to government-run nursing homes was used for other ends. Public-sector hospitals and clinics, all of which are struggling economically, have also been short-changed. Despite the growth of Medicaid enrollees and uninsured families who have been forced to seek health services from such providers, in several places across the nation policymakers simply substitute national resources for their own rather than augment services or improve the quality of care.[12]

The states continue to develop new, often problematic strategies to manipulate federal welfare medicine money to their advantage. As soon as the central government blocks one course of action, "creative states have always been able to pull another out of their hats."[13] Many of them, for example, have kept Medicaid dollars that were intended to finance school-based health services for eligible students, including diagnostic screening, physical therapy, speech therapy, and psychological counseling. A U.S. Government Accountability Office (GAO) study found that several states retained up to 85 percent of the money allocated to local school districts for these purposes; in a few instances, the services were not even provided. Georgia and Massachusetts even began using consultants in their efforts to garner more federal cash. Increasing from ten states in 2002 to thirty-four in 2004, more jurisdictions are using such advisors to develop innovative methods of substituting federal for state funding in their ongoing tug-of-war over who will pay the welfare medicine bill.[14]

In addition, because Medicaid is intertwined with all other aspects of state commitments, local officials have turned to the program, whenever possible, as a means of support for social provisions that had been or would have been financed exclusively out of their own budgets. By "Medicaiding" these provisions, as James Fossett and Courtney Burke fittingly put it, they can cash in on federal resources.[15] For example, in the 1980s, as the states jostled to fill the financial hole left by declining national subsidies for foster care, job training, home assistance to seniors, counseling, child protection, and chemical dependency treatments, many of them transferred these services to their low-income health plans. In a parallel movement, they increasingly utilized Medicaid to pay for the newly deinstitutionalized developmentally and mentally disabled population, a group that they previously had funded mainly on their own.[16] The program now provides a greater portion of the assistance to people with mental illnesses as well, most of whom had previously been state subsidized.[17] Local policymakers also have increasingly targeted their mental health initiatives to Medicaid recipients and Medicaid-eligible services in order to obtain a federal match.[18]

Such maneuvers are ongoing, including Pennsylvania's recent effort to render its county juvenile detention centers Medicaid eligible.[19] Alaska similarly sought a waiver to reorganize its health facilities for Alaskan

Natives so as to maximize contributions from the national government. Wisconsin, Indiana, Colorado, Maryland, and Massachusetts have secured federal welfare medicine subsidies for their previously state-funded aid to children with autism. Most prominently, state officials have transferred to the national government much of their Medicaid coverage expansion costs over the years, thus allowing them to serve more constituents at the least possible expense to their own budgets.

The central government not only defends itself against state efforts to capitalize on federal revenues, but periodically has initiated measures to shrink its own obligations to them. Both the Ronald Reagan and George W. Bush administrations, for example, energetically sought and achieved reductions in the growth of national welfare medicine outlays to the detriment of local budgets.[20] President Bush also embarked on one of the most vigorous financial assaults against the states in an attempt to eliminate, to the fullest extent possible, any of their "inappropriate" claims to Medicaid funds. Augmenting oversight activities of sixty-five regional analysts, the Centers for Medicare and Medicaid Services (CMS) hired ninety specialists whose main purpose, among other goals, was to slash the outflow of federal grants to the states.[21] Since 2001, CMS also has performed focused financial reviews, along with audits by the Office of Inspector General, to locate and prevent practices that allow the localities to maximize their federal match improperly. Conducting twenty intensive assessments each year, the agency identified millions of dollars in questionable disbursements, all of which the Bush administration forcefully endeavored to recover.

In squeezing the states monetarily, however, the Bush administration conspicuously did not take into account their financial situation or the implications for low-income households. As just one case in point, one of the audits discovered that although under federal law disabled children were allowed to stay in group homes for only up to 180 days, 500 children in Kansas had been reimbursed by Medicaid for longer stays. Local officials were told that they had to pick up the cost or throw the children out of the homes. However, states have few options to compensate for their loss of federal money. Unless they increase taxes, a politically untenable solution in most places, they are forced to cut back their welfare medicine plans or reduce other vital programs. Reductions in state grants certainly jeopardize any anticipated expansion in their coverage of the medically uninsured.

Medicare and Welfare Medicine

Medicare, too, has shifted costs to state Medicaid plans, especially because the federally financed program has high recipient cost-sharing requirements and lacks comprehensive services. In particular, welfare medicine has been forced to compensate for many of the unmet needs of dually eligible older and disabled low-income people who have not only steadily increased in number, but are an expensive population to care for. Totaling 7.5 million individuals, they represent 15 percent of Medicaid recipients but account for 42 percent of all spending.[22] The low-income program subsidizes a portion of or fully covers their Medicare Part A and Part B premiums, deductibles, and other coinsurance requirements. In addition, Congress allowed—and in 1988 mandated—the payment of Medicare Part B out-of-pocket charges for older and disabled Medicaid beneficiaries living at or below the federal poverty level (FPL) (Qualified Medicare Beneficiaries). Two years later, Congress required the states to "buy into" Part B premiums for the elderly and disabled having incomes up to 120 percent of the poverty threshold (Specified Low-Income Medicare Beneficiaries).[23] These monthly fees alone, which have steadily increased over the years, reached $96.40 per person in 2008.

Most significantly, however, the vast majority (about 85 percent) of dual eligibles qualifies for full Medicaid benefits, and so the states have been obligated to fund the "gaps" in Medicare services for them, especially for long-term care (LTC). Over the years, the localities have underwritten nursing home expenses, which, due to their enormous and mounting price tag, national policymakers have been unwilling to assign to Medicare. Today, about one-fifth of dual eligibles resides in institutional facilities.[24] Indeed, because Medicare does not cover LTC costs for anyone, only short stays after an acute episode in the hospital,[25] even older people who are not dually eligible eventually may turn to state Medicaid programs for their care after impoverishing themselves.

Medicaid and Medicare policies are interconnected in other ways; alterations to either program tend to affect the other, at times considerably. For example, so as to control costs in the federal program, Congress implemented a prospective payment method, based on diagnosis-related groups, for reimbursing hospitals in the mid-1980s; as the medical facilities neared their maximum allowable fees, they immediately began transferring as many of their patients as possible to nursing homes, obliging Medicaid plans to pick up the tab. As another case in point, when Congress transferred drug coverage for the dual eligibles to Medicare Part D, beginning in 2006, it required the states to subsidize most of the outlays but did not give them any leverage over prices.[26] Even worse, these medication charges are no longer subject to Medicaid rebates. State officials also have less ability now to demand discounts for their millions of other welfare medicine clients who do not participate in Medicare. Needless to say, local officials across party lines were dissatisfied with the situation, and nearly one-third of the states sued the federal government, arguing that the "clawback" provision was unconstitutional under the Tenth Amendment. However, it was upheld by the Supreme Court.

But the states are not shy about shifting their Medicaid liabilities to Medicare when they can. According to Edward Miller and William Weissert, when a member of their research team suggested a revised program design that would have lessened the hospitalization rate of older Medicaid recipients living at home, "The official retorted in all earnestness, 'Why would we want to do that? Those are Medicare dollars. For us that's development money. We don't want to reduce Medicare expenditures in our state.'" The localities take full advantage of any opportunity to minimize welfare medicine costs at the expense of Medicare.[27]

Combat Within and Among the States

A few states have handed over a portion of their Medicaid commitments to their counties, although rarely without provoking discord. For instance, New Hampshire requires counties to pay the entire state obligation (50 percent) for LTC costs, and in Florida they must contribute a portion of such outlays, up to a ceiling.[28] To varying degrees, other places, including Ohio, Pennsylvania, and Arizona, depend on county-generated revenues for selected Medicaid services. In New York and North Carolina, counties had been expected, until recently, to finance a fixed percentage of the entire price tag. In the latter state, where the local portion averaged 15 percent, the situation was highly contentious as innumerable "trades" were offered and rejected over the years. An agreement was recently reached: the legislature will gradually assume full Medicaid costs in exchange for some local revenues.

New York, which imposed the highest cost-sharing requirements on its local governments (initially 25 percent of total program outlays), also has experienced divisive clashes over who should shoulder the burden of welfare medicine. Operating the costliest program in the nation, with much of the expenses generated by New York City, the state has battled hard with its localities. Almost immediately after Medicaid was enacted, New York City was demanding a state takeover of its share of program outlays. County officials, too, blaming Medicaid for their financial woes and escalating property taxes, wanted relief but were averse to being saddled with any more of New York City's economic difficulties. In 1981, the controversy even held up passage of the state budget for more than a month. Since that time, assorted proposals emerged, with a succession of governors offering to pay some or all of the program costs, along with various "swap" arrangements. Such deals, which inevitably generated intense conflict as the various entities defended their respective financial interests, also were mired in party politics: Republicans dominated the Senate, representing upstate county interests, but Democrats controlled the lower chamber, acting on behalf of city concerns. The issue was resolved, at least temporarily, by capping local Medicaid liabilities in 2006.[29]

Financial squabbles among the states also have been commonplace, especially regarding their federal match, which is determined by a formula that compares each locality's per capita income with the national average. Thirteen states currently receive the minimum Federal Medical Assistance Percentage, which ranges from 50 to 83 percent; six of them obtain more than 70 percent. Many governors have complained over the years that current calculations do not take into account the disproportionate burdens that their states must bear, such as comparatively greater shares of people in poverty, more frail elders or individuals with disabilities, or larger numbers of immigrants. Even a slight revision in a state's federal percentage would have a considerable impact on its welfare medicine outlays.

Encumbering the Poor

Throughout the years, states have attempted to shift Medicaid expenses to recipients, but until the enactment of the Deficit Reduction Act (DRA) in 2005, cost-sharing had been circumscribed: federal law did not allow premiums, and copayments had to be "nominal"—for example, a $3.00 maximum for adults. For the most part, national regulations had prohibited any beneficiary payments for children, pregnant women, and the elderly or disabled who received Supplemental Security Income or were institutionalized. Certain types of services, such as family planning and emergency care, also were exempt from charges. Nevertheless, states that expanded Medicaid through waivers began using cost sharing more consistently and extensively as a means of picking up the tab.

Since 2006, armed with "new flexibilities" and convoluted justifications, nearly all local officials have been curbing their welfare medicine outlays or compensating for lower federal grants by requiring or increasing premiums, enrollment fees, and copayments on services, especially for medications. Because prescription drug costs are soaring, they are the target of choice:[30] more than 80 percent of the states now charge adults a fee for their medications, sometimes applying different amounts for generic or preferred brand and nonpreferred brand-name medicines. In twenty-six states, adults pay at least some of the costs for each inpatient hospital stay, and in a few places these sums are sizeable. Children, too, have become subject to more cost-sharing obligations, including premiums and copayments.[31] At the end of 2008, the Bush administration published new rules giving the states sweeping authority to impose even more extensive cost-sharing requirements.[32]

State officials typically contend that such fees will force participants to become more "engaged" in their health care and make them cost-conscious medical consumers. The reality, of course, is that policymakers are merely shifting expenses from state treasuries to low-income beneficiaries and their families. Some places such as South Carolina, Kentucky, and Rhode Island took advantage of the DRA's permission not only to institute higher premiums and copayments, but also to make it enforceable: providers were allowed to deny services to those who did not—or could not—pay. In addition, about one-fifth of the Medicaid and State Children's Health Insurance Program plans included a "lock-out" period on children in families that failed to pay their premiums, thus preventing them from reentering the program for a time ranging from sixty days to six months.[33] As a result, these youngsters had to do without health services, regardless of their medical needs.

+ +

Dodging Responsibility: The Private Sector

Private-sector stakeholders also scramble to transfer as many of their costs as they can to other players. Over the decades, proprietary hospitals have sought to minimize their care of the poor, regardless of the amount of public-sector support they obtain. For example, under the Hill-Burton Act of 1946 they were supposed to treat uninsured patients in exchange for government subsidies that assisted in the construction of more than one-third of the nation's hospital beds. Instead, a significant number of the "Hill Burton" hospitals handed indigent families over to state and local facilities. Attempting to restrain such practices, Congress mandated in 1986 that all hospitals participating in Medicare must provide a medical examination and stabilize any person who arrives with severe, acute symptoms. Nonetheless, a torrent of uninsured patients dumped by the for-profit institutions still floods the wards of the insufficiently funded public facilities and clinics.[34] The evidence suggests that hospitals also have shifted at least some of their Medicaid-related and uncompensated charity care expenses to commercial health plans, fostering a rise in premiums for businesses and consumers alike. In turn, state Medicaid plans have to subsidize more families because they are now priced out of the private insurance market.

Nursing homes, too, pass on their financial responsibilities elsewhere whenever feasible. For example, instead of treating patients who become ill, they send them to high-priced hospitals, paid for by Medicare. Such transfers are commonplace; one research group found that within any given six-month period, about 15 percent of all long-term stay residents are hospitalized for some period of time. The investigators suggest that with better staffing, therapy, and other clinical resources, about 40 percent of relocations could have been handled within the nursing home. They calculate that potentially avoidable hospitalizations[35] cost New York about $1.24 billion (in 2004 money) from 1999 to 2004.[36]

However, it is not in the interest of nursing homes to care for their sick inhabitants. Investigators who studied "bed-hold" regulations, for example, discovered that proprietors paid by the state to reserve places for their hospitalized residents were 36 percent more likely to send these patients away. The facility saves money while boosting government expenditures: Medicare now funds the care, and Medicaid pays for retaining the bed. In fact, nursing homes that invest in medical services and equipment that allow them to lower hospitalization rates may save the government programs money but add to their own overhead. Therefore, neither the facilities nor their state Medicaid funding partners have any financial incentive to keep patients in place, which would in actuality add to a frail elder's overall well-being.[37]

In a similar vein, large-scale employers endeavor to transfer their health costs to others. Beginning in the 1980s but intensifying during the 1990s, corporate America, supported by many elected officials, blamed high labor costs for weakening American competitiveness in the international marketplace.[38] Viewing escalating health premiums as their fundamental encumbrance, companies steadily demanded—and received—concessions that chipped away at medical benefits. They steadily imposed higher deductibles, copayments, and a greater share of premium costs on their workers and, in an increasing number of cases, dropped coverage for spouses and offspring. Many of them shut down their retiree health benefit plans, and a few places even excluded high-priced diseases, such as AIDS or cancer, from their insurance packages.

At the same time, the U.S. manufacturing sector has progressively been supplanted by small businesses and a low-wage service sector, which conspicuously do not provide medical coverage or offer affordable plans. Industrial jobs have gradually moved overseas, and the U.S. economy has experienced surges of acquisitions and mergers at home, leaving rising numbers of displaced workers in their wake. Many of these workers, along with women dropped from cash-assistance programs, are forced into poorly paying jobs that today are the fastest-growing occupational opportunities. Nonstandard workers, who compose one-fourth of the workforce (part-time employees, independent contractors, and contingent workers), along with the more than 3 million underpaid migrant farmers, also are far less likely to obtain medical insurance through their jobs.[39] As a consequence, the share of labor covered by employer-sponsored plans has been continuously declining; only about 62 percent of the nonaged population (including both workers and their dependents) still receive such medical benefits.

In some instances, firms in the service sector are exploiting Medicaid as part of an overall strategy to keep their operating costs low at the expense of taxpayers.[40] Large retail businesses, in particular, have shifted their health insurance obligations to welfare medicine. Wal-Mart is the archetypical company that, despite enormous profits, pays its sales personnel inordinately low wages and limits their benefits.[41] Its unwillingness to offer affordable medical coverage allows the corporation to carry low merchandise prices on the backs of employees, both in the United States and abroad. In many states, Medicaid fills the gap, especially for children. In 2005, nearly half of Wal-Mart's 1.3 million American workers was either uninsured or participating in welfare medicine. Fast-food chains, supermarkets, banks, and drug stores are also subsidized by the low-income health program. In Pennsylvania, for example, Wal-Mart is the largest private-sector employer, but 16 percent of its labor force participate in Medicaid at a cost to the state of more than $15 million annually. A high and increasing percentage of workers in Pennsylvania's other leading companies rely on the program as well, including Weiss markets (13.4 percent) and Giant (11.8 percent). Likewise, in Arizona Wal-Mart is the foremost employer of workers who depend on Medicaid (slightly more than 5 percent of its labor force), but McDonald's, Bashas' grocery chain, Target, Safeway, Fry's, Taco Bell, KFC, and Pizza Hut follow suit. The situation is similar in many other localities.[42]

A few state policymakers are fighting back, but with mixed success. The Maryland legislature, for example, passed the Fair Share Healthcare Bill in 2005, requiring all companies with more than 10,000 employees to spend at least 8 percent of its payroll on health benefits or contribute an equal amount to the state's Medicaid program; only Wal-Mart had that many workers. Governor Robert Ehrlich Jr. (R) promptly vetoed the bill, calling it an assault on business, but his veto was overridden by the legislature. A federal court subsequently struck down the so-called Wal-Mart Law.[43] Nonetheless, several states are pursing other strategies (i.e., "play or pay" employer mandates) aimed at corporations that hire large numbers of minimum-wage workers who must then rely on welfare medicine for their health insurance.

Because Medicaid is interconnected with nearly all aspects of health care in the United States, actions by one stakeholder to control its medical expenditures often generate ripples throughout the system. To illustrate, as employers increasingly turned to MCOs, it became more difficult for hospitals to shift their uncompensated care costs to commercial plans, thereby forcing some institutions to compensate for their losses at the expense of patient services or to squeeze more money from the government health programs. As the MCOs spread, there was less demand for inpatient care generally, fostering low occupancy levels that led, in some measure, to hospital closures, mergers, and the loss of jobs; in a few communities, the economic effects were devastating. In addition, by squeezing practitioner fees, managed care in the privately insured market also has made it more difficult for doctors to transfer their Medicaid shortfalls to other patients, further discouraging providers' participation in welfare medicine. At the same time, the shortage of physicians, due in part to inadequate Medicaid rates, has forced enrollees to seek their routine medical care in high-cost emergency rooms.[44]

States seeking to stem the flow of welfare medicine dollars by restricting program eligibility or increasing cost-sharing inevitably generate higher levels of medically uninsured families, who also must now rely on expensive emergency rooms for nonemergency care. In Oregon, after the legislature authorized larger out-of-pocket payments for enrollees, both the number of families without coverage and the use of hospital emergency services rose simultaneously.[45] Medicaid participants who are burdened with more cost-sharing responsibilities for their health services also may forgo early diagnosis of or treatment for their diseases, ultimately requiring more expensive therapies later on.

Domino effects reverberate throughout the health system in other ways, and the states have at times taken legal action against the perpetrators. For instance, cigarette companies, through their promotion of smoking, have contributed to the incidence of lung cancer, the treatment expenses for which are borne by everyone, including welfare medicine. Beginning in the late 1990s, the states sought and won billions of dollars from tobacco firms to compensate, in part, for their Medicaid outlays on smoking-related illnesses. Local policymakers have correspondingly endeavored to recoup millions of dollars in medical bills stemming from deceptive practices by drug manufacturers. In one case, Eli Lilly's antipsychotic drug Zyprexa engendered diabetes among a significant number of its users, a side effect that cost low-income health plans millions of dollars to treat. In another instance, officials initiated a class-action lawsuit against Purdue Pharma, the manufacturer of the prescription pain killer OxyContin, for misleading the public about the drug's risk of addiction. They sought reimbursement not only for Medicaid's purchase of the drug, but for the cost of addiction treatment centers and other associated expenses. Clearly, the American people in general, along with commercial and government health insurance plans, ultimately pay the price for companies that improve their bottom line at the expense of consumers.

Conclusion: Paying the Bill

Although health care for the poor, unlike federally assisted income-maintenance programs, has sustained support among large sectors of society, nobody actually wants to pay the bill. From national, state, and local officials to employers and contractors, everyone wants to pass the expenses to someone else. State policymakers progressively have engaged in numerous strategies to maximize federal dollars, supported by the health industries, whereas the federal government periodically seeks to lower its share of the costs. Squeezing Medicaid payments at one end, however, tends to increase outlays in other places. Indeed, cost shifting has been endemic both to welfare medicine and to medical care at large, often generating domino-like effects throughout the political economy. Welfare medicine is integrally connected to all other aspects of health care in so many respects that modifications in other policies, programs, or medical plans, whether enacted by private or government officials, inevitably will affect it and vice versa. As Medicaid providers, big business, and the government shift as many expenses as they can elsewhere, however, the low-income population—and increasingly the middle class—are paying the price.

10

CONCLUSION:
MEDICAID AND THE FUTURE OF
HEALTH CARE IN THE
UNITED STATES

Medicaid emerged in the shadow of Medicare but has developed into the largest medical insurance plan in the United States. It also ranks as a leading social program in general, slightly surpassing Social Security in the number of people served.[1] Welfare medicine is the fourth most expensive item on the federal budget, 7 percent of the total, and for nearly all of the states it represents the second-largest category of spending from their general revenue dollars, second only to elementary and secondary education. This book, by painting a picture of the social, economic, and political dynamics that have shaped the program over the decades, has attempted both to explain its inexorable growth and to explore the extent to which it meets the needs of low-income families. I have concluded that, given Medicaid's enormous and escalating price tag, we can do far better in serving them.

The initial goals were relatively modest because they emanated from a program that was conservative, sparse, uneven, and means tested. Its most significant promise was to ensure that eligible poor families had access to adequate health services. They accordingly were to receive similar treatment as people paying privately, underscored by the freedom-of-choice requirement enacted in 1967. Over the decades, Medicaid has functioned as the primary means of funding medical care for economically deprived households. In its origins, it also contained seeds for expansion, an objective of many early liberal reformers. Indeed, through incremental growth it now serves a substantial segment of low-income children, disabled individuals, pregnant women, and elders—people characterized as the "worthy" poor. In recent years, as employer-sponsored plans contract, a number of state officials have been resorting to welfare medicine as a vehicle for extending coverage to medically uninsured low-wage workers, especially their children. In 2008, two-thirds of state governors proposed an enlargement of the program to some degree.[2] In effect, the states tend to fall back on Medicaid whenever certain aspects of our privatized medical marketplace fall short.

The program also originally sought to reduce at least some of the financial burdens for needy households, many of whom have been economically ruined as a result of crushing medical bills. It has been somewhat successful in protecting eligible individuals, mostly children, against devastating hospital and prescription drug expenses. Welfare medicine also finances a large proportion of the nation's nursing home tab and a small measure of in-home care, thereby assisting frail elders and their families with their long-term care (LTC) financial burdens, even if they have to deplete all of their resources to qualify. In addition, it funds half of all state mental health services and, as the only game in town, has gradually taken on additional, worthwhile responsibilities not intended at the time of the program's enactment. Nevertheless, despite these limited accomplishments, the low-income health plan not only has failed to satisfy a significant portion of its original objectives or to provide effectively for low-income families, but also has acquired additional vested interests, many of them with aims unrelated to the health and well-being of the poor.

Throughout the book, I have shown how powerful stakeholders, each with its own and interconnected turf, both benefit from the program and have pushed for its expansion. After the passage of Medicaid, nearly every conceivable category of health care provider and vendor, despite initial opposition, had its hand in the program's piggy bank. Hospitals, nursing homes (and now Health Care Real Estate Investment Trusts), clinicians, insurance firms, drug companies, pharmacists, durable medical equipment suppliers, home health agencies, and others, all angling for a bigger piece of the lucrative Medicaid pie, have secured and fiercely defended their economic gains. As such, they tend to support the Medicaid-based Band-Aid approach to extending health services to the medically uninsured, albeit with enhanced reimbursement fees for themselves. They also have been instrumental in fashioning welfare medicine to meet their preferences: lobbyists affiliated with the thriving Medicaid medical industrial complex have separately and jointly warded off regulations, fought for higher fees, and assured themselves "comfortable" profits. As a consequence, welfare medicine has served to buttress these entrenched interests, many of which are now dependent on the program for their financial viability.

Middle-class elders, the disabled, and their families, who view the low-income health plan as a "safety net" for LTC, are vitally concerned with preserving the program as well. Probably one of the most intractable problems plaguing Medicaid has been the expensive but seriously deficient nursing home services that have long been a central force driving its expenditures, accounting for roughly one-third of the total. Many older people qualify as a result of medical indigence, a basic component of the program early on, although not envisioned as a seed for its dramatic growth.[3] Having been given the option to extend eligibility to the medically needy, state policymakers typically offered nursing home coverage to more of their newly impoverished frail and disabled middle-class residents. As a result, the low-income health plan became the mainstay of the nursing home industry as well as of older and disabled people requiring LTC.

However, officials have proven incapable of ameliorating the generally shoddy, often abusive conditions in these facilities or of controlling their escalating costs. In order to squeeze spending, they are increasingly turning to home- and community-based services, but for the most part to the detriment of Medicaid participants and their families: without a sufficient commitment of resources, the states are imposing greater, often overwhelming burdens on unpaid caregivers, mainly women. Together with national leaders, they also have restricted qualification criteria in yet another attempt to save money by chipping away at the program's ambiguous entitlement status.

Notwithstanding their interest in reining in expenditures, the states, too, have been seduced by the "pot of gold" emanating from the federal treasury and by the positive impact of the funding match on their local economies. Seeking to garner more national dollars, a motivating factor in the establishment of their programs in the first place, they increasingly have searched for ways to substitute outside money for their own, to maximize their grants, and even to expand their plans to cover more families. At times, federal congressional representatives, anxious to appease their constituents, have assented to these machinations.

A confluence of forces, then, has buoyed welfare medicine, rendering it relatively resilient to the periodic and concerted efforts to slash its funding over the decades. In the final analysis, compared to federally assisted cash welfare payments, the low-income health program has fared reasonably well, surviving the determination of Presidents Reagan and George W. Bush, as well as of congressional Republican majorities in the mid-1990s and once more in the early twenty-first century, to alter it into a more financially limited block grant; time and again Medicaid has emerged relatively intact. But escalating taxpayer dollars does not signify that the program has met the clients' requirements or is compatible with their preferences or circumstances. Regardless of how much money is lavished on it, there are no guarantees that the enrollees will be the primary beneficiaries. As shown in this volume, there is a palpable disjuncture between expenditures and the extent of benefits delivered. Steven Gold bitingly writes: "An individual Medicaid recipient did not receive 20% more service just because the state and federal governments spent 20% more on him or her."[4]

In actual fact, the persistent endeavors to contain overall expenditures, although decidedly unsuccessful, have had detrimental effects on beneficiaries. Economizing measures, a priority for elected officials across the political spectrum, have tended to trump all other concerns, rendering Medicaid sorely deficient as a health insurance system for needy families. From the start, cost considerations have engendered frequent and often injurious trade-offs between and among vital issues, including qualification criteria; number and types of services; provider fee levels; access to care; program efficiency, adequacy, effectiveness, equity, and quality; and patient rights.

Financial issues have always dominated policy discussions, thus precluding the participation of a significant number of low-income families in welfare medicine. The program does not even cover a majority of the federally defined poverty population, for the most part disregarding childless adults, many parents, middle-age men and women, low-wage workers, and some measure of children. Because Medicaid is not an entitlement, at least in the same sense as Medicare, its history has been a cycle of adding new eligibility groups and services while simultaneously cutting off existing ones. In the 1990s, for example, even as Congress included more children, it supported the disenrollment of countless cash-assistance welfare recipients. More recently, as states began extending coverage to additional families, they tended to scale back benefit packages.

It also is not surprising that inadequate access to doctors and dentists, especially private practices, is ubiquitous across the nation. Rather than offer mainstream medicine, as initially promised, Medicaid has sustained a second-rate medical system for its clients, composed of underfunded and poorly equipped public hospitals and clinics and inferior private practices. Poor quality of care is endemic to the program, whether owing to inadequate reimbursement rates or its secondary importance among policymakers. Enrollees suffer from greater undiagnosed illnesses, fewer treatments, and poorer health outcomes than privately insured patients. Frail elderly recipients, too, are subject to substandard care, whether in nursing homes or in other LTC settings.

Part and parcel of the overriding emphasis on reducing outlays, policymakers have steadily handed over Medicaid plans (and medical decisions) to managed-care companies. Although this approach is based on the premise that the commercial insurance firms will deliver decent services at lower costs, the evidence suggests that they ration services instead, boosting their earnings at their consumers' expense. To be sure, the more successful a firm, the lower its medical loss ratio (or proportion of earnings devoted to health services). Additional market-based initiatives and the catchwords shoring them up have increasingly informed welfare medicine policies and politics. The steady promotion of Health Savings Accounts (HSAs), Health Opportunity Accounts, and reward or bonus incentive programs—retrenchment measures enacted under the guise of "reform," "consumer choice," "empowerment," and "personal responsibility"—do not work to the advantage of low-income people. The rhetoric notwithstanding, families experience the actual impact of enhanced commercialization and stingy state policies; the unwelcome reality is that these strategies translate into service offerings that are unconnected to a client's particular health status or needs.

Beneficiaries are paying a price in other respects as elected officials impose increasingly onerous premium costs, deductibles, and copayments on them, forcing some clients to forgo services or to drop from the program entirely. Such cost shifting is a foremost Medicaid sport, as each player labors to obtain as much as is feasible from the program while transferring the expenses elsewhere. The national government reduces its outlays to the detriment of the states, and the latter in turn work to maximize their share of federal dollars. Providers, too, capitalize on the program and each other, a number of them engaging in fraud to do so. Although a wide range of contractors exploits Medicare as well, Medicaid has always experienced even greater problems because it consists of a much broader range of services, confusion over which level of government will or can control deceptive practices, and fifty different state plans to deal with. Moreover, enforcement activities have been aimed primarily at recouping the ill-gotten gains, often ignoring the negative impact of financial abuse on the delivery, effectiveness, and safety of services.

Finally, as the history of Medicaid demonstrates, because the program is not a clear-cut entitlement or premised on standards that place patients first, it has proven inadequate and for many people unreliable. Even families who obtain coverage are not assured that they can retain it or that their access to a particular service they require will last. Over the decades, welfare medicine has been subjected to cycles of protection and assault by various presidents, congressional leaders, governors, and state legislatures, depending on the economic and political winds of the times. Operating within a vacillating environment, including which party is in control, it has been susceptible to brutal discord, spurious arguments, uncertainty, and arbitrariness. Such volatility intensifies the incomplete and discontinuous nature of Medicaid coverage for low-income families. The State Children's Health Insurance Program (SCHIP), too, has been tossed around as a large number of congressional Republicans have sought to restrict eligibility and Democrats to expand it; as a result, many youngsters in need of medical treatment are hostage to the vagaries of the moment.

Devolution: The Fiscal and Political Incapacity of States

Despite complex intergovernmental funding and regulatory arrangements, Medicaid is firmly anchored in the states, even more so as a result of the ongoing devolution of power since 1980. States' rights advocates—and most governors—maintain that the localities are best suited for addressing the assorted health issues affecting low-income and medically uninsured families. They contend that local ingenuity not only generates innovative solutions, but also stimulates "best practices," thereby offering opportunities for different places to share the most efficient and effective methods and procedures with each other. According to this viewpoint, a "one size fits all" philosophy precludes states from implementing policies that suit their unique needs and conditions. Besides, the local approach is alleged to be more democratic, empowering consumers and their communities. These arguments have increasingly gained sway, coloring Medicaid policies and policymaking. Even some liberal reformers insist that we can best advance the cause of universal insurance through state-by-state experimentation, using Medicaid as a base of support. Indeed, as Michael Sparer points out, the principal of state influence and responsibility in health care is deeply ingrained in the United States.[5]

Nonetheless, as shown in the book's chapters, neither Medicaid nor the states are suitable means for insuring low-income families or advancing universal health care. Localities' glaring inability to lead the way is most evident in their fiscal constraints: compared to the federal government, virtually all of them require balanced budgets, depend on regressive and restrictive tax structures, and are more vulnerable to the exigencies of the political economy. During dire financial times, unemployment, the number of uninsured households, and welfare medicine caseloads rise simultaneously, just when the states confront declines in their revenues, thereby fostering deficits that short-circuit even the most liberal and ambitious plans proposed or enacted by governors and legislators.[6] For a variety of reasons, locally elected officials are decidedly reluctant to raise income, sales, or corporate taxes; they often desperately turn to lotteries, gambling casinos, and duties on alcohol and cigarettes.

In most places, recurrent economic "crises" have led to fewer services, reduced coverage, and lower provider fees. In the twenty-first century alone, financially strapped states have had to grapple with severe budgetary shortfalls from 2001 to 2004 and again beginning in 2008, when more than 60 percent could not discharge their welfare medicine commitments. Responses to their fiscal woes have ranged from slashing provider fees or freezing them (leading to less access to services) to trimming eligibility and benefit packages. As the economic situation worsened in 2009, and despite the $87 billion, two-year national stimulus package, more states cut programs.[7] Nearly all states that have attempted to cover more of their medically uninsured residents have experienced severe setbacks. However, even in "better" times, welfare medicine is a source of continuing financial strain. It is easier to expand coverage and services at the state level than to sustain them.[8] Despite fluctuations in the business cycle, people's actual medical needs remain the same.

Moreover, the vicissitudes of economic life do not affect the states in the same way, engendering sharp inequalities among them. Even during economic downturns, when most states are struggling to balance their budgets while fulfilling their Medicaid obligations, a few places may be thriving. Indeed, the states that are the most encumbered with low-income and medically uninsured populations tend to have the least capacity to serve them. Different jurisdictions also vary widely in immigrant status (legal and undocumented),[9] amount and growth of older people, size of their rural population, degree of medical inflation, extent of poverty, and per capita income.

Nor are states alike in their political will to care for low-income and other medically uninsured households, a factor that contributes to unequal access to Medicaid services across the nation. Racial and ethnic disparities play a role as well: several studies have found a link between the level of population diversity and welfare medicine spending, eligibility levels, and benefits, with the most homogeneous jurisdictions boasting the least parsimonious plans.[10] States diverge in other ways, including their historical approach to social provision, public opinion, political culture, and type and level of permissible taxation—all factors affecting the unevenness in welfare medicine policies and practices. As a consequence, the services individuals obtain—and whether they receive any at all—depend entirely on their geographic location or, as suggested earlier, on which party or governor is in power at any particular moment in time. Welfare medicine's state-by-state approach to insuring the poor has produced an inequitable, haphazard distribution of health care rather than local innovation, ingenuity, democracy, or empowerment, as argued by devolution advocates.

Medicaid and its state-based resources, procedures, and practices plainly cannot be a substitute for or a back-door approach to universal health care. The program has too many separate and distinct administrative arrangements, power relationships, budgetary means, and provider availability, among other drawbacks. Most critically, the states do not have the fiscal or political capacity to sustain comprehensive coverage. In addition, although they differ somewhat in the relative influence of their disparate Medicaid stakeholders, in the main a greater devolution of power has placed health policymaking squarely in the hands of elected officials, who are the most susceptible to pressure by special interests.[11] Thus, building on the low-income health program would only intensify current dilemmas, crises, and inequities in the health system at large. The question is not how we can expand Medicaid to cover more uninsured people, but rather what we must do to render the United States more capable of fulfilling the real health care needs of everyone in our society. This goal can be accomplished only through a national approach, not by piecemeal community-by-community programs.

The U.S. Health Care System: Broken and Dysfunctional

Medicaid is only a piece of the health care puzzle in American society and therefore inevitably suffers from the deficiencies of the larger medical system in which it is embedded. It not only reflects the problematic broader arrangements, but also helps to sustain them. The underlying structures have engendered severe income, racial, ethnic, and gender disparities in care, maldistribution of practitioners and facilities, uneven access to quality services, countless inefficiencies, and spiraling costs everywhere—shortcomings that are exacerbated for public-aid patients. Welfare medicine enrollees encounter innumerable obstacles in their quest for quality care, nearly all of which stem from failures in the system as a whole. Within this context, any attempts to improve Medicaid, extend coverage to additional groups, or even control outlays must address the root causes of the problems.

The configuration, delivery, and funding of American health care are complex, haphazard, and for the most part inequitable. Families who can afford it are offered state-of-the-art technologies, procedures, and equipment, skilled professionals, and modern facilities. The "haves," generally individuals with high-paying jobs or independent sources of wealth, have access to medical interventions that may provide early detection of diseases, allowing them a greater chance of preventing or delaying certain conditions, controlling serious complications, enhancing their well-being, and even saving their lives. These services are generally paid for through employer-sponsored plans, the cornerstone of American health insurance.[12] Grounded in the ideas, principles, and strategies of the marketplace, the basic framework of health care in the United States has been shaped over the years to accommodate the needs and preferences of multifarious health industries, professionals, and other pressure groups.

Piggy-backed atop this illogical, uncoordinated "system" of care and its fragmented funding sources are the government health care programs, each serving specially chosen segments of the American population. Medicare guarantees the elderly (and certain disabled people) access to medical services, even if entrée to the "best" care is not evenly distributed among racial, ethnic, or income groups, and many benefit and financial gaps exist.[13] Medicaid, as demonstrated in this book, is a more uncertain entitlement, with eligibility based on a random mix of such factors as household income and assets, geography, the presence of children, age, level of disability, type of medical condition, and immigrant status. At the lowest end of the spectrum are the medically uninsured; they must make due with "crisis" care in hospital emergency rooms, poorly funded and ill-equipped public hospitals and crowded clinics, and at times, no care at all. They are most often the working poor who are not eligible for Medicaid but are financially incapable of paying the exorbitant and soaring costs of health insurance premiums, even if their employers offer a plan.[14]

Because the system is an inefficient hodgepodge of services and payment mechanisms with irregular and irrational coverage and is dominated by profit-making vendors and professionals, it has triggered the runaway costs that we have experienced over the past several decades. Health care is privately and publicly one of the most expensive enterprises in the nation, vastly outpacing economic growth. By 2006, total U.S. outlays on medical-related services represented 16 percent of the gross domestic product, or $2.1 trillion, up from 5 percent the year Medicaid was enacted.[15] Although medical inflation may be due in part to an aging population and the proliferation of technological innovations, it stems mainly from, as Robert Kuttner cogently puts it, "our unique, pervasive commercialization."[16] Not only do certain industries siphon off up to one-third of U.S. health care outlays for non-health-related purposes (including administration, marketing, lobbying, high executive salaries, and the like), but the system also produces counterproductive incentives: resources are invested for financial gain rather than to address medical needs. Services and treatments are viewed as yet another commodity in the marketplace, at hand to maximize income for practitioners, vendors, and shareholders. Profit-maximizing behavior is intrinsic to the current organizational arrangements and is evident even among voluntary agencies, thereby escalating expenses and perverting the allocation of health dollars.

The situation is compounded by the fee-for-service approach that induces suppliers to engender their own demands, thereby promoting overutilization of treatments (with inherent risks to health and well-being). Conversely, the cost-saving alternative to this payment method, managed care, fosters underutilization of services (with even more dire consequences for health and well-being). The steady takeover of the health care system by managed-care organizations (MCOs) also has led to these organizations' greater control over physicians and medical decisions, along with reduced fees for their services, all of which has vastly increased the profitability of the insurance industry. Because of lower payments, along with pressures from MCOs, physicians have steadily increased the number of patients they treat on a daily basis. According to one source, they now average less than eight minutes per client, a considerable reduction from a decade ago.[17]

As political leaders debate whether to implement health insurance for everyone in the United States, and radical conservatives condemn it as "socialism," the paradoxical reality is that we already have expansive government involvement but without universal coverage. In 2006, the national government paid slightly more than one-third of total health care expenditures, mostly through Medicare ($378.6 billion) and Medicaid ($180.6 billion). Together with the states and their localities, which contributed another 13 percent (mostly for Medicaid), public-sector financing accounted for fully 46 percent of all health spending in the nation.[18] American taxpayers also contribute measurably to health care costs through tax subsidies. Federal income tax expenditures accounted for at least $141.5 billion through an assortment of exclusions, credits, and deductions from individual and corporate tax liabilities.[19] The states similarly lost revenues, amounting to $67 billion.[20] Whether paid for directly through the budget-making process or indirectly by means of tax expenditures, the government contributed roughly $1.2 trillion in 2006 for medical insurance and services.

Certainly, since at least the 1970s, the United States has committed a greater share of its gross domestic product to health care than has the rest of the industrialized world, including the thirty Organization for Economic Cooperation and Development (OECD) nations.[21] It also spends more per capita through the government; nonetheless, more than 47 million people are still medically uninsured. Even families who have decent insurance are subjected to expensive and increasingly unaffordable cost-sharing provisions. Many policies exclude mental health or dental services or limit other types of essential treatments. Because of frequent job changes or unemployment, individuals also risk disruptions in their care or loss of coverage entirely. Still others are underinsured and may be forced to face a sudden, devastating illness without adequate protection and thus experience financial ruin; crushing medical bills are a major cause of bankruptcy in the United States.[22] Such an approach to financing health care—at far greater costs than those incurred by any other prosperous industrial nation—is an illogical, unsound, and ineffective means of meeting America's health insurance needs.

In fact, despite outspending other nations, we do not fare particularly well in terms of health outcomes and quality measures.[23] In comparison to other places, the United States ranks 21st in infant mortality and 17th in life expectancy at birth.[24] We also are lower than the average of the OECD countries in the per capita number of physicians, nurses, hospital beds, and diagnostic imaging equipment.[25] In a ranking of 191 nations on a wide range of health indicators, we placed 37th.[26] For example, the United States consistently underperformed against other nations on such crucial measures as injury rates and death from medical errors; prevention of unnecessary, sometimes harmful treatments; coordination of chronic care; and waiting time for physician visits.[27] Equally disturbing, relative to other OECD members, we have one of the highest percentages of "amenable mortalities," defined as individuals whose lives could have been saved with effective and timely medical intervention.[28] Among the key factors contributing to our poor record are the relatively high percentage of uninsured and underinsured families, poor-quality services, and racial and socioeconomic inequities.

Unlike the United States, all of the Western industrialized countries share the view that health care is a basic right; they not only guarantee coverage, but also offer comprehensive benefits. Although their financing and delivery systems vary widely, they all rely on government protection to a greater extent than does the United States and disallow premiums that are related to risk status. Some nations have restructured their health systems in recent years, but they remain committed to universal access to services.[29] Moreover, the number of nations providing collective responsibility for LTC is growing (e.g., Germany and Japan). Moreover, in no other Western country are the frail elderly subjected to the substandard quality of care that is prevalent in American nursing homes.

If It's Broke, Fix It: The Need for National Health Care

In the end, after exploring the question of whether Medicaid is better than nothing, I have concluded that it depends on one's vantage point. From the perspective of low-income claimants, despite their difficulty in accessing high-quality services, for the most part they tend to be better off than medically uninsured families. More children and pregnant women now have the opportunity to obtain preventive care and treatments for their illnesses. The aged poor also have benefited, especially from the coverage of their Medicare premiums and other cost-sharing requirements. However, for frail elders who are forced into sorely deficient nursing homes, the answer is less certain. At best, their relatives are relieved of heavy financial burdens, but at a huge price, given that older people must first divest themselves of all resources. Even though funding for services in noninstitutional settings is seriously restricted, more younger disabled adults and some older people have been able to hire attendants, at least part-time, allowing them to achieve enhanced mobility, independence, and a better quality of life. Local communities, too, have gained, securing additional outside revenues to spur their economies and feed their budgets, along with greater employment opportunities for their residents.

Nevertheless, from the taxpayers' standpoint, the thorny issue is whether we are getting our money's worth in actual medical services for needy families, especially in light of the vast national and state resources devoted to the program. In my view, although welfare medicine is better than nothing for scores of individuals, it clearly does not suffice for meeting low-income families' needs overall, many of whom help support it financially through their tax dollars. That is not to say we should abandon health insurance for economically disadvantaged households or, for that matter, anyone else. As I discuss later, only deep systemic changes in the entire health care infrastructure will allow the poor and all uninsured families access to adequate medical services. This radical restructuring must be accompanied by the implementation of affordable universal coverage, a politically challenging task.

The failure to institute national health care in the United States has a long and well-established history. It can be attributed to a number of factors, but at least one crucial dynamic has been the enduring but shifting strength of opposition interest groups.[30] Early on, when the federal government came forward in the depths of the Great Depression to quell political unrest and avert financial disaster through a vast array of social programs, Franklin Delano Roosevelt surrendered at once to the powerful opponents of comprehensive medical insurance; less acquiescent, Harry Truman was nonetheless equally unsuccessful. Since that time, whenever national health care has been proposed—including through President Clinton's Health Security Act of 1993—its supporters have been forced to capitulate to the commanding medical interests of the day, who relentlessly pursue their cause with massive and disproportionate amounts of political and financial resources.[31]

National health care has once again burst upon the national agenda as states, in the midst of the current recession, scramble to contend with the needs of their uninsured working residents, escalating health costs, declining revenues, and budget imbalances. Opinion polls show that the vast majority of the population consistently views the large percentage of medically uninsured Americans as an important and serious problem, and a sizeable percentage of people wants the federal government to guarantee health insurance for all citizens; significant numbers are even willing to pay more taxes for expanded coverage. Not surprisingly, nearly everyone is concerned over the high and growing costs of health services and insurance premiums. There appears to be considerable backing for basic revision of the existing system as well.[32]

Notwithstanding these views, the most recent fiscal crisis—engendered by the irresponsible banking and investment industries—has put considerable financial obstacles in the path of health care reform. Along with state budgetary shortfalls across the nation, hundreds of billions of dollars have been drained from the federal treasury to bail out the financial and automobile industries and to fund the stimulus package, over and above our costly war spending—all of it adding to the ever-rising federal deficit.[33] Policymakers at every level of government are straining just to maintain existing public-sector health programs. Even without the current economic downturn, however, supporters of national health care would have to muster the political will to confront the ongoing, persistent, and powerful forces of the medical industries.

Although there is general agreement that the system is broken and must be revamped, partisanship and ideological divisions remain strong, as in other areas of social welfare. Central to the Republican approach is a revision of current health care arrangements through a mix of tax-based proposals, vouchers, and HSAs that are intended to lower government involvement, promote more self-financing of medical services, and place even greater control in the hands of the insurance industry.[34] Some contemporary conservatives envision a continuation of Medicaid as the mainstay of health insurance for the very poor, and most of them support the ongoing state-based restructuring that has fostered leaner benefit packages and greater beneficiary cost sharing, strategies that have weakened the program's ability to serve its clients effectively.

Nearly all Republicans are zealously pressing for further marketization, extreme individualism, more competition, and greater deregulation—generally preferring to rely on the same market forces that not only have conspicuously failed to meet the American population's health needs, but also have caused many of the problems in the first place. What is more, programs steeped in personal responsibility jargon—a central tenet of both their Medicaid and their larger health care reform initiatives—confound facts, logic, and decency. The demand for medical services is for the most part irregular and unpredictable, based on a chance assortment of genetic, socioeconomic, and environmental factors. The annual costs of health care for individual households, too, is indiscriminate and cannot be saved for. We accordingly need to pool both risks and expenditures among all Americans.

As the 2008 presidential election suggests and despite the raucous town hall meetings, more Americans have become weary of radical conservative precepts that have restricted and shaped the terms of the health care debate and Medicaid policies. Nonetheless, in their latest round of proposals for the twenty-first century, most—but not all—Democrats have abandoned the idea of a single-payer system as politically unachievable, falling back instead on weaving new approaches into existing ones.[35] The president, although pushing for comprehensive insurance for everyone and offering broad guiding principles and goals, has left the details to the congressional Democratic leadership, for whom reform is a moving target.

The employer-based system remains at the core of their approach to universal coverage. They, along with the Obama administration, envision a play-or-pay model whereby companies must offer health insurance to their employees or pay a financial penalty; small firms, which are exempt, would be induced to establish plans through tax incentives. The various Democratic proposals, including the Affordable Health Care for America Act of 2009 (H.R. 3962) and the Senate's Patient and Affordable Care Act (H.R. 3690) also incorporate a mandate that would require individuals to purchase insurance or pay a penalty, thereby rendering health care a personal responsibility rather than a right. They also call for greater regulation of commercial insurance, which, among other provisions, would prohibit the denial of coverage and higher premium costs for individuals with preexisting conditions or who are terminally ill, eliminate lifetime limits on payment for services, and set minimum standards for benefit packages.

Under both Obama's guidelines and the America's Affordable Health Choices Act, people who are not eligible for welfare medicine or who are not covered by an employer-sponsored scheme would have access to a newly established national health insurance exchange that would offer a government-run insurance option, alongside a number of market-based alternatives. Premium and cost-sharing subsidies, based on income, would be available for qualifying households. The Senate, responding to the growing and bitter aversion to the "public option," fuelled by the insurance industry and other vested interests, decided instead on state-based exchanges that must offer at least two national health plans, of which one must be a nonprofit entity.

Although all of the Democratic proposals would extend coverage to a much greater number of uninsured families at more affordable prices and put forward marginal improvements in current funding and delivery arrangements, they basically build on a fundamentally flawed system. For example, an employer mandate and the structures it relies on are not efficient or effective means of insuring working Americans and their families.[36] Company-sponsored insurance is hit and miss, especially for low-wage earners experiencing intermittent employment and for a growing number of other people whose jobs are subject to the ebb and flow of the economy. At the same time, the existing multipayer arrangements rely almost entirely on insufficiently controlled commercial markets—which foster needlessly excessive spending, particularly for non-medical-related purposes—as well as cost-shifting, misplaced priorities, an uneven distribution of services, and class-based medical care, all compounded by gender, race, ethnicity, and age issues.

Congressional Democrats are relying on an expansion of welfare medicine to a greater number of households as essential to achieving more comprehensive coverage, although with somewhat less fervor than the Republicans' for bare-bones offerings. Income thresholds would be raised nationwide to 150 percent of the federal poverty level (FPL) under H.R. 3962 and 133 percent of the FPL under the Senate bill, allowing more than 11 million additional people to qualify for the low-income health plan.[37] However, newly insured people will still face the same state-based, second-class medical care, access impediments, and other wide-ranging failings outlined in these pages. In addition, because welfare medicine is so deeply embedded in the jumble of public and private arrangements and funding sources, any serious reform of the program would reverberate throughout the system, generating problems elsewhere.

Likewise, ripple effects from alterations in other parts of the system would impinge on Medicaid. Fragmentation inhibits the effectiveness of measures to contain expenditures, enhance quality of care, or improve access to services. Each of the numerous payers, both private and public, establish their own regulations, criteria, service standards, benefit packages, and copayment levels.[38] Cost controls, for example, will be successful only if they affect all population groups uniformly. Coordinated reimbursement policies, too, are necessary for equal access to decent services. In other words, unless provider fees are the same for all consumers, policymakers cannot materially improve the availability of health professionals for low-income clients. Nor can wider Medicaid coverage work effectively under current conditions, given the maldistribution of medical services and resources, the inadequate number of nurses and nursing aides, and the insufficient availability of generalist doctors, especially relative to specialists. In fact, one of the many perverse facets of our current system is that despite an overabundance of specialists, Medicaid enrollees have inordinate difficulty in finding one who will treat them. [39]

Moreover, few proposals, including the president's, seriously address the issue of LTC, one of the most considerable challenges facing Medicaid and frail elders alike. Despite solid public support for a restructuring of and more rational funding mechanisms for assisting older and disabled people, policymakers have been highly reluctant to identify this extremely expensive component of health care as a major piece of their insurance initiatives. As noted in chapter 6, the main line of attack has been to promote individual responsibility through the purchase of private LTC insurance, induced through various forms of tax breaks, and to introduce piecemeal reforms that emphasize alternatives to institutionalization and better training for caregivers. Fierce opposition by the Health Insurance Association of America, allied with other vested interests, also has helped prevent any serious attempt to place a comprehensive publicly supported LTC system on the national agenda.[40]

Political officials must move beyond an approach that cobbles together the deficient Medicare and Medicaid programs and the unsound, erratic employer-sponsored system and that merely adds new mechanisms to pick up the pieces. For the most part, the president and the Democratic leadership are suggesting more of the same, inequities and all, but for a greater number of people. There are no basic revisions in the organization and funding of medical practice, but rather timid initiatives that tinker with the status quo. They certainly will not control costs or enhance quality of care.[41] Most important, the current proposals do not guarantee health care as a basic right. They may be a good, even impressive start, especially given political realities, but are not a substitute for national health care. Underlying real reform must be the assumption that quality health care is a basic right.

Rather than an employer mandate or an individual mandate, we need a national government guarantee that recognizes health care as a collective responsibility. That guarantee also must be informed by the premise that medical services are not just another commercial product, but a social good that is fundamental to human life and well-being. Given the irrationality and inefficiencies inherent in multiple funding sources, including unproductive cost shifting, a single payer is a necessary component of any restructuring of medical insurance, including Medicaid itself. Like most other affluent nations, we must enact a nationally funded system of affordable universal health care that offers continuous and seamless comprehensive services. And, as part of this program, we should include a system of LTC that takes into account the dignity of frail elders and disabled younger people as well as the multiple needs of their caregivers, whether family, friends, or paid assistants. Such a fundamental overhaul of our health care system is a simple matter of social justice.

AVERAGE MANUFACTURER PRICE: The average price that wholesalers pay in the United States for drugs distributed to retail pharmacies.

AVERAGE WHOLESALE PRICE: The average price at which wholesalers sell drugs to physicians, pharmacies, and other customers.

BOREN AMENDMENT: As part of the Omnibus Budget Reconciliation Act of 1980, this amendment required that Medicaid nursing home rates be "reasonable and adequate to meet the costs which must be incurred by efficiently and economically operated facilities in order to provide care and services in conformity with applicable state and federal laws, regulations, and quality and safety standards." The federal Balanced Budget Act of 1997 repealed the Boren amendment, giving states far greater freedom in setting nursing home payment rates.

CAPITATED PLANS: See *managed-care plans.*

CATEGORICALLY ELIGIBLE GROUPS: Five specific population groups that states are allowed to cover under federal law: children up to age nineteen; pregnant women; parents (and other caretakers of children) in families with dependent children; individuals with severe and permanent disabilities; and the elderly.

CENTERS FOR MEDICARE AND MEDICAID SERVICES: Federal agency under the U.S. Department of Health and Human Services that administers Medicare, Medicaid, and the State Children's Health Insurance Program.

CERTIFIED NURSE'S AIDE: A person certified by a state agency who assists individuals with activities of daily living and provides bedside care—including basic nursing procedures—all under the supervision of a registered nurse or licensed practical nurse.

COINSURANCE: A medical insurance policy provision under which the insurer and the insured share costs incurred after the deductible is met, according to a specific formula.

COPAYMENT: See *coinsurance.*

COMMUNITY HEALTH CENTERS: Facilities that provide comprehensive primary health care and supportive services to medically underserved communities and low-income and uninsured people, either without charge or with fees based on ability to pay.

CORPORATE INTEGRITY AGREEMENTS: Agreements, usually lasting four to five years, imposed on providers by the Office of Inspector General when serious misconduct (fraudulent or abusive activities) is discovered through an audit or self-disclosure. They include instituting training requirements, designating a compliance officer, and implementing a communications hotline or other initiatives that are designed to ensure that the wrongful behavior does not occur again.

DIAGNOSIS-RELATED GROUPS: Medical claims reimbursements developed by Medicare for hospitals as part of its prospective payment system developed in the mid-1980s, whereby predetermined fees are set for roughly 500 listed procedures.

DISPROPORTIONATE SHARE HOSPITAL (DSH) PAYMENTS: Special funding to hospitals that serve a significant percentage of indigent patients, as determined by special formulas under both Medicare and Medicaid. Under federal law, "A hospital is deemed to be a DSH hospital if its Medicaid utilization rate is at least one standard deviation above the mean rate for hospitals receiving Medicaid payments in the state or if the hospital's low-income utilization rate exceeds 25 percent" (U.S.C. §1396r-4 [b] [2000]).

DUAL ELIGIBLES: Individuals who are entitled to Medicare Part A or Part B or both and are also eligible for full Medicaid benefits.

EARLY AND PERIODIC SCREENING, DIAGNOSTIC, AND TREATMENT: A required benefit for all "categorically needy" children younger than age twenty-one (e.g., those who have poverty-level income, receive Supplemental Security Income, or receive federal foster care or adoption assistance). It must cover certain screening, diagnostic, and treatment services that must be furnished at both age-appropriate periodic intervals and when needed.

FALSE CLAIMS ACT: Legislation that allows people who are not affiliated with the government to file actions against federal contractors who are fraudulently billing or overcharging the government for goods and services. Persons filing under the act ("whistle-blowers") stand to receive a portion (usually about 15 to 25 percent) of any recovered damages.

FEDERALLY QUALIFIED HEALTH CENTERS: Public and private nonprofit health care organizations that meet certain criteria under the Medicare and Medicaid programs.

FEDERALLY QUALIFIED HEALTH CENTER LOOK-ALIKES: Health centers identified by the Health Resources Services Administration and certified by the Centers for Medicare and Medicaid Services as meeting the definition of health center, although they do not receive grant funding.

FEDERAL MEDICAL ASSISTANCE PERCENTAGE: The formula that determines the federal match for state Medicaid plans and is based on the state's per capita income relative to the national average.

FEE FOR SERVICE: In health care, a payment mechanism in which a provider is paid for each service rendered to a patient.

FORMULARY: A listing of prescription drugs, brand name and generic, that are available for payment through a particular health plan.

HEALTH CARE FINANCING ADMINISTRATION: The part of the U.S. Department of Health and Human Services that is responsible for administering Medicare and Medicaid.

HEALTH OPPORTUNITY ACCOUNT: A limited government-funded savings account for Medicaid beneficiaries to pay their own health care expenses, including a substantial deductible, before they are eligible for their regular welfare medicine benefits. Demonstration projects were first authorized under the Deficit Reduction Act of 2005.

HEALTH SAVINGS ACCOUNT: A vehicle for saving money for qualified medical expenses, on a tax-free basis, for people who are enrolled in high-deductible health plans. They were established as part of the Medicare Prescription Drug Improvement and Modernization Act of 2003. They were previously called *Medical Savings Accounts*.

HOME- AND COMMUNITY-BASED SERVICES: Services provided to frail and dependent people in the home or in community settings. Allowable services include but are not limited to personal assistance, homemaker and chore services, home health services, case management, medical transportation, respite care, adult day care, rehabilitation, minor home repairs, caregiver training, and nutrition counseling.

INTERMEDIATE CARE FACILITIES FOR THE MENTALLY RETARDED: Institutions (four or more beds) for people with mental retardation and related conditions. They are required to provide "active treatment" to their clients, including aggressive rehabilitation therapies that enable individuals to function with as much self-determination and independence as possible and that prevent or decelerate the regression or loss of current optimal functional status.

LONG-TERM CARE: Services of long duration that are provided to frail and dependent people in the home, community, or institutional facilities.

LOOK-BACK PERIOD: The time preceding a person's application for Medicaid (currently five years) during which any asset transfers may prevent her or him from receiving Medicaid long-term care benefits until that period expires.

MANAGED-CARE ORGANIZATIONS: Insurance companies that offer health plans to individuals, employers, or the government on a prepaid basis. The firms in turn contract with certain health care providers and medical facilities that form the restricted network from which participants can receive services.

MANAGED-CARE PLANS: Health plans that are offered by managed-care organizations. In this book, the terms *managed-care plan, capitated plan, prepaid plan*, and *risk-based plan* are used interchangeably.

MEDICAID MANAGED-CARE PLANS: Managed-care plans where the state governments pay set premiums to insurance companies serving Medicaid clients.

MANDATORY POPULATION GROUPS: Categorical population groups that the states are required to cover under federal law that include families with dependent children who are eligible for a state's cash assistance program (Temporary Assistance for Needy Families and previously Aid to Families with Dependent Children); children younger than age six whose family income is at or less than 133 percent of the federal poverty level (FPL); children up to eighteen years old in families with incomes at or less than the FPL; pregnant women whose family income is below 133 percent of the FPL (services to women are limited to those related to pregnancy, complications of pregnancy, delivery, and postpartum care); elderly and disabled Supplemental Security Income recipients; and children who are adopted or are in foster care.

MEDICAID FRAUD CONTROL UNITS (MFCUS): State law enforcement entities, first created in 1977, that investigate and prosecute provider fraud and violations of state law pertaining to fraud in the administration of the Medicaid program. In addition, the MFCUs are required to review complaints of resident abuse or neglect in nursing homes and other health care facilities.

MEDICAL LOSS RATIO: In health insurance, the fraction of revenue from a plan's premiums that goes to pay for medical services.

"MEDICAID MILLS": Medical and dental practices as well as pharmacies that provide high-volume services; unnecessary examinations, tests, and procedures; and shoddy care exclusively to welfare medicine patients for the purpose of profiting from the low-income health programs.

MEDICALLY NEEDY POPULATION: People who are able to pay everyday living expenses but cannot afford their health care bills. They must spend down their resources to meet program eligibility levels.

MEDICAL SAVINGS ACCOUNT: See *Health Savings Account.*

OPTIONAL POPULATION GROUPS: Categorically related population groups that the states are allowed to cover under federal law. These optional groups share the characteristics of the mandatory groups, but the eligibility criteria for them are somewhat more liberally defined. These groups include infants up to age one and pregnant women not covered under the mandatory rules whose family income is less than 185 percent of the federal poverty level (the percentage is set by each state); optional targeted low-income children; certain aged, blind, or disabled adults who have incomes up to 300 percent of the federal Supplemental Security Income (SSI) benefit; children younger than age twenty-one who meet income and resources requirements for Aid to Families with Dependent Children (AFDC), but who otherwise are not eligible for AFDC; people who are medically needy, as defined by each state; recipients of state SSI supplementary payments; tuberculosis-infected persons who would be financially eligible for Medicaid at the SSI level (only for tuberculosis-related ambulatory services and drugs); and low-income, uninsured women screened and diagnosed through the Centers for Disease Control Breast and Cervical Cancer Early Detection Program and determined to be in need of treatment for breast or cervical cancer.

PREPAID PLANS: See *managed-care plans.*

PROSPECTIVE PAYMENT SYSTEM: In health care, a payment system where reimbursement rates to health providers are set, for a given period of time, prior to the medical conditions generating the reimbursement claims.

PROVIDER TAXES AND DONATIONS: Surcharges on health providers, whether voluntary or mandatory, that states often use to generate an additional federal match for their Medicaid programs.

QUALIFIED MEDICARE BENEFICIARIES: Individuals who are entitled to Medicare Part A, have incomes at or below the federal poverty level, own assets under a specified federal limit, and are not otherwise eligible for Medicaid. Medicaid pays their Medicare Part A and Part B premiums and, depending on the state plan, their Medicare deductibles and coinsurance for services supplied by Medicare providers. Qualified Medicare Beneficiaries who are fully entitled to Medicaid must meet similar requirements and receive the same benefits, but they receive services by Medicaid providers, as stipulated under their state Medicaid plan.

QUALIFIED INDIVIDUALS: See *Specified Low-Income Medicare Beneficiaries.*

REBATE AGREEMENTS: Money that pharmaceutical firms must give back to the state based on either the difference between a drug company's best price (lowest charge to providers, managed-are organizations, and nonprofit or government entities) and the average manufacturer price (the mean price paid by wholesalers for drugs distributed to retail pharmacies), or 15.1 percent, whichever is greater.

REAL ESTATE INVESTMENT TRUSTS (REITS): In health care, small trusts that buy, develop, and manage hospitals, nursing homes, medical office buildings, and assisted-living residences. Some health REITs also finance these properties and sometimes keep the mortgages in their portfolios.

RISK-BASED PLANS: See *managed-care plans.*

SECTION 1115 WAIVERS: These waivers allow states to disregard certain Medicaid regulations as part of any experimental, pilot, or demonstration project that promotes the program's overall goals.

SECTION 1915(B) WAIVERS: These waivers permit states to waive Medicaid's "freedom-of-choice" requirement, thereby allowing them to implement managed care or other limits to an individual's choice of provider.

SECTION 1915(C) HOME- AND COMMUNITY-BASED SERVICE WAIVERS: These waivers allow states to substitute limited amounts of at-home and other assistance in lieu of institutional care.

SPECIFIED LOW-INCOME MEDICARE BENEFICIARIES: Individuals who are entitled to Medicare Part A have incomes between 100 and 120 percent of the federal poverty level, own assets under a specified federal limit, and are not otherwise eligible for Medicaid. Medicaid pays their Medicare Part B premiums only. Specified Low-Income Medicare Beneficiaries who are fully entitled to Medicaid must meet similar requirements, obtain payment for Medicare Part B premiums, and receive full Medicaid benefits under their state plan. The federal government provides the states with additional but limited funds to assist elders with incomes from 120 percent to 135 percent of the federal poverty level (qualified individuals).

++

SPEND DOWN: People with higher incomes can qualify for Medicaid if they have medical bills equal to or greater than the amount by which their income exceeds the medically needy income levels in participating states.

UPPER PAYMENT LIMITS: Nationally mandated ceilings on state Medicaid expenditures that are eligible for federal matching funds for certain types of services.

1. Introduction

1. Throughout this book, I use the terms *Medicaid, welfare medicine,* and *low-income health program* interchangeably.

2. Some of the more outstanding books include Robert Stevens and Rosemary Stevens, *Welfare Medicine in America: A Case Study of Medicaid* (New Brunswick, N.J.: Transaction, 2003); Theresa A. Coughlin, Leighton Ku, and John Holahan, *Medicaid Since 1980: Costs, Coverage, and Shifting Alliance Between the Federal Government and the States* (Washington, D.C.: Urban Institute, 1994); Jonathan Engel, *Poor People's Medicine: Medicaid and American Charity Care Since 1965* (Durham, N.C.: Duke University Press, 2006); Michael S. Sparer, *Medicaid and the Limits of State Health Reform* (Philadelphia: Temple University Press, 1996); David G. Smith and Judith D. Moore, *Medicaid Politics and Policy: 1965–2007* (New Brunswick, N.J.: Transaction, 2008).

3. In 2007, Medicaid was estimated to cover between 49 million and 62 million people, depending on the month. In contrast, Medicare served an average of 44 million people (37 million elderly and 7 million disabled adults). U.S. Department of Health and Human Services, Centers for Medicare and Medicaid Services, Office of the Actuary, *2008 Actuarial Report: On the Financial Outlook for Medicaid* (Washington, D.C.: U.S. Government Printing Office, October 17, 2008).

In 2008, another 6.6 million children and their parents participated in SCHIP at a cost of some $6 billion annually. In 2009, Congress added another $65 billion over ten years to extend the program to roughly 4 million more children.

4. Victoria Wachino, *The New Medicaid Integrity Program: Issues and Challenges in Ensuring Program Integrity in Medicaid* (Menlo Park, Calif.: Henry J. Kaiser Family Foundation, Kaiser Commission on Medicaid and the Uninsured, June 2007), available at http://www.kff.org.

5. Cindy Mann, "The Flexibility Factor: Finding the Right Balance," *Health Affairs* 22, no. 1 (January–February 2003): 62–76.

6. In 2007, the federal outlays were: Social Security, $586.2 billion; national defense, $552.6 billion; Medicare, $375.4 billion; and Medicaid, $190.6 billion.

7. In 2008, Medicaid averaged roughly 21 percent of state budgets. National Governors Association and National Association of Budget Officers, *The Fiscal Survey of States* (Washington, D.C.: U.S. Government Printing Office, June 2008).

8. Martin Gilens, *Why Americans Hate Welfare: Race, Media, and the Politics of Antipoverty Policy* (Chicago: University of Chicago Press, 1999). In 1996, AFDC was replaced with the more limited TANF.

9. The term *medical industrial complex* was first introduced by Barbara Ehrenreich and John Ehrenreich in their book *The American Health Empire: Power, Profits, and Politics* (New York: Random House, 1970).

10. Other influential groups at the state level include utility companies and lawyers.

11. Clive S. Thomas and Ronald J. Hrebenar, "Interest Groups in the States," in Virginia Gray and Russell L. Hanson, eds., *Politics in the American States: A Comparative Analysis*, 8th ed., 100–129 (Washington, D.C.: Congressional Quarterly Press, 2004).

12. Younger disabled adults utilize HCBS primarily as opposed to nursing homes.

13. Thomas and Hrebenar, "Interest Groups in the States"; Mann, "The Flexibility Factor"; Alan Rosenthal, *The Third House: Lobbyists and Lobbying in the States*, 2d ed. (Washington, D.C.: Congressional Quarterly Press, 2001).

14. In 2006, 36.5 million people (12.3 percent of the U.S. population) were living in poverty; about 42 percent of them had a household income below half of the official FPL. The average weighted poverty threshold for a family of four was $20,614 per annum. For individuals sixty-five or older and younger single adults, the threshold was $9,669 and $10,488, respectively. Carmen DeNavas-Walt, Bernadette Proctor, and Jessica Smith, *Income, Poverty, and Health Insurance Coverage in the U.S.: 2006*, U.S. Census Bureau Current Population Report, P60-233 (Washington, D.C.: U.S. Government Printing Office, 2007); U.S. Bureau of the Census, *Income, Poverty, and Health Insurance Coverage in the United States: 2004*, 2005 and Earlier Annual Social and Economic Supplements to the Current Population Survey (Washington, D.C.: U.S. Government Printing Office, 2005).

15. Henry J. Kaiser Family Foundation, Kaiser Commission on Medicaid and the Uninsured, *Health Insurance Coverage in America: A 2005 Data Update* (Menlo Park, Calif.: Henry J. Kaiser Family Foundation, Kaiser Commission on Medicaid and the Uninsured, November 2006), available at http://www.kff.org.

16. Throughout the book, the term *managed-care organizations* is used to represent all types of capitated arrangements, including health-maintenance organizations.

17. Laura Katz Olson, *The Not-So-Golden Years: Caregiving, the Frail Elderly, and the Long-Term Care Establishment* (Lanham, Md.: Roman and Littlefield, 2003).

18. At birth, men have a life expectancy of 75.2 years, compared to 80.4 for women. The disparity for blacks is even greater: 69.8 years and 76.5 years for black men and black women, respectively, compared to 75.7 years and 80.8 years for white men and white women. U.S. Department of Health and Human Services, National Center for Health Statistics, *Life Expectancy at Birth*, National Vital Statistics Report 54, no. 19 (Hyattsville, Md.: Centers for Disease Control and Prevention, June 28, 2006).

19. DeNavas-Walt, Proctor, and Smith, *Income, Poverty, and Health Insurance Coverage in the U.S.*

20. Henry J. Kaiser Family Foundation, Kaiser Commission on Medicaid and the Uninsured, *An Update on Women's Health Policy, Medicaid's Role for Women*, issue brief (Menlo Park, Calif.: Henry J. Kaiser Family Foundation, Kaiser Commission on Medicaid and the Uninsured, May 2006), available at http://www.kff.org.

21. Of all women in 2004, 10 percent participated in Medicaid, 17 percent in Medicare, 58 percent in employer-sponsored insurance, and 15 percent in no program (uninsured). Ibid.

22. Of the nonelderly women participating in Medicaid, 49 percent are white, 24 percent black, 21 percent Latina, 4 percent Asian/Pacific Islander, and 1 percent American Indian/Aleutian Eskimo. Another 1 percent is considered multiracial. Ibid.

23. In 2006, the poverty rate for various groups was: non-Latino whites, 8.2 percent; blacks, 24.3 percent; Latinos, 20.6 percent; and Asians, 10.3 percent. DeNavas-Walt, Proctor, and Smith, *Income, Poverty, and Health Insurance Coverage in the U.S.*

24. In 2005, 9.3 percent of non-Latino whites, 25.2 percent of blacks, 21.6 percent of Latinos, 8.6 percent of Asians/Pacific Islanders, and 19.7 percent of American Indians/ Alaskan Natives participated in Medicaid. Henry J. Kaiser Family Foundation, *Health Insurance Coverage in America*.

Coverage of Hispanics, however, varies widely by ethnicity: the percentage of Puerto Ricans participating in Medicaid is the highest (33 percent), as compared to Mexicans (18 percent), Cubans (15 percent), and Central or South Americans (13 percent). Institute of Medicine, *Unequal Treatment: Confronting Racial and Ethnic Disparities in Health Care* (Washington, D.C.: National Academies Press, 2003).

25. Henry J. Kaiser Family Foundation, Kaiser Commission on Medicaid and the Uninsured, *The Uninsured: A Primer. Key Facts About Americans Without Health Insurance* (Menlo Park, Calif.: Henry J. Kaiser Family Foundation, Kaiser Commission on Medicaid and the Uninsured, October 2006), available at http://www.kff.org.; Henry J. Kaiser Family Foundation, *Health Insurance Coverage in America*.

26. Institute of Medicine, *Unequal Treatment*.

27. Ibid.; U.S. Department of Health and Human Services (DHS), Agency for Healthcare Research and Quality (AHRQ), *National Healthcare Disparities Report, 2007*, Publication no. 08-0040 (Rockville, Md.: AHRQ, February 2008), available at http://www. ahrq.gov/QUAL/nhqr07/nhdr07.pdf; Amal N. Trived, Alan Zaslausky, Eric Schneider, and John Ayanian, "Relationship Between Quality of Care and Racial Disparities in Medicare Health Plans," *Journal of the American Medical Association* 296, no. 16 (October 25, 2006): 1998–2003.

28. Institute of Medicine, *Unequal Treatment*.

29. U.S. DHS AHRQ, *National Healthcare Disparities Report, 2007.*

30. Kant Patel and Mark E. Rushefsky, *Health Care in America: Separate and Unequal* (Armonk, N.Y.: M. E. Sharpe, 2008).

31. In April 2005, a survey by Princeton Survey Research Associates International asked: "Next, I have a few general questions about the Medicaid program. First I would like to read you a definition of Medicaid that I will read to everyone who is taking our survey. Medicaid is a government program for low-income people whose costs are shared by both the federal government and state governments. It provides health insurance and long term care assistance to eligible children and their parents, elderly, and people with disabilities. . . . During the past year, how much, if anything, have you personally seen, heard, or read about the issue of Medicaid? A lot, some, only a little, or nothing at all?" Nearly two-thirds of the respondents had some (30 percent) or only a little (34 percent) awareness of the program, and another 14 percent knew nothing at all about it. Henry J. Kaiser Family Foundation, *National Survey on the Public's Views About Medicaid*, methodology: conducted by Princeton Survey Research Associates International, April 1–May 1, 2005, with a national adult sample of 1, 201 (Menlo Park, Calif.: Henry J. Kaiser Family Foundation, 2005).

32. Fay Lomax Cook and Meredith B. Czaplewski, "Public Opinion and Social Insurance: The American Experience," paper presented at the 2008 Annual Meeting of the American Political Science Association, August 29, 2008, Boston.

33. Henry J. Kaiser Family Foundation, *National Survey on the Public's Views About Medicaid.*

34. Ibid.; Mark E. Rushefsky and Kant Patel, *Politics, Power, and Policy Making: The Case of Health Care Reform in the 1990s* (Armonk, N.Y.: M. E. Sharpe, 1998); Fay Lomax Cook and Edith J. Barrett, *Support for the American Welfare State: The Views of Congress and the Public* (New York: Columbia University Press, 1992); Coughlin, Ku, and Holahan, *Medicaid Since 1980.*

35. Cook and Barrett, *Support for the American Welfare State.* According to the authors, researchers who identify social programs as *welfare*—a term that has negative connotations—on their questionnaires tend to produce more negative results. Certain policymakers, self-serving groups, and complicit members of the mass media have rendered *welfare*—like *women's liberation* and *liberal*—a dirty word in American society; however, although the public may abhor the term, they generally support the underlying goal of assisting needy segments of society.

36. Cook and Barrett found that more than 95 percent supported preserving or enlarging funding to Social Security, Medicare, and SSI; only 3 percent wanted reductions. Ibid., 62.

37. For example, a Harris poll in April 1990 asked: "If you had to choose, would you prefer to see sharp cuts in . . . Medicaid benefits . . . or in defense spending?" Fully 82 percent of the respondents chose to cut defense spending, another 15 percent to cut other programs, and 3 percent to cut both or neither program. Louis Harris and Associates, *Harris Poll on Medicaid, April 1990*, survey, methodology: conducted April 26–May 2, 1990, with a national adult sample of 1,255 (Hamden: Roper Center for Public

Opinion Research, University of Connecticut, 1990), retrieved from the iPoll Databank, September 2, 2008, available at http://www.kff.org/kaiserpolls/healthpolls.cfm.

In May 1995, during the mayhem between Clinton and Congress, voters were asked: "A number of spending reductions have been proposed in order to balance the federal budget and avoid raising taxes. Would you favor or oppose making major spending reductions in . . . Medicaid?" Fully 65 percent of those polled were against cutting welfare medicine. Henry J. Kaiser Family Foundation and Harvard School of Public Health, *National Survey of Public Knowledge of the Medicare Program and Public Support for Medicare Policy Proposals*, methodology: conducted by Louis Harris and Associates, May 31–June 5, 1995, with a national adult sample of 1,383, available at http://www.kff .org/kaiserpolls/healthpoll.cfm.

In November 1996, respondents were asked: "I'm going to read you some areas in which the federal government spends most of its money. Keeping in mind that the federal government now has a budget deficit, please tell me if you think federal spending should be increased, decreased, or kept about the same as it is now in each of the following areas. What about federal spending for . . . Medicaid?" In this survey, 78 percent of those polled showed support for the program: 26 percent chose to increase funding, and 52 percent to keep it as is. Henry J. Kaiser Family Foundation and Harvard School of Public Health, *Health Care Agenda for the Next Congress*, survey, methodology: conducted by Princeton Survey Research Associates, November 6–10, 1996, with national self-described voters in the 1996 election sample of 1,000 (Storrs: Roper Center for Public Opinion Research, University of Connecticut, 1996), retrieved from the iPoll Databank, September 2, 2008, available at http://www.kff.org/kaiserpolls/ healthpolls.cfm.

38. The survey also found that 90 percent of the public viewed their state as having budget problems or experiencing a crisis situation and that 38 percent of them attributed the fiscal problems to Medicaid. Nevertheless, slightly more than 70 percent of the respondents did not favor cutting Medicaid to balance the budget. Moreover, nearly 80 percent of the people polled preferred maintaining current federal spending levels on Medicaid (44 percent) or increasing them (36 percent). Henry J. Kaiser Family Foundation, *National Survey on the Public's Views About Medicaid.*

39. Eighty-five percent of the respondents described the state's fiscal condition as either poor or fair. When asked which of the two largest expenditures in the state budget should be cut (education or heath care), 26 percent said health care, and 24 percent indicated education. However, 21 percent proposed that neither of them should be reduced, 10 percent said to decrease something else, 4 percent suggested lowering salaries, and another 4 percent wanted to cut both education and health care. Health Care Association of New York State, *New York Monthly Survey*, methodology: conducted by Siena Research Institute, August 11–24, 2008, with a New York State registered voter sample of 627 (Loudonville, N.Y.: Siena Research Institute, 2008).

40. AARP, *Opinions on the Budget Among U.S. Adults*, survey, methodology: conducted by International Communications Research, January 4–9, 2006, with a national adult sample of 1,026 (Washington, D.C.: AARP, 2006).

An earlier AARP poll (2005) produced similar results: when asked about current state funding levels, 57 percent of respondents said that there was not enough money in the Medicaid budget to pay for health and LTC in their state. AARP, *Medicaid Poll*, survey, methodology: conducted by International Communications Research, April 20–24, 2005, with a national adult sample of 1,011 (Washington, D.C.: AARP, 2005).

41. Cook and Czaplewski, "Public Opinion and Social Insurance."

42. In addition, the divergent approval ratings were somewhat larger than those for Social Security (Democrats, 90 percent; Independents, 87 percent; and Republicans, 89 percent), and Medicare (91 percent, 82 percent, and 78 percent, respectively). Henry J. Kaiser Family Foundation, *National Survey on the Public's Views About Medicaid.*

43. There also was a notable gender divide within Republicans: 62 percent of women as compared to 46 percent of men supported the SCHIP reauthorization and expansion act. Survey by the Henry J. Kaiser Family Foundation, Harvard School of Public Health, and National Public Radio, *Views and Opinions of State Health Insurance Program (SCHIP)*, methodology: conducted October 8–13, 2007, with a national adult sample of 1,527 (Menlo Park, Calif.: Henry J. Kaiser Family Foundation, 2007).

44. For example, in a May 2008 poll of registered voters by Quinnipiac University, when asked, "Do you think that it's the government's responsibility to make sure that everyone in the United States has adequate health care, or don't you think so?" 81 percent of Democrats, 59 percent of Independents, and 34 percent of Republicans responded that they "think it is." Quinnipiac University Polling Institute, *Quinnipiac University Poll, May 2008*, methodology: conducted May 8–17, 2008, with a national registered voter sample of 1,745 (Hamden: Roper Center for Public Opinion Research, University of Connecticut, 2008), retrieved from the iPoll Databank, September 4, 2008, available at http://www.pollingreport.com/health3.htm.

In an earlier poll, Quinnipiac University researchers asked: "If you had to say, which do you think is a more serious problem right now: keeping health care costs down for average Americans, or providing health insurance for Americans who do not have any insurance?" Seventy-one percent of Democrats, as compared to 53 percent of Independents and 33 percent of Republicans, indicated that it was more important to cover the uninsured than to keep costs down. Quinnipiac University Polling Institute, *Quinnipiac University Poll, October 2007*, survey, Methodology: conducted October 23–29, 2007, with a national registered voter sample of 1,636 (Hamden, Conn.: Roper Center for Public Opinion Research, University of Connecticut, 2007), retrieved from the iPoll Databank, September 4, 2008, available at http://www.pollingreport.com/health3.htm.

45. Fully 82 percent of the respondents thought it essential that Medicaid coverage include nursing home care, nearly as many as the 87 percent who viewed hospital stays and prescription drugs as vital components of the program. Henry J. Kaiser Family Foundation, *National Survey on the Public's Views About Medicaid.*

46. Of 12.9 million people participating in AFDC in 1996, 38 percent were white; 37 percent black; 19 percent Latino; 3 percent Asian American; 1 percent American Indian; and 2 percent other race/ethnicity.

2. The Launching of Medicaid

1. E. Richard Brown, *Rockefeller Medicine Men: Medicine and Capitalism in America* (Berkeley and Los Angeles: University of California Press, 1979).

2. Emily Friedman, "The Compromise and the Afterthought: Medicare and Medicaid After 30 Years," *Journal of the American Medical Association* 274, no. 3 (July 19, 1995): 278–282.

3. Brown, *Rockefeller Medicine Men.*

4. Jill Quadagno, *One Nation Uninsured: Why the U.S. Has No National Health Insurance* (Oxford, U.K.: Oxford University Press, 2005).

5. Vigorous lobbying by the AHA—then representing nonprofits for the most part—engendered the Hill-Burton Act in 1946. Subsidizing the construction of hospitals up to one-third of their costs, this act soon became the national government's primary involvement in health issues. In 1954, Congress amended the legislation to authorize federal money for the construction of certain public and nonprofit nursing homes. Robert Stevens and Rosemary Stevens, *Welfare Medicine in America: A Case Study of Medicaid* (New Brunswick, N.J.: Transaction, 2003). This book is the most comprehensive early account of Medicaid to date.

6. At the time, there were nearly 12.3 million aged persons in the United States, representing 8.1 percent of the population. Theodore R. Marmor, *The Politics of Medicare* (Chicago: Alpine, 1970).

7. Ibid.

8. Laurene A. Graig, *Health of Nations: An International Perspective on U.S. Health Care Reform* (Washington, D.C.: Congressional Quarterly Press, 1999), 177.

9. The legislation had been Mills's attempt to prevent health care insurance for all elders.

10. Quadagno, *One Nation Uninsured.*

11. The blind and disabled were included two years later.

12. Stevens and Stevens, *Welfare Medicine in America.*

13. "Care Plan Begun in Pennsylvania; Payments for Aged Patients Based on Kerr-Mills Law, Other Costs Included," *New York Times*, special edition, March 18, 1962.

14. Stevens and Stevens, *Welfare Medicine in America.*

15. Marmor, *The Politics of Medicare.*

16. Representative John Byrnes (R–Wisc.) had sponsored the initial Republican substitute legislation. Ibid.

17. Quadagno, *One Nation Uninsured.*

18. Stevens and Stevens, *Welfare Medicine in America.*

19. Ibid., 73.

20. Optional services included prescription drugs, eyeglasses, in-patient psychiatric care for the aged and children under age twenty-one, physical therapy, dental care, and other services.

21. After the enactment of SSI for the elderly and the disabled, their eligibility for Medicaid was tied to this national income standard.

22. Colleen M. Grogan and Eric M. Patashnik, "Universalism Within Targeting: Nursing Home Care, the Middle Class, and the Politics of the Medicaid Program," *Social Service Review* 77, no. 1 (March 2003): 51–71.

23. From a statement by Dr. Willging, director of the 1976 National Governors Association's Medicaid Task Force, in Nancy Hicks, "Governors Discuss Medicaid Reforms," *New York Times*, September 23, 1976, 19.

24. During the 1960s and 1970s, the percentage of general practitioners per 100,000 people in the United States actually declined. The AMA prevented the establishment of additional medical schools, encouraged the rise of specialists, and endorsed a growing focus on research. Jonathan Engel, *Poor People's Medicine: Medicaid and American Charity Care Since 1965* (Durham, N.C.: Duke University Press, 2006).

25. Ibid.; U.S. Congress, Congressional Budget Office (CBO), *Background Paper: Health Differentials Between White and Nonwhite Americans* (Washington, D.C.: U.S. Government Printing Office, September 1977).

26. Stevens and Stevens, *Welfare Medicine in America.*

27. Quadagno, *One Nation Uninsured.*

28. Section 1115 waivers allow states to disregard certain Medicaid regulations as part of any experimental, pilot, or demonstration project that promotes the program's overall goals. They initially had to apply to HEW—and later to the Department of Health and Human Services—for such waivers.

29. Optional services could include: prescription drugs; optometrist services and eyeglasses; emergency hospitalization; clinic services; dental services and dentures; prosthetic devices; hospice care; services by podiatrists, chiropractors, or other licensed health professionals; psychological services; private-duty nurses; personal care services; case management; and physical, occupational, and speech therapy. In 1971, Congress authorized states to offer in-patient psychiatric services for beneficiaries younger than twenty-one. It also allowed funding for care of the mentally disabled in ICFs-MR, an option that nearly all of the states rapidly adopted because they had been the primary payers of such services. By 1984, ICF services for the mentally disabled grew to 12 percent of total welfare medicine spending, although the percentage subsequently declined to 7.7 percent by 1992. Theresa A. Coughlin, Leighton Ku, and John Holahan, *Medicaid Since 1980: Costs, Coverage, and Shifting Alliance Between the Federal Government and the States* (Washington, D.C.: Urban Institute, 1994).

30. Colleen Grogan and Eric Patashnik, "Between Welfare Medicine and Mainstream Entitlement: Medicaid at the Political Crossroads," *Journal of Health Politics, Policy, and Law* 28, no. 1 (October 2003): 821–858.

31. Engel, *Poor People's Medicine.*

32. Under Medicaid managed-care plans, the state pays insurance companies a set premium to provide for the medical needs of the companies' welfare medicine clients. The companies, in turn, contract with certain health providers and medical facilities, which form the restricted network from which participants can receive services. In this book, the terms *managed care, capitated plans, prepaid plans,* and *health-maintenance organizations* are used interchangeably.

33. In 1977, President Carter put forward the Child Health Assessment Program, which proposed to increase federal grants for the EPSDT Program, extend coverage to needy children from families with two working parents, and include more prenatal care. Engel, *Poor People's Medicine.*

34. An estimated 35 to 40 million persons were potentially eligible for medical assistance. "Free Medicine Out of Hand in the U.S.," *U.S. News & World Report* 64 (April 8, 1968): 86–88.

35. The Federal Medical Assistance Percentages, used to determine the amount of federal matching funds to each state, are calculated annually using a formula in section 1905(b) of the Social Security Act. It is also based on a state's comparative per capita income.

36. Stevens and Stevens, *Welfare Medicine in America,* 79, 81.

37. Ronald Sullivan, "New York Seeking Medicaid Patients," *New York Times,* October 28, 1976.

38. Quadagno, *One Nation Uninsured.* These states included New York, California, Connecticut, and Massachusetts.

39. For example, Vermont, which had been paying large sums for institutional care out of its own pocket, was anxious to subsidize these costs through federal dollars. Stevens and Stevens, *Welfare Medicine in America,* 106 n. 66.

40. Sharing costs with its counties, New York had paid medical expenses for its needy residents since 1929. Its relatively heavy health care outlays would now be shared by the federal government, which would allow the state to be even more generous. Indeed, Governor Rockefeller touted his state's expansive Medicaid program as one for which Washington would bear the brunt of the cost. Ibid.

California's Medi-Cal program, also sizeable, provided comprehensive benefits and covered all of the groups allowed under federal guidelines. Prior to Medi-Cal, California had a relatively generous health care program for the indigent population, including an extensive public county-based hospital system. Michael S. Sparer, *Medicaid and the Limits of State Health Reform* (Philadelphia: Temple University Press, 1996).

41. "Medicare: Expensive and Successful; Medicaid, Chaotic but Irrevocable," *Time* magazine 90 (October 6, 1967): 96–97; Friedman, "The Compromise and the Afterthought"; "What the Doctor Ordered: Problems of Medicare and Medicaid," *Time* magazine 88 (August 26, 1966): 13.

With its income eligibility first set at $6,000 per annum for a family of four, New York's program provoked the greatest controversy. In its first year of operation, nearly 6 million people—fully one-third of the population—could potentially meet the requirements, including a significant number of low-wage workers. Similarly, Massachusetts established its level at $5,400, the second highest in the nation, followed by Rhode Island at $4,300. The rest of the states participating in 1966 and 1967 set their ceiling at between $3,000 and $4,000, with a low of $2,448 in Oklahoma. "Medicaid in the Billions—Getting out of Hand," *U.S. News & World Report* 63 (October 16, 1967): 32–34; "More Federal Billions for Medicaid Bills," *U.S. News & World Report* 61 (November 28, 1966): 13.

42. Wyoming, for example, offered the least services allowable under the legislation. "The Mess in Medicaid," *Time* magazine 95 (January 12, 1970): 32–33.

Other states with narrow programs included Hawaii, Illinois, Minnesota, North Dakota, Oklahoma, and Pennsylvania. Stevens and Stevens, *Welfare Medicine in America*.

A few places, however reluctant to join Medicaid, enhanced somewhat their existing health services for the poor. Idaho, for instance, inserted a new category for children under the age of twenty-one, and Louisiana added services such as X rays, emergency rooms, clinical laboratories, and at-home care. Engel, *Poor People's Medicine*.

43. For example, South Carolina, ranking at the bottom of the states in per capita expenditures for social welfare programs in general, put into effect its bare-bones Medicaid program at a cost of only $3.2 million to the state, garnering $12.8 million from Washington. "The Mess in Medicaid."

The other sixteen states with only public-assistance Medicaid recipients were Georgia, Idaho, Louisiana, Maine, Missouri, Montana, Nevada, New Mexico, Ohio, Oregon, South Carolina, South Dakota, Texas, Vermont, West Virginia, and Wyoming. "Free Medicine Out of Hand in the U.S."

44. The later-joining states included Alabama, Arkansas, Colorado, Florida, Indiana, Mississippi, New Jersey, North Carolina, Tennessee, and Virginia. "Breaking the Bank," *Science News* 95 (May 1969): 497–498; "Free Medicine Out of Hand."

45. The latter two, concerned that costs associated with American Indians, Aleuts, and Eskimos would be much greater than their current outlays for low-income health services, chose to sit on the sidelines for a while. A few years later, in 1974, Alaska established a program. Arizona did not launch its Medicaid program until 1982, and, as discussed later, it was the first plan allowed to mandate managed care statewide.

46. Congress had predicted that its initial portion of Medicaid outlays would be only $238 million more than Kerr-Mills, yet it rose to $770 million by the end of 1966; its share of New York's program alone proved to be $217 million, followed by California ($210 million), Pennsylvania ($100 million), Illinois ($40 million), and Minnesota ($39 million). Stevens and Stevens, *Welfare Medicine in America*, 106.

The following year, 1967, overall spending rose 57 percent. Grogan and Patashnik, "Between Welfare Medicine and Mainstream Entitlement."

47. Under the amendments, the states would not be allowed to set their medically needy levels higher than a certain percentage of their cash-assistance programs (i.e., 150 percent, 140 percent, and 133 percent of their AFDC programs in 1968, 1969, and 1970, respectively).

48. Quadagno, *One Nation Uninsured*.

49. U.S. Congress, Senate, Committee on Labor and Human Resources, Special Subcommittee on Aging, *Extended Care Services and Facilities for the Aging*, 91st Cong., 2d sess., May 18, 1970.

50. At the time, these health providers accounted for about 29 percent of total welfare medicine outlays. "Breaking the Bank."

51. The 1972 legislation also federalized aid to the elderly, blind, and disabled poor under the new SSI program and permitted states to include these groups under their

Medicaid programs. David G. Smith, *Entitlement Politics: Medicare and Medicaid 1995–2001* (New York: De Gruyter, 2002).

52. Deductibles were initially allowed only on noninstitutional services for the medically needy.

53. "Medicaid Patients Face New Charges," *New York Times*, July 2, 1973, 60.

54. Hospital costs increased at about 15 percent annually—at times reaching 18 percent— during the 1970s.

55. The number of clients nationwide rose from 4 million people in 1966 to more than 11 million in 1980.

56. Quadagno, *One Nation Uninsured*.

57. Grogan and Patashnik, "Between Welfare Medicine and Mainstream Entitlement." By the end of the 1970s, six states continued to dominate the Medicaid program financially—New York, California, Pennsylvania, Illinois, Michigan, and Massachusetts—representing 51 percent of total outlays.

58. By January 1968, 3.5 million people had enrolled, about 58 percent of the eligible population. "Free Medicine out of Hand."

59. Governor Rockefeller strongly supported the program, although he had to defend it against fellow Republicans and upstate political leaders of both parties, all of whom became increasingly alarmed by the escalating outlays.

60. In 1966, for example, the legislators enacted a bill requiring families with incomes between $4,500 and $7,500 to pay at least 1 percent of their medical bills, with the exception of hospital services, before receiving any assistance. Before long, supported by requirements of the 1967 congressional amendments, the legislators gradually lowered eligibility levels from $6,000 per year for a family of four to $5,000 by 1970. All employed adults younger than age sixty-five also were disqualified from the program, unless their medical costs exceeded 25 percent of their net income. As a result, more than a million people lost their Medicaid coverage the first year the cuts went into effect.

61. In its first sixteen months, Medi-Cal amounted to $130 million more than budgeted. By 1971, the program costs reached $1 billion.

62. "Medicaid: A Big Headache in Some Areas," *U.S. News & World Report* 62 (April 17, 1967): 10.

63. "Free Medicine Out of Hand."

64. Maryland had the third-largest program in the nation, with the medically needy representing 70 percent of overall costs. Grogan and Patashnik, "Between Welfare Medicine and Mainstream Entitlement."

After being forced to resort to emergency funds, Maryland governor Spiro Agnew cut the eligible population considerably. However, the incoming governor, Democrat Marvin Mandel, reinstated some beneficiaries the following year; he insisted that despite ongoing budget problems, he would not abandon the needy. "Free Medicine Out of Hand."

Oklahoma both reduced its medically needy caseload and slashed overall benefits. Iowa, which had offered comprehensive services to a limited indigent population prior to launching Medicaid and now included the medically needy in its new plan, would drop them from its rolls by mid-1969. "State Medicine in Trouble in U.S.," *U.S. News & World Report* 62 (May 22, 1967): 75–76.

Utah also temporarily curtailed its program because of insufficient funds. As suggested earlier, New Mexico suspended Medicaid entirely when the plan's annual budget was depleted three-quarters through 1969, stranding 63,000 people; nearly 1,500 patients were forced to leave their nursing homes. In a short while, the state established a revised program at a lower level of services. "Breaking the Bank."

65. In New Jersey, for instance, Medicaid had reached 7 percent of the state's total expenditures by 1972, up from only 1 percent in its first year of operation. Martin Waldron, "Costs of Welfare Soar," *New York Times*, April 25, 1976, 1.

66. Hicks, "Governors Discuss Medicaid Reforms."

67. "The Federal Health Care Programs: Medicare and Medicaid," *Congressional Digest* 53 (June 1974): 164–165.

68. Nancy Hicks, "Governors Will Vote on Medicaid Reform," *New York Times*, February 27, 1977. In addition to the section 1115 waiver allowing the states to disregard selected federal Medicaid regulations such as limits on copayments, the section 1915(b) waiver permitted them to put aside the "freedom-of-choice" requirement and to mandate managed care.

69. Political leaders' assault on New York's liberal program continued unabated throughout the 1970s. At first, policymakers emphasized utilization issues alone, but by the middle of the decade Governor Hugh Carey (D) announced what he identified as a "new era" of government retrenchment. Indeed, in 1975, major U.S. cities, especially New York, teetered on the brink of financial collapse, generating massive layoffs and cutbacks in all departments and programs. The severe fiscal crisis led to austere economic policies by both the state and the city. However, eligibility and benefit reductions in Medicaid, along with cuts in hospital and nursing home reimbursement rates, were again met with fierce resistance, and many of them were delayed or reversed.

California governor Ronald Reagan didn't spare anyone: in 1970, he imposed the maximum reductions allowed by law: he ordered a 10 percent slash in fees to providers; postponed most elective surgery; limited the number of allowable physician, clinic, and dental visits; and required prior approval for eye examinations and entrance into nursing homes. The following year he requested a federal waiver to allow small copayments on doctor appointments, drugs, and glasses for all Medicaid participants. Reagan was intent on taking advantage of the section 1115 waiver provision, intended for small-scale experiments, to establish a wholesale, statewide revision in California's plan.

Facing a deficit in 1975 that required emergency funds, New Jersey endeavored over the next several years to force the substitution of generic drugs for brand names; mandate an across-the-board 10 percent reduction in provider fees, including physicians, dentists, psychologists, and pharmacists; freeze hospital reimbursements; and eliminate some or all of its optional services. An initiative to impose copayments on beneficiaries for prescription drugs, dental care, psychological services, and medical supplies was ultimately postponed. State officials also sought to meet Medicaid's growing budgetary outlays through an increase in the cigarette tax and, after its defeat in the legislature, a higher gasoline tax.

+ +

Experiencing a $100 million Medicaid deficit in 1976 alone, mostly from reduced state income, Georgia attempted to impose some of the more severe cost-cutting measures, including copayments for recipients through a section 1115 waiver; decreased reimbursements to nursing homes; and "provider agreements," signed by doctors, to control fraud. Peter Ross Range, "Medicaid in Georgia," *The Nation* (November 22, 1975): 529–530.

North Carolina, which was viewed as a potential model for other states, even attempted to privatize Medicaid. In 1975, it contracted with a Bergen Brunswick Corp. subsidiary to operate its program for two years at a fixed fee of $405 million; three-fourths of the expected profit would be returned to the state. The state's secretary of human services triumphantly declared: "We've finally put a cap on it." By the following year, however, the company ran out of money and terminated its contract, and North Carolina had to pick up the pieces. "Private Management for Medicaid," *Business Week*, May 19, 1975, 45–46.

Other states experiencing particularly challenging budgetary problems, such as Illinois and Connecticut, also attempted diverse strategies aimed at beneficiaries and providers alike.

70. Section 1915(b) of the Social Security Act permits states to waive Medicaid's "freedom-of-choice" requirement, thereby allowing them to implement managed care or other limits to an individual's choice of provider.

In 1974, New Jersey established a relatively large but voluntary demonstration project for its Newark participants (the Newark Comprehensive Health Plan), the largest of its kind to date. It was open not only to all of Newark's 113,000 current Medicaid recipients, but also to others who had slightly higher annual incomes—$6,000 for a family of four, up from $4,400 for the state's traditional Medicaid program.

New York City launched a sizeable Medicaid managed-care scheme a few years later, offering 100,000 recipients the opportunity to enroll in its city employees' program, the Health Insurance Plan of Greater New York. However, a full year after the plan had been put forward, only 11,000 people had signed up.

California, too, pioneered in such prepaid plans, attempting to shift half of its welfare medicine population into them by 1975, but succeeded in transferring less than 10 percent. California had begun prepayments for physician services in 1968 and by 1975 had forty-seven plans. That year, $84 million of the state's $2 billion Medicaid budget supported such health plans. Engel, *Poor People's Medicine*.

71. At the end of the decade, the number of individuals receiving AFDC nationally reached 11.4 million. Engel, *Poor People's Medicine*.

72. A hospital was deemed eligible for Medicare and Medicaid as long as it was accredited by the Joint Commission on Accreditation, a private agency empowered by Congress to survey and certify hospitals.

73. Stevens and Stevens, *Welfare Medicine in America*, 188; "Medicare in Trouble: Senate Study of High Costs, Abuses," *U.S. News & World Report* 68 (February 16, 1970): 70–72.

74. Although many hospitals in overserved areas had surplus beds, other places—especially rural areas—had insufficient capacity to meet its residents' needs.

75. In an attempt to limit new investment in health care infrastructure, hospitals in particular, Congress enacted the National Health Planning Development Act in 1974. It

required a certificate of need, granted through a local health systems agency, for any new construction or purchase of expensive medical equipment.

76. Engel, *Poor People's Medicine.*

77. At the turn of the twentieth century, New York City had the largest municipal hospital system in the United States. By the 1930s, it was also reimbursing private hospitals that cared for the poor. Sparer, *Medicaid and the Limits of State Health Reform.*

Charity wards and clinics run by large teaching hospitals and supported by philanthropists also provided indigent care. With the enactment of Medicaid, certain hospitals—both private and public—began relying on welfare medicine as a major source of its revenues, especially in low-income neighborhoods.

78. "State Medicine in Trouble." In due course, the county hospitals in California were reorganized and their facilities upgraded, financed in part by Medicaid, so as to compete more effectively with the private sector. However, as the state sliced reimbursements over the years, proprietary hospitals again shifted Medicaid patients to the public institutions, thereby overloading them.

79. These states were West Virginia, Kentucky, South Carolina, North Carolina, Tennessee, and Arkansas.

80. Engel, *Poor People's Medicine.*

81. Some doctors had formerly treated the needy for little or no fees, with many using a sliding scale. The AMA, which had bitterly opposed Medicaid (and Medicare), soon changed its tune. One study found that between 1966 and 1968, physicians on average had an after-tax gain in income of between $5,400 and $7,400 because of Medicare and Medicaid. Bruce C. Stuart, "Who Gains from Public Health Services?" *Annals of the American Academy of Political and Social Sciences* 399 (January 1972): 145–150.

82. After New York City finally attained an amendment to state health regulations requiring the licensing and control of these entities in 1974, the Association of Health Care Facilities took the state to court. After a two-year fight, the regulation was held illegal. As one reporter pointed out, the city had no idea how many Medicaid mills there were or who owned them, and the court would not even let it find out. John Hess, "'Medicaid Mills' Are Generally Cloaked in Anonymity," *New York Times*, September 21, 1976. In 1977, however, a bill calling for the certification and inspection of these Medicaid Mills was eventually enacted.

83. Some of their dubious care practices included "ping-ponging" patients (sending them from one specialist to another), "churning" (unnecessarily requiring people to return for additional treatments), and "family ganging" (insisting that several members of a family come in for services even if they did not need them).

84. The number of institutions grew from roughly 12,800 facilities in 1963 to 17,700 by 1980; nearly 81 percent were for-profit institutions, up from 65 percent in 1969. Bradford H. Gray, ed., *For-Profit Enterprise in Health Care* (Washington, D.C.: Institute on Medicine and National Academy Press, 1986).

85. By 1975, barely 114,000 people, one-third of them elderly, were receiving any home care under Medicaid nationally. Sparer, *Medicaid and the Limits of State Health Reform.*

Although home care agencies had to be licensed to serve as Medicaid providers, only eleven states had such provisions by 1975.

With three separate Medicaid-funded home care programs, New York State had the most expansive offerings in the nation during this period, especially its Nursing Homes Without Walls, a program that allowed Medicaid recipients to receive at-home services at a cost of up to 75 percent of the average nursing home rate. Even here, however, the programs were rather small: care was available only to the frail elderly who would otherwise be institutionalized. It was administered entirely by voluntary agencies because HEW prohibited profit-making organizations from participating. The national agency soon reversed course, allowing commercial companies meeting federal standards to provide home care services.

Although New York governor Hugh Carey was wary about opening up yet another source of public funds to the private sector, in 1977 the legislature permitted proprietary agencies to join the program. Across the nation, home health care groups, especially the growing number of emerging chains, supported these efforts: Homemaker Upjohn was one of the larger chains, serving half a million people in 1974.

86. Local policymakers also pursued Community Mental Health Centers Act funds, which provided money to the states for the construction of special health clinics to serve the deinstitutionalized population. There were 330 such centers in 1969, but their number reached more than 600 by 1980. Engel, *Poor People's Medicine*. Nonetheless, mentally impaired adults were cared for mainly by their families, and some of them found themselves on the street.

87. John Hess, "State Audit Finds Wide Overbilling by Nursing Homes," *New York Times*, September 6, 1974.

88. Charges to the government included a profit based on a percentage of their "costs." Under New York's cost-plus reimbursement system, nursing homes received compensation for all their operating expenses, including debt interest, taxes, depreciation, and a return on investment based on current market interest rates. They also were remunerated for such activities as lobbying, professional and trade association dues, advertising, and, until 1975, litigation, which was mostly against the very government that was paying the bills. Rates were readjusted in the mid-1970s and were now set by "reasonable" costs for facilities of similar size and services, plus a significant return on owner equity. Operators earned even more from salaries paid to themselves and relatives, some of whom never showed up for work. As might be expected, LTC costs escalated commensurately. John Hess, "Care of Aged Poor a Growing Scandal," *New York Times*, October 7, 1974; John Hess, "2 State Inquiries Ordered on Nursing Home Control," *New York Times*, October 17, 1974.

89. As discussed later in the chapter, there was only limited enforcement of whatever regulations managed to materialize at either the national level or the state level. From the first, providers tended to develop advantageous, sometimes overly friendly relationships with the local government agencies charged with overseeing them. One body was usually designated for administering Medicaid, in general the Department of Welfare, and another for enforcing standards of care, most often the Department of Health. These units tended to be passive enforcers of policies at best. Regulators recognized besides

that any insistence on implementing controls over vendors would inevitably lead to costly and prolonged litigation.

90. In many places, nursing home owners injected substantial amounts of money into local and state elections. For instance, in Texas the Nursing Home Association contributed about $65,000 to eighty-three state legislators for the 1976 campaign. Most of the money was given to members of the two committees responsible for Medicaid nursing home reimbursement rates. The legislators afterward approved $44 million more for the facilities than state welfare officials had requested. Two years later, although at least one-third of the nursing homes in the state were in violation of federal standards, few of them were penalized or shut down. Howie Kurtz, "Politicians Find Nursing Homes a Good Investment, and Vice Versa: Green from Gray," *New Republic* 178 (June 24, 1978), 18.

At the national level, the American Nursing Home Association acknowledged that it annually contributed $500 each to key people in Congress, notably members of the Senate Finance Committee and the House Ways and Means Committee. John Hess, "Nursing Home Promoters Get Political Helping Hand," *New York Times*, October 21, 1974.

The dues of the national and state organizations, which paid for these donations, ironically derived to a large extent from the low-income health care program itself: federal Medicaid policy allowed such expenses, at least until 1975, to be included in the calculation of reimbursement fees. Robert McFadden, "State Studying Health Unit Dues," *New York Times*, February 16, 1975.

91. In Texas, Bill Moore (D)—the most powerful state legislator at the time—owned a nursing home in which considerable violations affected patient services. Representative Tim Von Dohlen (R), who opened a facility in Texas during his tenure as a state legislator, not only helped destroy a bill requiring more training for nurse's aides, but also pushed through a law requiring a hearing before the state could cut funds to violators. Kurtz, "Politicians Find Nursing Homes a Good Investment," 19.

In another instance, shortly after leaving the governorship in Pennsylvania, George Leader established the highly profitable Leader Nursing Homes, Inc., in 1959 and later Country Meadows and Providence Place Retirement Communities. Such conflict of interest was prevalent everywhere, particularly in New York.

92. Stevens and Stevens, *Welfare Medicine in America*.

93. Medical societies, dental associations, pharmacists, nursing homes, and other stakeholders nationwide often achieved their ends through such tactics. In 1975, for example, members of the New Jersey Federation of Physicians and Dentists threatened to turn away Medicaid recipients unless the state restored its recently enacted 10 percent reduction in provider fees. Shrewdly conflating their own interests with those of their clients, the group warned that the cutbacks would compromise the quality of care for the poor. "Cuts in Medicaid Prompt Anxiety over Health Care," *New York Times*, August 1, 1975.

In reaction to the proposed cuts for their services that year, New Jersey pharmacists gave notice that they would stop filling Medicaid prescriptions; the Pharmaceutical Association also successfully challenged the measure in court. State legislators faced a legal battle with the New Jersey Hospital Association when it proposed a reduction in hospital payments. Also dissatisfied with their fees, a few nursing homes in the state threatened to throw out its Medicaid residents. Joan Cook, "Twenty-one Medicaid Patients in Nursing Home in a Holiday Reprieve on Transfer," *New York Times*, November 26, 1975.

Indeed, skilled nursing homes in several states organized effective boycotts of Medicaid. Endeavoring to increase their reimbursement levels, sixty-one North Carolina facilities voted to withdraw from the program in 1971. Tipton's nursing home in Charlotte became the first to begin an actual eviction of residents. Florida too—both in 1971 and 1975—faced a boycott by its institutions. Similar actions in other places, including Massachusetts, California, and Georgia, frustrated officials' efforts to control nursing home rates.

Moreover, Georgia's beneficiary copays and physician "provider agreements," put forward in 1975, met similar resistance: almost half of the doctors refused to sign, withdrawing from the program instead; the Georgia Medical Association also sued the state over the requirement. Nursing homes threatened to pull out of the program. Range, "Medicaid in Georgia."

94. Over the years, the AMA contained the number of physicians by using its influence to limit the expansion of medical schools; by 1966, there were only ninety-three medical schools nationwide. E. T. Chase, "Crisis in Medicine: Impact of Medicare and Medicaid," *Commonweal* 85 (March 10, 1967): 650–652.

95. For example, when in the early 1970s the governor of Illinois attempted, among other efforts, to freeze provider fees, reduce services to the medically needy, and control the length of hospital stays, he faced not only entrenched bureaucrats, a hostile legislature, and the threat of hospital closings, but also antagonistic welfare rights groups. What is more, the state's hospital association and recipient organizations warned that they would sue; most of the cutbacks were eventually restored. Stevens and Stevens, *Welfare Medicine in America*, 298.

In a few instances, Medicaid participants and their advocates prevailed on their own. As a case in point, welfare rights groups forced Connecticut to reinstate its 1975 cutback in services, through court action and without any assistance from the more influential stakeholders.

96. However, such coalitions have always been short-lived and commonly encounter divisions among its members. For example, when faced with a choice between provider and recipient needs, unions generally have been in favor of regulating fees and charges rather than cutting eligibility levels and services.

97. "Breaking the Bank."

98. In 1969, HEW promulgated its guidelines for utilization review, required under the 1967 amendments. Two years later the agency issued a series of modest regulations that included a requirement that states spot-check clients to ensure they actually were receiving services. HEW continued to concentrate on dishonest beneficiaries.

99. Stevens and Stevens, *Welfare Medicine in America*.

100. The Finance Committee is responsible for overseeing Medicaid in the U.S. Senate. The committee's working group turned over to the Internal Revenue Service the names of 10,000 people whose annual earnings from Medicaid were particularly exorbitant. Robert E. Burger, "Medicare and Medicaid: Commercializing the Aged," *The Nation* (May 11, 1970): 557–560.

101. Sandra Salmans and Henry McGee, "Physician, Heal Thyself," *Newsweek* (August 9, 1976): 24.

102. In the U.S. House, for example, one committee found excessive surgery performed on Medicaid recipients as compared to the general population.

103. The Senate Finance Committee's Subcommittee on Health, headed by Senator Herman Talmadge (D–Ga.), also held hearings where witnesses disclosed dishonest conduct and scams among a variety of contractors. According to one account, doctors were among the more prominent perpetrators. Additional committee hearings provided more evidence that doctors and other medical professionals across the country were enriching themselves by providing "bad or indifferent care" and by draining the public treasury. Salmans and McGee, "Physician, Heal Thyself"; Richard Lyons, "Fraud and Waste in Medicaid Found in Senate Report," *New York Times*, August 30, 1976; "Medicaid Investigation: Senate Sleuths Sniff Snootful of Swindles and Shams," *Retirement Living* 16 (October 16, 1976): 12; "Medicaid's Bad Record," *New York Times*, September 5, 1976.

104. Testimony of Dr. Lester Breslow, dean of the School of Public Health at the University of California, quoted in Nancy Hicks, "Senate Inquiry Scans Charges Against Health Plans on Coast," *New York Times*, March 14, 1975.

105. "H.E.W. Issues Rules for States to Curb Fraud in Medicaid," *New York Times*, March 27, 1971; "Billions in Medicaid Ripoffs: Special Report," *U.S. News & World Report* 80 (March 22, 1976): 18–20; "Waste in Medicaid Is Estimated at 9% in Study by HEW," *New York Times*, April 30, 1977.

106. "Congress Catches Up with Medicaid Ripoff," *U.S. News & World Report* 81 (September 13, 1976): 55.

107. As an example, of the sixty physicians who had been convicted nationwide up to that time period, only fifteen of them were jailed, and only two had their medical licenses revoked; in general, convicted doctors merely had to repay the money they pocketed. Salmans and McGee, "Physicians, Heal Thyself."

108. Nevertheless, by the end of the decade only twenty-four states had actually created such agencies. Donald C. Bacon, "Medicaid Abuse: Even Worse Than Feared," *U.S. News & World Report* 86 (June 4, 1979): 43–45.

109. The department now had 1,000 auditors from its various units and 100 investigators working on health care fraud.

In 1975, after requesting money from Congress to investigate Medicaid fraud, the prior HEW secretary, David Matthews, had embarked on a federal–state campaign to reduce abuse of the program. Matthews began his state operation in Massachusetts, in collaboration with Governor Michael Dukakis (D), and a short time later progressed to Ohio, working with its governor, James Rhodes (R). Both Massachusetts and Ohio were among the top ten states in Medicaid spending at the time. "Congress Catches Up with Medicaid Ripoff."

110. A six-month investigation by Senator Frank Moss's subcommittee of the Senate Special Committee on Aging had found a prevalence of kickbacks to doctors by a monopoly of clinical labs, along with fraudulent or unnecessary lab work.

111. By the end of 1979, there were only 22 convictions, 346 administrative sanctions, and $5 million in restitution; an additional 296 cases were still under investigation. "U.S. Lists the Doctors Convicted for Fraud in Medicare-Medicaid," *New York Times*, June 14, 1979.

112. Launched with a probe of fifty New York hospitals, headed by the state's special prosecutor, Charles Hynes, the hospital investigations eventually spread to other states across the nation.

113. In order to push states into action, Congress offered them incentives, including money to design and operate the automated Management and Information Retrieval System, put forward under the 1972 Welfare Reform Law. Nevertheless, by the end of the decade fewer than half of the states were using computers; in many places, they were still processing claims by hand. Bacon, "Medicaid Abuse."

114. "Free Medicine Out of Hand." At the time, California's attorney general estimated that approximately $8 million had been lost to Medi-Cal because of unethical behavior. Stevens and Stevens, *Welfare Medicine in America*, 161.

115. In Chicago, Medicaid was steeped in financial deception and graft. Probes in New Jersey documented sizeable violations by physicians, pharmacies, nursing homes, hospitals, and other health-related suppliers. New Mexico uncovered excessive gains by vendors ranging from physicians to taxicab companies. "Breaking the Bank."

In 1969, Maryland's attorney general began the state's first investigations and prosecutions of Medicaid swindlers. Massachusetts discovered early on that many physicians, dentists, and optometrists had been paid not only more than once for the same service, but at fees higher than those allowed by state law. Frequent disclosures and scandals also erupted in Florida, Kentucky, and Georgia, among other places.

116. Between July 1975 and March 1976, there were some 6,000 investigations of Medicaid fraud and 47 convictions at the state level, up from roughly 1,500 investigations and 10 convictions during the same time period the previous year. Most of these concerted efforts, however, ensued in relatively few states. David Rosenbaum, "The Medicaid Scandal," *New York Times*, September 2, 1976.

As a case in point, the New Jersey Commission of Investigations, after an eighteen-month inquiry, exposed widespread cheating among physicians, dentists, hospitals, pharmacists, and Medicaid mills; the state legislature shortly thereafter passed a bill mandating triple monetary damages plus interest for any providers convicted of defrauding the program.

With its four-year-old team of twenty-nine auditors and investigators, Michigan was reputed to have one of the more aggressive antifraud efforts in the country by 1976. Nevertheless, just as national and state officials were congratulating themselves on Michigan's accomplishments, the *Detroit News* uncovered massive, previously unidentified criminal misconduct; the paper emphasized that there had not been one successful prosecution in years. Michigan subsequently established the Special Investigative Committee, which immediately began holding hearings. Edwin E. Chen, "Model for Fraud: Michigan's Medicaid Rip-Off," *The Nation* (February 26, 1977): 242–244.

117. John Hess, "New York Officials Put Fraud in Medicaid at 10 to 20 percent," *New York Times*, August 31, 1976.

118. These investigations initially centered their attention on questions of ineligibility, overutilization of services, sharing of Medicaid cards among friends and neighbors, and the illegal acquisition of drugs by addicts and dealers.

In response to a federal mandate, the Temporary State Commission to Revise the Social Services Law initiated a year-long investigation of Medicaid in 1975, concluding that many medically needy recipients were concealing income and assets and that hospitals were lax in checking their credentials. "New York State Audit Finds Improper Medicaid Payments," *New York Times*, February 25, 1977, 35.

Another inquiry uncovered financial abuse by most of the state's hospitals, problems that had abounded since the beginning of the program. These abuses included needless admissions in order to fill beds, bills for patients who had long departed, and unnecessarily lengthy stays. Viewing the state's antifraud efforts as sorely inadequate, HEW threatened in 1977 to withdraw Medicaid funds as well as to send in federal inspectors to check for excessive and inappropriate hospital services.

119. Hess, "State Audit Finds Wide Overbilling by Nursing Homes."

120. The Four Seasons Company in Oklahoma City, for example, which owned fifty homes nationwide and grossed more than $6 million in 1968, filed for bankruptcy two years later. "Nursing Homes a U.S. Challenge," *New York Times*, November 8, 1970.

121. In 1973, there were 200 applications for the transfer of ownership of 378 private nursing homes in New York, all supported by Medicaid. A few of the facilities changed hands up to twenty times from 1965 to 1974. In one instance, nursing home ownership turned over four times in one day. John Hess, "Study Denounces Nursing Home Deals as Costing State and Medicaid Millions," *New York Times*, October 31, 1974; John Hess, "Two State Inquiries Ordered on Nursing Home Control," *New York Times*, October 17, 1974.

Complicated deals and financial fraud abounded in other states as well. For example, in New Jersey, investors buying shares of nursing homes, often denominated in "beds" or even fractions of beds, were reaping huge profits while defrauding the state.

122. These machinations included sales and leasebacks, accelerated depreciation, excessive mortgages, and use of nursing facilities as collateral for other financial dealings.

123. The Senate Special Committee on Aging discovered that the majority of nursing homes demanded kickbacks from their various medical suppliers, sometimes as high as 25 percent. Kurtz, "Politicians Find Nursing Homes a Good Investment"; "H.E.W. Issues Rules for States to Curb Fraud in Medicaid."

124. Despite a 1972 federal law requiring an annual review of LTC facilities, nursing homes receiving Medicaid funding in twenty states had still never been audited five years later.

125. In New Jersey, though it had become increasingly apparent that there were rampant violations of Medicaid regulations by nursing homes, until the mid-1970s few attempts had been made to contend seriously with the problem; many of the facilities had never even been inspected. Pressure from lobbyists accounted for at least some of the

+ +

inaction. Moreover, those places that had been audited generally were given at least a two-months notice, allowing them to present an artificially acceptable front. As in other places, however, the industry increasingly came under more scrutiny. At the end of 1974, the New Jersey State Commission of Investigations was established to address fraud in the Medicaid program, and it began its work by focusing on LTC facilities. At the same time, the Joint Legislative Committee on Nursing Homes, established early in 1975, conducted the first of a series of public hearings. Among other findings, the hearing revealed issues ranging from financial deception to inhumane care. The committee found that Medicaid-certified homes were funded even when they were not in compliance with state standards; some of them had appalling conditions. As part of a larger series of state inquiries, a national task force also began an investigation into Medicare and Medicaid fraud in New Jersey, focusing on nursing homes. This task force was assisted by the U.S. Department of Justice and four other federal agencies. Similar to the results in other states, the first indictment of a nursing home operator did not occur until 1975. Because it was often difficult to track down a nursing home's real proprietors, New Jersey's governor proposed legislation requiring disclosure of ownership. He also called for criminal penalties and triple civil damages. "Legislature Will Discuss Stopping Medicaid Abuse," *New York Times*, September 3, 1976; Joan Cook, "Bergen Inquiry Begun by New Jersey," *New York Times*, January 4, 1975; Martin Waldron, "Medicaid Cost $1 Billion Since 1966," *New York Times*, September 5, 1976.

126. After gaining control over regulations from New York City in 1973, the state legislature established several special investigative bodies. The Moreland Act Commission on Nursing Homes, appointed by Governor Carey and chaired by Morris Abram, pursued one of the more well-known investigations. Its main goals were not only to seek evidence of misdoings, but also to come up with recommendations. During 1975, it held a series of televised hearings and shortly thereafter proposed a package of reforms, some of which were enacted by the legislature. For instance, until that time, when nursing homes were found guilty of "overcharging," the only penalty they faced was to return the money. Operators who defrauded Medicaid in New York would now have to pay triple damages. Overall, however, given the enormity of the problems, the proposals offered by the Moreland Commission (which was terminated in 1976) were not sweeping enough to rein in the industry's exploitive activities.

Another inquiry by the Temporary State Commission on Living Costs (known as the Stein Commission), also in 1975, documented widespread nursing home fraud, interlocking networks of nursing home owners, no-show jobs, syndicate operations, and numerous other ways in which the industry bilked taxpayers as well as neglected patients. It concluded that 21 percent of nursing home bills were "unwarranted" and that the facilities "overbilled" Medicaid by more than $400 million. The Stein Commission notably detailed instances of political abuse as well: it provided substantial evidence of conflicts of interest, linking many legislators and judges to nursing home concerns. John Hess, "Overbilling Laid to Nursing Home," *New York Times*, March 9, 1975.

127. Hess, "Care of Aged Poor a Growing Scandal."

128. One of the most notorious operators, Bernard Bergman, generously helped himself to Medicaid money and by 1974 had a nursing home empire worth around $24

million. At that time, he was linked to nearly seventy facilities in New York, New Jersey, and Connecticut. Although residents at his institutions encountered egregious conditions, including filth and neglect, he developed relationships with political leaders of both parties. Thus, "unfavorable inspection reports tended to be forgotten, rate increases were granted despite objections, and licenses to operate were not revoked despite recommendations for revocations." Samuel A. Klurman, chair of Medi-Home Enterprises, Inc., a chain of thirty-six facilities in 1975, had organized a cartel with Bernard Bergman that controlled most nursing homes in New York through partnerships. Edith Asbury, "Bergman Became Involved in Nursing Homes in '39," *New York Times*, March 12, 1976.

129. Charles Hynes, the special prosecutor, had an initial auditing staff of 16 people, which was increased to almost 200 by 1977. The following year he became head of New York State's first Medicaid Fraud Control Unit.

130. As a matter of fact, a few operators who had been found guilty of various nursing home crimes continued to run their facilities. Eugene Hollander, a past president of the Metropolitan Nursing Home Association, owned a significant number of places, and despite his conviction for defrauding Medicaid of $5.8 million, he was allowed to carry on with the business. Albert Christiano, president of the New York State Health Facilities Association and a member of New York's Hospital Review and Planning Council, was indicted for illegal welfare medicine activities.

Several prominent state officials were charged as well: both New York's Speaker of the House Assembly, Stanley Steingut, and its majority leader, Al Blumenthal, were accused of using their influence on behalf of Bergman. After taking a substantial bribe, Steingut had pressured his colleagues not to investigate the Bergman nursing homes, nearly all of which had atrocious conditions. John Hess, "Bergman Pleads Guilty to 1.2 Million Medicaid Fraud," *New York Times*, March 12, 1976.

131. U.S. Congress, Senate, Committee on Finance, *Medicare and Medicaid, Part 2,* hearings, 91st Cong., 2d sess., April 14–15, May 26–27, and June 2–3, 15–16, 1970.

132. Burger, "Medicare and Medicaid."

133. A 1973 HEW study found that more than half of the 7,000 nursing homes funded under Medicaid had code violations but were certified anyway, the vast majority with ongoing "correctable deficiencies."

134. See, for example, U.S. GAO, *Many Medicare and Medicaid Nursing Homes Do Not Meet Federal Fire Safety Requirements*, MWD-75-46 (Washington, D.C.: U.S. Government Printing Office, March 18, 1975); U.S. GAO, *Increased Compliance Needed with Nursing Home Health and Sanitary Standards*, MWD-76-8 (Washington, D.C.: U.S. Government Printing Office, August 18, 1975); U.S. GAO, *Federal Fire Safety Requirements Do Not Insure Life Safety in Nursing Home Fires*, MWD-76-136 (Washington, D.C.: U.S. Government Printing Office, June 3, 1976).

135. Some states had long waiting lists. By 1977, for example, New Jersey had an annual waiting list as high as 1,600 patients a month. Joan Cook, "Ruling by State Sought to Require Medicaid Care in Nursing Home," *New York Times*, February 10, 1977.

Social service agencies often sent Medicaid clients to the nearest place with a vacancy, regardless of its care record. John Hess, "How Referrals to Nursing Homes Are Made," *New York Times*, May 12, 1975.

136. "38 States Warned on Nursing Homes," *New York Times*, December 1, 1971, 24.

137. Stevens and Stevens, *Welfare Medicine in America*, 190.

138. Like other places, New York faced formidable legal challenges when it attempted to implement any sanctions on nursing homes. In 1973, whenever officials tried to shut down an unsafe facility, the state nursing home association typically obtained an injunction against the action until a hearing could be held. In another case, the association acquired an injunction to prevent the health commissioner from holding a hearing because it claimed he had shown prejudice against them. At issue was whether property rights would take precedence over recipients' needs; clearly, "in New York property rights wins nearly every time." John Hess, "Regulating Medicaid," *New York Times*, April 25, 1975.

In 1977, Michigan enacted the Administrative Procedures Act, which mandated a right to administrative hearings and court appeals for any provider accused of defrauding the public health care systems. Cleverly taking advantage of the law, proprietors of grossly substandard homes could in this way prevent their facilities from being shut down for nearly two years, if ever. Chen, "Model for Fraud."

3. From Reagan to Clinton

1. President Reagan sought severe reductions in Medicaid in real dollar amounts. Total outlays had been rising rapidly, averaging about 18 percent between 1977 and 1981, despite the fact that enrollment in most states was either steady or declining. During that period, general inflation averaged 8.4 percent. John D. Klemm, "Medicaid Spending: A Brief History," *Health Care Financing Review* 22, no. 1 (Fall 2000): 105–112.

2. For instance, according to the U.S. Census Bureau, 90 percent of Medicare recipients were white in 1980, compared to only 68 percent of people on Medicaid being white. "Census Finds U.S. Benefits Reach 1 out of 3 Families," *New York Times*, March 13, 1981.

3. Colleen Grogan and Eric Patashnik, "Between Welfare Medicine and Mainstream Entitlement: Medicaid at the Political Crossroads," *Journal of Health Politics, Policy, and Law* 28, no. 1 (October 2003): 821–858.

4. Fay Lomax Cook and Edith Barrett, *Support for the American Welfare State: The Views of Congress and the Public* (New York: Columbia University Press, 1992), 28.

5. Grogan and Patashnik, "Between Welfare Medicine and Mainstream Entitlement."

6. Enacted under OBRA 1981, states whose Medicaid growth surpassed specific targets would have their federal share of Medicaid funding lowered by 3 percent, 4 percent, and 4.5 percent, respectively, over three years, amounting to a total of roughly $1 billion. The legislation also provided for other, smaller cuts, including the elimination of the state option to include in their plans dependent children from ages nineteen to twenty-one.

7. One early Reagan proposal recommended that the federal government take over the Medicaid program entirely; his intention was to control eligibility levels and provide

only the minimum benefits required under federal law. In return, the states would have to fund the AFDC and food stamp programs on their own. "Shift in Federal–State Roles Seen as Curbing Medicaid and Welfare," *New York Times*, January 21, 1982.

Another idea was to have the national government take over the LTC portion of welfare medicine in exchange for divesting itself of the cash-assistance and food stamp programs. The administration later offered to transfer most obligations for LTC to the states, along with a federal block grant of $18.5 billion. Irvin Molotsky, "White House Revises 'New Federalism' Proposals," *New York Times*, June 24, 1983.

Over the years, including his last one in office, Reagan also recommended lowering federal matching rates for optional services and capping the national share of Medicaid grants indefinitely.

8. The administration estimated that it could save $1.1 billion over five years. States also would have had to cover everyone with incomes less than the FPL. Milt Freudenheim, "Serving the Poor Private Insurance," *New York Times*, October 9, 1990. Congress adopted this proposal several decades later, but without the mandate to serve all indigent families.

9. The enlargements were forced through mostly by Democrats in the House of Representatives, despite opposition by the Reagan and George H. W. Bush administrations and by a large number of congressional Republicans. David G. Smith, *Entitlement Politics: Medicare and Medicaid 1995–2001* (New York: De Gruyter, 2002).

Through a variety of methods, the following laws endeavored to cover a greater number of vulnerable mothers and their offspring and to increase services to them: the Deficit Reduction Act of 1984, the Consolidated Omnibus Reconciliation Act of 1985, OBRA 1986 and 1987, the Medicare Catastrophic Coverage Act of 1988, and OBRA 1989 and 1990. Teresa A. Coughlin, Leighton Ku, and John Holahan, *Medicaid Since 1980: Costs, Coverage, and the Shifting Alliance Between the Federal Government and the States* (Washington, D.C.: Urban Institute, 1994).

10. Emily Friedman, "The Compromise and the Afterthought: Medicare and Medicaid After 30 Years," *Journal of the American Medical Association* 274, no. 3 (July 19, 1995): 278–282; Grogan and Patashnik, "Between Welfare Medicine and Mainstream Entitlement"; Smith, *Entitlement Politics*. The Consolidated Budget Reconciliation Act of 1985 mandated coverage of all pregnant women who were eligible for AFDC.

11. Karl Kronebusch, "Children's Medicaid Enrollment: The Impacts of Mandates, Welfare Reform, and Policy Delinking," *Journal of Health Politics, Policy, and Law* 26, no. 6 (December 2001), 1227.

12. Underscoring Congress's retrenchment endeavors was its passage of the 1985 Balanced Budget and Emergency Deficit Control (Gramm-Rudman-Hollings) Act, which mandated annual deficit-reduction targets, effectively limiting national spending on an assortment of social benefits.

13. President Reagan did initially manage to get penalties removed from those states that refused to implement the EPSDT Program. Smith, *Entitlement Politics*.

14. The goal was to increase enrollments from an average of 39 percent of eligible children to 80 percent by 1995.

15. Smith, *Entitlement Politics*; Coughlin, Ku, and Holahan, *Medicaid Since 1980.*

16. For instance, Pennsylvania was sued in 1991 for enrolling fewer than 25 percent of the state's eligible children; failing to publicize the program; erecting barriers to participation; neglecting to assess and treat young beneficiaries for poisoning, hearing and vision impairments, and mental health disorders; and falling short on the provision mandating physical and speech therapies. Michael De Courcy Hinds, "Suit Charges Pennsylvania Failed to Meet Medicaid Plan for Youth," *New York Times*, November 14, 1991.

17. Grogan and Patashnik, "Between Welfare Medicine and Mainstream Entitlement."

18. The alliance prevailed over opposition from President George H. W. Bush and most governors. Robert Pear, "Deficit or No Deficit, Unlikely Allies Bring About Expansions in Medicaid," *New York Times*, November 4, 1990.

19. OBRA 1986 gave the states the option to finance part A and part B premiums, along with other cost-sharing requirements, of qualified Medicare beneficiaries whose incomes are at or below the FPL. The Medicare Catastrophic Act of 1988 required the states to pay their premiums, but still allowed the option of financing the other cost-sharing requirements. In 1993, Congress mandated the states to subsidize Medicare Part B premiums for specified low-income Medicare beneficiaries, individuals whose income is greater than the FPL, but less than 110 percent of that level; two years later the upper ceiling was raised to 120 percent of the FPL. In 1997, through a block grant, the federal government provided the states with additional but limited funds to assist older people (qualified individuals) having incomes from 120 percent to 135 percent of the FPL with their Part B Medicare premiums.

20. In 1989, forty-nine governors signed a letter insisting on a moratorium of any additional national Medicaid mandates. The following year, the National Conference on State Legislatures made a similar appeal. Coughlin, Ku, and Holahan, *Medicaid Since 1980.*

Because many of these enactments were to be delayed or phased in over several years, the full extent of their impact would not be experienced for many years hence. Caseloads rose from 21.4 million in 1989 to 28.9 million by 1992, an increase of 39 percent. Three years later they jumped another 16 percent to 33.4 million.

21. Individuals up to age sixty-five who receive SSI because of a medical condition that keeps them from working are eligible for Medicaid, as are children who have severe functional limitations that are expected to last at least twelve months.

Indeed, the blind and disabled were the fastest-growing Medicaid population, averaging 5.4 percent annually between 1984 and 1992; in the latter year, nearly 55 percent of the disabled poor were served by the program, representing about 37 percent of total program expenditures. Coughlin, Ku, and Holahan, *Medicaid Since 1980.*

22. Smith, *Entitlement Politics.*

23. For instance, from 1981 to 1982 the consumer price index rose by only 3 percent, but hospital charges and doctor fees grew by 20 percent and 11 percent, respectively. Jill Quadagno, *One Nation Uninsured: Why the U.S. Has No National Health Insurance* (Oxford, U.K.: Oxford University Press, 2005).

24. Lawrence D. Brown and Michael Sparer, "Poor Program's Progress: The Unanticipated Politics of Medicaid Policy," *Health Affairs* 22 (January–February 2003): 31–44; U.S. HHS, Health Care Financing Administration, *Health Care Programs, Medicaid*, annual statistical supplement (Washington, D.C.: U.S. Government Printing Office, 2005), table 8.E2: "Unduplicated Number of Recipients, Total Vendor Payments, and Average Payment, by Type of Eligibility Category, Selected Fiscal Years 1972–2002."

According to an analysis by one research group, larger enrollments accounted for about 36 percent of the growth in costs from 1988 to 1992, whereas medical inflation and greater utilization/higher reimbursement rates represented 29 percent and 33 percent, respectively. Coughlin, Ku, and Holahan, *Medicaid Since 1980*.

25. Rising from 2.5 percent of the federal budget ($17 billion) in 1981, Medicaid expenditures climbed to 3.3 percent ($41 billion) by 1990 and to 5.9 percent ($89 billion) by 1995.

26. Steven Gold, "State Fiscal Problems and Policies," in Steven Gold, ed., *The Fiscal Crisis of the States: Lessons for the Future*, 6–40 (Washington, D.C.: Georgetown University Press, 1995).

27. However, as Coughlin, Ku, and Holahan caution, "sometimes shortfalls are partly political in nature; spending projections or appropriations can be deliberately set low to ease initial budget negotiations." *Medicaid Since 1980*, 85.

28. Ibid. Certain states, especially those in the Northeast and California, experienced the fiscal crisis of the early 1990s both more protractedly and more severely than others. In a few places, such as Minnesota, the recession was comparatively mild, but Medicaid costs still grew rapidly, from 7 percent of the budget in 1991 to 15 percent in 1995. Gold, "State Fiscal Problems and Policies"; Thomas Luce, "Minnesota: Innovation in an Era of Constraint," in Gold, ed., *The Fiscal Crisis of the States*, 326–363.

29. In some locations, Medicaid absorbed even higher fractions: the 1993 budget percentages in California, Connecticut, Florida, Massachusetts, Michigan, and Minnesota were 13.1, 11.7, 13.1, 14.5, 13.7, and 12.9, respectively. Steven Gold, "Spending Policies and Revenue Trends Compared," in Gold, ed., *The Fiscal Crisis of the States*, 67–80.

In 1970, Medicaid had averaged only 3 percent of state general funds. "Stress Points in the State Budgets," *New York Times*, December 30, 1990.

30. Michael S. Sparer, *Medicaid and the Limits of State Health Reform* (Philadelphia: Temple University Press, 1996); Coughlin, Ku, and Holahan, *Medicaid Since 1980*.

In New York, by 1994, Medicaid spending had grown to $20.4 billion, or 20 percent of the state's spending from all revenue sources. Indeed, New York continued to consume a significant percentage of overall Medicaid dollars: its plan covered 9 percent of recipients (second only to California), but expended 14 percent of all federal Medicaid funds. Kevin Sack, "Albany Faces Hard Choices in Cash Quest," *New York Times*, January 20, 1992; Joyce Purnick, "Medicaid Myths Linger in Wake of Campaign," *New York Times*, November 17, 1994.

31. Only 1.4 percent of the welfare medicine population was covered under managed-care plans in 1981. Jonathan Engel, *Poor People's Medicine: Medicaid and American Charity Care Since 1965* (Durham, N.C.: Duke University Press, 2006); Robert B.

Hackey, *Rethinking Health Care Policy: The New Politics of State Regulation* (Washington, D.C.: Georgetown University Press, 1998).

32. Arizona's experimental statewide plan (Arizona Health Care Cost Containment System)—permitted through a three-year waiver and at a slightly lower matching formula than the state would have received otherwise—mandated managed-care contracts for all health services. It also specifically excluded LTC, home health benefits, and family planning.

33. Grogan and Patashnik, "Between Welfare Medicine and Mainstream Entitlement."

34. By the mid-1980s, although twenty-two states had instituted at least a small degree of home-based care, by the end of the decade only about a million recipients were being served. Engel, *Poor People's Medicine.*

35. Colleen Grogan, "The Influence of Federal Mandates on State Medicaid and AFDC Decision-Making," *Publius: The Journal of Federalism* 29, no. 3 (1999): 1–30. For example, when the Arkansas program faced its financial crises, Governor Bill Clinton tightened program eligibility from 185 percent to 133 percent of the FPL and eliminated many optional services; he also reduced payments to doctors and dentists by 20 percent. Robert Pear, "Arkansas Struggles to Deal with Rising Health Care Costs," *New York Times*, October 19, 1992.

36. Sparer, *Medicaid and the Limits of State Health Reform.* South Carolina and Oregon, for example, limited annual hospital stays to twelve days and eighteen days, respectively.

37. Eight states—Arkansas, Florida, Kansas, Massachusetts, New York, Tennessee, Vermont, and Washington—curbed physician visits. By the mid-1980s, fourteen states had adopted caps on the number of drugs. New Hampshire limited the total to three prescriptions per month, generating a 28 percent decrease in the use of essential prescription medications for such disorders as diabetes and heart disease. As a result, the state abandoned the ceiling and in 1987 imposed a one-dollar copay per drug instead. "Move to Cut Medicaid Spending on Drugs Is Called Harmful," *New York Times*, August 30, 1987.

38. Coughlin, Ku, and Holahan, *Medicaid Since 1980*; Grogan, "The Influence of Federal Mandates on State Medicaid and AFDC Decision-Making"; Gold, "Spending Policies and Revenue Trends Compared."

39. "Broad Access and Many Services," *New York Times*, April 14, 1991.

40. A few states temporarily withheld payments altogether. Coughlin, Ku, and Holahan, *Medicaid Since 1980.*

41. As part of OBRA 1980, the Boren amendment disregarded the congressional mandate that fees to skilled nursing homes and ICFs must be "cost related." Now they had to be "reasonable and adequate to meet the costs which must be incurred by efficiently and economically operated facilities." The following year it applied a similar directive for hospitals, adding a provision that any new rates had to take into account facilities caring for a "disproportionate share" of uninsured, special needs, or other nonpaying patients as well as to ensure that Medicaid recipients have access to quality services.

42. In 1981, forty states had paid hospitals' actual costs, equivalent to Medicare fees, but by 1991 only seven continued to do so, and three of these states capped the total allowable amount. Twenty-two states ultimately adopted prospective methods—based on diagnostically related groups—similar to the method later mandated under Medicare in the mid-1980s; sixteen states developed a fixed daily rate, regardless of diagnosis; and four states negotiated their rates with the hospitals. Engel, *Poor People's Medicine*; Sparer, *Medicaid and the Limits of State Health Reform*.

43. These costs include skilled nursing and ICFs-MR. John K. Iglehart, "Medicaid," *New England Journal of Medicine* 328, no. 12 (March 25, 1993): 896–900.

44. Sparer, *Medicaid and the Limits of State Health Reform*.

45. These provisions were provided for under OBRA 1987, which, among other things, set minimum criteria for services, staffing, and patient rights.

46. Smith, *Entitlement Politics*; Engel, *Poor People's Medicine*; "Many States Seeking to Cut Medicaid Costs," *New York Times*, October 14, 1984.

47. According to a reporter for the *New York Times*, the fees for nonelderly Medicaid patients averaged 65 percent of private and 69 percent of Medicare payments across the nation. Don Terry, "As Medicaid Fees Push Doctors Out, Chicago Patients Find Fewer Choices," *New York Times*, April 12, 1991.

Roughly forty-two states utilized a fee schedule; other places applied a formula based on prevailing costs. Sparer, *Medicaid and the Limits of State Health Reform*; Iglehart, "Medicaid."

48. To be sure, physician complaints about low remuneration and their consequent unwillingness to treat Medicaid patients in many areas of the nation generated a growing concern that the newly covered children and pregnant women would have insufficient access to medical services. Therefore, under yet another congressional mandate, OBRA 1989, states were required "to demonstrate that obstetrical and pediatric services are available to Medicaid beneficiaries at least to the extent that they are available to the general population. Thus a number of states [moved] to increase their rates of reimbursements to pediatricians and obstetricians." Iglehart, "Medicaid," 898.

49. Sparer, *Medicaid and the Limits of State Health Reform*. For instance, in February 1990 a federal judge ordered Pennsylvania to increase reimbursements to Temple University Hospital, the state's principal provider of services to the indigent, by 35 percent. Four months later legislators were forced to boost Medicaid payments to all other hospitals by at least 13 percent. Robert Pear, "Ruling May Lead to Big Rise in States' Medicaid Costs," *New York Times*, July 5, 1990.

50. Robert Pear, "Ruling Likely to Increase Strains on Medicaid," *New York Times*, June 15, 1990.

51. Sparer, *Medicaid and the Limits of State Health Reform*.

52. Coughlin, Ku, and Holahan, *Medicaid Since 1980*; Smith, *Entitlement Politics*.

53. The Boren amendment was rescinded under BBA 1997.

54. According to one source, the figures would be much higher if the money contributed through provider taxes were taken into account, 21.4 percent in 1991 and 34.4 percent in 1992. Gold, "State Fiscal Problems and Policies."

55. Vermont and Wyoming are the exceptions. However, many states can circumvent this requirement if spending "unexpectedly" exceeds revenues. They have used a number of gimmicks for political purposes, such as effecting funding delays and shifts, purposely overestimating revenues, underestimating expenditures, making one-time revenue infusions, and using creative accounting methods. Jeffrey Chapman, "California: The Enduring Crisis," in Gold, ed., *The Fiscal Crisis of the States*, 104–140; Robert Kleine, "Michigan: Rethinking Fiscal Priorities," in Gold, ed., *The Fiscal Crisis of the States*, 296–325.

56. Gold, "State Fiscal Problems and Policies"; Smith, *Entitlement Politics*; Coughlin, Ku, and Holahan, *Medicaid Since 1980*.

California faced dramatically rising Medicaid budgets, along with deficits of $2.9 billion in 1991 and $2.2 billion at the end of 1992. Its financial stress was compounded by a large number of illegal immigrants, base closings, and Proposition 13, which limited property taxes. Its elected officials responded to the budget deficits with repeated assaults on AFDC, including cuts in benefit levels (amounting to 15 percent between 1991 and 1994), more stringent eligibility rules, and a temporary suspension of cost-of-living adjustments; Medicaid, in contrast, was left relatively intact. Gold, "State Fiscal Problems and Policies"; Chapman, "California."

Michigan, in reaction to its dire financial situation, which was intensified by the steady loss of manufacturing jobs, chose to slash its overall budget across the board by 9.2 percent and to eliminate the state's general assistance welfare program for single adults and childless couples.

Massachusetts, one of the more generous Medicaid states in terms of optional benefits, endured annual program increases of 15 percent from 1988 to 1992. Facing huge budget overruns for a number of years, officials at one point had to borrow money to pay its Medicaid providers. By 1994, the program had become the largest item in the Massachusetts budget, reaching 21 percent. The legislature pursued aggressive revisions in its rates for hospitals and nursing homes, created a mandatory managed-care program and sought a 1915(c) HCBS waiver to slow down LTC expenditures. However, it eventually had to enact large cuts in both higher education and the state's general relief income-support program. Bruce Wallin, "Massachusetts: Downsizing State Government," in Gold, ed., *The Fiscal Crisis of the States*, 252–295; Hackey, *Rethinking Health Care Policy*.

Florida, which was affected particularly hard by both the recession and federal Medicaid mandates, also had an exceptionally high and steady growth in its older population as well as in its population of indigent immigrants with children (both documented and undocumented). Between 1990 and 1993, the state's Medicaid outlays grew by 99.6 percent, putting intense pressure on its resources. In response, among other initiatives, policymakers tightened eligibility for the medically needy program, limiting many older people's access to nursing homes; decreased funding for hospitals providing charity care; and reduced financial support for public education. Gold, "Spending Policies and Revenue Trends Compared"; Susan MacManus, "Florida: Reinvention Derailed," in Gold, ed., *The Fiscal Crisis of the States*, 197–251.

57. The National Association of State Budget Officers complained at its annual meeting in 1993 that Medicaid was now the main financial concern among the states. Coughlin, Ku, and Holahan, *Medicaid Since 1980.*

58. However, James Fossett and James Wuckoff tested whether the growth of Medicaid during the 1980s actually fostered lowered spending for education but did not find any significant correlation. Rather, the researchers attributed the reduction in such education funding to declining state revenues and other factors unrelated to Medicaid. James Fossett and James Wuckoff, "Has Medicaid Growth Crowded Out State Education Spending?" *Journal of Health Politics, Policy, and Law* 21 (Fall 1996): 409–432.

59. Between 1990 and 1993, twenty-seven states had initiated at least one sizeable tax increase; New Hampshire, Montana, Rhode Island, and Vermont had enacted two during this period. Gold, "State Fiscal Problems and Policies."

60. For example, for the first time in 1990, New York placed a ceiling on the number of allowable Medicaid services for childless adults, restricting them to fourteen physician visits and eighteen laboratory tests per year; however, an attempt to extend upper limits to all recipients that would also include hospital services and apply copayments for services was quickly thwarted by the courts: a suit against the state had been brought by Legal Services for the Elderly and Legal Services of the Cardoza Law School. Initiatives to control provider costs also proved futile. Recommending $1 billion in reduced hospital reimbursements, the governor was forced to rescind the proposal in response to protests by the Greater New York Hospital Association, Local 1199 of the state's health care union, religious leaders, and recipient organizations. In the end, there were few reductions for clients or contractors in the state. "Broad Access and Many Services."

61. Klemm, "Medicaid Spending."

62. Coughlin, Ku, and Holahan, *Medicaid Since 1980.*

63. Although the total amount of donations and taxes was not legally restricted at the time, they generally did not exceed 10 percent of a state's annual Medicaid spending. "States Using Donations to Get Medicaid Money," *New York Times,* May 12, 1991, 19.

64. After calculating the causes of accelerating Medicaid outlays between 1989 and 1992, one research group concluded that such expenditures were heavily influenced by the increasing state use of provider taxes and donations, disproportionate-share payments, and intergovernmental transfers. Coughlin, Ku, and Holahan, *Medicaid Since 1980.*

65. Robert E. Mechanic, *Medicaid's Disproportionate Share Hospital Program: Complex Structure, Critical Payments,* National Health Policy Forum Background Paper (Washington, D.C.: National Health Policy Forum, George Washington University, September 14, 2004).

66. Teresa A. Coughlin and David Liska, *The Medicaid Disproportionate Share Hospital Payment Program: Background and Issues,* Series A, no. A-14 (Washington, D.C.: Urban Institute, October 1997), 1–8.

67. Ibid. Maryland, for example, retained more than 45 percent of the new revenue it netted from DSH payments. Faced with severe financial difficulties in 1991, the state turned to DSH payments that amounted to 12 percent of its total Medicaid

expenditures that year, earning it more than $264 million in additional money. Hackey, *Rethinking Health Care Policy*.

68. Coughlin, Ku, and Holahan, *Medicaid Since 1980*. For example, in 1990 the newly elected governor of Massachusetts, William Weld (R), relied on the infusion of DSH money just to maintain the current level of services in the state, including Medicaid. Wallin, "Massachusetts."

69. Coughlin and Liska, *The Medicaid Disproportionate Share Hospital Payment Program*, 5.

70. Hackey, *Rethinking Health Care Policy*.

71. "States Using Donations to Get Medicaid Money."

72. These provisions were enacted under the Medicaid Voluntary Contributions and Provider-Specific Tax Amendments of 1991. Despite the stipulation that the provider taxes could no longer be a pretense simply for reaping additional federal dollars, the states began using them more aggressively for that purpose; by 1997, at least seventeen states were engaged in disputes with the national government about how they were raising their share of Medicaid money. As with the previous administration, President Clinton argued that the states were "gaming" the system, and he fought hard to eliminate such maneuvers.

73. Alan Weil, "There's Something About Medicaid," *Health Affairs* 22, no. 1 (January–February 2003), 13–23. President Clinton attempted to disallow the provision, using his new line-item veto authority for the first time, but the Supreme Court subsequently ruled the line-item veto unconstitutional.

74. The Democrats called these efforts "program cuts," whereas Republicans dubbed them "slower growth rates."

75. Although in general supporting the idea of block grants, five Republican senators and many House Republicans from the Northeast were opposed to the distribution formula, which they viewed as shifting federal money away from their geographical area to the South and the West. They also sought, but did not achieve, a release from the state matching requirements.

76. With the 1994 election, Republicans not only captured the majority rule of Congress but also thirty governorships, gaining eleven states, including eight of the nine most populous ones.

77. Grogan and Patashnik, "Between Welfare Medicine and Mainstream Entitlement," 844.

78. Smith, *Entitlement Politics*, 40.

79. Adam Clymer, "Governors Try to Find Unity on Medicaid," *New York Times*, July 31, 1995.

80. Smith, *Entitlement Politics*.

81. These reductions were estimated at about $115 billion over five years.

82. Along with the Taxpayers' Relief Act, signed into law at the same time, Congress mandated a balanced budget by 2002, while incongruously also rolling back tax rates, especially for upper-income households.

83. For example, BBA 1997 created Medicare+Choice, Part C, which allowed beneficiaries to sign up for managed-care plans (and added preferred-provider organizations

to the mix). It also slowed the growth of provider payments, sharply in some cases (although most of the reductions were rescinded in later legislation), and extended prospective payments to include outpatient and subacute care in rehabilitation hospitals, LTC hospitals, and skilled nursing homes, along with services through home health agencies.

84. Congress and President Clinton agreed to an estimated $17 billion decrease in federal contributions to Medicaid over five years and $61 billion over ten years. As usual, however, there was substantial disagreement about the actual size of the savings, with some experts estimating it as low as $14 billion over five years and $53.9 over ten years. Robert Green, *A Look at the Details of the New Budget Legislation* (Washington, D.C.: Center on Budget and Policy Priorities, August 12, 1997).

85. It was anticipated that repeal of the Boren amendment would generate the remaining savings.

86. A 75/25 percent rule had previously mandated that Medicaid-dominant MCOs had to serve at least 25 percent private-pay clients. Although the BBA recommended some controls over MCOs, including protections for recipients, the rules enforcing them were delayed until 2001, and even then they were weakened under the presidency of George W. Bush.

87. Engel, *Poor People's Medicine.*

88. In 2000, the United States spent only 17 percent of its GDP on social welfare programs that were directly paid for out of tax dollars, as compared to about 30 percent in Germany, Sweden, Italy, the Netherlands, and Denmark. Jeff Madrick, "Health for Sale," *New York Review of Books* 50, no. 20 (December 18, 2003): 71–74.

However, as Jack Hacker points out, we spend considerably more on such benefits if private sources are added in, much of them paid for indirectly through tax exemptions. Jack Hacker, *The Divided Welfare State: The Battle over Public and Private Benefits in the U.S.* (New York: Cambridge University Press, 2002).

89. Under conditions of economic catastrophe, such as the Great Depression in the 1930s and the 2008 recession, blame is spread more widely to include such captains of industry as bankers and automobile executives, especially when they, too, are explicitly on the dole.

90. "Stress Points in the State Budgets."

91. Coughlin, Ku, and Holahan, *Medicaid Since 1980.*

92. From 1992 to 1995, notwithstanding the continuing growth of households covered under the program, total AFDC outlays remained constant. Gold, "State Fiscal Problems and Policies"; Clymer, "Governors Try to Find Unity on Medicaid."

93. Sheila Zedlewski and Linda Giannarelli, *Diversity Among State Welfare Programs: Implications for Reform,* Assessing New Federalism: Issues and Options for States no. A-1 (Washington, D.C.: Urban Institute, January 1, 1997), available at http://www.urban.org/url.cfm.

94. States had to provide one year of coverage for families who lost their eligibility because of the new standards.

95. Case loads had been climbing steadily during the fiscal crisis of the early 1990s, but because of a stronger economy they declined about 13 percent between 1994 and

August 1996. Christopher Conte, "Welfare, Work, and the States: Can States Move Welfare Recipients into Jobs?" *CQ Researcher* 6, no. 45 (December 6, 1996): 1057–1080; Robert Pear, "Clinton to Expand Medicaid for Some of the Working Poor," *New York Times*, August 4, 1998.

96. Engel, *Poor People's Medicine.*

97. Conte, "Welfare, Work, and the States."

98. Mark E. Rushefsky and Kant Patel, *Politics, Power, and Policy Making: The Case of Health Care Reform in the 1990s* (Armonk, N.Y.: M. E. Sharpe, 1998). However, individuals who met state AFDC eligibility and other criteria in 1996 would still be entitled to Medicaid benefits.

99. As a case in point, the number of poor people covered under Medicaid in New York declined 26 percent between 1995 and 1998. Nina Bernstein, "Medicaid Rolls Have Declined in Last Three Years," *New York Times*, August 17, 1998.

States were allowed to provide transitional benefits—for up to twelve months—for individuals who were in school or found employment. According to Jill Quadagno, about one-third of the people who left welfare continued to receive Medicaid benefits; another third obtained some limited private coverage, mainly through work; and the rest were left uninsured. Quadagno, *One Nation Uninsured.*

100. Engel, *Poor People's Medicine*; Ronald J. Angel, Laura Lein, and Jane Henrici, *Poor Families in America's Health Care Crisis* (New York: Cambridge University Press, 2006).

101. Grogan and Patashnik, "Between Welfare Medicine and Mainstream Entitlement."

102. One researcher found that the low-income health program served from 926,000 to 1.3 million fewer children from 1995 to 1998. Karl Kronebusch, "Medicaid for Children: Federal Mandates, Welfare Reform, and Policy Backsliding," *Health Affairs* 20, no. 1 (January–February 2001): 97–112.

103. Rather than SCHIP's being implemented as an open-ended program, it was established as a block grant to the states in order to obtain the support of certain conservatives. Smith, *Entitlement Politics.*

Moreover, because SCHIP was established as part of an effort to balance the budget, the grants to the states were to be reduced by 26 percent in 2002 and subsequent years. Edwin Park, Leighton Ku, and Matthew Broaddus, *Congress Could Extend the Availability of Expanding SCHIP Funds and Undo the Reduction in SCHIP Funding Levels to Avert a Large Enrollment Decline* (Washington, D.C.: Center on Budget and Policy Priorities, November 7, 2002).

104. As of 2005, eighteen states had separate SCHIP programs; eleven states included it as part of their Medicaid plan; and twenty-one states had a combination of both. U.S. GAO, *States' SCHIP Enrollment and Spending Experiences and Considerations for Reauthorization* (Washington, D.C.: U.S. Government Printing Office, February 15, 2007).

105. States differ considerably in their SCHIP cost-sharing provisions. As of 2007, only seven states did not charge children anything under the program. U.S. GAO, *Children's Health Insurance: State Experiences in Implementing SCHIP and Considerations*

for Reauthorization, statement of Katherine G. Allen, director of Health Care, GAO, before the Committee on Finance, U.S. Senate, 110th Cong., 1st sess., February 1, 2007, GAO-07-447T (Washington, D.C.: U.S. Government Printing Office, 2007).

106. From a high of 28.6 percent in 1991, the annual increase in outlays fell to just less than 10 percent between 1992 and 1995 and dropped to 1.8 percent the following year. Expenditures remained relatively steady throughout the rest of the decade, increasing an average of 6.2 percent per year. U.S. HHS, Health Care Financing Administration, *Total Current Expenditures, Benefits, and Administrative Expenditures, Federal and State Shares*, Medicaid Financial Management Reports (CMS-64 and predecessors) (Washington, D.C.: U.S. Government Printing Office, 1990–99).

107. Grogan and Patashnik, "Between Welfare Medicine and Mainstream Entitlement." Only $200 million and $600 million, respectively, of national funds were spent during the first two years. New York, as usual, took full advantage of the program. In 1990, the state had created Child Health Plan Plus, providing limited services to low-income children ages thirteen and younger, and a few years later it raised the age limit to nineteen. With the enactment of SCHIP and the availability of enhanced federal dollars, the legislature added more benefits (e.g., dental, vision, hearing, speech, and inpatient mental health services) and raised the income eligibility level. Between 1997 and 2002, the number of children participating in the program increased by nearly 400 percent. Jeffrey Kraus, "Health Care in the Empire State," in Robert Pecorella and Jeffrey Stonecash, eds., *Governing New York State*, 5th ed., 331–431 (Albany: State University of New York Press, 2006).

A few other states were slightly less generous, such as Colorado's Child Health Plan Plus, which fixed its eligibility at 185 percent of the FPL. Colorado Health Institute (CHI), *Colorado Medicaid* (Denver: CHI, March 2005).

108. Grogan and Patashnik, "Between Welfare Medicine and Mainstream Entitlement."

109. Smith, *Entitlement Politics*.

110. Donna Ross, Laura Cox, and Caryn Marks, *Resuming the Path to Health Coverage for Children and Parents: A 50-State Update on Eligibility Rules, Enrollment and Renewal Procedures, and Cost-Sharing Practices in Medicaid and SCHIP in 2006* (Menlo Park, Calif.: Henry J. Kaiser Family Foundation, Kaiser Commission on Medicaid and the Uninsured, January 2007), available at http://www.kff.org.

111. In 1998, the administration issued a new rule that would allow more two-parent working families to participate in Medicaid: states could eliminate or raise the 100-hour per month limit on employment for the principal worker in order to qualify for the program. Twenty states already had permission to dispense with the 100-hour rule through waivers. Pear, "Clinton to Expand Medicaid for Some of the Working Poor"; Smith, *Entitlement Politics*.

112. For example, in 1996 Congress enacted the Health Insurance Portability and Accountability Act, which, among other provisions, authorized small-business purchasing pools; the portability of medical insurance; and a limited number of Medical Savings Accounts (up to 750,000 by December 2000 and restricted to persons who are self-employed or who work for small firms).

113. In order to "encourage" more of the 16.9 million adults with disabling conditions in the nation to seek employment, many of whom feared losing their Medicaid coverage, BBA 1997 and later the Ticket to Work and Work Incentives Improvement Act of 1999 gave the states the option of including in their plans a buy-in program for working people with disabilities whose earnings exceeded Medicaid eligibility levels. Such individuals could now increase their income without losing their welfare medicine benefits; they would pay premiums based on a sliding scale. Today, however, less than half of the states offer the program, and nearly all of these jurisdictions have long waiting lists.

114. As one researcher found, "The result was a barrage of proposals from states and 17 comprehensive Medicaid demonstration approvals between 1994 and 1999." Jennifer M. Ryan, *1115 Ways to Waive Medicaid and SCHIP Rules*, Issue Brief no. 777 (Washington, D.C.: National Health Policy Forum, George Washington University, June 13, 2002), 3. Each project was initially approved for at least five years, with opportunities for renewal.

115. Coughlin, Ku, and Holahan, *Medicaid Since 1980*.

116. Freudenheim, "Serving the Poor Private Insurance."

117. Hackey, *Rethinking Health Care Policy*.

118. Clarke Cagey, "Health Reform, Year Seven: Observations About Medicaid Managed Care," *Health Care Financing Review* (Fall 2000), 127.

119. Thomas R. Oliver, "The Collision of Economics and Politics in Medicaid Managed Care: Reflections on the Course of Reform in Maryland," *Milbank Quarterly 76*, no. 1 (1998): 59–101.

120. Anyone with earnings higher than the poverty threshold had to pay a premium, a deductible, and copayments on a sliding scale, based on total household income. By 1998, the coverage of people at or below 200 percent of the FPL had increased to 38 percent, up from 30 percent in 1993. Vernon Smith, Kathleen Gifford, Eileen Ellis, and Amy Wiles, *Results from a 50-State Survey: Medicaid Budgets, Spending, and Policy Initiatives in State Fiscal Years 2005 and 2006* (Menlo Park, Calif.: Henry J. Kaiser Family Foundation, Kaiser Commission on Medicaid and the Uninsured, October 2005), available at http://www.kff.org.

121. Providing eligibility for everyone at or below the poverty line, Oregon moved all participants into one of thirteen MCOs. By 1996, the medically uninsured population was reduced from 17 percent to 11 percent of the state's residents. As part of the revision, policymakers set up a prioritized system of medical and surgical procedures, ranked according to their effectiveness based on cost-benefit ratios; they would allow as many of them annually as they deemed financially feasible (which turned out to be a little more than 82 percent during the initial years). However, in limiting some medical procedures, the revision was subject to criticism as an immoral rationing of services.

The Oregon legislature also established the Family Health Assistance Program, which offered premium subsidies on a sliding scale to low-income residents not eligible for Medicaid, allowing them to purchase private insurance. Funded solely by the state at the time, the annual amount was capped. In addition, lawmakers added a "play or pay" mandate, requiring employers to cover their workers in a plan that was at least as generous as Medicaid; otherwise, they had to deposit funds into a state insurance pool. However, as shown in chapter 4, any enhancements were short-lived. Jonathan Oberlander, "Health Reform Interrupted: The Unraveling of the Oregon Health Plan," *Health Affairs* 26, no. 1 (January–February 2007): 96–105.

122. Hawaii has pursued its goal of providing at least some form of health insurance to its residents through two government programs. QUEST (the acronym used commonly instead of the very long full name: Quality Care Universal Access Efficient Utilization Stabilizing Costs Transforming the Way Health Care Is Provided) covers low-income families who do not have access to employer-sponsored plans. Since its establishment it has relied entirely on MCOs, except for children's dental services (eligibility for adults and children is at 100 percent and 200 percent, respectively, of the FPL). In contrast, the state's traditional Medical Assistance Program serving the elderly, disabled, and blind was until 2009 a fee-for-service plan. At that time, lawmakers obtained a section 1115 waiver mandating managed care for these clients.

Hawaii also had enacted "pay or play" regulations in 1974, requiring certain employers to cover the state's full-time workers or to contribute money into a system for those with incomes of up to 150 percent of the FPL. The state also caps employees' out-of-pocket expenses at 1.5 percent of their salary. National Conference of State Legislatures, *State Programs to Subsidize or Reduce the Cost of Health Insurance for Small Businesses and Individuals* (Washington, D.C.: National Conference of State Legislators, May 2007); Engel, *Poor People's Medicine.*

123. By the mid-1990s, other places, including Pennsylvania, Colorado, and Rhode Island, achieved nearly statewide MCO penetration for their welfare medicine clients. New York, which had only a small, voluntary capitated program in the 1980s, enacted the Medicaid Managed Care Act in 1991, which set targets for enrolling one-half of its welfare medicine population in MCOs over a five-year period. Its governor at the time, Mario Cuomo, had intended to compel participation gradually. In contrast, George Pataki, elected governor in 1995, wanted to force recipients into MCOs more rapidly, even before there were adequate services available. As a result, the state's waiver application was uncharacteristically delayed until he consented to slow down the pace. HHS gave its final approved in 1997, rendering the state's managed-care program the largest in the nation. Joyce Purnick, "Cutting Medicaid Will Not Be Crazy," *New York Times*, November 21, 1994; Ian Fisher, "Plan to Spread Pain of Medicaid Cuts Draws Wide but Tempered Criticism," *New York Times*, January 29, 1995; Elizabeth Rosenthal, "U.S. Sets Terms for State to Shift Medicaid to Managed Care," *New York Times*, August 15, 1996.

Beginning in the early 1990s, California required increasing numbers of recipients to join prepaid plans; the enrollment rate rose from less than 12 percent of its welfare medicine population in 1993 to fully 51 percent by 1999. Bonnie Austin, "Findings Brief: Managed Care Mandates Fall Short of Curbing California Medicaid Costs," *Academy Health* 8, no. 2 (March 2005): 1–3.

Selecting certain subsets of their Medicaid population starting in 1997, Oklahoma's SoonerCare and Maryland's HealthChoice engaged in large-scale shifts to mandatory managed-care plans as well. Smith et al., *Results from a 50-State Survey.*

Massachusetts used waivers to force all AFDC recipients into prepaid plans, and later, after broadening its Medicaid criteria to cover additional low-income populations (workers, children, the disabled, and persons with preexisting conditions), it energetically moved them into managed care, too. Hackey, *Rethinking Health Care Policy*.

124. Cagey, "Health Reform, Year Seven."

125. Medicaid enrollment growth in the early 1990s was due largely to the expanding eligibility of the blind and disabled, thus catching the attention of state legislators intent on cutting costs. By the end of the decade, about one-fourth of the states were employing waivers for this purpose, enrolling nearly 25 percent of Medicaid's younger disabled population. Cagey, "Health Reform, Year Seven."

A few states transferred a limited number of dually eligible frail older people into Programs of All Inclusive Care for the Elderly, permitted as a state option under BBA 1997.

126. Smith et al., *Results from a 50-State Survey*.

127. States that had more than 80 percent of their Medicaid clients covered through MCOs include Arizona (92 percent), Colorado (90 percent), Georgia (96 percent), Iowa (90 percent), Kentucky (81 percent), Maryland (81 percent), Michigan (100 percent), Oregon (83 percent), South Dakota (93 percent), Tennessee (100 percent), Utah (90 percent), and Washington State (100 percent).

128. U.S. HHS, Centers for Medicare and Medicaid Services, *National Summary of Medicaid Managed Care Programs and Enrollment* (Washington, D.C.: U.S. Government Printing Office, June 30, 2001); Laurene A. Graig, *Health of Nations: An International Perspective on U.S. Health Care Reform* (Washington, D.C.: Congressional Quarterly Press, 1999).

129. Grogan and Patashnik, "Between Welfare Medicine and Mainstream Entitlement."

4. Welfare Medicine in the Twenty-first Century

1. Rising to a record $378 billion in fiscal year (FY) 2003 and $412 billion in FY 2004, the annual federal deficit dropped to $319 billion in FY 2005, $248 billion in FY 2006, and $163 billion in FY 2007. However, it rose sharply to more than $400 billion in FY 2008 and reached $1.7 trillion at the end of 2009. The actual amounts, of course, are much greater because the federal government siphons surpluses from its off-budget accounts (mostly Social Security), replacing the money with IOUs, thus concealing the real debt.

2. David G. Smith, *Entitlement Politics: Medicare and Medicaid 1995–2001* (New York: De Gruyter, 2002).

3. The states also would have had the option to continue current arrangements, but without any additional federal assistance in future years.

4. Under HIFA, Medicaid could be extended to households with incomes up to 200 percent of the FPL. States had to retain mandatory populations and offer them the

federally established minimum benefit package. Except for children, optional groups could be given fewer services, have restrictions placed on their utilization, and be subject to cost sharing at the will of the state.

5. The governors opposed the president's severe cuts to welfare medicine; as usual, they were interested in greater control over Medicaid, but without sacrificing federal dollars.

6. In 2005, the administration had recommended $12.8 billion in Medicaid cuts over five years and more than $60 billion over ten years (a 2 percent decrease from projected spending). After interparty wrangling about the size of the reductions, Congress eventually whittled them down to $10 billion over five years. Policymakers expected most of the saving to come from lower payments to pharmacies; a crackdown on state financing maneuvers, including intergovernmental transfers and DSH payments; and stricter controls over asset transfers by the elderly.

In 2006, President Bush asked for another $14 billion in net federal Medicaid savings (and $35.9 billion for Medicare) over five years.

7. Several of these directives were revised rules from the previous year. The administration proposed an overall $25.7 billion reduction in the growth of Medicaid over five years, of which more than $12 billion would be achieved through the new regulations. At $66 billion, the cuts envisioned for Medicare were even higher. Henry J. Kaiser Family Foundation, Kaiser Commission on Medicaid and the Uninsured, *President's FY 2008 Budget and Medicaid*, fact sheet (Menlo Park, Calif.: Henry J. Kaiser Family Foundation, Kaiser Commission on Medicaid and the Uninsured, April 2007), available at http://www.kff.org.

8. These cuts included a decrease in allowable provider taxes; removal of state grants related to administration and transportation expenses for Medicaid-eligible children relying on school-based health clinics; curbs on certain medical, social, educational, and other ancillary services covered by "targeted case-management" plans; and the lowering of payments to government providers of services, such as public hospitals and nursing homes, which were now limited to documented costs. Other proposed regulations eliminated federal money for graduate medical education at teaching hospitals, reduced patient benefits covered in outpatient settings (dental, preventive, laboratory, and ambulance services), restricted the types of covered rehabilitative services for people with disabilities (including participants with mental illnesses), and cut pharmacy fees for generic drugs.

9. In violation of the congressional moratorium, President Bush had issued "emergency" regulations in an attempt to implement the $5 billion reduction in Medicaid reimbursements to public hospitals. Hospital trade associations filed a lawsuit, and in May 2008 a U.S. District Court in Washington, D.C. temporarily stopped the execution of these regulations.

10. The White House anticipated a reduction of from $13 to $17.8 billion in federal Medicaid funding over five years because of these directives; the states estimated the cuts at $50 billion. In his budget proposal for 2009, the president also recommended a $91 billion to $178.2 billion reduction in Medicare over five years that would be achieved mostly through a 0.4 percent cut to health care providers.

11. A provision of the American Recovery and Reinvestment Act encouraged the Department of Health and Human Services not to promulgate the rest of the Bush rules. The permanently rescinded rules, if left in place, would have removed state grants for certain school-based health services, curbed case-management payments, reduced patient benefits covered in outpatient settings, and decreased allowable provider taxes.

12. As part of its 2005 budget measure reducing the growth of Medicaid spending by $10 billion over five years, Republicans had called for the creation of a bipartisan commission, appointed by HHS secretary Mike Leavitt, to advise them on options for achieving the savings and to provide long-term solutions to rising welfare medicine costs. The resultant Federal Medicaid Advisory Commission, cochaired by former Tennessee governor Don Sundquist (R–Tenn.) and former Maine governor Angus King (Independent), was boycotted by Democratic legislators as well as by all but two governors. Notwithstanding these protests, its proposals were incorporated into the DRA.

In January 2007, the commission presented its long-term recommendations for restructuring the program. It predictably promoted state flexibility, especially in their ability to tailor plans to particular participant groups; premium assistance to recipients for purchasing health insurance in the private market; greater provision of LTC at home and in the community, whenever feasible (along with tax breaks for family caregivers and the use of home equity to finance privately delivered services); personal responsibility for health care decisions; rewards for healthy behavior; tax breaks for LTC insurance; and a Medicaid Advantage plan for dual eligibles, modeled after Medicare. Medicaid Commission, *Final Report and Recommendations*, presented to Michael O. Leavitt, secretary, Department of Health and Human Services (Washington, D.C.: U.S. Government Printing Office, December 29, 2006).

13. Because of some opposition from Republican moderates, the Senate initially had been somewhat adverse to such a severe undermining of federal standards and oversight of the program.

14. Premiums could be imposed on households with an income more than 150 percent of the FPL. Total cost sharing had to be kept to less than 5 percent of family earnings for children as well as for other groups that the states were federally required to cover.

15. It specifically lifted the moratorium on the Long-Term Care Partnership Programs, which had been limited to five states, for the purpose of persuading families to purchase private LTC insurance policies.

16. According to one study, for every one percent increase in unemployment, an additional 470,000 children and 387,000 nondisabled adults younger than age sixty-five become qualified for Medicaid. Stan Dorn, Barbara Markham Smith, and Bowen Garrett, *Medicaid Responsiveness, Health Coverage, and Economic Resilience: A Preliminary Analysis* (Washington, D.C.: Health Policy Institute of the Joint Center for Political and Economic Studies, September 27, 2005).

James Fossett and Courtney Burke have estimated the consequent growth in Medicaid eligibility somewhat higher, at about 1.6 million. James W. Fossett and Courtney E.

Burke, *Managing Medicaid: Take-Up, Is Medicaid Retrenching? State Budgets and Medicaid Enrollment in 2002* (Albany, N.Y.: Federalism Research Group, Rockefeller Institute of Government, February 2003), 15.

17. In both 2002 and 2003, enrollment grew by nearly 9 percent.

18. Medicaid costs averaged an astounding 12 percent annual growth in 2001 and 2002, 6.9 percent in 2003, and 7.6 percent in 2004. Lisa Dubay, Christina Moylan, and Thomas Oliver, "Advancing Toward Universal Coverage: Are States Able to Take the Lead?" *Journal of Health Care Law and Policy* 7, no. 1 (2004): 1–41; Donald Boyd and Victoria Wachino, *Medicaid and the Uninsured: Is the State Fiscal Crisis Over? A 2004 State Budget Update* (Menlo Park, Calif.: Henry J. Kaiser Family Foundation, Kaiser Commission on Medicaid and the Uninsured, January 2004), 1–15, available at http://www.kff.org.

19. In 1994, Medicaid had averaged 15 percent of total state budgets, but by 2004 it had grown to nearly 20 percent. Jurisdictions spending the most as a percentage of their overall budget included Tennessee (33.3 percent), Missouri (30.7 percent), Pennsylvania (29.5 percent), Maine (29 percent), New York (28.3 percent), Illinois (28.1 percent), Vermont (27.5 percent), New Hampshire (26.4 percent), Mississippi (26.3 percent), and Rhode Island (25.5 percent). Averages for other items as a percentage of the states' overall budget included: elementary and secondary education (23 percent), higher education (11 percent), transportation (9 percent), corrections (4 percent), and cash assistance (2 percent). U.S. GAO, *Medicaid: Strategies to Help States Address Increased Expenditures During Economic Downturns* (Washington, D.C.: U.S. Government Printing Office, October 2006); Dianne Rahm, *United States Public Policy: A Budgetary Approach* (Belmont, Calif.: Wadsworth, 2004).

State-financed Medicaid also varies widely. In 2001, it averaged 12 percent nationwide but accounted for a high of 20.5 in Connecticut and a low of 4.4 percent in Alaska. Donald Boyd, *The Current State Fiscal Crisis and Its Aftermath* (Menlo Park, Calif.: Henry J. Kaiser Family Foundation, Kaiser Commission on Medicaid and the Uninsured, September 2003), available at http://www.kff.org.

20. Mark Rushefsky has pointed out to me that during the late 1990s a number of states, including his own (Missouri), had enacted tax cuts, thereby rendering them even less capable of coping with the economic downturn.

21. In 2002, for instance, proceeds averaged a 7.5 percent decline in real per capita tax revenues. U.S. GAO, *Medicaid: Strategies to Help States.*

22. Boyd and Wachino, *Medicaid and the Uninsured.*

23. Under the Jobs and Growth Tax Relief Reconciliation Act of 2003, the states received $10 billion in general fiscal relief and another $10 billion for their Medicaid programs through the end of FY 2004. In 2009, they were granted $87 billion in federal reimbursements for welfare medicine alone over an eighteen-month period.

24. In their study of ten states, James Fossett and Courtney Burke found that, on average, Medicaid cutbacks were less than 7 percent of the total gap-filling and budget-balancing measures and 12 percent of overall expenditure reductions. However, the extent of damage to the program varied, depending on the will of the state's political leaders. These authors point out that in West Virginia, Kansas, Michigan, and Arizona,

+ +

for example, the governors decided to protect Medicaid and were "largely able to sustain this position even under challenge." James Fossett and Courtney Burke, *Medicaid and State Budgets in FY 2004: Why Medicaid Is Hard to Cut* (Albany, N.Y.: Federalism Research Group, Rockefeller Institute of Government, July 2004), 15.

25. Dubay, Moylan, and Oliver, "Advancing Toward Universal Coverage"; Donna Ross, Laura Cox, and Caryn Marks, *Resuming the Path to Health Coverage for Children and Parents: A 50-State Update on Eligibility Rules, Enrollment and Renewal Procedures, and Cost-Sharing Practices in Medicaid and SCHIP in 2006* (Menlo Park, Calif.: Henry J. Kaiser Family Foundation, Kaiser Commission on Medicaid and the Uninsured, January 2007), available at http://www.kff.org.

26. Smith, *Entitlement Politics*.

27. U.S Congress, Joint Economic Commission, *Highlights from the Census Bureau's Update on U.S. Health Insurance Coverage*, fact sheet delivered to Senator Charles E. Schumer, chair, and Congresswoman Carolyn B. Maloney, vice chair (Washington, D.C.: U.S. Government Printing Office, August 29, 2007).

28. Carmen DeNavas-Walt, Bernadette Proctor, and Jessica Smith, *Income, Poverty, and Health Insurance Coverage in the U.S.: 2006*, U.S. Census Bureau Current Population Report, P60-233 (Washington, D.C.: U.S. Government Printing Office, 2007).

29. Two-thirds of the medically uninsured population are poor, although most of them reside in families with at least one member who works full-time (70 percent) or part-time (11 percent). Roughly 55 percent of employees from low-income families have no access to employer-sponsored insurance, compared to only 4 percent of those from higher-income households. Henry J. Kaiser Family Foundation, Kaiser Commission on Medicaid and the Uninsured, *The Uninsured: A Primer. Key Facts About Americans Without Health Insurance* (Menlo Park, Calif.: Henry J. Kaiser Family Foundation, Kaiser Commission on Medicaid and the Uninsured, October 2006), available at http://www.kff.org.

30. Only about 5 percent of families participate in the nongroup private-sector market.

31. Increases in caseloads averaged 4 percent in 2005 and 1.6 percent in 2006; the growth in program outlays averaged 6 percent and 2.8 percent, respectively. Vernon Smith, Kathleen Gifford, Eileen Ellis, and Amy Wiles, *Low Medicaid Spending Growth amid Rebounding State Revenues: Results from a 50-State Medicaid Budget Survey Fiscal Years 2006 and 2007*, executive summary (Menlo Park, Calif.: Henry J. Kaiser Family Foundation, Kaiser Commission on Medicaid and the Uninsured, October 2006), available at http://www.kff.org; Vernon Smith, Kathleen Gifford, Eileen Ellis, and Amy Wiles, *Results from a 50-State Survey: Medicaid Budgets, Spending, and Policy Initiatives in State Fiscal Years 2005 and 2006* (Menlo Park, Calif.: Henry J. Kaiser Family Foundation, Kaiser Commission on Medicaid and the Uninsured, October 2005), available at http://www.kff.org.

In the first six months of 2007, Medicaid expenditures significantly shifted direction: they escalated by 10.7 percent, whereas state revenues rose only 5 percent. Dennis Cauchon, "Medicaid Spending Jumps Sharply," *USA Today*, October 8, 2007.

32. Health Policy Tracking Service, *What the States Said, Did, and Plan to Do* (Eagan, Minn.: Thompson Corporation, October 5, 2005).

33. Ross, Cox, and Marks, *Resuming the Path to Health Coverage for Children and Parents*; National Association of State Budget Offices and the National Governors Association, *The Fiscal Survey of States* (Washington, D.C. : U.S. Government Printing Office, December 2007).

34. For example, South Carolina relies on the cigarette tax for the program Working Families, Healthy Families, and Colorado passed a referendum for assisting pregnant women and children through more money from smokers. Oregon voters increased cigarette tax rates in 1996 and 2002 and considered it again in 2006 for welfare medicine purposes. That year, Amendment 3 in Missouri and Proposition 86 in California—both tobacco measures—were placed on the ballot to raise money for improvements to welfare medicine; the initiatives failed. However, a similar proposal passed in South Dakota. The governors of Iowa, Kansas, Maryland, Mississippi, and Vermont, among others, also have shown an interest in using greater cigarette taxes to expand Medicaid.

35. Smith et al., *Low Medicaid Spending Growth amid Rebounding State Revenues*. In 2007, twenty-two states improved physician fees, and in 2008 thirty-three states planned to do so. In Connecticut, fees were raised from 45 percent of Medicare reimbursement levels to 80 percent. In most other states, however, the increase was much more modest. Forty-six states boosted nursing home rates for 2008. Vernon Smith, Kathleen Gifford, Eileen Ellis, Robin Rudowitz, Molly O'Malley, and Caryn Marks, *As Tough Times Wane, States Act to Impose Medicaid Coverage and Quality: Results from a 50-State Medicaid Budget Survey for State Fiscal Years 2007 and 2008* (Menlo Park, Calif.: Henry J. Kaiser Family Foundation, Kaiser Commission on Medicaid and the Uninsured, October 2007), available at http://www.kff.org.

36. In early 1980, Congress had enacted legislation that allowed states to override this rule as long as the changes saved money and did not produce second-class medicine for the poor.

37. Georgia, for example, is one of the leanest states in terms of scope of services. Its governor, Sonny Perdue (R), intent on curbing Medicaid costs, has centered most of his waiver revisions on forcing more families into one of three commercial insurance companies: Amerigroup, Peach State Health Plan (Centene), and WellCare.

38. Henry J. Kaiser Family Foundation, Kaiser Commission on Medicaid and the Uninsured, *Medicaid and SCHIP* (Menlo Park, Calif.: Henry J. Kaiser Family Foundation, Kaiser Commission on Medicaid and the Uninsured, 2007), available at http://www.statehealthfacts.org.

In 1991, 2.7 million people, or 9.5 percent of the Medicaid population, were covered under MCOs; the proportion steadily climbed to 50 percent in 2000 and 59 percent by 2003. Penelope Lemov, "Critical Condition," in John R. Baker, ed., *The Lanahan Readings in State and Local Government*, 457–464 (Baltimore: Lanahan, 2001).

Slightly more than 70 percent of SCHIP clients are currently enrolled in managed care, 14 percent participate in primary-care management, and 16 percent receive fee-for-service care. Stan Dorn and John Holahan, *Are We Heading Toward Socialized Medicine?* (Washington, D.C.: Urban Institute, April 16, 2008).

39. Under his Louisiana Health First Plan, Governor Jindal is seeking a waiver to pilot a mandated managed-care program in four parts of the state, based on the Florida model. His ultimate goal is to institute the capitated medical plans statewide.

40. Other states that expanded eligibility but also with a marked undercutting of federal regulations were Arkansas, Indiana, Iowa, and New Mexico.

41. Eligibility was limited to people with incomes less than 150 percent of the FPL.

42. Jennifer M. Ryan, *1115 Ways to Waive Medicaid and SCHIP Rules*, Issue Brief no. 777 (Washington, D.C.: National Health Policy Forum, George Washington University, June 13, 2002); Samantha Artiga, David Rousseau, and Barbara Lyons, "Can States Stretch the Medicaid Dollar Without Passing the Buck? Lessons from Utah," *Health Affairs* 25, no. 2 (March–April 2006): 532–540.

43. Despite the facts that 116,000 uninsured people in Utah were eligible for PCN by 2006 and that the state was experiencing a record budget surplus, estimated at between $70 million and $1 billion, officials maintained an enrollment ceiling of 19,000 participants.

44. Artiga, Rousseau, and Lyons, "Can States Stretch the Medicaid Dollar Without Passing the Buck?"

45. As part of the waiver, Oregon's governor, John Kitzhaber (D), was able to procure a federal match to enhance the Family Health Insurance Assistance Program that subsidized private insurance for low-income residents not eligible for Medicaid; it had previously been financed solely by the state. Jonathan Oberlander, "Health Reform Interrupted: The Unraveling of the Oregon Health Plan," *Health Affairs* 26, no. 1 (January–February 2007): 96–105.

46. Ibid., 102. By 2005, there were only 27,000 recipients left, from a high of 92,000 in 2003. A ceiling of 24,000 was subsequently placed on the plan, which was now funded entirely by beneficiary premiums and provider taxes.

47. Joan Alker, *Premium Assistance Programs: How Are They Financed and Do States Save Money?* (Menlo Park, Calif.: Henry J. Kaiser Family Foundation, Kaiser Commission on Medicaid and the Uninsured, October 2005), available at http://www.kff.org; Pam Silberman, Laura Brogan, and Charity Moore, *Premium Assistance Programs for Low Income Families: How Well Does It Work in Rural Areas?* (Chapel Hill: Cecil G. Sheps Center for Health Services Research, University of North Carolina, January 24, 2006); Thomas McAuliffe, *Supporting Private Insurance Through Premium Assistance*, fact sheet (St. Louis: Missouri Foundation for Health, January 2007).

48. Silberman, Brogan, and Moore, *Premium Assistance Programs for Low Income Families*.

49. Alker, *Premium Assistance Programs*. For example, in 2007 newly elected Arkansas governor Mike Beebe (D) established a bare-bones, "safety-net" package, the ARHealthNet insurance plan, for low-income workers (in businesses with 500 or fewer employees) who have not had medical coverage for at least a year. Participants must pay an annual deductible and copayments and are limited to only six physician visits, seven inpatient hospital days, two outpatient procedures, and two monthly drug prescriptions per year. The state expected its share of the costs to come from its $18 million tobacco settlement money.

50. For instance, Oklahoma's Employer/Employee Partnership for Insurance Coverage is funded by a tobacco tax that was instituted in 2005. The program, which offers a state-defined basic benefit package to firms hiring fifty or fewer workers with incomes at or less than 185 percent of the FPL, subsidizes up to 60 percent of the premium. The employer is required to contribute a minimum of 25 percent for each employee; the worker pays up to 15 percent, subject to a cap of 3 percent of his or her gross annual family income. McAuliffe, *Supporting Private Insurance Through Premium Assistance*; National Conference of State Legislatures, *State Programs to Subsidize or Reduce the Cost of Health Insurance for Small Businesses and Individuals* (Washington, D.C.: National Conference of State Legislators, May 2007).

The state share of South Carolina's new premium assistance program similarly derived mostly from an increase in the cigarette tax. As part of the state's market-based waiver initiatives, Governor Mark Sanford (R) linked Medicaid to a buy-in program, Working Families, Healthy Families, which supports the purchase of private insurance by low-income employees of small businesses consisting of seventy-five workers or less. Available to people earning up to 200 percent of the FPL, Medicaid covers 60 percent of the cost.

Montana's small-business purchasing pool, which includes subsidized premiums on a sliding scale based on family income, is also funded by a tobacco tax.

51. New Mexico's New Health Plan Initiative, launched in 2005, relies most heavily on federal SCHIP money, about 74 percent of the total. Each month companies must pay $75 per employee; workers, who contribute up to $35 (based on family income), are responsible for copayments. National Conference of State Legislatures, *State Programs to Subsidize or Reduce the Cost of Health Insurance*; Institute for Health Policy, *Comparing the Dirigo Choice Program Experience with Other State Initiatives Targeted to Small Business and Individuals* (Portland: Muskie School of Public Service, University of Southern Maine, August 2006).

52. In Nevada, for example, the state contributes only $100 per month to cover a portion of the worker's 50 percent share of premium expenses for a bare-bones plan.

In Kentucky, the state pays employers who are participating in its 2006 Insurance Coverage Affordability and Relief to Small Employers Program $40 per month for each qualified worker, an amount that is reduced by $10 per year. What is more, the legislature committed itself to just two years of funding.

The Montana program, which has incurred substantial growth, capped its enrollments; as of August 2007, there was a waiting list.

53. McAuliffe, *Supporting Private Insurance Through Premium Assistance*.

54. As a case in point, Maryland's new premium-assisted program was not available to any employers who already offered health insurance to its workers. The Working Families and Small Business Coverage Act, signed by Governor Martin O'Malley (D) at the end of 2007, both raised Medicaid eligibility levels and provided funds to subsidize pensions in the private market for workers in small companies (employing from two to nine people). Employees must earn less than $50,000 per year.

55. National Conference of State Legislatures, *State Programs to Subsidize or Reduce the Cost of Health Insurance*.

56. As a case in point, in 2005 the programs in Utah and New Jersey served only 73 and 791 people, respectively. New Mexico's plan enrolled just 4,837. Maine's Dirigo Choice, established in 2005, covered slightly more than 11,000 people that year; it is available for companies with fifty or fewer employees. Institute for Health Policy, *Comparing the Dirigo Choice Program Experience.*

Oklahoma's Employer/Employee Partnership for Insurance Coverage had assisted 731 businesses and 664 individuals as of January 2007. McAuliffe, *Supporting Private Insurance Through Premium Assistance.*

Healthy New York, created as part of the state's Health Care Reform Act of 2000, subsidizes premiums for high-cost participants and provides reinsurance subsidies for other low-income working residents. Although its enrollment numbers are relatively high, the approximately 107,000 participants represent less than 6 percent of employees without any health care coverage.

57. Joan Alker found that a typical full-time Wal-Mart employee, earning roughly $14,400 annually, would have to spend $181 per month for herself and one child to enroll in the company's plan. Under the Illinois subsidized program for children, she would pay $106 per month, a sum that still represents nearly 9 percent of her earnings. Before receiving any benefits, she must contribute another $350 for the deductible. Alker, *Premium Assistance Programs.*

58. Massachusetts, for example, had earlier endeavored to establish universal coverage through its 1988 Health Security Act, but because of its subsequent fiscal crisis it was forced to postpone and ultimately repeal the legislation three years later. Its "pay or play" employer mandate was also delayed before being rescinded in 1996. Robert B. Hackey, *Rethinking Health Care Policy: The New Politics of State Regulation* (Washington, D.C.: Georgetown University Press, 1998).

Similarly, in 1994 Minnesota had attempted to insure all of its residents who had no access to employer-based insurance for at least eighteen months. Its 1997 implementation deadline was postponed to 2000, but the program collapsed before then because of insufficient revenues, among other factors.

Washington State's initial attempt at universal coverage in 1993 also became mired in problems, including huge premium increases, a withdrawal of the employer mandate by its newly elected Republican legislative officials the following year, and abandonment of the market by companies offering individual insurance. Teresa A. Coughlin, Leighton Ku, and John Holahan, *Medicaid Since 1980: Costs, Coverage, and the Shifting Alliance Between the Federal Government and the States* (Washington, D.C.: Urban Institute, 1994); Michael S. Sparer, *Medicaid and the Limits of State Health Reform* (Philadelphia: Temple University Press, 1996); Lemov, "Critical Condition."

Nevertheless, today Washington State has one of the lowest uninsured populations (slightly under 10 percent) and has been steadily attempting to cover even more people.

59. Individuals who refuse to purchase health care insurance must pay a penalty. The maximum amount was $912 in 2008, up from $219 the previous year.

60. These policies are called Commonwealth Connector Health Insurance Plans.

61. Households having earnings up to the FPL are fully subsidized.

62. The researchers do warn, however, that even the top plans are sorely lacking in at least some aspects of their coverage, benefit packages, cost-sharing requirements, and quality of care. Annette B. Ramirez and Sidney M. Wolfe, *Unsettling Scores: A Ranking of State Medicaid Programs*, Public Citizen Health Research Group (PCHRG) Publication no. 1807 (Washington, D.C.: PCHRG, April 2007).

63. Few of the medically insured nonelderly adults participate in Medicaid (15 percent). Most (roughly 80 percent) rely on employer-based plans; the remainder (5 percent) depend on Medicare.

64. Robert Steinbrook, "Health Care Reform in Massachusetts—Expanding Coverage, Escalating Costs," *New England Journal of Medicine* 358, no. 26 (June 26, 2008): 2757–2760.

65. Ramirez and Wolfe, *Unsettling Scores.*

66. Dr. Dinosaur serves children living in households with income less than 300 percent of the FPL, pregnant women with income less than 200 percent of the FPL, and parents less than 185 percent of the FPL. The Vermont Health Access Plan is available to adults living in households with income less than 150 percent of the FPL.

67. The program relies partially on increased tobacco taxes. Individuals must be uninsured for at least twelve months to be eligible for the subsidies, a provision that was added to deter companies from dropping their health care plans.

68. These changes include increased premiums for Dr. Dinosaur and the Vermont Health Access Plan, lowered reimbursement rates for certain physicians, and higher deductibles for the state's Catamount Health Plan.

69. For example, the rate of uninsured residents dropped from approximately 11 percent in 2007 to only 10.7 percent at the end of 2008.

70. Eligibility was extended to parents and childless adults with family incomes up to 200 percent and 125 percent of the FPL, respectively. The program, which already covered roughly one-fifth of all residents, had been scheduled to increase another 10 percent by 2009.

71. Enacted under Maine's Dirigo Health Reform Act of 2003, the program is available to people with incomes up to 300 percent of the FPL who are employed in companies with fifty or fewer workers.

72. BadgerCare Plus, launched in 2008, is available to children under the age of nineteen whose parents are not covered by an employer-sponsored plan. Households with up to 300 percent of the FPL pay a premium from $10 to $90 per month for each child, depending on their income. Those with earnings higher than that ceiling can purchase coverage at full cost. Parents with incomes up to 200 percent of the FPL also can enroll in BadgerCare Plus.

Children in families with an income less than 200 percent of the FPL, who are fully subsidized, are placed in the Standard Plan, which is similar to Wisconsin's traditional Medicaid benefits package. Higher-income enrollees are covered under a more limited Benchmark Plan (modeled on the state's largest commercial low-cost plan). Since early 2009, childless adults with incomes up to 200 percent of the FPL are eligible for even more basic services; the BadgerCare Plus Core Plan offers only primary and preventive physician care and generic drugs. As in other states, Wisconsin lawmakers are expecting to pay for the expansions primarily through cost-saving measures, such as its managed-care mandate, income accruing from the hefty cost-sharing provisions, a hospital tax, and money from its uncompensated care pool.

73. Emily Wagler Pettus, "Moody: Medicaid Tightening up on Providers and Recipients," *Sun Herald* (Biloxi, Miss.), August 17, 2005, available at http://www.sunherald .com/.

74. Governor Bredesen achieved 59 percent of his original goal of 323,000 people. Two years later, the state reopened its medically needy program, renamed "Standard Spend Down," with a more restrictive benefit package, and an enrollment cap of 100,000 participants.

75. The report is cited in John Reichard, "Learning from Tennessee's Medicaid Cuts," *CQ Health Beat*, April 23, 2007.

76. Republicans had taken over the House in 2001 and the Senate in 2002; Blunt began his term after twelve years of Democrats in the governor's office.

77. In January 2006, endowed with a slight budget surplus, Governor Blunt proposed placing some of these disabled workers in a revised, pared-down program, Medical Assistance for Employed Persons with Disabilities. However, because he tied the legislation to fraud control, including financial incentives for whistle-blowers and tougher penalties for Medicaid cheaters, it failed to pass.

78. A suit was brought against Missouri by individuals who had lost coverage for their medical equipment; the court ruled that under federal law the state does not have to cover any durable medical equipment, but it cannot pick and choose which ones will be included in the Medicaid benefits package.

79. Intent on achieving a major overhaul of welfare medicine, especially through greater privatization, Governor Blunt had established the Medicaid Reform Commission to design a replacement plan. According to Blunt, "And we must unleash the power of the free market by empowering individuals to be more informed and active customers." Quoted in Jason Rosenbaum, "Blunt: Medicaid a Relic," *Columbia Daily Tribune* (Mo.), January 25, 2007, available at http://archives.columbiatribune.com/2007/jan/ 20070125news003.asp.

80. Ramirez and Wolfe, *Unsettling Scores*.

81. The plan allowed only two brand-name and three generic medications per year. An exemption was eventually made for participants with HIV.

82. By 2006, 15,000 people (4,000 of them children) had been dropped from the rolls. Joe Rutherford, "Medicaid Issues," *Northeast Mississippi Daily Journal*, April 29, 2007.

83. In 2008, the Mississippi deficit reached from $90 million to $100 million. Among other alternatives, policymakers debated an increase in the cigarette tax, by how much, and whether to impose a hospital tax.

84. The restructured Medicaid plan was opposed by Rhode Island's Congressional Delegation and all Democrats in the state legislature.

85. The federal Medicare Prescription Drug Improvement and Modernization Act of 2003 authorized tax exemptions for individuals and their employers who contribute to HSAs (previously called Medical Savings Accounts). These exclusions appear to be used

primarily by high-income households as a vehicle for reducing their tax obligations rather than for their medical needs. U.S. GAO, *Health Savings Accounts: Participation Grew and Many HSA-Eligible Plan Enrollees Did Not Open HSAs While Individuals Who Did Had Higher Incomes*, testimony before the Subcommittee on Health, Committee on Ways and Means, U.S. House of Representatives, 110th Cong., 2d sess., May 14, 2008 (Washington, D.C.: Government Printing Office, 2008).

86. Ten states were given approval, beginning in January 2007, to implement HOAs as demonstrations under the DRA. However, they were not allowed to include the elderly, disabled, pregnant women, or anyone who was institutionalized. Regardless, the Bush administration's intention was to expand HOAs nationwide and to open the programs to more groups of people.

South Carolina was one of the first states to apply. Determined to privatize its already sorely limited and deficient Medicaid program, Governor Mark Sanford (R) earlier had forwarded thirty separate waiver proposals to HHS. Under his overall plan, South Carolina Medicaid Choice, most recipients would be given Personal Health Accounts, with a fixed dollar amount, to purchase their medical services. When the Bush administration opened up the HOA pilot projects to the states, Governor Sanford redirected this piece of his program to the new demonstration, with the intention of spreading it throughout the state in five years. Lawmakers also launched another pilot program, the high-deductible Benchmark Plan, currently offered to South Carolina government employees: up to 1,000 Medicaid recipients could join. The state, with less than 10 percent of its Medicaid population enrolled in commercial plans, also began automatically moving nearly everyone into managed care.

87. Under federal law, the HOAs are capped at $2,500 per adult and $1,000 per child annually. Participants must meet a large deductible ($250 for adults and $100 for children) before they are eligible for any Medicaid benefits and must pay substantial copayments, using their HOA debit cards for at least partial defrayal of these costs. Families are responsible for any medical services beyond the maximum allowable amount.

88. Recipients can graduate from Team Care after a year of "good behavior."

89. Since 2007, Idaho helps offset premiums for children who go for an annual checkup and receive their immunizations. The state also provides financial rewards (vouchers) to enable clients to participate in weight-management or smoking-cessation programs. "FAMIS-ly Fit" in Virginia, a pilot program for overweight children on Medicaid, includes guidance on exercising, psychological counseling related to overeating, and rewards for those who stay on a healthy path. Wisconsin has included incentives for healthful activities in its SCHIP expansion waiver. Jessica Greene, *State Approaches to Consumer Direction in Medicaid: Issue Brief* (Hamilton, N.J.: Center for Health Care Strategies, July 2007).

In December 2007, Indiana received a section 1115 waiver to launch its Healthy Indiana Plan, available to uninsured adults with incomes up to 200 percent of the FPL and who lack the opportunity to participate in an employer-sponsored plan. They will have access to a high-deductible Personal Wellness and Responsibility Account, worth $1,100, that is funded through their own premium contributions (from 2 percent to 5 percent of a household's gross income, depending on total earnings) and through state money, financed by a cigarette tax. Any balances can be rolled over to the next year as long as individuals obtain preventive services, such as smoking-cessation programs, as required by the plan; enrollees can receive up to $500 per year for these wellness activities. If participants exceed the money in their personal account, they also are eligible for a basic commercial benefits package for additional medical expenses.

90. The program began in March 2007 as a pilot in three counties and was expanded statewide eight months later.

91. Michael Hendryx, Carol Irvin, James Mulligan, Sally Richardson, Johanna Beanet, and Margo Rosenbach, *Evaluation of Mountain Health Choices: Implementation Challenges and Recommendations* (Morgantown: Institute for Health Policy Research at West Virginia University and Mathematica Policy Research, March 2009); Joan Alker, *West Virginia's Medicaid Redesign: What Is the Impact on Children?* (Washington, D.C.: Health Policy Institute, Center for Children and Families, Georgetown University, August 2008); Pat Redmond, Judith Solomon, and Mark Lin, *Can Incentives for Healthy Behavior Improve Health and Hold Down Medicaid Costs?* (Washington, D.C.: Center on Budget and Policy Priorities, June 1, 2007), 4–5.

92. The program was enacted under Oklahoma's Medicaid Reform Act in 2006. Governor Brad Henry (D) intends to extend the program statewide.

93. HHS approved an even more problematic market-based approach, GraniteCare Select, in June 2007, but the New Hampshire legislature subsequently put it on hold. The program would have put certain procedures, such as ambulatory surgery and diagnostic radiology, out to bid to hospitals throughout the state. Recipients thus not only would have to run the risk of low-quality care, but would have to travel long distances for their medical services. Lauren R. Dorgan, "HHS Wants Low Bidder for Medicaid—Women, Children Could Travel for Care," *Concord Monitor*, June 30, 2007.

94. Initiated by former governor Tom Vilsack (D), the new IowaCare Program replaced the State Papers/Indigent Care plan for these enrollees beginning in the summer of 2005.

95. Quoted in Victoria Wallack, "Maine's Medicaid Program Deemed Unsustainable," *Lincoln County News Online* (Maine), October 19, 2005, available at http://lincolncountynewsonline.com/main.asp?search=1&articleID=22250&sectionID=8&subsectionID=8&5=1.

96. With 2.2 million beneficiaries and total program expenditures of $15 billion in 2006, Florida's Medicaid program was the fourth largest in the United States. The governor had received approval for his plan from the state legislature, composed of Republican majorities in both houses; most Democrats were opposed to it.

97. Douglas M. Cook, director of the Florida Agency for Health Care Administration, which administers the Florida Medicaid program, lamented at the time: "We didn't realize how difficult it was going to be. We see abuses every day that are egregious." Quoted in Robert Pear, "Florida's Struggles to Lift Burden of Medicaid Serves as Model and Warning," *New York Times*, April 24, 1995.

By 1995, twenty-nine insurance companies, some of them set up mainly or exclusively for welfare medicine clientele, served 440,000 enrollees. They generated huge profits, especially through a succession of buying and selling their firms over the years.

98. Children and pregnant women were exempt.

99. From \$15 to \$25 in credit is placed in an Enhanced Benefits Account for individuals who engage in nineteen approved activities, including annual checkups, immunizations and cancer screenings, compliance with medication regimens, and participation in alcohol, drug, exercise, or weight loss treatment programs. Greene, *State Approaches to Consumer Direction in Medicaid*.

100. For example, patients cannot be treated by specialists who accept Medicaid but are outside the plan's immediate network, thereby often causing long and possibly fatal delays.

101. As a case in point, the largest insurer, WellCare Health Plans Inc., pulled out of the pilot programs in 2009, forcing thousands of its clients to scramble for coverage.

102. In a letter to HHS secretary Michael Leavitt and congressional leaders, the GAO general counsel noted that in approving the Florida governor's waiver, HHS had set aside certain mandatory requirements for private plans enrolling Medicaid recipients. U.S. GAO, *Medicaid Demonstration Projects in Florida and Vermont Approved Under Section 115 of the Social Security Act*, letter from Gary L. Kepplinger, general counsel, GAO, to Michael O. Leavitt, secretary, U.S. HHS, July 24, 2007, B-309734 (Washington, D.C.: U.S. Government Printing Office, 2007), available at http://www. gao.gov/decisions/other/309734.pdf.

103. According to investigators at the Georgetown University Health Policy Institute, who surveyed medical providers and clients in 2007, half of the responding doctors indicated that new restrictions and requirements imposed by the MCOs rendered it more difficult to provide medically necessary services to children. Medicaid participants claimed that they found it difficult to negotiate through the maze of health plans, each offering a different benefits package. Joan Alker and Jack Hoadley, *Waving Cautionary Flags: Initial Reactions from Doctors and Patients to Florida's Medicaid Changes*, Briefing no. 2, commissioned by the Jessie Ball du Pont Fund (Washington, D.C.: Health Policy Institute, Georgetown University, May 2007).

In a study of Florida's Broward and Duval counties, other researchers concluded that despite the hype about greater competition, expanded choices, and consumer-driven systems of care, participants had limited awareness or understanding of the reform: approximately one-third of the enrollees did not even know that they had been switched to a new plan, and roughly half of the total had played no role in choosing their own coverage. Teresa Coughlin, Sharon Long, Timothy Triplett, Samantha Artiga, Barbara Lyons, R. Paul Duncan, and Allyson Hall, "Florida's Medicaid Reform? Informed Consumer Choice?" *Health Affairs* 27, no. 6 (November–December 2008): 523–532.

104. "Medicaid 'Reform' Adds New Problems to Old," editorial, *Palm Beach Post*, November 3, 2007.

105. When Florida officials attempted to add the three counties (Baker, Clay, and Nassau) to the ongoing demonstration projects in Broward and Duval counties, one of the commissioners petitioned the newly elected governor, Charlie Crist (R), to postpone the addition. The chief executive of Baker County Medical Services and a top administrator of Ed Fraser Memorial Hospital (a nonprofit, charity medical center) also vehemently objected to the extension of the experiment, arguing that "it will funnel

public money to Medicaid HMOs instead of helping poor people. . . . We will subsidize the state of Florida. We will not subsidize a private company. . . . These people are destroying the health care system." Quoted in J. Taylor Rushing, "Nassau Resists Medicaid Reform," *Florida Times-Union* (Jacksonville), July 5, 2007.

Regardless of the disastrous impact of the pilots on clients to date, Republicans in the Florida House of Representatives and the Florida Agency for Health Care Administration pushed for an expansion of the "experiment" to at least twenty more counties in 2009.

Lawmakers had also implemented a two-year dental managed-care pilot (Medicaid Pre-Paid Dental Pilot) in Miami-Dade County, through Atlantic Dental Inc. At the end of the demonstration in 2006, the University of Florida Institute for Child Health Policy and the College of Dental Medicine at Columbia University evaluated its effectiveness. The researchers learned that the state did not reap any financial advantage but did receive a lower quality of care for its money: the percentage of eligible children with at least one dental visit declined from 37 percent to 22 percent, and fewer dentists participated in the program. Despite the negative findings, the legislature extended the program for at least three more years. Burton Edelstein, *Miami-Dade County Prepaid Dental Health Plan Demonstration: Less Value for State Dollars* (Miami: Collins Center for Public Policy and Community Voices Miami, August 2006).

106. By the end of 2006, Idaho had joined in. Already rated by the Public Citizen Health Research Group as having the second-worst welfare medicine program in the nation (Ramirez and Wolfe, *Unsettling Scores*), Idaho was ready to chip away at federal guarantees by parceling out services to different categories of recipients. Promoted by former governor Dirk Kempthorne (R), the revamped, pared-down plan (which began in 2006) divided clients into three groups, each provided with a separate benefits package: healthy adults and children (the basic plan); people with disabilities, mental illnesses, and other chronic needs (an enhanced plan); and the dually eligible elderly (Medicare-Medicaid Coordinated Plan). With a goal of disciplining certain participants (labeled "empowerment"), the state offered them limited extra dollars (in voucher points) for healthy behavior (smoking cessation, dieting, and child immunizations); the money could be used for counseling, nicotine gum, and other wellness activities. When Idaho encountered budget shortfalls as a result of the 2008 recession, its new governor, C. L. "Butch" Otter (R), ordered large across-the-board agency cuts for 2009, with an even greater deduction in Medicaid outlays.

107. Henry J. Kaiser Family Foundation, Kaiser Commission on Medicaid and the Uninsured, *KyHealth Choices Medicaid Reform: Key Program Changes and Questions*, fact sheet, (Menlo Park, Calif.: Henry J. Kaiser Family Foundation, Kaiser Commission on Medicaid and the Uninsured, July 2006), available at http://www.kff.org.

108. Cost sharing is subject to out-of-pocket maximums. In addition, mandatory children and pregnant women are not liable for any of these charges.

109. Henry J. Kaiser Family Foundation, *KyHealth Choices Medicaid Reform*.

110. Governor Fletcher expected reductions of up to $120 million per year and $1 billion over seven years as a result of his overhaul. To the contrary, welfare medicine costs rose by $42 million during 2007. Fletcher was defeated that year in his attempt to seek another term.

111. Slightly more than one-third of the states had either raised their income eligibility to at least 250 percent of the FPL or planned to do so; a few nudged it up even higher in a decided effort to include middle-class children. For example, Connecticut, Hawaii, Maryland, Missouri, New Hampshire, New York, Ohio, Vermont, and New Jersey have set their SCHIP income-eligibility levels at 300 percent of the FPL or more. Iowa, which has the second-lowest percentage of medically uninsured children in the nation (5.2 percent), recently raised the ceiling of its Hawk-1 SCHIP program to 300 percent of the FPL, beginning July 2009.

112. Henry J. Kaiser Family Foundation, Kaiser Commission on Medicaid and the Uninsured, *SCHIP Reauthorization: Key Questions in the Current Debate*, issue brief (Menlo Park, Calif.: Henry J. Kaiser Family Foundation, Kaiser Commission on Medicaid and the Uninsured, July 2007), available at http://www.kff.org.

Pennsylvania began its efforts toward universal insurance by offering free, subsidized, or inexpensive health insurance to all of its children, regardless of income, through Cover All Kids, enacted at the end of 2006. However, it would appear from Governor Edward Rendell's (D) annual budget proposals that he intends to expand enrollments by materially cutting back on their services.

Hawaii supported universal coverage for children by launching Keiki Care in 2008. In partnership with Hawaii Medical Service Association, a private firm, it offered free basic care to all uninsured youngsters who were not eligible for any other federal or state program. Citing state budgetary problems, however, Governor Linda Lingle (R) dropped the plan—which already had 2,000 children enrolled—seven months later. Nevertheless, the state still has relatively high Medicaid coverage for children; expansions in 2006 and 2008 raised their eligibility levels to 300 percent of the FPL.

113. Families must pay premiums based on their annual income (in 2006, from $40 to $100 per month for each child) and make a copayment on services.

114. From its establishment in 2000 to 2005, as income eligibility requirements were loosened, the FamilyCare program steadily increased its enrollment of the uninsured population, reaching 300,000 people. In 2006, the second phase began, and another 100,000 adults were added. Illinois, however, has been plagued with backlogs in its payments to providers; according to a report by the state's auditor general, unpaid bills have averaged $1.5 billion from 2005 to 2007. Illinois Office of the Auditor General, *Performance Audit of the Department of Healthcare and Family Services' Prompt Payment Act Compliance and Medicaid Payment Process* (Springfield: State of Illinois, May 2008).

115. Although the enrollment of children in the low-income health programs had risen 31 percent from 1996 to 2002, the proportion of them insured privately fell by 5 percent and has continued to drop. The number of those covered under SCHIP increased from 1.9 million in 1999 to 3.3 million in 2000, 4.6 million in 2001, 5.4 million in 2002, and 6 million in 2003, where it remained relatively constant over the next two years. In 2004, 28 million youngsters participated in Medicaid, and another 6 million in SCHIP. The U.S. GAO warns, however, that these numbers are inflated because many children cycle in and out of the program. For example, at any one point in time, there were only 4 million children enrolled in SCHIP during 2003, 2004, and 2005. U.S. GAO, *States' SCHIP Enrollment and Spending Experiences and Considerations for*

+ +

Reauthorization (Washington, D.C.: U.S. Government Printing Office, February 15, 2007); Lynn Blewett, Michael Davern, and Holly Rodin, "Covering Kids: Variation in Health Insurance Coverage Trends by State, 1996–2002," *Health Affairs* 23, no. 6 (November–December 2004): 170–180; Ross, Cox, and Marks, *Resuming the Path to Health Coverage for Children and Parents.*

In 2005, roughly 8.4 million children younger than eighteen were uninsured in the Untied States, increasing to 9 million in 2006. They represent roughly 11.7 percent of all children in the country, ranging from 5.6 percent in Vermont to 20.4 percent in Texas. Jonathan Engel, *Poor People's Medicine: Medicaid and American Charity Care Since 1965* (Durham, N.C.: Duke University Press, 2006); Henry J. Kaiser Family Foundation, *SCHIP Reauthorization*; U.S. GAO, *States' SCHIP Enrollment and Spending Experiences.*

116. In 2007, the Bush White House did not even include enough dollars for the states to maintain their current participants. The Congressional Budget Office had documented that $33 billion would be required over five years just to retain the same number of current beneficiaries; in reality, $39 billion would be needed for states to protect all of the children actually eligible for the program, and even higher amounts would be required to expand coverage. Henry J. Kaiser Family Foundation, *SCHIP Reauthorization*; Leighton Ku, Andy Schneider, and Judy Solomon, *The Administration Again Proposes to Shift Federal Medicaid Costs to States* (Washington, D.C.: Center on Budget and Policy Priorities, February 14, 2007).

117. Twelve states received an additional $283 million in grants in 2006. The following year, even more states had exhausted their annual allotments early on. U.S. GAO, *States' SCHIP Enrollment and Spending Experiences.*

118. Roughly three-quarters of the children enrolled in the program are insured through MCOs. Henry J. Kaiser Family Foundation, *SCHIP Reauthorization*; U.S. GAO, *States' SCHIP Enrollment and Spending Experiences*; Ku, Schneider, and Solomon, *The Administration Again Proposes to Shift Federal Medicaid Costs to States.*

119. Because Medicaid is not capped, several states were shifting their lowest-income children into the program from their SCHIP plans; the idea was to use any freed-up dollars to extend coverage to youngsters at higher income levels. Sonya Schwartz and John McInerney, *Examining a Major Policy Shift: New Federal Limits on Medicaid Coverage for Children* (Portland, Me.: National Academy for State Health Policy, April 2008).

120. The GAO concluded in May 2008 that the CMS rules must be submitted to Congress and the comptroller general before they can take effect. Nonetheless, the Bush administration carried on unimpeded. U.S. GAO, *Congressional Review Act: Applicability to CMS Letter on State Children's Health Insurance Program*, statement of Dayna K. Shah, managing associate general counsel, GAO, before the Subcommittee on Health, Committee on Energy and Commerce, U.S. House of Representatives, 110th Cong., 2d sess., May 15, 2008, GAO-08-785T (Washington, D.C.: Government Printing Office, 2008).

121. The new rules included unrealistic coverage expectations (states had to achieve a 95 percent enrollment of children in households with incomes less than 200 percent

of the FPL before they could expand eligibility to higher-income groups—a rule applicable to new expansion proposals as well as to already established ones); a decrease in the federal match to states insuring children in families with an income higher than 200 percent of the FPL or any parents covered under SCHIP; cost sharing that mirrored commercial insurance amounts; and a one-year waiting period after becoming uninsured.

122. Health Policy Institute, Georgetown University, *SCHIP Funding in the Year Ahead: Implications of the Medicare, Medicaid, and SCHIP Extension Act* (Washington, D.C.: Center for Children and Families, March 2008). CMS, however, never enforced the limit, and President Barack Obama rescinded it shortly after taking office in 2009.

123. President Bush endorsed tax credits and deductions for households who buy private policies on their own. In 2007, he even supported tax increases for people who have plans offering benefits beyond the national average. In one of his radio addresses, he cautioned: "[the current system] unwisely encourages workers to choose overly expensive, gold-plated plans, driving up the overall cost of coverage and care." Quoted in Henry J. Kaiser Family Foundation, Kaiser Commission on Medicaid and the Uninsured, *The Affordable Choices Initiative: An Overview* (Menlo Park, Calif.: Henry J. Kaiser Family Foundation, Kaiser Commission on Medicaid and the Uninsured, May 2007), available at http://www.kff.org.

5. Better Than Nothing?

1. Carmen DeNavas-Walt, Bernadette Proctor, and Jessica Smith, *Income, Poverty, and Health Insurance Coverage in the U.S.: 2006*, U.S. Census Bureau Current Population Report P60-233 (Washington, D.C.: U.S. Government Printing Office, 2007).

As of 2006, in their regular Medicaid program twenty-two states covered children ages six to nineteen whose families had incomes at the FPL; five states at 133 percent to 140 percent of the FPL; six states at 150 percent; six states at 175 to 185 percent; six states at 200 percent; one state at 235 percent; one state at 250 percent; and three states at 275 percent to 300 percent. Donna Ross, Laura Cox, and Caryn Marks, *Resuming the Path to Health Coverage for Children and Parents: A 50 State Update on Eligibility Rules, Enrollment and Renewal Procedures, and Cost-Sharing Practices in Medicaid and SCHIP in 2006* (Menlo Park, Calif.: Henry J. Kaiser Family Foundation, Kaiser Commission on Medicaid and the Uninsured, January 2007), available at http://www.kff.org, table 3, "Income Threshold for Parents Applying for Medicaid."

2. Eighteen states had upper limits of 35 percent of the FPL, with several as low as 23 percent of the FPL. Only fourteen jurisdictions allowed parents access to their regular programs at 100 percent or more of the FPL. Four of them had a threshold at 100 percent; four between 115 percent and 150 percent; and six between 185 percent and 275 percent. The ceiling for nonworking parents tended to be lower nearly everywhere, averaging 42 percent of the FPL. Ross, Cox, and Marks, *Resuming the Path to Health Coverage for Children and Parents.*

3. Henry J. Kaiser Family Foundation, Kaiser Commission on Medicaid and the Uninsured, *The Uninsured: A Primer. Key Facts About Americans Without Health Insurance* (Menlo Park, Calif.: Henry J. Kaiser Family Foundation, Kaiser Commission on Medicaid and the Uninsured, October 2006), available at http://www.kff.org.

4. Ibid.

5. In 2006, there were 36.5 million people with incomes less than the FPL, or 12.3 percent of the population. The poverty rate was just 8 percent for non-Latino whites and 10 percent for Asians, but 24 percent for blacks and 21 percent for Latinos. Moreover, a significant percentage of children younger than age eighteen lived in officially defined poverty: 17 percent as against 11 percent of people ages eighteen to sixty-four and 9 percent of the sixty-five or older population.

Overall, 28 percent of female-headed families were considered impoverished, as compared to 13 percent of male-headed households (no female adult present).

The FPL, of course, does not embody the full extent of financial deprivation. In 2006, the threshold was $10,294 for a single adult, $13,167 for a family of two, $16,079 for a family of three, and $20,614 for a family of four. These measures also vary by age. The threshold, for example, was $9,669 for a single person age sixty-five or older and $10,488 for a younger adult. DeNavas-Walt, Proctor, and Smith, *Income, Poverty, and Health Insurance Coverage in the U.S.*

According to researchers at the Maine Center for Economic Policy, a single person, a parent with one child, and a household composed of two workers and two children would require earnings of about $21,000, $34,000, and $59,000, respectively, just to meet their basic living expenses in Maine. Ed Cervone, Judy Ward, and Lisa Pohlmann, *Getting By: Maine Livable Wages in 2006* (Augusta: Maine Center for Economic Policy, June 26, 2007).

6. In 2004, only 27 percent of all nonelderly adults living at the FPL and 13 percent with incomes from 100 percent to 199 percent of the FPL participated in Medicaid. Among all nonelderly adults, 21 percent are uninsured. Henry J. Kaiser Family Foundation, Kaiser Commission on Medicaid and the Uninsured, *Health Insurance Coverage in America: A 2005 Data Update* (Menlo Park, Calif.: Henry J. Kaiser Family Foundation, Kaiser Commission on Medicaid and the Uninsured, November 2006), available at http://www.kff.org.

7. Teresa A. Coughlin, Leighton Ku, and John Holahan, *Medicaid Since 1980: Costs, Coverage, and the Shifting Alliance Between the Federal Government and the States* (Washington, D.C.: Urban Institute, 1994).

8. Karl Kronebusch, "Medicaid for Children: Federal Mandates, Welfare Reform, and Policy Backsliding," *Health Affairs* 20, no. 1 (January–February 2001): 97–112.

9. Under federal law, Medicaid transitional benefits continue for a year after cash-assistance welfare recipients enter the labor force. Most adults lose their benefits after that period, but their children may still be eligible for SCHIP, depending on the state. In 1996, AFDC was replaced with the more restrictive TANF.

10. According to a recent study, nearly 75 percent of children lacking health insurance (slightly more than 6 million youngsters) were eligible for Medicaid or SCHIP but were not enrolled in either program. Henry J. Kaiser Family Foundation, *The Uninsured.*

Similarly, nearly 85 percent of Specified Low-Income Beneficiaries, 22 percent of Qualified Medicare Beneficiaries, and roughly half of all parents eligible for welfare medicine were not enrolled in the program. Alan Weil, "There's Something About Medicaid," *Health Affairs* 22, no. 1 (January–February 2003): 13–23.

11. Ronald J. Angel, Laura Lein, and Jane Henrici, *Poor Families in America's Health Care Crisis* (New York: Cambridge University Press, 2006); Health Policy Analysis Program (HPAP), *The Costs of Enrollment Instability in Washington State's Medicaid Program*, prepared for the Health Improvement Partnership of Spokane (Seattle: University of Washington, March 5, 2004); Ian Hill and Amy Lutzky, *Is There a Hole in the Bucket? Understanding SCHIP Retention*, Occasional Paper no. 67 (Washington, D.C.: Urban Institute, May 2003).

12. Benjamin D. Sommers, "Why Millions of Children Eligible for Medicaid and SCHIP Are Uninsured: Poor Retention Versus Poor Take-up," *Health Affairs* 26, no. 5 (September–October 2007): 560–567, available at http://www.healthaffairs.org.

13. Amy Davidoff, Bowen Garrett, and Alshadye Yemane, *Medicaid-Eligible Adults Who Are Not Enrolled* (Washington, D.C.: Urban Institute, 2005).

14. As of 2007, fifteen states had SCHIP waivers to cover adults, but together they served less than 700,000 people. Adults can participate in SCHIP only if the states can prove that it is cost effective to include them. Moreover, DRA 2005 prohibits any new section 1115 SCHIP waivers for nonpregnant, childless adults. U.S. GAO, *Children's Health Insurance: State Experiences in Implementing SCHIP and Considerations for Reauthorization*, statement of Katherine G. Allen, director, of health care, GAO, before the Committee on Finance, U.S. Senate, 110th Cong., 1st sess., February 1, 2007, GAO-07-447T (Washington, D.C.: U.S. Government Printing Office, 2007); Henry J. Kaiser Family Foundation, Kaiser Commission on Medicaid and the Uninsured, *SCHIP Reauthorization: Key Questions in the Current Debate*, issue brief (Menlo Park, Calif.: Henry J. Kaiser Family Foundation, Kaiser Commission on Medicaid and the Uninsured, July 2007), available at http://www.kff.org.

15. Certain politicians intermittently target Medicaid recipients for fraudulently participating in the program and institute harsh preventive measures, even though studies suggest that such activities represent a relatively insignificant portion of program costs.

16. In 2004, New Mexico began requiring biannual recertification but immediately canceled the new regulation after more than 10,000 recipients lost coverage in only one year.

17. Florida increased the reenrollment period from six to twelve months in 2005. Donna Ross and Laura Cox, *In a Time of Growing Need State Choices Influence Health Coverage Access for Children and Families: A 50-State Update on Eligibility Rules, Enrollment and Renewal Procedures, and Cost-Sharing Practices in Medicaid and SCHIP for Children and Families* (Menlo Park, Calif.: Henry J. Kaiser Family Foundation, Kaiser Commission on Medicaid and the Uninsured, October 2005), available at http://www.kff .org; HPAP, *The Costs of Enrollment Instability in Washington State's Medicaid Program*.

18. Angel, Lein, and Henrici, *Poor Families in America's Health Care Crisis*; Michael Perry, Susan Kannel, R. Burciaga, and Christina Chang, *Medicaid and Children: Over-*

coming *Barriers to Enrollment* (Menlo Park, Calif.: Henry J. Kaiser Family Foundation, Kaiser Commission on Medicaid and the Uninsured, January 2000), available at http://www.kff.org.

19. Ross and Cox, *In a Time of Growing Need*. In 2005, when Mississippi switched from recertification by mail to on-site meetings, about 50,000 people, many of them income-eligible for the program, were dropped from the Medicaid rolls. Emily Wagler Pettus, "Moody: Medicaid Tightening Up on Providers and Recipients," *SunHerald.com* (Biloxi, Miss.), August 17, 2005, at http://www.sunhearald.com.

20. The survey was conducted by the Kaiser Family Foundation in 2000: see Perry and Kannel, *Medicaid and Children*.

21. In Georgia, families now have to prove their income eligibility prior to receiving benefits; the state had previously utilized a system of self-declaration (although officials later verified the information).

22. HPAP, *The Costs of Enrollment Instability in Washington State's Medicaid Program*, 17.

23. In a 2002 Commonwealth Fund examination of SCHIP, investigators found that a substantial number of parents had difficulty coping with the renewal notices and forms and that many of them lacked sufficient literacy skills. Among those mothers who did not renew coverage for their children, about half indicated that they were unaware that they had to do so. Leighton Ku and Donna Cohen Ross, *Staying Covered: The Importance of Retaining Health Insurance for Low-Income Families* (New York and Washington, D.C.: Commonwealth Fund and Center on Budget and Policy Priorities, December 2002).

24. Perry and Kannel, *Medicaid and Children*.

25. Angel, Lein, and Henrici, *Poor Families in America's Health Care Crisis*.

26. Families USA, *Cost-Sharing in Medicaid: It's Not About "Skin in the Game"—It's About Lives on the Line*, fact sheet (Washington, D.C.: Families USA, September 2005).

27. Victoria Wachino, Leighton Ku, Edwin Park, and Judith Solomon, *An Analysis of the National Governors Association's Proposals for Short-Run Medicaid Reform* (Washington, D.C.: Center on Budget and Policy Priorities, October 14, 2005), 2.

28. Families USA, *Cost-Sharing in Medicaid*, 2.

29. Leighton Ku and Teresa Coughlin, *The Use of Sliding Scale Premiums in Subsidized Insurance Programs* (Washington, D.C.: Urban Institute, March 1997).

30. In 2005, the Oregon legislature prohibited premiums for families with income less than 10 percent of the FPL. Oregon Center for Public Policy (OCPP), *Considerations in Medicaid Cost Sharing Policy: Fact Sheet* (Silverton: OCPP, September 16, 2005).

31. Bill Wright, Matthew Carlson, and Jeanene Smith, *Impact of Changes to Premiums, Cost-Sharing, and Benefits on Adult Medicaid Beneficiaries: Results from an Ongoing Study of the Oregon Health Plan* (New York: Commonwealth Fund, July 29, 2005).

32. Samantha Artiga and Molly O'Malley, *Increasing Premiums and Cost Sharing in Medicaid and SCHIP: Recent State Experiences* (Menlo Park, Calif.: Henry J. Kaiser Family Foundation, Kaiser Commission on Medicaid and the Uninsured, May 2005), available at http://www.kff.org.

33. Soon after Vermont raised its Medicaid and SCHIP premiums, participation in these programs declined 11 percent. Ibid.

Likewise, when Missouri established a SCHIP premium for households with income greater than 150 percent of the FPL, about 22,000 families (representing about half of the affected children) withdrew from the program. Ross and Cox, *In a Time of Growing Need*.

34. Medicaid funds are available for emergency services if the undocumented immigrant otherwise would have qualified for the program. In 2005, Congress offered additional money for families who are not income eligible.

Nevertheless, the definition of the term *emergency* can be murky. In 2007, for example, a struggle ensued between the federal government and at least two states (New York and Georgia) over "questionable" reimbursements for "emergency" services provided to illegal immigrants.

35. For example, North Carolina denied chemotherapy to an undocumented immigrant diagnosed with leukemia, and the Supreme Court supported the state's decision.

36. Certain states such as New York and Maryland did pay for pregnant women and children out of their own budgets. However, when Maryland ceased doing so in 2005, the Maryland Legal Aid Bureau sued the state, demanding that the participants be reinstated.

37. At state option, dual eligibles, people receiving SSI, and, as of December 2006, foster children may be exempted from the verification rules.

38. In an ongoing analysis of the issue in six states, the Center on Budget and Policy Priorities found that they all experienced considerable losses in enrollment. For example, in the first six months after implementation of the DRA directive, Iowa's caseload decreased by 5,700 people; marked reductions also were experienced in Kansas (18,000 to 20,000 people) and Ohio (39,000 people). Despite the sharp increase in applications anticipated for the September–October back-to-school period, there were nearly 15,000 fewer youngsters on the Medicaid rolls in Louisiana, and 13,300 less on the rolls in Virginia. Donna Cohen Ross, *New Medicaid Citizenship Documentation Requirement Is Taking a Toll: States Report Enrollment Is Down and Administrative Costs Are Up* (Washington, D.C.: Center on Budget and Policy Priorities, March 13, 2007), 1–10.

By 2007, other places, including New Mexico, Georgia, and Florida, reported declines in Medicaid coverage because of the new rules: in the latter state, fully 63,000 children were disenrolled from July 2006 to January 2007. Robert Pear, "Lacking Papers, Citizens Are Cut From Medicaid," *New York Times*, March 12, 2007.

39. Ross, *New Medicaid Citizenship Documentation Requirement*, 1.

40. Quoted in ibid.

41. Peter Shin, Brad Finnegan, Lauren Hughes, and Sara Rosenbaum, *An Initial Assessment of the Effects of Medicaid Documentation on Health Centers and Their Patients* (Washington, D.C.: School of Public Health and Health Services, George Washington University, May 7, 2007).

42. For example, in March 2007 there were 3,500 cases pending approval in Virginia. Ross, *New Medicaid Citizenship Documentation Requirement*; Center on Budget and Policy Priorities, *The New Medicaid Citizenship Documentation: A Brief Overview* (Washington, D.C.: Center on Budget and Policy Priorities, September 28, 2006).

43. In a survey of 800 Virginia parents who are citizens but had difficulty in proving it, the Virginia Health Care Foundation and the Virginia Department of Medical Assistance Services found that nearly 25 percent of the affected children skipped medical services for an illness and 40 percent for a dental problem; nearly one-fifth was forced to forgo a necessary prescription; and half of the babies under the age of two did not receive immunizations. The researchers emphasized that nearly 60 percent of eligible children whose parents applied for Medicaid in the state did not regain coverage for long periods of time because their documents were not easily available. The survey is discussed in Chris Jenkins, "Medicaid Wait Rising for Virginia Children Study Says," *Washington Post*, June 7, 2007.

Likewise, according to the Oregon Department of Human Services, 1,000 citizens (two-thirds of them children) had to go without medical care from September 2006 to February 2007 because of the DRA regulations. Oregon Center for Public Policy (OCPP), *Oregon Study Finds That Federal Medicaid Rules Aimed at Illegal Immigrants Harm Vulnerable Citizens* (Silverton: OCPP, May 11, 2007).

44. Shin et al., *An Initial Assessment of the Effects of Medicaid Documentation*.

45. Peter J. Cunningham and Len M. Nichols, "The Effects of Medicaid Reimbursement on the Access to Care of Medicaid Enrollees: A Community Perspective," *Medical Care Research and Review* 62, no. 6 (December 2005), 678.

46. State Plans for Medical Assistance, 42 U.S.C. § 1396a(a)(30)(A).

47. Colleen Grogan and Eric Patashnik, "Between Welfare Medicine and Mainstream Entitlement: Medicaid at the Political Crossroads," *Journal of Health Politics, Policy, and Law* 28, no. 1 (October 2003): 821–858.

48. Jonathan Engel, *Poor People's Medicine: Medicaid and American Charity Care Since 1965* (Durham, N.C.: Duke University Press, 2006).

49. Stuart E. Eizenstat, "How to Make Medicaid Popular," *New York Times*, September 4, 1991.

50. E. Hing and C. W. Burt, *Characteristics of Office-Based Physicians and Their Practices: United States, 2003–2004*, Series 13, no. 164 (Hyattsville, Md.: National Center for Health Statistics, 2007).

51. Peter J. Cunningham and Jessica H. May, *Medicaid Patients Increasingly Concentrated Among Physicians*, Tracking Report no. 16 (Washington, D.C.: Center for Studying Health System Change, August 2006).

52. Phil Galewitz, "Medicaid Patients Find Care Limited," *Palm Beach Post*, November 26, 2006.

53. Kristen Stewart, "Where Are the Doctors Who Accept Medicaid?" *Salt Lake City Tribune*, September 16, 2007.

54. Marian Uhlman, "Specialist Care Waning for People on Medicaid," *Philadelphia Inquirer*, March 27, 2005.

55. A consultant group hired by the State of Connecticut found that only 25 percent of new Medicaid patients were able to get appointments because there were so few doctors. The state Freedom of Information Commission ruled that the MCOs must make the physician fees public, and this ruling was upheld by a superior court judge in December 2006,

but the firms appealed the case to the state supreme court. "Lawmakers Seek Medicaid Spending Information from HMOs," *Hartford Advocate* (Conn.), December 1, 2006.

Several lawmakers in Connecticut have more recently been endeavoring to ease state Freedom of Information Act regulations, an action opposed by Governor M. Jodi Rell (R).

56. For example, with the second-largest public hospital system in the nation, California's twenty county-owned and operated facilities (representing only 6 percent of the hospitals in the state) deliver almost three-fourths of all outpatient care to the medically indigent and more than one-half of the total to the uninsured.

57. The figures are 80.3 per 100 persons with Medicaid or SCHIP; 47.1 per 100 persons with Medicare; 20.3 per 100 persons with private insurance; and 44.6 per 100 persons with no insurance. Linda F. McCaig and Eric N. Nawar, *National Hospital Ambulatory Medical Care Survey, 2004*, Emergency Care Summary, advance data from Vital and Health Statistics, no. 372 (Hyattsville, Md.: National Center for Health Statistics, 2006).

58. Ibid.

59. Even more than doctors, dentists complain of inordinately low reimbursement rates, administrative hurdles (eligibility verification and prior authorization requirements), and an excessive number of broken appointments. Stephen A. Eklund, James L. Pittman, and Sarah J. Clark, "Michigan Medicaid's Healthy Kids Dental Program: An Assessment of the First Twelve Months," *Journal of the American Dental Association* 134 (November 2003): 1509–1515.

60. S. Gehshan, P. Hauck, and J. Scales, *Increasing Dentists' Participation in Medicaid and SCHIP*, issue brief (Washington, D.C.: Forum for State Health Policy Leadership, National Conference of State Legislatures, 2001).

As usual, the situation varies considerably across the states and in some places is worsening over time. For example, from 2000 to 2007 Utah experienced a 14 percent drop in the number of dentists who accept welfare medicine. Stewart, "Where Are the Doctors Who Accept Medicaid?"

In Maine, where there is an overall shortage of dentists throughout the state, about one-third of the total number participates in Medicaid. Josi Huang, "Dental Community Scrambles to Fill Dentist to Patient Gap," *Kennebec Journal* (Augusta, Me.), October 14, 2007.

The Illinois registry lists 25 percent of the state's dentists as participating in welfare medicine, but only about 10 percent actually treat patients. Stephanie Sievers, "Medicaid Patients Face Hardest Time Finding Dentists," *Springfield Times* (Ill.), March 15, 2007, available at http://www.MyWebTimes.com.

However, after South Carolina increased its reimbursement rate so that it would equal the seventy-fifth percentile of commercial fees in 2000, the percentage of children receiving at least one dental service annually increased from 26 percent to 38.5 percent by 2006. Indiana implemented similar changes in the late 1990s, and utilization of dental services rose from 18 percent of Medicaid participants in 1997 to nearly 40 percent by 2005. Fees in both states have been frozen since the original rate increases, though, and the gains most likely will deteriorate over time. Don Schneider, *CDHP*

State Summary: South Carolina Dental Medicaid (Washington, D.C.: Children's Dental Health Project, American Dental Association, 2007); Don Schneider, *CDHP State Summary: Indiana Dental Medicaid* (Washington, D.C.: Children's Dental Health Project, American Dental Association, 2007).

61. This finding is even more troubling given that Congress specifically mandated dental screenings and diagnostic, preventive, and treatment services for children in 1989.

62. U.S. GAO, *Medicaid: Extent of Dental Disease in Children Has Not Decreased, and Millions Are Estimated to Have Untreated Tooth Decay*, GAO-08-1121 (Washington, D.C.: U.S. Government Printing Office, September 2008).

CMS data show that 30 percent of covered youngsters saw a dentist at least once a year, 25 percent had a preventive office visit, and 16 percent received services for their problem. U.S. Congress, House, Committee on Energy and Commerce, Subcommittee on Health, *Insuring Bright Futures: Improving Access to Dental Care and Providing a Healthy Start for Children*, testimony of Burton Edelstein, professor of dentistry and health policy, Columbia University, 110th Cong., 1st sess., March 27, 2007; U.S. Congress, House, Committee on Oversight and Government Reform, Subcommittee on Domestic Policy, *Oversight Adequacy of the Pediatric Dental Program for Medicaid Eligible Children*, testimony of Jane Perkins, legal director, National Law Program, 110th Cong., 1st sess., May 2, 2007.

63. Wendy Mouradian, Elizabeth Wehr, and James Crall, "Disparities in Children's Oral Health and Access to Dental Care," *Journal of the American Medical Association* 284, no. 20 (November 22–29, 2000): 2625–2631.

64. U.S. Congress, House, *Insuring Bright Futures*, Edelstein testimony.

65. Meg Booth and Burton Edelstein, *State Children's Health Insurance (SCHIP): A Decade of Optional Dental Coverage for Kids* (Washington, D.C.: Children's Dental Health Project, November 2006).

66. For example, in 2002 Massachusetts eliminated adult dental benefits and eyeglasses from Medicaid as one way of coping with its fiscal distress that year.

67. U.S. Congress, House, *Insuring Bright Futures*, testimony of Nicholas Mosca, American Dental Education Association.

68. U.S. Congress, House, *Insuring Bright Futures*, testimony of Kathleen Roth, president, American Dental Association.

69. In 2005, for instance, Virginia initiated a fee-for-service program (Smiles for Children) for its Medicaid and SCHIP recipients. In addition to handing the program over to a private company (Doral Dental, Inc.), the state increased provider fees. After a year, only 25 percent of dentists had joined in, and treatment rates had increased from 24 percent to only 29 percent. Tennessee, which "carved out" its dental program from other TennCare health services, in 2002 also had contracted with Doral Dental; by 2006, the percentage of children receiving at least one dental service rose from 26 percent to a mere 37 percent. Don Schneider, *CDHP State Summary: Virginia Dental Medicaid* (Washington, D.C.: Children's Dental Health Project, American Dental Association, 2005); Don Schneider, *CDHP State Summary: Tennessee's TennCare Program* (Washington, D.C.: Children's Dental Health Project, American Dental Association, 2005).

Despite only limited gains for public-aid clients, these states were now supporting Doral Dental USA, LLC (a division of Dental Quest Ventures, Inc., which, in turn, is a subsidiary of Dental Services of Massachusetts). It is a dental benefits–management company that provides services exclusively to people participating in Medicaid, SCHIP, and Medicare Advantage. It serves 7 million recipients in eighteen states.

70. David Satcher, *Oral Health in America: A Report of the Surgeon General, U.S. Department of Health and Human Services (HHS)* (Washington, D.C.: U.S. Government Printing Office, May 2000).

71. U.S. GAO, *Medicaid: Extent of Dental Disease.*

72. Mouradian, Wehr, and Crall, "Disparities in Children's Oral Health and Access to Dental Care," 2627.

73. In Maryland, services are provided through United Health Care's subsidiary AmeriChoice.

74. U.S. Congress, House, *Oversight Adequacy of the Pediatric Dental Program.*

75. Of the 918 dentists listed as Medicaid providers in nineteen of the twenty-three counties in the state, nearly 20 percent of them were duplicated entries, and only 23 percent of the rest accepted new Medicaid patients. Ibid.

76. U.S. Congress, House, *Oversight Adequacy of the Pediatric Dental Program,* testimony of Dr. Frederick Clark, dental practitioner.

77. A survey taken by the Texas Medical Association indicated that from 1993 to 1996 fewer doctors were serving Medicaid patients. See Elliot Jaspin, "Austin No Hot Spot for Medicaid Patients," *Austin American-Statesman,* August 6, 2007.

78. Doctors and dentists who treat children obtained a raise of 25 percent and 50 percent, respectively. Reimbursements to physicians serving adults were augmented by only 10 percent.

79. Jack Kresnak, "State Health Standards for Kids Upheld in Settlement," *Detroit Free Press,* August 23, 2007.

80. In 2004, a U.S. District Court accepted a consent decree between New Hampshire Legal Assistance (on behalf of Medicaid-eligible children) and the state, ruling that most youngsters were not receiving the basic dental care that they had been promised under federal law. The legislature accordingly had to spend an additional $1.2 million annually for at least five years. "Lawsuit: New Hampshire Failing in Dental Care for Kids on Medicaid," *Boston Herald,* February 7, 2007, available at http://www.Bostonherald.com.

81. Diane Strand, "Options Dwindle for New Medicaid Patients," *De Kalb Midweek,* November 22, 2006.

82. For instance, the Florida Pediatric Society and the Academy of Pediatric Dentistry are arguing that 75 percent of children participating in the state's Medicaid plan received no dental care in 2005 and that 500,000 enrollees lacked physician services. Greater Hartford Legal Aid took Connecticut to court, also over access issues: the group contends that although the state's Health Care for Uninsured Kids and Youth Program has a high level of allowable medical services, few specialists and dentists are willing to treat welfare medicine patients. In yet another case, the American Civil Liberties Union sued Indiana because the state would not pay for dentures and related procedures for adults.

83. Annette B. Ramirez and Sidney M. Wolfe, *Unsettling Scores: A Ranking of State Medicaid Programs*, Public Citizen Health Research Group (PCHRG) Publication no. 1807 (Washington, D.C.: PCHRG, April 2007).

84. For example, the governor of Ohio, Robert Taft (R), eliminated dental services for adults in 2005. Although the subsequent governor, Ted Strickland (D), pledged during his gubernatorial campaign to restore these benefits, he failed to do so after he assumed office.

85. U.S. Department of Health and Human Services, Agency for Healthcare Research and Quality (AHRQ), "Medicaid Pays for More than One-Third of $10 Billion Bill for Drug Abuse," *AHRQ News and Numbers* (Rockville, Md.) (October 24 , 2007), available at http://www.ahrq.gov/news/nn/nn103107.htm.

86. Richard Perez-Pena, "Revolving Door for Addicts Adds to Medicaid Cost," *New York Times*, April 17, 2007.

87. Natalie Angier, "Study Finds Uninsured Receive Less Hospital Care," *New York Times*, September 12, 1990.

88. Ramirez and Wolfe, *Unsettling Scores*.

89. In 1998, President Clinton ordered the states to fund drugs for the treatment of erectile dysfunction, such as Viagra, Cialis, and Levitra. By 2005, Medicaid was paying $38 million annually for impotence medication nationwide. Registered sex offenders were then discovered using these government-funded medications, thus stirring even more controversy over the issue. Robert Salladay, "Governor Says No to Viagra for Sex Offenders," *Los Angeles Times*, May 27, 2005; "Sex Offenders in New York Getting Viagra—Paid for by Medicaid," *Chicago Tribune*, May 23, 2005.

90. A few states—including Pennsylvania, Utah, Louisiana, and Arkansas—only reluctantly accepted the rape or incest exemptions and have forced Medicaid recipients to prove the circumstances of their pregnancy.

91. Sara Sills and Sue Frietsche, *Removing Barriers to Medicaid-Funded Abortion* (New York and Philadelphia: Women's Law Project and Institute for Productive Health Access, 2004); Marlene Gerber Fried, *The Hyde Amendment: 30 Years of Violating Women's Rights* (Washington, D.C.: Center for American Progress, October 6, 2006).

92. The question of Medicaid-funded abortions is obviously far from settled. In 2008, for example, more than forty bills related to the issue were introduced in the West Virginia legislature. In another instance, the Oklahoma legislature banned funding for "elective" abortions, but the governor vetoed the bill. In Kansas, the state attorney general endeavored but failed to eliminate all Medicaid-funded abortions, arguing that a fetus is a person at conception and thus entitled to protection under the Fourteenth Amendment. Maine, in contrast, was debating whether to add abortion to its Medicaid options.

At the same time, the George W. Bush administration extended SCHIP coverage to unborn children in 2002, and several states—including Texas, Illinois, Rhode Island, Michigan, Mississippi, Massachusetts, and Washington—expanded their SCHIP programs accordingly.

93. The comparable figures for privately insured individuals were 12 percent (did not visit a doctor), 18 percent (did not have a breast examination), 20 percent (did not have

a Pap test), 17 percent (delayed care they thought was needed), and 17 percent (did not fill a prescription). Henry J. Kaiser Family Foundation, Kaiser Commission on Medicaid and the Uninsured, *An Update on Women's Health Policy, Medicaid's Role for Women*, issue brief (Menlo Park, Calif.: Henry J. Kaiser Family Foundation, Kaiser Commission on Medicaid and the Uninsured, May 2006), available at http://www.kff.org.

94. The Henry J. Kaiser Family Foundation estimates that the annual number of such deaths is about 18,000 adults between the ages of twenty-five and sixty-four. Henry J. Kaiser Family Foundation, *The Uninsured*.

95. Ibid.

96. Angel, Lein, and Henrici, *Poor Families in America's Health Care Crisis*.

97. U.S. Congress, House, *Insuring Bright Futures*, Edelstein and Mosca testimony; Don Schneider, *State Innovations to Improve Access to Oral Health Care for Low Income Children* (Washington, D.C.: American Dental Association, 2005).

98. In some states, including Arkansas, Arizona, Louisiana, New Mexico, Mississippi, and Vermont, Medicaid finances fully half of all births. Henry J. Kaiser Family Foundation, *An Update on Women's Health Policy*.

99. These services and supplies include contraceptives, Pap smears, counseling, and testing for sexually transmitted diseases. Family-planning services are mandated by federal law, and states receive a 90 percent match for each state dollar spent. According to the Henry J. Kaiser Family Foundation, twenty-three states cover family-planning services to low-income women who do not otherwise qualify for Medicaid. Ibid.

100. U.S. Congress, House, *Insuring Bright Futures*, testimony of Chris Koyanagi, policy director, Bazelon Center for Mental Health Law.

6. Long-Term Care

1. Ellen O'Brien tells us that about 85 percent of LTC spending is discretionary, whether paying for elective services (i.e., HCBS) or nonobligatory populations (i.e., the medically needy). Ellen O'Brien, *Long-Term Care: Understanding Medicaid's Role for the Elderly and Disabled* (Menlo Park, Calif.: Henry J. Kaiser Family Foundation, Kaiser Commission on Medicaid and the Uninsured, November 2005), available at http://www.kff.org.

2. Children and nonaged adults compose 76 percent of Medicaid recipients, but only 29 percent of total costs. In contrast, the elderly and young disabled populations represent 9 percent and 15 percent of total enrollees, respectively, but together consume 71 percent of the Medicaid budget (26 percent for older people and 45 percent for the disabled). Jennifer Jenson, *Health Care Spending and the Aging Population*, report for the U.S. Congress (Washington, D.C: Library of Congress, March 13, 2007); Elicia S. Herz, *Medicaid: A Primer*, report for the U.S. Congress (Washington, D.C.: Library of Congress, Congressional Research Service, December 22, 2005).

In 2003, the average national cost per nondisabled younger adult or child participating in Medicaid was $1,823, compared to $14,079 for the elderly, blind, and disabled. U.S. GAO, *Medicaid: Strategies to Help States Address Increased Expenditures*

During Economic Downturns (Washington, D.C.: U.S. Government Printing Office, October 2006).

3. Roughly 79 percent of women and 58 percent of men currently turning sixty-five will eventually be forced to seek assistance from others due to functional limitations. They will be reliant on them for an average of three years; nearly one-third of the women and 11 percent of the men will need help for more than five years. Howard Gleckman, *Medicaid and Long-Term Care: How Will Rising Costs Affect Services for an Aging Population?* Issue Brief no.7-4 (Boston: Center for Retirement Research, Boston College, April 2007); P. Kemper, H. L. Komisar, and L. Alecixth, "Long-Term Care over an Uncertain Future: What Can Current Retirees Expect?" *Inquiry* 42, no. 4 (Winter 2005): 335–350.

4. These activities include both activities of daily living, such as eating, bathing, dressing, toileting, and getting into or out of a bed or chair, and instrumental activities of daily living, such as shopping, doing chores, cleaning, cooking, managing money, and using a telephone.

5. Minorities represent about 18 percent of the sixty-five and older population (blacks, 8 percent; Hispanics, 6 percent; Asians or Pacific Islanders, 3 percent; and American Indians or Native Alaskans, 1 percent), but by 2030 they are expected to reach more than 26 percent. U.S. HHS, Administration on Aging, *A Profile of Older Americans: 2005* (Washington, D.C.: U.S. Government Printing Office, 2005).

6. Average life expectancy at age 65 has been extended 18.5 years (19.8 for women and 16.8 for men), about 6.7 years longer than in 1900. About half of the oldest elders (85 years and older) requires assistance with activities of daily living and instrumental activities. Sheila Burke, Judith Feder, and Paul Van de Water, *Developing a Better Long-Term Care Policy: A Vision and Strategy for America's Future*, report of the Long-Term Care Study Panel (Washington, D.C.: National Academy of Social Insurance, November 2005).

7. It is estimated that the number of seniors in the United States will nearly double by 2030, to 71.5 million; multiplying at four times the rate of other age groups, they will represent about 20 percent of the population. U.S. HHS, *A Profile of Older Americans*.

8. More than 83 percent of people receiving LTC live at home or in community-based settings. Robert B. Friedland, *Caregivers and Long-Term Care Needs in the 21st Century: Will Public Policy Meet the Challenge?* issue brief (Washington, D.C.: Health Policy Institute, Georgetown University, July 2004).

9. Frail elderly women face a 50 percent greater likelihood of institutionalization than men. Moreover, nearly half of nursing home residents have some form of dementia. Ari N. Houser, *Nursing Homes*, research report (Washington, D.C.: AARP Policy and Research, October 2007).

In addition to long-stay residents, many others (about one-third of older people) will encounter at least some nursing home care in their lifetime, although most of the stays will be relatively brief (less than three months). However, about 18 percent of individuals who enter an institution will remain there for at least a year, and 5 percent for about five years or more. Kemper, Komisar, and Alecixth, "Long-Term Care over an Uncertain Future."

10. The younger disabled population includes individuals with mental and developmental disabilities, mental illnesses, traumatic brain or spinal cord injuries, debilitating

disorders such as Parkinson's disease and multiple sclerosis, AIDS, and severe physical or mental impairments or both at birth. Between 1975 and 2007, the number of this group enrolled in Medicaid grew from 2.5 million to 8.5 million. U.S. HHS, Centers for Medicare and Medicaid Services, Office of the Actuary, *2008 Actuarial Report: On the Financial Outlook for Medicaid* (Washington, D.C.: U.S. Government Printing Office, October 17, 2008).

Of the total LTC costs for this younger group, HCBS account for about 50 percent; ICFs-MR, 30 percent; and nursing homes, 20 percent. O'Brien, *Long-Term Care.*

11. Harriet Komisar and Lee S. Thompson, *National Spending for Long-Term Care*, fact sheet, Long Term Care Financing Project (Washington, D.C.: Health Policy Institute, Georgetown University, February 2007).

12. For example, the cost of a single-occupancy room ranged from $43,000 per year in Louisiana to $197,000 in Alaska. The typical annual cost for private quarters in an assisted-living facility was about $33,000, varying from $19,000 in Montana to $57,000 in Massachusetts. Genworth Financial, Inc., *2007 Cost of Living Survey* (March 31, 2007), available at http://www.longtermcare.Genworth.com.

13. Ibid.

14. Individuals and their families contribute another $37.4 billion (18.1 percent) out of pocket, followed by LTC insurance and commercial health plans ($14.9 billion or 7.2 percent), additional private sources ($5.6 billion or 2.7 percent), and other public programs ($5.3 billion or 2.6 percent). Komisar and Thompson, *National Spending for Long-Term Care.*

15. The rest of nursing home costs derive from Medicare (17 percent); residents and their families out of pocket (25 percent); private LTC insurance (7 percent); and other public or private sources, such as the Veterans Administration (6 percent). Ibid.

16. Medicare, which severely restricts nursing home coverage, paid only about 20 percent of LTC costs in 2005. The program funds 100 days of institutional services, but only for older people who require skilled nursing care or rehabilitative therapy subsequent to a hospital stay of at least three days. Moreover, after twenty days, there is a daily copayment, $124 in 2007. Even though home health care is not tied to a hospitalization, and there are no limits on the number of days or visits a beneficiary can receive, eligibility for such assistance is rigidly controlled: a person must be "homebound," need "intermittent" skilled nursing or therapy services, and be under the care of a physician who puts together a rehabilitation plan. Moreover, the patient must show improvement or lose her benefits.

17. Ellen O'Brien, *Options to Broaden Role of Medicare in Long-Term Care*, Long Term Care Financing Project (Washington, D.C.: Health Policy Institute, Georgetown University, February 2007); Anna Sommers and Mindy Cohen, *Medicaid's Long-Term Care Beneficiaries: An Analysis of Spending Patterns* (Menlo Park, Calif.: Henry J. Kaiser Family Foundation, Kaiser Commission on Medicaid and the Uninsured, November 2006), available at http://www.kff.org.

The 7.5 million dual eligibles account for 24 percent of Medicare spending. About 20 percent of the dually eligible population resides in institutional facilities as compared with 3 percent of Medicare recipients at large. David Grabowski, "Medicare and Medicaid: Conflicting Incentives for Long-Term Care," paper presented at the 2007 Annual Research Meeting of Academy Health, June 3–5, Orlando, Florida.

18. O'Brien, *Long-Term Care.*

19. States with particularly large older populations include Florida, Pennsylvania, West Virginia, Iowa, and North Dakota. The sixty-five and older population, however, is projected to grow dramatically over the next decade in Nevada, Arizona, Colorado, Utah, Oregon, Idaho, Georgia, Alaska, and Washington. Virginia Gray, "The Socioeconomic and Political Context of States," in Virginia Gray and Russell L. Hanson, eds., *Politics in the American States: A Comparative Analysis,* 8th ed., 1–30 (Washington, D.C.: Congressional Quarterly Press, 2004).

As a percentage of Medicaid budgets, LTC costs vary widely: the states with the highest proportions include North Dakota (57.8 percent), Connecticut (50.9 percent), Minnesota (45.5 percent), Wyoming (44.3 percent), Montana (42.5 percent), Nebraska (42.3 percent), Pennsylvania (42.1 percent), Iowa (41.9 percent), Wisconsin (41.8 percent), Ohio (40.4 percent), Kansas (40.1 percent), New York (38.9 percent), and New Hampshire (38.7 percent). Among the states with the lowest percentages are Tennessee (21.2 percent), Texas (21.6 percent), Mississippi (23.1 percent), Nevada (23.1 percent), South Carolina (23.3 percent), Georgia (23.5 percent), California (24.0 percent), and Kentucky (24.2 percent). O'Brien, *Long-Term Care.*

20. Colleen M. Grogan and Eric M. Patashnik, "Universalism Within Targeting: Nursing Home Care, the Middle Class, and the Politics of the Medicaid Program," *Social Service Review* 77, no. 1 (March 2003): 51–71.

21. Several states even began imposing certificate-of-need mandates to control the rapid spread of nursing homes. Regardless, nursing homes continued to expand during the next two decades: from 1990 to 1996 alone, the number of freestanding skilled nursing facilities increased by 49 percent, and hospital-based nursing homes increased by 82 percent. Although the total number of institutions has decreased in recent years (in 1985, there were 19,100 nursing homes, but only 16,400 by 2006), the facilities themselves have grown larger and contain more beds, totaling about 1.7 million today. The number of people living in the mostly for-profit institutions also has decreased slightly (to about 1.5 million residents as of May 2008), with consequent declines in occupancy rates (from 92 percent in the mid-1980s to about 86 percent today). Houser, *Nursing Homes;* U.S. GAO, *Nursing Homes: Federal Monitoring Surveys Demonstrate Continued Understatement of Serious Care Problems and CMS Oversight Weaknesses,* report to congressional requesters, GAO-08-517 (Washington, D.C.: U.S. Government Printing Office, May 2008).

22. Komisar and Thompson, *National Spending for Long-Term Care.* In some states, the amount is even higher. For example, more than 75 percent of nursing home residents in New York and South Carolina are subsidized through the low-income health program; Tennessee finances about 83 percent of its 35,000 institutionalized residents. Candice Choi, "Health Department Seeks to Trim Medicaid Waste in Nursing Homes," *New York Times,* September 21, 2005; John C. Goodman, Michael Bond, Devon Herrich, Joe Barnett, and Pamela Villarreal, *Medicaid Empire: Why New York Spends So Much on Health Care for the Poor and How the System Can Be Reframed,* Policy Report no. 284 (Dallas: National Center for Policy Analysis, March 20, 2006).

23. There were about 300,000 nursing home beneficiaries in 1965. Jonathan Oberlander, *The Political Life of Medicare* (Chicago: University of Chicago Press, 2003).

24. As of 2008, the SSI income-eligibility level for individuals and couples was $623 and $934 per month, respectively. Thus, elders could be qualified for nursing home care at monthly income thresholds of up to $1,869 and $2,802, respectively. The corresponding allowable upper limits for assets are $2,000 and $3,000.

25. Enid Kassner, *Medicaid Financial Eligibility for Older People: State Variations in Access to Home and Community-Based Waiver and Nursing Home Services* (Washington, D.C.: AARP Public Policy Institute, April 2002).

By the mid-1980s, about two-thirds of the states had adopted a "medically needy" program for the elderly and people with disabilities; thirty-three states currently have such programs, and most of these states also employ the special-income rule. Around sixteen states that do not have a "medically needy" program use the special-income rule exclusively. Most of the thirty-eight states that rely on the special-income rule allow the full 300 percent of SSI. Teresa A. Coughlin, Leighton Ku, and John Holahan, *Medicaid Since 1980: Costs, Coverage, and the Shifting Alliance Between the Federal Government and the States* (Washington, D.C.: Urban Institute, 1994); Enid Kassner, *Private Long-Term Care Insurance: The Medicaid Interaction*, Issue Brief no. 68 (Washington, D.C.: AARP Public Policy Institute, 2004); Citizens for Long-Term Care, *Long-Term Care Financing Reform: An Integral Part of Social Security and Medicare Reform* (Washington, D.C.: Citizens for Long-Term Care, June 2002).

26. Coughlin, Ku, and Holahan, *Medicaid Since 1980*.

27. Colleen Grogan and Eric Patashnik, "Between Welfare Medicine and Mainstream Entitlement: Medicaid at the Political Crossroads," *Journal of Health Politics, Policy, and Law* 28, no. 1 (October 2003): 821–858.

28. Ibid., 844.

29. Grogan and Patashnik, "Universalism Within Targeting," 58.

30. The allowable personal needs allowance ranged from $30 to $100 per month in 2007.

31. Judith Kasper, Barbara Lyons, and Molly O'Malley, *Long-Term Services and Supports: The Future Role and Challenges for Medicaid* (Menlo Park, Calif.: Henry J. Kaiser Family Foundation, Kaiser Commission on Medicaid and the Uninsured, September 2007), available at http://www.kff.org.

32. U.S. Congress, Senate, Committee on Finance, *Medicaid Waste, Fraud, and Abuse: Threatening the Health Care Safety Net*, hearings, testimony of Julie Stone-Axelrod, Congressional Research Service, Domestic Social Policy Division, Library of Congress, 109th Cong., 1st sess., June 29, 2005.

33. In most states, the maximum allowable assets for an individual and couple—excluding a home, burial expenses, life insurance, household goods, and personal items up to a certain value—are $2,000 and $3,000, respectively.

34. Gleckman, *Medicaid and Long-Term Care*; U.S. Congress, Senate, *Medicaid Waste, Fraud, and Abuse*, testimony of Judith Feder, professor and dean, Public Policy Institute, Georgetown University.

35. The option was first given to the states under the Tax Equity and Fiscal Responsibility Act (the Katie Beckett Program) of 1982.

36. Robert Pear, "Protecting Family Assets: A New Breed of Medicaid Counselors Steps In," *New York Times*, November 26, 1987.

Prior to the passage of Medicaid, at least thirty-five states expected adult children to contribute money to their parents as a condition of receiving old-age assistance, including LTC. Several states (e.g., Indiana, Virginia, Mississippi) subsequently required contributions from adult children of Medicaid recipients in nursing homes, although this requirement was rarely enforced.

37. Jerry Gray, "Governors Seek to Shed Burdens of Medicaid," *New York Times*, August 4, 1992.

38. However, heirs can request a delay if there is a disabled child or a child younger than twenty-one.

39. Prior to 1988, the community spouse could keep only $2,000 in countable assets, excluding the primary residence, one car, household goods and personal property, and $1,500 for burial expenses. He or she generally was allowed to retain the institutionalized spouse's income up to the SSI threshold, an amount that was less than the FPL.

Since then, each state still sets the exact amount that a healthy spouse can keep, but within a higher range established by the federal government. He or she is allowed half of the joint assets, with a minimum of $20,328 to $101,640 in 2007, and from $1,650 to $2,541 per month of their shared income.

40. U.S. GAO, *Medicaid Long-Term Care: Few Transferred Assets Before Applying for Nursing Home Coverage; Impact of DRA on Eligibility Is Uncertain*, GAO-07-280 (Washington, D.C.: U.S. Government Printing Office, March 2007).

41. Ellen O'Brien, *Medicaid's Coverage of Nursing Home Costs: Asset Shelter for the Wealthy or Essential Safety Net?* issue brief, Long Term Care Financing Project (Washington, D.C.: Health Policy Institute, Georgetown University, May 2005), 11.

42. Timothy Waidmann and Korbin Liu, *Asset Transfer and Nursing Home Use: Empirical Evidence and Policy Significance* (Menlo Park, Calif.: Henry J. Kaiser Family Foundation, Kaiser Commission on Medicaid and the Uninsured, April 2006), available at http://www.kff.org.

43. Jinkook Lee, Hyungsoo Kim, and Sandra Tannenbaum, "Medicaid and Family Wealth Transfer," *Gerontologist* 46, no. 1 (February 2006): 6–13.

44. Jonathan Feinstein and Chich-Chin Ho, *Elderly Asset Management and Health: An Empirical Analysis*, Working Paper no. W7814 (Cambridge, Mass.: National Bureau of Economic Research, July 2000); Donald Taylor, Frank Sloan, and Edward Norton, "Formation of Trusts and Spend Down to Medicaid," *Journal of Gerontology: Social Sciences* 54B, no. 4 (1999): S194–S201.

45. U.S. Congress, Senate, *Medicaid Waste, Fraud, and Abuse*, Feder testimony.

46. O'Brien, *Medicaid's Coverage of Nursing Home Costs*; Jonathan Feinstein and Chich-Chin Ho, "Elderly Asset Management and Health," in William Gale, James Hines, and Joel Slemrod, eds., *Rethinking Estate and Gift Taxation*, 457–498 (Washington, D.C.: Brookings Institution, 2001).

47. The AARP reported spending millions on lobbying: $105.3 million from 1998 to 2006 at the national level ($23 million in 2006 alone). Center for Responsive Politics Web site at http://www.opensecrets.org.

48. Christine Day, *What Older Americans Think: Interest Groups and Aging Policy* (Princeton, N.J.: Princeton University Press, 1990), 33.

49. Clive S. Thomas and Ronald J. Hrebenar, "Interest Groups in the States," in Gray and Hanson, eds., *Politics in the American States*, 100–129.

50. Supported by more than 100 national organizations, AARP and the Villers Foundation (now Families USA) launched a campaign for LTC legislation but failed to achieve its inclusion in the Medicare Catastrophic Coverage Act of 1988. Oberlander, *The Political Life of Medicare.*

51. Day, *What Older Americans Think*; Colleen Grogan, "Political-Economic Factors Influencing State Medicaid Policy," *Political Research Quarterly* 47, no. 3 (September 1994): 589–622.

52. Colleen Grogan describes how in 1995 Republicans in Congress proposed to force adult children to take financial responsibility for their parents' nursing home care. The bill was solidly opposed by voters across the political aisle and "quickly dropped" by the lawmakers. Colleen Grogan, "Medicaid: Health Care for You and Me?" in James A. Morone, Theodore Litman, and Leonard S. Robins, eds. *Health Politics and Policy*, 4th ed., 329–354, Delmar Series in Health (Albany, N.Y.: Delmar, 2008).

53. The 1915(c) waivers serve about 40 percent of all people receiving Medicaid HCBS today, but represent two-thirds of such costs due mainly to the high price tag of serving the mentally and developmentally disabled population. O'Brien, *Long-Term Care*; Martin Kitchener, Terrence Ng, Charlene Harrington, and Molly O'Malley, *Medicaid 1915 (c) Home and Community Based Service Programs: Data Update* (Menlo Park, Calif.: Henry J. Kaiser Family Foundation, Kaiser Commission on Medicaid and the Uninsured, December 2006), available at http://www.kff.org.

54. In the first year (1982) of the HCBS waiver program, only six states participated, spending $3.8 million. Paul Saucier, Brian Burwell, and Kerstin Gerst, *The Past, Present, and Future of Managed Long-Term Care* (Washington, D.C.: Office of Disability, Aging, and Long-Term Care Policy, U.S. Department of Health and Human Services, and the MEDSTAT Group, April 2005); Citizens for Long-Term Care, *Long-Term Care Financing Reform.*

55. Citizens for Long-Term Care, *Long-Term Care Financing Reform.*

56. Heidi Reester, Raad Missmar, and Anne Tumlinson, *Recent Growth in Medicaid and Community-Based Service Waivers* (Menlo Park, Calif.: Henry J. Kaiser Family Foundation, Kaiser Commission on Medicaid and the Uninsured, April 2004), available at http://www.kff.org.

57. By 2005, in thirty states, 260,000 people were on such lists for 102 waivers, up from 156,000 individuals in 2002, with average waiting times ranging from thirteen months for the aged and disabled to twenty-six months for mentally and developmentally disabled populations. Kitchener et al., *Medicaid 1915 (c) Home and Community Based Service Programs*; Jeffrey Crowley, *Medicaid Long-Term Services Reforms in the Deficit Reduction Act* (Menlo Park, Calif.: Henry J. Kaiser Family Foundation, Kaiser

+ +

Commission on Medicaid and the Uninsured, April 2006), 1–19, at http://www.kff.org; Kasper, Lyons, and O'Malley, *Long-Term Services and Supports*.

For example, during 2006, the Wisconsin Family Care program had more than 11,000 seniors and disabled people waiting for services. Indiana's waiver for children with autism and developmental disabilities, which provides assistance to 5,400 youngsters in apartments, group homes, and elsewhere in the community, had 15,000 on its wait list.

58. In Ohio, for example, the number of slots for people with developmental disabilities was cut by one-third in 2005. At the time, there already was a substantial waiting list for services. In another typical example, in 2009 the governor of Rhode Island, Donald Carcieri (R), was seeking to eliminate dental coverage for low-income parents enrolled in the state's Rite Care Plan.

59. O'Brien, *Long-Term Care*; Komisar and Thompson, *National Spending for Long-Term Care*. The proportion of Medicaid LTC expenses ($89.3 billion in 2004) are: ICFs-MR (13 percent); personal care (8 percent); HCBS waivers (24 percent); home health (4 percent); and skilled nursing homes (51 percent). Enid Kassner, *Medicaid and Long-Term Care Services and Supports for Older People* (Washington, D.C.: AARP Public Policy Institute, April 2006).

The amount of money, extent of services, and type of programs devoted to such care vary dramatically among the states. For example, the percentage of home and community-based assistance relative to their overall LTC costs ranges from more than 60 percent in Oregon, Alaska, and New Mexico to less than 15 percent in Louisiana and Mississippi. Citizens for Long-Term Care, *Long-Term Care Financing Reform*; Coughlin, Ku, and Holahan, *Medicaid Since 1980*.

60. In 2005, 1.2 million people participated in 1915(c) HCBS waiver programs. Kitchener et al., *Medicaid 1915 (c) Home and Community Based Service Programs*.

61. Richard Johnson, Desmond Toohey, and Joshua Wiener, *Meeting the Long-Term Care Needs of the Baby Boomers: How Changing Families Will Affect Paid Helpers and Institutions*, the Retirement Project, Discussion Paper 07-04 (Washington, D.C.: Urban Institute, May 2007).

For the nation as a whole, 75 percent of the overall Medicaid LTC budget still funds nursing home care for frail older people and adults with physical disabilities. Only seven states spent 40 percent or more of their LTC budgets on HCBS for these sectors of the population: Alaska, Oregon, Washington, New Mexico, California, Minnesota, and Texas. Enid Kassner, Susan Reinhard, Wendy Fox-Grage, Ari N. Houser, Jean C. Accius, Barbara Coleman, and Dann Milne, *In Brief: A Balancing Act, State Long-Term Care Reform, Research Report* (Washington, D.C.: AARP Public Policy Institute, September 5, 2008).

Moreover, because states tend to be wary of potential lawsuits by the low-income disabled population or their advocates, the shift to community-based services has been more extensive for that group relative to the frail elderly.

62. Kassner, *Medicaid Financial Eligibility for Older People*, 10. States allow a small maintenance allowance, and any income above that amount is subject to cost sharing. Under the new DRA guidelines, if the disabled spouse stays at home, the couple is allowed only $5,400 in combined assets and $900 per month in income, 20 percent less than the FPL.

63. In a telling study of three hypothetical individuals requiring LTC, representing diverse ages, disabilities, and needs, but all income eligible for Medicaid, Laura Summer describes the diverse prospects for each one in four states. Depending on his or her location, each experiences a vastly different mix and quantity of available benefits or equipment, access to providers, waiting lists, and limits on services. Laura Summer, *Choices and Consequences: The Availability of Community-Based Long-Term Care Services to the Low-Income Population*, Long-Term Care Financing Project (Washington, D.C.: Health Policy Institute, George Washington University, May 2003).

64. By 1989, with nearly 6 percent of its welfare medicine recipients receiving in-home care, New York had the most expensive offerings in the nation. That year the state had less than 8 percent of the nation's population but accounted for 20 percent of total Medicaid spending, predominantly because of LTC. Michael S. Sparer, *Medicaid and the Limits of State Health Reform* (Philadelphia: Temple University Press, 1996); Sam Howe Verhovek, "Legislators Resist Cuomo on Medicaid Cuts," *New York Times*, February 24, 1989; Anne Martin, Lekha Whittle, Katherine Levit, Greg Won, and Lindy Minman, "Health Care Spending During 1991–1998: A Fifty-State Review," Exhibit 4, *Health Affairs* 21, no. 4 (July–August 2002): 112–126.

65. Public Policy Institute of New York, *Just the Facts: Key Economic and Social Indicators for New York State: 2006 Medicaid Spending on Home Health Care and Personal Care* (Albany: Public Policy Institute of New York, 2006), available at http://www.ppinys.org; Public Policy Institute of New York, *2006 Medicaid Spending on Long-Term Care Facilities* (Albany: Public Policy Institute of New York, 2006), available at http://www.ppinys.org.

Only seventeen other states fund "personal care," and fifteen offer private-duty nursing. Goodman et al., *Medicaid Empire*.

66. Laura Summer, *Community-Based Long-Term Services Financed by Medicaid: Managing Resources to Provide Appropriate Medicaid Services*, issue brief, Long-Term Care Financing Project (Washington, D.C.: Health Policy Institute, George Washington University, June 2007).

67. In eligibility criteria for HCBS waivers, 74 percent of states use 300 percent of SSI; 3 percent use from 101 to 299 percent of SSI; and 23 percent use 100 percent of SSI. Kitchener et al., *Medicaid 1915 (c) Home and Community Based Service Programs*.

68. Prior to the DRA, functional eligibility criteria for institutional and at-home services in most states were equally stringent. Kasper, Lyons, and O'Malley, *Long-Term Care Services and Supports*.

69. Nursing home transition programs, funded with federal dollars, had been established in the late 1990s. Florida, for example, created the Florida Diversion Program for four counties in 1998. However, only a small number of people was deinstitutionalized under the several state programs. Judy Kasper and Molly O'Malley, *Nursing Home Transition Programs: Perspectives of State Medicaid Officials* (Menlo Park, Calif.: Henry J. Kaiser Family Foundation, Kaiser Commission on Medicaid and the Uninsured, April 2006), available at http://www.kff.org.

70. Under the Family Opportunity Act of 2005 (or Dylan Lee James Act), parents of disabled children can now buy into Medicaid if their family income is less than 300

percent of the FPL. The legislation not only offers states the option of covering such children, but allows them to charge premiums, along with copayments, of up to 5 percent of income for households with earnings less than 200 percent of the FPL and up to 7.5 percent for those having between 200 and 300 percent of the FPL. If employer-sponsored health insurance is available, and the company pays at least 50 percent of the premium, parents must choose that alternative in order to receive the Medicaid subsidy.

In addition, the Tax Equity and Fiscal Responsibility Act (the Katie Beckett Program) of 1982 allows the states to waive parental income when assessing Medicaid eligibility for children with severe disabilities who live at home. In order to receive coverage, however, the youngsters must otherwise require institutionalization, and the cost of care cannot exceed that of nursing home or hospital services. Less than half of the states offer the program, and, nearly all of those that do, have long waiting lists.

71. Under the projects, the recipient must have resided in an institution from six months to two years, depending on the state plan. The grants can be used for personal assistance, home modifications, respite services, assistive devices, and the like. Moreover, the Medicaid enrollee can receive a set amount of money for self-directed care that includes an ability to hire and fire a caregiver.

72. Texas, Utah, and Vermont already had their own Money Follows the Person programs but had established them without the enhanced federal payments. Crowley, *Medicaid Long-Term Services Reforms in the Deficit Reduction Act.*

73. Ibid. In the first year, seventeen states received only $23.8 million to deinstitutionalize about 20,000 people.

74. Kasper and O'Malley, *Nursing Home Transition Programs.*

75. Colleen Grogan and Vernon Smith, "From Charity Care to Medicaid: Governors, States, and the Transformation of American Health Care," in Ethan Sribnick, ed., *A More Perfect Union*, 353–401 (Philadelphia: University of Pennsylvania Press, 2008).

76. And as Ronald Angel, Laura Lein, and Jane Henrici note, "Survival in low-income resource-poor neighborhoods requires a mutual interdependence, and many women find themselves responsible not only for their own families but for others in extended networks of kin and close friends." Ronald J. Angel, Laura Lein, and Jane Henrici, *Poor Families in America's Health Care Crisis* (New York: Cambridge University Press, 2006), 137.

77. O'Brien, *Long-Term Care.*

78. Metlife Mature Market Institute, *The Metlife Caregiving Cost Study: Productivity Losses to U.S. Business* (Westport, Conn.: Metlife Mature Market Institute, National Alliance for Caregiving, July 2006).

At the end of 2006, Congress passed the Lifespan Respite Care Act to assist family members with respite services, regardless of the recipient's age, income level, or condition severity. However, it was not funded until 2009, at which time the program received $2.5 million. In 2000, the National Family Caregiver Program, funded through the federal Older Americans Act, provides limited assistance to caregivers of the frail elderly.

79. AARP, *Caregiving in the U.S.* (Washington, D.C.: AARP, National Alliance for Caregiving, April 2004).

80. May Jo Gibson and Ari N. Houser, *Valuing the Invaluable: A New Look at the Economic Value of Family Caregiving*, issue brief (Washington, D.C.: AARP Public Policy Institute, June 2007).

81. For example, in a study of 888 elderly participants using Michigan's HCBS waiver program, Lydia Li found that although family assistance initially dropped, it had stabilized by the third year, averaging fully eighteen hours per week. Lydia W. Li, "Longitudinal Changes in the Amount of Informal Care Among Publicly Paid Home Care Recipients," *Gerontologist* 45 (2005): 474–485.

82. Metlife Mature Market Institute, *The Metlife Caregiving Cost Study*.

83. Saucier, Burwell, and Gerst, *The Past, Present, and Future of Managed Long-Term Care*. PACE was originally authorized under OBRA 1986 as a demonstration program with ten sites. Under BBA 1997, it became a regular part of the Medicare program, with a limited number of site expansions available each year. The legislation also allowed states to include it as an optional benefit in their Medicaid plan. PACE targets the highly disabled fifty-five and older population who meet Medicaid nursing home eligibility criteria and reside within a PACE service area. Integrating Medicare and Medicaid financing, it covers all primary, acute, and LTC services, including doctors, hospitals, nursing home, therapies, pharmaceuticals, equipment, adult day care, and home care. David C. Grabowski, "The Cost Effectiveness of Noninstitutional Long-Term Care Services: Review and Synthesis of the Most Recent Evidence," *Medical Care Research and Review* 63, no. 1 (February 2006): 3–28. As of February 2006, there were more than twenty-four PACE sites serving 17,000 people.

84. Arizona's Long-Term Care System was first authorized as a demonstration program in 1989 through a section 1115 waiver. Contractors provide services within specified geographic areas.

85. Saucier, Burwell, and Gerst, *The Past, Present, and Future of Managed Long-Term Care*.

86. There is a number of small, voluntary prepaid LTC managed-care plans nationwide. For example, New York State has had such waiver demonstration projects since 1994. Today there are fifteen of them in the state, but each includes fewer than 500 members. Minnesota implemented the Minnesota Senior Health Options in 1997, an optional demonstration program that integrates acute and LTC for dually eligible older participants, and in 2001 the state established the Minnesota Disability Health Option for people with physical disabilities. Wisconsin's Family Care, which now includes about twenty-four counties, also is an elective program. And in 2004, Massachusetts implemented the Senior Care Options program, offering three separate plans.

A few states have more recently begun requiring many of their frail elderly and disabled residents to join such programs. Texas cautiously began its demonstration for integrating acute and LTC Medicaid services for the aged and disabled through its Star+Plus program in 1998. Beginning with one county, the program is now mandatory for most eligible people who live in about twenty-nine counties. Shortly after his 2005 election, Indiana governor Mitch Daniels (R) resolved to hold the growth in Medicaid outlays to 5 percent a year, primarily by gradually forcing everyone, including pregnant women and children, into capitated plans. In 2007, the state mandated its blind, aged, and disabled clients to sign up as well. In another case, Ohio began moving almost all Medicaid-eligible children and parents, as well as about one-third of its elders and people with disabilities, into three commercial MCOs. Beginning with a pilot program in selected counties, Florida Senior Care has not only forced its frail population into managed care, but has given the firms power to decide which services, whether nursing home or community care, Medicaid enrollees will receive. Grabowski, "The Cost Effectiveness of Noninstitutional Long-Term Care Services"; Brian Burwell, "Medicaid Long-Term Care Expenditures in FY 2000," *Gerontologist* 41, no. 5 (October 2001): 687–691; Saucier, Burwell, and Gerst, *The Past, Present, and Future of Managed Long-Term Care.*

87. Saucier, Burwell, and Gerst, *The Past, Present, and Future of Managed Long-Term Care.*

88. About seventy-two firms began selling policies; however, with no federal regulations in place until 1990, not only had many of them engaged in unscrupulous sales practices, but their plans tended to be even more sorely inadequate than they are today. Jill Quadagno, *One Nation Uninsured: Why the U.S. Has No National Health Insurance* (Oxford, U.K.: Oxford University Press, 2005).

89. The original states were California, Connecticut, Indiana, and New York.

90. In New York, consumers are required to purchase the cost of three years of institutional care, but they can shelter all of their assets. About 45,000 people currently hold Partnership for Long-Term Care Program policies in the state. Goodman et al., *Medicaid Empire.*

91. U.S. GAO, *Long-Term Care Insurance: Partnership Programs Include Benefits That Protect Policyholders and Are Unlikely to Result in Medicaid Savings,* GAO-07-231 (Washington, D.C.: U.S. Government Printing Office, May 2007).

92. U.S. Congress, Senate, *Medicaid Waste, Fraud, and Abuse,* Feder testimony.

93. Most policyholders in the four initial participating states have assets of more than $350,000. In these localities, there are only about 172,000 active policies, less than 3 percent of their combined sixty-five and older population. U.S. GAO, *Overview of the Long-Term Care Partnership Program,* letter to Senator Charles E. Grassley, ranking minority member, Committee on Finance, and Senator John D. Rockefeller, September 9, 2005, GAO-05-021R (Washington, D.C.: U.S. Government Printing Office, 2005), available at http://www.gao.gov/newitems/d051021r.pdf.

94. For example, premium assistance is available only to households who itemize deductions and whose overall qualifying health care outlays are more than 7.5 percent of their adjusted gross income. The self-employed can fully deduct their LTC insurance premiums without having to meet these requirements.

95. Joshua M. Wiener, Jane Tilly, and Susan M. Goldevson, "Federal and State Initiatives to Jump Start the Market for Private Long-Term Care Insurance," *Elder Law Journal* 8 (2000): 57–102; Brenda Spillman, "Consumer Preparedness for Long-Term Care: Personal Financing Options for Long-Term Care," paper presented at the LTC colloquium "Building Bridges: Making a Difference in Long-Term Care," June 2, 2007, Orlando, Florida.

96. Kassner, *Private Long-Term Care Insurance*; O'Brien, *Long-Term Care.*

+ +

97. See the *Consumer Reports* site at http://www.consumerreports.orh/cro/money/ insurance/longterm-care-insurance-1103/htm, November 2003.

98. Spillman, "Consumer Preparedness for Long-Term Care."

99. CNA Financial Corporation increased its charges by 50 percent. Laura Benko, "Medicaid Woes, Aging Population Have Insurers Thinking Long-Term," *Crain's Detroit Business*, September 19, 2005; U.S. GAO, *Federal Program Compared Favorably with Other Products, and Analysis of Claims Trend Could Inform Future Decisions*, report to congressional committees on long-term care insurance, GAO-06-401 (Washington, D.C.: U.S. Government Printing Office, March 2006); *Consumer Reports* Web site (see note 97).

100. Participants in the federal plan—whether employees, retirees, or their families—must pay for their own premiums out of pocket.

101. Less than 10 percent of the fifty-five and older population own policies, and sales have been decreasing since 2002. Overall, in 2005 slightly more than a million people paid out about $7 billion in premiums. Benko, "Medicaid Woes"; U.S. Congress, Senate, *Medicaid Waste, Fraud, and Abuse*, testimony of the American Council of Life Insurers.

7. Quality of Care

1. John S. O'Shea, *More Medicaid Means Less Quality Health Care*, Center for Health Policy Studies, Web Memo no. 1402 (Washington, D.C.: Heritage Foundation, March 21, 2007), available at http://www.heritage.org/research/healthcare/wm1402.cfm.

2. In 1987, New York, Minnesota, and Wisconsin had the best Medicaid programs in the nation, whereas Mississippi, Wyoming, and Arizona had the worst ones. Public Citizen Health Research Group (PCHRG), *Poor Medicine for Poor People* (Washington, D.C.: PCHRG, 1987).

3. The highest-ranking states, in descending order, were Massachusetts, Nebraska, Vermont, Alaska, Wisconsin, Rhode Island, Minnesota, New York, Washington, and New Hampshire. The most inadequate were Mississippi, Idaho, Texas, Oklahoma, South Dakota, Indiana, South Carolina, Colorado, Alabama, and Missouri. Annette B. Ramirez and Sidney M. Wolfe, *Unsettling Scores: A Ranking of State Medicaid Programs*, Public Citizen Health Research Group (PCHRG) Publication no. 1807 (Washington, D.C.: PCHRG, April 2007).

4. The limited number of expectant women in the state who paid for the birth of their child out of pocket (about 4 percent) surprisingly fared even worse. Dr. Albert Wool and colleagues, *Method of Payment for Delivery*, report (Montgomery: Center for Health Statistics, Alabama Department of Health, 2005).

5. Interestingly, the disparities between individuals covered commercially and older people enrolled in Medicare were considerably less. James E. Calvin, Matthew Roe, and Anita Chen, "Insurance Coverage and Care of Patients with Non-St-Segment Elevation Acute Coronary Syndrome." *Annals of Internal Medicine* 145, no. 10 (November 21, 2006): 739–748.

6. Amy Chen, Nicole Schrag, Michael Halpern, Andrew Stewart, and Elizabeth Ward, "Health Insurance and Stage at Diagnosis of Laryngeal Cancer: Does Insurance Type Predict Stage at Diagnosis?" *Archives of Otolaryngology–Head and Neck Surgery* 133 (August 2007), 788–789.

7. Indeed, the widest variations were among cancers that are more easily identified through early, standard testing or symptom assessment, including breast, colorectal, melanoma, and lung cancers. Michael Halpern, Elizabeth Ward, Alexandre Pauluck, Nicole Schrag, John Brian, and Amy Chen, "Association of Insurance Status and Ethnicity with Cancer Stage at Diagnosis for 12 Cancer Sites: A Retrospective Analysis," *The Lancet Oncology* 9, no. 3 (March 2008): 222–231.

8. Cathy J. Bradley, Jan P. Clement, and Chunchieh Lin, "Absence of Cancer Diagnosis and Treatment in Elderly Medicaid-Insured Nursing Home Residents," *Journal of the National Cancer Institute* 100 (February 11, 2008): 4–5.

9. Among patients with diabetes, for instance, only 42 percent had a vital test for blood sugar control (glycosylated hemoglobin). David Zingmond, Kathleen Wilber, Catherine Maclean, and Neil Wenger, "Measuring the Quality of Care Provided to Community Dwelling Vulnerable Elders Dually Enrolled in Medicare and Medicaid," *Medical Care* 45, no. 10 (October 2007): 931–938.

10. Arnold Epstein, "Medicaid Managed Care and High Quality: Can We Have Both?" *Journal of the American Medical Association* 278, no. 19 (November 19, 1997): 1617–1621.

11. Bruce Landon, Eric Schneider, and Sharon-Lise Normand, "Quality of Care in Medicaid Managed Care and Commercial Plans," *Journal of the American Medical Association* 208, no. 14 (October 10, 2007): 1674–1681.

12. Then again, the evaluators were quick to point out that none of the MCOs, regardless of whether they were privately or publicly funded, reliably functioned up to par on any of the measures. Joseph Thompson, Kevin Ryan, Sathiska Pinidiya, and James Bost, "Quality of Care for Children in Commercial and Medicaid Managed Care," *Journal of the American Medical Association* 290, no. 4 (September 17, 2004), 1492.

13. To illustrate, commercial patients obtained at least 15 percent more cervical cancer screenings and diabetes-management services; they also received 4.9 percent more assistance in the control of hypertension, and 24.5 percent more appropriate postpartum care than did Medicaid enrollees. Landon, Schneider, and Normand, "Quality of Care in Medicaid Managed Care and Commercial Plans."

14. Anna Aizer, Janet Currie, and Enrico Moretti, "Does Managed Care Hurt Health? Evidence from Medicaid Mothers," *Review of Economics and Statistics* 89, no. 3 (2007), 386.

15. Epstein, "Medicaid Managed Care and High Quality," 1617.

16. Congress eventually set some standards for the industry, including a few consumer protections. Nonetheless, these regulations were not finalized until 2002, at which time they were markedly weakened by the Bush administration. David G. Smith, *Entitlement Politics: Medicare and Medicaid 1995–2001* (New York: De Gruyter, 2002).

One federal initiative intended to enhance the MCOs' quality of care was the 1996 Quality Improvement System for Managed Care; federal administrators have used the ensuing guidelines to assess Medicare MCOs, but states were not obligated to follow them for their Medicaid plans. U.S. GAO, *Medicaid Managed Care: Access and Quality Requirements Specific to Low-Income and Other Special Needs Enrollees* (Washington, D.C.: U.S. Government Printing Office, December 8, 2004).

17. These provisions were enacted under BBA 1997.

18. Roughly eleven states had enacted legislation that allowed patients to sue MCOs for malpractice damages. However, these laws were invalidated in 2004 when the U.S. Supreme Court struck down a Texas statute holding the insurance firms accountable for negligence.

19. A fine of $3.7 million was imposed by the legislature on the Peach State Health Plan for inadequate service provision. Dave Williams, "Managed Care Companies Defend Medicaid Services," *Henry Daily Herald* (McDonough, Ga.), August 29, 2007; Dave Williams, "Medicaid HMO Hit with Fine," *Henry Daily Herald* (McDonough, Ga.), July 16, 2007.

20. In June 2009, WellCare agreed to pay more than $90 million to settle the Florida Medicaid fraud cases, thereby resolving the federal and state investigations in that state.

21. Ann Marie Somma, "Managed Care Group Comes Under Fire—Health Net of Connecticut Accused of Sending Misleading Messages to Pharmacies," *Hartford Courant*, November 15, 2007.

22. The company eventually settled the charges for $225 million. Bethany McClean, "The Big Money in Medicaid," *Fortune*, June 11, 2007.

23. Mark Duggan, "Does Contracting Out Increase the Efficiency of Government Programs? Evidence from Medicaid HMOs," *Journal of Public Economics* 88, no. 12 (December 2004): 2549–2572.

24. As a case in point, Minnesota devoted far fewer tax dollars to patients after handing its Medicaid program over to private insurers. An audit of Medica, the state's largest MCO, discovered that it spent from 18 percent to 19 percent of its revenues on overhead; such expenses had previously cost Minnesota less than 5 percent. Kip Sullivan, "HMO Profits on Medical Assistance Hurt Many in State," *Minneapolis Star Tribune*, May 28, 2005.

25. David L. Shern, Kristine Jones, Huey Jen Chen, Neil Jordon, Josefa Ramoni-Perazzi, and Roger Boothroyd, "Medicaid Managed Care and the Distribution of Societal Costs for Persons with Severe Mental Illness," *American Journal of Psychiatry* 165, no. 2 (2008): 254–260.

26. In one state, more than 30 percent of its HCBS waiver participants did not obtain any of their authorized assistance, and 49 percent received only half of them. U.S. GAO, *Federal Oversight of Growing Medicaid Home and Community-Based Waivers Should Be Strengthened*, report to congressional requesters, GAO-03-576 (Washington, D.C.: U.S. Government Printing Office, June 2003).

27. Ibid.

28. Jane Gross, "Under One Roof, Aging Together Yet Alone," *New York Times*, January 28, 2005. In this chapter, the terms *assisted-living facilities, board-and-care homes,* and *residential facilities* are used interchangeably.

The two largest assisted-living companies in 2003 were Sunrise Senior Living and Emeritus Assisted Living, both national chains, followed by Alterra Healthcare, Atria

Senior Living, and Merrill Gardens. "Assisted Living: How Much Assistance Can You Really Count On?" *Consumer Reports* 70, no. 7 (July 2005): 28–33. Alterra filed for bankruptcy that year and subsequently was acquired by Emeritus, whose stock rose 52 percent in 2003, 57 percent in 2004, and 50 percent in 2005. Sunrise, whose share of the assisted-living market has steadily enlarged over the past several years, began entering into other types of elder care as well, including in-home, respite, institutional, and rehabilitative services. Its shares increased 55 percent in 2003, 20 percent in 2004, and 44 percent in 2005.

29. In 2006, for example, Ohio implemented a waiver allowing a small number of individuals who were already receiving Medicaid-funded LTC services to transfer to assisted-living facilities. In other places, such as New York's recently established "right-sizing demonstration plan," nursing home owners experiencing high vacancy rates are pushing legislators to allow them to convert their empty beds into assisted-living slots, financed by welfare medicine. Candice Choi, "Health Department Seeks to Trim Medicaid Waste in Nursing Homes," *New York Times*, September 21, 2005; "Assisted Living: How Much Assistance Can You Really Count On?"; Gross, "Under One Roof, Aging Together Yet Alone."

30. "Assisted Living: How Much Assistance Can You Really Count On?"

31. The investigators reviewed inspection data in seven states. Kevin McCoy, "Job Applicants Not Always Screened" (series on assisted-living facilities), *USA Today*, May 26, 2004; Kevin McCoy, "Poor Training Shows During Emergencies" (series on assisted-living facilities), *USA Today*, May 26, 2004; Kevin McCoy and Julie Appleby, "Many Facilities Accept People Who Are Too Ill" (series on assisted-living facilities), *USA Today*, May 27, 2004; Kevin McCoy and Julie Appleby, "Problems with Staffing Can Cost Lives, Money" (series on assisted-living facilities), *USA Today*, May 26, 2004.

32. David S. Fallis, "Virginia Rarely Prosecutes Cases of Neglect, Abuse: Lack of Expertise, Victims' Disabilities Hamper Investigations" (series on assisted-living facilities), *Washington Post*, May 26, 2004; David S. Fallis, "Weak Laws Let Deficient Facilities Stay Open: Demand for Assisted Living Care Pushes Virginia to Emphasize Improvement, Not Punishment" (series on assisted-living facilities), *Washington Post*, May 26, 2004.

33. "Assisted Living Horrors," editorial (series on assisted-living facilities), *Washington Post*, May 28, 2004.

34. For example, Assisted Living Concepts, Inc., which operates more than 200 homes in seventeen states, began withdrawing its facilities from Medicaid in 2007 and evicting Medicaid-funded residents. However, elders living in eight New Jersey facilities alleged that although they were promised that they could stay after their resources were depleted, the administrators were pushing them to leave now that they were enrolled in Medicaid. Guy Boulton, "Caregiver Puts Out Medicaid Recipients: Milwaukee Firm Runs Assisted-Living Centers," *Milwaukee Journal Sentinel*, May 19, 2007; Trish G. Graber, "Were More Medicaid Patients Evicted"? *Bridgetown News* (N.J.), June 12, 2008; Gross, "Under One Roof, Aging Together Yet Alone."

At the end of 2006, Assisted Living Concepts was converted into Extendicare Real Estate Investment Trust, and its new wholly owned subsidiary in the United States,

Extendicare Health Services, Inc., now operates its varied elder care facilities, including assisted-living facilities and nursing homes.

35. U.S. GAO, *Nursing Homes: Quality of Care More Related to Staffing Than Spending*, letter to congressional requesters, June 13, 2002, GAO-02-431R (Washington, D.C.: Government Printing Office, 2002), available at http://www.gao.gov/new.items/d02431r .pdf; J. F. Schnelle, S. F. Simmons, C. Harrington, M. Cadogan, E. Garcia, and B. M. Bates-Jensen, "Relationship of Nursing Home Staffing to Quality of Care," *Health Services Research* 39, no. 2 (2004): 225–250; Robert B. Hackey, *Rethinking Health Care Policy: The New Politics of State Regulation* (Washington, D.C.: Georgetown University Press, 1998).

36. ABT Associates, *Appropriateness of Nurse Staffing Ratios in Nursing Homes*, Phase 11 Final Report (Cambridge, Mass.: Centers for Medicare and Medicaid Services, 2002).

The evidence suggests that a minimum threshold of staffing hours is required to prevent serious risk to the frail elder's safety and well-being. CMS holds that patients ought to have at least 2.4 to 2.8 hours of care per day by CNAs; 1.15 to 1.3 hours by licensed practical nurses; and 0.55 to 0.75 hours by registered nurses. Others propose somewhat higher levels.

37. National Citizens' Coalition for Nursing Home Reform, *The Faces of Neglect: Behind the Closed Doors of Nursing Homes* (Washington, D.C.: National Citizens' Coalition for Nursing Home Reform, April 28, 2006).

38. PayScale, Inc., *PayScale Reports* (Seattle: PayScale, Inc., 2007), available at http://www.payscale.com; Kristin Smith and Reagan Baughman, "Caring for America's Aging Population: A Profile of the Direct-Care Workforce," *Monthly Labor Review* (September 2007): 20–26.

In an attempt to improve the situation, several states have enacted wage pass-through measures, targeting additional dollars for CNA salaries and benefits. However, these endeavors have been plagued with problems of accountability, rendering it difficult to track whether the funds are actually paid out to the workers. At any rate, because the add-ons tend to be "one-shot" arrangements and generally consist of minimal amounts of money (fifty cents or less per hour), they have not appreciably enhanced the financial standing of direct-care assistants. Steven L. Dawson, *Long-Term Care Financing and the Long-Term Care Workforce Crisis: Causes and Solutions*, report prepared for Citizens for Long-Term Care (Washington, D.C.: ParaProfessional Health Care Institute, November 2002).

39. Dawson, *Long-Term Care Financing and the Long-Term Care Workforce Crisis*.

40. Smith and Baughman, "Caring for America's Aging Population."

41. Ibid.; National Conference of State Legislators, *Better Jobs, Better Care: Retaining Long-Term Care Workers* (Washington, D.C.: National Conference of State Legislators, June 2007); PayScale, Inc., *PayScale Reports*; Dawson, *Long-Term Care Financing and the Long-Term Care Workforce Crisis*.

42. The U.S. Bureau of Labor Statistics identifies three main categories of direct-care workers: (1) home health aides; (2) nursing aides, orderlies, attendants; and (3) personal and home care aides.

+ +

43. This number represents an increase of more than 2 percent annually at a time when the working-age population is expected to increase by only 0.3 percent. Robert B. Friedland, *Caregivers and Long-Term Care Needs in the 21st Century: Will Public Policy Meet the Challenge?* issue brief (Washington, D.C.: Health Policy Institute, Georgetown University, July 2004).

44. Forty-one percent of female caregivers (1.1 million) worked in nursing homes, 41 percent (1.1 million) in home and community care, and 18 percent (0.5 million) in hospitals.

Among nursing home aides, 51 percent are white; 35 percent, black; 10 percent, Latino; and 4 percent, other minorities. Among home health aides, 48 percent are white; 24 percent, black; 21 percent, Latino; and 7 percent, other minorities. Nearly one-fifth of the direct-care workforce is foreign born. Smith and Baughman, "Caring for America's Aging Population."

45. According to the U.S. GAO, in the first few years of the twenty-first century Medicare's "improper" payments totaled nearly 15 percent of the program's outlays. U.S. GAO, *Health Care Fraud and Abuse Control Program: Results of Review of Annual Reports for FY 2002 and 2003*, report to congressional committees (Washington, D.C.: U.S. Government Printing Office, April 2005).

46. U.S. Congress, Senate, Committee on Finance, *Medicaid Waste, Fraud, and Abuse: Threatening the Health Care Safety Net*, hearings, Chuck Grassley, chair, Opening Statement, 109th Cong., 1st sess., June 28, 2005.

47. Clifford J. Levy and Michael Luo, "New York Medicaid Fraud May Reach into Billions," Program Disorder, Exploiting a Safety Net series, *New York Times*, July 18, 2005. Under the Improper Payments Information Act of 2002, the Bush administration endeavored to review every federal program to assess the risk of wrongful payments, estimate the extent to which such expenditures were occurring in the more precarious programs, put procedures in place to prevent it, and assess the effect of these deterrents annually. In 2001, CMS established Payment Accuracy Measurement to calculate improper state Medicaid payments and ultimately to reduce them. In 2006, this assessment approach was transformed into a mandatory program and renamed the Payment Error Rate Measurement initiative. Effective October 2007, CMS contractors must measure the extent of erroneous expenditures every three years, and the states have to determine eligibility error rates. The goal was to develop a national Medicaid payment error rate and force the states to reduce inappropriate billings. U.S. GAO, *Medicaid Financial Management: Steps Taken to Improve Federal Oversight but Other Actions Needed to Sustain Efforts*, report to the chairman, Committee on Finance, U.S. Senate, GAO-06-705 (Washington, D.C.: U.S. Government Printing Office, June 22, 2006).

48. Federal regulations require that each Medicaid agency maintain a Medicaid Management Information System, which is a claims payment and information retrieval system that must include a Surveillance and Utilization Review Subsystem. The subsystem is supposed to safeguard against overpayments by identifying aberrant billing patterns among providers as well as unnecessary and inappropriate utilization among recipients.

49. MFCUs were first instituted in 1978; the federal government funds 75 percent of their administrative costs. If an MFCU discovers improper payments, it sends its

recommendation back to the Medicaid agency for recovery of the money. If it determines that a claim is fraudulent, the MFCU can impose restitution, fines, penalties, a corporate integrity agreement, or jail.

In 2007, the fifty state MFCUs achieved 1,205 convictions and roughly $1.1 billion in court-ordered restitution, fines, civil settlements, and penalties in cases connected to the FCA, falsified bills, and patient abuse and neglect. U.S. Department of Justice, Office of the Inspector General (OIG), *OIG Semi-annual Report* (Washington, D.C.: U.S. Government Printing Office, October 1, 2007–March 31, 2008).

50. Federal law allows whistle-blowers to collect up to 30 percent of the recovery from perpetrators, although the amount generally has been about 17 percent. Cases also can be filed in state courts under state false claims acts, where they exist. Victoria Wachino, *The New Medicaid Integrity Program: Issues and Challenges in Ensuring Program Integrity in Medicaid* (Menlo Park, Calif.: Henry J. Kaiser Family Foundation, Kaiser Commission on Medicaid and the Uninsured, June 2007), available at http://www.kff.org.

51. Victoria Wachino and Robin Rudowitz, *Key Issues and Opportunities: Implementing the New Medicaid Integrity Program* (Menlo Park, Calif.: Henry J. Kaiser Family Foundation, Kaiser Commission on Medicaid and the Uninsured, July 2006), available at http://www.kff.org.; Wachino, *The New Medicaid Integrity Program.*

In New York, the number of people dedicated to fighting Medicaid fraud declined dramatically, from a staff of 200 in the late 1980s to only 50 by 2005. Michael Luo and Clifford Levy, "As Medicaid Balloons, Watchdog Force Shrinks," *New York Times*, July 19, 2005.

Florida's efforts became so lax that in 2003 HHS deemed the state a "high-risk" recipient of federal Medicaid money, a label that was later removed.

52. To illustrate, a 2005 investigation by Ohio's inspector general "found that health officials in that state prefer to 'educate' doctors, hospitals, and others who overbill Medicaid rather than refer cases for investigation and possible prosecution." Steven Malanga, "How to Stop Medicaid Fraud," *City Journal* (Manhattan Institute, N.Y.), April 21, 2006, available at http://www.city-journal.org/html/16_2_medicaid_fraud.html.

53. U.S. HHS, Office of the Inspector General (OIG), Daniel R. Levinson, Inspector General, *Suspected Medicaid Fraud Referrals*, report OEi-07-04-00181 (Washington, D.C.: U.S. Government Printing Office, January 2007).

54. U.S. Congress, Senate, *Medicaid Waste, Fraud, and Abuse*, hearings, testimony of Nicholas Messuri, president of the National Association of Medicaid Fraud Control Units, June 28, 2005.

55. Michael Luo, "Hospital Agrees to Repay State $76.5 million," *New York Times*, May 18, 2005.

56. The state created the Inspector General's Office; added more employees, computer experts, and prosecutors; acquired the latest software; and even forced Medicaid clients to use a "smart card" with their fingerprints on it so that they could not share it with others. U.S. Congress, Senate, *Medicaid Waste, Fraud, and Abuse*, hearings, testimony of Patrick O'Connell, chief, Civil Medicaid Fraud Section, Office of the Attorney General of

Texas, June 29, 2005; Steven Malanga, "How to Stop Medicaid Fraud," *City Journal* (Manhattan Institute, N.Y.) (Spring 2006), available at http://City-Journal.org/html.

57. Using computer analyses of several million records, interviews with state and local officials, and other key data, the newspaper embarked on a year-long investigation. Luo and Levy, "As Medicaid Balloons"; Levy and Luo, "New York Medicaid Fraud May Reach into Billions."

58. To that end, one county hired a Medicaid commissioner and two associates. Another paid $200,000 for new software that costs $30,000 in annual maintenance expenses. The counties share with the state a percentage of any money reclaimed. "N.Y. in the News: Feds to Audit New York State Medicaid Fraud Prevention Unit," *Empire Journal* (New York), September 3, 2005.

59. New York also had to accept and act on the findings of its newly established Commission on Health Care Facilities in the 21st Century, thereby setting in motion the closing of at least nine hospitals and seven nursing homes and the restructuring of many more.

60. In Ohio, Auditor of State Betty Montgomery identified $42 million in unwarranted payments to nursing homes, hospitals, and others, at times for patients who were deceased. Among other innovations, she called for a new inspector general, arguing that the state could save $400 million if it followed her recommendations. "Find Common Ground to Cure Medicaid's Ills," editorial, *Cleveland News-Herald*, December 27, 2006, available at http://www. News-Herald.com.

61. People convicted of fraud in New Jersey face up to ten years in prison as well as fines that are five times the amount swindled. Malanga, "How to Stop Medicaid Fraud."

62. DRA 2005 provides financial incentives: states with an approved FCA are allowed to keep a greater amount of any money recouped. Taxpayers Against Fraud, *What Is the False Claims Act and Why Is It So Important?* (Washington, D.C.: False Claims Act Legal Center, 2006), available at http://www.taf.org.

63. The Health Care Fraud and Abuse Program was established under the Health Insurance Portability and Accountability Act of 1996. Administered by both the HHS—through the OIG—and the Department of Justice, it provides about $240 million a year (2003) to combat fraud through an account set up within the Medicare trust fund. The OIG, the FBI, and the Medicare Integrity Program all receive a set amount of money from the account. For Medicaid, however, officials must specifically request an allocation from its discretionary funds, competing with other HHS programs, such as the Administration on Aging and the Office of the General Counsel. U.S. GAO, *Medicaid Financial Management.*

64. From 2003 to 2005, CMS received about $46 million from the Health Care Fraud and Abuse Program account for Medicaid projects, including OIG state audits; preliminary Medicare-Medicaid Data Match programs to share and analyze Medicare and Medicaid data (limited to a few states); and the Post Approval Monitoring Program. Beginning in 2004, it also received $12 million for ninety funding specialists to concentrate on improper state practices. Ibid.

65. Not only did the CMS have only eight full-time-equivalent employees to assist states with their fraud and abuse work, but its overall resources devoted to addressing

the issue had been steadily decreasing. U.S. Congress, Senate, *Medicaid Waste, Fraud, and Abuse,* hearings, statement by Kathryn Allen, director, Health Care, GAO, June 29, 2005; U.S. GAO, *Medicaid Integrity: Implementation of New Program Provides Opportunities for Federal Leadership to Combat Fraud, Waste, and Abuse,* statement of Leslie G. Aronovitz, director, Health Care, GAO, before the Subcommittee on Federal Financial Management, Government Information, and International Security and Government Affairs, 109th Cong., 2d sess., March 28, 2006, GAO-06-578T (Washington, D.C.: U.S. Government Printing Office, 2006).

66. Congress added 100 new full-time-equivalent employees and gave the Medicaid Integrity Program $255 million in funding over five years, along with another $25 million annually for the OIG. U.S. GAO, *Medicaid Integrity*; Wachino and Rudowitz, *Key Issues and Opportunities.*

67. DRA 2005 promoted other antifraud activities as well, including an expansion of and greater resources for the Medicare-Medicaid Data Match project. Funding for data match programs would steadily rise from $12 million annually in 2006 to $60 million in 2011 and beyond. The act also supported state efforts to enhance the efficiency and fiscal integrity of their Medicaid programs and strengthened efforts to seek payment from third parties, thus ensuring welfare medicine as the payer of last resort. Called Medicaid Transformation Grants, $75 million was available for these activities in both 2007 and 2008. Wachino, *The New Medicaid Integrity Program*; Wachino and Rudowitz, *Key Issues and Opportunities*; U.S. GAO, *Medicaid Integrity.*

68. In its 2006 annual report on MFCUs, for example, the OIG emphasized the units' huge recoveries, $1.1 billion in restitution, fines, civil settlements, and penalties, relative to the $159 million in administrative costs. U.S. HHS, Office of Inspector General (OIG), Daniel R. Levinson, Inspector General, *State Medicaid Fraud Control Units: Annual Report, Fiscal Year 2006* (Washington, D.C.: U.S. Government Printing Office, 2006).

In fact, the DRA mandates CMS to compile annual "return on investment" measures for the new Medicaid Integrity Program initiative. Wachino, *The New Medicaid Integrity Program.*

69. Levy and Luo, "New York Medicaid Fraud May Reach into Billions."

70. All the same, many of these large recoveries represent only a portion of the amount stolen. Taxpayers Against Fraud, *FY 2005 False Claims Act Settlements* (Washington, D.C.: False Claims Act Legal Center, 2006), available at http://www.taf.org.; Taxpayers Against Fraud, *FY 2006 False Claims Act Settlements (as of September 30, 2006)* (Washington, D.C.: False Claims Act Legal Center, 2006), available at http://www.taf.org.

71. U.S. Congress, Senate, *Medicaid Waste, Fraud, and Abuse,* hearings, testimony of James W. Moorman, president and CEO, Taxpayers Against Fraud, June 28, 2005.

As a case in point, roughly half of the $62.5 million recovered in 2004 by the New York MFCU accrued from the state's share of major nationwide settlements with two pharmaceutical corporations. Levy and Luo, "New York Medicaid Fraud May Reach into Billions."

Texas, too, concentrates mostly on drug companies because cases against them vastly dwarf, at least financially, cases against other types of contractors. U.S. Congress, Senate, *Medicaid Waste, Fraud, and Abuse,* hearings, O'Connell testimony.

72. The Medicaid rebate program was established under OBRA 1990. Rebate agreements are based on either the difference between a drug company's best price (lowest charge to providers, health-maintenance organizations, and nonprofit or government entities) and average manufacturer price (the mean price paid by wholesalers for drugs distributed to retail pharmacies) or 15.1 percent, whichever is greater.

73. In 2001, for example, TAP (Tapeda) pharmaceutical products resolved court action against the company for $875 million, the largest amount paid up to that time. U.S. Congress, Senate, *Medicaid Waste, Fraud, and Abuse*, hearings, testimony of Timothy Coleman, senior counsel to the deputy attorney general, U.S. Department of Justice, June 28, 2005.

Between 2002 and 2006, the drug firms paid about $3.8 billion to settle Medicare and Medicaid lawsuits against them. Wachino, *The New Medicaid Integrity Program*. For instance, Schering-Plough agreed in 2004 to pay $292 million to state Medicaid programs for concealing its "best price" for the drug Claritin. According to the whistle-blower, Beatrice Manning (a former Schering-Plough manager), although the deception was unmistakably criminal, with company senior officers keeping two sets of books, "Nobody was held personally responsible for their actions. No executives were pursued either civilly or criminally." U.S. Congress, Senate, *Medicaid Waste, Fraud, and Abuse*, hearings, testimony of Beatrice Manning, June 28, 2005; Taxpayers Against Fraud, *Total FY 2004 False Claims Act Fraud Settlements and Judgments* (Washington, D.C.: False Claims Act Legal Center, 2006), available at http://www.taf.org.

Bayer had concealed the deeply discounted prices it offered managed-care plans, thereby underpaying its Medicaid rebates; it settled in 2001 for $14 million. Two years later, the company had to pay another $257.2 million, this time for deceptive "private labeling" of its products and an attempt to cover up its illegal practices. U.S. Congress, Senate, *Medicaid Waste, Fraud, and Abuse*, hearings, Moorman and O'Connell testimony.

Similarly, in 2005 GlaxoSmithKline paid $150 million for a "private labeling" scheme to avoid paying the government its lowest price. Instead of undergoing criminal prosecution, corporate officials in both the Bayer and GlaxoSmithKline cases had to enter into a corporate integrity agreement. Taxpayers Against Fraud, *FY 2005 False Claims Act Settlements*.

In 2006, King Pharmaceuticals, Inc., settled for $124 million plus interest for concealment practices from 1994 to 2002 that short-changed Medicaid rebate programs in forty-nine states. It, too, had to sign a corporate integrity agreement. Baxter International had to pay $8.5 million to the Texas Medicaid system for similar deceptive actions. Taxpayers Against Fraud, *FY 2006 False Claims Act Settlements (as of September 30, 2006)*.

Alabama's attorney general filed lawsuits against seventy pharmaceutical companies in 2005, settling with Pharmaceuticals North America and DEY. In 2008, a jury ordered AstraZeneca, the first one to go to trial, to pay $215 million for fraudulently overstating its drug prices. At least twenty other states were looking into taking similar action. Merck Serono International, which has repaid $649 million as of mid-2008 to several states for its dishonest calculations on rebates for Zocor and Vioxx, settled with

Missouri for $8.7 million later that year. Also in 2008, Aventis Pharmaceuticals, Inc., agreed to a civil settlement of $22.7 million to the federal government and thirty-eight states for augmenting the wholesale price of its drug Anzemet and marketing it unlawfully. The company had to enter a corporate integrity agreement.

74. U.S. HHS, OIG, *State Medicaid Fraud Control Units.*

75. Taxpayer's Against Fraud, *FY 2006 False Claims Act Settlements (as of September 30, 2006).*

76. "N.Y. In the News: Rochester Hospital Repays Medicaid Overbilling," *Empire Journal* (N.Y.), August 31, 2005.

77. Taxpayer's Against Fraud, *FY 2005 False Claims Act Settlements.*

78. Ibid.

79. Taxpayer's Against Fraud, *Total FY 2004 False Claims Act Settlements and Judgments.*

80. In January 2009, Lilly settled the civil suits for $1.4 billion ($438 million to the federal government and $362 million to the states). A monetary payment of $615 million put an end to the criminal investigation; the company pleaded guilty of a misdemeanor but did not acknowledge any wrongdoing. About 30,000 affected individuals, who were left to fight on their own either by themselves or through class-action lawsuits, had settled earlier for $1.2 billion in product liability claims.

81. Lilly paid $36 million in its settlement of the Evista case for violating the Food, Drug, and Cosmetics Act.

82. Pfizer paid $240 million in criminal fines and $190 million in civil fines to the federal and state Medicaid programs. It also signed a corporate integrity agreement. U.S. Congress, Senate, *Medicaid Waste, Fraud, and Abuse*, hearings, Coleman and Moorman testimony.

83. Merck Serono was fined $704 million, and Schering-Plough paid out $435 million. Taxpayer's Against Fraud, *FY 2006 False Claims Act Settlements (as of September 30, 2006).*

84. U.S. HHS, OIG, *State Medicaid Fraud Control Units*, 3.

85. U.S. GAO, *Nursing Home Deaths: Arkansas Coroner Referrals Confirm Weaknesses in State and Federal Oversight of Quality of Care*, report to congressional requesters, GAO-05-78 (Washington, D.C.: U.S. Government Printing Office, November 2004); Evelyn Pringle, "Nursing Home Industry—Breeding Ground for Whistleblowers," Legal Marketing Ltd. (June 2, 2006), available at http://www.lawyersandsettlements .com/articles/00210/Beverly_Enterprises_Fraud.html.

86. Pringle, "Nursing Home Industry—Breeding Ground for Whistleblowers."

87. Wrongful death claims also tend to produce more punitive financial outcomes. In one case highlighted in the *New Orleans Times-Picayune* investigation, a Louisiana nursing home deemed negligent by state regulators in the death of a patient was fined only $1,500; after initiating a wrongful death lawsuit against the nursing home, however, the patient's family was awarded $840,000 by a jury. Jeffrey Meitrodt and Steve Ritca, "State of Neglect" (series on nursing home abuse), *New Orleans Times-Picayune*, April 17, 2005.

Such lawsuits have increased since 2000, as much as 51 percent in 2003 and 18 percent in 2004, along with the exploding costs of malpractice insurance. In response, some states are enacting legislation to protect nursing home owners, including caps on allowable monetary awards.

88. Other federal FCA cases, settled in 2005, include Harbor Healthcare (Delaware), Hillcrest Healthcare, Inc. (Connecticut), and Life Care Center of Lawrenceville (Georgia). Despite appalling conditions in the facilities, none of the responsible individuals was jailed in these instances. Harbor Healthcare, charged with inadequate care provided to severely disabled children in the 1990s, received a $150,000 penalty; Hillcrest was accused of submitting false claims because of its disturbingly inadequate care in Hillcrest Healthcare Center that led to a resident's death. Connecticut's attorney general, Richard Blumenthal, noted: "This company had such gross disregard for human life and the law—fatally neglecting patients, while at the same time billing the state for the very services it failed to provide." The nursing home had to pay a civil fine amounting to $200,000 for the deficient services. Incredibly, the company (rather than the actual perpetrators) was convicted of manslaughter, resulting in only $10,000 in additional penalties. U.S. Attorney's Office, District of Connecticut, "Nursing Home Agrees to Pay $750,000 to Settle Allegations Under the False Claims Act," press release, May 18, 2005, available at http://usdoj.gov/usao/ct/Press2005/.

Life Care Center, its owner, and two investor companies agreed to $2.5 million in fines to resolve allegations that they billed the low-income health programs for services that were either withheld from or were worthless to the nursing home residents because of their poor quality, in a few cases leading to premature death. U.S. Attorney's Office, Northern District of Georgia, "Lawrenceville Nursing Home to Pay $2.5 million to Settle Allegations of Gross Neglect of Residents," press release, December 22, 2005, available at http://usdoj.gov/usas/gan/press/2005.

89. Jeffrey Meitrodt, "Fighting Abuse" (series on nursing home abuse), *New Orleans Times-Picayune*, April 20, 2005.

90. New York State Attorney General's Office, Eliot Spitzer, news release, March 25, 2004.

91. Among other maladies, residents experienced dehydration, malnutrition, unhygienic conditions, and life-threatening preventable bedsores. After nine years of litigation, the CEO and the nursing home's associated firms had to pay fines of $750,000, in addition to $2 million in civil penalties that had been levied earlier. Robert Patrick, "'Worthless Services' Amount to Fraud: A New Tactic Prosecutors Are Going After Nursing Homes over Billing for Care That Was Not Provided," *St. Louis Post-Dispatch*, March 1, 2007.

92. David Mendell, "Nursing Home Lawsuit Settled: Whistle-blowers Alleged Fraud, Patient Abuse," *Chicago Tribune*, November 23, 2004.

8. The Energizer Bunny

1. Jonathan Oberlander, *The Political Life of Medicare* (Chicago: University of Chicago Press, 2003), 104.

2. Fyyor 2004 and 2006, the $655 million excludes any money donated to state and local party committees. Including professionals, pharmaceutical firms, hospitals,

MCOs, nursing homes, and related services, they spent $97.2 million in 2006 and $109 million in 2007. They gave to nearly every member of the U.S. House of Representatives and Senate. The top spenders were the AMA, the AHA, the ADA, PhRMA, Pfizer, Inc., the American Health Care Association, and GlaxoSmithKline. See also Center for Responsive Politics (CRP) Web site at http://www.opensecrets.org, in particular the section "Politicians and Elections."

3. Health groups' federal lobbying costs amounted to $2.3 billion between 1998 and 2006, with $338 million paid out in the latter year. Ibid.

Among eighty-four possible issues, Medicare and Medicaid are in the tenth position as far as the number of lobbying disclosure reports in the ten years since 1998. Daniel Gitterman, John Scott, and Judie Svihula, *Medicaid and Lobbying Groups*, report prepared for DPG Associates (Washington, D.C.: Office of the Assistant Secretary for Planning and Evaluation, U.S. Department of Health and Human Services, 2009).

4. New York State Temporary Commission on Lobbying, *2002 Annual Report* (Albany: State of New York, 2002). The New York Public Interest Group found that fully one-third of the $6 million spent by the state's top sixteen political action committees in 2004 came from groups that benefit from Medicaid dollars, including Local 1199. Nicole Gelinas, "Spitzer's Radical Medicaid Surgery? It's Really a Placebo, but You Wouldn't Know It from Union Screaming," *City Journal* 17, no. 1 (Winter 2007), available at http://www.city-journal.org/html/econ2007-02-08ng.html.

In another characteristic example, nine of the eleven members of a Utah task force established to study the effects of Medicaid on the state budget received a total of $68,125 from the health care industry for their 2006 campaigns, amounting to 20 percent of their total intake that year. Hospitals, doctors, dentists, and therapists contributed $39,325; drug companies gave $21,200; and medical equipment companies provided $7,600. Kirsten Stewart, "Medicaid Task Force a Lucrative Gig," *Salt Lake Tribune*, December 9, 2006.

5. In 2009, of course, these self-serving words take on a new meaning, given the $50 billion taxpayer bailout of General Motors and the direct government ownership of a portion of the company's stock.

6. In addition to various health industries, the coalition included advocates for other businesses, labor, consumers, the elderly, the disabled, and children. Among other initiatives, Health Policy Agenda for the American People proposed extending Medicaid coverage and raising fees to physicians and hospitals. "Coalition Recommends an Expansion of Medicaid," *New York Times*, February 17, 1989.

7. The Children's Medicaid Coalition included the U.S. Chamber of Commerce, the National Association of Manufacturers, the AMA, the AHA, the American Academy of Pediatricians, the National Association of Children's Hospitals, the Children's Defense Fund, the ADA, the Health Insurance Association of America, and the Blue Cross Blue Shield Association.

Among the reasons for these groups' active involvement in the campaign, health insurers were defending against potential national health care legislation; hospitals, doctors, and dentists sought to gain reimbursements for their hitherto uncompensated care; and business leaders were looking to contain the cost shifting that was steadily augmenting their medical insurance premiums.

8. Congressional representatives were besieged by advocates for drug companies, physicians, hospitals, MCOs, the elderly, the disabled, children, medical equipment firms, nurses, and the service employees' union.

9. BBA 1997 had reduced reimbursements under Medicare and, to a lesser extent, Medicaid. But powerful sectors of the health care industry soon achieved extensive legislative victories. Under the Balanced Budget Refinement Act of 1999, which rescinded or delayed many of the provisions of BBA 1997—including regulations—providers recovered billions of dollars. Hospitals received the most money, followed by MCOs, home health agencies, and nursing homes. Again in 2000, under the Medicare/Medicaid and SCHIP Benefits Improvement and Protection Act, they retrieved even more public dollars, totaling $35 billion over five years. Hospitals once more were the largest winners ($13 billion), followed by MCOs ($10.3 billion). Nursing homes received temporary, across-the-board rate increases (4 percent in 2001 and 2002), along with other boosts in payments, totaling $2.4 billion. David G. Smith, *Entitlement Politics: Medicare and Medicaid 1995–2001* (New York: De Gruyter, 2002); U.S. GAO, *Skilled Nursing Facility Payments*, GAO-03-183 (Washington, D.C.: U.S. Government Printing Office, December 2002); U.S. Congress, Senate, Special Committee on Aging, *Nursing Homes: Aggregate Medicare Payments Are Adequate Despite Bankruptcies*, hearings, testimony of Laura Dunmit, associate director of health financing and public-health issues, Department of Health and Human Services, 106th Cong., 2d sess., September 5, 2000.

10. The American Nurses Association represents 2.7 million registered nurses and has fifty-four constituent member organizations.

11. AARP was concerned primarily with the LTC asset-transfer penalties.

12. The Coalition for Meaningful Medicaid Reform represented mostly community pharmacists and chain drug stores who were angry over cuts to their fees.

13. The Health Coverage Coalition for the Uninsured signatory list included AARP, America's Health Insurance Plans, American Academy of Family Physicians, AHA, AMA, American Public Health Association, Blue Cross Blue Shield Association, Catholic Health Association, Families USA, Federation of American Hospitals, Healthcare Leadership Council, Johnson and Johnson, Kaiser Permanente, Pfizer, Inc., UnitedHealth Group, and U.S. Chamber of Commerce.

Seeking "significant new federal funds" for the states, the coalition lobbied for greater coverage of children in the first phase of its plan, followed by an extension of the program to more low-income adults. It also aimed to expand health care insurance through a new tax credit for households with income up to 300 percent of the FPL and not eligible for public-sector coverage; families could purchase insurance through their employers or the private market. See http://www.familiesusa.org.

14. About 28 percent of nursing homes are nonprofit, and another 5 percent are government institutions. U.S. HHS, Centers for Medicare and Medicaid Services, *Statistics: Information About Persons Covered by Medicare, Medicaid, or SCHIP* (Washington,

D.C.: U.S. Government Printing Office, 2006), table 20: "Selected Facilities/Type of Control."

15. AHCA's federal campaign contributions totaled $7.6 million between 1990 and 2006. CRP, "Politicians and Elections."

16. For instance, in 2007 Kindred Healthcare and the Alliance for Quality Nursing Home Care paid out $1 million and $2.7 million, respectively, to lobby national officials. The alliance represents seventeen national Medicaid LTC contractors. Ibid.; Gitterman, Scott, and Svihula, *Medicaid and Lobbying Groups.*

17. Andrew Schneider and Philip O'Connor, "Nursing Home Industry Wields Clout in State Capitals—in Missouri and Illinois, Lobby Has Helped Defeat Reform Legislation," *St. Louis Post-Dispatch*, October 17, 2002.

In Illinois that year, the industry contributed more than $1 million to local political candidates; Governor Rod Blagojevich (D) received $211,250. Moreover, the executive director of the Illinois Health Care Association, William Kempiners, is a former state representative; he also headed the Illinois Department of Public Health, the agency that regulates the facilities. Carolyn Tuft, "Industry Donated $1 Million in Illinois Election," *St. Louis Post-Dispatch*, December 22, 2002.

18. The investigation discovered that nursing home owners and their representatives contributed $615,000 to state legislators and $245,995 to the Louisiana governor, Kathleen Blanco. The money reached 130 state representatives (out of a total of 144), with most of it going "to lawmakers whose leadership posts put them in the best position to influence the nursing homes' Medicaid-dependent budgets." Louisiana House Speaker Charlie DeWitt (D) received $110,550 (nearly one-third of his total campaign chest that year); Senate president John Hainkel was given $40,100. Both men were active on behalf of the industry, including successful proposals to protect it against lawsuits by victims of negligence. As a result of substantial campaign contributions, lobbying, and cronyism, spending on institutional care in Louisiana rose 59 percent from 1999 to 2005, more than two and a half times the rate of inflation. Indeed, nursing home advocates were instrumental in the establishment of a special state trust fund, which paid a portion of the rate increases. The industry in the state has maintained very healthy profit margins: a study commissioned by the Louisiana Department of Health and Hospitals found that nursing home profit margins averaged 15 percent in 2001 and 2002. Facility owners have other concerns besides funding issues, of course, and use their considerable influence to achieve these goals as well. For example, state senator Donald Cravins (D) complained that the industry is so strong that he could not even get a committee hearing on his proposed bill to boost minimum staffing requirements. Jan Moller, "Money = Clout," *New Orleans Times-Picayune*, April 19, 2005.

19. The nursing home industry challenged the rates by arguing that they were not "reasonable and adequate" to meet their costs, as required under the Boren amendment.

In his study of nursing home litigation under the Boren amendment, Edward Miller determined that between 1981 and 2001 eighty-four cases dealt with reimbursement issues; most states had at least one lawsuit. His study found that of the total cases, nursing homes prevailed in 38 percent, the states in 46 percent, both parties (depending on the issue) in 13 percent, and neither in 2 percent. Edward Alan Miller, "Federal Oversight, State Policy Making, and the Courts: An Empirical Analysis of Nursing Facility Litigation Under the Boren Amendment," *Journal of Empirical Legal Studies* 3, no. 1 (March 2006): 145–173.

20. In 2002, the AHCA sponsored a thirty-seven-state survey and, based on self-reported nursing home figures, substantiated its claims: the study concluded, not surprisingly, that expenses for Medicaid patients exceeded Medicaid rates an average of $10 per resident each day; in some states, it was even higher. U.S. GAO, *Medicaid Nursing Home Payments: States' Payment Rates Largely Unaffected by Recent Fiscal Pressures* (Washington, D.C.: U.S. Government Printing Office, October 2003).

21. For example, in 2005 the *SeniorCare Investor* warned that because of Florida's "unhealthy" liability environment, most nursing home chains most likely would leave the state if the situation were not "improved" for them. *SeniorCare Investor* (February 2005).

22. In an attempt to control the number of hospital and nursing home beds, the certificate-of-need planning program was enacted under the Health Act of 1974. Although federal financial support was terminated in 1986, many states and local communities fund their own schemes for assessing and regulating health care–related capital projects.

23. As a case in point, during 1983 a backlog of 4,200 people languished in New York City hospitals because nursing homes began rejecting Medicaid beneficiaries, contending that reimbursements were too low. The Greater New York Nursing Home Association began a public-relations campaign, broadcasting that 7 percent of the city's costly hospital beds were filled with these patients.

24. In 1997, the federal government revised the Medicare reimbursement policy. Moving from a "cost-based" formula, it established a prospective payment system whereby nursing homes receive a fixed per diem fee for each beneficiary that includes all services, is case-mix adjusted, and reflects geographic differences. The initial compensation was based on a facility's actual earlier costs, along with temporary higher dollar amounts to ease the transition.

In a nineteen-state study of Medicaid nursing home fees, the GAO found that states with a cost-based approach tended to develop fees specific to each facility, updated annually, and generally imposed ceilings on the total allowable amounts. GAO, *Medicaid Nursing Home Payments.*

25. The federal government uses the skilled nursing facility market basket index to measure changes in costs for nursing homes in its rate setting for Medicare. According to the GAO, Arkansas (1998–2000), South Dakota (1998–2000), Connecticut (2001–2003), and Massachusetts (2001–2003) had for short periods rates below the market basket index; California, New York, and Illinois paid lower amounts for both the 1998–2000 and 2001–2003 periods. Ibid.

26. The study was carried out by the Michigan Senate Fiscal Agency. Its staff noted that Michigan nursing homes always received fee increases that were greater than those for other Medicaid providers. John S. Walker, Steve Angelotti, and Dana Patterson, *Medicaid Funding for Nursing Homes Services: A Historical Perspective* (Lansing: Michigan Senate Fiscal Agency, June 2000).

27. About half of all nursing homes are part of national or regional chains.

28. "The New Math of Old Age: Why the Nursing Home Industry's Cries of Poverty Don't Add Up," *U.S. News & World Report* 133 (September 30, 2002): 66–67, 70–74.

29. Cited in ibid.

30. Ibid.

31. *New York Times* reporters obtained this information when inspecting the state's health department records, which they accessed through the Freedom of Information Act. Clifford Levy and Michael Luo, "New York Medicaid Fraud May Reach into Billions," Program Disorder; Exploiting a Safety Net series, *New York Times*, July 18, 2005.

32. They gained 7 percent in salary and 48 percent in bonuses. Among the highest paid were the chief executives of Manor Care ($3.1 million), Kindred Healthcare ($2.5 million), Beverly Enterprises ($2.4 million), and NeighborCare ($2.2 million). Irving Levin Associates, Inc., *Who's Making What in Health Care: The Irving Levin Health Care Executive Compensation Report* (New Canaan, Conn.: Irving Levin Associates Inc., 2004), available at http://www.levinassociates.com/publications/mam/mamprem/04execcomp.pdf.

33. The chains went into Chapter 11 bankruptcy, which allowed them to continue to care for patients while restructuring their debts and streamlining operations. U.S. Congress, Senate, *Nursing Homes*, Dunmit testimony.

Among the chains that declared bankruptcy were Genesis Health Ventures, Vencor, Inc., Centennial Health Care, Integrated Health Services, Mariner Health Care, and Sun Healthcare.

34. From the mid-1980s to 1997, Medicare costs for skilled nursing homes had increased, on average, 30 percent per year—from $578 million to $13.6 billion. The operators, especially large chains, had cashed in on some of Medicare's overly generous features, such as unlimited reimbursements for ancillary services. U.S. GAO, *Skilled Nursing Facility Payments*; U.S. Congress, Senate, Special Committee on Aging, *Skilled Nursing Facilities: Medicare Payment Changes Require Adjustments but Maintain Access*, report from the GAO to the chairman and ranking minority member (Washington, D.C.: U.S. Government Printing Office, December 1999).

35. U.S. Congress, Senate, *Skilled Nursing Facilities*; U.S. Congress, Senate, *Nursing Homes*.

36. During this seven-year period, Formation Capital affiliates purchased 186 nursing homes from various companies for $660 million, in addition to its acquisition of Genesis HealthCare. In turn, General Electric bought 186 nursing homes from Formation for $1.4 billion in 2006. Beverly Enterprises (the nation's second-largest nursing home chain, with 342 facilities) was obtained in 2006 for $1.8 billion by Fillmore Strategic Investors LLC (a private real estate equity firm whose parent firm is Fillmore Capital Partners). In 2000, Warburg Pincus procured approximately 100 nursing homes from Centennial HealthCare for $65.5 million, and in 2004 National Senior Care picked up 274 facilities for $1 billion from Mariner Health Care. At the end of 2007, the Carlyle Group acquired more than 500 nursing homes from HCR Manor Care at a price tag of $6.3 billion. "Just Who Is Buying Beverly?" *Business Week Online*, November 21, 2005, available at http://www.businessweek.com; Carlyle Group, *The Carlyle Group Completes*

Transaction with Manor Care; Temporary Restraining Order Dissolved in Michigan, News Report no. 2007-154 (Washington, D.C.: Carlyle Group, December 21, 2007), available at http://www.carlyle.com; Charles Duhigg, "At Many Homes, More Profit and Less Nursing," *New York Times,* September 23, 2007.

The largest REIT, Health Care Property Investors, owns 144 nursing homes, which represent 28 percent of the firm's properties; its overall compounded annual stockholder return was 18 percent since its inception in 1985, and 43.9 percent in 2003. Another firm, Health Care REIT, owns 550 properties in thirty-seven states, of which 220, or 40 percent, are skilled nursing facilities; its shareholder return was 44 percent in 2003. With 30 percent of its 400 property holdings in nursing homes, Nationwide Health Properties stock had a return of 44.9 percent that year. The CEOs of these top health care REITs in 2003 earned between $0.9 and $1.8 million in cash compensation alone. Irving Levin Associates, *Who's Making What in Health Care.*

37. In 2007, using CMS data, the *New York Times* investigated 1,200 nursing homes purchased by REITs from 2000 to 2006, weighing them against 14,000 other facilities. Duhigg, "At Many Homes, More Profit and Less Nursing,"

38. The remainder of this section is based on an account of their findings by *New York Times* reporter Charles Duhigg. Ibid.

39. The *New York Times* investigators found that in 2002, Formation Properties 1 had bought forty-eight facilities in the state (the land and buildings) but leased the homes (for rent and other fees) to Florida Health Care Properties (which was renamed Epsilon Health Care Properties), an affiliate of Warburg Pincus (one of the largest private-equity firms in the world). Florida Health Care Properties then subleased management of the nursing homes to yet another company, which held the license; that company, in turn, subcontracted to other firms that were responsible for other aspects of the business, such as supplies and equipment (and these companies are actually owned by Formation Properties 1, or Warburg Pincus).

40. In the case of Vencor, Inc., which was established in 1985, the company grew rapidly through acquisitions, especially with the purchase of the Hillhaven nursing home chain in 1995, a company four times its size. Just a year before declaring Chapter 11 in 1999, Vencor had split into two parts, a REIT (Ventas) and an operating company (Vencor), which now leased from Ventas. Not only did the nursing home operator (Vencor) funnel public money away from patient services through high rental fees (four times their previous costs) paid to itself through the new REIT, but its capital assets were protected when Vencor went into bankruptcy. Emerging from Chapter 11 protection two years later under a new name, Kindred Healthcare, the chain's nursing home operations continued to enrich the REIT with high nursing home rentals. In fact, Ventas offered a total average annual shareholder return of 36.2 percent from 2001 to 2006. See the Ventas, Inc., Web site at http://www.ventasreit.com.

In another example, after Beverly Enterprises was acquired by Fillmore Strategic Investors LLC, the company was split in two: an operating firm (renamed Golden Gate National Senior Care Holdings) that manages 262 facilities (roughly 80 of which are leased by Golden Gate from Geary Property Holdings and are still run under the Beverly Health Care name) and a new REIT (Geary Property Holdings), which now owns the land and buildings. At the time of the acquisition, the chief officers at Beverly received a total of $109 million in severance packages, with its chairman, CEO, and president, William Floyd, attaining $40 million. Evelyn Pringle, "Beverly Enterprises—Poster Child of Fraud and Neglect in Nursing Home Industry," Legal Marketing Ltd., June 1, 2006, available at http://www.lawyersandsettlements.com.

Genesis Health Ventures provides yet another instance of REIT takeovers of facilities. Established in 1985, the company expanded dramatically over the next fifteen years (from a $32 million company to one earning $2.4 billion) through the acquisition of additional nursing homes and service-related firms. The company weighed itself down in such heavy debt that it could no longer pay interest payments when Medicare reimbursements were cut in 1997. Although its facilities were at nearly full capacity and earning money, Genesis, like many of the other large for-profit chains, went into Chapter 11 protection in 2000. Emerging from bankruptcy at the end of 2001, the company spun off its skilled nursing homes, assisted-living facilities, independent communities, and rehabilitation therapy centers into a new entity, Genesis Healthcare Corp, with Genesis Health Ventures (renamed NeighborCare Pharmacy) retaining the pharmaceutical services. As of 2008, Genesis Healthcare Corp owned, leased, managed, or jointly held more than 200 skilled nursing homes and assisted-living facilities in thirteen states. It has experienced strong financial performance from its nursing home and assisted-living facilities; by 2004, its stock had increased by 54 percent. In 2005, Zacks Investment Research, Inc., ranked this chain as a "number one," solid stock. Two years later the corporation was acquired jointly by Formation Capital, LLC (an equity-investment and asset-management company) and JER Partners (a real estate investment–management company) for $1.5 billion: the $63 per share price was about one-third more than the stock's average trading value during the preceding month. Genesis Healthcare Corp still operates the facilities as a tenant under its new real estate company owners. See its Web site at http://www.Genesishcc.com. See also U.S. Congress, Senate, Special Committee on Aging, *Nursing Home Bankruptcies: What Caused Them*, 106th Cong., 2d sess., September 5, 2000 (Washington, D.C.: U.S. Government Printing Office, 2000); and Formation Capital, LLC, *What We Do: Our Investments and Portfolios* (Alpharetta, Ga.: Formation Capital, LLC, 2006), available at http://www.formationcapital.com.

41. For example, Senators Charles Grassley (R–Iowa) and Herb Kohl (D–Wisc.) and Representative Eddie Johnson (D–Tex.) introduced the Nursing Home Transparency and Improvement Act of 2008, which would have mandated disclosure of nursing home ownership patterns and provided measures for improving quality of care, including increased penalties for patient abuse. Led by the influential Carlyle Group REIT, however, the industry has successfully halted the legislation's progress. In the House, Representative Johnson had no cosponsors, and in the Senate there were only eleven. Introduced in 2008, H.R. 5799 and S. 2641 languished in House and Senate committees after their introduction. Gitterman, Scott, and Svihula, *Medicaid and Lobbying Groups*; see also the Web sites at http://www.opencongress.org/bill/110-h5799/show and http://www.opencongress.org/bill/110-s2641/show.

42. In 2004, other government sources accounted for another 5 percent; private insurance, 38 percent; and patient out of pocket, only 6 percent. U.S. Bureau of the Cen-

sus, *Current Business Reports (B5/2004), Service Annual Survey: 2004* (Washington, D.C.: U.S. Government Printing Office, 2006), tables 8.1 and 8.11.

However, there is significant variation among and within states. Rural hospitals, for example, tend to be more reliant on Medicare than urban facilities (50 percent versus 37 percent of total patient discharges), but the reverse is true for Medicaid (17 percent versus 26 percent). Mustafa Younis, "Comparative Study of Urban and Small Rural Hospitals Financial and Economic Performance," *Journal of Rural Nursing and Health Care Online* 3, no. 1 (spring 2003), available at http://www.rno.org/journal/index.php/online-journal/article/viewFile/110/106.

43. AHA and allied individuals, subsidiaries, and affiliates reported spending $129.1 million in lobbying expenses between 1998 and 2006 and $13.5 million in contributions to federal candidates and parties between 1990 and 2006. CRP Web site and its sections "Influence and Lobbying," "Lobbying Database," "Hospitals and Nursing Homes," and "Politicians and Elections."

44. For example, when congressional Republicans proposed their deep cuts in Medicare and Medicaid in 1995, Karen Heller of the Greater New York Hospital Association threatened: "We will really, truly have to cut services. . . . We are very dependent on Medicare and Medicaid." Quoted in Bob Herbert, "The Republican Way," *New York Times*, October 27, 1994.

45. The very notion of what renders a Medicaid reimbursement rate "inadequate" is murky in the health care sector overall, although the various industries tend to frame it in terms of a percentage of their charges to other customers. For hospitals, whose prices vary from patient to patient, it is often unclear whether this rate denotes their highest fees, ones that have been negotiated with assorted insurance companies, Medicare's prospective payment system, the amount paid by MCOs, or just simply their average price. In a study of Utah's annual hospital cost reports, health officials found that their Medicaid reimbursements "cover far more than their actual costs—which make up an average of 42 percent of what they charge." The state, which pays hospitals based on a percentage of their charges, has the third most profitable hospital industry in the nation. Kirsten Stewart, "Hospitals Want More Cash from Medicaid," *Salt Lake Tribune*, November 13, 2006.

46. Robert B. Hackey, *Rethinking Health Care Policy: The New Politics of State Regulation* (Washington, D.C.: Georgetown University Press, 1998).

47. At the time, the president had recommended a cut of $40 billion over five years. "House and Senate Budget Plans Reject Medicare, Medicaid Cuts to Hospitals," AHANEWS.com, April 2, 2007.

48. Ohio Hospital Association, "Hospitals Fight Medicaid Cut at JCARR," news release, testimony of John Callender before the Ohio Department of Job and Family Services, September 12, 2005, Columbus, Ohio, available at http://www.ohanet.org/media/news_release/jcarr.pdf.

49. John Callender, senior vice president of the Ohio Hospital Association, quoted in Reginald Fields, "Hospitals Assail Medicaid Plan, Jobs Threatened, Association Says," *Cleveland Plain Dealer*, September 9, 2005.

In another typical example, because of hospitals' complaints about the burdens of low Medicaid payments in Connecticut, the General Assembly increased their rates by

$46 million in 2008 and promised another $76 million by the summer of 2009. The governor had earlier set up a task force to assess the industry's financial situation. It found that the salaries paid to the state's hospital executives nearly doubled between 2002 and 2006 and that their fringe benefits rose even higher. According to the Connecticut Hospital Association's executive director, "Competition for good administrators is driving up salaries." "Executives' Pay Nearly Doubles at Hospitals, Task Force Finds," *Newsday Online*, January 27, 2008, available at http://www.Newsday.com/news.

50. Jonathan Engel, *Poor People's Medicine: Medicaid and American Charity Care Since 1965* (Durham, N.C.: Duke University Press, 2006).

51. Steve Angelotti, *Medicaid and Michigan Hospitals: A Look Behind the Numbers*, Senate Fiscal Agency Issue Paper, requested by Senator Joel Gougeon, chairman of the Senate Appropriations Subcommittee on the Fiscal Status of Michigan Medicaid Health Providers (Lansing: State of Michigan, March 2000).

52. The Michigan Senate Fiscal Agency did find that *Medicare* rates contributed, in some measure, to the weak economic condition of some Michigan hospitals. Ibid.

53. Research shows that hospitals located in areas with high levels of uninsured families or with relatively greater eligibility-restricted Medicaid plans, or both, tend to have more uncompensated care costs as a percentage of their patient operating expenses. U.S. Congress, House, Committee on Ways and Means, *Nonprofit, For-Profit, and Government Hospitals: Uncompensated Care and Other Community Benefits*, testimony of David Walker, U.S. comptroller general, 109th Cong., 1st sess., May 26, 2005.

54. In recent years, traditional hospitals in many places have confronted fiscal pressures because of competition from short-term acute care specialty hospitals that treat specific medical conditions and surgical procedures, along with the rise of small, ambulatory, and diagnostic treatment centers. Primarily owned by doctors, these places drain off the more lucrative patients and services, forcing some hospitals—generally nonprofit and government facilities—to care for more Medicaid-eligible and uninsured people.

55. "Children's Hospitals: A Healthy Future?" *New Scientific Magazine*, May 14, 2005. In 2005, there were eighty-one children's hospitals nationwide. U.S. HHS, Centers for Medicare and Medicaid, *Statistics*, table 15: "Inpatient Hospitals/Trends."

56. In 1975, the Community Health Centers Program replaced the Neighborhood Health Centers that had been created ten years earlier. In 1989, they were redesignated Federally Qualified Health Centers. Established in severely impoverished, underserved areas, they receive enhanced payments from Medicaid (and Medicare) for services rendered to eligible families. In the 1990s, these clinics received about half of their income from Medicaid, allowing them to subsidize the uninsured.

President Bush's 2001 Health Center Initiative and his 2005 High Poverty Counties Initiative proposed to open or expand 1,200 Federally Qualified Health Centers, an objective met at the end of 2007. Nevertheless, 43 percent of medically underserved areas still lack a community health center. Today, roughly 3,700 sites serve 14 million patients, of which roughly 5 million are enrolled in Medicaid; welfare medicine currently accounts for 37 percent of the clinics' total revenues. U.S. GAO, *Health Centers and Rural Clinics: State and Federal Implementation Issues for Medicaid's New Payment System*,

+ +

report to congressional committees (Washington, D.C.: U.S. Government Printing Office, June, 2005); U.S. GAO, *Many Underserved Areas Lack a Health Center Site. And the Health Center Program Needs More Oversight*, report to ranking member, Subcommittee on Oversight and Investigations, Committee on Energy and Commerce, U.S. House of Representatives (Washington, D.C.: U.S. Government Printing Office, August 2008); Peter Shin, Brad Finnegan, Lauren Hughes, and Sara Rosenbaum, *An Initial Assessment of the Effects of Medicaid Documentation on Health Centers and Their Patients* (Washington, D.C.: School of Public Health and Health Services, George Washington University, May 7, 2007); U.S. Office of Management and Budget, *Budget of the U.S., FY 2007: Analytical Perspectives* (Washington, D.C.: U.S. Government Printing Office, 2007), 104.

57. Under federal law, "a hospital is deemed to be a DSH hospital if (A) the hospital's medicaid [*sic*] inpatient utilization rate is at least one standard deviation above the mean Medicaid inpatient utilization rate for hospitals receiving medicaid [*sic*] payments in the state; or (B) if the hospital's low-income utilization rate exceeds 25 percent." "Safety-net" hospitals and clinics receive DSH funding from both Medicaid and Medicare. UU.S.C. §1396r-4 (b) (2000).

58. For example, 60 percent of the New York Health and Hospital Corporation's $5 billion annual budget, the nation's largest public health care system, come from Medicaid. About one-third of its patients are uninsured. California's twenty-two public hospitals also are highly dependent on Medicaid.

59. Engel, *Poor People's Medicine*. Safety-net hospitals overall provided two-thirds of all uncompensated care reported by hospitals in 2002. Robert E. Mechanic, *Medicaid's Disproportionate Share Hospital Program: Complex Structure, Critical Payments*, National Health Policy Forum Background Paper (Washington, D.C.: National Health Policy Forum, George Washington University, September 14, 2004).

60. Safety-net facilities may suffer in other ways when Medicaid reimbursement levels are in danger. For instance, when the Republican majority in Congress attempted to impose deep cuts on Medicare and Medicaid in 1995, Moody's Investors Service, Inc., threatened to downgrade the credit ratings of hospitals with the greatest reliance on Medicare/Medicaid clients; such an action would have forced higher interest rates on the hospitals' future borrowing needs and therefore created greater financial instability. Holcomb B. Noble, "Credit Agency Says Hospitals Face Hazards from Proposed Cuts," *New York Times*, November 3, 1995.

61. In 1996 alone, one in twelve hospitals was involved in a merger or acquisition, generating large chains across the nation, including Columbia/Health Care Association Healthcare Corporation and Tenet Healthcare Corporation. In April 2007, Tenet created a special board seat for former Florida governor Jeb Bush, including the usual fee for a director (from $97,700 to $129,222), plus $260,000 in stock. One of the largest hospital chains in the United States, Tenet has lost money since 2003; among other problems, it had to pay Medicare $900 million to settle charges that the company had overbilled the program.

By the end of 2005, there were approximately 3,800 nonfederal, short-term acute care general hospitals in the United States, of which 60 percent were nonprofit, 20 percent for profit, and 20 percent state and local institutions, with the lowest concentration of nonprofits in the South. U.S. HHS, Centers for Medicare and Medicaid, *Statistics*, table 20: "Selected Facilities, Type of Control."

62. In their investigation of private Medicaid-dependent hospitals (those averaging 26 percent of their gross revenues from the program) in California, researchers found that as reimbursement levels declined from 1983 to 1992, the extent of services decreased for all patients, but the reductions were more severe for those on Medicaid. In addition, many of these hospitals shut down. David Dranove and William White, "Medicaid- Dependent Hospitals and Their Patients: How Have They Fared?" *Health Services Research* 33 (1998): 163–185.

Even more problematic was the situation of state and local hospitals; as Jonathan Engel indicates, there were mass closings of these institutions across the nation in the early 1990s, a pattern that continues today. Engel, *Poor People's Medicine.*

63. Nonprofit hospitals receive considerable funding from Medicaid. They receive generous tax exemptions as well. However, in recent years many leading ones "have transformed into profit machines." The net income of the fifty largest nonprofit hospitals rose eightfold between 2001 and 2006, and the money has often been used for new elaborate facilities, fancy upgrades, and high executive salaries, perks, and bonuses. At the same time, there is no minimum amount of charity care required of them. Some nonprofits even count the difference between their "list" prices and what they receive from Medicare and Medicaid as their contribution to the community. John Carreyrou, "Nonprofit Hospitals, Once for the Poor, Strike It Rich," *Wall Street Journal*, April 4, 2008.

64. In 1990, the pharmaceutical industry's top ten establishments had profits of nearly 25 percent and, except for a short period of time, continued at comparatively high rates of return throughout the decade and into the twenty-first century: average returns for the firms were 18.5 percent of sales in 2001 (as compared to 3.3 percent for other Fortune 500 companies) and 14.3 percent in 2003 (as compared to 4.6 percent for other Fortune 500 companies).

Total cash compensation for CEOs of pharmaceutical companies averaged $2 million in 2003, with a high of $6.92 million for the head of Pfizer. Shareholder returns that year were: Abbott Lab, 19.3 percent; Allergan, 34 percent; Alpharma, 70.5 percent; Amgen, 27.8 percent; Bristol-Myers Squibb, 29 percent; Eli Lilly, 13 percent; Forest Lab, 25.8 percent; GlaxoSmithKline, 28.7 percent; Ivax, 96.9 percent; Johnson & Johnson, 2.1 percent; Merck, 11.4 percent; Pfizer, 17.8 percent; Schering-Plough, 19 percent; Watson Pharmaceuticals, 62.7 percent; Wyeth, 16.1 percent. Marcia Angell, *The Truth About the Drug Companies: How They Deceive Us and What to Do About It* (New York: Random House, 2004); Irving Levin Associates, *Who's Making What in Health Care*; Jeff Madrick, "Health for Sale," *New York Review of Books* 50, no. 20 (December 18, 2003): 71–74.

65. U.S. Congress, Senate, Committee on Finance, *Medicaid Waste, Fraud, and Abuse: Threatening the Health Care Safety Net*, hearings, testimony of James W. Moorman, president and CEO, Taxpayers Against Fraud, 109th Cong., 1st sess., June 28, 2005.

In 2005, out-of-pocket outlays, private health insurance, and Medicare had represented 29.9 percent, 47.8 percent, and 1.6 percent of payment sources, respectively.

William G. Weissert and Edward Alan Miller, "Punishing the Pioneers: The Medicare Modernization Act and State Pharmacy Assistance Programs," paper presented at the 2005 Annual Meeting of the American Political Science Association, September 1–4, Washington, D.C.

66. Unlike the United States, other OECD nations control drug prices through a variety of mechanisms, including ceilings, maximum prices for medications that are therapeutically similar, and profit limits. As a consequence, their spending on drugs rose an average of only 6 percent a year from 1998 to 2003. U.S. Congress, Senate, Committee on Finance, *Prescription Drugs: An Overview of Approaches to Negotiate Drug Prices Used by Other Countries and U.S. Private Payers and Federal Programs*, testimony of John E. Dicken, director of health care, GAO, 110th Cong., 1st sess., January 11, 2007.

67. In her research on the subject, Marcia Angell found that from 1997 to 2002 pharmaceutical manufacturers employed about 675 lobbyists annually. Angell, *The Truth About the Drug Companies*, 198.

68. Between 1998 and 2006, PhRMA reported $104.3 million in federal-level lobbying costs. Pfizer, Inc.—one of the five largest pharmaceutical manufacturers—reported spending $12.2 million in 2006 to lobby federal officials, and GlaxoSmithKline and Eli Lilly paid out a little less than $1.0 million and $3.7 million, respectively. The trade association also contributes substantially to political campaigns; from 1990 to 2006, it reported more than $92 million in funding for national elections ($16.4 million directly from individuals, $37 million from political action committees, and $39 million in soft money). Again, many of the conglomerates donate millions more individually. CRP Web site and its sections "Influence and Lobbying," "Lobbying Database," "Pharmaceuticals/Health Products," and "Politicians and Elections."

69. See http://www. Phrma.org/issues/. In reality, research and development accounts for only 14 percent of pharmaceutical companies' operating expenses, whereas marketing accounts for fully 34 percent of the total. Angell, *The Truth About the Drug Companies.*

70. As a case in point, Mark McClellan, who consistently defended drug company interests, was made commissioner of the FDA in 2002. Among other industry viewpoints, he was opposed to "stringent" price regulations, arguing that drug companies require "sufficient" money for research and development that improves the health and comfort of all Americans. In 2004, McClellan was chosen to head the CMS. Ibid.

In another instance, Thomas Scully, the CMS administrator from mid-2001 to December 2003, resigned to join a law firm (Alston and Bird) that lobbies national officials for hospitals, drug companies, and other firms in the health care industry. Tommy Thompson, HHS secretary at the time, gave Scully a waiver to exempt him "from certain parts of the federal ethics law" while Scully was simultaneously negotiating the new Medicare drug bill in 2003 and his employment options. Robert Pear, "Medicare Chief Joins Firm with Health Clients," *New York Times*, December 19, 2003.

71. From 1983 to 1993, Medicaid outpatient drug spending rose from $2 billion to $8.3 billion, averaging 41 percent annually. In subsequent years, it represented more than twice the rate of increases in total program spending. Rising from 7 percent of

program costs in 1990 and nearly 11 percent in 2000, prescription drugs represented nearly 14 percent of welfare medicine expenditures, or fully $40 billion, by 2004. In 2006, when dual eligibles were shifted to Medicare Part D, Medicaid drug spending decreased by 34 percent. U.S. HHS, Centers for Medicare and Medicaid, Office of the Actuary, *2008 Actuarial Report: On the Financial Outlook for Medicaid* (Washington, D.C.: U.S. Government Printing Office, October 17, 2008); Steven Holmes, "Drug Makers and Black Groups Fight Prescription Controls," *New York Times*, November 20, 1994; U.S. GAO, *Medicaid: States' Payments for Outpatient Prescription Drugs* (Washington, D.C.: U.S. Government Printing Office, October 31, 2005).

There also has been greater use of the more expensive, newer classes of drugs, a rise in the number of prescriptions per person, and a growth in the number of disabled adult participants in the program, including people with serious mental illnesses, many of whom rely on multiple medications.

72. Under provisions of OBRA 1990, drug companies must give states the difference between the best price that they offer to their other customers and the average manufacturer price, or 15.1 percent of the average manufacturer price, whichever is greater. Teresa A. Coughlin, Leighton Ku, and John Holahan, *Medicaid Since 1980: Costs, Coverage, and the Shifting Alliance Between the Federal Government and the States* (Washington, D.C.: Urban Institute, 1994); Weissert and Miller, "Punishing the Pioneers."

For a covered drug to be eligible for federal matching funds, the manufacturer must enter into a rebate agreement with CMS and pay rebates to the states.

73. A few of the states that have taken drug manufacturers to court have forced companies to pay millions in additional rebates. U.S. Congress, House, Committee on Oversight and Government Reform, *Prescription Drugs: Oversight of Drug Pricing in Federal Programs*, hearings, statement of John E. Dicken, Director of Health Care, GAO, 110th Cong., 1st sess., February 9, 2007, GAO-07-481T (Washington, D.C.: U.S. Government Printing Office, 2007); U.S. Congress, House, Committee on Energy and Commerce, Subcommittee on Health, *Medicaid Drug Rebate Program: Inadequate Oversight Raises Concerns About Rebates Paid to States*, hearings, statement of Kathleen King, director of health care, GAO, 109th Cong., 1st sess., June 22, 2005.

In an analysis of Medicaid drug costs in five states, based on actual sales data, the GAO found large differences between state payments and manufacturer prices. In each state, the average Medicaid reimbursement for brand-name drugs was 12 percent higher than the average manufacturer price and 36 percent greater than the "best price" offered to other customers. U.S. GAO, *Medicaid: States' Payments for Outpatient Prescription Drugs*.

74. Although OBRA 1990 initially prevented the states from using formularies, this provision was repealed in 1993. As of 2006, about two-thirds of the states had preferred drug lists. Some places even demand discounts from the drug companies as a precondition for being placed on them.

75. Weissert and Miller, "Punishing the Pioneers."

76. Other beneficiaries of the Medicare Prescription Drug Improvement and Modernization Act include employers, rural health care providers, and teaching hospitals, all of which will receive billions in subsidies. Thomas R. Oliver, Philip Lee, and Helene

Lipton, "A Political History of Medicare and Prescription Drug Coverage: Missed Opportunities and Muddled Outcomes," paper presented at the 2004 Annual Meeting of the American Political Science Association, September 2–5, Chicago.

77. The Medicare Prescription Drug Improvement and Modernization Act also prohibits HHS from intervening in any price discussions between insurers, drug companies, and pharmacies. U.S. Congress, Senate, *Prescription Drugs*, Dicken testimony.

78. From 2006 to 2008, the additional prescription drug costs paid by the government for the dual eligibles amounted to $3.7 billion. U.S. Congress, House, Committee on Oversight and Government Reform, *Medicare Part D: Drug Pricing and Manufacturer Windfalls*, report prepared by Majority Staff (Washington, D.C.: U.S. Government Printing Office, July 2008).

At the same time, the dual eligibles have experienced innumerable problems in obtaining their medications. Because many of them are randomly assigned to contractors, there is no guarantee that their drugs will be included in their plan's formulary. With the exception of nursing home residents, for the first time they also have copayments. Moreover, although they receive a subsidy that covers the full cost of their monthly premium, there is a ceiling. If they select a plan more expensive than the allowable amount, they must pay the difference out of pocket. There have been large annual premium increases, averaging 8.7 percent in stand-alone plans from 2007 to 2008; Humana's standard plan, with the second-highest enrollment, raised its premiums by 69 percent. After United Health Medicare RX AARP (with the largest market share) raised its prices, the fees rose higher than the upper threshold for dual-eligible participants, forcing their reassignment to another plan—and a new formulary. The following year, premiums rose another 22 percent. U.S. Congress, Senate, Committee on Finance, *Medicare Part D: Enrolling New Dual Eligible Beneficiaries in Prescription Drug Plans*," hearings, statement of Kathleen M. King, director of health care, GAO, 110th Cong., 1st sess., May 8, 2007; U.S. Congress, House, Committee on Oversight and Government Reform, letter from Henry Waxman, chair, to Kerry Weems, acting administrator, CMS, October 14, 2008. available at http://oversight.house.gov/documents/20081014164341.pdf.

79. Although each state determines its own method, the federal government has established certain requirements for reimbursing pharmacies for the drugs they acquire, together with a "reasonable" dispensary fee. States must pay pharmacies either *(a)* the lower of their acquisition cost for a drug or *(b)* the federal upper payment limit, set by CMS for multiple-source drugs based on the average manufacturer's price (required under OBRA 1990, the limit is 150 percent of the lowest average manufacturer's price from among a drug's therapeutically equivalent types) or *(c)* a state's maximum allowable cost, if it has established one. Daniel Levinson, *Comparison of Medicaid Federal Upper Limit Amounts to Average Manufacturers Prices (AMPS)* (Washington, D.C.: Office of the Inspector General, U.S. Department of Health and Human Services, June 2005).

80. Mostly using the average wholesale price as their measure of acquisition costs, local policymakers have to estimate the amounts by using published list prices; they do not have access to the confidential sales data. U.S. GAO, *Medicaid: States' Payments for Outpatient Prescription Drugs.*

The OIG and GAO found in separate studies that these average wholesale prices were significantly higher than the actual prices paid to manufacturers by retail pharmacies, thereby boosting the latter's markup and thus their profits considerably. According to the OIG, federal upper payment limits, on average, were five times higher than the published average manufacturer's price charges for generic drugs (some were nineteen times higher). As a consequence, in 2005 Congress began utilizing an alternative method for reimbursing pharmacies under Medicare, but state Medicaid programs persisted in employing the inflated list prices. U.S. Congress, Senate, *Medicaid Waste, Fraud, and Abuse*, testimony of Robert A. Vito, regional inspector general for calibration and inspections, Pennsylvania Department of Health and Human Services; Levinson, *Comparison of Medicaid Federal Upper Limit Amounts to Average Manufacturers Prices*.

81. By the pharmacist industry's own account, chains now operate 36,000 U.S. retail pharmacies, employ 112,000 pharmacists, fill about 70 percent of the nation's total 3.2 billion annual prescriptions, and bring in more than $221 billion in revenue from the sale of prescription medicine. See http://www.nacd.org.

82. In 2006, the 24,000 NCPA members filled about 1.5 billion prescriptions, representing $85 billion in sales.

83. Quoted in "Pharmacists Seek Better Reimbursements," *Business First of Louisville* (Kentucky), February 1, 2007, available at http://www.bizjournals.com/Louisville.

84. "Proposed Medicaid Cuts Would Hurt Pharmacies," Naplenews.com, March 17, 2007.

85. For example, through court action in early 2009, Walgreens and other drug store chains successfully thwarted Washington State's attempt to cut reimbursement rates for brand-name medications. In another case at the time, a U.S. District Court issued an injunction that temporarily blocked California's attempt to reduce pharmacy fees by 5 percent, arguing that the cuts could significantly curtail Medicaid clients' access to prescription drugs.

86. U.S. HHS, *Statistics*, table 32: "Medicaid/Type of Service."

87. In 2004, Anthem Inc. acquired Wellpoint Health Networks of California, which then adopted the Wellpoint name. With 2 million members in 2006, the firm operates Anthem Blue Cross/Blue Shield in fourteen states and has exclusive contracts in a few localities. Its stock has grown measurably—for example, 24 percent during 2004.

88. Welfare medicine represents about 10 percent of the parent company's total enrollment as of 2005. Americhoice serves 1.4 million Medicaid and SCHIP participants in at least thirteen states. Overall, UnitedHealth Group divisions that concentrate on the state programs had combined revenues of $9.32 billion in 2005, up 44 percent from the previous year. "Increase in Quarterly Earnings for United Health Group," *Bloomberg News*, January 21, 2005.

Since 2000, UnitedHealth Group has acquired Lifemark Corporation (2001), AmeriSource Corp. (2002), Mid Atlantic Medical Services (2004), and Oxford Health Plans, Inc. (2004). Standard and Poor's, *United Health Group, Inc.: Corporate Actions* (New York: Standard and Poor's, April 28, 2005).

89. Since 1996, AmeriHealth Mercy has been an alliance between Independence Blue Shield and Mercy Health Systems.

90. WellCare has the largest number of enrollees, about 2.4 million in 2009; despite ongoing probes for financial fraud in three states, it has continued to boost its welfare medicine clientele, with a sizeable stake in a few places, including Georgia and Florida. Florida is WellCare's single largest Medicaid customer; it has nearly half of the state's business, which accounts for 39 percent of the company's total welfare medicine clients. Marley Seaman, "WellCare Drops on Florida Expansion Halt," *Business Week*, October 30, 2007. Amerigroup, too, has extended the scope of its services to more and more localities and now serves well more than 1.7 million Medicaid participants in eleven states. Centene, with a total of more than 1.2 million welfare medicine clients, has steadily gained market shares in such states as Texas, Georgia, Florida, South Carolina, Indiana, New Jersey, Ohio, and Wisconsin. Molina serves 1.3 million people in California, Michigan, Missouri, Ohio, New Mexico, Texas, Utah, and Washington.

Amerigroup and Centene Corporation grew steadily by acquiring smaller plans at bargain-basement prices. Amerigroup's revenues have risen enormously in the past several years, along with generally impressive growth in its stock. In September 2006, for example, profits were up 35.4 percent for the year. Centene grew from a $200 million company in 1999 to a $1.5 billion company at the end of 2007. Its profits more than doubled to $25.6 million, or fifty-seven cents per share, from the first quarter of 2007 to the first quarter of 2008. WellCare Health Plans, Inc. was purchased by venture capitalist George Soros's private-equity fund in 2002, and it too was progressively enlarged. The company, which also has a substantial Medicare business, experienced the highest stock-market gains of the four firms, more than three times its initial stock offering by 2004; the following year its shares soared another 68 percent. Its 2008 annual income dropped from the previous year for a variety of reasons that included Medicaid rate changes. Molina Healthcare Inc. was launched in 1980 by a physician and was later expanded by his son. Its stock has risen 160 percent since it went public in 2003, with a particularly notable performance in 2007. By 2005, all four of the government-only MCOs had become public companies. Bethany McClean, "The Big Money in Medicaid," *Fortune*, June 11, 2007; Barbara Martinez, "Health-Care Goldmines: Middlemen Strike It Rich," *Wall Street Journal*, November 15, 2006; Barbara Martinez, "In Medicaid, Private HMOs Take a Big and Profitable Role," *Wall Street Journal*, November 15, 2006; Lisa LaMotta, "Centene Jumps on Earnings Beat," *Forbes*, April 22, 2008, available at http://www.Forbes.com.

91. AHIP's predecessor organizations included the American Association of Health Plans and Health Insurance Association of America.

92. CRP Web site and its sections "Influence and Lobbying," "Lobbying Database," and "Insurance."

93. For instance, with 92,000 welfare medicine beneficiaries in Illinois, WellCare subsidiaries provided $125,000 to the state's now infamous former governor Rod Blagojevich for his reelection campaign in 2005, along with a donation of $100,000 for President Bush's inaugural gala and another $34,000 to the Republican Governors Association.

Martinez, "Health-Care Goldmines"; Martinez, "In Medicaid, Private HMOs Take a Big and Profitable Role"; McClean, "The Big Money in Medicaid."

In 2006, WellCare executives and their families, along with a company-sponsored political action committee, contributed $1.5 million to Florida candidates for state and federal offices, including the president of the state Senate. Moreover, that year a Well-Care board member, Dr. Andrew Agwunobi, resigned to become secretary of Florida's Agency for Health Care Administration, which administers Medicaid. McClean, "The Big Money in Medicaid."

94. Ignagni's statements come from several AHIP press releases, all available at http://www.AHIP.org: "Statement on HHS Medicaid Managed Care Regulation" June 14, 2002; "Analysis Shows Medicaid Managed Care Provides Value," August 6, 2004; "New Report Details How Dynamic Medicaid Managed Care Programs Are Improving Health of Beneficiaries," March 8, 2005.

95. From 2002 to 2003, average total cash compensation for MCO executives grew by 19 percent, reaching $2.4 million. For the second year in a row, Leonard Schaffer, chairman and CEO of WellPoint Health Networks, was the most highly paid, receiving $12 million in total compensation. The chief officer of UnitedHealth Group received $8 million in salary and bonuses. His complete compensation package was even greater. Irving Levin Associates, *Who's Making What in Health Care.*

Since WellCare's initial public offering, its CEO Doug Farha has sold more than $37 million of his personal company stock but still owns shares valued at roughly $100 million. He was paid nearly $3.5 million in cash compensation from 2004 to 2007. During that same period, Amerigroup CEO Jeff McWaters obtained $6.5 million in salary, and Centene CEO Michael Neidorff collected $6.75 million; both men were given millions more in stocks and options. In 2006, Towerbrook Capital Partners, L.P., Soros's renamed investment firm, sold the last of its Wellcare stock, garnering between $650 and $900 million in profit from its initial outlay in 2002. Martinez, "Health-Care Goldmines"; McClean, "The Big Money in Medicaid."

96. It is also called the medical cost ratio.

97. Philip M. Seligman, *Healthcare: Managed Care*, Standard and Poor's Industry Survey (New York: Standard and Poor's, March 31, 2005).

98. Martha Roherty, director of the National Association of State Medicaid Directors, quoted in Martinez, "Health-Care Goldmines"; see also McClean, "The Big Money in Medicaid," and Martinez, "In Medicaid, Private HMOs Take a Big and Profitable Role."

99. As a case in point, "In Illinois, the state and the Justice Department asserted in a lawsuit that Amerigroup spent only $131 million on medical care from 2000 to 2004, despite taking in $243 million from the state"; its medical loss ratio was less than 50 percent. The jury agreed, ordering the company to pay back $144 million. Martinez, "In Medicaid, Private HMOs Take a Big and Profitable Role."

100. For example, in 2008, dissatisfied with the rates in Nevada, Anthem notified officials that it was abandoning the program; the company served more than 80 percent of the state's welfare medicine clients and nearly one-third of the children participating

in the Nevada Check-up plan. WellPoint recently exited the Ohio and Connecticut Medicaid markets.

101. About 15 percent of doctors do not accept any welfare medicine patients (up from 13 percent in 1997), and slightly more than 20 percent will not take on any new ones. Among practitioners who do treat low-income health plan recipients, about 60 percent receive less than one-fifth of their practice revenue from Medicaid. However, fully 25 percent of doctor's offices receive one-third or more of their income from the program. Overall, in 2004, doctors received roughly 6.9 percent of their $290.8 billion in total 2004 earnings from the program. U.S. Bureau of the Census, *Current Business Reports (B5/2004)*, tables 8.1 and 8.11; Peter J. Cunningham and Jessica H. May, *Medicaid Patients Increasingly Concentrated Among Physicians*, Tracking Report no. 16 (Washington, D.C.: Center for Studying Health System Change, August 2006).

102. The health professionals industry together reported contributing more than $359 million to federal candidates and parties from 1990 to 2006. During that period, the AMA donated $24.2 million, along with spending $156.2 million on federal lobbying. CRP Web site and its sections "Influence and Lobbying," "Lobbying Database," "Health Professionals," and "Politicians and Elections."

103. U.S. Bureau of the Census, *Current Business Reports (B5/2004)*, tables 8.1 and 8.11.

104. The Federation of Pediatric Organizations includes among its several member organizations the American Academy of Pediatrics and the American Pediatric Society. Because so many more children than adults are covered by welfare medicine, pediatricians have less opportunity to opt out of Medicaid or SCHIP and so are among those who are most concerned with welfare medicine funding practices and policies.

105. The ADA has reported federal campaign contributions of $13.5 million between 1990 and 2006 ($1.9 million in 2006) and lobbying expenditures of $3.3 million ($0.2 million in 2006). CRP Web site and its sections "Health Professionals," "Influence and Lobbying," "Lobbying Database," and "Politicians and Elections."

106. Slightly more than half of dentists' income is derived from private insurance; patient out-of-pocket payments account for another 44 percent. U.S. Bureau of the Census, *Current Business Reports (B5/2004)*, tables 8.1 and 8.11.

However, individual companies such as Doral Dental actively work to gain contracts at the state level. A for-profit dental benefits–management firm (and subsidiary of DentaQuest Ventures, Inc.), Doral is one of the largest administrators of government dental benefits programs in the United States. It serves more than 9 million Medicaid participants in twenty states. In 2008, it bought Atlantic Dental, which is the primary server of Medicaid participants in Miami-Dade County, Florida. Atlantic Dental is controlled by MBF Healthcare Partners, L.P., a Miami investment group.

107. Lisa Rathke, "Low Reimbursement Rates Hinder Dental Care for Poor," *Boston Globe*, February 3, 2007.

108. At the end of 2005, proprietary, nonprofit, and government agencies accounted for 62 percent, 27 percent, and 11 percent of home health agencies, respectively. The four largest proprietary home care agencies are Gentiva Health Services, Inc.; Amedisys, Inc.; LHC Group; and Almost Family. Together, they receive about 15 percent of

industry revenue. Citizens for Long-Term Care, *Defining Common Ground: Long-Term Care Financing Reform in 2001* (Washington, D.C.: Citizens for Long-Term Care, February 2001); Enid Kassner, *Medicaid and Long-Term Care Services and Supports for Older People* (Washington, D.C.: AARP Public Policy Institute, April 2006); U.S. HHS, Centers for Medicare and Medicaid Services, *Statistics*, table 20: "Selected Facilities/Type of Control."

109. The National Association for Home Care and Hospice has reported spending $5.7 million since 1998 and $0.7 million in 2006 to lobby federal elected officials. The American Association for HomeCare reported $0.3 million in national lobbying expenses for 2006. CRP Web site and its sections "Health Professionals," "Influence and Lobbying," "Lobbying Database."

110. These affiliates include the Hospice Association of America, Private Duty Homecare Association of America, Center for Health Care Law, HomeCare University, Caring Photography, Home Care Technology Association, Home Care and Hospice Financial Managers Association, the Caring Institute, Home Healthcare Nurses Association, Home Care Aide Association of America, National Association for Physicians in Home Care, World Homecare and Hospice Organization, Pediatric Home Care Association of America, Hospital Home Care Association of America, Proprietary Home Care Association of America, Voluntary Home Care Association of America, and Home Medical Equipment Association of America.

111. Accenture services also include enrollment screening for SCHIP, food stamps, and TANF. Because of the company's many errors, SCHIP enrollment dropped in 2006. Among other myriad problems, the company had huge backlogs in its workload. As a result, the state reduced its compensation and ended the contract two years early.

112. In 2006, Electronic Data Systems had more than 117,000 employees, total sales of $21.3 billion, and profits of $470 million. Among other recent financially rewarding agreements, the company signed a $100.8 million contract in 2007 to design, develop, and install a new Medicaid technology system for Ohio, a $91.7 million, three-year contract extension in Kansas, and a $59.1 million contract extension in Oklahoma.

113. Electronic Data Systems was North Carolina's fiscal agent for years but lost the $171 million contract to Affiliated Computer Services in 2004. Across the nation, however, the latter company has been beset with delays in its efforts, cost overruns, and problems with the function of the systems themselves.

114. Unisys received an additional $14 million from West Virginia in 2007 because the company had "miscalculated" the project's costs. Tom Breen, "Lawmakers: Co. Controls West Virginia Medicaid," *Business Week Magazine*, April 18, 2007, available at http://www.BusinessWeek.com.

115. In Maine, the project was supposed to be completed in 2002 but was not implemented until 2005, at which time it completely malfunctioned. The original contract of $15 million eventually cost the state an additional $55 million to work through the problems. Victoria Wallack, "Report: Plenty of Blame for Medicaid Software Debacle," Village Soup Media Services, December 20, 2006, available at http://www.waldo.villagesoup.com/news.

116. As just one typical example, CGI Group, Inc. (a subsidiary of CGI Federal, Inc.), a customer of CMS since 1998, signed a $27 million medical records contract with the agency in 2008.

117. Providence Service Corporation acquired LogistiCare at the end of 2007.

118. Dan Burrows, "Small Contractor Finds Niche Fixing Medicaid Errors," *Smartmoney.com*, March 2, 2007, available at http://www.smartmomey.com. HMS Holdings also recently purchased its main rival, Benefits Solutions Practice Area.

119. Steven Rathgeb Smith, "Medicaid Funding of Social Services: Implications for Social and Health Policy," paper presented at the 2007 Annual Meeting of the American Political Science Association, August 30–September 2, Chicago.

120. Paul Krugman and Robin Wells, "The Health Care Crisis and What to Do About It," *New York Review of Books* 50, no. 5 (March 23, 2006): 38–43; U.S. Congress, House, Committee on Appropriations, Subcommittee on Military Construction, Veterans Affairs, and Related Agencies, *Health Care Spending: Public Payers Face Burden of Entitlement Program Growth, While All Payers Face Rising Prices and Increasing Use of Services*, hearings, statement of A. Bruce Steinwald, director of health care, GAO, 110th Cong., 1st sess., February 15, 2007.

In 2006, hospitals represented 33 percent of the total, followed by physicians (23 percent), drug companies (11 percent), nursing homes (7 percent), and providers of other health services and supplies (26 percent).

121. According to the AHA, hospitals support 10 percent of all U.S. jobs, totaling 12.9 million, and because of the ripple effect generate 8 million more.

122. Daniel Gitterman, Joanne Spetz, and Matthew Fellowes, *The Other Side of the Ledger: Federal Health Spending in Metropolitan Economies*, discussion paper (Washington, D.C.: Metropolitan Policy Program, Brookings Institution, September 2004).

123. Gardiner Harris, "The Nation, Medicaid's Tentacles: Gee, Fixing Welfare Seemed Like a Snap," *New York Times*, June 19, 2005.

124. The Family USA researchers estimated that the more than $132 billion that states expected to spend on welfare medicine in 2005 would generate a $367.5 billion increase in their local output of goods and services and 3.4 million new jobs, with wages of more than $133 billion. The boost to business activity per million of state Medicaid money ranges from a high of $6.2 million in Mississippi, $5.5 million in Arkansas and Utah, and $5.6 million in New Mexico to less than $2.2 million in Delaware, Colorado, Connecticut, Maryland, Massachusetts, Minnesota, New Hampshire, New York, Virginia, and Washington.

In 2004, a few states had particularly large increases in Medicaid-related employment. In New York, there were 396,600 more jobs, followed by California (314,800), Texas (214,600), Pennsylvania (175,100), Florida (173,700), and Ohio (160,000). Rachel Klein, Kathleen Stoll, and Adele Bruce, *Medicaid: Good Medicine for State Economies, 2004 Update* (Washington, D.C.: Families USA Foundation, May 2004), available at http://www.familiesusa.org.

125. In 2007, the federal matching rate ranged from 50 percent to 76 percent; twelve states received a 50 percent match.

126. James Fossett and Courtney E. Burke, *Is Medicaid Retrenching? State Budgets and Medicaid Enrollment in 2002* (Albany, N.Y.: Nelson A. Rockefeller Institute of Government, February 12, 2003).

127. U.S. Office of Management and Budget, *Budget of the U.S., FY 2007.* It is expected that Medicaid and SCHIP funds will account for $215.7 billion of the $476.1 billion in federal grants to the states in 2009. U.S. Office of Management and Budget, *Budget of the U.S., FY 2009: Analytical Perspectives* (Washington, D.C.: U.S. Government Printing Office, 2009), 109.

128. Don Boyd, "Medicaid Spending—New York Versus Other States," presentation to the New York Health Care Task Force, September 5, 2003, Albany, New York.

129. Moore Business School, Division of Research, *Economic Impact of Medicaid on South Carolina*, report developed for the South Carolina Department of Health and Human Services (Columbia: University of South Carolina, January 2002), available at http://www.research.moore.sc.edu/research/studies/Medicaid/Medicaideconimpact.pdf.

130. Anand Desai, Yushim Kim, and Robert Greenbaum, *Health Data Brief: Study Estimates Economic Effects of Medicaid Spending Changes in Ohio* (Columbus: Health Policy Institute of Ohio, December 15, 2005).

131. For example, Kerry Kilpatrick and his colleagues looked into the impact of reductions in North Carolina's Medicaid program in 2002. They found that if the state cut its contributions by 6 percent (or $129.7 million in 2003), federal receipts would fall by $278.6 million, resulting in a $706.3 million loss in the output of goods and services and 9,700 fewer jobs; the federal share alone would lead to a shortfall of $479.9 in economic output and 6,590 in employment opportunities. Kerry Kilpatrick, Joshua Olinick, Michael Luger, and Jun Koo, *The Economic Impact of Proposed Reductions in Medicaid Spending in North Carolina* (Chapel Hill: Institute for Public Health, University of North Carolina, April 11, 2002).

Similarly, a Colorado Health Institute inquiry established that the $1.3 billion in state Medicaid money multiplies into $3 billion of new business activity, 28,356 more jobs, and $1.1 billion additional wages. Colorado Health Institute, *Colorado Medicaid* (Denver: Colorado Health Institute, March 2005).

132. John Goddeeris and Yong Li, *Effects of Changes in Medicaid on Income and Jobs in Michigan: Estimates from the RIMS II Model* (East Lansing: Institute for Health Care Studies and the Institute for Public Policy and Social Research, Michigan State University, February 2005).

According to Spencer Johnson, president of the Michigan Hospital Association, "Medicaid is one reason health care is Michigan's top private sector employer, providing more than 472,300 direct jobs and 254,340 indirect jobs that pump $29.8 billion a year in wages and salaries into the state's economy." Spencer Johnson, "Medicaid Cuts Will Rebound on Everyone," *Detroit Free Press*, August 29, 2005.

133. The economic stimulus plan was enacted under the American Recovery and Reinvestment Act of 2009.

134. Lawrence D. Brown and Michael Sparer, "Poor Program's Progress: The Unanticipated Politics of Medicaid Policy," *Health Affairs* 22, no. 1 (January–February 2003), 38.

135. James Fossett and Courtney Burke, *Medicaid and State Budgets in FY 2004: Why Medicaid Is Hard to Cut* (Albany, N.Y.: Federalism Research Group, Nelson A. Rockefeller Institute of Government, July 2004).

9. The Buck Stops Where?

1. UPLs are nationally mandated ceilings on the allowable amount states can pay for certain services in order to be eligible for federal matching funds. They generally are based on what Medicare pays for an equivalent service. However, because DSH schemes were initially exempt from UPLs, the states were able to use them as an opportunity to garner extra federal funding for their Medicaid programs.

The DSH program was established to provide higher fees to hospitals that care for a disproportionate percentage of Medicaid and uninsured patients. The states, however, have employed it to capture additional federal money. First, they demand a tax or donation of money from private or government providers. Second, they give the vendor a payment, which includes the original contribution plus additional money. Third, they receive a federal match, based on the full amount handed over to the provider. As an example, a nursing home donates $10,000 to the state, which, in turn, gives the facility a $12,000 payment. If a 50 percent match is assumed, the state receives $6,000 from the federal government. The end result is that the nursing home keeps $2,000, and the state nets $4,000.

As Congress imposed restrictions on using provider taxes and donations for their DSH funding, the states began taking more advantage of intergovernmental transfer loopholes, especially with regard to government-run hospitals and nursing homes. (Intergovernmental transfers can occur between the various units of government, including the state, cities, counties, and their agencies.) For the purpose of maximizing their federal match, states pay the locally owned facilities far more than the facilities' costs, but up to the allowable UPL. The federal government pays its match on the "gap" between the two amounts. The government institutions are then obligated to return all or most of these enhanced payments to the state through intergovernmental transfers, which, along with the additional national match, are deposited in the state's general treasury. As an example, the state pays a county nursing home $7,000 in excess payments. Assuming a 50 percent match, the state receives $3,500 from the federal government. The nursing home then returns $6,000 to the state, which nets $2,500; the nursing home gains $1,000.

2. Congressional legislation in 1991, 1993, 1997, and 2000—urged on by Presidents George H. W. Bush and Bill Clinton—endeavored, in part, to control the excessive use of disproportionate share payments.

3. In 2001, DSH payments as a percentage of Medicaid funding ranged from a high of 21 percent in Louisiana, 18 percent in New Hampshire, 16 percent in Indiana, and 16 percent in New Jersey to negligible amounts in Montana, Wyoming, and Utah. Robert E. Mechanic, *Medicaid's Disproportionate Share Hospital Program: Complex Structure, Critical Payments*, National Health Policy Forum Background Paper (Washington, D.C.: National Health Policy Forum, George Washington University, September 14, 2004).

4. Michael Sparer, "Medicaid, Federalism, and National Health Insurance," paper presented at the 2007 Annual Meeting of the American Political Science Association, August 30–September 2, Chicago.

Congressional support for its home districts, despite the financial ramifications, has been evidenced on many occasions. For example, the George W. Bush administration had proposed to lower the cap on allowable state provider taxes, thereby saving the federal government billions in matching Medicaid grants, but costing the states substantial losses of money. West Virginian officials estimated that if the ceiling were lowered to 3 percent, the state would forfeit about $45 million annually; Missouri anticipated a $1.3 billion per year shortfall. When Congress refused to enact the measure, Bush determined to push it through by administrative rule instead, spurring intense bipartisan opposition that included a letter signed by 263 U.S. House members and 62 senators, the National Governors Association, and the National Association of Public Hospitals and Health Systems. Tom Searis, "West Virginia Could Lose Millions in Medicaid," *Charlestown Gazette* (Virginia), December 6, 2006; T. J. Greaney, "Medicaid Funding Likely to Avoid Ax," *Missourian*, December 9, 2006.

In another example, when the Bush administration attempted to curb the federal share of Medicaid reimbursements to "safety-net" and government hospitals, local officials pushed Congress to maintain the extra funding. The president later endeavored to restrict federal reimbursements to publicly run institutions by limiting their Medicaid payments to the incurred cost of providing care. After much controversy, the rules were delayed—along with several others—after Congress added the moratorium to its 2009 supplemental spending bill.

5. Karen Matherlee, *The Federal-State Struggle over Medicaid Matching Funds: An Update*, National Health Policy Forum Background Paper (Washington, D.C.: National Health Policy Forum, George Washington University, May 31, 2001).

National policymakers ultimately reduced DSH payments to roughly 6 percent of Medicaid costs by 2007, down from 14 percent in 1992, but total outlays were still sizable ($16 billion). Allotments had been raised in 2004 under the Medicare Modernization Act of 2003 but were capped at that level and, since then, can increase only at the annual rate of the consumer price index. U.S. HHS, Centers for Medicare and Medicaid Services, Office of the Actuary, *2008 Actuarial Report: On the Financial Outlook for Medicaid* (Washington, D.C.: U.S. Government Printing Office, October 17, 2008).

6. For example, the number of UPL schemes grew from twenty-eight in 2000 to forty-five in 2004. U.S. Congress, Senate, Committee on Finance, *Medicaid Waste, Fraud, and Abuse: Threatening the Health Care Safety Net*, hearings, statement by Kathryn Allen, director of health care, GAO, 109th Cong., 1st sess., June 28, 2005.

7. U.S. GAO, *Medicaid: Improved Federal Oversight of State Financing Schemes Is Needed*, report to the Committee on Finance, U.S. Senate (Washington, D.C.: U.S. Government Printing Office, February 2004).

8. Teresa Coughlin, Brian Bruen, and Jennifer King, "States' Use of Medicaid UPL and DSH Financing Mechanisms in 2001," *Health Affairs* 23, no. 2 (January–February 2003): 245–257.

9. Mechanic, *Medicaid's Disproportionate Share Hospital Program.*

10. In their 2001 survey, Teresa Coughlin, Brian Bruen, and Jennifer King found that more of the DSH funding was accruing to hospitals, but the states still retained a considerable share of the grants. At the same time, they observed that the states kept, on average, 80 percent of the inflated UPL dollars. Coughlin, Bruen, and King, "States' Use of Medicaid UPL and DSH Financing Mechanisms in 2001."

In Pennsylvania, the schemes involved mainly county-run nursing homes. According to one source, the state has amassed $1 billion annually since 1990 through enhanced federal payments; it has not used any of the money to improve conditions for institutionalized residents, depositing the money in the state coffers instead. However, a few places, such as Washington, used the extra DSH and UPL subsidies to meet their citizenry's health care needs. U.S. HHS, Office of the Inspector General, Daniel R. Levinson, Inspector General, *Review of the Commonwealth of Pennsylvania's Use of Intergovernmental Transfers to Finance Medicaid Supplementation Payments to County Nursing Facilities* (Washington, D.C.: U.S. Government Printing Office, January 2001); Amy Schneider and David Rousseau, *Upper Payment Limits: Reality and Illusions in Medicaid Financing* (Menlo Park, Calif.: Henry J. Kaiser Family Foundation, Kaiser Commission on Medicaid and the Uninsured, February 2002), available at http;//www.kff.org.

11. Schneider and Rousseau, *Upper Payment Limits.*

12. Teresa A. Coughlin, Leighton Ku, and John Holahan, *Medicaid Since 1980: Costs, Coverage, and the Shifting Alliance Between the Federal Government and the States* (Washington, D.C.: Urban Institute, 1994).

13. Matherlee, *The Federal-State Struggle over Medicaid Matching Funds*, 2.

14. From 2000 to 2004, Georgia received $1.5 billion and Massachusetts about $570 million in extra national Medicaid reimbursements at a cost of $82 million and $11 million, respectively, in consultant fees. U.S. Congress, Senate, *Medicaid: States' Efforts to Maximize Federal Reimbursements*, Allen statement.

15. James Fossett and Courtney E. Burke, *Medicaid and State Budgets in FY 2004: Why Medicaid Is Hard to Cut* (Albany, N.Y.: Federalism Research Group, Nelson A. Rockefeller Institute of Government, July 2004).

16. In 1977, 57 percent of expenditures on services for the developmentally and mentally disabled were unmatched state and local dollars. By 2004, this total had declined to 14 percent. Steven Rathgeb Smith, "Medicaid Funding of Social Services: Implications for Social and Health Policy," paper presented at the 2007 Annual Meeting of the American Political Science Association, August 30–September 2, Chicago.

17. Moreover, in the early 1990s, because treatment for mental illnesses was not reimbursable by Medicaid in a psychiatric institution but was covered in general hospitals, certain states simply moved patients or designated their mental health institutions as DSH institutions. Bruce Wallin, "Massachusetts: Downsizing State Government," in Steven Gold, ed., *The Fiscal Crisis of the States: Lessons for the Future*, 252–295 (Washington. D.C.: Georgetown University Press, 1995); Alan Weil, "There's Something About Medicaid," *Health Affairs* 22, no. 1 (January–February 2003): 13–23.

18. Colleen Grogan, Michael Gusmano, and Patricia King, "Medicaid Policymaking: The Role of Nonprofit Providers and Medicaid Advocates," paper prepared for the 2007

Annual Meeting of the American Political Science Association, August 30–September 2, Chicago.

19. In 2001, the Pennsylvania Department of Public Welfare began eyeing Medicaid as a more lucrative source of funding.

20. For example, OBRA 1981 mandated, among other provisions, a three-year reduction in the federal Medicaid match. More than twenty years later, President George W. Bush achieved sizeable cutbacks as well, amounting to $4.9 billion over five years and $26.5 billion over ten years, as part of DRA 2005. The president had put forward larger reductions: researchers calculated that more than 80 percent of his requests would have benefited the national treasury "by shifting costs directly from the federal government to the states." Andy Schneider, Leighton Ku, and Judith Solomon, *The Administration's Medicaid Proposals Would Shift Federal Costs to States* (Washington, D.C.: Center on Budget and Policy Priorities, February 14, 2006).

21. In 2004, the ninety funding specialists cost $12 million. They also were directed to ferret out reimbursement "errors" to providers. Their activities were centralized through a new unit, the Division of Reimbursement and State Financing. U.S. GAO, *Medicaid Financial Management: Steps Taken to Improve Federal Oversight but Other Actions Needed to Sustain Efforts*, report to the chairman, Committee on Finance, U.S. Senate, GAO-06-705 (Washington, D.C.: U.S. Government Printing Office, June 22, 2006).

22. Among the dual eligibles in 2005, 4.2 million were age sixty-five and older, and 2.6 million were the younger disabled population. The two groups account for 15 percent of Medicare enrollees as well. U.S. HHS, Centers for Medicare and Medicaid Services, *Statistics: Information About Persons Covered by Medicare, Medicaid, or SCHIP* (Washington, D.C.: U.S. Government Printing Office, 2006), table 14: "State Buy-Ins for Dual Eligible Medicaid Beneficiaries/State Buy-Ins for Medicare"; U.S. Congress, Senate, Committee on Finance, *Medicare Part D: Enrolling New Dual Eligible Beneficiaries in Prescription Drug Plans*, hearings, statement of Kathleen M. King, director of health care, GAO, 110th Cong., 1st sess., May 8, 2007; Brian Bruen and John Holahan, *Shifting the Cost of Dual Eligibles: Implications for States and the Federal Government* (Menlo Park, Calif.: Henry J. Kaiser Family Foundation, Kaiser Commission on Medicaid and the Uninsured, February 2002), available at http://www.kff.org.

23. The Qualified Medicare Beneficiary and Specified Low-Income Medicare Beneficiary requirements were enacted under the Medicare Catastrophic Coverage Act of 1988 and OBRA 1990, respectively.

24. In comparison, only 3 percent of all Medicare beneficiaries live in a nursing home. Bruen and Holahan, *Shifting the Cost of Dual Eligibles*.

25. Not only do Medicare patients have coverage for only 100 lifetime days in a skilled facility, but they must be "making progress" toward "recovery" in order to receive paid services under the program.

26. William G. Weissert and Edward Alan Miller, "Punishing the Pioneers: The Medicare Modernization Act and State Pharmacy Assistance Programs," paper presented at the 2005 Annual Meeting of the American Political Science Association, September 1–4, Washington, D.C., 29, 30.

In the first year, states had to refund 90 percent of their 2003 drug costs for dual eligibles (about $6 billion), a proportion that will decline to 75 percent by 2014.

27. Edward Alan Miller and William G. Weissert, "Strategies for Integrating Medicare and Medicaid Design Features and Incentives," *Medical Care Research and Review* 60, no. 2 (June 2003), 153.

28. In 1998, New Hampshire counties had agreed to split the nonfederal costs of HCBS. However, in 2007 the state demanded that the counties pay the full nonfederal share of LTC expenses, phased in over several years. In exchange, the state would take over other costs, such as treatment for delinquent youths, which they had previously shared with the counties. The New Hampshire Association of Counties and the ten localities individually sued, arguing that they had not given their approval for the swap. In 2009, the New Hampshire Supreme Court sided with the state.

In Florida, because the cap has not changed since it was imposed in the 1970s, the rate for the counties has steadily diminished from its original 10.6 percent to 1.8 percent by 2001. In 2007, the legislature proposed to increase the counties' Medicaid contribution substantially.

29. In 1991, for instance, Governor Cuomo offered to take over all Medicaid payments but demanded that New York City and all of the counties give up some of their revenues from income and sales taxes. The controversies (and diverse "swap" proposals) continued into the twenty-first century, with Governor Pataki taking the lead. Beginning in 2009, increases in the counties' Medicaid costs will be held at 3 percent.

30. Nearly all of the states also sought to control prescription drug coverage by imposing preferred drug lists. Vernon Smith, Kathleen Gifford, Eileen Ellis, and Amy Wiles, *Low Medicaid Spending Growth amid Rebounding State Revenues: Results from a 50-State Medicaid Budget Survey Fiscal Years 2006 and 2007*, executive summary (Menlo Park, Calif.: Henry J. Kaiser Family Foundation, Kaiser Commission on Medicaid and the Uninsured, October 2006), available at http://www.kff.org

31. As of 2006, eleven states required premiums for children in households with earnings at 101 percent of the FPL; twenty-six states, at 151 percent; and twenty-eight states, at 200 percent. For those states with premiums at 101 percent of the FPL, the annual amount of premiums ranged from $52 in Utah to a high of $480 in Tennessee. Donna Ross, Laura Cox, and Caryn Marks, *Resuming the Path to Health Coverage for Children and Parents: A 50 State Update on Eligibility Rules, Enrollment and Renewal Procedures, and Cost-Sharing Practices in Medicaid and SCHIP in 2006* (Menlo Park, Calif.: Henry J. Kaiser Family Foundation, Kaiser Commission on Medicaid and the Uninsured, January 2007), available at http://www.kff.org

In addition, about 40 percent of the states require youngsters to pay a copayment for nonpreventive physician services, emergency-room care, inpatient hospital care, and prescription drugs. Donna Ross and Laura Cox, *In a Time of Growing Need State Choices Influence Health Coverage Access for Children and Families: A 50-State Update on Eligibility Rules, Enrollment and Renewal Procedures, and Cost-Sharing Practices in Medicaid and SCHIP for Children and Families* (Menlo Park, Calif.: Henry J. Kaiser Family Foundation, Kaiser Commission on Medicaid and the Uninsured, October 2005), available at http://www.kff.org.

32. For families with income lower than the FPL, the maximum copay is up to $3.40 per service and will be updated annually to inflation. The states can charge up to 10 percent of service costs for people with incomes from 100 percent to 150 percent of the FPL and up to 20 percent of the charges for those with incomes higher than that. Total out-of-pocket costs cannot exceed 5 percent of household earnings.

33. Ross and Cox, *In a Time of Growing Need State Choices Influence Health Coverage Access for Children and Families.*

34. The provision was enacted under the Emergency Medical Treatment and Active Labor Act as part of the Consolidated Omnibus Budget Reconciliation Act of 1986. Jonathan Engel, *Poor People's Medicine: Medicaid and American Charity Care Since 1965* (Durham, N.C.: Duke University Press, 2006).

35. The most common avoidable conditions included pneumonia, kidney/urinary tract infections, congestive heart failure, dehydration, and chronic obstructive pulmonary disease.

36. David Grabowski, A. James O'Malley, and Nancy Barhydt, "The Costs and Potential Savings Associated with Nursing Home Hospitalizations," paper given at the 2007 Annual Research Meeting of Academy Health, June 3–5, Orlando, Florida.

37. Orna Intrator, David Grabowski, Jacqueline Zinn, Mark Schleinitz, Zhanlian Feng, Susan Miller, and Vince Mor, "Hospitalization of Nursing Home Residents: The Effects of States' Medicaid Payment and Bed-Hold Policies," *Health Services Research* 42, no. 4 (August 2007): 1651–1671.

38. However, according to Marie Gottschalk, the burden of medical inflation rests firmly on workers and their families, and not on employers per se. In fact, the cost of escalating health expenses for American business is less than that shouldered by advanced industrial nations; many European and Japanese firms encounter "relatively higher corporate and personal income taxes they must pay to support more extensive welfare states." In Germany, for example, employer outlays for health care, which is financed through a payroll tax, are in general higher than "what even the most generous U.S. firms spend on health care for their employees." Marie Gottschalk, *The Shadow Welfare State: Labor, Business, and the Politics of Health Care in the U.S.* (Ithaca, N.Y.: Cornell University Press, 2000), 134.

39. Roughly 20 percent of nonstandard employees and 5 percent of migrant and seasonal farmworkers obtain any job-related health benefits. Michael Doyle, "Farm Workers' Study in Limbo," *Kansas City Star*, November 23, 2006; Elaine Ditsler, Peter Fisher, and Colin Gordon, *On the Fringe: The Substandard Benefits of Workers in Part-Time, Temporary, and Contract Jobs* (Iowa City: Iowa Policy Project, December 2005).

40. Andrew Spano, *Medicaid: The Best Business Subsidy Your Tax Dollars Can Buy* (New York City: Westchester County, New York, November 1, 2006).

Elaine Ditsler, Peter Fisher, and Colin Gordon argue that many firms "routinely refer low-wage, part-time, and nonstandard workers to public sources of individual or family health coverage. In doing so, such employers are relying on public programs to subsidize inadequate benefits." Ditsler, Fisher, and Gordon, *On the Fringe*, 9.

41. In 2005, Wal-Mart had $315 billion in sales and earned $12.2 billion in profits, up 10 percent from the previous year.

42. A study in Illinois, for instance, revealed that between August 2005 and March 2006 there were 363,000 workers participating in welfare medicine at a cost of $335.7 million to the state. The companies with the most employees receiving publicly subsidized medical services were Wal-Mart, McDonald's, Burger King, Target, Jewel, Manpower, and Kelly Service. "Low-Wage Workers' Health Care Costs State Millions," *Register-Mail Online* (Galesburg, Ill.), October 17, 2006, available at http://www.Gales burg.com.

In Florida, more than 22,000 individuals working at the state's top ten companies are on Medicaid. In addition to Wal-Mart, these firms include Publix, Wendy's, and McDonald's. Fully 22 percent of all Ohio's workers employed by either Wal-Mart or McDonald's depend on welfare medicine for their family's medical needs. In Washington State, Safeway, McDonald's, Jack in the Box, Del Monte, and Snokist had more than 200 people on Medicaid. Similarly, a recent study by the Rhode Island Department of Human Resources determined that Wal-Mart, the Bank of America, Citizens Financial Group, the City of Providence, C-U-S, and S-and-S Credit Company each employed more than 250 people who relied on the program. "Study: Some State Workers Relying on Medicaid," *Boston Globe*, March 30, 2007.

43. The law was judged as violating the Employee Retirement Income Security Act of 1974.

44. Peter Cunningham, "Medicaid/SCHIP Cuts and Hospital Emergency Department Use," *Health Affairs* 25, no. 1 (January–February 2006): 237–247.

45. Bill Wright, Matthew Carlson, and Jeanene Smith, *Impact of Changes to Premiums, Cost-Sharing, and Benefits on Adult Medicaid Beneficiaries: Results from an Ongoing Study of the Oregon Health Plan* (New York: Commonwealth Fund, July 29, 2005).

10. Conclusion

1. In 2007, Medicare and the Social Security program assisted 44.1 and 48.8 million older and disabled people per month, respectively, as compared to between 49 and 62 million people served by Medicaid. U.S. HHS, Centers for Medicare and Medicaid Services, Office of the Actuary, *2008 Actuarial Report: On the Financial Outlook for Medicaid* (Washington, D.C.: U.S. Government Printing Office, October 17, 2008).

2. In at least half of these states, the governors either fully or partially enacted or implemented the measures through administrative order. National Governors Association and National Association of Budget Officers, *The Fiscal Survey of States* (Washington, D.C.: U.S. Government Printing Office, June 2008).

3. Colleen M. Grogan and Vernon K. Smith, "From Charity Care to Medicaid: Governors, States, and the Transformation of American Health Care," in Ethan Sribnick, ed., *A More Perfect Union*, 353–401 (Philadelphia: University of Pennsylvania Press, 2008).

4. Steven Gold, "A Framework for Viewing State Policies," in Steven Gold, ed., *The Fiscal Crisis of the States: Lessons for the Future* (Washington, D.C.: Georgetown University Press, 1995), 49.

5. Michael Sparer, "States in a Reformed Health System: Lessons from Nursing Home Policy," *Health Affairs* 12, no. 1 (Spring 1993): 7–20.

6. According to Rockefeller Institute estimates, for every increase in unemployment, 1.6 million more people are eligible for Medicaid or SCHIP. James W. Fossett and Courtney E. Burke, *Managing Medicaid: Take-Up, Is Medicaid Retrenching? State Budgets and Medicaid Enrollment in 2002* (Albany, N.Y.: Federalism Research Group, Nelson A. Rockefeller Institute of Government, February 2003).

7. In their 2010 budgets that began in July 2009, at least twenty-one states reduced eligibility or access to services, and twenty-two states curbed assistance to the low-income elderly and disabled populations. Many jurisdictions are targeting optional services, in particular adults' dental and vision care and various types of therapies. At least one-fourth of the states are cutting reimbursements to providers. Cash-strapped states, including Kansas and New Mexico, are now seeking ways to cut Medicaid drastically in their next budget cycle. Pauline Vu, "States Make Deep Cuts to Health," August 23, 2009, available at http://www.stateline.org/live/details/story?contentId=417167; Susan Haigh, "States Slash Health Care Programs in Budget Crisis," July 29, 2009, available at http://www.kirotv.com/health/20216250/detail/html.

The situation would have been worse, however, without the stimulus money, which allowed some states to maintain their Medicaid programs and to expand them in a few cases. For example, in 2007 the governor of Maryland, Martin O'Malley (D), signed the Working Families and Small Business Coverage Act, which extended Medicaid coverage to more than 100,000 working parents with annual incomes of 115 percent of the FPL or less, up from 30 percent in prior years. The expansion was supposed take place over several years, beginning with coverage of parents, followed by single, childless adults. After enrolling more than 30,000 more individuals, O'Malley indicated in early 2009 that he might not be able to fund any additional people because of recession-induced budget deficits. The Working Families and Small Business Coverage Act expansions resumed as a result of the stimulus money and intense pressure by local health care advocates. However, in its 2010 budget, the Maryland state legislature enacted other reductions, including lower reimbursements for hospital stays.

In other cases, South Carolina used the stimulus money to restore most scheduled benefit and eligibility reductions, including hospice care, adult dental and vision services, home health nurse visits, admission to an HIV/AIDs waiver program, and services to autistic children. Wisconsin proceeded with its planned extension of BadgerCare Plus to childless adults. Alaska and North Dakota also increased welfare medicine benefits because of the stimulus dollars. Vu, "States Make Deep Cuts to Health"; Haigh, "States Slash Health Care Programs in Budget Crisis."

Under the American Recovery and Reinvestment Act, states are not allowed to put Medicaid stimulus money in their "rainy day" reserve accounts or to lower beneficiary coverage that was in place as of July 2008.

8. Jonathan Oberlander, "Health Reform Interrupted: The Unraveling of the Oregon Health Plan," *Health Affairs* 26, no. 1 (January–February 2007): 96–105.

9. Immigrants account for a large percentage of the uninsured population, 10 million strong in 2006. Sixty percent of them live in four states (California, Texas,

New York, and Florida). See the Web site of the Tax Policy Center of the Urban Institute and the Brookings Institution, Washington, D.C., at http://www.taxpolicycenter.org; Paul Fronstin, "The Impact of Immigration on Health Insurance Coverage in the United States," *Employee Benefit Research Institute (EBRI) Notes* 26, no. 6 (June 2005): 2–8.

10. Rodney E. Hero, *Faces of Inequality: Social Diversity in American Politics* (New York: Oxford University Press, 1998); Rodney E. Hero and Caroline J. Tolbert, "A Racial/Ethnic Diversity Interpretation of Politics and Policy in the States of the U.S.," *American Journal of Political Science* 40 (1996): 851–871.

11. Clive S. Thomas and Ronald J. Hrebenar, "Interest Groups in the States," in Virginia Gray and Russell L. Hanson, eds., *Politics in the American States: A Comparative Analysis*, 8th ed., 100–129 (Washington, D.C.: Congressional Quarterly Press, 2004).

12. Of the 258 million Americans with at least some type of insurance, 159 million were covered through their employers (62 percent), 17 million paid individually out of pocket (6.5 percent), 38 million participated in Medicaid or SCHIP (14.5 percent), and 43.6 million were enrolled in Medicare Part A (16.9 percent). Out of the 305 million Americans overall, the percentages were 52, 5.6, 12.5, and 14.3, respectively.

13. Medicare, for example, has vital gaps in its benefits package, including for dental services, eyeglasses, hearing tests and hearing aids, at-home assistance for personal care and chores, routine annual checkups, LTC, and prescription drug coverage (in which there may be an interruption, or "donut hole"), along with high and, for many, onerous deductibles, copayments, and other out-of-pocket expenses. Nearly two-thirds of beneficiaries pay privately for expensive "medigap" insurance policies.

The "donut hole" most likely will gradually be cut in half because the pharmaceutical companies have offered to pay $8 billion annually, up to eight years, to subsidize Medicare beneficiaries who temporarily lose their funding. These industry-sponsored discounts, however, are only for brand-name drugs and may induce consumers to purchase these higher-priced medications, thus benefiting Big Pharma. The companies will gain in other ways, particularly if these subsidies forestall price controls over their products or prevent the importation of prescription drugs from Canada, as promised by the Obama administration.

14. By 2006, annual premiums for a family of four covered through an employer-sponsored plan averaged $11,500 ($4,200 for a single worker). National Coalition on Health Care, *Health Care Costs* (Washington, D.C.: National Coalition on Health Care, January 2007), available at http://www.nchc.org/facts/costs.shtml.

15. Expected to remain among the fastest-expanding component of the gross domestic product, total health care spending is projected to grow to 20 percent by 2015. U.S. Congress, House, Committee on Appropriations, Subcommittee on Military Construction, Veterans Affairs, and Related Agencies, *Health Care Spending: Public Payers Face Burden of Entitlement Program Growth, While All Payers Face Rising Prices and Increasing Use of Services*, hearings, statement of A. Bruce Steinwald, director of health care, GAO, 110th Cong., 1st sess., February 15, 2007.

16. Robert Kuttner, "Market-Based Failure—a Second Opinion on U.S. Health Care Costs," *New England Journal of Medicine* 358 (February 7, 2008), 549.

17. Simon Head, "They're Micromanaging Your Every Move," *New York Review of Books* 49, no. 13 (August 16, 2007): 42–44.

18. In 2006, federal costs for other health programs included: SCHIP ($6 billion), veteran's medical benefits ($29.9 billion), the Defense Health Program ($38 billion), and other endeavors ($74.4 billion), including the National Institutes of Health ($28.3 billion). Unlike in other industrialized nations, in the United States 54 percent of total health care spending in 2006 were derived from private sources ($723 billion, insurance; $256.5 billion, out of pocket; and $120.1 billion, other private funds). Meena Seshamani, Jeanne M. Lambrew, and Joseph Antos, *Financing the U.S. Health System: Issues and Options for Change* (Washington, D.C.: Leaders Project, June 2008), available at http://www.bipartisanpolicy.org.; Executive Office of the President, Council of Economic Advisors, *Economic Report of the President, FY 2009*, transmitted to Congress together with the annual report of the Council of Economic Advisors (Washington, D.C.: U.S. Government Printing Office, February 2008); U.S. Office of Management and Budget, *Budget of the United States, FY 2008: Analytical Perspectives* (Washington, D.C.: U.S. Government Printing Office, 2008).

19. Tax expenditures are defined under federal law as "revenue losses attributable to provisions of the Federal tax laws which allow a special exclusion, exemption, or deduction from gross income or which provides a special credit, a preferential tax rate, or a deferral of liability." The government views tax expenditures "as alternatives to other policy instruments, such as spending or regulatory programs." Federal health care tax expenditures for 2006 include: employer contributions for medical premiums and medical care ($125 billion); self-employed medical insurance premiums ($4 billion); Medical Savings Accounts and HSAs ($280 million); medical expenses, including LTC insurance premiums that exceed 7.5 percent of adjusted gross income ($3.8 billion); interest on hospital construction bonds ($3.4 billion); health-related charitable contributions ($4.2 billion); credits for orphan drug research ($230 million); and special Blue Cross Blue Shield withholdings ($620 million). U.S. Office of Management and Budget, *Budget of the United States, Fiscal Year 2008*, 285.

The national government loses an additional estimated $58 billion in exclusions because of payroll tax exclusions for employer-sponsored plans. Seshamani, Lambrew, and Antos, *Financing the U.S. Health System*.

20. Seshamani, Lambrew, and Antos, *Financing the U.S. Health System*.

21. OECD nations include Australia, Austria, Belgium, Canada, the Czech Republic, Denmark, Finland, France, Germany, Greece, Hungary, Iceland, Ireland, Italy, Japan, Korea, Luxembourg, Mexico, the Netherlands, New Zealand, Norway, Poland, Portugal, Slovak Republic, Spain, Sweden, Switzerland, Turkey, the United Kingdom, and the United States. Today, the share of gross domestic product that each devotes to health care averages 8.5 percent: Switzerland (10.9 percent) and Germany (10.7 percent) have the highest share, followed by Norway (10.1 percent), Canada (9.9 percent), France (9.5 percent), Sweden (9.3 percent), Australia (9.2 percent), Netherlands (9.1 percent), Italy (8.4 percent), Japan (8 percent), and the United Kingdom (7.8 percent). Henry J. Kaiser Family Foundation, Kaiser Commission on Medicaid and the Uninsured, *Snapshots: Health Care Spending in the U.S. and OECD Countries* (Menlo Park, Calif.: Henry J.

Family Foundation, Kaiser Commission on Medicaid and the Uninsured, January 2007), available at http://www.kff.org.; Carlos Angrisano, Diana Farrell, Bob Kocher, and Sara Parker, *Accounting for the Cost of Health Care in the U.S.* (Washington, D.C.: McKinsey Global Institute, January 2007); National Coalition on Health Care, *Health Care Costs.*

22. Since 2003, the number of families who are underinsured has risen by 60 percent. Meredith King Ledford, Jeanne Lambrew, David Rothman, and John Podesta, "Introduction," in Meredith King Ledford, Jeanne Lambrew, David Rothman, and John Podesta, eds., *The Health Care Delivery System: A Blueprint for Reform*, 1–30 (Washington, D.C.: Center for American Progress and the Institute on Medicine as a Profession, October 2008).

23. Some experts argue that the high U.S. costs and relatively low values stem primarily from supply-driven care, based on availability of practitioners and facilities rather than on need, and from waste, two factors that account for 30 percent or more of total health spending. Donald Berwick and Chiquita Brooks-LaSure, "Quality of Care," in Ledford et al., eds., *The Health Care Delivery System*, 50–79.

24. U.S. Bureau of the Census, *International Database* (Washington, D.C.: U.S. Government Printing Office, 2007).

25. Gerard Anderson and Hugh Waters, *Achieving Universal Coverage Through Medicare Part E*, Policy Brief no. 2007-10 (Washington, D.C.: Hamilton Project, Brookings Institution, July 2007).

26. The ranking was determined by authorities on health care for the World Health Organization. Joseph Shapiro, *Health Care Lessons from France*, National Public Radio, August 21, 2008, available at http://www.npr.org.

27. Berwick and Brooks-LaSure, "Quality of Care."

28. Two studies (one in 1997, the other in 2002) measured avoidable deaths of people younger than age seventy-five among OECD members. In the 2002 inquiry, the United States had the highest rates for both men and women, far higher than France, Japan, and Australia. In addition, the researchers found that the United States had started at a relatively high rate of premature, preventable deaths in 1997 and had experienced the smallest reductions over the five years. Among the conditions most responsive to treatment are bacterial infections, certain cancers, diabetes, cardiovascular and cerebrovascular disease, and complications of common surgical procedures. Ellen Nolte and C. Martin McKee, "Measuring the Health of Nations: Updating an Earlier Analysis," *Health Affairs* 27, no. 1 (January–February 2008): 58–71.

29. Laurene A. Graig, *Health of Nations: An International Perspective on U.S. Health Care Reform* (Washington, D.C.: Congressional Quarterly Press, 1999).

30. Jill Quadagno, *One Nation Uninsured: Why the U.S. Has No National Health Insurance* (Oxford, U.K.: Oxford University Press, 2005). Other factors include the lack of support by unions, which had negotiated their own insurance systems with employers; an insufficient popular drive, especially among middle-class Americans who enjoy relatively decent coverage; the nature of American institutional structures; and anti-statist values, generally fueled by conservative shouts of "socialism." Daniel Hirschfield, *The Last Reform: The Campaign for Compulsory Health Insurance in the United States*

from 1932–1943 (Cambridge, Mass.: Harvard University Press, 1970); Daniel Fox, *Health Policies, Health Politics: The British and American Experience, 1911–1965* (Princeton, N.J.: Princeton University Press, 1986); Paul Starr, *The Social Transformation of American Medicine* (New York: Basic Books, 1982); Jonathan Engel, *Doctors and Reformers: Discussion and Debate over Health Policy, 1925–1950* (Columbia: University of South Carolina Press, 2002).

31. During the 1950s and 1960s, the AMA held sway, along with its allies in the AHA and big business. In the 1970s and 1980s, the budding insurance industry emerged as the central powerhouse (the Health Insurance Association of America), aided by the National Federation of Independent Business in the following decade. Jill Quadagno points out that because of their incompetence, deceptive practices, and greed, many insurance firms experienced economic setbacks in the 1980s; nevertheless, through a jumble of financial schemes and ineffectual state government insurance departments, in the 1990s they came out as the "unchallenged master of the health care financing system" and crushed any proposals for national health insurance, including for LTC. Joined by pharmaceutical firms, large companies, small businesses, the Republican Party, the AHA, and sectors of the AMA, they lobbied vigorously against the Health Security Act of 1993. Hundreds of millions of dollars were spent to defeat it: "The campaign against health care reform was virtually indistinguishable from presidential campaigns in the scale of field organizing, sophistication, and public relations tactics." The "Harry and Louise" ads, in particular, utilized highly effective but false scare tactics, seriously undermining any backing for national health care: in 1993, 67 percent of the public approved of national health care, but by February 1994, support dropped to 44 percent. By the end of that year, President Clinton's scheme, along with various congressional and other proposals, again faded away. Quadagno, *One Nation Uninsured.*

32. In one poll, a nationwide sample of adults was asked, "How serious a problem is it for the United States that many Americans do not have health insurance?" Nearly everyone viewed the problem as either "very serious" (76 percent) or "somewhat serious" (16 percent). CBS News, *CBS News Poll*, methodology: conducted by CBS News, February 23–27, 2007, with a national sample of 706 adults, available at http://www.pollingreport.com/health3.htm.

In January 2006, another survey asked: "Do you think the federal government should guarantee health insurance for all Americans, or isn't this the responsibility of the federal government?" Nearly two-thirds of the participants selected a national guarantee (63 percent), whereas only one-third was opposed (30 percent); the rest were unsure (7 percent). CBS News and the *New York Times, CBS News/NY Times Poll*, methodology: conducted January 20–January 25, 2006, with a national adult sample of 1,229, available at http://www.pollingreport.com/health3.htm.

In an August 2009 survey, the following question was posed to a sample of adults nationwide: "Would you be willing to pay more—either in higher health insurance premiums or higher taxes—in order to increase the number of Americans who have health insurance, or not?" Although a majority of the respondents disagreed with the assertion (55 percent), fully 42 percent indicated that they would be willing to pay higher taxes to support greater health care coverage. Henry J. Kaiser Family Foundation, *Kaiser Health*

Tracking Poll, survey, methodology: conducted by Princeton Survey Research Associates International, August 4–11, 2009, with a national adult sample of 1,207 (Menlo Park, Calif.: Henry J. Kaiser Family Foundation, 2009), available at http://www.kff.org/kaiserpolls/healthpoll_question.cfm?qid=1745.

In a typical poll about the cost of health care, the 2006 CBS News and *New York Times* researchers asked: "How concerned are you about the health care costs you are facing now or will face in the future: a lot, some, or not at all?" Nearly two-thirds (61 percent) said "a lot," and 26 percent answered "some"; relatively few people selected "not much" (8 percent) or "not at all" (5 percent). CBS News and the *New York Times*, CBS *New/NY Times Poll*.

In another survey, when queried about the price of health care, nearly everyone was either "extremely concerned" (39 percent) or "very concerned (45 percent); only a few were "not very concerned" (12 percent) or "not at all concerned" (3 percent). Fox News, *Opinion Dynamics Poll*, survey, methodology: conducted by Opinion Dynamics, based on data provided by the Roper Center for Public Opinion Research, University of Connecticut, September 8–September 9, 2008, with a national registered voter sample of 900, available at http://www.pollingreport.com/health3.htm.

A late August 2009 CBS News survey asked, "Which of the following three statements comes closest to expressing your overall view of the health care system in the United States? On the whole, the health care system works pretty well and only minor changes are necessary to make it work better. OR, There are some good things in our health care system, but fundamental changes are needed. OR, Our health care system has so much wrong with it that we need to completely rebuild it." Fully 55 percent of the participants chose fundamental changes, and another 27 percent opted to completely rebuild it. Only 17 percent viewed the system as requiring minor changes. CBS News, *CBS News Poll*, survey, methodology: conducted August 27–31, 2009, with a national adult sample of 1,097, available at http://www.kff.org/kaiserpolls/healthpoll_question.cfm?qid=1746.

33. During George W. Bush's term in office, he added more than $4 trillion to the overall deficit, leaving a whopping $11.2 trillion for the incoming Obama administration. By the end of 2009, it reached $12.1 trillion.

34. For example, one Republican proposal, the Empowering Patients First Act, extends the income tax deduction on health premiums to people purchasing insurance in the nongroup market and offers a refundable low-income tax credit for premiums, based on household income. Among the measure's provisions related to Medicaid, the states would be required to cover 90 percent of individuals qualifying for SCHIP before they would be allowed to raise their eligibility levels, offer some form of premium assistance for employer-sponsored insurance as part of their welfare medicine plans, and provide incentives aimed at enlarging the number of health professionals working in community health centers. The Empowering Patients First Act also would encourage an expansion of the private market through vouchers and HSAs in lieu of Medicaid and SCHIP and reduce federal Medicaid and Medicare DSH payments to the states. Republican Study Committee for Access to Affordable, Quality Care for All Americans, *Empowering Patients First Act: Putting Patients First!* (July 2009), available at http://rsc .tomprice.house.gov/Solutions/EmpoweringPatientsFirstAct.htm.

35. In 2007, Representative John Conyers (D–MI) introduced the United States National Health Insurance Act (H.R. 676), a single-payer plan that would provide coverage for every citizen through a Medicare-like public insurance system. It uniquely would not allow any commercial insurance or for-profit providers—the latter would have to convert to nonprofit companies. Although the bill currently has ninety-three cosponsors, it has never been reported out of committee.

36. There are notable problems with an employer mandate per se. For example, if the employer assessment is set low, some firms would just simply pay, which would exacerbate the erosion of employer-based insurance. In any case, participating employers just pass through additional medical costs on to employees. According to researchers, rather than coming out of corporate profits, growing premium payments have been at the expense of wage increases over the past three decades. Ezekiel Emanuel and Victor Fuchs, "Who Really Pays for Health Care? The Myth of 'Shared Responsibility,'" *Journal of the American Medical Association* 299, no. 9 (March 5, 2008): 1057–1059.

37. Governors across party lines are determined to fight any enlargement of welfare medicine unless the federal government pays the entire bill. The Affordable Health Care for America Act would provide 100 percent federal funding, but an amendment by the House Energy and Commerce Committee limited full support only until 2014, at which time the match would drop to 90 percent. In the Senate proposal, the maximum eligibility level would rise to 130 percent of the FPL, with the federal government paying the full cost of the expansion for three years and an 82 percent to 95 percent match thereafter.

38. Ledford et al., "Introduction."

39. About 60 percent of all physicians are currently specialists. Ibid. The Affordable Health Care for America Act would increase physician fees for primary-care services to match Medicare rates but specialist rates would remain as is.

40. Over the past several decades, a few members of Congress have put forward various LTC proposals. One bill, introduced in 1987 by Claude Pepper (D–Fla.), would have provided comprehensive LTC insurance for disabled persons of all ages, financed under Medicare by removing the payroll tax cap. However, the proposal was never even brought to a vote. Quadagno, *One Nation Uninsured.*

President Clinton's 1994 Health Security Act included a community-based LTC benefit (with eligibility based on level of impairment rather than on age), paired with tax credits to support the expansion of private LTC insurance. Marty Lynch and Carroll L. Estes, "The Underdevelopment of Community-Based Services in the U.S. Long-Term Care System: A Structural Analysis," in Carroll L. Estes, ed., *Social Policy and Aging: A Critical Perspective*, 122–146 (Thousand Oaks, Calif.: Sage, 2001); Joshua M. Wiener, Jane Tilly, and Susan M. Goldevson, "Federal and State Initiatives to Jump Start the Market for Private Long-Term Care Insurance," *Elder Law Journal* 8 (2000): 57–102.

More recently, in 2007, Senators Edward Kennedy (D–Mass.) and Tom Harkin (D–Iowa), along with Representatives John Dingell (R–Mich.) and Frank Pallone (D–N.J.), introduced the Community Living Assistance Services and Supports Act of 2007. The legislation would have established some form of national LTC insurance, financed by a voluntary payroll tax of $30 per month. After five years of contributions, individuals who became functionally impaired would be entitled to a $50 to $100 per day cash benefit that would partially fund institutional services, at-home care, or other forms of assistance. As a senator, Barack Obama was a cosponsor of the legislation. However, the measure was never reported out of the House or Senate committees.

41. Despite Obama's mandate that any health care legislation enacted by Congress must be budget neutral, the current proposals conspicuously lack reliable cost controls for the ever-spiraling health care outlays. Nor do they impede the billions of dollars that are siphoned off by commercial interests for nonmedical expenses. In order to improve the likelihood of political success, the White House and Democrats are mostly highlighting measures that do not antagonize the health industries, including disease prevention, better management of chronic illnesses, greater use of electronic medical records, a redirection of federal spending on DSH programs, and the development of data to assess the effectiveness of specific medical interventions. Jonathan Oberlander, "Great Expectations: The Obama Administration and Health Care Reform," *Northeast Journal of Medicine* 360, no. 4 (January 22, 2009): 321–323.

What is more, none of the initiatives provides for dedicated tax revenues that would help safeguard any expansions against future onslaughts by antagonists. Much of the $630 billion president Obama has asked Congress to set aside over the next ten years, for example, is expected to come from squeezing money from the projected growth of Medicare and Medicaid costs, especially from a reduction in the excessive payments for Medicare Advantage plans and the curtailment of fraud, as well as from the expiration of Bush's tax cuts for the wealthy. In 2001, the Bush administration–sponsored tax cuts significantly reduced high-income rates (the top two brackets, paid by about 2 percent of the population, declined from 39.6 percent to 35 percent and from 36 percent to 33 percent, respectively). Revisions in the estate tax added another $7 million in annual exemptions for wealthy families. In 2002, the president and his supporters in Congress added tax breaks for new businesses and, in 2003, cutbacks in rates for dividends and capital gains. If not reauthorized, these breaks and cutbacks are scheduled to end in 2011. Although Obama's cost-cutting recommendations are commendable, including his intent to let the Bush tax cuts for affluent households expire, these measures certainly cannot be a substitute for ongoing, dedicated tax sources.

BIBLIOGRAPHY

Books, Journal Articles, and Nongovernmental Reports

AARP. *Caregiving in the U.S.* Washington, D.C.: AARP and National Alliance for Caregiving, April 2004.

ABT Associates. *Appropriateness of Nurse Staffing Ratios in Nursing Homes.* Phase 11 Final Report, prepared for the Centers for Medicare and Medicaid Services. Cambridge, Mass.: ABT Associates, 2002.

Aizer, Anna, Janet Currie, and Enrico Moretti. "Does Managed Care Hurt Health? Evidence from Medicaid Mothers." *Review of Economics and Statistics* 89, no. 3 (2007): 385–399.

Alker, Joan. *Premium Assistance Programs: How Are They Financed and Do States Save Money?* Menlo Park, Calif.: Henry J. Kaiser Family Foundation, Kaiser Commission on Medicaid and the Uninsured, October 2005. Available at http://www.kff.org.

——. *West Virginia's Medicaid Redesign: What Is the Impact on Children?* Washington, D.C.: Health Policy Institute, Center for Children and Families, Georgetown University, August 2008.

Alker, Joan and Jack Hoadley. *Waving Cautionary Flags: Initial Reactions from Doctors and Patients to Florida's Medicaid Changes.* Briefing no. 2, commissioned by the Jessie Ball du Pont Fund. Washington, D.C.: Health Policy Institute, Georgetown University, 2007.

Anderson, Gerard and Hugh Waters. *Achieving Universal Coverage Through Medicare Part E.* Policy Brief no. 2007-10. Washington, D.C.: Hamilton Project, Brookings Institution, July 2007.

Angel, Ronald J., Laura Lein, and Jane Henrici. *Poor Families in America's Health Care Crisis.* New York: Cambridge University Press, 2006.

Angell, Marcia. *The Truth About the Drug Companies: How They Deceive Us and What to Do About It.* New York: Random House, 2004.

Angrisano, Carlos, Diana Farrell, Bob Kocher, and Sara Parker. *Accounting for the Cost of Health Care in the U.S.* Washington, D.C.: McKinsey Global Institute, January 2007.

Artiga, Samantha and Molly O'Malley. *Increasing Premiums and Cost Sharing in Medicaid and SCHIP: Recent State Experiences.* Menlo Park, Calif.: Henry J. Kaiser Family Foundation, Kaiser Commission on Medicaid and the Uninsured, May 2005. Available at http://www.kff.org.

Artiga, Samantha. David Rousseau, and Barbara Lyons. "Can States Stretch the Medicaid Dollar Without Passing the Buck? Lessons from Utah." *Health Affairs* 25, no. 2 (March–April 2006): 532–540.

"Assisted Living: How Much Assistance Can You Really Count On?" *Consumer Reports* 70, no. 7 (July 2005): 28–33.

Austin, Bonnie. "Findings Brief: Managed Care Mandates Fall Short of Curbing California Medicaid Costs." *Academy Health* 8, no. 2 (March 2005): 1–3.

Berwick, Donald and Chiquita Brooks-LaSure. "Quality of Care." In Meredith King Ledford, Jeanne Lambrew, David Rothman, and John Podesta, eds., *The Health Care Delivery System: A Blueprint for Reform*, 50–79. Washington, D.C.: Center for American Progress and the Institute on Medicine as a Profession, October 2008.

Blewett, Lynn, Michael Davern, and Holly Rodin. "Covering Kids: Variation in Health Insurance Coverage Trends by State, 1996–2002." *Health Affairs* 23, no. 6 (November–December 2004): 170–180.

Booth, Meg and Burton Edelstein. *State Children's Health Insurance (SCHIP): A Decade of Optional Dental Coverage for Kids.* Washington, D.C.: Children's Dental Health Project, November 2006.

Boyd, Donald. *The Current State Fiscal Crisis and Its Aftermath.* Menlo Park, Calif.: Henry J. Kaiser Family Foundation, Kaiser Commission on Medicaid and the Uninsured. September 2003. Available at http://www.kff.org.

Boyd, Donald and Victoria Wachino. *Medicaid and the Uninsured: Is the State Fiscal Crisis Over? A 2004 State Budget Update.* Menlo Park, Calif.: Henry J. Kaiser Family Foundation, Kaiser Commission on Medicaid and the Uninsured, January 2004. Available at http://www.kff.org.

Bradley, Cathy J., Jan P. Clement, and Chunchieh Lin. "Absence of Cancer Diagnosis and Treatment in Elderly Medicaid-Insured Nursing Home Residents." *Journal of the National Cancer Institute* 100 (February 2008): 4–5.

Brown, E. Richard. *Rockefeller Medicine Men: Medicine and Capitalism in America.* Berkeley and Los Angeles: University of California Press, 1979.

Brown, Lawrence D. and Michael Sparer. "Poor Program's Progress: The Unanticipated Politics of Medicaid Policy." *Health Affairs* 22, no. 1 (January–February 2003): 31–44.

Bruen, Brian and John Holahan. *Shifting the Cost of Dual Eligibles: Implications for States and the Federal Government.* Menlo Park, Calif.: Henry J. Kaiser Family

Foundation, Kaiser Commission on Medicaid and the Uninsured, February 2002. Available at http://www.kff.org.

Burke, Courtney. *Medicaid Funding for Nonprofit Health Care Organizations.* Albany: Rockefeller Institute of Government, State University of New York, and the Aspen Institute, June 2007.

Burke, Sheila, Judith Feder, and Paul Van de Water. *Developing a Better Long-Term Care Policy: A Vision and Strategy for America's Future.* Report of the Long-Term Care Study Panel. Washington, D.C.: National Academy of Social Insurance, November 2005.

Burwell, Brian. "Medicaid Long-Term Care Expenditures in FY 2000." *Gerontologist* 41, no. 5 (October 2001): 687–691.

Cagey, Clarke. "Health Reform, Year Seven: Observations About Medicaid Managed Care." *Health Care Financing Review* (Fall 2000): 127–133.

Calvin, James E., Matthew Roe, and Anita Chen. "Insurance Coverage and Care of Patients with Non-St-Segment Elevation Acute Coronary Syndrome." *Annals of Internal Medicine* 145, no. 10 (November 21, 2006): 739–748.

Carlyle Group. *The Carlyle Group Completes Transaction with Manor Care; Temporary Restraining Order Dissolved in Michigan.* News Report no. 2007-154. Washington, D.C.: Carlyle Group, December 21, 2007. Available at http://www.carlyle.com.

Center for Responsive Politics (CRP). Web site at http://www.opensecrets.org.

Center on Budget and Policy Priorities. *The New Medicaid Citizenship Documentation: A Brief Overview.* Washington, D.C.: Center on Budget and Policy Priorities, September 28, 2006.

Cervone, Ed, Judy Ward, and Lisa Pohlmann. *Getting By: Maine Livable Wages in 2006.* Augusta: Maine Center for Economic Policy, June 26, 2007.

Chapman, Jeffrey. "California: The Enduring Crisis." In Steven Gold, ed., *The Fiscal Crisis of the States: Lessons for the Future,* 104–140. Washington. D.C.: Georgetown University Press, 1995.

Chase, E. T. "Crisis in Medicine: Impact of Medicare and Medicaid." *Commonweal* 85 (March 10, 1967): 650–652.

Chen, Amy, Nicole Schrag, Michael Halpern, Andrew Stewart, and Elizabeth Ward. "Health Insurance and Stage at Diagnosis of Laryngeal Cancer: Does Insurance Type Predict Stage at Diagnosis?" *Archives of Otolaryngology–Head and Neck Surgery* 133 (August 2007): 784–790.

Citizens for Long-Term Care. *Defining Common Ground: Long-Term Care Financing Reform in 2001.* Washington, D.C.: Citizens for Long-Term Care, February 2001.

——. *Long-Term Care Financing Reform: An Integral Part of Social Security and Medicare Reform.* Washington, D.C.: Citizens for Long-Term Care, June 2002.

Colorado Health Institute. *Colorado Medicaid.* Denver: Colorado Health Institute, March 2005.

Conte, Christopher. "Welfare, Work, and the States: Can States Move Welfare Recipients into Jobs?" *Congressional Quarterly Researcher* 6, no. 45 (December 6, 1996): 1057–1080.

Cook, Fay Lomax and Edith Barrett. *Support for the American Welfare State: The Views of Congress and the Public.* New York: Columbia University Press, 1992.

Coughlin, Teresa, Brian Bruen, and Jennifer King. "States' Use of Medicaid UPL and DSH Financing Mechanisms in 2001." *Health Affairs* 23, no. 2 (January–February 2003): 245–257.

Coughlin, Theresa A., Leighton Ku, and John Holahan. *Medicaid Since 1980: Costs, Coverage, and the Shifting Alliance Between the Federal Government and the States.* Washington, D.C.: Urban Institute, 1994.

Coughlin, Teresa A. and David Liska. *The Medicaid Disproportionate Share Hospital Payment Program: Background and Issues.* Series A, no. A-14. Washington, D.C.: Urban Institute, October 1997.

Coughlin, Teresa, Sharon Long, Timothy Triplett, Samantha Artiga, Barbara Lyons, R. Paul Duncan, and Allyson Hall. "Florida's Medicaid Reform? Informed Consumer Choice?" *Health Affairs* 27, no. 6 (November–December 2008): 523–532.

Crowley, Jeffrey. *Medicaid Long-Term Services Reforms in the Deficit Reduction Act.* Menlo Park, Calif.: Henry J. Kaiser Foundation, Kaiser Commission on Medicaid and the Uninsured, April 2006. Available at http://www.kff.org.

Cunningham, Peter. "Medicaid/SCHIP Cuts and Hospital Emergency Department Use." *Health Affairs* 25, no. 1 (January–February 2006): 237–247.

Cunningham, Peter J. and Jessica H. May. *Medicaid Patients Increasingly Concentrated Among Physicians.* Tracking Report no. 16. Washington, D.C.: Center for Studying Health System Change, August 2006.

Cunningham, Peter J. and Len M. Nichols. "The Effects of Medicaid Reimbursement on the Access to Care of Medicaid Enrollees: A Community Perspective." *Medical Care Research and Review* 62, no. 6 (December 2005): 676–696.

Davidoff, Amy, Bowen Garrett, and Alshadye Yemane. *Medicaid-Eligible Adults Who Are Not Enrolled.* Washington, D.C.: Urban Institute, 2005.

Dawson, Steven L. *Long-Term Care Financing and the Long-Term Care Workforce Crisis: Causes and Solutions.* Report prepared for Citizens for Long-Term Care. Washington, D.C.: ParaProfessional Health Care Institute, November 2002.

Day, Christine. *What Older Americans Think: Interest Groups and Aging Policy.* Princeton, N.J.: Princeton University Press, 1990.

Desai, Anand, Yushim Kim, and Robert Greenbaum. *Health Data Brief: Study Estimates Economic Effects of Medicaid Spending Changes in Ohio.* Columbus: Health Policy Institute of Ohio, December 15, 2005.

Ditsler, Elaine, Peter Fisher, and Colin Gordon. *On the Fringe: The Substandard Benefits of Workers in Part-Time, Temporary, and Contract Jobs.* Iowa City: Iowa Policy Project, December 2005.

Dorn, Stan and John Holahan. *Are We Heading Toward Socialized Medicine?* Washington, D.C.: Urban Institute, April 16, 2008.

Dorn, Stan, Barbara Markham Smith, and Bowen Garrett. *Medicaid Responsiveness, Health Coverage, and Economic Resilience: A Preliminary Analysis.* Washington, D.C.: Health Policy Institute of the Joint Center for Political and Economic Studies, September 27, 2005.

Dranove, David and William White. "Medicaid-Dependent Hospitals and Their Patients: How Have They Fared?" *Health Services Research* 33 (1998): 163–185.

Dubay, Lisa, Christina Moylan, and Thomas Oliver. "Advancing Toward Universal Coverage: Are States Able to Take the Lead?" *Journal of Health Care Law and Policy* 7, no. 1 (2004): 1–41.

Duggan, Mark. 2004. "Does Contracting Out Increase the Efficiency of Government Programs? Evidence from Medicaid HMOs." *Journal of Public Economics* 88, no. 12 (December 2004): 2549–2572.

Edelstein, Burton. *Miami-Dade County Prepaid Dental Health Plan Demonstration: Less Value for State Dollars.* Miami: Collins Center for Public Policy and Community Voices Miami, August 2006.

Eklund, Stephen A., James L. Pittman, and Sarah J. Clark. "Michigan Medicaid's Healthy Kids Dental Program: An Assessment of the First Twelve Months." *Journal of the American Dental Association* 134 (November 2003): 1509–1515.

Emanuel, Ezekiel and Victor Fuchs. "Who Really Pays for Health Care? The Myth of 'Shared Responsibility.'" *Journal of the American Medical Association* 299, no. 9 (March 5, 2008): 1057–1059.

Engel, Jonathan. *Doctors and Reformers: Discussion and Debate over Health Policy, 1925–1950.* Columbia: University of South Carolina Press, 2002.

——. *Poor People's Medicine: Medicaid and American Charity Care Since 1965.* Durham, N.C.: Duke University Press, 2006.

Epstein, Arnold. "Medicaid Managed Care and High Quality: Can We Have Both?" *Journal of the American Medical Association* 278, no. 19 (November 19, 1997): 1617–1621.

Families USA. *Cost-Sharing in Medicaid: It's Not About "Skin in the Game"—It's About Lives on the Line.* Fact sheet. Washington, D.C.: Families USA, September 2005.

"The Federal Health Care Programs: Medicare and Medicaid." *Congressional Digest* 53 (June 1974): 164–165.

Feinstein, Jonathan and Chich-Chin Ho. "Elderly Asset Management and Health." In William Gale, James Hines, and Joel Slemrod, eds., *Rethinking Estate and Gift Taxation*, 457–498. Washington, D.C.: Brookings Institution, 2001.

——. *Elderly Asset Management and Health: An Empirical Analysis.* Working Paper no. W7814. Cambridge, Mass.: National Bureau of Economic Research, July 2000.

Formation Capital, LLC. *What We Do: Our Investments and Portfolios.* Alpharetta, Ga.: Formation Capital, LLC, 2006. Available at http://www.formationcapital.com.

Fossett, James and Courtney E. Burke. *Is Medicaid Retrenching? State Budgets and Medicaid Enrollment in 2002.* Albany, N.Y.: Nelson A. Rockefeller Institute of Government, February 12, 2003.

——. *Managing Medicaid: Take-Up, Is Medicaid Retrenching? State Budgets and Medicaid Enrollment in 2002.* Albany, N.Y.: Federalism Research Group, Rockefeller Institute of Government, February 2003.

——. *Medicaid and State Budgets in FY 2004: Why Medicaid Is Hard to Cut.* Albany, N.Y.: Federalism Research Group, Nelson A. Rockefeller Institute of Government, July 2004.

Fossett, James and James Wuckoff. "Has Medicaid Growth Crowded Out State Education Spending?" *Journal of Health Politics, Policy, and Law* 21 (Fall 1996): 409–432.

Fox, Daniel. *Health Policies, Health Politics: The British and American Experience, 1911–1965*. Princeton, N.J.: Princeton University Press, 1986.

Fried, Marlene Gerber. *The Hyde Amendment: 30 Years of Violating Women's Rights*. Washington, D.C.: Center for American Progress, October 6, 2006.

Friedland, Robert B. *Caregivers and Long-Term Care Needs in the 21st Century: Will Public Policy Meet the Challenge?* Issue brief. Washington, D.C.: Health Policy Institute, Georgetown University, July 2004.

Friedman, Emily. "The Compromise and the Afterthought: Medicare and Medicaid After 30 Years." *Journal of the American Medical Association* 274, no. 3 (July 19, 1995): 278–282.

Fronstin, Paul. "The Impact of Immigration on Health Insurance Coverage in the United States." *Employee Benefit Research Institute (EBRI) Notes* 26, no. 6 (June 2005): 2–8.

Gehshan, S., P. Hauck, and J. Scales. *Increasing Dentists' Participation in Medicaid and SCHIP*. Issue brief. Washington, D.C.: Forum for State Health Policy Leadership, National Conference of State Legislatures, 2001.

Gibson, May Jo and Ari N. Houser. *Valuing the Invaluable: A New Look at the Economic Value of Family Caregiving*. Issue brief. Washington, D.C.: AARP Public Policy Institute, June 2007.

Gilens, Martin. *Why Americans Hate Welfare: Race, Media, and the Politics of Antipoverty Policy*. Chicago: University of Chicago Press, 1999.

Gitterman, Daniel, Joanne Spetz, and Matthew Fellowes. *The Other Side of the Ledger: Federal Health Spending in Metropolitan Economies*. Discussion paper. Washington, D.C.: Metropolitan Policy Program, Brookings Institution, September 2004.

Gleckman, Howard. *Medicaid and Long-Term Care: How Will Rising Costs Affect Services for an Aging Population?* Issue Brief no. 7-4. Boston: Center for Retirement Research, Boston College, April 2007.

Goddeeris, John and Yong Li. *Effects of Changes in Medicaid on Income and Jobs in Michigan: Estimates from the RIMS II Model*. East Lansing: Institute for Health Care Studies and Institute for Public Policy and Social Research, Michigan State University, February 2005.

Gold, Steven. "A Framework for Viewing State Policies." In Steven Gold, ed., *The Fiscal Crisis of the States: Lessons for the Future*, 43–51. Washington. D.C.: Georgetown University Press, 1995.

——. "Spending Policies and Revenue Trends Compared." In Steven Gold, ed., *The Fiscal Crisis of the States: Lessons for the Future*, 67–80. Washington. D.C.: Georgetown University Press, 1995.

——. "State Fiscal Problems and Policies." In Steven Gold, ed., *The Fiscal Crisis of the States: Lessons for the Future*, 6–40. Washington, D.C.: Georgetown University Press, 1995.

Goodman, John C., Michael Bond, Devon Herrich, Joe Barnett, and Pamela Villarreal. *Medicaid Empire: Why New York Spends So Much on Health Care for the Poor and How the System Can Be Reframed*. Policy Report no. 284. Dallas: National Center for Policy Analysis, March 20, 2006.

Gottschalk, Marie. *The Shadow Welfare State: Labor, Business, and the Politics of Health Care in the U.S.* Ithaca, N.Y.: Cornell University Press, 2000.

Grabowski, David. "The Cost Effectiveness of Noninstitutional Long-Term Care Services: Review and Synthesis of the Most Recent Evidence." *Medical Care Research and Review* 63, no. 1 (February 2006): 3–28.

Graig, Laurene A. *Health of Nations: An International Perspective on U.S. Health Care Reform.* Washington, D.C.: Congressional Quarterly Press, 1999.

Gray, Bradford H., ed. *For-Profit Enterprise in Health Care.* Washington, D.C.: Institute on Medicine and National Academy Press, 1986.

Gray, Virginia. "The Socioeconomic and Political Context of States." In Virginia Gray and Russell L. Hanson, eds., *Politics in the American States: A Comparative Analysis*, 8th ed., 1–30. Washington, D.C.: Congressional Quarterly Press, 2004.

Green, Robert. *A Look at the Details of the New Budget Legislation.* Washington, D.C.: Center on Budget and Policy Priorities, August 12, 1997.

Greene, Jessica. *State Approaches to Consumer Direction in Medicaid: Issue Brief.* Hamilton, N.J.: Center for Health Care Strategies, July 2007.

Grogan, Colleen M. "The Influence of Federal Mandates on State Medicaid and AFDC Decision-Making." *Publius: The Journal of Federalism* 29, no. 3 (1999): 1–30.

——. "Medicaid: Health Care for You and Me?" In James A. Morone, Theodore Litman, and Leonard S. Robins, eds. *Health Politics and Policy*, 4th ed., 329–354, Delmar Series in Health. Florence, Ky.: Delmar Centage Learning, 2008.

——. "Political-Economic Factors Influencing State Medicaid Policy." *Political Research Quarterly* 47, no. 3 (September 1994): 589–622.

Grogan, Colleen M. and Eric M. Patashnik. "Between Welfare Medicine and Mainstream Entitlement: Medicaid at the Political Crossroads." *Journal of Health Politics, Policy, and Law* 28, no. 1 (October 2003): 821–858.

——. "Universalism Within Targeting: Nursing Home Care, the Middle Class, and the Politics of the Medicaid Program." *Social Service Review* 77, no. 1 (March 2003): 51–71.

Grogan, Colleen M. and Vernon K. Smith. "From Charity Care to Medicaid: Governors, States, and the Transformation of American Health Care." In Ethan Sribnick, ed., *A More Perfect Union*, 353–401. Philadelphia: University of Pennsylvania Press, 2008.

Hacker, Jack. *The Divided Welfare State: The Battle over Public and Private Benefits in the U.S.* New York: Cambridge University Press, 2002.

Hackey, Robert B. *Rethinking Health Care Policy: The New Politics of State Regulation.* Washington, D.C.: Georgetown University Press, 1998.

Halpern, Michael, Elizabeth Ward, Alexandre Pauluck, Nicole Schrag, John Brian, and Amy Chen. "Association of Insurance Status and Ethnicity with Cancer Stage at Diagnosis for 12 Cancer Sites: A Retrospective Analysis." *The Lancet Oncology* 9, no. 3 (March 2008): 222–231.

Head, Simon. "They're Micromanaging Your Every Move." *New York Review of Books* 49, no. 13 (August 16, 2007): 42–44.

Health Policy Analysis Program. 2004. *The Costs of Enrollment Instability in Washington State's Medicaid Program.* Prepared for the Health Improvement Partnership of Spokane. Seattle: University of Washington, March 5, 2004.

Health Policy Institute, Georgetown University. *SCHIP Funding in the Year Ahead: Implications of the Medicare, Medicaid, and SCHIP Extension Act*. Washington, D.C.: Center for Children and Families, March 2008.

Health Policy Tracking Service. *What the States Said, Did, and Plan to Do*. Eagan, Minn.: Thompson Corporation, October 5, 2005.

Hendryx, Michael, Carol Irvin, James Mulligan, Sally Richardson, Johanna Beanet, and Margo Rosenbach. *Evaluation of Mountain Health Choices: Implementation Challenges and Recommendations*. Morgantown: Institute for Health Policy Research of West Virginia University and Mathematica Policy Research, March 2009.

Henry J. Kaiser Family Foundation, Kaiser Commission on Medicaid and the Uninsured. *The Affordable Choices Initiative: An Overview*. Menlo Park, Calif.: Henry J. Kaiser Family Foundation, Kaiser Commission on Medicaid and the Uninsured, May 2007. Available at http://www.kff.org.

——. *Health Insurance Coverage in America: A 2005 Data Update*. Menlo Park, Calif.: Henry J. Kaiser Family Foundation, Kaiser Commission on Medicaid and the Uninsured, November 2006. Available at http://www.kff.org.

——. *KyHealth Choices Medicaid Reform: Key Program Changes and Questions*. Fact sheet. Menlo Park, Calif.: Henry J. Kaiser Family Foundation, Kaiser Commission on Medicaid and the Uninsured, July 2006. Available at http://www.kff.org.

——. *Medicaid and SCHIP*. Menlo Park, Calif.: Henry J. Kaiser Family Foundation, Kaiser Commission on Medicaid and the Uninsured, 2007. Available at http://www.statehealthfacts.org.

——. *President's FY 2008 Budget and Medicaid*. Fact sheet. Menlo Park, Calif.: Henry J. Kaiser Family Foundation, Kaiser Commission on Medicaid and the Uninsured, April 2007. Available at http://www.kff.org.

——. *SCHIP Reauthorization: Key Questions in the Current Debate*. Issue brief. Menlo Park, Calif.: Henry J. Kaiser Family Foundation, Kaiser Commission on Medicaid and the Uninsured, July 2007. Available at http://www.kff.org.

——. *Snapshots: Health Care Spending in the U.S. and OECD Countries*. Menlo Park, Calif.: Henry J. Kaiser Family Foundation, Kaiser Commission on Medicaid and the Uninsured, January 2007. Available at http://www.kff.org.

——. "State Medicaid Developments." *Kaiser Daily Health Policy Report Highlights*, July 27, 2007. Available at http://www.kaisernetwork.org/daily-reports/rep-hpolicy.cfm.

——. *The Uninsured: A Primer. Key Facts About Americans Without Health Insurance*. Menlo Park, Calif.: Henry J. Kaiser Family Foundation, Kaiser Commission on Medicaid and the Uninsured, October 2006. Available at http://www.kff.org.

——. *An Update on Women's Health Policy, Medicaid's Role for Women*. Issue brief. Menlo Park, Calif.: Henry Kaiser Family Foundation, Kaiser Commission on Medicaid and the Uninsured, May 2006. Available at http://www.kff.org.

Hero, Rodney. *Faces of Inequality: Social Diversity in American Politics*. New York: Oxford University Press, 1998.

Hero, Rodney E. and Caroline J. Tolbert. "A Racial/Ethnic Diversity Interpretation of Politics and Policy in the States of the U.S." *American Journal of Political Science* 40 (1996): 851–871.

Hill, Ian and Amy Lutzky. 2003. *Is There a Hole in the Bucket? Understanding SCHIP Retention.* Occasional Paper no. 67. Washington, D.C.: Urban Institute, May 2003.

Hing, E. and C. W. Burt. *Characteristics of Office-Based Physicians and Their Practices: United States, 2003–2004.* Series 13, no. 164. Hyattsville, Md.: National Center for Health Statistics, 2007.

Hirschfield, Daniel. *The Last Reform: The Campaign for Compulsory Health Insurance in the United States from 1932–1943.* Cambridge, Mass.: Harvard University Press, 1970.

Houser, Ari N. *Nursing Homes.* Research report. Washington, D.C.: AARP Policy and Research, October 2007.

Iglehart, John K. "Medicaid." *New England Journal of Medicine* 328, no. 12 (March 25, 1993): 896–900.

Illinois Office of the Auditor General. *Performance Audit of the Department of Health-care and Family Services' Prompt Payment Act Compliance and Medicaid Payment Process.* Springfield: State of Illinois, May 2008.

Institute for Health Policy. *Comparing the Dirigo Choice Program Experience with Other State Initiatives Targeted to Small Business and Individuals.* Portland: Muskie School of Public Service, University of Southern Maine, August 2006.

Institute of Medicine. *Unequal Treatment: Confronting Racial and Ethnic Disparities in Health Care.* Washington, D.C.: National Academies Press, 2003.

Intrator, Orna, David Grabowski, Jacqueline Zinn, Mark Schleinitz, Zhanlian Feng, Susan Miller, and Vince Mor. "Hospitalization of Nursing Home Residents: The Effects of States' Medicaid Payment and Bed-Hold Policies." *Health Services Research* 42, no. 4 (August 2007): 1651–1671.

Irving Levin Associates, Inc. *Health Care M&A Info Service.* New Canaan, Conn.: Irving Levin Associates, 2004. Available at http://www.levinassociates.com/publicarions.

——. *Who's Making What in Health Care: The Irving Levin Health Care Executive Compensation Report.* New Canaan, Conn.: Irving Levin Associates, 2004. Available at http://www.levinassociates.com/publications/mam/mamprem/04execcomp.pdf.

Johnson, Richard, Desmond Toohey, and Joshua Wiener. *Meeting the Long-Term Care Needs of the Baby Boomers: How Changing Families Will Affect Paid Helpers and Institutions.* The Retirement Project. Discussion Paper 07-04. Washington, D.C.: Urban Institute, May 2007.

Kasper, Judith, Barbara Lyons, and Molly O'Malley. *Long-Term Care Services and Supports: The Future Role and Challenges for Medicaid.* Menlo Park, Calif.: Henry J. Kaiser Family Foundation, Kaiser Commission on Medicaid and the Uninsured, September 2007. Available at http://www.kff.org.

Kasper, Judith and Molly O'Malley. *KyHealth Choices Medicaid Reform: Key Program Changes and Questions.* Fact sheet. Menlo Park, Calif.: Henry J. Kaiser Family Foundation, July 2006. Available at http://www.kff.org.

——. *Nursing Home Transition Programs: Perspectives of State Medicaid Officials.* Menlo Park, Calif.: Henry J. Kaiser Family Foundation, Kaiser Commission on Medicaid and the Uninsured, April 2006. Available at http://www.kff.org.

Kassner, Enid. *Medicaid and Long-Term Care Services and Supports for Older People.* Washington, D.C.: AARP Public Policy Institute, April 2006.

——. *Medicaid Financial Eligibility for Older People: State Variations in Access to Home and Community-Based Waiver and Nursing Home Services.* Washington, D.C.: AARP Public Policy Institute, April 2002.

——. *Private Long-Term Care Insurance: The Medicaid Interaction.* Issue Brief no. 68. Washington, D.C.: AARP Public Policy Institute, 2004.

Kassner, Enid, Susan Reinhard, Wendy Fox-Grage, Ari N. Houser, Jean C. Accius, Barbara Coleman, and Dann Milne. *In Brief: A Balancing Act, State Long-Term Care Reform, Research Report.* Washington, D.C.: AARP Public Policy Institute, September 5, 2008.

Kemper, P., H. L. Komisar, and L. Alecixth. "Long-Term Care over an Uncertain Future: What Can Current Retirees Expect?" *Inquiry* 42, no. 4 (Winter 2005): 335–350.

Kilpatrick, Kerry, Joshua Olinick, Michael Luger, and Jun Koo. *The Economic Impact of Proposed Reductions in Medicaid Spending in North Carolina.* Chapel Hill: Institute for Public Health, University of North Carolina, April 11, 2002.

King, Martha P. *Medicaid: A Snapshot of State Legislatures.* Washington, D.C.: National Conference of State Legislatures, 2004.

Kitchener, Martin, Terrence Ng, Charlene Harrington, and Molly O'Malley. *Medicaid 1915 (c) Home and Community Based Service Programs: Data Update.* Menlo Park, Calif.: Henry J. Kaiser Family Foundation, Kaiser Commission on Medicaid and the Uninsured, December 2006. Available at http://www.kff.org.

Klein, Rachel, Kathleen Stoll, and Adele Bruce. *Medicaid: Good Medicine for State Economies, 2004 Update.* Washington, D.C.: Families USA Foundation, May 2004. Available at http://www.familiesusa.org.

Kleine, Robert. "Michigan: Rethinking Fiscal Priorities." In Steven Gold, ed., *The Fiscal Crisis of the States: Lessons for the Future,* 296–325. Washington, D.C.: Georgetown University Press, 1995.

Klemm, John D. "Medicaid Spending: A Brief History." *Health Care Financing Review* 22, no. 1 (Fall 2000): 105–112.

Komisar, Harriet and Lee S. Thompson. *National Spending for Long-Term Care.* Fact sheet. Long-Term Care Financing Project. Washington, D.C.: Health Policy Institute, Georgetown University, February 2007.

Kraus, Jeffrey. "Health Care in the Empire State." In Robert Pecorella and Jeffrey Stonecash, eds., *Governing New York State,* 5th ed., 331–431. Albany: State University of New York Press, 2006.

Kronebusch, Karl. "Children's Medicaid Enrollment: The Impacts of Mandates, Welfare Reform, and Policy Delinking." *Journal of Health Politics, Policy, and Law* 26, no. 6 (December 2001): 1223–1260.

——. "Medicaid for Children: Federal Mandates, Welfare Reform, and Policy Backsliding." *Health Affairs* 20, no. 1 (January–February 2001): 97–112.

Krugman, Paul and Robin Wells. "The Health Care Crisis and What to Do About it." *New York Review of Books* 50, no. 5 (March 23, 2006): 38–43.

Ku, Leighton and Donna Cohen Ross. *Staying Covered: The Importance of Retaining Health Insurance for Low-Income Families*. New York and Washington, D.C.: Commonwealth Fund and Center on Budget and Policy Priorities, December 2002.

Ku, Leighton and Teresa Coughlin. *The Use of Sliding Scale Premiums in Subsidized Insurance Programs*. Washington, D.C.: Urban Institute, March 1997.

Ku, Leighton, Andy Schneider, and Judy Solomon. *The Administration Again Proposes to Shift Federal Medicaid Costs to States*. Washington, D.C.: Center on Budget and Policy Priorities, February 14, 2007.

Kurtz, Howie. "Politicians Find Nursing Homes a Good Investment, and Vice Versa: Green from Gray." *New Republic* 178 (June 24, 1978): 17–19.

Kuttner, Robert. "Market-Based Failure—A Second Opinion on U.S. Health Care Costs." *New England Journal of Medicine* 358 (February 7, 2008): 549–551.

Lambrew, Jeanne M. "Making Medicaid a Block Grant Program: An Analysis of the Implication of Past Proposals." *Milbank Quarterly* 83, no. 1 (2005): 1–23.

Landon, Bruce, Eric Schneider, and Sharon-Lise Normand. "Quality of Care in Medicaid Managed Care and Commercial Plans." *Journal of the American Medical Association* 208, no. 14 (October 10, 2007): 1674–1681.

Ledford, Meredith King, Jeanne Lambrew, David Rothman, and John Podesta. "Introduction." In Meredith Ledford King, Jeanne Lambrew, David Rothman, and John Podesta, eds., *The Health Care Delivery System: A Blueprint for Reform*, 1–30. Washington, D.C.: Center for American Progress and the Institute on Medicine as a Profession, October 2008.

Lee, Jinkook, Hyungsoo Kim, and Sandra Tannenbaum. "Medicaid and Family Wealth Transfer." *Gerontologist* 46, no. 1 (February 2006): 6–13.

Lemov, Penelope. "Critical Condition." In John R. Baker, ed., *The Lanahan Readings in State and Local Government*, 457–464. Baltimore: Lanahan, 2001.

Lewis, Carol. "Connecticut: Surviving Tax Reform." In Steven Gold, ed., *The Fiscal Crisis of the States: Lessons for the Future*, 141–196. Washington. D.C.: Georgetown University Press, 1995.

Li, Lydia W. "Longitudinal Changes in the Amount of Informal Care Among Publicly Paid Home Care Recipients." *Gerontologist* 45 (2005): 474–485.

Long-Term Care Financing Project. *Medicaid's Spousal Impoverishment Protections*. Fact sheet. Washington, D.C.: Public Policy Institute, Georgetown University, 2007.

Luce, Thomas. "Minnesota: Innovation in an Era of Constraint." In Steven Gold, ed., *The Fiscal Crisis of the States: Lessons for the Future*, 326–363. Washington. D.C.: Georgetown University Press, 1995.

Lynch, Marty and Carroll L. Estes. "The Underdevelopment of Community-Based Services in the U.S. Long-Term Care System: A Structural Analysis." In Carroll L. Estes, ed., *Social Policy and Aging: A Critical Perspective*, 122–146. Thousand Oaks, Calif.: Sage, 2001.

MacManus, Susan. "Florida: Reinvention Derailed." In Steven Gold, ed., *The Fiscal Crisis of the States: Lessons for the Future*, 197–251. Washington. D.C.: Georgetown University Press, 1995.

Madrick, Jeff. "Health for Sale." *New York Review of Books* 50, no. 20 (December 18, 2003): 71–74.

Mann, Cindy. "The Flexibility Factor: Finding the Right Balance." *Health Affairs* 22, no. 1 (January–February 2003): 62–76.

Marmor, Theodore R. *The Politics of Medicare*. Chicago: Alpine, 1970.

Martin, Anne, Lekha Whittle, Katherine Levit, Greg Won, and Lindy Minman. "Health Care Spending During 1991–1998: A Fifty-State Review." Exhibit 4. *Health Affairs* 21, no. 4 (July–August 2002): 112–126.

Matherlee, Karen. *The Federal-State Struggle over Medicaid Matching Funds: An Update*. National Health Policy Forum Background Paper. Washington, D.C.: National Health Policy Forum, George Washington University, May 31, 2001.

McAuliffe, Thomas. *Supporting Private Insurance Through Premium Assistance*. Fact sheet. St. Louis: Missouri Foundation for Health, January 2007.

Mechanic, Robert E. *Medicaid's Disproportionate Share Hospital Program: Complex Structure, Critical Payments*. National Health Policy Forum Background Paper. Washington, D.C.: National Health Policy Forum, George Washington University, September 14, 2004.

Metlife Mature Market Institute. *The Metlife Caregiving Cost Study: Productivity Losses to U.S. Business*. Westport, Conn.: Metlife Mature Market Institute and National Alliance for Caregiving, July 2006.

Miller, Edward Alan. "Federal Oversight, State Policy Making, and the Courts: An Empirical Analysis of Nursing Facility Litigation Under the Boren Amendment." *Journal of Empirical Legal Studies* 3, no. 1 (March 2006): 145–173.

Miller, Edward Alan and William G. Weissert. "Strategies for Integrating Medicare and Medicaid Design Features and Incentives." *Medical Care Research and Review* 60, no. 2 (June 2003): 123–157.

Moore Business School. Division of Research. *Economic Impact of Medicaid on South Carolina*. Report developed for the South Carolina Department of Health and Human Services. Columbia: University of South Carolina, January 2002. Available at http://www.research.moore.sc.edu/research/studies/Medicaid/Medicaideconimpact.pdf.

Mouradian, Wendy, Elizabeth Wehr, and James Crall. "Disparities in Children's Oral Health and Access to Dental Care." *Journal of the American Medical Association* 284, no. 20 (November 22–29, 2000): 2625–2631.

National Citizens' Coalition for Nursing Home Reform. *The Faces of Neglect: Behind the Closed Doors of Nursing Homes*. Washington, D.C.: National Citizens' Coalition for Nursing Home Reform, April 28, 2006.

National Coalition on Health Care. 2007. *Health Care Costs*. Washington, D.C.: National Coalition on Health Care, January 2007. Available at http://www.nchc.org/facts/costs.shtml.

National Conference of State Legislators. *Better Jobs, Better Care: Retaining Long-Term Care Workers*. Washington, D.C.: National Conference of State Legislators, June 2007.

——. *State Programs to Subsidize or Reduce the Cost of Health Insurance for Small Businesses and Individuals*. Washington, D.C.: National Conference of State Legislators, May 2007.

Nolte, Ellen and C. Martin McKee. "Measuring the Health of Nations: Updating an Earlier Analysis." *Health Affairs* 27, no. 1 (January–February 2008): 58–71.

Oberlander, Jonathan. "Great Expectations: The Obama Administration and Health Care Reform." *Northeast Journal of Medicine* 360, no. 4 (January 22, 2009): 321–323.

——. "Health Reform Interrupted: The Unraveling of the Oregon Health Plan." *Health Affairs* 26, no. 1 (January–February 2007): 96–105.

——. *The Political Life of Medicare.* Chicago: University of Chicago Press, 2003.

O'Brien, Ellen. *Long-Term Care: Understanding Medicaid's Role for the Elderly and Disabled.* Menlo Park, Calif.: Henry J. Kaiser Family Foundation, Kaiser Commission on Medicaid and the Uninsured, November 2005. Available at http://www.kff.org.

——. *Medicaid's Coverage of Nursing Home Costs: Asset Shelter for the Wealthy or Essential Safety Net?* Issue brief. Long-Term Care Financing Project. Washington, D.C.: Health Policy Institute, Georgetown University, May 2005.

——. *Options to Broaden Role of Medicare in Long-Term Care.* Long-Term Care Financing Project. Washington, D.C.: Health Policy Institute, Georgetown University, February 2007.

Oliver, Thomas R. "The Collision of Economics and Politics in Medicaid Managed Care: Reflections on the Course of Reform in Maryland." *Milbank Quarterly* 76, no. 1 (1998): 59–101.

Olson, Laura Katz. *The Not-So-Golden Years: Caregiving, the Frail Elderly, and the Long-Term Care Establishment.* Lanham, Md.: Rowman and Littlefield, 2003.

Oregon Center for Public Policy (OCPP). *Considerations in Medicaid Cost Sharing Policy: Fact Sheet.* Silverton: OCPP, September 16, 2005.

——. *Oregon Study Finds That Federal Medicaid Rules Aimed at Illegal Immigrants Harm Vulnerable Citizens.* Silverton: OCPP, May 11, 2007.

O'Shea, John S. *More Medicaid Means Less Quality Health Care.* Center for Health Policy Studies, Web Memo no. 1402. Washington, D.C.: Heritage Foundation, March 21, 2007. Available at http://www.heritage.org/research/healthcare/wm1402.cfm.

Park, Edwin, Leighton Ku, and Matthew Broaddus. *Congress Could Extend the Availability of Expanding SCHIP Funds and Undo the Reduction in SCHIP Funding Levels to Avert a Large Enrollment Decline.* Washington, D.C.: Center on Budget and Policy Priorities, November 7, 2002.

Patel, Kant and Mark E. Rushefsky. *Health Care in America: Separate and Unequal.* Armonk, N.Y.: M. E. Sharpe, 2008.

PayScale, Inc. *PayScale Reports.* Seattle: PayScale, Inc., 2007. Available at http://www.payscale.com.

Perry, Michael, Susan Kannel, R. Burciaga, and Christina Chang. *Medicaid and Children: Overcoming Barriers to Enrollment.* Menlo Park, Calif.: Henry J. Kaiser Family Foundation, Kaiser Commission on Medicaid and the Uninsured, January 2000. Available at http://www.kff.org.

Pringle, Evelyn. "Beverly Enterprises—Poster Child of Fraud and Neglect in Nursing Home Industry." Legal Marketing Ltd., June 1, 2006. Available at http://www.lawyersandsettlements.com/articles/00210/Beverly_Enterprises_Fraud.html.

——. "Nursing Home Industry—Breeding Ground for Whistleblowers." Legal Marketing Ltd., June 2, 2006. Available at http://www.lawyersandsettlements.com/articles/00210/Beverly_Enterprises_Fraud.html.

Public Citizen Health Research Group (PCHRG). *Poor Medicine for Poor People.* Washington, D.C.: PCHRG, 1987.

Public Policy Institute of New York. *Just the Facts: Key Economic and Social Indicators for New York State: 2006 Medicaid Spending on Home Health Care and Personal Care.* Albany: Public Policy Institute of New York, 2006. Available at http://www.ppinys.org.

——. *Just the Facts: Key Economic and Social Indicators for New York State: 2006 Medicaid Spending on Long-Term Care Facilities.* Albany: Public Policy Institute of New York, 2006. Available at http://www.ppinys.org.

Quadagno, Jill. *One Nation Uninsured: Why the U.S. Has No National Health Insurance.* Oxford, U.K.: Oxford University Press, 2005.

Rahm, Dianne. *United States Public Policy: A Budgetary Approach.* Belmont, Calif.: Wadsworth, 2004.

Ramirez, Annette B. and Sidney M. Wolfe. *Unsettling Scores: A Ranking of State Medicaid Programs.* Public Citizen Health Research Group (PCHRG) Publication no. 1807. Washington, D.C.: PCHRG, April 2007.

Redmond, Pat, Judith Solomon, and Mark Lin. *Can Incentives for Healthy Behavior Improve Health and Hold Down Medicaid Costs?* Washington, D.C.: Center on Budget and Policy Priorities, June 1, 2007.

Reester, Heidi, Raad Missmar, and Anne Tumlinson. *Recent Growth in Medicaid and Community-Based Service Waivers.* Menlo Park, Calif.: Henry J. Kaiser Family Foundation, Kaiser Commission on Medicaid and the Uninsured, April 2004. Available at http://www.kff.org.

Rosenthal, Alan. *The Third House: Lobbyists and Lobbying in the States.* 2d ed. Washington, D.C.: Congressional Quarterly Press, 2001.

Ross, Donna. *New Medicaid Citizenship Documentation Requirement Is Taking a Toll: States Report Enrollment Is Down and Administrative Costs Are Up.* Washington, D.C.: Center on Budget and Policy Priorities, March 13, 2007.

Ross, Donna and Laura Cox. *In a Time of Growing Need State Choices Influence Health Coverage Access for Children and Families: A 50-State Update on Eligibility Rules, Enrollment and Renewal Procedures, and Cost-Sharing Practices in Medicaid and SCHIP for Children and Families.* Menlo Park, Calif.: Henry J. Kaiser Family Foundation, Kaiser Commission on Medicaid and the Uninsured, October 2005. Available at http://www.kff.org.

Ross, Donna, Laura Cox, and Caryn Marks. *Resuming the Path to Health Coverage for Children and Parents: A 50 State Update on Eligibility Rules, Enrollment and Renewal Procedures, and Cost-Sharing Practices in Medicaid and SCHIP in 2006.* Menlo Park, Calif.: Henry J. Kaiser Family Foundation, Kaiser Commission on Medicaid and the Uninsured, January 2007. Available at http://www.kff.org.

Rushefsky, Mark E. and Kant Patel. *Politics, Power, and Policy Making: The Case of Health Care Reform in the 1990s.* Armonk, N.Y.: M. E. Sharpe, 1998.

Ryan, Jennifer M. *1115 Ways to Waive Medicaid and SCHIP Rules.* Issue Brief no. 777. Washington, D.C.: National Health Policy Forum, George Washington University, June 13, 2002.

Schneider, Amy and David Rousseau. *Upper Payment Limits: Reality and Illusions in Medicaid Financing.* Menlo Park, Calif.: Henry J. Kaiser Family Foundation, Kaiser Commission on Medicaid and the Uninsured, February 2002. Available at http://www.kff.org.

Schneider, Andy, Leighton Ku, and Judith Solomon. *The Administration's Medicaid Proposals Would Shift Federal Costs to States.* Washington, D.C.: Center on Budget and Policy Priorities, February 14, 2006.

Schneider, Don. *CDHP State Summary: Indiana Dental Medicaid.* Washington, D.C.: Children's Dental Health Project, American Dental Association, 2005.

——. *CDHP State Summary: South Carolina Dental Medicaid.* Washington, D.C.: Children's Dental Health Project, American Dental Association, 2005.

——. *CDHP State Summary: Tennessee's TennCare Program.* Washington, D.C.: Children's Dental Health Project, American Dental Association, 2005.

——. *CDHP State Summary: Virginia Dental Medicaid.* Washington, D.C.: Children's Dental Health Project, American Dental Association, 2005.

——. *State Innovations to Improve Access to Oral Health Care for Low-Income Children: A Compendium Update.* Washington, D.C.: American Dental Association, 2005.

Schnelle, J. F., S. F. Simmons, C. Harrington, M. Cadogan, E. Garcia, and B. M. Bates-Jensen. "Relationship of Nursing Home Staffing to Quality of Care." *Health Services Research* 39, no. 2 (2004): 225–250.

Schwartz, Sonya and John McInerney. *Examining a Major Policy Shift: New Federal Limits on Medicaid Coverage for Children.* Portland, Me.: National Academy for State Health Policy, April 2008.

Seligman, Philip M. *Healthcare: Managed Care.* Standard and Poor's Industry Survey. New York: Standard and Poor's, March 31, 2005.

Seshamani, Meena, Jeanne M. Lambrew, and Joseph Antos. *Financing the U.S. Health System: Issues and Options for Change.* Washington, D.C.: Leaders Project, June 2008. Available at http://www.bipartisanpolicy.org.

Shapiro, Joseph. 2008. *Health Care Lessons from France.* National Public Radio, August 21, 2008. Available at http://www.npr.org.

Shern, David L., Kristine Jones, Huey Jen Chen, Neil Jordon, Josefa Ramoni-Perazzi, and Roger Boothroyd. "Medicaid Managed Care and the Distribution of Societal Costs for Persons with Severe Mental Illness." *American Journal of Psychiatry* 165, no. 2 (2008): 254–260.

Shin, Peter, Brad Finnegan, Lauren Hughes, and Sara Rosenbaum. *An Initial Assessment of the Effects of Medicaid Documentation on Health Centers and Their Patients.* Washington, D.C.: School of Public Health and Health Services, George Washington University, May 7, 2007.

Silberman, Pam, Laura Brogan, and Charity Moore. *Premium Assistance Programs for Low Income Families: How Well Does It Work in Rural Areas?* Chapel Hill: Cecil G. Sheps Center for Health Services Research, University of North Carolina, January 24, 2006.

Sills, Sara and Sue Frietsche. *Removing Barriers to Medicaid-Funded Abortion*. New York and Philadelphia: Women's Law Project and Institute for Productive Health Access, 2004.

Smith, David G. *Entitlement Politics: Medicare and Medicaid 1995–2001*. New York: De Gruyter, 2002.

Smith, David G. and Judith D. Moore. *Medicaid Politics and Policy: 1965–2007*. New Brunswick, N.J.: Transaction, 2008.

Smith, Kristin and Reagan Baughman. "Caring for America's Aging Population: A Profile of the Direct-Care Workforce." *Monthly Labor Review* (September 2007): 20–26.

Sommers, Anna and Mindy Cohen. *Medicaid's Long-Term Care Beneficiaries: An Analysis of Spending Patterns*. Menlo Park, Calif.: Henry J. Kaiser Family Foundation, Kaiser Commission on Medicaid and the Uninsured, November 2006. Available at http://www.kff.org.

Sommers, Benjamin D. "Why Millions of Children Eligible for Medicaid and SCHIP Are Uninsured: Poor Retention Versus Poor Take-Up." *Health Affairs* 26, no. 5 (September–October 2007): 560–567. Available at http://www.healthaffairs.org.

Spano, Andrew. *Medicaid: The Best Business Subsidies Your Tax Dollars Can Buy*. New York: Westchester County, New York, November 1, 2006.

Sparer, Michael S. *Medicaid and the Limits of State Health Reform*. Philadelphia: Temple University Press, 1996.

——. "States in a Reformed Health System: Lessons from Nursing Home Policy." *Health Affairs* 12, no. 1 (Spring 1993): 7–20.

Standard and Poor's. *United Health Group, Inc.: Corporate Actions*. New York: Standard and Poor's, April 28, 2005.

Starr, Paul. *The Social Transformation of American Medicine*. New York: Basic Books, 1982.

Steinbrook, Robert. "Health Care Reform in Massachusetts—Expanding Coverage, Escalating Costs." *New England Journal of Medicine* 358, no. 26 (June 26, 2008): 2757–2760.

Stevens, Robert and Rosemary Stevens. *Welfare Medicine in America: A Case Study of Medicaid*. New Brunswick, N.J.: Transaction, 2003.

Stuart, Bruce C. "Who Gains from Public Health Services?" *Annals of the American Academy of Political and Social Sciences* 399 (January 1972): 145–150.

Summer, Laura. *Choices and Consequences: The Availability of Community-Based Long-Term Care Services to the Low-Income Population*. Long-Term Care Financing Project. Washington, D.C.: Health Policy Institute, George Washington University, May 2003.

——. *Community-Based Long-Term Services Financed by Medicaid: Managing Resources to Provide Appropriate Medicaid Services*. Issue brief. Long-Term Care Financing Project. Washington, D.C.: Health Policy Institute, George Washington University, June 2007.

Taxpayers Against Fraud. *FY 2005 False Claims Act Settlements*. Washington, D.C.: False Claims Act Legal Center, 2006. Available at http://www.taf.org.

———. *FY 2005 False Claims Act Settlements and Judgments.* Washington, D.C.: False Claims Act Legal Center, 2006. Available at: http://www.taf.org.

———. *FY 2006 False Claims Act Settlements (as of September 30, 2006).* Washington, D.C.: False Claims Act Legal Center, 2006. Available at http://www.taf.org.

———. *Total FY 2004 False Claims Act Fraud Settlements and Judgments.* Washington, D.C.: False Claims Act Legal Center, 2006. Available at http://www.taf.org.

———. *What Is the False Claims Act and Why Is It So Important?* Washington, D.C.: False Claims Act Legal Center, 2006. Available at http://www.taf.org.

Taylor, Donald, Frank Sloan, and Edward Norton. "Formation of Trusts and Spend Down to Medicaid." *Journal of Gerontology: Social Sciences* 54B, no. 4 (1999): S194–S201.

Thomas, Clive S. and Ronald J. Hrebenar. "Interest Groups in the States." In Virginia Gray and Russell L. Hanson, eds., *Politics in the American States: A Comparative Analysis*, 8th ed., 100–129. Washington, D.C.: Congressional Quarterly Press, 2004.

Thompson, Joseph, Kevin Ryan, Sathiska Pinidiya, and James Bost. "Quality of Care for Children in Commercial and Medicaid Managed Care." *Journal of the American Medical Association* 290, no. 4 (September 17, 2004): 1486–1493.

Trived, Amal N., Alan Zaslausky, Eric Schneider, and John Ayanian. "Relationship Between Quality of Care and Racial Disparities in Medicare Health Plans." *Journal of the American Medical Association* 296, no. 16 (October 25, 2006): 1998–2003.

Wachino, Victoria. *The New Medicaid Integrity Program: Issues and Challenges in Ensuring Program Integrity in Medicaid.* Menlo Park, Calif.: Henry J. Kaiser Family Foundation, Kaiser Commission on Medicaid and the Uninsured, June 2007. Available at http://www.kff.org.

Wachino, Victoria, Leighton Ku, Edwin Park, and Judith Solomon. *An Analysis of the National Governors Association's Proposals for Short-Run Medicaid Reform.* Washington, D.C.: Center on Budget and Policy Priorities, October 14, 2005.

Wachino, Victoria and Robin Rudowitz. *Key Issues and Opportunities: Implementing the New Medicaid Integrity Program.* Menlo Park, Calif.: Henry J. Kaiser Family Foundation, Kaiser Commission on Medicaid and the Uninsured, July 2006. Available at http://www.kff.org.

Waidmann, Timothy and Korbin Liu. 2006. *Asset Transfer and Nursing Home Use: Empirical Evidence and Policy Significance.* Menlo Park, Calif.: Henry J. Kaiser Family Foundation, Kaiser Commission on Medicaid and the Uninsured, April 2006. Available at http://www.kff.org.

Wallin, Bruce. "Massachusetts: Downsizing State Government." In Steven Gold, ed., *The Fiscal Crisis of the States: Lessons for the Future*, 252–295. Washington, D.C.: Georgetown University Press, 1995.

Weil, Alan. "There's Something About Medicaid." *Health Affairs* 22, no. 1 (January–February 2003): 13–23.

Wiener, Joshua M., Jane Tilly, and Susan M. Goldevson. "Federal and State Initiatives to Jump Start the Market for Private Long-Term Care Insurance." *Elder Law Journal* 8 (2000): 57–102.

Wool, Dr. Albert and colleagues. *Method of Payment for Delivery.* Report. Montgomery: Center for Health Statistics, Alabama Department of Health, 2005.

Wright, Bill, Matthew Carlson, and Jeanene Smith. *Impact of Changes to Premiums, Cost-Sharing, and Benefits on Adult Medicaid Beneficiaries: Results from an Ongoing Study of the Oregon Health Plan.* New York: Commonwealth Fund, July 29, 2005.

Younis, Mustafa. "Comparative Study of Urban and Small Rural Hospitals' Financial and Economic Performance." *Journal of Rural Nursing and Health Care Online* 3, no. 1 (spring 2003). Available at http://www.rno.org/journal/index.php/online-journal/article/viewFile/110/106.

Zedlewski, Sheila and Linda Giannarelli. 1997. *Diversity Among State Welfare Programs: Implications for Reform.* Assessing New Federalism: Issues and Options for States no. A-1. Washington, D.C.: Urban Institute, January 1, 1997. Available at http://www.urban.org/url.cfm.

Zingmond, David, Kathleen Wilber, Catherine Maclean, and Neil Wenger. "Measuring the Quality of Care Provided to Community Dwelling Vulnerable Elders Dually Enrolled in Medicare and Medicaid." *Medical Care* 45, no. 10 (October 2007): 931–938.

Newspaper and Magazine Articles

"38 States Warned on Nursing Homes." *New York Times*, December 1, 1971.

Angier, Natalie. "Study Finds Uninsured Receive Less Hospital Care." *New York Times*, September 12, 1990.

Asbury, Edith. 1976. "Bergman Became Involved in Nursing Homes in '39." *New York Times*, March 12, 1976.

"Assisted Living Horrors," editorial (series on assisted-living facilities). *Washington Post*, May 28, 2004.

Bacon, Donald C. "Medicaid Abuse: Even Worse Than Feared." *U.S. News & World Report* 86 (June 4, 1979): 43–45.

Benko, Laura. "Medicaid Woes, Aging Population Have Insurers Thinking Long-Term." *Crain's Detroit Business*, September 19, 2005.

Bernstein, Nina. "Medicaid Rolls Have Declined in Last Three Years." *New York Times*, August 17, 1998.

"Billions in Medicaid Ripoffs: Special Report." *U.S. News & World Report* 80 (March 22, 1976): 18–20.

Boulton, Guy. "Caregiver Puts Out Medicaid Recipients: Milwaukee Firm Runs Assisted-Living Centers." *Milwaukee Journal Sentinel*, May 19, 2007.

"Breaking the Bank." *Science News* 95 (May 1969): 497–498.

Breen, Tom. "Lawmakers: Co. Controls West Virginia Medicaid." *Business Week*, April 18, 2007. Available at http://www.BusinessWeek.com.

"Broad Access and Many Services." *New York Times*, April 14, 1991.

Burger, Robert E. Census. "Medicare and Medicaid: Commercializing the Aged." *The Nation* (May 11, 1970): 557–560.

Burrows, Dan. "Small Contractor Finds Niche Fixing Medicaid Errors." Smartmoney.com, March 2, 2007. Available at http://www.smartmoney.com.

"Care Plan Begun in Pennsylvania; Payments for Aged Patients Based on Kerr-Mills Law, Other Costs Included." *New York Times*, special edition, March 18, 1962.

Carreyrou, John. "Nonprofit Hospitals, Once for the Poor, Strike It Rich." *Wall Street Journal*, April 4, 2008.

Cauchon, Dennis. "Medicaid Spending Jumps Sharply." *USA Today*, October 8, 2007.

"Census Finds U.S. Benefits Reach 1 out of 3 Families." *New York Times*, March 13, 1981.

Chen, Edwin E. "Model for Fraud: Michigan's Medicaid Rip-Off." *The Nation* (February 26, 1977): 242–244.

"Children's Hospitals: A Healthy Future?" *New Scientific Magazine*, May 14, 2005.

Choi, Candice. "Health Department Seeks to Trim Medicaid Waste in Nursing Homes." *New York Times*, September 21, 2005.

Clymer, Adam. "Governors Try to Find Unity on Medicaid." *New York Times*, July 31, 1995.

"Coalition Recommends an Expansion of Medicaid." *New York Times*, February 17, 1989.

"Congress Catches Up with Medicaid Ripoff." *U.S. News & World Report* 81 (September 13, 1976): 55.

Cook, Joan. "Bergen Inquiry Begun by New Jersey." *New York Times*, January 4, 1975.

——. "Ruling by State Sought to Require Medicaid Care in Nursing Home." *New York Times*, February 10, 1977.

——. "Twenty-one Medicaid Patients in Nursing Home in a Holiday Reprieve on Transfer." *New York Times*, November 26, 1975.

"Cuts in Medicaid Prompt Anxiety over Health Care." *New York Times*, August 1, 1976.

De Courcy Hinds, Michael. "Suit Charges Pennsylvania Failed to Meet Medicaid Plan for Youth." *New York Times*, November 14, 1991.

Dorgan, Lauren R. "HHS Wants Low Bidder for Medicaid—Women, Children Could Travel for Care." *Concord Monitor*, June 30, 2007.

Doyle, Michael. "Farm Workers' Study in Limbo." *Kansas City Star*, November 23, 2006.

Duhigg, Charles. "At Many Homes, More Profit and Less Nursing." *New York Times*, September 23, 2007.

Eizenstat, Stuart E. "How to Make Medicaid Popular." *New York Times*, September 4, 1991.

"Executives' Pay Nearly Doubles at Hospitals, Task Force Finds." *Newsday Online*, January 27, 2008. Available at http://www.Newsday.com/news.

Fallis, David S. "Virginia Rarely Prosecutes Cases of Neglect, Abuse: Lack of Expertise, Victims' Disabilities Hamper Investigations" (series on assisted-living facilities). *Washington Post*, May 26, 2004.

——. "Weak Laws Let Deficient Facilities Stay Open: Demand for Assisted Living Care Pushes Virginia to Emphasize Improvement, Not Punishment" (series on assisted-living facilities). *Washington Post*, May 26, 2004.

Fields, Reginald. "Hospitals Assail Medicaid Plan, Jobs Threatened, Association Says." *Cleveland Plain Dealer*, September 9, 2005.

"Find Common Ground to Cure Medicaid's Ills," editorial. *Cleveland News-Herald*, December 27, 2006. Available at http://www. News-Herald.com.

Fisher, Ian. "Plan to Spread Pain of Medicaid Cuts Draws Wide but Tempered Criticism." *New York Times*, January 29, 1995.

"Free Medicine out of Hand in the U.S." *U.S. News & World Report* 64 (April 8, 1968): 86–88.

Freudenheim, Milt. "Serving the Poor Private Insurance." *New York Times*, October 9, 1990.

Galewitz, Phil. "Medicaid Patients Find Care Limited." *Palm Beach Post*, November 26, 2006.

Gelinas, Nicole. "Spitzer's Radical Medicaid Surgery? It's Really a Placebo, but You Wouldn't Know It from Union Screaming." *City Journal* 17, no. 1 (Winter 2007). Available at http://www.city-journal.org/html/eon2007-02-08ng.html.

Graber, Trish G. "Were More Medicaid Patients Evicted?" *Bridgetown News* (N.J.), June 12, 2008.

Gray, Jerry. "Governors Seek to Shed Burdens of Medicaid." *New York Times*, August 4, 1992.

Greaney, T. J. "Medicaid Funding Likely to Avoid Ax." *Missourian*, December 9, 2006.

"The Great Medicaid Scandal." *Time* magazine 105 (May 26, 1975): 55–56.

Gross, Jane. "Under One Roof, Aging Together Yet Alone." *New York Times*, January 28, 2005.

Haigh, Susan. "States Slash Health Care Programs in Budget Crisis." July 29, 2009. Available at http://www.kirotv.com/health/20216250/detail/html.

Harris, Gardiner. "The Nation, Medicaid's Tentacles: Gee, Fixing Welfare Seemed Like a Snap." *New York Times*, June 19, 2005.

Herbert, Bob. "The Republican Way." *New York Times*, October 27, 1994.

Hess, John. "2 State Inquiries Ordered on Nursing Home Control." *New York Times*, October 17, 1974, 45.

——. "Bergman Pleads Guilty to 1.2 Million Medicaid Fraud." *New York Times*, March 12, 1976.

——. "Care of Aged Poor a Growing Scandal." *New York Times*, October 7, 1974.

——. "How Referrals to Nursing Homes Are Made." *New York Times*, May 12, 1975.

——. "'Medicaid Mills' Are Generally Cloaked in Anonymity." *New York Times*, September 21, 1976.

——. "New York Officials Put Fraud in Medicaid at 10 to 20 Percent." *New York Times*, August 31, 1976.

——. "Nursing Home Promoters Get Political Helping Hand." *New York Times*, October 21, 1974.

——. "Overbilling Laid to Nursing Home." *New York Times*, March 9, 1975.

——. "Regulating Medicaid." *New York Times*, April 25, 1975.

——. "State Audit Finds Wide Overbilling by Nursing Homes." *New York Times*, September 6, 1974.

——. "Study Denounces Nursing Home Deals as Costing State and Medicaid Millions." *New York Times*, October 31, 1974.

"H.E.W. Issues Rules for States to Curb Fraud in Medicaid." *New York Times*, March 27, 1971.

Hicks, Jonathan. "Spitzer Counterpunches with Ad Defending Health Care Overhaul." *New York Times*, March 1, 2007.

Hicks, Nancy. "Governors Discuss Medicaid Reforms." *New York Times*, September 23, 1976.

——. "Governors Will Vote on Medicaid Reform." *New York Times*, February 27, 1977.

——. "Senate Inquiry Scans Charges Against Health Plans on Coast." *New York Times*, March 14, 1975.

Holmes, Steven. "Drug Makers and Black Groups Fight Prescription Controls." *New York Times*, November 20, 1994.

Huang, Josi. "Dental Community Scrambles to Fill Dentist to Patient Gap." *Kennebec Journal* (Augusta, Me.), October 14, 2007.

Hunter, Desiree. "Data Links Infant Mortality with Lack of Insurance." *Decatur Daily* (Montgomery, Ala.), September 5, 2007.

"Increase in Quarterly Earnings for United Health Group." *Bloomberg News*, January 21, 2005.

"In Medicaid, Private HMOs Take a Big and Profitable Role." *Wall Street Journal*, November 15, 2006.

Jaspin, Elliot. "Austin No Hot Spot for Medicaid Patients" *Austin American-Statesman*, August 6, 2007.

Jenkins, Chris. "Medicaid Wait Rising for Virginia Children, Study Says." *Washington Post*, June 7, 2007.

Johnson, Avery and John Carreyrou. "Lilly Is in Talks to Settle Zyprexa Allegations." *Wall Street Journal*, January 31, 2008.

Johnson, Spencer. "Medicaid Cuts Will Rebound on Everyone." *Detroit Free Press*, August 29, 2005.

"Just Who Is Buying Beverly?" *Business Week Online*, November 21, 2005. Available at http://www.businessweek.com.

Kresnak, Jack. "State Health Standards for Kids Upheld in Settlement." *Detroit Free Press*, August 23, 2007.

LaMotta, Lisa. "Centene Jumps on Earnings Beat." *Forbes*, April 22, 2008. Available at http://www.Forbes.com.

"Lawmakers Seek Medicaid Spending Information from HMOs." *Hartford Advocate* (Conn.), December 1, 2006.

"Lawsuit: New Hampshire Failing in Dental Care for Kids on Medicaid." *Boston Herald*, February 7, 2007. Available at http://www.Bostonherald.com.

"Legislature Will Discuss Stopping Medicaid Abuse." *New York Times*, September 3, 1976.

Levy, Clifford J. and Michael Luo. "New York Medicaid Fraud May Reach into Billions" (Program Disorder; Exploiting a Safety Net series). *New York Times*, July 18, 2005.

"Low-Wage Workers' Health Care Costs State Millions." *Register-Mail Online* (Galesburg, Ill.), October 17, 2006. Available at http://www.Galesburg.com.

Luo, Michael. "Hospital Agrees to Repay State $76.5 million." *New York Times*, May 18, 2005.

Luo, Michael and Clifford Levy. "As Medicaid Balloons, Watchdog Force Shrinks." *New York Times*, July 19, 2005.

Lyons, Richard. "Fraud and Waste in Medicaid Found in Senate Report." *New York Times*, August 30, 1976.

Malanga, Steven. "How to Stop Medicaid Fraud." *City Journal* (Manhattan Institute, N.Y.), April 21, 2006. Available at http://city-journal.org/html/16_2_medicaid_fraud.html.

"Many States Seeking to Cut Medicaid Costs." *New York Times*, October 14, 1984.

Martinez, Barbara. "Health-Care Goldmines: Middlemen Strike It Rich." *Wall Street Journal*, November 15, 2006.

McClean, Bethany. "The Big Money in Medicaid." *Fortune*, June 11, 2007.

McCoy, Kevin. "Job Applicants Not Always Screened" (series on assisted-living facilities). *USA Today*, May 26, 2004.

——. "Poor Training Shows During Emergencies" (series on assisted-living facilities). *USA Today*, May 26, 2004.

McCoy, Kevin and Julie Appleby. "Many Facilities Accept People Who Are Too Ill" (series on assisted-living facilities). *USA Today*, May 27, 2004.

——. "Problems with Staffing Can Cost Lives, Money" (series on assisted-living facilities). *USA Today*, May 26, 2004.

McFadden, Robert D. "Health System in New York Faces Big Cuts." *New York Times*, February 23, 1991.

——. "State Studying Health Unit Dues." *New York Times*, February 16, 1975.

"Medicaid: A Big Headache in Some Areas." *U.S. News & World Report* 62 (April 17, 1967): 10.

"Medicaid in the Billions—Getting Out of Hand." *U.S. News & World Report* 63 (October 16, 1967): 32–34.

"Medicaid Investigation: Senate Sleuths Sniff Snootful of Swindles and Shams." *Retirement Living* 16 (October 16, 1976): 12.

"Medicaid Patients Face New Charges." *New York Times*, July 2, 1973.

"Medicaid 'Reform' Adds New Problems to Old," editorial. *Palm Beach Post*, November 3, 2007.

"Medicaid's Bad Record." *New York Times*, September 5, 1976.

"Medicare: Expensive and Successful; Medicaid, Chaotic but Irrevocable." *Time* magazine 90 (October 6, 1967): 96–97.

"Medicare in Trouble: Senate Study of High Costs, Abuses." *U.S. News & World Report* 68 (February 16, 1970): 70–72.

Meitrodt, Jeffrey. "Fighting Abuse" (series on nursing home abuse). *New Orleans Times-Picayune*, April 20, 2005.

——. "Making the Grade" (series on nursing home abuse). *New Orleans Times-Picayune*, April 17, 2005.

——. "Tightening Closure" (series on nursing home abuse). *New Orleans Times-Picayune*, April 17, 2005.

Meitrodt, Jeffrey and Steve Ritca. "State of Neglect" (series on nursing home abuse). *New Orleans Times-Picayune*, April 17, 2005.

Mendell, David. "Nursing Home Lawsuit Settled: Whistle-blowers Alleged Fraud, Patient Abuse." *Chicago Tribune*, November 23, 2004.

"The Mess in Medicaid." *Time* magazine 95 (January 12, 1970): 32–33.

Moller, Jan. "Culture Change" (series on nursing home abuse). *New Orleans Times-Picayune*, April 21, 2005.

———. "Money = Clout" (series on nursing home abuse). *New Orleans Times-Picayune*, April 19, 2005.

Moller, Jan and Steve Titea. "A Position of Power" (series on nursing home abuse). *New Orleans Times-Picayune*, April 19, 2005.

Molotsky, Irvin. "White House Revises 'New Federalism' Proposals." *New York Times*, June 24, 1983.

"More Federal Billions for Medicaid Bills." *U.S. News & World Report* 61 (November 28, 1966): 13.

"Move to Cut Medicaid Spending on Drugs Is Called Harmful." *New York Times*, August 30, 1987.

"The New Math of Old Age: Why the Nursing Home Industry's Cries of Poverty Don't Add Up." *U.S. News & World Report* 133 (September 30, 2002): 66–67, 70–74.

"New York State Audit Finds Improper Medicaid Payments." *New York Times*, February 25, 1977.

New York State Attorney General's Office. Eliot Spitzer, news release, March 25, 2004.

Noble, Holcomb B. "Credit Agency Says Hospitals Face Hazards from Proposed Cuts." *New York Times*, November 3, 1995.

"Nursing Homes a U.S. Challenge." *New York Times*, November 8, 1970.

"N.Y. in the News: Feds to Audit New York State Medicaid Fraud Prevention Unit." *Empire Journal* (N.Y.), September 3, 2005.

"N.Y. in the News: Rochester Hospital Repays Medicaid Overbilling." *Empire Journal* (New York), August 31, 2005.

Patrick, Robert. "'Worthless Services' Amount to Fraud: A New Tactic Prosecutors Are Going After Nursing Homes over Billing for Care That Was Not Provided." *St. Louis Post-Dispatch*, March 1, 2007.

Pear, Robert. "Arkansas Struggles to Deal with Rising Health Care Costs." *New York Times*, October 19, 1992.

———. "Clinton to Expand Medicaid for Some of the Working Poor." *New York Times*, August 4, 1998.

———. "Deficit or No Deficit, Unlikely Allies Bring About Expansions in Medicaid." *New York Times*, November 4, 1990.

———. "Florida's Struggles to Lift Burden of Medicaid Serves as Model and Warning." *New York Times*, April 24, 1995.

———. "Lacking Papers, Citizens Are Cut from Medicaid." *New York Times*, March 12, 2007.

———. "Medicare Chief Joins Firm with Health Clients." *New York Times*, December 19, 2003.

———. "Nursing Home Penalties Criticized: Many Facilities Cycle in and out of Compliance." *New York Times*, April 22, 2007.

———. "Protecting Family Assets: A New Breed of Medicaid Counselors Steps In." *New York Times*, November 26, 1987.

———. "Ruling Likely to Increase Strains on Medicaid." *New York Times*, June 15, 1990.

———. "Ruling May Lead to Big Rise in States' Medicaid Costs." *New York Times*, July 5, 1990.

Perez-Pena, Richard. "Revolving Door for Addicts Adds to Medicaid Cost." *New York Times*, April 17, 2007.

Pettus, Emily Wagler. "Moody: Medicaid Tightening Up on Providers and Recipients." *Sun Herald* (Biloxi, Miss.), August 17, 2005. Available at http://www.sunherald.com/.

"Pharmacists Seek Better Reimbursements." *Business First of Louisville* (Ky.), February 1, 2007. Available at http://www.bizjournals.com/Louisville.

"Private Management for Medicaid." *Business Week*, May 19, 1975, 45–46.

"Proposed Medicaid Cuts Would Hurt Pharmacies." Naplenews.com, March 17, 2007.

Purnick, Joyce. "Cutting Medicaid Will Not Be Crazy." *New York Times*, November 21, 1994.

——. "Cutting Nursing Home Profits, Not Care." *New York Times*, March 16, 1995.

——. "Medicaid Myths Linger in Wake of Campaign." *New York Times*, November 17, 1994.

Range, Peter Ross. "Medicaid in Georgia." *The Nation*, November 22, 1975, 529–530.

Rathke, Lisa. "Low Reimbursement Rates Hinder Dental Care for Poor." *Boston Globe*, February 3, 2007.

Reichard, John. "Learning from Tennessee's Medicaid Cuts." *CQ Health Beat*, April 23, 2007.

Ritea, Steve. "Front-Line Caregivers" (series on nursing home abuse). *New Orleans Times-Picayune*, April 17, 2005.

Rosenbaum, David. "The Medicaid Scandal." *New York Times*, September 2, 1976.

Rosenbaum, Jason. "Blunt: Medicaid a Relic." *Columbia Daily Tribune* (Mo.), January 25, 2007. Available at http://archives.columbiatribune.com/2007/jan/20070125news003.asp.

Rosenthal, Elizabeth. "U.S. Sets Terms for State to Shift Medicaid to Managed Care." *New York Times*, August 15, 1996.

Rushing, J. Taylor. "Nassau Resists Medicaid Reform." *Florida Times-Union* (Jacksonville), July 5, 2007.

Rutherford, Joe. "Medicaid Issues." *Northeast Mississippi Daily Journal*, April 29, 2007.

Sack, Kevin. "Albany Faces Hard Choices in Cash Quest." *New York Times*, January 20, 1992.

Salladay, Robert. "Governor Says No to Viagra for Sex Offenders." *Los Angeles Times*, May 27, 2005.

Salmans, Sandra and Henry McGee. "Physician, Heal Thyself." *Newsweek* (August 9, 1976): 24.

Schneider, Andrew and Philip O'Connor. "Nursing Home Industry Wields Clout in State Capitals—in Missouri and Illinois, Lobby Has Helped Defeat Reform Legislation." *St. Louis Post-Dispatch*, October 17, 2002.

Seaman, Marley. "Well Care Drops on Florida Expansion Halt." *Business Week*, October 30, 2007.

Searis, Tom. "West Virginia Could Lose Millions in Medicaid." *Charlestown Gazette* (Virginia), December 6, 2006.

++

"Sex Offenders in New York Getting Viagra—Paid for by Medicaid." *Chicago Tribune*, May 23, 2005.

"Shift in Federal–State Roles Seen as Curbing Medicaid and Welfare." *New York Times*, January 21, 1982.

Sievers, Stephanie. "Medicaid Patients Face Hardest Time Finding Dentists." *Spring-field Times* (Ill.), March 15, 2007. Available at http://www.MyWebTimes.com.

Somma, Ann Marie. "Managed Care Group Comes Under Fire—Health Net of Connecticut Accused of Sending Misleading Messages to Pharmacies." *Hartford Courant*, November 15, 2007.

"State Medicine in Trouble in U.S." *U.S. News & World Report* 62 (May 22, 1967): 75–76.

"States Using Donations to Get Medicaid Money." *New York Times*, May 12, 1991, 19.

Stewart, Kirsten. "Hospitals Want More Cash from Medicaid." *Salt Lake Tribune*, November 13, 2006.

——. "Medicaid Task Force a Lucrative Gig." *Salt Lake Tribune*, December 9, 2006.

——. "Where Are the Doctors Who Accept Medicaid?" *Salt Lake City Tribune*, September 16, 2007.

Strand, Diane. "Options Dwindle for New Medicaid Patients." *De Kalb Midweek*, November 22, 2006.

"Stress Points in the State Budgets." *New York Times*, December 30, 1987.

"Study: Some State Workers Relying on Medicaid." *Boston Globe*, March 30, 2007.

Sulivan, Kip. "HMO Profits on Medical Assistance Hurt Many in State." *Minneapolis Star Tribune*, May 28, 2005.

Sullivan, Ronald. "New York Seeking Medicaid Patients." *New York Times*, October 28, 1976.

Terry, Don. "As Medicaid Fees Push Doctors Out, Chicago Patients Find Fewer Choices." *New York Times*, April 12, 1991.

Thomas, Ralph. "Union, Nursing Home Alliance Team." *Seattle Times*, March 5, 2007.

Tuft, Carolyn. "Industry Donated $1 Million in Illinois Election." *St. Louis Post-Dispatch*, December 22, 2002.

Uhlman, Marian. "Specialist Care Waning for People on Medicaid." *Philadelphia Inquirer*, March 27, 2005.

"U.S. Lists the Doctors Convicted for Fraud in Medicare-Medicaid." *New York Times*, June 14, 1979.

Verhovek, Sam Howe. "Curbs on 'Medicaid Mills' Draw Criticism." *New York Times*, September 30, 1989.

——. "Legislators Resist Cuomo on Medicaid Cuts." *New York Times*, February 24, 1989.

Vu, Pauline. "States Make Deep Cuts to Health." August 23, 2009. Available at http://www.stateline.org/live/details/story?contentId=417167.

Waldron, Martin. "Costs of Welfare Soar." *New York Times*, April 25, 1976.

——. "Medicaid Cost $1 Billion Since 1966." *New York Times*, September 5, 1976.

Wallack, Victoria. "Maine's Medicaid Program Deemed Unsustainable." *Lincoln County News* (Me.), October 19, 2005.

——. "Report: Plenty of Blame for Medicaid Software Debacle." Village Soup Media Services, December 20, 2006. Available at http://www.waldo.villagesoup.com/news.

"Waste in Medicaid Is Estimated at 9% in Study by HEW." *New York Times*, April 30, 1977.

"What the Doctor Ordered: Problems of Medicare and Medicaid." *Time* magazine 88 (August 26, 1966): 13.

Williams, Dave. "Managed Care Companies Defend Medicaid Services." *Henry Daily Herald* (McDonough, Ga.), August 29, 2007.

——. "Medicaid HMO Hit with Fine." *Henry Daily Herald* (McDonough, Ga.), July 16, 2007.

Paper Presentations

Boyd, Donald. "Medicaid Spending—New York Versus Other States." Presentation to the New York Health Care Task Force, September 5, 2003, Albany, New York.

Cook, Fay Lomax and Meredith B. Czaplewski. "Public Opinion and Social Insurance: The American Experience." Paper presented at the 2008 Annual Meeting of the American Political Science Association, August 29, Boston.

Grabowski, David. "Medicare and Medicaid: Conflicting Incentives for Long-Term Care." Paper presented at the 2007 Annual Research Meeting of Academy Health, June 3–5, Orlando, Florida.

Grabowski, David, A. James O'Malley, and Nancy Barhydt. "The Costs and Potential Savings Associated with Nursing Home Hospitalizations." Paper presented at the 2007 Annual Research Meeting of Academy Health, June 3–5, Orlando, Florida.

Grogan, Colleen, Michael Gusmano, and Patricia King. "Medicaid Policymaking: The Role of Nonprofit Providers and Medicaid Advocates." Paper prepared for the 2007 Annual Meeting of the American Political Science Association, August 30–September 2, Chicago.

Oliver, Thomas R., Philip Lee, and Helene Lipton. "A Political History of Medicare and Prescription Drug Coverage: Missed Opportunities and Muddled Outcomes." Paper presented at the 2004 Annual Meeting of the American Political Science Association, September 2–5, Chicago.

Smith, Steven Rathgeb. "Medicaid Funding of Social Services: Implications for Social and Health Policy." Paper presented at the 2007 Annual Meeting of the American Political Science Association, August 30–September 2, Chicago.

Sparer, Michael S. "Medicaid, Federalism, and National Health Insurance." Paper presented at the 2007 Annual Meeting of the American Political Science Association, August 30–September 2, Chicago.

Spillman, Brenda. "Consumer Preparedness for Long-Term Care: Personal Financing Options for Long-Term Care." Paper presented at the long-term care colloquium "Building Bridges: Making a Difference in Long-Term Care," June 2, 2007, Orlando, Florida.

Weissert, William G. and Edward Alan Miller. "Punishing the Pioneers: The Medicare Modernization Act and State Pharmacy Assistance Programs." Paper presented at the 2005 Annual Meeting of the American Political Science Association, September 1–4, Washington, D.C.

Surveys and Government Documents

AARP. *Medicaid Poll.* Survey. Methodology: conducted by International Communications Research, April 20–24, 2005, with a national adult sample of 1,011. Press release available at http://www.aarp.org/presscenter/pressrelease/articles/Medicaid_cuts.html.

——. *Opinions on the Federal Budget Among U.S. Adults.* Survey. Methodology: conducted by International Communications Research, January 4–9, 2006, with a national adult sample of 1,026. Washington, D.C.: AARP, 2006.

Angelotti, Steve. *Medicaid and Michigan Hospitals: A Look Behind the Numbers.* Senate Fiscal Agency Issue Paper, requested by Senator Joel Gougeon, chairman of the Michigan Senate Appropriations Subcommittee on the Fiscal Status of Michigan Medicaid Health Providers. Lansing: State of Michigan, March 2000.

CBS News. *CBS News Poll.* Survey. Methodology: conducted August 27–31, 2009, with a national adult sample of 1,097. Available at http://www.kff.org/kaiserpolls/health-poll_question.cfm?qid=1746.

——. *CBS News Poll.* Survey. Methodology: conducted by CBS News, February 23–27, 2007, with a national sample of 706 adults. Available at http://www.pollingreport.com/health3.htm.

CBS News and the *New York Times. CBS News/New York Times Poll.* Survey. Methodology: conducted January 20–January 25, 2006, with a national adult sample of 1,229. Available at http://www.pollingreport.com/health3.htm.

DeNavas-Walt, Carmen, Bernadette Proctor, and Jessica Smith. *Income, Poverty, and Health Insurance Coverage in the U.S.: 2006.* U.S. Census Bureau Current Population Report P60-233. Washington, D.C.: U.S. Government Printing Office, 2007.

Executive Office of the President. Council of Economic Advisors. *Economic Report of the President, FY 2009.* Transmitted to Congress together with the annual report of the Council of Economic Advisors. Washington, D.C.: U.S. Government Printing Office, February 2008.

Fox News. *Opinion Dynamics Poll.* Survey. Methodology: conducted by Opinion Dynamics, based on data provided by the Roper Center for Public Opinion Research, University of Connecticut, September 8–September 9, 2008, with a national registered voter sample of 900. Available at http://www.pollingreport.com/health3.htm.

Genworth Financial, Inc. *2007 Cost of Living Survey.* March 31, 2007. Available at http://www.longtermcare.Genworth.com.

Gitterman, Daniel, John Scott, and Judie Svihula. *Medicaid and Lobbying Groups.* Report prepared for DPG Associates. Washington, D.C.: Office of the Assistant Secretary for Planning and Evaluation, U.S. Department of Health and Human Services, 2009.

Grassley, Chuck, Chair, Committee on Finance, U.S. Senate. Letter to Mark McClellan, Administrator, Centers for Medicare and Medicaid Services, July 7, 2004, Washington,

D.C. Available at http://www.canhr.org/newsroom/newdev_archive/past/Grassley letter.html.

Health Care Association of New York State. *New York Monthly Survey.* Survey. Methodology: conducted by Siena Research Institute, August 11–24, 2008, with a New York State registered voter sample of 627. Loudonville, N.Y.: Siena Research Institute, 2008.

Henry J. Kaiser Family Foundation. *Kaiser Health Tracking Poll.* Survey. Methodology: conducted by Princeton Survey Research Associates International, August 4–11, 2009, with a national adult sample of 1,207. Menlo Park, Calif.: Henry J. Kaiser Family Foundation, 2009. Available at http://www.kff.org/kaiserpolls/healthpoll_ques tion.cfm?qid=1745.

Henry J. Kaiser Family Foundation, Kaiser Commission on Medicaid and the Uninsured. *National Survey on the Public's Views About Medicaid.* Kaiser Health Poll Report. Methodology: conducted by Princeton Survey Research Associates International, April 1–May 1, 2005, with a national adult sample of 1,201. Menlo Park, Calif.: Henry J. Kaiser Family Foundation, Kaiser Commission on Medicaid and the Uninsured, 2005.

Henry J. Kaiser Family Foundation and Harvard School of Public Health. *Health Care Agenda for the Next Congress.* Survey. Methodology: conducted by Princeton Survey Research Associates, November 6–10, 1996, with national self-described voters in the 1996 election sample of 1,000. Storrs: Roper Center for Public Opinion Research, University of Connecticut, 1996. Retrieved from the iPoll Databank, September 2, 2008. Available at http://www.kff.org/kaiserpolls/healthpolls.cfm.

——. *National Survey of Public Knowledge of the Medicare Program and Public Support for Medicare Policy Proposals.* Survey. Methodology: conducted by Louis Harris and Associates, May 31–June 5, 1995, with a national adult sample of 1,383. Available at http://www.kff.org/kaiserpolls/healthpolls.cfm.

Henry J. Kaiser Family Foundation, Harvard School of Public Health, and National Public Radio. *Views and Opinions of State Health Insurance Program (SCHIP).* Survey. Methodology: conducted October 8–13, with a national adult sample of 1,527. Menlo Park, Calif.: Henry J. Kaiser Family Foundation, 2007.

Herz, Elicia S. *Medicaid: A Primer.* Report for the U.S. Congress. Washington, D.C.: Library of Congress, Congressional Research Service, December 22, 2005.

Jenson, Jennifer. *Health Care Spending and the Aging Population.* Report for the U.S. Congress. Washington, D.C: Library of Congress, March 13, 2007.

Levinson, Daniel. *Comparison of Medicaid Federal Upper Limit Amounts to Average Manufacturers Prices (AMPS).* Washington, D.C.: Office of the Inspector General, U.S. Department of Health and Human Services, June 2005.

Louis Harris and Associates. *Harris Polls on Medicaid, April 1990.* Methodology: conducted April 26–May 2, 1990, with a national adult sample of 1,255. Hamden: Roper Center for Public Opinion Research, University of Connecticut, 1990. Retrieved from the iPoll Databank, September 2, 2008. Available at http://www.kff.org/kaiser polls/healthpolls.cfm.

McCaig, Linda F. and Eric N. Nawar. *National Hospital Ambulatory Medical Care Survey, 2004.* Emergency Care Summary. Advance data from Vital and Health Statistics, no. 372. Hyattsville, Md.: National Center for Health Statistics, 2006.

Medicaid Commission. *Final Report and Recommendations.* Presented to Michael O. Leavitt, secretary, Department of Health and Human Services. Washington, D.C.: U.S. Government Printing Office, December 29, 2006.

National Association of State Budget Offices and the National Governors Association. *The Fiscal Survey of States.* Washington, D.C.: U.S. Government Printing Office, December 2007.

National Governors Association and National Association of Budget Officers. *The Fiscal Survey of States.* Washington, D.C.: U.S. Government Printing Office, June 2008.

NBC News and the *Wall Street Journal. NBC News/Wall Street Journal Poll.* Survey. Methodology: conducted by the polling organization of Peter Hart (D) and Bill McInturff (R), January 17–20, 2007, with a national adult sample of 1,007. Available at http://www.pollingreport.com/health3.htm.

New York State Temporary Commission on Lobbying. *2002 Annual Report.* Albany: State of New York, 2002.

Quinnipiac University Polling Institute. *Quinnipiac University Poll, May 2008.* Survey. Methodology: conducted May 8–17, 2008, with a national registered voter sample of 1,745. Hamden: Roper Center for Public Opinion Research, University of Connecticut, 2008. Retrieved from the iPoll Databank, September 4, 2008. Available at http://www.pollingreport.com/health3.htm.

——. *Quinnipiac University Poll, October 2007.* Survey. Methodology: conducted October 23–29, 2007, with a national registered voter sample of 1,636. Hamden: Roper Center for Public Opinion Research, University of Connecticut, 2007. Retrieved from the iPoll Databank, September 4, 2008. Available at http://www.pollingreport.com/health3.htm.

Republican Study Committee for Access to Affordable, Quality Care for All Americans. *Empowering Patients First Act: Putting Patients First!* July 2009. Available at http://rsc.tomprice.house.gov/Solutions/EmpoweringPatientsFirstAct.htm.

Satcher, David. *Oral Health in America: A Report of the Surgeon General, U.S. Department of Health and Human Services (HHS).* Washington, D.C.: U.S. Government Printing Office, May 2000.

Saucier, Paul, Brian Burwell, and Kerstin Gerst. *The Past, Present, and Future of Managed Long-Term Care.* Washington, D.C.: Office of Disability, Aging, and Long-Term Care Policy, U.S. Department of Health and Human Services, and MEDSTAT Group, April 2005.

Smith, Vernon, Kathleen Gifford, Eileen Ellis, Robin Rudowitz, Molly O'Malley, and Caryn Marks. *As Tough Times Wane, States Act to Impose Medicaid Coverage and Quality: Results from a 50-State Medicaid Budget Survey for State Fiscal Years 2007 and 2008.* Menlo Park, Calif.: Henry J. Kaiser Family Foundation, Kaiser Commission on Medicaid and the Uninsured, October 2007. Available at http://www.kff.org.

Smith, Vernon, Kathleen Gifford, Eileen Ellis, and Amy Wiles. *Low Medicaid Spending Growth amid Rebounding State Revenues: Results from a 50-State Medicaid Budget Survey Fiscal Years 2006 and 2007.* Executive summary. Menlo Park, Calif.: Henry J. Kaiser Family Foundation, Kaiser Commission on Medicaid and the Uninsured, October 2006. Available at http://www.kff.org.

——. *Results from a 50-State Survey: Medicaid Budgets, Spending, and Policy Initiatives in State Fiscal Years 2005 and 2006.* Menlo Park, Calif.: Henry J. Kaiser Family Foundation, Kaiser Commission on Medicaid and the Uninsured, October 2005. Available at http://ww.kff.org.

U.S. Attorney's Office. District of Connecticut. "Nursing Home Agrees to Pay $750,000 to Settle Allegations Under the False Claims Act." Press release, May 18, 2005. Available at http://usdoj.gov/usao/ct/Press2005/.

——. Northern District of Georgia. "Lawrenceville Nursing Home to Pay $2.5 Million to Settle Allegations of Gross Neglect of Residents." Press release, December 22, 2005. Available at http://usdoj.gov/usas/gan/press/2005.

U.S. Bureau of the Census. *Current Business Reports (BS/2004), Service Annual Survey: 2004.* Washington, D.C.: U.S. Government Printing Office, 2006.

——. *Income, Poverty, and Health Insurance Coverage in the United States: 2004.* 2005 and Earlier Annual Social and Economic Supplements to the Current Population Survey. Washington, D.C.: U.S. Government Printing Office, 2005.

——. *International Database.* Washington, D.C.: U.S. Government Printing Office, 2007.

U.S. Congress. "The Federal Health Care Programs: Medicare and Medicaid." *Congressional Digest* 53 (June 1974): 164–165.

U.S. Congress. Congressional Budget Office. *Background Paper: Health Differentials Between White and Nonwhite Americans.* Washington, D.C.: U.S. Government Printing Office, September 1977.

U.S. Congress. House. Committee on Appropriations. Subcommittee on Military Construction, Veterans Affairs, and Related Agencies. *Health Care Spending: Public Payers Face Burden of Entitlement Program Growth, While All Payers Face Rising Prices and Increasing Use of Services.* Hearings. Statement of A. Bruce Steinwald, director of health care, Government Accountability Office. 110th Cong., 1st sess., February 15, 2007.

——. Committee on Energy and Commerce. Subcommittee on Health. *Insuring Bright Futures: Improving Access to Dental Care and Providing a Healthy Start for Children.* Testimony of Burton Edelstein, professor of dentistry and health policy, Columbia University; Nicholas Mosca, American Dental Education Association; Kathleen Roth, president, American Dental Association; and Chris Koyanagi, policy director, Bazelon Center for Mental Health Law. 110th Cong., 1st sess., March 27, 2007.

——. Committee on Energy and Commerce. Subcommittee on Health. *Medicaid Drug Rebate Program: Inadequate Oversight Raises Concerns About Rebates Paid to States.* Hearings. Statement of Kathleen King, director of health care, Government Accountability Office. 109th Cong., 1st sess., June 22, 2005.

———. Committee on Oversight and Government Reform. Letter from Henry Waxman, chair, to Kerry Weems, acting administrator, CMS, October 14, 2008. Available at http://oversight.house.gov/documents/20081014164341.pdf.

———. Committee on Oversight and Government Reform. *Medicare Part D: Drug Pricing and Manufacturer Windfalls.* Report prepared by majority staff, 110th Cong., 2d sess. Washington, D.C.: U.S. Government Printing Office, July 2008.

———. Committee on Oversight and Government Reform. *Prescription Drugs: Oversight of Drug Pricing in Federal Programs.* Hearings. Statement of John E. Dicken, director of health care, Government Accountability Office. 110th Cong., 1st sess., February 9, 2007. GAO-07-481T. Washington, D.C.: U.S. Government Printing Office, 2007.

———. Committee on Oversight and Government Reform. Subcommittee on Domestic Policy. *Oversight Adequacy of the Pediatric Dental Program for Medicaid Eligible Children.* Testimony of Jane Perkins, legal director, National Law Program; and Dr. Frederick Clark, dental practitioner. 110th Cong., 1st sess., May 2, 2007.

———. Committee on Ways and Means. *Nonprofit, For-Profit, and Government Hospitals: Uncompensated Care and Other Community Benefits.* Testimony of David Walker, U.S. comptroller general. 109th Cong., 1st sess., May 26, 2005.

U.S. Congress. Joint Economic Commission. *Highlights from the Census Bureau's Update on U.S. Health Insurance Coverage.* Fact sheet delivered to Senator Charles E. Schumer, chair, and Congresswoman Carolyn B. Maloney, vice chair. Washington, D.C.: U.S. Government Printing Office, August 29, 2007.

U.S. Congress. Senate. Committee on Finance. *Medicaid Waste, Fraud, and Abuse: Threatening the Health Care Safety Net.* Hearings. Opening statement of Senator Chuck Grassley, chair. Testimony of Kathryn Allen, director of health care, Government Accountability Office; Timothy Coleman, senior counsel to the deputy attorney general, U.S. Department of Justice; James W. Moorman, president and CEO, Taxpayers Against Fraud; Patrick O'Connell, chief, Civil Medicaid Fraud Section, Office of the Attorney General of Texas; Nicholas Messuri, president, National Association of Medicaid Fraud Control Units; Julie Stone-Axelrod, Congressional Research Service, Domestic Social Policy Division, Library of Congress; Judith Feder, professor and dean, Public Policy Institute, Georgetown University; the American Council of Life Insurers; Robert A. Vito, regional inspector general for calibration and inspections, Pennsylvania Department of Health and Human Services; Beatrice Manning, former Schering-Plough manager. 109th Cong., 1st sess., June 28–29, 2005.

———. Committee on Finance. *Medicare and Medicaid, Part 2.* Hearings. 91st Cong., 2d sess., April 14–15, May 26–27, and June 2–3, 15–16, 1970.

———. Committee on Finance. *Medicare Part D: Enrolling New Dual Eligible Beneficiaries in Prescription Drug Plans.* Hearings. Statement of Kathleen M. King, director of health care, Government Accountability Office. 110th Cong., 1st sess., May 8, 2007.

———. Committee on Finance. *Prescription Drugs: An Overview of Approaches to Negotiate Drug Prices Used by Other Countries and U.S. Private Payers and Federal Programs.* Testimony of John E. Dicken, director of health care, Government Accountability Office. 110th Cong., 1st sess., January 11, 2007.

——. Committee on Labor and Human Resources, Special Subcommittee on Aging. *Extended Care Services and Facilities for the Aging.* 91st Cong., 2d sess., May 18, 1970. Washington, D.C.: U.S. Government Printing Office, 1970.

——. Special Committee on Aging. *Nursing Home Bankruptcies: What Caused Them.* 106th Cong., 2d sess., September 5, 2000. Washington, D.C.: U.S. Government Printing Office, 2000.

——. Special Committee on Aging. *Nursing Homes: Aggregate Medicare Payments Are Adequate Despite Bankruptcies.* Hearings. Testimony of Laura Dunmit, associate director of health financing and public-health issues, Department of Health and Human Services. 106th Cong., 2d sess., September 5, 2000.

——. Special Committee on Aging. *Skilled Nursing Facilities: Medicare Payment Changes Require Adjustments but Maintain Access.* Report from the Government Accounting Office to the chairman and ranking minority member. Washington, D.C.: U.S. Government Printing Office, December 1999.

U.S. Department of Health and Human Services (HHS). Administration on Aging. *A Profile of Older Americans: 2005.* Washington, D.C.: U.S. Government Printing Office, 2005.

——. Agency for Healthcare Research and Quality (AHRQ). "Medicaid Pays for More Than One-Third of $10 Billion Bill for Drug Abuse." *AHRQ News and Numbers* (Rockville, Md.) (October 24, 2007). Available at http://www.ahrq.gov/news/nn/nn/03107.htm.

——. Agency for Healthcare Research and Quality (AHRQ). *National Healthcare Disparities Report, 2007.* Publication no. 08-0040. Rockville, Md.: AHRQ, February 2008. Available at http://www.ahrq.gov/QUAL/nhqr07/nhdr07.pdf.

——. Centers for Medicare and Medicaid Services. *National Summary of Medicaid Managed Care Programs and Enrollment.* Washington, D.C.: U.S. Government Printing Office, June 30, 2001.

——. Centers for Medicare and Medicaid Services. *Statistics: Information About Persons Covered by Medicare, Medicaid, or SCHIP.* Washington, D.C.: U.S. Government Printing Office, 2006.

——. Centers for Medicare and Medicaid Services. Office of the Actuary. *2008 Actuarial Report: On the Financial Outlook for Medicaid.* Washington, D.C.: U.S. Government Printing Office, October 17, 2008.

——. Health Care Financing Administration. *Health Care Programs, Medicaid.* Annual Statistical Supplement. Washington, D.C.: U.S. Government Printing Office, 2005.

——. Health Care Financing Administration. *Medicaid Statistical Data (2082/MSIS Reports), FY 1989 to 1995.* Washington, D.C.: U.S. Government Printing Office, December 1996.

——. Health Care Financing Administration. *Total Current Expenditures, Benefits, and Administrative Expenditures, Federal and State Shares.* Medicaid Financial Management Reports (CMS-64 and predecessors). Washington, D.C.: U.S. Government Printing Office, 1990–99.

——. National Center for Health Statistics. *Life Expectancy at Birth.* National Vital Statistics Report 54, no. 19. Hyattsville, Md.: Centers for Disease Control and Prevention, June 28, 2006.

——. Office of the Inspector General. Daniel R. Levinson, Inspector General. *Review of the Commonwealth of Pennsylvania's Use of Intergovernmental Transfers to Finance Medicaid Supplementation Payments to County Nursing Facilities.* Washington, D.C.: U.S. Government Printing Office, January 2001.

——. Office of the Inspector General. Daniel R. Levinson, Inspector General. *State Medicaid Fraud Control Units: Annual Report, Fiscal Year 2006.* Washington, D.C.: U.S. Government Printing Office, 2006.

——. Office of the Inspector General. Daniel R. Levinson, Inspector General. *Suspected Medicaid Fraud Referrals.* Report OEi-07-04-00181. Washington, D.C.: U.S. Government Printing Office, January 2007.

U.S. Department of Justice. Office of the Inspector General (OIG). *OIG Semi-annual Report.* Washington, D.C.: U.S. Government Printing Office, October 1, 2007–March 31, 2008.

U.S. Government Accountability Office (GAO). *Children's Health Insurance: State Experiences in Implementing SCHIP and Considerations for Reauthorization.* Statement of Katherine G. Allen, director of health care, GAO, before the Committee on Finance, U.S. Senate, 110th Cong., 1st sess., February 1, 2007. GAO-07-447T. Washington, D.C.: U.S. Government Printing Office, 2007.

——. *Congressional Review Act: Applicability to CMS Letter on State Children's Health Insurance Program.* Statement of Dayna K. Shah, managing associate general counsel, GAO, before the Subcommittee on Health, Committee on Energy and Commerce, U.S. House of Representatives, 110th Cong., 2d sess., May 15, 2008. GAO-08-785T. Washington, D.C.: U.S. Government Printing Office, 2008.

——. *Federal Fire Safety Requirements Do Not Insure Life Safety in Nursing Home Fires.* MWD-76-136. Washington, D.C.: U.S. Government Printing Office, June 3, 1976.

——. *Federal Oversight of Growing Medicaid Home and Community-Based Waivers Should Be Strengthened.* Report to congressional requesters. GAO-03-576. Washington, D.C.: U.S. Government Printing Office, June 2003.

——. *Federal Program Compared Favorably with Other Products, and Analysis of Claims Trend Could Inform Future Decisions.* Report to congressional committees on long-term care insurance. GAO-06-401. Washington, D.C.: U.S. Government Printing Office, March 2006.

——. *Centers and Rural Clinics: State and Federal Implementation Issues for Medicaid's New Payment System.* Report to congressional committees. Washington, D.C.: U.S. Government Printing Office, June, 2005.

——. *Health Care Fraud and Abuse Control Program: Results of Review of Annual Reports for FY 2002 and 2003.* Report to congressional committees. Washington, D.C.: U.S. Government Printing Office, April 2005.

——. *Health Savings Accounts: Participation Grew and Many HSA-Eligible Plan Enrollees Did Not Open HSAs While Individuals Who Did Had Higher Incomes.* Testimony before the Subcommittee on Health, Committee on Ways and Means, U.S. House of Representatives. 110th Cong., 2d sess., May 14, 2008. Washington, D.C.: U.S. Government Printing Office, 2008.

———. *Increased Compliance Needed with Nursing Home Health and Sanitary Standards.* MWD-76-8. Washington, D.C.: U.S. Government Printing Office, August 18, 1975.

———. *Long-Term Care Insurance: Partnership Programs Include Benefits that Protect Policyholders and Are Unlikely to Result in Medicaid Savings.* GAO-07-231. Washington, D.C.: U.S. Government Printing Office, May 2007.

———. *Many Medicare and Medicaid Nursing Homes Do Not Meet Federal Fire Safety Requirements.* MWD-75-46. Washington, D.C.: U.S. Government Printing Office, March 18, 1975.

———. *Many Underserved Areas Lack a Health Center Site. And the Health Center Program Needs More Oversight.* Report to ranking member, Subcommittee on Oversight and Investigations, Committee on Energy and Commerce, U.S. House of Representatives. Washington, D.C.: U.S. Government Printing Office, August 2008.

———. *Medicaid Demonstration Projects in Florida and Vermont Approved Under Section 115 of the Social Security Act.* Letter from Gary L. Kepplinger, general counsel, GAO, to Michael O. Leavitt, secretary, U.S. Department of Health and Human Services, July 24, 2007. B-309734. Washington, D.C.: U.S. Government Printing Office, 2007. Available at http://www.gao.gov/decisions/other/309734.pdf.

———. *Medicaid: Extent of Dental Disease in Children Has Not Decreased, and Millions Are Estimated to Have Untreated Tooth Decay.* GAO-08-1121. Washington, D.C.: U.S. Government Printing Office, September 2008.

———. *Medicaid Financial Management: Steps Taken to Improve Federal Oversight but Other Actions Needed to Sustain Efforts.* Report to the chairman, Committee on Finance, U.S. Senate. GAO-06-705. Washington, D.C.: U.S. Government Printing Office, June 22, 2006.

———. *Medicaid: Improved Federal Oversight of State Financing Schemes Is Needed.* Report to the Committee on Finance, U.S. Senate. Washington, D.C.: U.S. Government Printing Office, February 2004.

———. *Medicaid Integrity: Implementation of New Program Provides Opportunities for Federal Leadership to Combat Fraud, Waste, and Abuse.* Statement of Leslie G. Aronovitz, director of Health Care, GAO, before the Subcommittee on Federal Financial Management, Government Information, and International Security and Government Affairs, 109th Cong., 2d sess., March 28, 2006. GAO-06-578T. Washington, D.C.: U.S. Government Printing Office, 2006.

———. *Medicaid Long-Term Care: Few Transferred Assets Before Applying for Nursing Home Coverage; Impact of DRA on Eligibility Is Uncertain.* GAO-07-280. Washington, D.C.: U.S. Government Printing Office, March 2007.

———. *Medicaid Managed Care: Access and Quality Requirements Specific to Low-Income and Other Special Needs Enrollees.* Washington, D.C.: U.S. Government Printing Office, December 8, 2004.

———. *Medicaid Nursing Home Payments: States' Payment Rates Largely Unaffected by Recent Fiscal Pressures.* Washington, D.C.: U.S. Government Printing Office, October 2003.

———. *Medicaid: States' Payments for Outpatient Prescription Drugs.* Washington, D.C.: U.S. Government Printing Office, October 31, 2005.

———. *Medicaid: Strategies to Help States Address Increased Expenditures During Economic Downturns.* Washington, D.C.: U.S. Government Printing Office, October 2006.

———. *Nursing Home Deaths: Arkansas Coroner Referrals Confirm Weaknesses in State and Federal Oversight of Quality of Care.* Report to congressional requesters. GAO-05-78. Washington, D.C.: U.S. Government Printing Office, November 2004.

———. *Nursing Homes: Federal Monitoring Surveys Demonstrate Continued Understatement of Serious Care Problems and CMS Oversight Weaknesses.* Report to Congressional Requesters. GAO-08-517. Washington, D.C.: U.S. Government Printing Office, May 2008.

———. *Nursing Homes: Quality of Care More Related to Staffing Than Spending.* Letter to congressional requesters, June 13, 2002. GAO-02-431R. Washington, D.C.: U.S. Government Printing Office, 2002. Available at http://www.gao.gov/new.items/d02431r.pdf.

———. *Overview of the Long-Term Care Partnership Program.* Letter to Senator Charles E. Grassley, ranking minority member, Committee on Finance, and Senator John D. Rockefeller, September 9, 2005. GAO-05-021R. Washington, D.C.: U.S. Government Printing Office, 2005. Available at www.gao.gov/newitems/d051021r.pdf.

———. *Skilled Nursing Facility Payments.* GAO-03-183. Washington, D.C.: U.S. Government Printing Office, December 2002.

———. *States' SCHIP Enrollment and Spending Experiences and Considerations for Reauthorization.* Washington, D.C.: U.S. Government Printing Office, February 15, 2007.

———. *Undocumented Aliens: Questions Persist About Their Impact on Hospitals' Uncompensated Care Costs.* Report to congressional requesters. Washington, D.C.: U.S. Government Printing Office, May 2004.

U.S. Office of Management and Budget. *Budget of the United States, FY 2007: Analytical Perspectives.* Washington, D.C.: U.S. Government Printing Office, 2007.

———. *Budget of the United States, FY 2008: Analytical Perspectives.* Washington, D.C.: U.S. Government Printing Office, 2008.

———. *Budget of the United States, FY 2009: Analytical Perspectives.* Washington, D.C.: U.S. Government Printing Office, 2009.

Walker, John S., Steve Angelotti, and Dana Patterson. *Medicaid Funding for Nursing Homes Services: A Historical Perspective.* Lansing: Michigan Senate Fiscal Agency, June 2000.

LTC, 138, 139, 149; and MCOs, 278n86; and Medicaid cuts, 77–81, 92, 93, 102–3, 184, 225, 284nn69; and pharmacies, 197; and poverty, 67; and quality of care, 323n16; and SCHIP, 71, 100–101, 107, 299n116, 309n92; and state *vs.* federal funding, 15, 210, 212, 356n4, 358n20; strategies of, 2, 83, 102–3; tax cuts by, 369n41; use of regulations by, 79–80
Bush, Jeb, 97, 343n61
Byrnes, John, 253n16

Califano, Joseph, 43
California: budget deficits in, 275n56; costs in, 35, 313n19, 337n25; demonstration projects in, 72; and DSH payments, 63; economy of, 272n28, 353n124; and federal funding, 255n40, 256n46, 257n57; fraud in, 43, 44, 169; HCBS in, 317n61; health insurance companies in, 349n90; hospitals in, 260n78, 306n56, 344n62; immigrants in, 362n9; LTC in, 313n19, 337n25; MCOs in, 58, 161, 282n123; Medicaid in, 30, 59, 91, 258n69, 272nn29,30, 353n124; Partnership for Long-Term Care Program in, 321n89; and pharmacies, 348n85; reimbursement rates in, 38, 263n93; taxes in, 57, 61, 288n34
campaign contributions, 206; and AMA, 200, 334n2; from hospitals, 190, 334n4; from insurance companies, 349n93; and MCOs, 198, 199; from nursing homes, 185, 262n90, 336nn17,18; from pharmaceutical companies, 334nn2,4, 345n68; from providers, 202, 351n102; in states, 185, 262n90, 334n4, 336nn17,18, 350n93
capitated plans. *See* managed-care organizations
Carcieri, Donald, 93, 317n58
caregivers, informal, 142, 147–48, 152, 240, 319n78; women as, 148, 166, 225, 319n76, 327n44; and "woodwork effect," 148. *See also* staff, health-care
Carey, Hugh, 258n69, 261n85, 267n126
Carter, Jimmy, 33–34, 43, 255n33
Cash and Counseling Option, 146
Catamount Health Plan (Vermont), 90, 292n68
Centene (MCO), 160, 198, 288n37, 349n90
Centers for Medicare and Medicaid Services (CMS), 79; and Congress, 299n120; and fraud, 169, 170, 327n47, 329nn64,65; and hospitals, 190; and information technology, 202; lobbying of, 182; and Medicare Part D, 196; and pharmaceutical

companies, 195, 345n70, 346n72; and pharmacies, 197; and quality of care, 156, 162, 164, 178, 326n36; and SCHIP, 300n122; and state *vs.* federal funding, 212
certified nurse's aides (CNAs), 164–65, 166, 326nn36,38
charity care, 22, 24, 27, 85, 260n77, 344n63; and cost shifting, 217; and Medicaid reimbursement, 37; by physicians, 260n81
Cheney, Dick, 80
childbirth, 310n98, 322n4
Child Health Assessment Program, 255n33
children: access for, 118, 119, 120, 227, 274n48; adult, 315n36, 316n52; advocacy groups for, 17; benefits for, 127, 234; and costs, 99, 300n121; and cost shifting, 216, 219; coverage for, 5, 15, 69–71, 75, 92, 93, 99–100, 126, 223, 226, 279n102, 298nn112,115, 299nn119,121; and cuts, 269n6, 284n8; dental care for, 117–19, 120, 201, 307nn61,62,69, 308nn80,82; disabled, 318n70; eligibility of, 100, 271n21, 301n5, 319n70; and fraud, 173; and health care reform, 99–100; of immigrants, 111, 112; lobbying for, 184, 335n13; in MCOs, 158, 296n103, 297n105, 299n118; and Medicaid expansion, 14, 55, 56; and medical industrial complex, 183; participation of, 7, 29, 105, 108; in poverty, 28, 29, 301n5; premiums for, 319n70, 359n31; and rationing, 98; and states, 83, 256n42, 292nn66,72, 294n89, 297n106, 298nn112,115, 299n119, 300nn1,2; uninsured, 299n115; and welfare reform, 69. *See also* Aid to Families with Dependent Children; State Children's Health Insurance Program
Children's Health Insurance Program Reauthorization Act (2008), 101
Children's Medicaid Coalition, 55, 184, 334n7
Christiano, Albert, 268n130
citizenship, 15, 107. *See also* immigrants
class, socioeconomic, 8, 27, 28, 34, 47
clinics, community health, 192, 226, 342n56; and access, 115, 116; and discontinuities in coverage, 112–13; and physicians, 200, 201
Clinton, Bill: and DSH payments, 355n2; as governor, 273n35; and health care reform, 235, 366n31, 368n40; and impotence medication, 309n89; and LTC, 136, 368n40; and MCOs, 73, 159; and Medicaid, 12, 14, 70, 75, 235, 251n37, 278n84; opposition to, 64–66, 251n37, 366n31; and states, 277nn72,73; and uninsured population, 72; and welfare reform, 66, 68

Coalition for Community Pharmacy Action, 196–97
Coalition for Meaningful Medicaid Reform, 184, 335n12
Coalition on Human Needs, 184
Colorado: cigarette tax in, 288n34; economy of, 353n124, 354n131; elderly population in, 313n19; MCOs in, 282n123, 283n127; Medicaid in, 120, 256n44, 322n3; outsourced services in, 202; SCHIP in, 280n107; and state *vs.* federal funding, 212
Commonwealth Health Insurance Connector Authority (Connector; Massachusetts), 89
Community Health Centers Program, 342n56
Community Living Assistance Services and Supports Act (2007), 368n40
Community Mental Health Centers Act, 261n86
Congress: and abortion, 124; and adult children of elderly, 316n52; and advocacy groups, 335n8; and Bush, 79–80; and Clinton, 64–66, 251n37; and CMS, 299n120; and computerization, 265n113; and cost control, 213, 214, 217, 226, 270n12, 278n84, 284n6, 285n12, 343n60; and dental care, 307n61; and DSH payments, 62, 355n1; and eligibility, 111–12, 257n60; and equal access, 114; and expansion of Medicaid, 54–56, 57, 270n9; and federal funding, 53, 210, 256n46, 356n4; and fraud, 42–43, 169–70, 264nn103,109, 330n66; and HCBS, 142; and health care reform, 237–38, 280n112, 369n41; and hospitals, 190, 191; and LTC, 138, 319n78, 368n40; and medical industrial complex, 182; New Right in, 14, 64–66, 75; and nursing homes, 186, 190, 262n90; and patient abuse, 47; and pharmacies, 197; and prescription drugs, 195, 348n80; and quality of care, 156, 323n16; and Reagan, 53–54; and REITs, 340n41; and SCHIP, 71, 100, 101, 228; and standards, 285n13; and taxes, 277n82. *See also* campaign contributions; Democratic Party; Republican Party; *particular acts and amendments*
Connecticut: and abortion, 124; costs in, 286n19, 313n19, 337n25; dental care in, 308n82; economy of, 353n124; litigation in, 263n95, 333n88; LTC in, 313n19, 321n89; and MCOs, 160–61; Medicaid in, 91, 259n69, 272n29, 286n19; nursing homes in, 268n128, 333n88, 337n25; physician shortage in, 116, 305n55; public education in, 61; reimbursement rates in, 288n35, 341n49; SCHIP in, 298n111

conservatives, 5, 49, 69, 101, 102–3, 123–25, 236. *See also* Bush, George W.; Reagan, Ronald; Republican Party
Consolidated Omnibus Reconciliation acts, 270nn9,10, 360n34
Conyers, John, 368n35
Cook, Douglas M., 295n97
Cook, Fay Lomax, 11
copayments: as behavioral controls, 110; and benefits, 276n60; and cost control, 36, 114, 216, 218; and coverage, 85, 86, 93, 94; and DRA, 80; increasing, 2, 227; for LTC, 312n16; as obstacle, 2, 88; for prescription drugs, 347n78, 359n31; and rationing, 98; in state plans, 82, 195, 258n69, 281n120, 289n49
costs, 2–4; and access, 4, 110–11, 113, 226; of AFDC, 61, 67–68, 278n92; for care of children, 99, 300n121, 364n18; for care of disabled, 131, 310n2, 311n10; for care of elderly, 131, 232, 310n2; causes of high U.S., 365n23; of dental care, 201; and economy, 17, 32, 36; escalating, 24, 31–37, 42, 44, 46–48, 53, 57, 61, 181, 186, 210, 231, 272n24, 276n64, 286n18; and fraud, 42, 44; of HCBS, 142, 143, 144, 146–47, 317n59; and health care reform, 90, 236; of hospitals, 24, 257n54, 274n42, 343n58; of ICF-MRs, 317n59; of ICFs, 135; of informal caregivers, 147–48; of lobbying, 232; of LTC, 136, 137, 147, 150, 152, 312n12, 313nn19,22, 317n59; of MCOs, 36, 149, 227, 232; and medical inflation, 2, 56, 66, 81, 229, 232, 271n23, 272n24, 360n38; of nursing homes, 135, 146–47, 187, 225, 337nn25,26; of pharmaceutical industry, 195, 345n69; of prescription drugs, 214, 216, 345n71, 346n73, 347n78; and provider participation, 36–40; public opinion on, 367n32; and quality of care, 46–48, 233; of SCHIP, 71, 364n18; of skilled nursing facilities, 186, 317n59, 337n25, 338n34; and staffing, 165; state, 34–36, 53, 56–57, 61, 91, 223, 228, 233, 235, 257n64, 258n65, 286n19, 287n31, 312n12, 313nn19,22, 317n59, 337nn25,26, 343n58
cost control, 14, 15; and benefits, 49, 59, 114; and Boren amendment, 273n41; and Bush strategy, 78; and children's coverage, 99; by Congress, 213, 214, 217, 226, 270n12, 278n84, 284n6, 285n12, 343n60; and DRA, 80, 285n12; and DSH system, 63–64, 75, 276nn64,67; and HCBS, 141, 143, 145; and health care reform, 88, 238, 239,

cost control (*continued*)
369n41; in hospitals, 33, 59, 60; and income eligibility, 31, 34, 35, 49, 59, 74, 114, 213, 220, 271n19, 285n14; and LTC, 132, 151, 285n12; and MCOs, 33, 158, 161, 232; and Medicare, 196, 213–14; and nursing homes, 32, 59–60; and pharmaceutical companies, 194; and pharmacies, 196; and poor, 34–35, 226; and privatization, 259n69, 285n12; and providers, 49, 114, 226; and quality of care, 155, 156, 226; and rationing, 2–3, 59, 96, 98–99, 281n121; and reimbursement rates, 49, 59, 60, 61, 75; and SCHIP, 279n103; and states, 31–33, 48, 49, 53, 57, 59–61, 74–75, 77, 203–6, 226, 257n64, 258n69, 263n95, 285n12, 286n24, 313n19; and taxes, 34, 61, 75, 215, 233; and waivers, 36, 74, 216, 283n125
cost sharing, with recipients, 17, 48, 209, 221, 233; and behavioral controls, 96, 102; and benefits, 121; and children, 99, 300n121; and coverage, 85, 86, 93; and dental care, 117; and DRA, 86, 215–16; and HCBS, 317n62; and health care reform, 236, 238; and HIFA, 283n4; and hospitals, 21, 87, 216; and income eligibility, 271n19, 285n14; and LTC, 131; and Medicare, 234, 271n19; as obstacle, 15, 107, 109–11, 126, 227; in private plans, 128; and SCHIP, 101, 279n105; in state plans, 49, 59, 110, 111, 220, 255n40, 292n62, 293n72, 297n108. *See also* copayments; premiums
cost shifting: by employers, 218–19; Medicare-Medicaid, 213–14, 217; within states, 214–15, 216, 359nn28,29
cost shifting, federal-state, 15, 28, 30–33, 62–64, 209–21, 358n20; and advocacy groups, 335n7; and children, 216, 219; and decline in services, 4–5; and employer-based health insurance, 218–19; and fraud, 227; and health care reform, 240; and hospitals, 210, 217, 219–20; and LTC, 36, 213, 214; and MCOs, 219–20; and national economy, 77, 218; and nursing homes, 213, 214, 217, 218; and private sector, 217–21; and reimbursement rates, 213–14; and states, 77, 79, 220, 227, 255n40; and uninsured population, 217, 220
coverage, Medicaid: *vs.* benefits, 85–86, 226; for childbirth, 310n98; for children, 5, 15, 69–71, 75, 92, 93, 99–100, 126, 223, 226, 279n102, 298nn112,115, 299nn119,121; and copayments, 85, 86, 93, 94; for dental care, 113, 117–19, 201; for disabled, 56, 72, 92–93, 223; discontinuities in, 105, 109,

112–13, 126, 158, 228; for elderly, 92–93, 94, 126, 223; and eligibility, 85–86, 93, 126; expansion of, 85–92, 223, 366n32; and HCBS, 94, 224; and health care reform, 238; and hospitals, 85, 112–13, 223; of immigrants, 111–12; of LTC, 93–94, 128, 224; by MCOs, 86, 88, 90, 93, 94, 99, 283n127; and national economy, 90, 94, 236; obstacles to, 105–13, 106–9, 126; and physicians, 200; for preexisting conditions, 237; for pregnant women, 223, 270n10, 304n36; of prescription drugs, 92, 93, 94, 110, 127, 195, 223, 363n13; reductions in, 92–99, 279n99; of SCHIP, 99–100, 247n3; in skilled nursing facilities, 263n93, 358n25; in state plans, 279n99, 292n62; and state *vs.* federal funding, 212; universal, 17, 22, 24, 33, 34, 49, 70, 73, 88–92, 99–100, 153, 228, 230–40, 291n58, 298n112; and waivers, 85–86, 90, 92–99, 100
coverage, Medicare, 128, 138, 141, 247n3, 270n9, 271n19, 316n50, 358n23
Cravins, Donald, 336n18
Crist, Charlie, 296n105
Cunningham, Peter, 115
Cuomo, Mario, 282n123, 359n29
Czaplewski, Meredith B., 11

Daniels, Mitch, 320n86
Deficit Reduction Act (DRA; 1984), 270n9
Deficit Reduction Act (DRA; 2005), 4, 15, 16; and citizenship requirements, 107, 108, 111, 112; and cost control, 80, 285n12; and cost sharing, 80, 86, 215–16; and enrollment, 304n38, 305n43; and federal funding, 358n20; and federal standards, 94; and fraud, 170, 329n62, 330n67; and HCBS, 80, 144–47, 317n62; and HOAs, 294n86; and LTC, 80, 81, 138, 139, 150; and rationing, 98; and SCHIP, 302n14; and states, 80–81, 83
Delaware, 353n124
Democratic Party, 11, 12; and cost control, 277n74, 285n12; and cost shifting, 215; and expansion of Medicaid, 55, 270n9; and health care reform, 13, 18, 21, 237–38, 239, 252n44, 369n41; and LTC, 136; and Medicare, 252n42; and SCHIP, 100, 228; and Social Security, 252n42; southern, 21, 22; and states, 65
dental care: access to, 113, 117–19, 127; for children, 117–19, 120, 201, 307nn61,62,69, 308nn80,82; and Congress, 307n61; costs of, 201; cuts in, 317n58; fraud in, 173; and MCOs, 297n105; and private sector,

dental care (*continued*)
  307n69, 351n106; quality of, 155;
  reimbursement rates for, 306nn59,60; in
  state plans, 117, 118, 307n66, 308nn80,82,
  309n84
dentists, 181, 201. *See also* American Dental
  Association
DeWitt, Charlie, 336n18
diagnosis-related groups (DRGs), 133, 213,
  274n42
Dingell, John, 368n40
Dirigo Choice Health Plan (Maine), 91,
  291n56, 292n71
disabled: advocacy groups for, 143; benefits for,
  28, 128, 234; costs for care of, 131, 310n2,
  311n10; and cost sharing, 216, 319n70;
  coverage for, 56, 72, 92–93, 223; and cuts,
  92–93, 284n8, 317n58, 362n7; and
  direct-care staff, 166; and DRA, 80;
  employment for, 281n113; and federal
  funding, 256n51; and fraud, 173; and
  HCBS, 142, 317n61; and health care
  reform, 240; increasing population of,
  271n21; and informal caregivers, 147; and
  LTC, 15, 133–34, 135, 152; and managed
  care, 84; and Medicaid expansion, 14,
  283n125; and medical industrial complex,
  183; and Medicare, 231; and PACE,
  320n83; and prescription drugs, 346n71;
  quality of care for, 161–66; and rationing,
  98; and resilience of Medicaid, 224; and
  SSI, 253n21; in state plans, 81, 90, 293n77,
  297n106; and waivers, 316n53
Disproportionate Share Hospital (DSH) system,
  192–93, 209–10, 343n57, 355n2; and Boren
  amendment, 273n41; and Clinton, 66; and
  Congress, 62, 355n1; and cost control,
  63–64, 75, 276nn64,67; and cuts, 284n6,
  356n5; and Empowering Patients First Act,
  367n34; and health care reform, 369n41; in
  state plans, 62–64, 276n67, 277n68, 355n3,
  357n10; UPLs in, 209, 355n1, 356n6, 357n10
Douglas, James, 90
Driver, Deamonte, 118
drug abuse, 122, 173
Duggan, Mark, 161
Dukakis, Michael, 264n109

Early and Periodic Screening, Diagnosis, and
  Treatment (EPSDT) Program (1967), 29,
  55, 127, 255n33; and access, 114, 119, 126;
  and dental care, 117; and Reagan, 270n13
economies, local, 235
economies, state, 17; and Medicaid, 203–6,
  272nn28,29,30, 301n9, 353n124,

354nn131,132; and national economy, 57,
  62, 81–82, 83, 92, 229, 272n28; public
  opinion on, 251nn38,39; and uninsured
  population, 82–83
economy, national, 66, 73; and cost shifting, 77,
  218; and coverage, 90, 94, 236; and health
  care costs, 17, 32, 36, 363n15; and health
  care reform, 90, 236, 238; and Medicaid
  expansion, 56, 70, 74; and medical
  industrial complex, 203–4; and nursing
  homes, 186, 353n120; and social programs,
  68, 77, 278n95; and state economies, 57, 62,
  81–82, 83, 92, 229, 272n28
Edelstein, Burton, 117
education, public, 61, 82, 211, 286n19; cuts in,
  275n56, 276n58
Ehrlich, Robert, Jr., 219
elderly: adult children of, 315n36, 316n52;
  advocacy groups for, 41, 140–41, 184;
  benefits for, 28–29, 123, 128, 234;
  care-givers for, 147, 166; costs for care of,
  131, 232, 310n2; and cost sharing, 216;
  coverage for, 92–93, 94, 126, 223; and cuts,
  92–93, 94, 362n7; early programs for,
  22–23; and eligibility, 106; and estate
  planning, 138–40; and federal funding,
  256n51; female, 311nn3,9; and fraud, 173;
  HCBS for, 123, 133, 261n85; and health
  care reform, 240; increasing population of,
  56, 132, 133, 165, 311n7; and Kerr-Mills,
  23, 24; life expectancies of, 311n6;
  low-income, 56; and LTC, 15, 144; and
  managed care, 84; and Medicaid
  expansion, 14, 55, 56; and medical
  industrial complex, 183; and Medicare, 40,
  231; middle-class, 136–37; in other
  countries, 234; public opinion on, 13, 28;
  quality of care for, 7–8, 161–66, 226; race
  of, 6, 13, 311n5; and rationing, 98; and
  resilience of Medicaid, 224; and SSI,
  253n21; in state plans, 22, 23, 81, 90, 229,
  297n106, 313n19. *See also* assets; women
eligibility: for AFDC, 26, 55, 279n98; barriers
  to, 15, 26, 105–6, 108–9, 126, 231; of
  children, 99, 100, 271n21, 301n5, 319n70;
  and Congress, 111–12, 257n60; and cost
  control, 31, 34, 35, 49, 59, 74, 114, 213, 220,
  271n19, 285n14; and cost sharing, 87,
  271n19, 285n14, 360n32; and coverage,
  85–86, 93, 126; and cuts, 92, 93, 275n56,
  362n7; and dental care, 118; dual, 56, 106,
  134, 157, 196, 213–14, 285n12, 304n37,
  312n17, 347n78, 358n22; and economy, 77;
  and employment, 204, 285n16, 301n9; and
  enrollment, 7, 298n114; expansion of, 184,

203, 280n111; and federal funding, 256n51;
and fraud, 327n47; and gender, 8, 9, 106; for
HCBS, 142, 144, 145, 318n67; and health
care reform, 238, 368n37; and HIFA,
283n4; of hospitals, 259n72; and Hurricane
Katrina, 126; of immigrants, 106, 231; and
Kerr-Mills, 23, 24; for LTC, 105, 132, 135,
147, 150, 152; and MCOs, 149; and
Medicaid expansion, 283n125; and
Medicare-Medicaid cost shifting, 213; for
nursing homes, 144, 314nn24,25; and
poverty, 49, 106, 248n14; and quality of
care, 156, 158; and race, 106, 230; and
Reagan, 269n7; and regulations, 289n40;
requirements for, 28, 305n43; restrictions
on, 92; for SCHIP, 71, 101, 112, 228,
280n107, 298n111; and SSI, 253n21,
271n21, 314n24, 318n67; in state plans, 26,
27, 30, 32, 82, 83, 89, 90, 91, 255n41,
256n43, 257n64, 273n35, 275n56, 280n107,
289n43, 290n54, 298n111, 300nn1,2,
303n21; and stimulus plan, 205; Supreme
Court on, 56; of uninsured population,
301nn6,10. *See also* assets
emergency rooms, 38, 47, 85, 95, 112, 116–17,
231; and physicians, 201, 220
Employee Retirement Income Security Act
(1974), 361n43
employers: cost shifting by, 218–19; and
informal caregivers, 148; insurance
provided by, 86–88, 92, 93, 97, 98, 100, 110,
121, 165, 218–219, 223, 231, 237, 239,
281n121, 287n29, 290nn50,52,54, 292n63,
319n70, 360nn38,39, 363nn12,14, 367n34,
368n36; and LTC insurance, 151; mandates
on, 92, 282n122, 291n58, 368n36; and
Medicaid-covered workers, 218–19,
291n57, 360n41, 361n42; and subsidized
premiums, 86–88
Empowering Patients First Act, 367n34
Engle, Jonathan, 27
enrollment, 2, 3, 11, 303n33; and DRA, 304n38,
305n43; and eligibility, 7, 298n114; in HCBS,
273n34; in MCOs, 272n31; Medicare,
363n12; and reenrollment, 107, 112, 302n17;
in SCHIP, 108, 298n115, 363n12; *vs.*
services, 298n112; by state, 107, 304n38,
305n43; and unemployment, 362n6
entitlements, 54, 77–78, 100
entitlement status of Medicaid, 5, 14, 65, 66,
136, 144, 152, 225, 226, 227

False Claims Act (FCA), 155, 167, 168, 169, 170,
175–77, 178
"familism," 2, 148, 152

Family Opportunity Act (Dylan Lee James
Act; 2005), 318n70
family planning, 123–24, 127, 273n32, 310n99
Feder, Judith, 150
Federal Drug Administration (FDA), 171, 175
Federal Medicaid Advisory Commission, 97,
285n12
Fletcher, Ernie, 99, 297n110
Florida: access in, 115; campaign contributions
in, 350n93; cost shifting within, 214,
359n28; dental care in, 308n82; elderly
population in, 313n19; fraud in, 44, 169,
265n115, 324n20, 328n51; health
insurance companies in, 349n90; health
insurance plan of, 295nn96,97,
296nn102,103,105; and Hurricane Katrina,
125; immigrants in, 363n9; litigation by
drug companies in, 195; LTC in, 149,
321n86; MCOs in, 84, 149, 160, 198,
289n39, 321n86; Medicaid-covered
workers in, 361n42; Medicaid employment
in, 353n124; Medicaid in, 107, 256n44,
272n29, 273n37, 275n56, 304n38; nursing
homes in, 337n21; outsourced services in,
202; privatization in, 3, 97–98; public
education in, 61; reenrollment in, 302n17;
REITs in, 189; taxes in, 61; threatened
withdrawals in, 263n93; transition
programs in, 318n69
Forand, Aime, 22
Ford, Gerald R., 33
Fossett, James, 204, 211, 276n58, 285n16,
286n24
fraud, 14, 41–46, 166–71; in assisted-living
facilities, 166–67; and CMS, 169, 170,
327n47, 329nn64,65; and Congress,
42–43, 169–70, 264nn103,109, 330n66;
controlling, 203, 264n109; and cost
shifting, 227; and DRA, 170, 329n62,
330n67; financial, 178; and health care
reform, 369n41; and health insurance
companies, 349n90; and HEW, 42, 43,
263n98, 266n118; in hospitals, 44, 166, 168,
171, 173, 265n112, 266n118; investigations
of, 264n110, 265nn112,115,116, 266n118;
by laboratories, 43–44, 173, 264n110; and
litigation, 167, 170–71, 172, 220–21; in
MCOs, 43, 159, 160, 167, 331n73; and
media, 41, 42, 168–69, 170; and Medicare,
42, 166, 167, 169, 174, 227, 329n63; in
nursing homes, 41, 44, 45–46, 49, 166,
168, 175–77, 187, 267nn126,128,
268nn128,130; and patient abuse, 171–77,
178; by pharmaceutical industry, 167, 171,
174–75,

campaign contributions, 336n18; and federal standards, 47, 48; financial gains from, 170–71, 174–78; and fraud, 167, 170–71, 172, 220–21; and HCBS, 143, 317n61; and MCOs, 161, 324nn18,20, 350n99; and Medicaid mills, 260n82; and nursing homes, 185, 269n138, 332n87, 333nn88,91, 336n19; and patient abuse, 172, 177; and pharmaceutical industry, 195, 220, 330n71, 331n73, 332n82; and pharmacies, 197, 348n85; and quality of care, 324n18; by recipients, 263n95; and regulations, 261n89; reimbursement for, 261n88; and reimbursement rates, 49, 276n60, 336n19; and REITs, 189–90; and SCHIP, 271n16; and states, 91, 195, 263n95, 271n16, 293n78, 332n87, 333n88, 337n21

lobbying, 3, 40, 55; by ADA, 351n105; by age-based groups, 140–41, 184, 316nn47,50; by AHA, 341n43, 366n31; by AMA, 184, 200, 366n31; for children, 184, 335n13; of CMS, 182; costs of, 232; for federal funding, 206, 335n13; and HCBS, 142, 352n109; by health insurance industry, 366n31; and Hill-Burton Act, 253n5; by hospitals, 190; and LTC, 185, 336n16; and MCOs, 198, 199; and medical industrial complex, 224; and Medicare, 334n3; by nursing homes, 185; by pharmaceutical industry, 194, 195, 345nn67,68,70, 366n31; and pharmacies, 196; by providers, 182, 185, 202, 203, 366n31; and regulations, 79, 185, 335n9; reimbursement for, 261n88; and reimbursement rates, 37, 49; and states, 5–6, 184, 185, 335n13

long-term care (LTC), 2, 6, 7, 11, 13, 131–53; and assets, 135, 136–40, 150, 234, 315n39, 321nn90,93; audits of, 266n124; and Congress, 368n40; costs of, 36, 214, 285n12; coverage of, 93–94, 128, 224; cuts in, 15–16, 103; direct-care workers in, 166, 326n42; and DRA, 80, 81, 138, 139, 150; and estate planning, 138–40; expansion of, 39–40; and health care reform, 239, 240; insurance for, 132, 134, 137, 149–52, 153, 285n15, 321n94; and lobbying, 185, 336n16; and MCOs, 131, 132, 149, 152, 320n86; and Medicare, 134, 137, 312n16; and Medicare-Medicaid cost shifting, 213; for mentally ill, 147; and middle class, 131, 135–41, 152; and Obama, 369n40; in other countries, 234; and private sector, 131, 149–53, 368n40; and quality of care, 16, 132, 147, 155; and rationing, 98; and

resilience of Medicaid, 224, 225; shortage of, 49; in states, 90, 135, 138, 149, 150, 270n7, 273n32, 312n12, 313n19, 315n36, 317nn57,59, 318n63, 320nn84,86, 321nn86,89, 325n34, 337n25; tax credits for, 132, 150, 151, 152–53, 368n40; and women, 132, 137, 152

Long-Term Care Partnership Programs, 16, 150, 285n15, 321nn89,90

Louisiana, 107, 256nn42,43, 304n38; abortion in, 309n90; campaign contributions in, 185, 336n18; childbirth in, 310n98; DSH payments in, 355n3; fraud in, 172, 176; and Hurricane Katrina, 125–26; and immigrants, 112; LTC costs in, 312n12, 317n59; MCOs in, 84, 160, 289n39; nursing homes in, 332n87; and SCHIP, 101

Maine, 87, 195, 256n43, 306n60; abortion in, 309n92; costs in, 286n19; fraud in, 169; health plan in, 91, 291n56, 292n71; Medicaid technology in, 352n115; outsourced services in, 202; poverty level in, 301n5

malpractice liability, 186, 190, 332n87

managed-care organizations (MCOs): and access, 16, 73, 113, 116, 158, 159, 199; and BBA, 66, 73, 277n83, 278n86; behavioral controls in, 95; and campaign contributions, 198, 199; children in, 99, 158, 296n103, 297n105, 299n118; and cost shifting, 219–20; costs of, 33, 36, 149, 158, 161, 227, 232; coverage by, 86, 88, 90, 93, 94, 99, 283n127; and cuts, 93, 94, 102, 103; and dental care, 118–19, 297n105; enrollment in, 272n31; expansion of, 86, 282n123; fraud in, 43, 159, 160, 167, 331n73; vs. freedom-of-choice requirement, 29, 73, 84; and funding, 2, 182, 206; "gag rules" in, 159; growth of, 73–74, 288n38, 289n39; and health insurance industry, 66, 84, 232; and HOAs, 294n86; and hospitals, 192; and litigation, 161, 324nn18,20, 350n99; lobbying by, 198, 199; for LTC, 131, 132, 149, 152, 320n86; mandatory, 73, 74, 75, 84, 275n56; and Medicaid recipients, 7, 16; and medical industrial complex, 197–200; for mental health services, 160, 161; and outsourcing of services, 202; and patient bill of rights, 199; and physician shortage, 305n55; power of, 181; and prescription drugs, 161, 199; and privatization, 84, 97–98; profits of, 198–99, 350n95; and quality of care, 14, 149, 155, 156, 158–61, 177, 199, 227,

171, 173, 174; generic, 194, 197, 216, 258n69, 284n8, 293n81, 348n80; for impotence, 309n89; and MCOs, 161, 199; and Medicare-Medicaid cost shifting, 214; and Medicare Part D, 195–96; price controls on, 196, 345n66, 346n72, 347n77, 348n80; reimbursement rates for, 347n79; reimportation of, 196, 363n13; restrictions on, 121, 293n81, 359n30; state funding of, 309n89. *See also* pharmaceutical industry

Primary Care Network (PCN; Utah), 85, 289n43

prisoners, 122

private sector, 21, 27, 28, 40, 50, 103, 209, 364n18; and ADA, 201; and cost control, 285n12; and cost shifting, 217–21; and dental care, 307n69, 351n106; and DSH payments, 63; and Empowering Patients First Act, 367n34; and LTC, 149–53, 368n40; and Medicaid employment, 354n132; and Medicare Part D, 196; and nursing homes, 184; and premium subsidies, 86–88. *See also* health insurance, private

privatization, 2–4, 8, 102; and Bush, 78, 300n123; and Clinton, 66; and cost control, 259n69, 285n12; and coverage, 85; and DRA, 81; of health insurance, 54, 97–98; and HOAs, 294n86; and LTC, 131; and MCOs, 84, 97–98; and Republicans, 64, 77; and SCHIP, 101; in states, 3, 97–98, 293n79; and subsidized premiums, 86–88

profit-maximizing behavior, 3, 28, 232

Program of All-Inclusive Care of the Elderly (PACE), 149, 320n83

providers, health care: campaign contributions by, 202, 351n102; and charity care, 22, 24, 27; and cost control, 49, 114, 226; and cost shifting, 216, 217–21, 227; and escalating costs, 34, 36; fees for, 2, 29, 32; foreign-educated, 27; fraud by, 41–46, 49, 166–67, 170, 172, 173, 178; and Kerr-Mills, 23; lobbying by, 182, 185, 202, 203, 366n31; and Medicaid, 28, 181–82, 206–7, 284nn8,10; and medical industrial complex, 200–203; and Medicare, 24; and national health insurance, 34, 49; outsourcing of services by, 202; participation of, 36–40, 262n93; political contributions from, 182; and political power, 40–41, 181, 182–83; private *vs.* public, 48; and privatization, 97; reimbursement rates for, 21–22, 23, 36–40; shortage of, 27, 46, 47, 49, 114–20, 126; specialist, 115–16, 159, 201, 239, 254n24,

296n100, 368n39; and states, 17, 41, 59, 202; taxes from, 209–10, 274n54, 276n64, 277n72, 284n8. *See also* hospitals; managed-care organizations; nursing homes; physicians; skilled nursing facilities

Pryor, David, 47

Quality Improvement System for Managed Care (1996), 323n16

quality of care, 2, 22, 27, 103, 155–78; and access, 4, 7, 10, 115, 156; in assisted-living facilities, 162–64, 177; and CMS, 156, 162, 164, 178, 326n36; and cost control, 46–48, 155, 156, 226, 233; and costs, 46–48, 233; for disabled, 161–66; for elderly, 7–8, 161–66, 226; *vs.* financial issues, 170–71, 174, 175–76, 177, 178; and fraud, 46–48, 155; in HCBS, 16, 157, 161–62, 177, 324n26; and health care reform, 238, 239; in LTC, 16, 132, 147, 155; in MCOs, 14, 149, 155, 156, 158–61, 177, 199, 227, 297n105, 323nn12,16, 324n24; in Medicaid mills, 260n83; for minorities, 9–10; in nursing homes, 7–8, 16, 59, 155, 156, 157, 162, 186, 188–89, 234; and privatization, 97, 98; and reimbursement rates, 156, 183, 226; and REITs, 188, 189, 340n41; in state plans, 120, 156–57, 211, 292n62, 322n3, 324n24; two levels of, 7, 9, 13, 16, 29, 47, 49, 105, 126, 226, 230–34, 238; in U.S., 234

race, 13, 27, 106, 311n5; and AFDC, 252n46; of caregivers, 166, 327n44; and Medicaid, 249nn22,24; and Medicaid *vs.* Medicare, 269n2; and poverty, 67, 249n23, 301n5; and quality of care, 9–10; and states' inequalities, 229–30; in U.S., 234

rationing, 2–3; and coverage, 85, 94; by MCOs, 16, 158, 200, 227, 281n121; of prescription drugs, 96, 98; by states, 59, 98–99, 281n121

Reagan, Ronald, 14, 35; and block grants, 64, 65; in California, 258n69; and cuts, 225, 269n1; and EPSDT, 270n13; and health care reform, 34; and LTC, 138; and MCOs, 159; and Medicaid, 55, 74, 212, 269n7, 270n9; and medical industrial complex, 183–84; and social services, 53–54, 78; and states rights, 56–57

recipients, Medicaid: and behavioral controls, 94–97; categories of, 98; deinstitutionalization of, 146; and fraud, 16, 168, 171–77, 220–21; fraud by, 42, 44, 45, 46, 263n98, 302n15; increases in, 198; limits on, 105–13; low-income, 15, 21–22,

South Carolina: cigarette tax in, 288n34; costs in, 216, 313nn19,22; cuts in, 273n36; dentists in, 306n60; eligibility in, 256n43; fraud in, 169; health insurance in, 290n50, 349n90; and HOAs, 294n86; hospitals in, 260n79; LTC in, 313nn19,22; MCOs in, 84, 198; Medicaid in, 120, 204–5, 256n43; 322n3; and stimulus, 362n7

South Dakota, 256n43, 283n127, 288n34, 322n3, 337n25

Sparer, Michael, 228

Spitzer, Eliot, 99

staff, health-care: in assisted-living facilities, 163, 166; and cost shifting, 217; direct-care, 166, 326n42; mandates for, 186; in nursing homes, 164–65, 166, 186, 187, 188, 189; quality of, 173, 177–78; and quality of care, 326nn36,38

standards, federal, 15, 85, 227, 285n13; and assisted-living facilities, 163; and HSAs, 94; and litigation, 47, 48; for nursing homes, 32, 60, 266n125; and patient abuse, 47; and quality of care, 323n16; and rationing, 98

State Children's Health Insurance Program (SCHIP), 7, 12, 14, 83, 279nn103,104,105, 299n119; and adults, 107, 302n14; and AMA, 200; and block grants, 70, 279n103; and Bush administration, 71, 100–101, 107, 299n116, 309n92; and Congress, 71, 100, 101, 228; and cost sharing, 101, 279n105; costs of, 71, 279n103, 364n18; coverage of, 99–100, 247n3; and dental care, 117, 307n69; dropout rates from, 107; eligibility for, 71, 101, 112, 228, 280n107, 298n111; and employment, 301n9; and Empowering Patients First Act, 367n34; enrollment in, 108, 298n115, 363n12; expansion of, 184; and health care reform, 99–100; and HIFA, 78; litigation on, 271n16; and MCOs, 198, 288n38; and Obama, 71, 101, 300n122; and outsourcing, 352n111; and quality of care, 155, 156; renewal of, 303n23; restrictions on, 300n122; and subsidized premiums, 87; and uninsured population, 126–27, 128, 301n10; and U.S. economy, 203

states: autonomy for, 77, 78; and Bush administration, 15, 78, 79; conflict between, 215; cost shifting within, 214–215, 216, 359nn28,29; devolution of responsibility to, 14, 64, 75, 77, 78, 80–81, 83–84, 182, 228–30; and DRA, 80–81, 83; and DSH payments, 62–64, 357n10; economies of, 5–6, 56–61, 81–82, 203–6, 272n28, 354n131, 362n7; employment in,

203–6; expansion of Medicaid by, 29, 55, 74, 368n37; "flexibilities" for, 83–84, 94, 102, 145, 159, 162, 216, 285n12; and fraud, 42, 43, 44–45, 166, 167–69; and health care reform, 235–36, 238; health insurance plans in, 290nn50,51,52,54, 291nn56,58, 292nn62,66,68,71,72, 294nn86,89; inequities among, 13, 49, 229; innovative financing by, 62–64; and medical industrial complex, 203–6; and Republicans, 64, 77, 78, 236; and uninsured population, 72, 82–83; variations among, 83, 318n63, 341n42. See also block grants; State Children's Health Insurance Program (SCHIP)

states' rights, 56–57, 74

Stein Commission (Temporary State Commission on Living Costs), 267n126

Steingut, Stanley, 268n130

Stevens, Robert, 27, 30

Stevens, Rosemary, 27, 30

stimulus plan, 205–6, 236, 354n133, 362n7

Strickland, Ted, 309n84

Sullivan v. Zebley (1990), 56

Sundquist, Don, 285n12

Supplemental Security Income (SSI), 56, 98, 256n51; and cost shifting, 216; and eligibility, 253n21, 271n21, 314n24, 318n67; and LTC, 135, 315n39; public opinion on, 11–12, 250n36

Supreme Court, 56, 60, 124, 142, 214, 304n35, 324n18

Taft, Robert, 309n84

Talmadge, Herman, 264n103

tax credits, 88, 93, 300n123, 367n34; and health care reform, 239; lobbying for, 335n13; for LTC, 132, 150, 151, 152–53, 368n40; and SCHIP, 101

Tax Equity and Fiscal Responsibility Act (Katie Beckett Program; 1982), 315n35, 319n70

taxes: and Congress, 277n82; and cost control, 34, 61, 75, 215, 233; and cost shifting within states, 215; cuts in, 286n20; and DSH payments, 63, 64, 355n1; and economy, 77; and federal funding, 62, 356n4, 364n19; and health care reform, 88, 89, 91, 236, 369n41; and health insurance, 360n38, 364n19, 366n32; as incentives, 16, 33; increases in, 276n59; and LTC, 369n40; and Medicaid, 207, 284n8; and Medicare, 24; and nursing-home fraud, 45; on providers, 209–10, 274n54, 276n64, 277n72, 284n8; and Republicans, 64, 77; and SCHIP, 101; "sin," 81, 84, 87, 88; and

taxes (*continued*)
  social services, 67, 278n88; on tobacco,
  288n34, 290n50, 293n83, 295n89; and
  trusts, 140
taxes, state, 84, 229, 258n69, 276n59, 286n20,
  293n83; in California, 57, 61, 275n56,
  288n34; and cost controls, 61; and
  economies, 57, 81; *vs.* federal funding, 210,
  212; and inequalities, 230; and insurance
  plans, 295n89; on tobacco, 292n67
Taxpayers' Relief Act, 277n82
Temporary Assistance for Needy Families
  (TANF), 68–69, 70, 109, 352n111; *vs.*
  AFDC, 301n9; *vs.* Medicaid, 6, 141
Tennessee, 256n44, 260n79, 286n19, 307n69;
  cuts in, 92, 273n37; LTC in, 313nn19,22;
  MCOs in, 73, 283n127
Texas, 119, 202, 256n43, 308n77, 322n3,
  349n90; fraud in, 168, 330n71, 331n73;
  HCBS in, 317n61; and Hurricane Katrina,
  125; immigrants in, 362n9; LTC in, 313n19,
  320n86; MCOs in, 84, 320n86; Medicaid
  employment in, 353n124; Money Follows
  the Person Program in, 319n72; nursing
  homes in, 262nn90,91; quality of care in,
  324n18; and SCHIP for unborn, 309n92;
  uninsured children in, 299n115
Thomas, Clive, 140
Thompson, Tommy, 345n70
Ticket to Work Act, 92, 281n113
transportation, 115, 119, 173, 203
Truman, Harry S., 21, 235

underinsured population, 365n22
uninsured population: and Bush, 103; children
  in, 299n115; and cost shifting, 217, 220;
  eligibility of, 301nn6,10; growth of, 71–72,
  109, 110, 233; and health care reform,
  88–89, 90, 235–36; and hospitals, 192, 193;
  immigrants in, 362n9; and loss of
  Medicaid, 109, 110; *vs.* MCOs, 160; *vs.*
  Medicaid recipients, 126–28, 157, 158,
  234–35; poverty of, 231, 287n29; and
  SCHIP, 126–27, 128, 301n10; and state
  economies, 82–83; and state plans, 83–84,
  90, 91, 123, 212, 223, 228, 229, 291n58,
  298n111; and subsidized premiums, 86, 88;
  and waivers, 72–73
unions, 17, 41, 55, 263n96; and health care
  reform, 34, 49, 365n30; lobbying by, 184;
  and medical industrial complex, 183
upper payment limits (UPLs), 209, 355n1,
  356n6, 357n10
Utah, 85, 258n64, 319n72, 341n45; abortion in,
  309n90; access to specialists in, 116;

campaign contributions in, 334n4; dentists
  in, 306n60; DSH payments in, 355n3;
  economy of, 353n124; elderly population
  in, 313n19; health insurance in, 291n56,
  349n90; MCOs in, 58, 283n127; and
  SCHIP, 71; uninsured in, 289n43

Varady, Des, 169
Vermont, 111, 275n55, 310n98; and federal
  funding, 255n39; health insurance plan of,
  292nn66,68; litigation in, 195; Medicaid
  in, 256n43, 273n37, 286n19, 322n3; Money
  Follows the Person Program in, 319n72; *vs.*
  Rhode Island, 93; SCHIP in, 298n111,
  303n33; taxes in, 276n59, 288n34;
  uninsured children in, 299n115; universal
  coverage in, 90
Vilsack, Tom, 295n94
Virginia, 256n44, 307n69; economy of,
  353n124; enrollment in, 304n38, 305n43;
  health insurance plan of, 294n89; LTC in,
  163, 315n36
Von Dohlen, Tim, 262n91

Wachino, Victoria, 3
Wagner-Murray-Dingell bills, 21
waivers, 75, 89, 289n45; 1115 (for targeted
  groups), 58, 72, 78, 83, 94, 97, 98, 146,
  254n28, 258nn68,69, 282n122, 294n89,
  302n14; 1915(b), 78, 258n68, 259n70;
  1915(c), 142, 143, 275n56, 316n53, 317n60;
  and assisted-living facilities, 163; and
  Bush strategy, 78, 100; and cost control,
  36, 74, 216, 283n125; and coverage, 85–86,
  90, 92–99, 100; and demonstration
  projects, 72–73, 78, 145, 149; on DSH
  payments, 64; of freedom-of-choice
  requirement, 58, 73, 259n70; for HCBS, 58,
  141–44, 145, 275n56, 316nn53,54,57; and
  HOAs, 94; and Hurricane Katrina, 125;
  and LTC, 147; and MCOs, 73–74, 84, 149,
  259n70, 283n123; and quality of care, 16,
  161–62; and rationing, 98; requirements
  for, 28; and SCHIP, 101, 302n14; and
  staffing, 165; and state plans, 14, 83–84,
  90, 294n89, 296n102; and subsidized
  premiums, 87; and uninsured population,
  72–73
Wal-Mart, 218–19, 291n57, 360n41,
  361n42
Washington state, 108, 110, 124, 322n3,
  348n85; benefits in, 59, 273n37; and DSH
  payments, 357n10; economy of, 353n124;
  elderly population in, 313n19; HCBS in,
  317n61; health insurance in, 291n58,